Hands-On Application Development with PyCharm

Build applications like a pro with the ultimate python development tool

Bruce M. Van Horn II

Quan Nguyen

BIRMINGHAM—MUMBAI

Hands-On Application Development with PyCharm

Group Product Manager: Kunal Sawant
Publishing Product Manager: Akash Sharma
Senior Editor: Kinnari Chohan
Technical Editor: Jubit Pincy
Copy Editor: Safis Editing
Project Coordinator: Manisha Singh
Proofreader: Safis Editing
Indexer: Rekha Nair
Production Designer: Ponraj Dhandapani
Development Relations Marketing Executive: Sonia Chauhan

First published: October 2019

Second edition: October 2023

Production reference: 1290923

Published by Packt Publishing Ltd.
Grosvenor House
11 St Paul's Square
Birmingham
B3 1RB

ISBN 978-1-83763-235-0

www.packtpub.com

For my daughters, Kitty and Phoebe, and my wife Karina. For my team at Visual Storage Intelligence. For my Lord and Savior, Jesus Christ. "As each has received a gift, use it to serve one another, as good stewards of God's varied grace." — 1 Peter 4:10.

– Bruce M. Van Horn II

To my two great teachers in life: my mother Chi Lan, and my father, Bang. In memory of my grandmother and my two dear grandfathers.

– Quan Nguyen

Contributors

About the authors

Bruce M. Van Horn II is the Lead Principal Software Engineer for Visual Storage Intelligence. He specializes in software engineering and web development in Python, C# and JavaScript. He's also in charge of DevOps, and is an Advanced Certified Scrum Master(A-CSM). With over 30 years of experience creating and shipping successful software, he also has 25 years of teaching experience gained by teaching evening classes at colleges and universities near his home in Dallas, Texas. Van Horn is the author of several books and video series published by Packt, Skillsoft, Lynda.com and LinkedIn Learning including LinkedIn's original video course on PyCharm. His projects over the years have won many auspicious awards, but his proudest achievement to date was his team's achievement winning the U.S. Navy's IS&T award. You can reach him at LinkedIn at `https://www.linkedin.com/in/brucevanhorn2/`

Quan Nguyen, the author of the first edition of this book, is a Python programmer with a strong passion for machine learning. He holds a dual degree in mathematics and computer science, with a minor in philosophy, earned from DePauw University. Quan is deeply involved in the Python community and has authored multiple Python books, contributing to the Python Software Foundation and regularly sharing insights on DataScience.com. Currently pursuing a Ph.D. in computer science at Washington University in St. Louis, you can find him on LinkedIn at `https://www.linkedin.com/in/quan-m-nguyen/`.

About the reviewers

Dr. Gowrishankar S Nath is a professor and dean of the Department of Computer Science and Engineering at Dr. Ambedkar Institute of Technology in Bengaluru, India. He earned a Ph.D. in engineering for Jadavpur University, Kolkata India in 2010, and an MTech in software engineering along with a BE in computer science and engineering from Visvesvaraya Technological University (VTU) in 2005 and 2003 respectively. His research interests include the applications of machine learning, data mining, and big data analytics in health care. You'll find him on LinkedIn at `https://www.linkedin.com/in/gowrishankarnath/`.

Walker Crystal is a creative tinkerer at heart who loves to listen and solve problems. Walker has a Bachelor's degree in Automotive Engineering Technology from Brigham Young University, Idaho and has worked as a system integration tester for an automotive manufacturer, software developer at a fortune 500 company, and DevOps Engineer/Software Developer for a large trucking company among jobs in other career fields. His keen attention to detail and natural curiosity help him to ask the right questions and develop innovative and creative solutions to problems. He believes that technology is a force multiplier that can amplify your efforts to do good and extend your positive impact to customers all across the globe. In his spare time he makes 3D CAD models and prints them on a 3D printer, plays with Legos, fixes old and new cars, explores new technologies and spends time with his family. You can find him on LinkedIn at `https://www.linkedin.com/in/nitrospaz/`.

Karina Van Horn has a dual degree in Political Science and Creative Writing from Southern Methodist University, as well as a Juris doctorate from Texas Wesleyan University. Despite disliking anything related to technology, she has a talent for taking good writing and making it great.

Table of Contents

Part 2: Improving Your Productivity

3

Customizing Interpreters and Virtual Environments   69

4

Editing and Formatting with Ease in PyCharm   111

5

Version Control with Git in PyCharm   159

6

Seamless Testing, Debugging, and Profiling   197

Part 3: Web Development in PyCharm

7

Web Development with JavaScript, HTML, and CSS   241

8

Building a Dynamic Web Application with Flask 275

9

Creating a RESTful API with FastAPI 305

10

More Full Stack Frameworks – Django and Pyramid   347

11

Understanding Database Management in PyCharm   379

Part 4: Data Science with PyCharm

12

Turning On Scientific Mode   429

13

Dynamic Data Viewing with SciView and Jupyter   455

14

Building a Data Pipeline in PyCharm   491

Part 5: Plugins and Conclusion

15

More Possibilities with Plugins   543

16

Your Next Steps with PyCharm   579

Preface

Welcome to the world of Python programming with PyCharm! In this book, we embark on a journey through the versatile and dynamic realm of Python development, empowered by the PyCharm integrated development environment. Whether you are a novice programmer just starting your coding adventure or an experienced developer looking to enhance your Python skills, this book is designed to be your trusted companion.

Python has emerged as one of the most popular and versatile programming languages, known for its simplicity and readability. With its rich ecosystem of libraries and frameworks, Python is used in a wide range of applications, from web development and data analysis to artificial intelligence and scientific computing. PyCharm, developed by JetBrains, is a leading Python IDE that empowers programmers with a robust set of tools and features for efficient code development, debugging, and collaboration.

In the following chapters, we will explore PyCharm's fundamentals, dive into advanced configuration capabilities, and leverage PyCharm's professional edition to streamline your coding workflow. Whether you aspire to build web applications, automate tasks, analyze data, or develop machine learning models, this book will equip you with the knowledge and skills to turn your ideas into reality.

Our aim is to make your Python programming journey not only educational but also enjoyable. Throughout the book, we provide practical examples, hands-on exercises, and real-world projects to reinforce your understanding and ignite your creativity. By the time you reach the final page, you will have the confidence and expertise to tackle Python projects of all scales and complexities using PyCharm as your single go-to tool.

So, let's embark on this exciting adventure together, as we unravel the beauty of Python programming and harness the power of PyCharm to transform your coding aspirations into tangible achievements. Happy coding!

Who this book is for

This book is designed for a diverse audience of individuals who are interested in Python programming and wish to leverage the PyCharm integrated development environment (IDE) to enhance their coding experience. Here are the primary groups of people for whom this book is tailored:

- **Beginner Programmers**: If you are new to programming or have limited coding experience, this book provides a gentle introduction to Python and PyCharm. By its very nature, PyCharm makes Python easier to learn by providing a great deal of help in setting up project templates, providing auto-completion, and automatic PEP-8 formatting for your code.

- **Intermediate Python Developers**: If you already have some experience with Python but want to deepen your knowledge and proficiency, this book along with PyCharm can help. PyCharm's configurable linter and code analysis technology will hold your work to the highest standards. Refactoring, a practice that is too often neglected, becomes trivial owing to PyCharm's indexing and refactoring tools. You'll learn to use integrated testing, coverage, and profiling tools to ensure your code runs swiftly and reliably.

- **Experienced Developers from Other Languages**: If you are an experienced programmer in another language and want to transition to Python or incorporate Python into your skillset, this book will help you bridge the gap and master Python programming using PyCharm. This is especially true if you've used other PyCharm IDEs. If you normally use IntelliJ Idea, WebStorm, Rider, or PHP Storm, you'll be right at home since you'll be using the same keyboard shortcuts. If you use Visual Studio, you can easily configure PyCharm to use the keyboard shortcuts you are used to, and we think you'll find common workflows, like working with Git, to be superior and more intuitive in PyCharm.

- **Students and Educators**: Python is a popular language for teaching and learning programming. This book can serve as a valuable resource for students studying Python as part of their coursework and educators looking for a comprehensive guide to teaching Python with PyCharm effectively.

- **Data Scientists and Analysts**: Python is widely used in the field of data analysis and machine learning. This book covers advanced libraries and tools for data exploration, manipulation, cleansing, and analysis, making it valuable for data professionals seeking to improve their Python skills within the context of PyCharm. PyCharm contains a powerful set of tools for working with relational and non-relational databases which are fully covered.

- **Web Developers**: If you are interested in web development using Python, this book covers web frameworks and tools, enabling you to create dynamic web applications with PyCharm as your development tool. You'll learn to create projects in popular web development frameworks like Flask, FastAPI, and Django. Most people don't realize it, by PyCharm professional contains a full IDE geared towards JavaScript and HTML development. This book covers this in great detail.

- **Anyone Interested in Python and PyCharm:** If you have a general interest in programming, technology, or Python in particular, this book offers an engaging exploration of Python's capabilities and PyCharm's features, making it accessible and informative for a wide range of readers.

No matter your background or level of expertise, this book is intended to be a valuable resource for anyone eager to learn Python programming and harness the power of PyCharm to write efficient, readable, and maintainable code.

What this book covers

Chapter 1, Introduction to PyCharm, the most popular IDE for Python: In this initial chapter, we discuss the road ahead.

Chapter 2, Installation and Configuration: This chapter presents the installation process along with instructions on customizing PyCharm to your particular development style.

Chapter 3, Customizing Interpreters and Virtual Environments: One very useful feature of the Python ecosystem is the ability to sandbox your projects. PyCharm provides a project-centered graphical tool to manage your projects and the related interpreters and virtual environments.

Chapter 4, Editing and Formatting with Ease in PyCharm: The heart of any great IDE its editor. This chapter provides a solid orientation.

Chapter 5, Version Control with Git in PyCharm: Everything you would normally do on the command line can be done graphically within the IDE. This chapter shows you how it's done.

Chapter 6, Seamless Testing, Debugging and Profiling: PyCharm supports a variety of unit testing frameworks directly within the IDE. You'll learn to write tests and visualize the results in PyCharm.

Chapter 7, Web Development with JavaScript, HTML, and CSS: PyCharm is a complete development environment for full-stack development. As such, you'll learn to develop HTML, JavaScript, and CSS in PyCharm. We'll briefly cover a few front-end frameworks like HTML Boilerplate, Bootstrap, and React.

Chapter 8, Building a Dynamic Web Application with Flask: Flask is an un-opinionated framework for building web applications capable of serving dynamic content. PyCharm makes this very easy.

Chapter 9, Creating a RESTful API with FastAPI: In this chapter you'll learn to create a RESTful API with FastAPI. You'll also learn to test the API using PyCharm's built-in HTTP request and testing framework.

Chapter 10, More full stack frameworks: Django and Pyramid: PyCharm contains specialized tooling for Django, one of the most popular web frameworks in Python. We'll also touch on Pyramid, a framework that aims to be less complex than Django, but more complete than Flask.

Chapter 11, Understanding Database Management in PyCharm: PyCharm contains a fully featured database IDE facilitating your work with dozens of relational and non-relational (NoSQL) data platforms.

Chapter 12, Turning on Scientific Mode: You'll learn the fundamentals of PyCharm's scientific mode which is the heart of its data science tooling.

Chapter 13, Dynamic Data Viewing with SciView and Jupyter: You'll learn to leverage the ability to see the data at each step during a multi-phase data pipeline is invaluable. PyCharm supports an advanced viewer that renders NumPy and Pandas data structures.

Chapter 14, Building a Data Pipeline in PyCharm: PyCharm has everything you need to perform advanced scientific data analysis. In this chapter, we analyze a scientific study designed to predict early-onset Alzheimer's disease.

Chapter 15, *More Possibilities with PyCharm Plugins*: A great deal of the features in JetBrains IDEs are implemented using plugins. The JetBrains marketplace allows you to soup up your PyCharm installation with even more specialized features.

Chapter 16, *Future Developments*: JetBrains isn't sitting still. PyCharm evolves rapidly. This chapter shows you some of the features that are in active development at the time of writing.

To get the most out of this book

I assume you understand basic Python programming along with basic command line skills for your favorite operating system. One thing to remember throughout is that we are covering PyCharm rather than deep development tutorials of frameworks mentioned in various chapters. For example, *Chapter 8* covers the PyCharm features designed for Flask development. It isn't meant to be a full tutorial on Flask.

Software/hardware covered in the book	Operating system requirements
Python 3	Windows, macOS, or Linux
PyCharm Professional	Windows, macOS, or Linux
Docker Desktop	Windows, macOS, or Linux
Git	Windows, macOS, or Linux

Most of the book requires the professional edition of PyCharm. The first six chapters will work with the Community edition, but after that, you must have the professional edition.

If you are using the digital version of this book, we advise you to type the code yourself or access the code from the book's GitHub repository (a link is available in the next section). Doing so will help you avoid any potential errors related to the copying and pasting of code.

Download the example code files

You can download the example code files for this book from GitHub at `https://github.com/PacktPublishing/Hands-On-Application-Development-with-PyCharm---Second-Edition`. If there's an update to the code, it will be updated in the GitHub repository. *Chapter 2* covers cloning the repository using PyCharm's integrated Git client.

We also have other code bundles from our rich catalog of books and videos available at `https://github.com/PacktPublishing/`. Check them out!

Conventions used

There are a number of text conventions used throughout this book.

`Code in text`: Indicates code words in text, database table names, folder names, filenames, file extensions, pathnames, dummy URLs, user input, and Twitter handles. Here is an example: "We compute the correlation matrix of this dataset using the `corr()` method."

A block of code is set as follows:

```
# Compute and show correlation matrix
corr_mat = df.corr()

plt.matshow(corr_mat)
plt.show()
```

Any command-line input or output is written as follows:

```
$ mkdir css
$ cd css
```

Bold: Indicates a new term, an important word, or words that you see onscreen. For instance, words in menus or dialog boxes appear in **bold**. Here is an example: "If you click on the **View as Array** link, which can also be activated by right-clicking the variable, you can see a spreadsheet-like table in the **Data** panel."

> **Tips or important notes**
> Appear like this.

Get in touch

Feedback from our readers is always welcome.

General feedback: If you have questions about any aspect of this book, email us at customercare@ packtpub.com and mention the book title in the subject of your message.

Errata: Although we have taken every care to ensure the accuracy of our content, mistakes do happen. If you have found a mistake in this book, we would be grateful if you would report this to us. Please visit www.packtpub.com/support/errata and fill in the form.

Piracy: If you come across any illegal copies of our works in any form on the internet, we would be grateful if you would provide us with the location address or website name. Please contact us at copyright@packt.com with a link to the material.

If you are interested in becoming an author: If there is a topic that you have expertise in and you are interested in either writing or contributing to a book, please visit authors.packtpub.com.

Share Your Thoughts

Once you've read *Hands-On Application Development with PyCharm*, we'd love to hear your thoughts! Scan the QR code below to go straight to the Amazon review page for this book and share your feedback.

https://packt.link/r/1837632359

Your review is important to us and the tech community and will help us make sure we're delivering excellent quality content.

Download a free PDF copy of this book

Thanks for purchasing this book!

Do you like to read on the go but are unable to carry your print books everywhere?

Is your eBook purchase not compatible with the device of your choice?

Don't worry, now with every Packt book you get a DRM-free PDF version of that book at no cost.

Read anywhere, any place, on any device. Search, copy, and paste code from your favorite technical books directly into your application.

The perks don't stop there, you can get exclusive access to discounts, newsletters, and great free content in your inbox daily

Follow these simple steps to get the benefits:

1. Scan the QR code or visit the link below

https://packt.link/free-ebook/9781837632350

2. Submit your proof of purchase
3. That's it! We'll send your free PDF and other benefits to your email directly

Part 1: The Basics of PyCharm

This part introduces the readers to PyCharm and offers a detailed walkthrough on how to download, install, and get started on using PyCharm for their Python projects.

This part has the following chapters:

- *Chapter 1, Introduction to PyCharm, the most popular IDE for Python*
- *Chapter 2, Installation and Configuration*

1

Introduction to PyCharm – the Most Popular IDE for Python

Welcome to the second edition of *Hands-On Application Development with PyCharm*! Most programmers have the objective to build robust, high-quality software that can stand the test of time. The most important step to reach this goal is choosing the correct language. With so many languages out there, which is the best one to choose? A stellar programmer will take many things about the language into consideration. One of the most important aspects of the programming language to consider is the support tools that are necessary for the development stages. The **Python** programming language is rumored to enable great productivity compared to many other languages. Python's famous *batteries included* philosophy embodies this idea by bundling a powerful standard library, a code editor, and a debugger. Everything is built into the language's normal installer, which is available from `https://www.python.org`. There's just one small problem, at least for me – Microsoft.

I know what you're thinking. You've just mentally prepared yourself for a protracted rant from one of those **Unix/Linux** guys complaining about the big, bad evil that is Microsoft. I'm not going to do that because I'm not sure I'm a Linux guy. I mean, I do have an awful lot of cargo pants in my closet. I can't help it. They're just so roomy and you can carry all of your stuff without dragging a bag around with you. I'll also admit to having a great many T-shirts with emblems, logos, or statements that maybe only 5% of the people I encounter will understand. These T-shirts are very funny, but the only grins I get are from my colleagues. The more I think about it, I'm not a Linux guy. To me, Linux is a tool. Sometimes, it's the right one, but sometimes, it isn't. Since I'm not a Linux fanboy, that can't be the reason for my statement that Microsoft is the problem. The real reason is quite the opposite. About 30 or so years ago, Microsoft did something massively right. They created the first really good commercially available **integrated development environment** (**IDE**).

In truth, it may have been more than 30 years ago, and there may have been others before it. However, many "senior developers" in the software business today got their start with a Microsoft product called **Visual Basic** (**VB**). OK; this is the part where the language snobs sneer and hold their noses as though they were just presented with a plate of Brussels sprouts, or maybe a dirty diaper, but let's reel it back in. 30 years ago, most people rocking home computers only had a handful of options. **Beginners All-Purpose Symbolic Instruction Code** (**BASIC**) shipped with just about every computer made from 1978 forward. It was an age when not even Apple had a **graphical user interface** (**GUI**) on their **operating system** (**OS**). That didn't happen until 1983 when Apple released Lisa. We had mice, and we could create programs capable of working with pointing devices, but the OS didn't have a windowing system. They didn't need a windowing system because back then, computers could only run one program at a time.

Writing desktop software for computers that lacked OS-level support for Windows was hard. There were no **software development kits** (**SDKs**) or **application programming interfaces** (**APIs**) to handle any of the heavy lifting. Writing software was mostly an exercise in tedium. You had to write hundreds of lines of box-drawing boilerplate code in a tool that was barely better than Notepad. Then, one day in 1991, the year I graduated from the University of Oklahoma, it all changed.

Microsoft released a version of BASIC that included the ability to create **desktop GUIs** right there in the development environment. They called it *Visual Basic*. The first versions ran in **Microsoft's Disk Operating System** (**MS-DOS**), but later, we got support for Windows, Windows 2, and then Windows 3.1. Windows 3.1 was significant because that's when we got true multitasking if our PC was equipped with an 80386 processor. PCs were no longer limited to running one program at a time, and the Windows OS made mouse-driven interaction ubiquitous.

Things got interesting with VB. Instead of coding an interface, you drew the interface. The IDE included a palette of components and a window. You could draw buttons, text boxes, and anything else you needed, directly onto the window. After you drew them, you would then "wire them together" with event handlers. What you drew was what showed up when you ran the program. The VB **user interface** (**UI**) was ultimately carried over into Microsoft's Visual Studio. Even today, Visual Studio 2022 continues with the same features that were so groundbreaking in 1991. *Figure 1.1* shows the toolkit used to draw visual UIs for Windows:

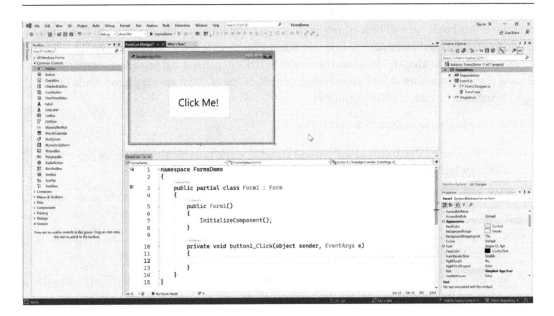

Figure 1.1: The Visual Studio IDE originated as a product called Visual Basic
in 1991. It defined the standards for what a good IDE should be

The VB3 IDE that began my career introduced even more ground-breaking features that my smug, cargo-pants-wearing Unix colleagues could only dream of. They were still fighting over vi's superiority over Emacs, or vice versa, depending on whom you asked. Meanwhile, VB3 had colored syntax highlighting, support for editing multiple files, a graphical interface editor for drawing buttons and other screen widgets, and a visual programming tool that tied code, events, and GUI elements together. It had a debugging system you could use by simply clicking a line number. Doing so would create a red dot – a breakpoint in the code where the execution would stop during a test run, allowing the developer to inspect the state of the running program. It was pure coder nerd-vana! Love them or hate them, Microsoft's VB IDEs defined what IDEs are supposed to be today. Nobody who has learned to code using a Microsoft IDE, whether it be a legacy language or a modern one, is willing to accept anything less than that experience.

With every language that I've learned since, the first thing I always do is find the very best IDE available that offers those features I can't live without. When I started working with Python 3 about six years ago, I found PyCharm. I used it to perform a full re-write on a complex **software-as-a-service (SaaS)** product, which took me about 18 months to complete. It was trial by fire. In this book, I intend to share what I learned, complete with scorch marks.

Throughout this book, we will be learning about the general interface of the PyCharm IDE, along with customizations and extensions to help you adapt your tools to the kind of work you'll be doing with Python. This first chapter discusses the merits of IDEs in general. I'll provide a comparison of the most common tools used for Python development. Some of them are very good while others, despite being widely used, are fairly primitive.

We'll cover the following main topics in this chapter:

- The purpose of PyCharm as a Python IDE and some notable details on its developing company, JetBrains

- The usage of PyCharm within the community and a breakdown of which professions tend to utilize PyCharm the most

- A comprehensive outline regarding the advantages and disadvantages of using PyCharm, in comparison to other Python editors/IDEs

- The differences between the Professional and Community editions of PyCharm and the additional functionalities that the paid edition offers

On the other hand, if you have already decided that PyCharm is the Python IDE for you, feel free to jump to *Chapter 2, Installing and Configuring PyCharm*, to go through the installation and registration process. If you have already downloaded and successfully set up PyCharm on your system, you might want to begin at the second section of this book, starting from *Chapter 3, Customizing Interpreters and Virtual Environments*.

Technical requirements

This chapter is introductory, so we won't be coding yet and the technical requirements are nil. It's *Chapter 1* and I know you're all fired up and ready to go and nil is boring. So, let's get moving!

First, here is what you will need to be successful with this book:

- A computer. I know! It's obvious, but I pride myself on being complete and leaving nothing to chance!

- An OS. This works best if it is installed on your computer already since we won't cover how to do that in this book. Windows, macOS, Linux – it's all the same as far as this book is concerned because PyCharm works in all three, and the UI is nearly identical in each environment.

- An installation of Python. We're going to be using Python 3 exclusively in this book. There are a few different "flavors" of Python 3 but for the most part, the plain old Python 3 from `https://www.python.org` will be fine. We'll get into those "flavors" later when we start talking about virtual environments in *Chapter 3, Customizing Interpreters and Virtual Environments*. If revision numbers give you comfort, the latest release at the time I'm writing this book is 3.11.1. The Python revision I'm using in that production SaaS app I mentioned earlier is 3.8. If your Python 3 installation is older than that, you should update it.

- At some point, a **GitHub** account might come in handy since I will be sharing the code from the book using a **Git** repository.

The continued success of Python

In the first edition of this book, the author titled this section *The recent rise of Python*. Time has passed and I'm picking up where he left off. I think it's important to point out that the *recent* rise has more or less continued since the first edition of this book was published. Python has continued to be one of the most popular and widely adopted languages for some very good reasons. One of those reasons is that Python stresses readability and uses a simple syntax. This allows newcomers to the language, and indeed to the field of software development, a quick path to success. Contrast that with the previously normal experience of forcing college and university students to learn C or C++ as their first language. These languages are terse and complicated and generally have a poor track record when it comes to developer productivity. Sure, C and C++ are powerful languages and can produce the most performant software available. However, in my experience, a language that can take you from "Hello World" to being able to produce useful software in a short period trumps the performance gains in all but the most extreme cases. **Guido van Rossum**, the creator of Python, compares the quickness of Python to other languages in his paper *OMG-DARPA-MCC Workshop on Compositional Software Architecture*. In the paper, van Rossum states that development in Python is estimated to be 3-5 times faster than that in Java, and 5-10 times faster than that in C/C++. Keeping this difference in mind, we can easily understand why Python is being so widely adopted. After all, time is money. You can find Guido van Rossum's complete essay here: `http://www.python.org/doc/essays/omg-darpa-mcc-position/`.

The comparison between Python and Java or C/C++ is a weak one since these languages are designed and used for different applications. C and C++ are used when very high performance is required. Most OSs are written in C++, as are real-time systems such as those you'd find in a Tesla automobile or modern spacecraft. It isn't necessarily fair to compare specific productivity between Python and C++ because they aren't used to make the same types of applications.

Java, on the other hand, is used to develop the same types of applications for which you might use Python: enterprise and web applications. Java, though, requires a lot of boilerplate. This means a developer has to create a lot of code and structures just to support the application's existence before they can even think about writing code for the application itself. This boilerplate is largely absent from Python. Furthermore, Java relies on a very rigid, static object-oriented paradigm. Python, in contrast, is far more flexible, offering a dynamic programming model. Even though the two languages are used to make the same type of application, Python gives you some serious shortcuts, owing to its more flexible paradigm.

These factors that comprise Python's strengths, along with many others, have coalesced to form a very accessible development language supported by a community of raving fans. That community is still growing by introducing coding to a gamut of fields and professions distinct from those of us who historically focus solely on traditional application development. At the time of writing, the **TIOBE Index**, a ranking system for the popularity of programming languages, ranks Python as the number one language, as seen in *Figure 1.2*:

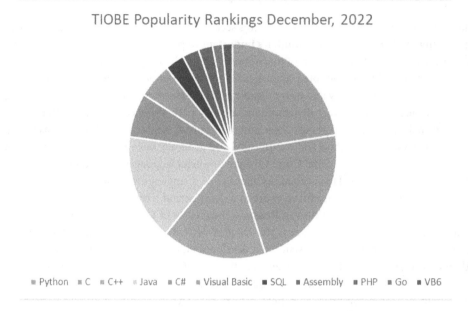

Figure 1.2: TIOBE rankings show Python to be the most popular language

Python has a huge standard library that provides anything you might need to build any kind of software you can imagine. If that statement proves false for your specific project, there is a vast third-party and largely open source ecosystem consisting of hundreds of thousands of libraries upon which you can build. You can find a catalog of these libraries at `https://pypi.org`. Taking all this together, a new software developer can go from idea and zero Python experience to a production application very quickly. This process can be greatly accelerated by a good IDE.

The philosophy of IDEs

Back when I was your age, things were different. That is, of course, unless we are the same age, in which case everything was the same. We didn't have the internet. When we wanted to learn new coding languages and techniques or understand the history of our craft, we were required to take a sacred pilgrimage. One year, I smuggled in a Polaroid. You can see the pictures I took in *Figure 1.3*. You should understand that all of what I am about to tell you is both true and a closely guarded industry secret. Just so we're clear, you didn't hear this from me.

Hidden somewhere in a mystic range of mountains, seekers of great coding wisdom would ascend the 10,000 stairs by the light of the full moon in search of the Master. The journey was not easy, and the wisdom imparted had to be hard-earned. It was on one such crusade that I learned why good IDEs are so important. The Master said, "If you know the language, and you know the IDE, you need not fear the result of a hundred deployments."

Figure 1.3: High in the sacred mountains, up the 10,000 stairs, lies the monastery where I learned to code

The Master often speaks in riddles, so let me explain. *Deployment* refers to a published iteration or an **increment** of your software. In most professional circumstances, the objective is to publish your software. If our objective is to publish, the next sticking point is that we must know a programming language. I assume you have at least a tacit understanding of programming in Python. That just leaves the Master's reference to the IDE.

There are several classes of tools a developer might use to develop Python code. The Python language can be considered an interpreted language. We could argue that when it runs, some of the code is optimized into C code and cached, but at this stage, we aren't worried about that level of detail. The point is that a Python program exists as simple plain text files and can be executed in that form. Contrast this with statically compiled languages such as C, C++, C#, Java, or Go. Those and many other languages require the code in the text files to undergo a compilation phase where a new executable file is produced. In C#, you can't simply execute a .cs file. You need to compile it into a binary, then execute the binary. Since Python executes its code directly via the Python interpreter, the level of tooling needed to work on Python can be very simple. Essentially, any text editor will do. There are three levels of editor capability to choose from.

The first is a simple text editor. Simple text editors are generally limited to opening, editing, and saving text. They are generic tools designed to work with any kind of text file, from grocery lists to `systemd` configurations. In Windows, you might know it as *Notepad*. On a Mac, you might use *TextPad*, and if you are rocking a Linux desktop such as **Ubuntu**, you'll easily find *Text Editor*. If you are not a fan of GUIs on your OS, then you have no doubt heard of editors such as vi, vim (vi improved), Emacs, and nano. All these programs fall into the category of simple text editors. If you're not sure what a `systemd` configuration is, don't sweat it; it's a system administration file on Linux. I just needed something that sounded complicated to characterize the more complex end of the text file gamut.

The second evolution of programming editors is called *enhanced editors*. These editors are purposefully designed to work with technical files. Some popular examples include the following:

- Visual Studio Code
- Atom
- Notepad++
- UltraEdit
- Sublime Text
- JetBrains Fleet
- Bluefish Editor
- IDLE (the editor that ships with Python)

These tools are designed to work with a wide range of programming languages and can generally be easily customized to add support for emerging languages. Enhanced editors offer some common features that make a developer's life a little nicer, such as these:

- Syntax highlighting, which color codes keywords and other semantic elements in your code.
- Macros, which allow the developer to record and play back common keystrokes
- Project and file organization to allow easy switching between multiple files that make up a project
- Rudimentary code completion to reduce the amount of typing needed to write your code
- Plugin support for other niceties such as linters, spell checkers, file previews for your code, and more

Over time, some of these enhanced editors have become very robust because you can customize and expand their capabilities. When you consider these tools as they are right out of the box, they are more useful and specialized than general text editors, but they fall short of qualifying as IDEs.

At the top of the code editor food chain is the **IDE**. If you were to look inside the cockpit of a fighter plane from the World War I era, you'd see a few simple controls and nothing more. If that's a text editor, the IDE is the cockpit of a Boeing 747 aircraft. Every tool a developer could ever desire or need is crammed into a comparably complex UI. IDEs contain all the features of an enhanced text editor, but usually offer the following additional enhancements:

- Some easy ways to run your code right from the editor.

- Tooling to help manage your source code repository, such as **Git** or **Subversion**.

- An integrated, easy-to-use debugger, which allows you to pause the execution of a running program and inspect or alter its current state.

- Tools to help you write automated tests such as unit tests and run and visualize the results.

- Complex code completion is based on the introspection or indexing of the code in your project. In modern IDEs, this is enhanced using **artificial intelligence (AI)**.

- Profiling tools to help you find execution bottlenecks.

- Integrated tooling to help with supplementary systems, such as databases.

- Tools for deploying your code to a server or cloud environment right from the IDE.

Some popular examples of IDEs include the following:

- Visual Studio (this is different from Visual Studio Code)

- PyCharm

- IntelliJ IDEA

- NetBeans

- Apple Xcode

- Xamarin Studio

- Eclipse

As you can see, the IDE is the most powerful weapon in your coding arsenal. It is important to use the best one available to you. If you are new to software development, or maybe even not-so-new, you might wonder why the enhanced editors are so popular. At the time of writing, roughly 50% of developers use Visual Studio Code, which is not on my list of IDEs.

Many developers prefer a more "lightweight" development environment. This is especially true of frontend web developers who swear by Sublime Text and Visual Studio Code. In truth, they need all the features of the IDE, and they use them, but they are spread out across different tools they use throughout the day. A frontend developer relies on profilers and debuggers that run in web browsers and they don't need those tools in an IDE. Instead, they can get a simpler editor that downloads quickly, installs simply, and runs instantly when they click the icon in their OS.

I submit that if you are doing full stack web development or mobile development, or you need to work servers or containers, an IDE is a better choice.

There exists a certain class of software developer who swears you should never use anything other than the simplest possible tools. They believe that reliance on a tool to do coding and related hard work diminishes the overall mastery and accomplishment needed to be considered proficient. I couldn't disagree more. One year, while at the monastery, the Master told me a story of a great swordsman from Japan named Miyamoto Musashi. In his day, every samurai knew of Musashi as the greatest living swordsman and all the samurai wanted to take a shot at defeating him. Back then, duels were usually fought to the death. One day, a dueling challenger met Musashi as he was getting off a boat. Musashi was unarmed. The challenger waited until Musashi could fashion a wooden sword, called a *bokken*, from one of the boat's oars, which he intended to use in the dual. Legend has it Musashi made a fool of that challenger and left him alive, much to the challenger's disgrace. Musashi, the Master said, was the finest warrior who ever lived, and his skill with a sword has never since been matched. However, if the objective were simply to defeat him, I could have easily done so with a machine gun.

In my opinion, limiting the tools you use owing to a sense of pride in your capability, or lack thereof, is foolish. The objective of a software developer is to ship software, usually on an unforgiving deadline. It isn't to waste time trying to prove yourself to someone else's standards, unless, of course, you're a degree-seeking student. I'm sure there are a few of you reading this book. Play the game and do what your professors say. You should realize that once you graduate, everything changes. You will be expected to produce code quickly, accurately, and consistently. This is best achieved via the automation available in a good IDE. You should choose the best tool for the job at hand. I found PyCharm helped me to become productive while I was learning the Python language. When you start, and you're not using an editor that corrects your line spacing and indents, you're going to make a lot of silly mistakes. It's frustrating. I'd think to myself, "If I were using C#, I'd be done by now." I was even tempted to abandon Python and PyCharm for something more comfortable. However, that's not what I wanted to do.

PyCharm will underline all those silly mistakes for you and correct them with the touch of a button! I learned, after seeing those mistakes underlined over and over, what to do when I'm using an editor without code inspection. Today, when I am working in other languages, I still use Python rules. Having learned Python with the help of PyCharm, I was able to ship faster, learn faster, and improve my code in other languages and tools. Do me a favor and never let anybody tell you you're not a *real developer* because you didn't do something their way. If they persist, tell them nano is better than vi or Emacs, and just walk away. Such a statement will probably cause their head to explode.

I'd like to make one more comment about Visual Studio Code. This editor has evolved through plugins to the point where it can compete with a fully featured IDE. However, this comes at a cost compared to a professionally developed IDE such as PyCharm. To get the identical features you'd find in PyCharm in Visual Studio Code, you'd need to install a large number of plugins. These plugins are all written by the community, which means they are all independent development efforts. These plugins will never work as cohesively as the base features you will find in an IDE such as PyCharm. This is also true when comparing Visual Studio with Visual Studio Code. Try creating a C# project in Visual

Studio versus Visual Studio Code and you'll find the process is dreamy and smooth in Visual Studio. Visual Studio Code, on the other hand, requires a lot of command-line work and lots of weird plugin installations. The experience just isn't the same. The same observation holds with other editors such as vim, which can be heavily customized. You'll spend a week messing with plugins and open source scripts to achieve, at best, partial parity with an IDE's out-of-the-box functionality.

PyCharm as a Python IDE

It's all well and good to talk about tool comparisons common to other languages. But we don't care about that, do we? We want to know our options for Python! The best IDEs are typically specialized. PyCharm is specialized in working with Python. That's it. When you create a new project in PyCharm, you'll see options for Python projects and nothing else. Contrast this experience with Visual Studio. In my opinion, Visual Studio is the only close competitor to PyCharm when it comes to working with Python projects. When a project is created in Visual Studio, you will most likely spend a good five minutes trying to wade through the myriad of options. The IDE supports dozens of languages, and that is compounded by a dozen project types such as web, desktop, and others. Visual Studio is trying to be all things to all developers. PyCharm only wants to play with Python developers.

PyCharm itself was created with a few design goals in mind:

- Intelligent coding assistance
- Streamlined programming tools
- Web development options
- Scientific computing support
- Visual debugging and performance profiling

We'll take a look at each of these design goals in turn, but first, I need to point something out. At the time I'm writing this, PyCharm is about to go through a big change. JetBrains is working on a brand-new user experience. By the time this book is published, there is a strong chance that this new UI will be the default. If you're new to PyCharm, you should understand that you're going to see it in two different ways for a while. The classic UI will continue to be available in the product for a time, allowing us to ease into the new experience. I've decided I'm going to embrace the new UI given the time between the first edition and this one is a few years. That said, it bears mentioning that you're going to see the classic UI alongside the new UI until probably late 2024 when the old UI is no longer maintained. It will become deprecated and one day will disappear into the sands of time like Shelley's fabled statue of Ozymandias:

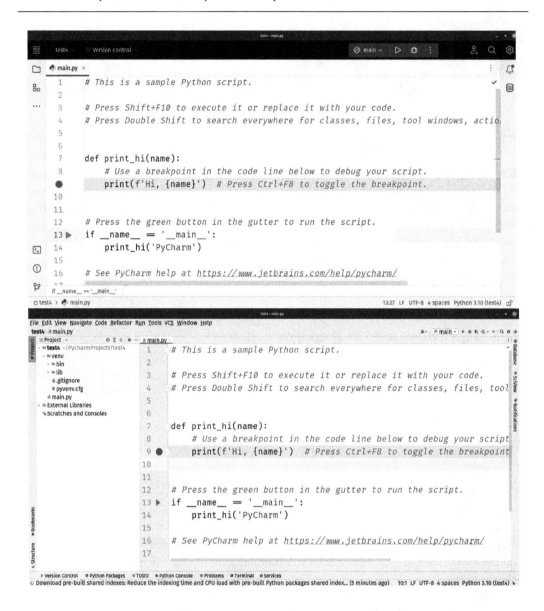

Figure 1.4: The new UI (top) compared to the classic UI (bottom)

Figure 1.4 shows the two UIs side by side. The design objective of the new UI is to reduce the clutter in the interface. They're not wrong on that point. As the tool has grown over the years, more and more features have been crammed into the menus, making the UI a little bit daunting for new users. The biggest thing to realize is that most of the things you'd find in the menu are still there, but the menu system itself is hidden beneath the hamburger icon in the top-left corner of the screen. Don't worry;

I'll cover this in detail later. As I write this, there is a setting we'll review in *Chapter 2, Installing and Configuring PyCharm*, that allows you to toggle between the classic and new UIs.

I wanted to point this out now because you're about to see some screenshots, and if you've seen the old UI, you might think you've picked up the wrong book. You haven't. Just the opposite. If I time this right, you'll be the only one with the right book.

Intelligent coding assistance

I'm going to tell you something my wife says all the time. I'm very lazy. Wait. That came out wrong. She is saying that I'm lazy. I'm not saying that she is saying she is lazy. Sheesh. Writing is hard! I almost dug a hole there, didn't I?

She's not wrong. As a developer, I am essentially very lazy. I refuse to spend hours or even minutes doing something the long way. The Greeks had a legend about a guy named Sisyphus who was cursed to push a stone up a steep hill. As soon as he reached the top, the stone would roll back down the hill. Sisyphus was stuck in an infinite loop with no *Cmd/Ctrl + C* option on his keyboard.

Here's one thing I know: Sisyphus was not a software developer! Any software developer would have rolled that stone exactly twice, after which they would have spent eternity devising a system of pulleys and cranes controlled by an IoT device. Naturally, the microcontroller would be running a Python script. I digress.

What *some* (I say in my head looking in my unsuspecting wife's direction) might call lazy, I call *efficient*! As a developer, I want to create maximum effect with minimal effort in everything I do. Writing code is complicated. You are writing instructions for the most stubborn and unintelligent object ever devised. Coding is worse than trying to teach a 2-year-old to tie their shoes. Trust me, I've done both! Coders must be extremely specific and verbose in their explanation of any operations they want to perform. Furthermore, things are made worse by the language developers out there who tend to want to force users to write a bunch of boilerplate code. I'm talking about the excise code that has nothing to do with the code you want to write or the problem you want to solve. Python generally avoids this, so let me give an example of possibly the worst offender: Java.

Back in the day when I was a wee lad, Java was all the rage. There was this caste of corporate programmers involved with Java who thought up something called **Enterprise Java Beans (EJBs)**. EJBs were supposed to be the epitome of module programming with reusable objects. It was an absolute beating to implement. Rather than simply making a class, which is all you need, you had to create a special file structure with various folders and manifest files to expose what was in the bean, and it was all compiled into a special format. It turned out that the special format was nothing more than a ZIP file. It took a lot of work just to make an EJB, which meant developers had to make a ton of files and write a lot of code just to get started on the functionality they needed to express to get their work done. That's what we mean by *boilerplate*. Boilerplate is generally useless but necessary because, without it, the code doesn't work.

All IDEs have evolved because of this phenomenon. PyCharm evolved from JetBrains' Java IDE, IntelliJ. Python doesn't usually have a lot of boilerplate required for your code to work, but it does come up. There are two kinds of boilerplate. The boilerplate needed to make old-school EJBs work is the bad kind. The boilerplate generated as a means to jumpstart your project is the good kind. As we'll see, PyCharm, as with most IDEs, generates a folder structure, a set of files, and some basic code to get you started. That can be considered boilerplate. But in this case, that code isn't retained. It is replaced by the real code for your project. The code generated by the IDE is just a mental prompt to get you going. It prevents you from having to create your project's starting point by hand.

All this is great, but boilerplate code generation isn't what we usually think about when we hear "intelligent coding assistance." We usually think of the feature pioneered by Microsoft called **IntelliSense**. If you'll allow me to anthropomorphize the IDE for a moment, this feature watches as you type your code. All the while, the IDE is thinking about what you're trying to do. When it sees a way it can help, such as by completing a word or line for you automatically, it presents that as an option. I have an intelligent person completing all my sentences for me: she's my wife. When she completes my sentences for me, they are usually more organized and intelligent than they would have been if I were on my own. (This might be another reason she thinks I'm lazy.)

I want to point out that not all tools with an IntelliSense-like feature are created equally. When you see this feature in an enhanced editor, it usually works differently than it would in an IDE. In enhanced editors, they use keyword lists to highlight and autocomplete the elements of a language. Really good enhanced editors might index your code and recognize variable and function names and use statistics to give you the most likely completion first. That option is generally followed by a long list of noise comprising every possibility that exists for a given completion. Code completion is becoming very advanced with the introduction of AI tools, and this makes the difference between IDEs and enhanced editors a little muddier, at least on this point. Tools such as GitHub's Copilot can not only autocomplete variable names and keywords but also write entire sections of your code automatically.

It is important to remember, at least as I write this, that those AI features are not part of the IDE or enhanced editor. They are implemented as plugins. Since this is true, I'll continue espousing the merits of IDEs, and PyCharm in particular, based solely on the merits of the software by itself. We'll discuss plugins in *Chapter 16, More Possibilities with PyCharm Plugins*.

While enhanced editors might present you with a long list of possibilities for your code completion, PyCharm can analyze your code and perform more intelligent autocompletion. You also get code analysis, such as duplicate code warnings. A common antipattern in software development is copying and pasting code across or even within the same project. It's a terrible but common thing to see. PyCharm will spot duplicate code and flag it for you so that you can be reminded to refactor the duplicated code into a function or module that can be reused and maintained in one location.

PyCharm can also perform a static analysis of your code. This type of analysis is looking for antipatterns within the code itself; for example, PyCharm will detect dead code like that shown in *Figure 1.5*. Concerning Python development, PyCharm will automatically format your indentations and give you critical feedback on how your code conforms to **PEP-8** conventions, which are stylistic requirements you must meet to be considered *pythonic* (that's a good thing).

For example, if you were to type the following code into a new file in PyCharm, you'd see PyCharm's warning that you have created unreachable code on line 13. The text on that line is highlighted. Hovering your mouse over this highlighted line reveals what is wrong:

```python
def print_hi(name):
    print(f'Hi, {name}')
    for x in range(25):
        print(str(x))
        if x == 12:
            return
        print("You'll never make it here")


if __name__ == '__main__':
    print_hi('PyCharm')
```

The `print_hi` function starts innocuously enough by printing to the console whatever is passed into the function within the `name` argument. After that, we create a loop that will run 25 times. On each run of the loop, we print out x, which contains the current iteration. When the counter variable, x, reaches 12, the loop exits via the `return` function, which, as luck has it, is on line 12. I assure you, this is purely a coincidence. Since the loop returns on line 12, the code on line 13 will never be reached:

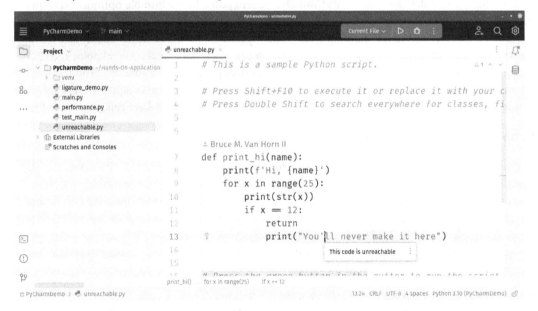

Figure 1.5: PyCharm will highlight many common coding mistakes such as this one. The code on line 13 is unreachable, which is indicated when you hover your mouse over the highlighted code

PyCharm also allows you to navigate between files in a complex project by helping you find where functions, variables, and classes are defined, as well as where they are used. Over time, you'll learn a set of keystrokes that will allow you to move anywhere in your project without your fingers leaving the keyboard.

In essence, PyCharm's intelligent coding assistance allows you to worry less about mistakes and more about your logic and requirements, which allows you to complete your code more quickly with fewer mistakes.

Streamlined programming tools

Writing code is but one activity a developer performs each day in pursuit of a project deadline. Great developers also spend time debugging, testing, and profiling their products to produce the best possible result. We also need to deal with pushing code to testing servers, refactoring (other people's) bad code, working with databases, and dealing with containers. There is tooling in PyCharm for each of these processes and more. When I write complicated web applications in PyCharm, the only tools I usually have open are PyCharm and a web browser: two tools each on their own monitor.

The PyCharm debugger

My favorite feature and the one that got me excited the first time I used PyCharm is the debugger. PyCharm's debugger is great. It is much better than the standard debugger you get with Python itself. Python ships with a debugger called **Python Debugger** (**pdb**). In my humble opinion, I'd rather eat bugs off the sidewalk than use this tool. I alluded to this earlier in this chapter. I grew up using Microsoft debuggers and simply nothing else will do. PyCharm's debugger works exactly as I would expect. Click your mouse at the line where you want execution to stop to make a breakpoint and click the debug button in the IDE, and the program runs and stops at the indicated line. You will get a screen where you can inspect both the state of the stack as well as the terminal output. It's very simple to use, and I'll be showing you how to do so in *Chapter 6, Seamless Testing, Debugging, and Profiling*.

Running tests with the graphical test runner

Testing tools are integrated in the form of test runners. PyCharm supports all the major testing frameworks, including **pytest**, **nose**, and the regular unit test features from the standard library. Again, I'm coming from experiencing some very good IDEs, and in this case, I'm remembering Eclipse and Visual Studio, which both include graphical test runners. The adage *If the bar is green, the code is clean* is visually implemented in PyCharm. You can see an example in *Figure 1.6*. You can run your tests and see a list display showing what passed and what failed, though it is a list rather than a bar. You can then rerun your failing tests until they work.

I'll give you a simple example. In `main.py` within this chapter's source code, I have one file called `main.py` and another called `test_main.py`. The content of `main.py` is a simple function that adds two numbers together:

```python
def add_two_numbers(a: int, b: int) -> int:
    return a + b
```

Within the `test_main.py` file, there is a simple unit test:

```python
from unittest import TestCase
from main import add_two_numbers

class Test(TestCase):
    def test_add_two_numbers(self):
        self.assertTrue(add_two_numbers(a=5, b=6) == 11, \
            "Should be 11")

    def test_show_a_fail(self):
        self.fail()
```

The `Test` class contains two tests: one that will pass and one that will automatically fail. I usually make the automatically failing test first just to make sure I have my test class set up properly. Then, later, I remove the fail because of my dopamine addiction, which is only satisfied by green checkmarks in the test runner, as seen in *Figure 1.6*. If I right-click on `test_main.py`, as seen in *Figure 1.5*, I'll get an option to run the tests within the file:

Figure 1.6: Right-click the test_main.py file and click Run 'Python tests in test...' to run the unit tests contained within the file

Look to the lower-left corner in *Figure 1.7*, which shows the test run's completion, and you'll see a list of tests that passed or failed with either a green check or a yellow X showing failure. Like all figures in this book, which are printed in black and white, you won't see the colors. Color ink is expensive, and your father is right, money doesn't grow on trees:

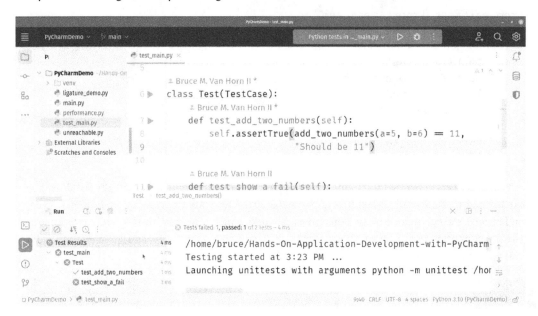

Figure 1.7: PyCharm's built-in test runner shows a traditional pass/
fail list (lower-left pane) to indicate passing and failing tests

PyCharm's profiling tools

Similarly, code profiling is built in and easy to use. You can click the **Profile** button to run the code. When the program exits, you will get a graph of each function call, along with the time and resources consumed by the call. This makes it easy to spot unrealized opportunities for improvement concerning the speed of execution and resource consumption.

Consider the possibility that you have an algorithm in your program that might not be performing as you'd like. I know, I know, it would never happen to you, so supposed you just got hired, and the person they fired wrote this horribly performing algorithm. Maybe pretend it is 1956, and the guy who got fired from your new employer, New York Life Insurance Company, was one **Edward Harry Friend**. Friend wrote a paper titled *Sorting on Electronic Computer Systems*, which is likely the first published instance of an algorithm we know today as **bubble sort**. If Friend had written his algorithm in Python 3, it might look a little like this:

```
def bubble_sort(input_array):
    length_of_array = len(input_array)
```

Friend has just created a function that accepts a list as an argument, which in our case will be an array of integers. The objective is to sort these numbers. To do this, let's create two loops, one inside the other:

```
for i in range(length_of_array):
    for j in range(0, length_of_array - i - 1):
        if input_array[j] > input_array[j + 1]:
            input_array[j], input_array[j + 1] = \
            input_array[j + 1], input_array[j]
```

Within these loops, each number is compared with the number before it. If it is determined those two numbers are out of order, they are swapped. In the next run of the loop, this happens again with the next two numbers, and this continues until it reaches the end of the list.

If you've studied algorithms at all, you've probably heard of bubble sort, and you've been warned as to why it is not used. It is very slow. We have a `for` loop within another `for` loop, which is fine if the size of your unsorted list is small. But this algorithm slows down at a logarithmic rate as the list of numbers grows. Algorithm performance is measured using **big O notation**. I don't want to turn this into an algorithm book, so I'll just tell you that a loop inside another loop will scale poorly in terms of performance. In big O notation, we classify this algorithm as $O(n^2)$. That's bad.

In plain English, this means that if you double the count of numbers to sort (n), then your algorithm will take 2^2 or 4 times longer to process. If you multiply your count's size by 5, then it becomes 5^2 or 25 times slower. The bigger the list, the slower it sorts.

To show off the performance tool, we're going to give this test run a list of 100,000 numbers to sort. Now is a good time to point out I'm running an Intel i9 processor. If you're a student or some other budget-constrained consumer rocking an i3 processor (or worse), you might want to take the list of numbers down a few zeros if you want to try this out. It takes a good while on my i9:

```
test_array = []
for x in range(100000):
    test_array.append(random.randint(1, 10000))
```

Let's finish the test code by calling the function and printing the results:

```
bubble_sort(test_array)
print("The result of the sort is:")
for i in range(len(test_array)):
    print(test_array[i])
```

We'll cover the profiling tool extensively in *Chapter 6, Seamless Testing, Debugging, and Profiling*, but for now, let's just run this code with the profiler and review the result. To run the profiler on the `performance.py` file, simply right-click the file and click **More Run/Debug**, then **Profile 'performance'**, as shown in *Figure 1.8*:

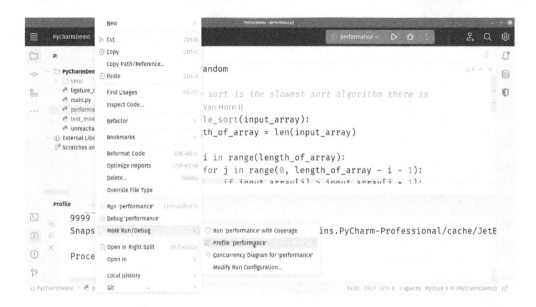

Figure 1.8: Right-click the file you'd like to profile and click More Run/
Debug | Profile 'performance' to see a performance profile

Remember, if you use the same code I did, this will take a long time to run, especially on a slower computer. Feel free to adjust the size of the list downward if it's taking too long to run. The result is a `.pstat` file that displays as a table in PyCharm. Again, we'll cover this more extensively in *Chapter 6, Seamless Testing, Debugging, and Profiling*. You can see the performance report in *Figure 1.9*:

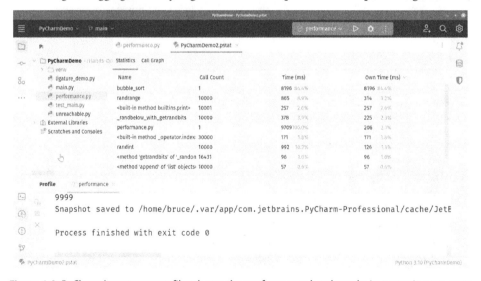

Figure 1.9: PyCharm's resource profiler shows the performance bottlenecks in a running program

As you can see, 84.4% of the program's time is spent in the `bubble_sort` function, which is the bottleneck. PyCharm has told you where to concentrate your refactoring efforts to improve the performance of your program.

Publishing from the IDE

When you need to publish your code to a testing server, and you aren't using a continuous integration system for that, you can use PyCharm. To be clear, you should use a continuous integration system, but I often use the PyCharm features early in a project before the continuous integration system is operational to get code up for stakeholders to play with. You can deploy using **file transfer protocol (FTP)** or **secure file transfer protocol (SFTP)**, or copy directly to a network share for a quick and easy way to share your progress with anyone who might want to review it.

Refactoring tools

PyCharm has robust refactoring tools you'd expect from a proper IDE. If you want to change a variable name, or even a method signature on a function, right-click and select the **Refactor** tool. Rest assured the changes you make will carry over to all related instances in your project, not just in the file you are editing. *Figure 1.10* shows an example of this in action:

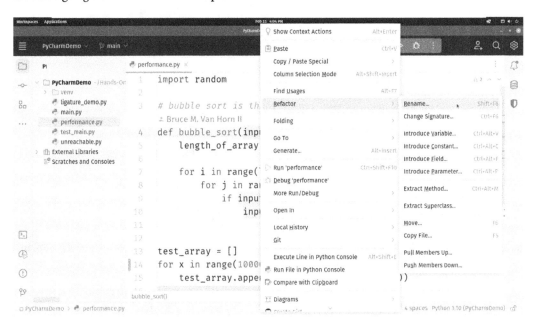

Figure 1.10: PyCharm has a full selection of refactoring tools available

In addition to renaming a variable or function, there are other actions you can perform, such as changing the method signature and changing the structure of your object-oriented classes.

Working with databases in PyCharm

If you work with databases, the Professional edition of PyCharm includes a graphical table editor and SQL support for dozens of popular databases. Check it out in *Figure 1.11*. I'll talk more about the Professional edition of PyCharm a little later in this chapter; we'll have a whole chapter on the database features in *Chapter 11, Understanding Database Management with PyCharm*:

Figure 1.11: PyCharm has a robust and complete set of tools for working with relational databases such as Oracle, SQL Server, Postgres, and many more

As you can see, a great many relational and NoSQL databases are directly supported.

Remote development, containers, and virtual machines

Finally, but not exhaustively, PyCharm has features for working with remote systems via **SSH**, local virtual machines using HashiCorp's **Vagrant**, and extensive support for **Docker** containers.

This isn't an exhaustive list of what PyCharm can do for you, but by now, you get the point. Every tool you might need is integrated into the development environment. That's probably why they called it an *integrated development environment*.

Web development options

I'd wager that more than half the developers working in Python need, at some point, a web project. Whether you're like me and you're making a SaaS offering as a fully realized web application, or you are doing rocket science and you need a way to visualize and interactively share your latest fast-Fourier transform on deep space radio emissions data, web projects are usually inevitable. I'm not a scientist and I made that up. If the last sentence made sense to anyone, it was pure coincidence.

Working with web projects offers a new and separate layer of complexity. Most use three-tier designs commonly expressed with the **model-view-controller** (**MVC**) pattern. If you're not sure what this means, stay tuned because there's a whole section of this book dedicated to web development. For now, this means the application has a frontend where the user can interact, a middle tier containing connective logic, and a database tier for structured data storage and retrieval. Only the middle tier is done in Python. We'll extensively cover web development in later chapters, but for now, I want to tell you about the level of tooling you get with PyCharm.

The company that made PyCharm, JetBrains, makes a variety of IDEs targeted at different languages. One of their IDEs is specifically targeted toward web development. It is called **WebStorm**. I said earlier that good IDEs target one language. WebStorm targets JavaScript; specifically, we're talking about full stack JavaScript. Modern JavaScript execution occurs in two places. Traditionally, JavaScript was always executed in the browser. About 10 years ago, **Node.js** was released and JavaScript was released from the confines of the browser window and allowed to run on the backend.

Earlier, I alluded to a robust set of features in PyCharm for working with databases. JetBrains also has an IDE that targets SQL database developers called **DataGrip**. As it happens, the Professional edition of PyCharm includes the entire feature set available in WebStorm and DataGrip. When you buy the Professional edition, you're getting three JetBrains products in one package: PyCharm, WebStorm, and DataGrip. When you use PyCharm to work on web projects, you need all three feature sets and they are there for you in the Professional edition.

Scientific computing support

The growth of the data science field has played an important role in the growth of Python itself, and Python is now the most common programming tool used in scientific projects (even more common than **R**). Notable functionalities included in PyCharm that facilitate data science work are the integration of **IPython**, **Jupyter** notebooks, and an interactive console. The support for scientific computing in PyCharm is detailed in section four of this book, starting from *Chapter 13*, *Turning On Scientific Mode*. PyCharm also provides a customized view that optimally organizes workspaces in a scientific project called **SciView**, which is shown in *Figure 1.12*:

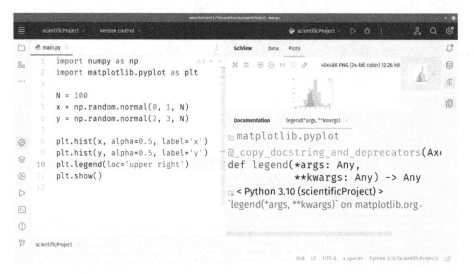

Figure 1.12: SciView in PyCharm grants access to scientific visualization tools via a slick interface

Understanding the Professional, Community, and Educational editions

There are three editions to PyCharm. I've alluded to two, because the third is a special version that is only useful to teachers, and the focus of this book is application development, not software development instruction. I'll tell you about each, but I know what you want is a feature comparison chart. You'll find it in *Figure 1.13*:

	PyCharm Professional	PyCharm Community
Cost	Paid	Free
Intelligent Python editor	✓	✓
Graphical debugger and test runner	✓	✓
Code navigation and refactor tools	✓	✓
Code inspection	✓	✓
Git, Subversion, and other source control tools	✓	✓

Scientific tools	✓	
Web development with HTML, JavaScript, CSS, and so on	✓	
Python web framework support	✓	
Performance profiling	✓	
Remote development, containers, and so on	✓	
Database and SQL support	✓	

Figure 1.13: A feature comparison chart showing the features contained in
the free Community edition versus the paid Professional version

The **Community edition** is free but only offers a limited set of features compared to the Professional edition. It is perfect for working on projects that only entail working with Python. The product I work on has a set of Python scripts that batch-process large amounts of data. Everything happens in Python and this is the perfect use case for the Community edition. If all you need is a terrific Python IDE, use the free version. The Community edition is also perfect if you are just working on automation scripts, such as graphics pipelines for 3D computer graphics, or general IT task automation.

The **Professional edition** has all the features of the free version but adds web development, database, remote development, containerization, and scientific project types. This is aimed at professionals who produce publishable software projects. While it is not free, JetBrains is pretty good about keeping it affordable with several pricing options, depending on how you are using the tool. Solo developers may obtain licenses at a lower price point than corporate developers. There are also ways to get the Professional edition free of charge, such as proving that you are using PyCharm on a **fully open source software** (FOSS) project. Start-up companies might be eligible for a 50% discount, and if you're teaching in a code boot camp or a university setting, you may also qualify for free professional licenses. Since these things can fluctuate over time, you should check the JetBrains website for full details at `https://www.jetbrains.com/pycharm/`.

I said earlier there are three editions of PyCharm, and we've only covered two. The **Educational edition** is aimed at teachers and university professors developing curricula to teach Python. This edition can create and play back interactive lessons right in the IDE. It is only valuable to teachers, instructors, and content creators.

In this book, I will focus on the features present in the Community edition and the Professional edition.

Summary

In this chapter, we introduced the Python language itself, as well as the background behind Python IDEs in general and, specifically, PyCharm.

We also discussed the usability of PyCharm for Python programmers. Specifically, to be able to take full advantage of all the features and functionalities that PyCharm offers without becoming too dependent on the IDE, a programmer should first master the fundamentals of the Python language and its core syntax. We also looked at comparisons between PyCharm itself and various other Python editors/IDEs and the reason why PyCharm is considered the best development environment of them all.

Finally, we compared the two editions of PyCharm that are available for download: the paid Professional edition and the free Community edition. If you are working with large, complex projects with many moving parts, including database management, web development languages, and viewability in scientific reports, then you will most likely benefit from using the Professional edition.

In the next chapter, you will learn how to download PyCharm, set it up on your system, and configure its environment for your Python projects. This will serve as the first step in getting started with PyCharm, after which we will start discussing the specific features PyCharm offers that this book covers.

Questions

Answer the following questions to test your knowledge of this chapter:

1. Programmers typically develop their code with an editor or an IDE. What is the difference between the two, and which one is PyCharm?

2. Why might some think that an IDE for Python development might be inappropriate or unnecessary?

3. What are some key features of PyCharm? Of those features, which give PyCharm an edge over other editors/IDEs?

4. What advantage does PyCharm have over editors such as Visual Studio Code or vim, which can be configured to perform many of the same features offered by PyCharm?

5. What are the three editions of PyCharm? What are the key differences between them?

Further reading

Be sure to check out the companion website for this book at `http://pycharm-book.com`. To learn more about the topics that were covered in this chapter, take a look at the following resources:

- Friend, Edward H. *Sorting on Electronic Computer Systems. Journal of the ACM (JACM)* 3.3 (1956): 134-168.

- Nguyen, Quan. *Hands-On Application Development with PyCharm: Accelerate your Python applications using practical coding techniques in PyCharm.* Packt Publishing Ltd, 2019.

- Shelley, Percy B. *Ozymandias.* `https://www.poetryfoundation.org/poems/46565/ozymandias`.

- Wikipedia contributors. (2022, December 19). *Bubble sort.* Wikipedia. `https://en.wikipedia.org/wiki/Bubble_sort`.

2

Installing and Configuring PyCharm

In the previous chapter, we looked at the most popular features of PyCharm and considered not only what makes PyCharm a great IDE but also what makes any IDE historically great. There is a base set of features we as developers need in order to be truly productive. In this chapter, we'll turn our focus toward installing PyCharm. You may be thinking that you simply download and install it. You can do that, but there are different ways to install PyCharm that you might like better. There are also different options based on your operating system.

Aside from the simple act of downloading the installer, running it, and mashing the next button until the installer's dialog boxes go away, there are other considerations for getting the tool properly installed and working. PyCharm is highly customizable, and you are presented with some of those customization options as soon as the program runs for the first time. Some of these options are interesting, and some of them can be troublesome if you're just picking every option and every customization during the process.

Here's what you can look forward to in this chapter:

- Downloading JetBrains Toolbox and using it to install and manage PyCharm. This is my recommended method of installation because you get an easy way to handle upgrades and uninstall. You can even install and manage several versions of PyCharm should you ever need to.

- We'll run PyCharm for the first time and go through the customization options the software presents on the first run. Naturally, you can change these at any time, and we'll cover that too.

- We'll clone this book's repository from GitHub using PyCharm's integrated **version control system (VCS)** tools.

Technical requirements

To be successful in this chapter, you will need the following:

- A computer. Just in case you missed this particular gag in *Chapter 1*, I pride myself on being complete and leaving nothing to chance! The computer should meet the following system requirements for PyCharm:

  - 64-bit versions of Microsoft Windows 8 or higher, macOS 10.14 or higher, or Linux running GNOME or KDE desktop.

  - The official system requirements list 4 GB RAM as the minimum and 8 GB as recommended. If you intend to do non-trivial work, and you're thinking about specs on a new computer, I wouldn't buy less than 16 GB RAM, and I'd prefer 32 GB. The lighter specs are just those needed to run PyCharm. Most developers run more than the IDE.

  - 2.5 GB hard disk space; SSD recommended. Again, that's PyCharm's low-end recommendation. If you're shopping, get an NVMe drive rather than an SSD. The performance is usually 10x greater and the cost is easily affordable.

  - 1,024 X 768 minimum screen resolution. That's the low-end specification, and it's a joke. You won't get much done on a screen that size, and even cheap computers today can easily support 1,920 X 1,080. For professional work, you really want 4K if possible, or failing that two (or more) 1,920 X 1,080 monitors. The more screen real estate you have, the more productive you will be with any IDE. On a 4K monitor, I can have PyCharm showing me my project explorer, two open code windows side by side, the database explorer, and a terminal session.

- An operating system. This works best if it is installed on your computer already since we don't cover how to do that in this book. Windows, macOS, Linux—it's all the same as far as this book is concerned because PyCharm works in all three environments, and the UI is nearly identical in each environment.

- A connection to the internet.

- An installation of Python 3. We're going to be using Python 3 exclusively in this book. There are a few different "flavors" of Python 3, but for the most part, the plain old Python 3 from `https://www.python.org` will be fine. We'll get into those "flavors" later when we start talking about virtual environments in *Chapter 3, Customizing Interpreters and Virtual Environments*. If revision numbers give you comfort, the latest release at the time I'm writing is 3.11.1. The Python revision I'm using in that production SaaS app I mentioned in *Chapter 1* is 3.8. If your Python 3 installation is older than that, you should update it.

- At some point, a **GitHub** account might become handy since I will be sharing the code from the book using a **Git** repository. Since you'll be cloning some code, but not pushing, it isn't strictly necessary to sign in—that is, unless you'd like to sign in, view the book's repository, and give it a star. That'd be peachy and prove to the world that you're a stand-up human being.

Downloading PyCharm the traditional way

First, I'm going to show the simplest, most direct, and most common way to install PyCharm. There's a decent chance you've already done this before you bought this book, and there's nothing wrong with that. After we cover this, I'll show you my preferred way to install using a free app from JetBrains called Toolbox. You can choose any of the installation methods you'd like, knowing the choice won't affect the outcome of anything we do in this book.

Note there is a 30-day free trial available for the Professional edition if you'd like to try it out. After 30 days, you'll have to pay for it or downgrade to the Community edition. Furthermore, don't get too hung up on the version number displayed in *Figure 2.1*. JetBrains releases updates to PyCharm quite often, and the number will probably change several times before this book even hits the shelves. It's hard to go wrong with the latest version.

To download and install PyCharm, direct your browser to `https://www.jetbrains.com/pycharm`. The site will detect your operating system and attempt to present you with the correct download option.

The download page has three main parts, as seen in *Figure 2.1*:

1. You can select the operating system (Windows, macOS, or Linux). If you want to use Linux, make sure you're running GNOME or KDE as those are supported window managers.

2. You can choose between the Professional edition or the Community edition.

3. Regardless of the first two options, make sure you take a look at the dropdown for the installer. Windows and Linux let you select between Intel and ARM. macOS lets you select between Intel and Apple Silicon:

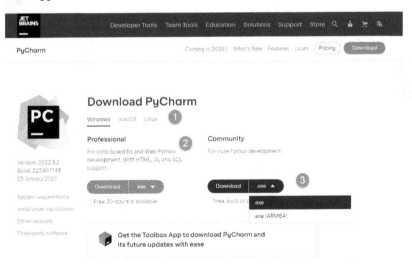

Figure 2.1: The download window on the JetBrains website; make sure
the correct operating system and processor are selected

Once you have downloaded the proper version, follow the regular installation procedure for your operating system. If you selected a Linux version, you aren't downloading an installer—you're downloading a gzipped `.tar` file. You can just extract it and run PyCharm from the resulting folder.

JetBrains Toolbox

I just presented the most common way people install software, including PyCharm, to their development computer. There is a different way, which I prefer, involving installing a separate product called JetBrains Toolbox. Toolbox is especially useful if you have multiple JetBrains products, as I do. I have a subscription to all their tools, and I regularly use many of them. My preferred C# IDE is JetBrains Rider, which I used exclusively in my book *Real-World Implementation of Design Patterns in C#*, available from Packt Publishing.

Even if you don't use multiple JetBrains products, Toolbox provides some useful features such as providing an easy way to install, uninstall, and update your PyCharm installation. You can even use it to install multiple versions of PyCharm should you ever need to, including **Early Access Program (EAP)** releases. EAP releases give you access to the most cutting-edge features from JetBrains before they are generally available. As a development lead, I like to take the newest IDEs for a test drive before I give the *all-clear* to my development team. Toolbox makes that very easy.

Toolbox is a separate download, and it is free. Let's start by revisiting the PyCharm download page. At the bottom, you'll find a link to JetBrains Toolbox, as shown in *Figure 2.2*:

Figure 2.2: Skip the usual download links we covered earlier and instead click the link to Toolbox

It is entirely possible that JetBrains will re-arrange its website. If there is no link at the bottom, you can simply search for *Toolbox* and find the most current download. You'll land on a page like the one shown in *Figure 2.3*:

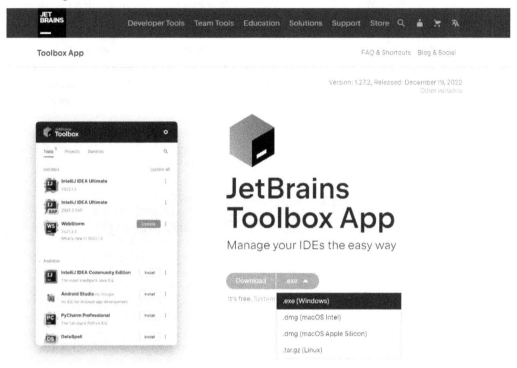

Figure 2.3: The Toolbox download screen

As with the normal PyCharm download we reviewed earlier, this web page will detect the operating system you are using. The options are a bit simpler, but if you're using a Mac, be sure to click the format button to select Intel versus Apple Silicon, as seen in *Figure 2.3*.

Installing Toolbox in Windows

The process for installing Toolbox is straightforward. It's a case where you run the installer and smash the **Next** button until the dialog goes away.

Note that when Toolbox is running, you can find it in the system tray in Windows.

Installing Toolbox in macOS

As with all things Mac, the macOS install is very easy. Having verified you downloaded the right version of the .dmg file (Intel versus Apple Silicon), find the downloaded .dmg file in the Downloads folder within your home folder. Double-click to open the .dmg file. Drag the Toolbox icon to the Applications folder. You're done!

Installing PyCharm with Toolbox

Regardless of how you got here—be it on a Mac, Windows, or Linux—you should now have Toolbox running. At this point, the experience is almost universal. On macOS, Toolbox is just a regular app like any other. On Windows, though, it runs in the system tray.

Running Toolbox for the first time brings a pretty standard **end user license agreement** (**EULA**). You know the drill. Read it and make sure that JetBrains isn't demanding the surrender of your firstborn, then make your selection to agree or disagree with the EULA. Naturally, if you disagree, our time together is at an end, unless you're tuning in for the occasional dad joke. I'll operate on the assumption you agreed to the EULA.

With Toolbox installed, you can install IDEs. You'll see a screen like the one shown in *Figure 2.4*, which lists all the available JetBrains products:

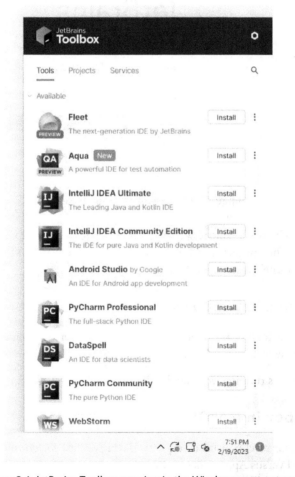

Figure 2.4: JetBrains Toolbox running in the Windows system tray

Naturally, we're only interested in PyCharm. *Figure 2.4* shows PyCharm Professional and PyCharm Community in the list. If you're interested in the PyCharm Educational edition, it's further down on the list.

To install an IDE, click the **Install** button and wait while Toolbox downloads and installs the IDE. Once it is installed, the Toolbox menu changes slightly to show you which tools you have installed. You can see mine after I installed PyCharm Professional in *Figure 2.5*:

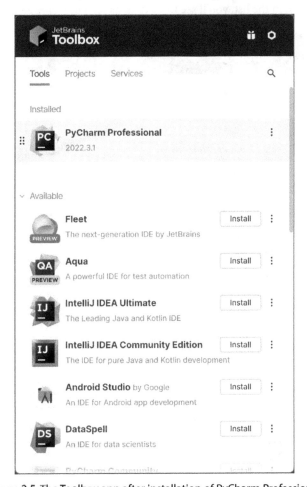

Figure 2.5: The Toolbox app after installation of PyCharm Professional

You'll notice Toolbox lists the applications you have installed at the top of the list, while those available for install are below. The advantage offered by Toolbox versus a normal install is the ability to launch, update, and uninstall your IDEs as well as easily experiment with different versions.

Launching PyCharm using Toolbox

After you've installed PyCharm, you can launch it or any installed IDE by simply clicking the entry in the menu. Before we leave Toolbox, let me show you some more interesting features.

Installing an alternate version or uninstalling

Next to each installed IDE in the list, you'll see three dots, as seen in *Figure 2.6*:

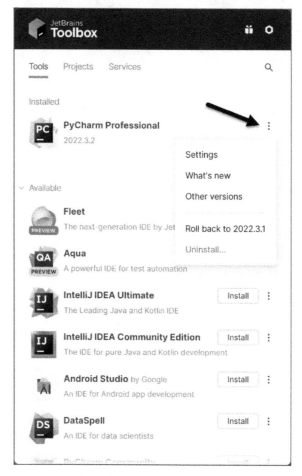

Figure 2.6: The three dots next to each app represent a menu

The dots are a menu. If you click them, you'll see some options. You can access the settings for PyCharm. We're going to do this later inside PyCharm itself, so we don't need to do that now. There's an option for viewing the latest news by clicking **What's new**. Below that, there is an option for installing different versions of PyCharm aside from the latest. You can easily roll back to the last install if you have problems with the latest. Finally, below the divider and rendered in a very intimidating red font is the option to uninstall. It even has a terrifying and mysterious ellipsis following the menu option. Hovering over the option usually instills a sense of foreboding in all who try it. You were warned.

Updating PyCharm using Toolbox

Toolbox will help you stay up to date with the latest version of PyCharm and any other IDEs you use. Toolbox itself has its own settings and its own update mechanism.

To get to these settings, click the hexagonal icon in the top-right corner of the Toolbox screen, as seen in *Figure 2.7*:

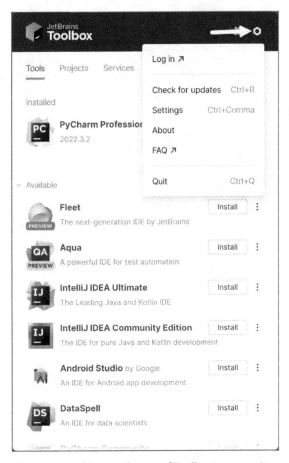

Figure 2.7: Use the hexagonal icon at the top of Toolbox to access its update options

The **Log in** option allows you to connect Toolbox to your JetBrains account. The **About** and **FAQ** options show information about the product. The latter takes you to a website where the product's **frequently asked questions** (**FAQ**) is maintained. The **Quit** option will close the Toolbox program.

Launching and registering PyCharm

Launching PyCharm, regardless of how you do it, shows you a splash screen, then takes you to a set of typical first-launch screens. If you installed the Professional edition, the first thing you'll see is the registration screen shown in *Figure 2.8*:

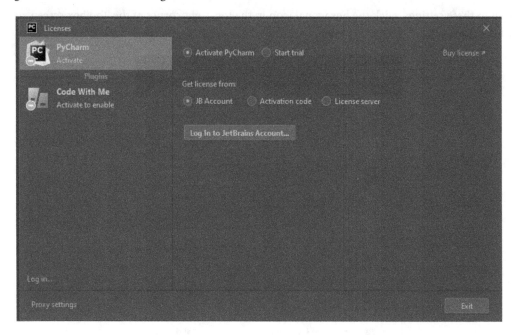

Figure 2.8: The licensing screen in PyCharm Professional appears on the first run

The most common way to proceed here is to log in to your JetBrains account. Clicking the button labeled **Log In to JetBrains Account…** will launch your browser. You can log in or create an account. If you have purchased a license, logging in will associate your copy with the license you purchased.

If you work for a company that owns many licenses, you might need to log in to a JetBrains license server. There is also an option for registering with a registration code. You'll find this code in your store account. This can be useful if you don't have good internet access.

Do you have more than one computer?

Note that it is legal to install on multiple computers so long as you aren't running two copies concurrently with the same license. The IDE will detect that and demand you shut one copy down.

If you don't have a license and you aren't ready to commit, you can select the **Start trial** option. You will still have to log in to a JetBrains account in order to activate your trial.

Setting up PyCharm

When you launch PyCharm for the first time, and you make it past the license and registration, the very next thing you see is a smallish window representing PyCharm without a loaded project. You can see the light color scheme version of this screen in *Figure 2.9*:

Figure 2.9: PyCharm with no loaded project

From this window, there are a few obvious options. I call them *obvious* because they are right in the middle of a big open space in the middle of the window. You can create a project, open an existing project, or clone a project from a VCS such as Git or **Subversion (SVN)**. However, my first stop is in the gray area to the left on the screen where you'll find the **Customize** menu option. Let's go ahead and review your options for customizing PyCharm to fit your working style. Clicking **Customize** brings you to the preferences screen, as seen in *Figure 2.10*:

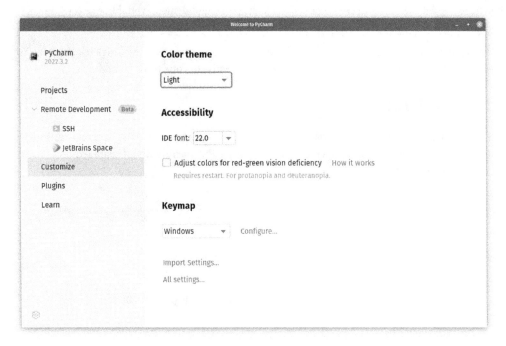

Figure 2.10: A small window for setting some of the important preferences in PyCharm

This screen allows us to change the most frequently accessed settings. We can change our color theme, the IDE font, and our keymap.

At the bottom, we can import our settings. This is useful when your boss finally springs for that new laptop, and you don't want to spend a bunch of time re-customizing your IDE. As we all know, a well-configured, personalized IDE is like your old couch. Everybody who tries to sit on it will be horribly uncomfortable. Also, it smells. Your friends won't tell you, but it does. To you, though, it's molded itself perfectly to your form via potentially years of sedentary satisfaction. That's your IDE. You might take years tweaking it to perfection only to be faced with having to start over every time you get a new machine. Not today, friends. Not with PyCharm. We can export, import, and even share our settings and easily bring them into new installations.

> **I like big fonts and I don't know why!**
>
> You might be noting my font sizes are gigantic in all these shots. I am from Texas, and everything is bigger in Texas. However, in this case, I did that for you. Screenshots are easy to read with exaggerated font sizes, so you'll see crazy settings in my preferences throughout this book.

You might be thinking at this point that PyCharm has a rather paltry set of customization options. You'd be wrong. This deceptively simple window is meant to ease you in by presenting the most changed settings. Many users stop here. But not you. No, not you. You're a Viking! Other developers see a deceptively diminutive **All settings…** button at the bottom of the screen and think *There be dragons!* You see a rich opportunity for adventure! So, click the **All settings…** button, if you dare, and we'll explore this brave new world together.

Appearance and behavior

Clicking the **All settings…** button brings you to the screen shown in *Figure 2.11*. I will mercifully not attempt to cover every available setting as the list of possibilities is extensive to the point of tedium. The takeaway as you move through the customization settings is that you can pretty much customize every pixel generated by the running IDE:

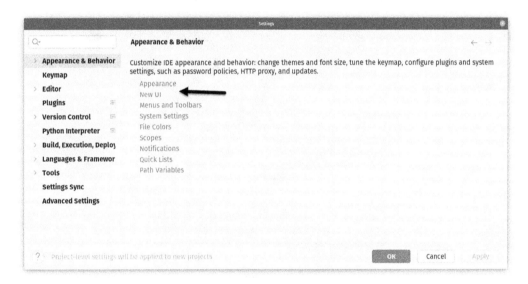

Figure 2.11: The Settings screen in PyCharm lets you change every
aspect of the user experience within PyCharm

Perhaps the most useful way to start is to point out there is a search box at the top of the settings categories list. It is usually more practical to search for the setting you want than it is to troll through all the screens trying to find it.

Before we go further, I want you to notice the arrow in *Figure 2.11* points to two items on the screen: **Appearance** at the top (which we'll talk about in just a moment) and a **New UI** setting. As this book is being written, the user experience for PyCharm is undergoing a complete overhaul. As the application has grown, the menus and toolbars have become increasingly crowded. To fix this, JetBrains is working on a simpler UI layout that will hopefully make the tool easier to learn and adopt. The classic UI will likely remain available through 2024, but the new UI will become the standard in late 2023, which should coincide with this book going to press. Everything I'm showing you in this book will be with the **New UI** setting turned on. It may even be that this option isn't even on the screen in later editions of PyCharm.

The first thing most developers want to do with a new IDE is to tweak the appearance. We've already found the setting for the color theme and the font size, but there are other settings you'll want to visit. Let's start by clicking on **Appearance**, as seen in *Figure 2.11*. This will open a menu on the left and display the appearance settings screen.

Appearance

Having opened the **Appearance** settings, you'll see a window resembling the one shown in *Figure 2.12*:

Figure 2.12: The Appearance settings for PyCharm

We have seen a few of these settings before. We can set the theme as we could in the simpler settings dialog we saw earlier. This window, however, gives you a link, labeled **Get more themes**, which will let you explore the JetBrains Marketplace for themes beyond the standard issue you have with the PyCharm install. We'll cover plugins toward the end of the book, but there's no harm in looking around if you'd like to find something a bit more unique.

> **Wait for it!**
>
> This is not where you set the font that appears in the code editor. This setting controls the fonts on the UI itself. It will affect the buttons, menu items, window titles, and so on rather than the editor, which is probably what you are wanting to change.

Don't worry—we'll customize the editor font in just a moment.

Editor settings

As with most of the sections within the **Settings** window, there are a lot of customization options. I'm just going to hit a few highlights. As we go through the screens, you'll see just how much customization is possible. If it's a pixel on your screen rendered by PyCharm, you can likely customize it in some way! *Figure 2.13* shows the **Editor** settings section of the **Settings** window:

Figure 2.13: The Editor settings in PyCharm's Settings window

Go through the options on the left side if you like, and see whether there's anything that makes sense for you to change. The **Color Scheme** section lets you customize the way the IDE colors your syntax. I'm going to jump to what I think is the most useful setting to modify. Click the **Font** section, as I have in *Figure 2.14*:

Figure 2.14: The Font settings for the editor in PyCharm

This screen does one thing: it controls the appearance of text in the IDE's editor window. The other font settings we've seen have generally applied to the whole IDE. This setting is the most important one for us as users of the tool. This is the setting for the part of the tool you'll be staring at all day long. You can set the font, the size, and the line height. I have my font size set high because I need nice, big fonts for all these screenshots, but to be honest, my daily driver on my work laptop is set to around 16 or 18. Bigger font sizes are easier to read depending on how far away your monitor is. Ideally, that shouldn't be much further than arm's length. If your font size is too small, you'll unknowingly squint at your monitor more often, and this could lead to fatigue.

There is a setting here for enabling font ligatures. These are enhancements to standard fonts that allow symbols that we use in our code to show up with a bit more elegance. For example, with font ligatures enabled, a conditional with a not equals sign such as if a != b will be rendered as seen in *Figure 2.15*:

```
1    # I have ligatures turned on
2    a = 5
3    b = 6
4
5    if a ≠ b:
6        print("They're not equal")
7
```

Figure 2.15: Turning on font ligatures allows you to express certain symbols that
are not normally available, such as the inequality symbol on line 5

In order for this to work, you have to select a font that supports ligatures. PyCharm ships with the *Fira Code* font specifically because it's a nice IDE font that supports ligatures. If you want to explore more fonts with ligatures, point your browser to `https://nerdfonts.com`. It has many fonts appropriate for editors, terminals, and consoles, many of which support ligatures.

Below the **Font** settings in the **Editor** settings lies **the color scheme**. You've seen this one before, but it's nice to know where it is since the last time we saw it, it was in the setup window.

If you'd like more customizations for the color scheme, twirl down the caret next to the **Color Scheme** menu item and you'll see, as I do in *Figure 2.16*, that there are many more options:

Figure 2.16: You can change the color of just about anything in PyCharm
using the options in the Color Scheme settings menu

You can control the colors for every window in the application in every context they are used. For example, you can have different color schemes for SQL files versus JavaScript files versus Python files.

Perhaps the most useful setting in this lot is the ability to customize the font that appears in PyCharm's integrated terminal window. You can see that in *Figure 2.17*:

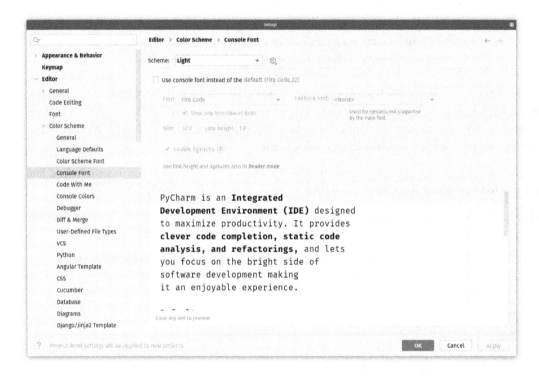

Figure 2.17: You can customize the font that appears in PyCharm's integrated terminal window

By default, the console uses the same font as the editor. If you'd like to change that, you can. You can further customize the appearance of the console using the **Console Colors** settings, as seen in *Figure 2.18*:

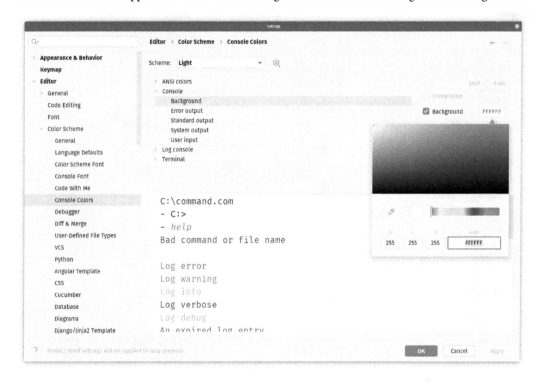

Figure 2.18: Console Colors settings in PyCharm

Personally, I spend a lot of time in the terminal, so I appreciate the level of customization available.

Close the **Color Scheme** menu and let's jump to the **Code Style** menu. You can see the menu in *Figure 2.19*:

Figure 2.19: The Code Style menu within PyCharm's Settings window

This one I find a little puzzling. The *PEP 8* standard states no Python line should be longer than 79 characters, yet the editor has a hard wrap set to 120. Thankfully, we can fix this. As I said, *PEP 8* says code lines should be limited to 79 columns or fewer. The standard goes on to recommend comment lines and docstrings should be limited to 72 columns. To make sure I follow these rules, I change my **Code Style** settings, as shown in *Figure 2.20*:

Figure 2.20: These are my recommended settings for wraps and guides, which honor PEP 8

I change the **Hard wrap at** setting to 79, and I check the wrap by typing in the checkbox. Then, I add 72 and 79 to the **Visual guides** setting so that I'll see lines in the right-hand gutter. Well-written Python code is always consistent with standards. Setting these visual guides helps me avoid those annoying red squiggly lines. I hate those.

If you don't know what I mean, Python has a built-in linter that will warn you when you break *PEP 8* rules. After a while, it's kind of like an annoying mother-in-law sitting in the backseat while you drive. Setting up the **Code Style** settings this way avoids code rage in a way that is unavoidable with actual backseat drivers, and perhaps mothers-in-law in general.

Applying these settings changes the look of the editor, as seen in *Figure 2.21*. We can see two lines on the right side showing our guides at 72 and 79 columns respectively:

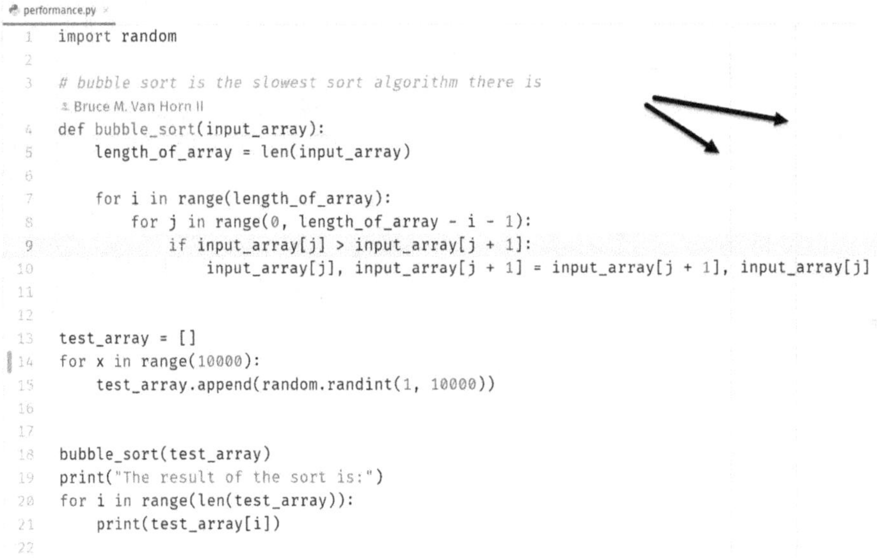

```
performance.py
1   import random
2
3   # bubble sort is the slowest sort algorithm there is
    ± Bruce M. Van Horn II
4   def bubble_sort(input_array):
5       length_of_array = len(input_array)
6
7       for i in range(length_of_array):
8           for j in range(0, length_of_array - i - 1):
9               if input_array[j] > input_array[j + 1]:
10                  input_array[j], input_array[j + 1] = input_array[j + 1], input_array[j]
11
12
13  test_array = []
14  for x in range(10000):
15      test_array.append(random.randint(1, 10000))
16
17
18  bubble_sort(test_array)
19  print("The result of the sort is:")
20  for i in range(len(test_array)):
21      print(test_array[i])
22
```

Figure 2.21: Code style has been applied and we can see our two faint gray lines on the right in the editor

If you remember, we also turned on a hard wrap at *line 79*. To demonstrate this, you'll note that *line 10* in the code, which was typed in before I changed the settings, clearly runs past our guide at 79 columns. To test the hard-wrap setting, I typed the line again immediately below *line 11*. Once I reached the hard-wrap limit, PyCharm inserted a line continuation (\) and dropped me to the next line down with an appropriate indent. It is now impossible for me to type a line of code that violates the *PEP 8* standard.

Note that changing the settings doesn't automatically re-format your code. There is a utility that does that. We will learn how to automatically format and re-format code in *Chapter 4*.

Other settings

There are more settings visible in the **Settings** window, including **Remote Development** and **Plugins**. These will be covered in later chapters.

Exporting customized settings

Customized settings are amazing! But it's always rough when you must switch to a new computer. You'd hate to have to redo all your customizations. Or maybe you want to share your settings with other developers on your team. PyCharm makes this easy. Just click the **File** menu and find the **Manage IDE Settings** option, as seen in *Figure 2.22*:

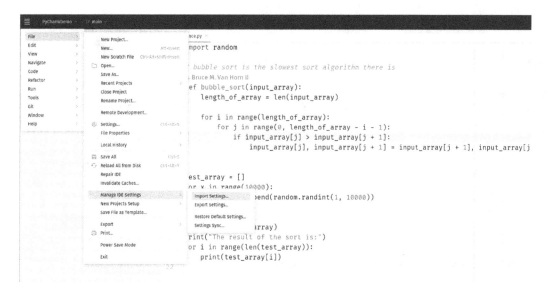

Figure 2.22: PyCharm lets you export and import your settings

You can import, export, and reset your settings as you wish.

Working with projects

Now that we have seen all the configuration options and we've tweaked some of the more popular settings, let's take PyCharm for a quick spin around the block. We'll create a quick Python project and learn how to run our main script within the UI.

At this point, you're going to need to have installed Python 3 on your computer. The Python documentation at https://docs.python.org/3/using/index.html explains the installation. I find this documentation to be complete, but you have to wade through a lot to get to the good part. To make this easier for beginners, I'll include some additional links in the *Further reading* section at the end of this chapter.

Creating a new project

You're probably starting to realize that PyCharm is a pretty powerful and flexible tool. There are several ways to configure it and several places in the application where you can start the configuration process. There is similar flexibility in creating projects.

If you've never created a project in PyCharm before, which is likely the case right now, you'll see a window like the one shown in *Figure 2.23*. This window offers a button to create a new project:

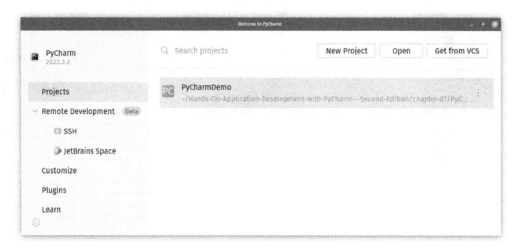

Figure 2.23: The opening screen for PyCharm has a button that can be used to create a new project

If you have created a project in PyCharm already, the PyCharm window will open with the last project it had loaded. This is the case I'm showing in *Figure 2.24*. Here, I have the demo project I've had open for our examples so far. A little later in this chapter, I'll show you how to clone this code using PyCharm's integrated Git client, but let's get back to creating a new project. In *Figure 2.24*, I already have a project open. In this case, you can use the **File** menu to create a new project. Click **File | New Project…**:

Figure 2.24: You can use the File menu to create a new project by clicking File | New Project…

Regardless of which vector you choose, the result is the same. You get the **New Project** window shown in *Figure 2.25*:

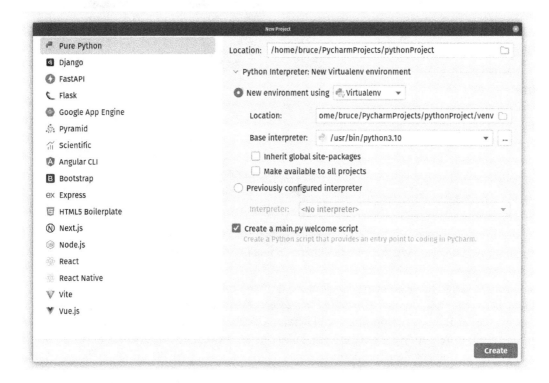

Figure 2.25: The New Project window in PyCharm Professional

Here is where you will notice a big difference between the Professional edition and the Community edition. In *Figure 2.26*, you'll see the **New Project** windows for the Professional edition (left) and the Community edition (right). Focus your attention on the left side of the Professional edition window. The Professional edition offers a lot more project types, versus only one option in the free edition. The Community edition only creates pure Python projects. It doesn't even give you an option, since that's all it can do:

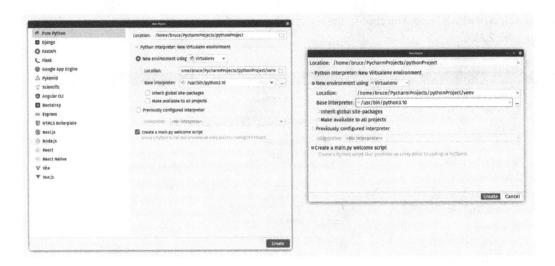

Figure 2.26: The project creation options in PyCharm Professional
(left) side by side with the Community edition (right)

It is important to note that it is not impossible to create projects of any type in the PyCharm Community edition. For example, if I wanted to create a Flask project to make a web application, I absolutely can do that in the Community edition. However, I'll have to do it manually from scratch. The Professional edition speeds things up with better tooling, but it doesn't prevent you from doing anything you couldn't do in any other editor, free or otherwise.

I'm going to choose a project common to both editions: a pure Python project. This is the default in both editions.

The first option at the top of the screen allows you to set the name and location of your project. I'm going to leave the default at pythonProject. Beneath that, there are a bunch of options for creating a Python virtual environment. This is the topic of *Chapter 3*, so I'll leave them as default for now.

Note

If you have not yet installed Python 3, or if PyCharm cannot detect your Python 3 installation, you may be prompted to install Python 3 automatically. Be advised that PyCharm might not install the latest version of Python 3, nor will it give you any control over where it is installed. It will also considerably slow down the time needed to create your first project.

Make sure the checkbox titled **Create a main.py welcome script** is checked, and click the **Create** button. If you had a project open already when you began the process of creating this new project, you'll see a dialog asking what you'd like to do with the currently open project, as seen in *Figure 2.27*:

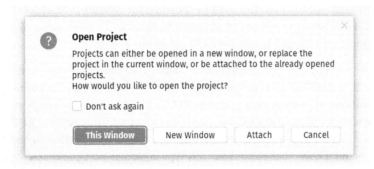

Figure 2.27: If you had a project open already, you have options on
what you'd like to do with it when creating a new project

For now, let's select the **This Window** button, which will close the project you have open and replace it with your new project. Naturally, your old project is still intact and can be re-opened using the **File | Open** menu option.

The result is a new Python 3 project with a single file. The file will contain a variant of the ubiquitous *Hello World* idiom, which spares me from having to include it in the book's source code. See? We all win! Let's take a look at our new project within the IDE in *Figure 2.28*:

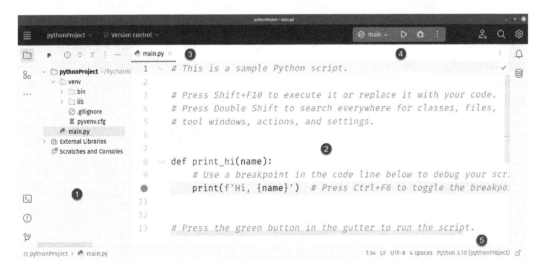

Figure 2.28: The new project is created; now, let's look around!

As you can see, PyCharm created a project structure for us in the project explorer (**1**). The project explorer allows you to see and interact with all the files in your project. You can see that it created a few folders for the virtual environment. We'll cover this in depth in *Chapter 3*.

The editor is clearly seen in the middle (**2**). We'll be spending a lot of time here, so let's point out that PyCharm, as with most IDEs and editors, uses a tabbed interface (**3**). There is a toolbar (**4**) to run, debug, test, and profile your program, which we will use in just a moment.

On the bottom right (**5**), you can see a few important settings with respect to the currently open file, and the project itself. We can see the text encoding for the file is UTF-8 since I'm running Windows, and my newline character is **carriage return line feed** (**CRLF**). This will likely be different on macOS and Linux. We are set to use four spaces for standard indentation, which is per the *PEP 8* specs. When you hit *Tab* on your keyboard, it will be interpreted as four spaces, thus putting an end to the battle between which is better. I'll say that again. You can't type an actual tab (\t) character in PyCharm unless you customize it that way. But why in the world would you go and do a thing like that?

> **Tip**
> If PyCharm is unresponsive, look down at the bottom of the window near *area 6*, and you'll probably see a progress bar indicating that PyCharm is performing some operation such as project file indexing. You might have to wait until it finishes before your IDE is fully responsive.

Running a PyCharm project

I kind of feel like an annoying car salesman who won't shut up about the features of the car. All you want to do is drive it already. Let me get you those keys and tell my non-existent manager that we have a fish on the hook. I'll be right back.

In the case of PyCharm, the keys are toward the top of the window: *area 4* shown in *Figure 2.28*. You can easily find it by locating the blue button with an arrow on it. I'll show you exactly which button in *Figure 2.29*. You'll have to trust me on the color. It's blue. This is the **Run** button. Click it:

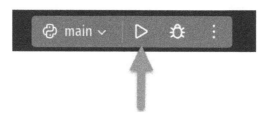

Figure 2.29: Click the blue arrow to run the main script

Now, let out a big old Texas YEEEE-HAW! Or, you can just do whatever passes for a hoot and holler wherever you're from. You just ran your program. We've taken a big step toward mastering a new IDE. The IDE window changes, as seen in *Figure 2.30*:

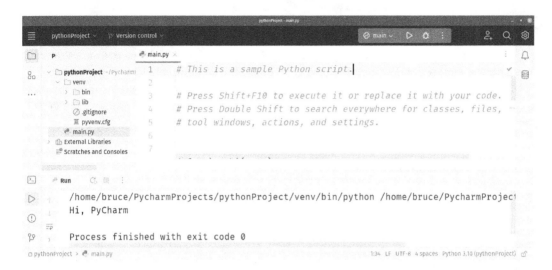

Figure 2.30: When you run your program, you can see the result of your run in the console

In addition to the run window itself, note that there are buttons on the tab that allow you to rerun the program or stop a program that is currently running.

In the next section, you'll learn how to clone a code project from GitHub. Before we do that, let's close the current project. Locate the **File** menu and click **File | Close Project**, as seen in *Figure 2.31*:

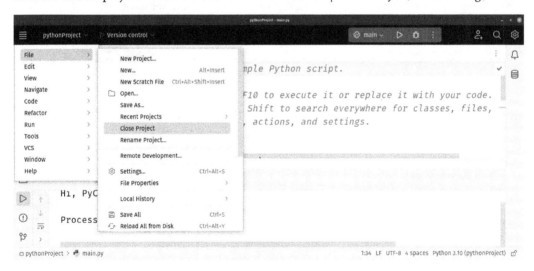

Figure 2.31: Close the project from the File menu

Excellent! You're ready for your next adventure! Let's go get the sample source code for the book from GitHub.

Cloning this book's code from GitHub

PyCharm has a robust set of features for working with VCSs such as Git, SVN, Mercurial, and Perforce. We're going to work with Git and GitHub throughout this book because they have become the de facto standard in the industry. If you use one of the other supported VCSs, the process is mostly the same. In fact, the user experience is mostly the same except for differences in how some of the VCSs operate. For example, Git uses a four-step process to commit and push files:

1. Stage your local changes (`git add`).
2. Commit your changes locally (`git commit`).
3. Pull from GitHub or your central repository to make sure you have the latest changes and fix any conflicts (`git pull`).
4. Push your changes to the central repository (`git push`).

In contrast, SVN only has two steps:

1. Pull the latest and fix any conflicts (`svn update`).
2. Commit your local changes to the central repository (`svn commit`).

My point is, the different VCSs might have different workflows that change the user experience in PyCharm. For this book, we'll only use Git.

Since you closed your project at the end of the last section, you should see a window similar to the one shown in *Figure 2.32*:

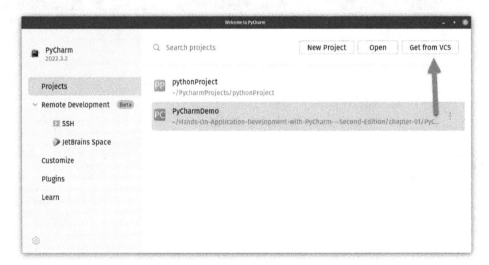

Figure 2.32: Locate the Get from VCS button

We're going to accomplish two things in this section. First, we're going to set up your GitHub account in PyCharm. This isn't strictly a requirement should you not currently have an account, but sooner or later in your career, you're going to need a GitHub account. You might as well rip off the proverbial band-aid. I won't cover how to create a GitHub account here. You can find instructions for this at https://github.com/signup.

Locate and click the **Get from VCS** button. You'll see a screen like the one shown in *Figure 2.33*:

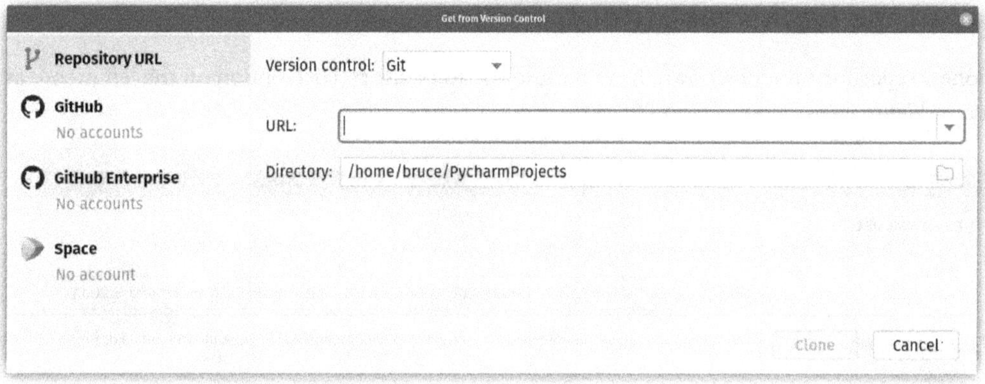

Figure 2.33: The Get from Version Control window in PyCharm

Setting up your GitHub account

Note that on the right side of the window, you can see all your accounts for GitHub, GitHub Enterprise, and JetBrains Space. I'm going to go ahead and set up my GitHub account. Click the **GitHub** item on the left menu. You'll see a screen like the one shown in *Figure 2.34*:

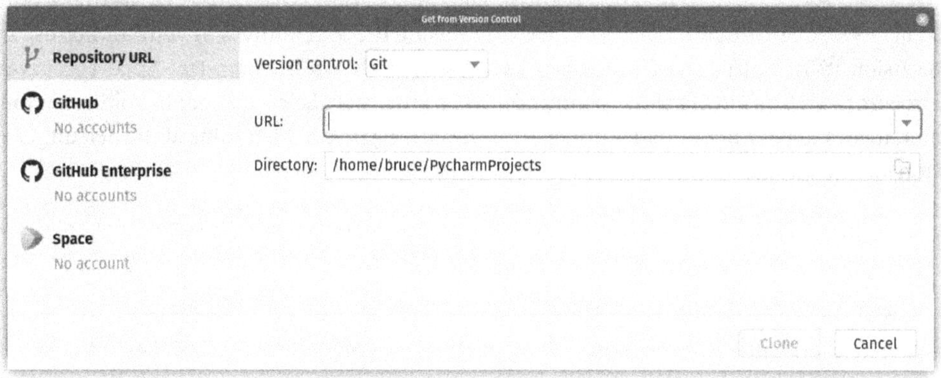

Figure 2.34: Logging in to GitHub is easy and only needs to be done one time

Locate and click the **Login via GitHub** button. Before you click it, I recommend you go ahead and log in to GitHub at `https://github.com/login` using your favorite browser. This process is more seamless if you've already logged in and cleared any **two-factor authentication (2FA)** hurdles.

Once authorized, you can close your browser and return to PyCharm. After a few minutes, you'll see all your GitHub repositories in the window. This makes working with your own repositories very easy. However, the repository we're going to clone isn't on your list, so we've got a little more work to do.

Cloning the book's repository

To clone a repository you don't own, head back to the **Repository URL** option on the left menu, as shown in *Figure 2.35*:

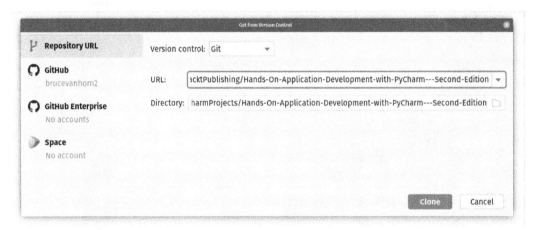

Figure 2.35: To clone a repository you don't own, click the Repository URL option on the left menu

Within the **Repository URL** section, you'll need to enter the URL for the repository, which is `git@github.com:PacktPublishing/Hands-On-Application-Development-with-PyCharm---Second-Edition.git`. Here, I'm using the SSH address. If you'd rather use the HTTPS version, it's `https://github.com/PacktPublishing/Hands-On-Application-Development-with-PyCharm---Second-Edition.git`. Select a folder to hold your clone. By default, it goes to your home folder under `PyCharmProjects`. I left mine at the default. Click the button labeled **Clone**.

Once cloned, you're given the usual paranoid dialog box pervasive in software development tools today, as seen in *Figure 2.36*:

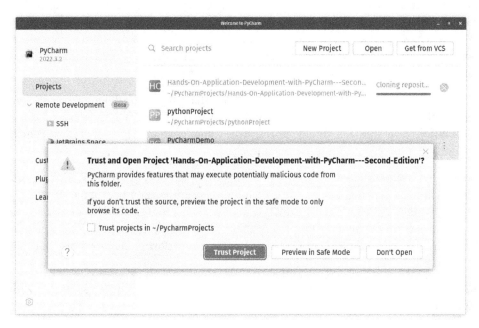

Figure 2.36: Do you trust me?

I know we just met and all, but if you really want the book's source code, you should click the **Trust Project** button. Once you do, you're all set. You now have all the sample code shown in the book.

Summary

This chapter was all about the preliminaries. We installed and configured your new instance of PyCharm on your computer. There are several ways you can install PyCharm. You can go the traditional route of just downloading the installer. My preferred way is to install the JetBrains Toolbox app and use that to install and manage PyCharm, along with any other JetBrains tools I might need or want. Using the Toolbox app allows us an easy way to update PyCharm or even perform a clean uninstall should the need arise.

We learned the differences between the three versions of PyCharm. The free Community edition is limited in the types of projects PyCharm supports with integrated tooling. When we created a new project, we were not afforded any project template options. Only "pure Python" projects are supported. This doesn't mean we can't create any kind of project; it simply means that the tedious part of setting up different kinds of projects isn't handled for you by the IDE.

The Professional edition supports a broader set of tools, including a full set of project templates and expanded tools for web development and scientific workloads. While the Professional edition isn't free, there are licensing options for individuals and a separate price for corporate developers. There also exist options to obtain a free professional license through an application process. Examples include Microsoft MVPs and other recognized professionals, open source developers, and university professors. There are often discount deals on JetBrains' website for start-ups, educational institutions, and others. Unfortunately, book authors aren't listed.

The third version of PyCharm is the Educational edition. This is a special edition that allows for the creation and playback of interactive lessons right in the IDE. If you teach Python using PyCharm, you probably don't want this. You should rather use the Community or Professional edition and take advantage of JetBrains' offer of free software for teachers.

Once we got PyCharm installed, we set out to configure the application. A number of important configuration options were highlighted. We can customize nearly every aspect of the way PyCharm works. Popular settings include setting the IDE's color theme, font size, and code development settings. In our case, we set up our editor to use a font with ligatures called Fira Code, which ships with PyCharm. We also configured our **Code Style** settings to perform a hard wrap at 79 characters to keep us compliant with *PEP 8* standards.

After we got everything set up, we kicked the proverbial tires by creating a simple pure Python project and running it using the IDE's **Run** button.

Finally, we set up PyCharm with our GitHub account and cloned this book's sample code repository. We've got a lot done in a short amount of time. At this point, you're all set to develop software using PyCharm, and we're only in *Chapter 2*!

Stick with me as we dive deeper into working with Python virtual environments in the next chapter. Virtual environments are considered a best practice, and they provide a way to segregate the requirements of your projects in your local development environment. As you'll see, PyCharm negates the need to remember a half-dozen or so commands as well as the installation of extra libraries to get your project up and running more quickly.

Questions

1. What are the benefits of using the JetBrains Toolbox app to install and manage PyCharm installations?

2. What are the main differences between the Community edition and the Professional edition of PyCharm?

3. What are the main limitations of PyCharm Community?

4. If you are using the PyCharm Community edition, can you still develop projects using frameworks such as Flask that are seemingly only supported in the Professional edition?

5. What are the benefits of linking your GitHub account to PyCharm?

6. Have you gone to the book's repository and given it a star yet? If you fork the repository, you'll be notified if I ever change anything. I doubt that will happen since, like yours, my code is often perfect on the first try. Nope. Couldn't keep a straight face. I tried.

Further reading

Be sure to check out the companion website for this book at `http://pycharm-book.com`.

Instructions for setting up Puthon: `https://www.maddevskilz.com/pages/python-landing-page`

PEP 8 – Style Guide for Python Code: `https://peps.python.org/pep-0008/#maximum-line-length`

Part 2: Improving Your Productivity

This part covers beginner to advanced concepts and techniques that facilitate productivity while working on Python projects in PyCharm. Readers will be able to learn about the dynamic options for the management of projects, Python interpreters, and virtual environments as well as know how to carry on good programming practices such as version control, testing, debugging, and profiling and how PyCharm streamlines those processes.

This part has the following chapters:

- *Chapter 3, Customizing Interpreters and Virtual Environments*
- *Chapter 4, Editing and Formatting with Ease in PyCharm*
- *Chapter 5, Version Control with Git in PyCharm*
- *Chapter 6, Seamless Testing, Debugging and Profiling*

3

Customizing Interpreters and Virtual Environments

The last chapter focused on configuration options. Configuration options are designed to help you customize your working environment to fit the project and also allow for customization to fit your personal tastes. These options are one of the many reasons that PyCharm is a great tool. Another great feature that makes PyCharm useful is the customization of interpreters and virtual environments.

This chapter will cover the following topics:

- The importance of working with virtual environments in Python
- How to create a virtual environment manually using `virtualenv`
- How to create a virtual environment using PyCharm
- How to work with an existing virtual environment in PyCharm
- How to add and remove third-party libraries using PyCharm
- How to import projects created outside PyCharm
- How to work with virtual environment settings within run configurations

At this point, many of you will have at least one installation of a Python interpreter installed. It either came with your system, as is the case with macOS or Linux, or you installed it, as is the case with Windows. Python is an **interpreted language**—this means the written code is not truly evaluated until it is run. Let's take a moment to describe what this means by comparing Python to a few other languages and how they are executed.

There are three common ways to execute written code on your computer, as follows:

- Compilation
- Interpretation
- Intermediate compilation with a runtime

Before we dig into these, let's take a short trip back through time. I know it is history but stick with me. In the year 1522, the predominant religion throughout most of Western Europe was Roman Catholicism. This was a time of great turmoil in that church's history, but we will put that aside for a moment. Instead, we will focus on a German priest named Martin Luther. In those days, the German people were completely reliant on the clerical establishment for their spiritual needs. The Bible, in 1522, was only available in Greek and Latin. Luther, who was imprisoned at the time, translated the Old Testament from Greek into the German Vulgate. This was a game changer for the Germans. Printers of the day snatched it up and printed hundreds of copies so that every family could read it. I'm going to use this as an analogy.

The first method of executing written code is *compilation*. This is similar to Martin Luther's translation from Greek into German. Most people who cannot code will see a programming language and scratch their heads and think to themselves: "This is Greek to me!" The same thing is happening with computers because the computer can't understand your code language either. Computers don't "speak" C or C++ or Java. Instead, a programmer has written something in a language that is simple and easy to translate as compared to human language. Compilation refers to a process where your textual code files are translated once into a binary format that is understood by the computer. Examples of compiled languages include C and C++. The code files are run through a compiler, which translates the code into a separate and new format only one time. The process produces a new file, separate from the code, which is useful only to the computer. To finalize our analogy, after translating Greek into German, the printed books became the result of the compilation step. The ability to read the Bible was useful to the Germans.

Contrast that with the second form of code execution: the *interpreted language*. Prior to Luther's translation, the Bible was translated on the fly in church. A priest would open the Bible and translate the text into German as he read it aloud. This is what happens with interpreted languages, including Python. The **interpreter** in our case is the Python interpreter—the Python executable you installed at some juncture earlier in your setup journey. When you execute your code with a command such as `python main.py`, the Python interpreter opens the code file, reads the code, translates (compiles) that code, and executes the instructions as it reads them line by line.

This might be an oversimplification for those of you deeply familiar with compiler theory, but for most of us, the analogy holds. Python does some extra work during the process by way of caching and optimizing some of the translation so that it can be used again. By and large, each run of the program presents a new interpretation. Examples of interpreted languages include Python, JavaScript, and Lua.

The last category of code execution involves a middle ground between the other two. Languages such as C# and Java use a *compilation* step. Unlike regular compilers, the result isn't a file that runs by itself on the bare metal of your computer. Instead, it produces an intermediate format that can be read by a **runtime**.

Think back to when you were in school. A common practice is for a professor or teacher to lecture the class and for the class to take notes. A good student can reproduce the lecture's content from the notes. Those notes are an abbreviated form of the lecture. In this analogy, the teacher is the programmer and the student is the intermediate compiler. The output of the compiler, hopefully, is a stellar set of notes that will allow the student to get a good grade on the test. Your code files (the lecture) are translated into a compact, binary version of the code (your notes). When that intermediate file is executed, a runtime essentially "looks at the notes" and enables that code to run on the computer. The upside to this method is that the intermediate compilation can run on a variety of platforms without having to be recompiled. Programs written in C will run on a variety of platforms, ranging from Intel and ARM to old platforms such as mainframes. To accomplish this, however, you must recompile the program on that platform. The executables only run on the platform that compiles them. In the runtime system, the runtime is translated and made to run on different platforms. The intermediate compilation then runs on any platform that supports the runtime. You can compile once and distribute anywhere.

Python, for our purposes, is an interpreted language, and we need an interpreter. Furthermore, PyCharm needs to know a little bit about the interpreter. This chapter is all about the means by which you can make introductions. PyCharm, meet interpreter. Interpreter, meet PyCharm.

Technical requirements

In order to proceed through this chapter, and indeed the rest of the book, you will need the following:

- An installed and working Python interpreter. I'll be using the latest from `https://python.org`.

- Installed copies of `pip` and `virtualenv`. You get these automatically when you install Python on Windows, and macOS has them included on every system. If you are using Linux, you need to install package managers, such as `pip`, and virtual environment tools, such as `virtualenv`, separately. Our examples will use `pip` and `virtualenv`.

- An installed and working copy of PyCharm. Installation was covered in *Chapter 2, Installation and Configuration*, in case you are jumping into the middle of the book.

- This book's sample source code from GitHub. We covered cloning the code in *Chapter 2, Installation and Configuration*. You'll find this chapter's relevant code at `https://github.com/PacktPublishing/Hands-On-Application-Development-with-PyCharm---Second-Edition/tree/main/chapter-03`.

There are several flavors of Python. I have used and referenced Python 3 from `https://www.python.org`. Remember—because it is an open source project, it is possible to create an alternative version of Python. This has been done many times with varying degrees of success. Some of these variants include the following:

- **Anaconda**—This is a variant of Python focused on scientific and big data work. Essentially, it is regular Python pre-bundled with the most popular and useful external libraries such as `numpy`, `matplotlib`, and `pandas` included in the installation. The downside is the amount of space on your drives consumed by this bigger installation, but given the price of storage these days, it is likely not much of a consideration. These libraries are probably the most important variant to consider if you intend to do data science work.

- **IronPython**—This is a variant of Python designed to run in the Microsoft .NET runtime. The implications of that are beyond the scope of this book. However, IronPython is interesting because, in addition to running in a .NET environment, this implementation isn't hobbled by a **global interpreter lock** (GIL). GILs prevent efficient multithreading in your code. If you're not aware of this limitation in Python, I'll leave a link in the *Further reading* section of this chapter.

- **Jython**—This variant allows your Python code to execute within a **Java Virtual Machine** (JVM).

- **MicroPython**—This variant is used to run Python code with microcontrollers for use in the **Internet of Things** (IoT) and potentially embedded projects.

- **ActiveState ActivePython**—This is a commercially supported implementation of Python, with special attention paid to Windows compatibility and execution. Traditionally, Python was designed with the assumption that it would be running in Unix or Linux environments. If you intend to run your Python code in production on a Windows server, you might consider this variant.

You'll find these documented officially at `https://www.python.org/download/alternatives/`. While any of these variants should work in PyCharm, most developers using the IDE are working in vanilla Python (the one from `python.org`) or Anaconda. As you work with virtual environments in Python, you will undoubtedly see different options for these alternative implementations. In general, I always use the vanilla version of Python 3.

Virtual environments

We oriented ourselves with respect to project creation in *Chapter 2, Installation and Configuration*; however, we glossed over the details around creating or setting up a **virtual environment**. Virtual environments are a feature of Python rather than of PyCharm. A virtual environment is a copy of a Python interpreter and its related files that is specific to a project. Most programming languages allow some way of segregating the requirements of one project from any other on your computer. At the outset of a project, you will typically create a virtual environment from your main, also called *global*, Python installation. The benefit comes when you are working on multiple projects with different requirements. It might be that one project requires Python 3.6, and the version is frozen there in order to comply with customer requirements around change control. Or maybe a library you need, such as `matplotlib`, only runs in Python 3.6 on your Mac, but in Windows, it's stable at Python 3.9. While that project is going on, another project starts that requires Python 3.10.

If you were strictly working with the global or system-wide installations of Python, it would be very hard to switch back and forth between those two projects. You would have to futz with environment variables and fix your computer's PATH environment variable. Then, you would have to try to remember which third-party libraries are installed globally and hope there isn't a clash between those library requirements for the separate projects. Yuck.

Virtual environments allow you to manage these problems easily. While using them is purely optional, it is considered a best practice to create a virtual environment for every project. Before we dive back into PyCharm, I thought it would be fun to create a virtual environment manually. You can skip this if you'd like, but if you haven't done this before, I think it will give you an appreciation for some of the work PyCharm takes off your plate at the onset of a new project.

Creating a virtual environment by hand

Open up your computer's terminal and find a spot on your drive where you can do a little temporary work. We won't be keeping this for later; we're just going to go through the process. We will then switch to PyCharm so that we can see a more automated version of the same workflow.

I'm running Windows, and I have a place in my home folder where I keep my projects; a folder simply called *Projects*. Having opened my computer's terminal program, which in this case is **Windows Terminal** running **PowerShell**, I can type the commands for this experiment. You do not have to use Windows, nor do you have to use PowerShell. The normal **zshell** (**zsh**) terminal prompt in macOS or the **Bourne Again Shell** (**Bash**) prompt in Linux works the same. Most of the commands are identical in all terminals and operating systems. I'll start by creating a new folder, as follows:

```
mkdir python-environment-demo
```

This creates a new folder called `python-environment-demo`. Next, I need to change directory (`cd`) into it, like so:

```
cd python-environment-demo
```

Now I'm inside that folder, I'll create my virtual environment. If you are using macOS or Linux, there's a good chance you have both Python 2 and 3 installed, and we want to be sure to make a virtual environment based on Python 3. In order to differentiate, you need to type the following:

```
python3 -m venv venv
```

If you're on Windows, you probably only have Python 3 installed, so the command is this:

```
python -m venv venv
```

Here, we're running the `python3` command, and we're passing a switch (`-m`) that will execute the `venv` package to create a new virtual environment based on Python 3 within a new folder called `venv`. Once the command finishes, I can make sure it worked on Windows with this:

```
dir
```

Or on macOS/Linux, I can use this:

```
ls -a
```

You should see your system's output. I'm using Windows, so mine appears as seen in *Figure 3.1*:

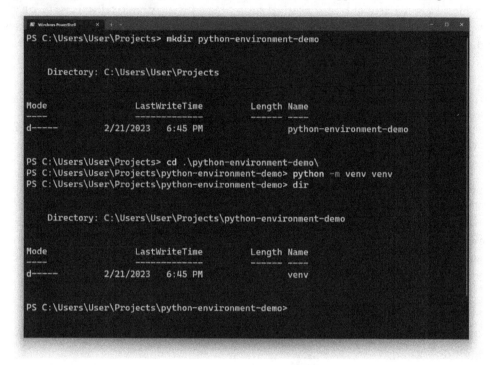

Figure 3.1: Terminal output checking whether my virtual environment creation was successful

It isn't necessary for your virtual environment to be in the same folder as the rest of your project, but I usually organize things this way to make the virtual environment easy to find later.

If I intend to use Git or some other revision control system, it would be appropriate for me to have the revision control system ignore this folder. You should *not* check this folder into your repository.

The final step in working with a virtual environment is to activate it. The command is a little different in Windows compared to macOS and Linux. The command to activate a virtual environment in Windows is this:

```
.\venv\Scripts\activate
```

While in macOS and Linux, it would be this:

```
source ./venv/bin/activate
```

If you successfully activated your virtual environment, the prompt should have changed to display the name of the virtual environment that is currently active. Bear in mind that if you have customized your terminal to prevent this, it might not work. You can see in *Figure 3.2* that everything worked for me, as indicated by (venv) appearing at the front of my prompt. The top example shows activation in Windows 11, while the lower example shows the activation command in Linux, which is the same as it would be in macOS:

Figure 3.2: My virtual environment has been activated

When I'm ready to stop working in my virtual environment, I can deactivate it by typing the following command in the terminal:

```
deactivate
```

That was a little bit of work. If you've been doing this for a while, it isn't too bad—maybe just a few minutes. However, if you do not do this very often, you will have to look everything up, and this may take time. You really only do this at the beginning of a new project. Some people might only do this a few times per year. Now, let's go back to PyCharm and see how this step is integrated into the new project creation workflow.

Creating a project in PyCharm (revisited)

If we go back to PyCharm and create a new pure Python project, you'll see where the process of creating a virtual environment happens. In PyCharm, let's create a new project by clicking **File** | **New Project…**, as seen in *Figure 3.3*:

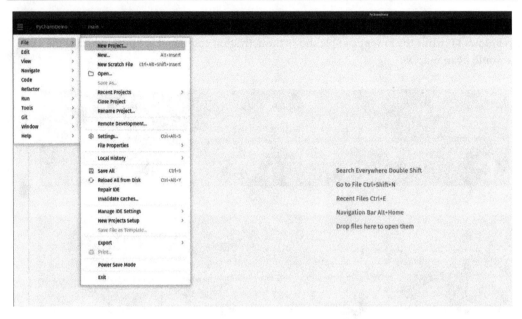

Figure 3.3: Creating a new project in PyCharm

This will be a pure Python project. The Professional edition is not necessary to follow along. The new project dialog is something we saw before in *Chapter 2, Installation and Configuration*, but this time we will focus on some of the details we skipped. *Figure 3.4* shows the Professional edition of PyCharm's new project window on the left. PyCharm Community lacks the project type menu since it can only create "pure Python" projects:

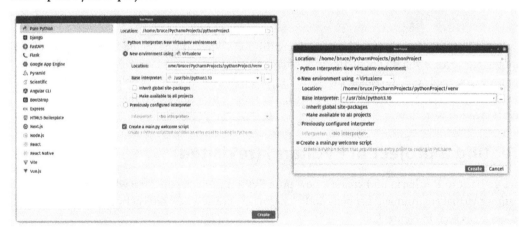

Figure 3.4: A side-by-side comparison of the New Project window for the
Professional edition (left) and the Community edition (right)

The section of the **New Project** dialog I'd like you to focus on is highlighted in *Figure 3.5*. It is this section of the screen that allows you to set up your virtual environment. In *Chapter 2, Installation and Configuration*, we breezed right past this and just accepted the defaults. As it happens, the defaults nearly match the manual process we completed in the last section:

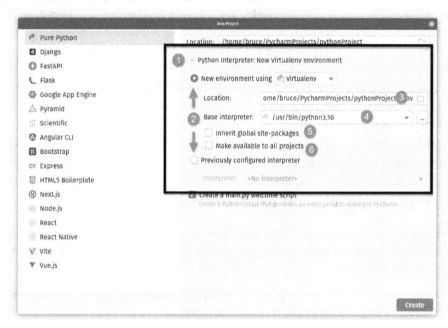

Figure 3.5: The virtual environment settings from PyCharm enumerated for explanation

Let's consider the numbered labels in *Figure 3.5*:

1. This is the Python interpreter settings section of the **New Project** window. You can hide it if you like by twirling the triangle next to the section label, though if we did that, we wouldn't be able to continue talking about what comes next.

2. There are two options at play here. You can either create a new virtual environment or point to one you've already created. Let's focus on creating a new one. The **New environment** option has a radio button next to it and a drop-down list allowing you to choose a mechanism for creating your virtual environment. In our manual example in the previous section, we used the Python `virtualenv` virtual environment feature. Changing the mechanism using the dropdown will change the contents of the screen to match the settings for the virtual environment script you pick. For now, let's leave it on **Virtualenv** since that is the oldest and likely the most widely used.

3. The **Location** field allows you to set the location for your virtual environment. It will default to a folder called `venv` within the folder for the project. You can set the location anywhere on your computer; it doesn't have to be in the project folder. If you have several projects that share a virtual environment because they share dependencies, it makes sense to create a central

location to hold the environment. Most of the time, I prefer to keep the virtual environment in the same folder as the project so that there is no question as to its location.

4. The **Base interpreter** field lets you choose which Python installation will be used to create the virtual environment. If you have more than one Python installation on your computer, PyCharm was probably able to find it automatically. The selection is presented as a drop-down list of the locations where PyCharm found a Python installation. If it somehow missed one, you can click the ellipsis button (…) and navigate to the Python installation you're interested in using. If you do this, you need to navigate all the way to the Python executable and double-click it.

5. The **Inherit global site-packages** checkbox deals with any third-party libraries you might have installed globally. Checking this box will copy those into your virtual environment so that they are available locally in your project.

6. The **Make available to all projects** checkbox allows you to easily find and reuse this virtual environment in other projects.

Using an existing virtual environment

Sometimes, you need to make a project with the exact same requirements used in another project. You can share or reuse a virtual environment easily in PyCharm. *Figure 3.5* shows the **New Project** dialog in PyCharm.

To use an existing virtual environment, you'd need to change the default setting from **New environment** using to **Previously configured interpreter**, as seen in *Figure 3.6*:

Figure 3.6: You can point your project to an existing virtual
environment by changing the setting for the project

Once you do that, your options for selecting an existing environment become active. There is a drop-down list available to pick the interpreter. It works the same as the **Base interpreter** dropdown we saw earlier when creating a new virtual environment. If you created the existing environment in PyCharm, the IDE would remember it. In this case, I previously created a virtual environment using PyCharm when I created the demo project code for *Chapter 1, Introduction to PyCharm – The Most Popular IDE for Python*. PyCharm will remember virtual environments created using PyCharm and will offer them in the list.

If you used a manual method or some other tool, you'll need to add the interpreter to the list using the **Add Interpreter** button. When you click the button, you'll notice some possibilities, as seen in *Figure 3.7*:

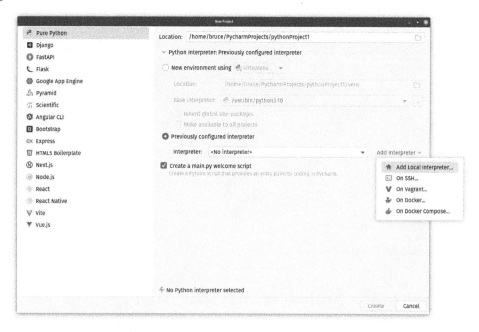

Figure 3.7: When you click Add Interpreter, you have a myriad of options
for the origin of the environment you might want to add

So far, we're strictly limiting our discussion to adding a virtual environment that exists on your local computer. It is possible to add an environment on a remote computer, **virtual machine (VM)**, **Windows Subsystem for Linux (WSL**, which is a VM), or a **Docker** container. We're going to talk about those options much later in the book.

Once you select **Add Local Interpreter…**, you are prompted to navigate to the Python executable in the virtual environment you want to use, as seen in *Figure 3.8*. Remember—the structure of virtual environments is different on Windows versus everywhere else. macOS and Linux virtual environments will have a `bin` folder containing the Python executable. In Windows, the virtual environment has a `Scripts` folder that will contain a file that points to the Python executable. Your goal in any case is to select the executable:

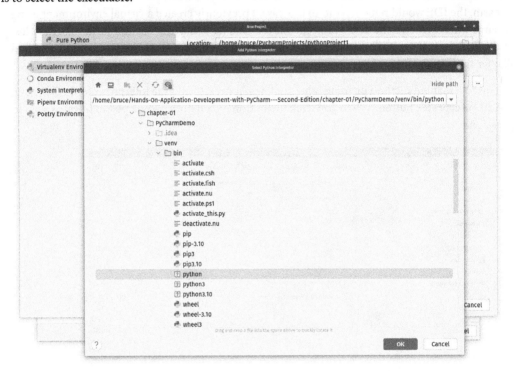

Figure 3.8: You need to select the Python executable within the virtual environment folder you'd like to use

Changing the interpreter for a project

One trick I employ when I'm working on a project that's been ongoing for 6 months or longer is to create a new virtual environment with fully updated packages. This way, I can test the program with updated dependencies without corrupting my production-ready virtual environment. We'll cover package management a little later in this chapter. For now, I want to show you where the setting for your project's interpreter exists independently of the project creation process. I find this to be a little bit non-intuitive. It's in **Settings**. The same **Settings** option you use to configure the IDE globally across all projects is used to set project-specific settings such as the interpreter settings.

Regardless of your reason, it is possible to change the interpreter, and by extension the virtual environment used in your project. You'll find the project settings by clicking the gear icon in the top-left corner of the UI, as seen in *Figure 3.9*:

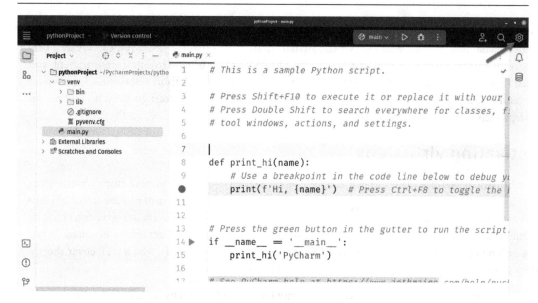

Figure 3.9: You'll find global and project settings by clicking the gear

Once you select **Settings**, you'll be taken to the global settings screen we studied in *Chapter 2, Installation and Configuration*. Project properties are also stored here, as shown in *Figure 3.10*:

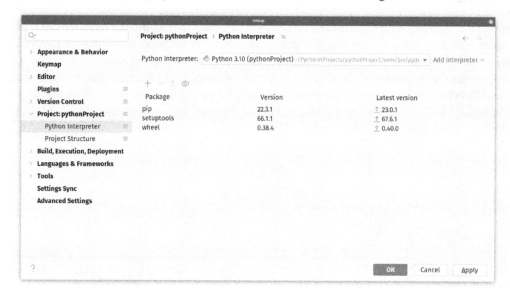

Figure 3.10: The project settings are in the middle of the list

Select the interpreter settings on the left side of the screen and change the interpreter using the same mechanism we used when we set the virtual environment the first time. You can create a new environment or browse to a new one. Don't forget that when you browse to a new environment, you need to select the Python executable and not the folder where the Python installation is located. I forget this sometimes, and I'm left wondering why the selection dialog won't go away. It's looking for a file, which is the Python executable, not a folder.

Activating virtualenv

In our manual exercise earlier in this chapter, we created a virtual environment from scratch using `virtualenv`. Once the environment is created, you must activate it in order to use it. An obvious question might be "*How do I activate the environment?*" Here's the beautiful answer: you don't have to. While you are in the IDE, the environment settings are always there and are always honored. When you add new third-party packages from the **Python Package Index** (**PyPI**), which we'll cover shortly, they automatically go to the right place per your environment settings.

When we run our program, we can override the **run configuration**, but by default, it uses the project's environment setting. Frankly, it's rare that the override in the run configuration is useful. With that said, I'll show you how to override the run configuration later in this chapter.

Using the integrated terminal

Another place to worry about the virtual environment being active is within the **terminal**. It's true PyCharm can't help you with your system terminal. However, PyCharm does have its own terminal window tab. If you use PyCharm's terminal, the project's interpreter settings are automatically applied. You will not have to manually activate anything. Since we are talking about it, let's look at the integrated terminal in PyCharm. You can find the menu item for showing the terminal in the **View** menu, as seen in *Figure 3.11*. Personally, I spend a lot of time in the terminal, so I have committed the keyboard shortcut to muscle memory:

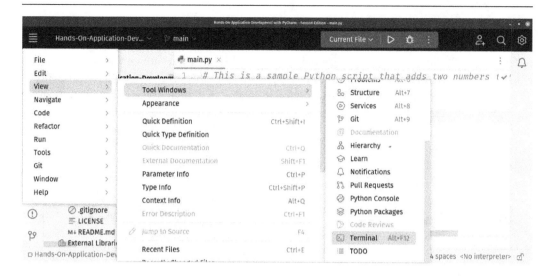

Figure 3.11: PyCharm's integrated terminal can be found buried within the View menu

Invoking the menu option brings up the terminal and, as promised, you can see in *Figure 3.12* it honors our project's virtual environment setting:

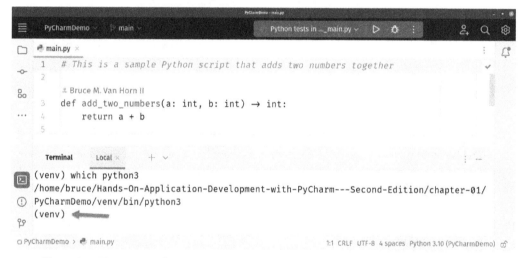

Figure 3.12: You can see the terminal comes up with your virtual environment already active

If the presence of (venv) in the prompt isn't proof enough that it worked, I provided more in *Figure 3.12*. If you use macOS or Linux, you can use the which command to find the path to any executable. Sorry, Windows users: there isn't an equivalent command on your OS. The result of the which command is that it shows when I run python3 it is using the one at the indicated path, rather than the system-wide installation, which is usually at /usr/bin/python3.

Working with the REPL in the console window

One final tool in PyCharm that might cause you to wonder whether or not your environment settings are being honored is the **console**. The console is different from the terminal. The terminal is just your operating system's shell. The console is a running version of Python based on your interpreter settings. You are presented with Python's **Read Execute Print Loop** (**REPL**) environment, which is handy for testing small pieces of syntax, or for testing imports. If you didn't have this tool, you could get the same functionality in the terminal by simply running `python3` by itself. PyCharm gives you an integrated tool so that you don't have to. To get to the console, use the same menu you used to get to the terminal. I've shown it to you in *Figure 3.13*:

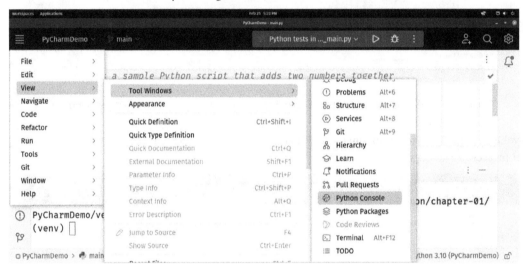

Figure 3.13: The Python console can be invoked via the View menu

Your console is not only aware of your interpreter settings, but it is also aware of the contents of your project. You can import and test anything in your project directly in the console. I find this useful when I'm tracking down the dreaded "*Module not found? Whaddya mean it's not found?! It's right there! I'm looking right at it!*" issues we sometimes face. It is also useful for experimenting with some of the terser syntax we find in Python, such as **regular expressions** (**regexes**) or list comprehensions. There's a small example in *Figure 3.14*:

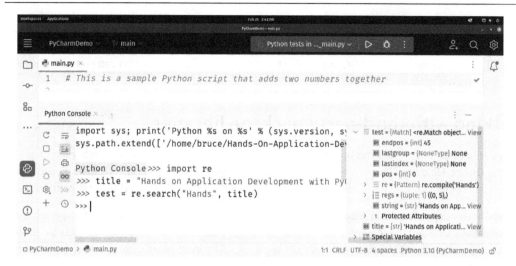

Figure 3.14: The console window in use to test a simple regex

The code I'm trying out in *Figure 3.14* isn't going to impress anyone in my big Python interview with Google:

```
import re
title = "Hands on Application Development with PyCharm"
test = re.search("Hands", title)
```

I type each line into the console. Remember—this is a live coding view, not a file that you execute. Every time I press *Enter*, the expression I just typed is evaluated, and the results appear in the debug-like window on the right side when appropriate. Think of it like a debugging session where you have a watch window on the right, and everything you type in next to the >>> prompt becomes an instant breakpoint.

Having pressed *Enter* to evaluate the third line, I can see that the `test` variable has a `re.Match` object as its value. Stare at the window a little longer, and you can see the characters were found at position (0, 5), or characters 0 through 5 represented in a single tuple (`regs`).

Trying out complicated bits of code in the console saves a little bit of time versus the usual process comprised of running the program, reading `print` statements, making a change, and trying again, which eats up most of our days as developers. Then, you forget to take out the print statements, and you should because they can seriously slow down a long-running script.

The console executes everything instantly and feeds the results back to you. It is far more detailed than a print statement because you can see the internals of any object using the debug-like window, rather than just seeing a string. After some tinkering in the console window, you can go back to your code and just use what worked.

Working with third-party package libraries

Python is famous for its "batteries included" philosophy, which is at odds with many other languages. Python's creator, Guido van Rossum, believes a robust and complete standard library is important and that the language ought to be able to complete nearly any task without using any third-party dependencies.

By third-party dependencies, I mean libraries external to Python designed to perform a specialized functionality that is not implemented in Python "out of the box." In other words, Python sets for itself a very lofty goal. It should be able to do literally anything all by itself using what is called the Python standard library.

Naturally, this goal can never be fully realized. The Python standard library is very complete. Eventually, though, you'll find something the standard library either can't do or the standard library's implementation isn't as easy to use as it could be. Let's look at a couple of quick examples of third-party libraries that are widely used, and talk about why you might want to use them.

Let's start with the `requests` library. This is a third-party library you'll find on PyPI at `https://pypi.org/project/requests/`. Every modern language has something similar. JavaScript has the **Node Package Manager** (**NPM**) at `https://npmjs.com`. **PHP** uses **Composer** to install packages from `https://packagist.org/`. The .NET languages use **NuGet** with packages registered at `https://nuget.org`. Python has `https://pypi.org`. It is a centralized listing of third-party modules and libraries you can add to your project, often free of charge. Metaphorically speaking, the idea is to prevent us from having to reinvent the wheel every time we want to build a new car. Since I work on a **software-as-a-service** (**SaaS**) project as my day job, I find myself needing an easy way to make **Hypertext Transfer Protocol** (**HTTP**) requests. The ability for my Python scripts to be able to make a call to some web service and process the results is crucial, and it is a very common task.

Python's standard library has a few options for accomplishing this. I think the most obvious is `urllib` from the standard library. Here is some example code from the `urllib2` documentation at `https://docs.python.org/3/howto/urllib2.html`:

```python
import urllib.parse
import urllib.request

url = 'http://www.someserver.com/cgi-bin/register.cgi'
values = {'name' : 'Michael Ford',
      'location' : 'Northampton',
      'language' : 'Python' }
```

```
data = urllib.parse.urlencode(values)
data = data.encode('ascii') # data should be bytes
req = urllib.request.Request(url, data)
with urllib.request.urlopen(req) as response:
  the_page = response.read()
```

First, we import two parts of the `urllib` package, remembering that is really `urllib2`. Next, we create a `url` variable. If you're wondering what the references to `cgi` are in the sample, that's a **common gateway interface** (**CGI**). Nobody has used that in production since around 1991, but it's still in the documentation and is still valid. CGI is the ancestor of modern web development. Basically, it refers to a program written in C that is executed by the web server in response to an endpoint having `cgi-bin` within the address. This style of development was supplanted long ago by the likes of **PHP**, classic **Active Server Pages** (**ASP**), **Java ServerPages** (**JSP**), and ColdFusion. Even those have since evolved into modern systems that use more sophisticated yet easier-to-code implementations of routing libraries that are very flexible. We'll cover these later in the book when we talk about the web application development features in PyCharm Professional.

Once we have our `url` variable established, we need some data. In this example, we are using HTTP `POST` to send data to our web server for processing. This is done with the `values` variable, which contains a dictionary that mimics the fields and values you might find in a **Hypertext Markup Language** (**HTML**) form.

Once we've set that up, we must parse that dictionary into a format suitable for transmission. That is done with `urllib.parse.urlencode`. Next, we need to further encode the data as **American Standard Code for Information Interchange** (**ASCII**). This is another anachronism in the documentation. Modern systems use the 8-bit universal text format (UTF-8) since ASCII only encodes letters from Romance languages such as English, French, German, Italian, or Portuguese. The rest of the world is out of luck. UTF-8 handles every alphabet in common global use today; this way, only the ancient Egyptians are snubbed, since UTF-8 doesn't support hieroglyphics —at least, not that I know of.

After we encode the text, we need to create a `request` object. We pass in our `url` variable and data to the constructor for `urllib.request.Request`. Only then are we ready to send the request in the last two lines of the sample.

We've established there is a way to make a `POST` request in Python's standard library. So far, though, we've only handled a very basic requirement. What if I need to present a request that is authenticated? How would I deal with sessions or cookies? Could we make this even simpler? We can with the `requests` library. Here is some sample code:

```
import requests

requests.post('https://httpbin.org/post', data={'key':'value'})
```

Our previous code from `urllib` could be expressed as a one-liner using `requests`! More advanced requirements such as sessions, cookies, and so on are equally easy. The documentation is modern and contains useful examples. Popular PyPI libraries such as `requests` are very well documented, with tutorials on sites such as `https://realpython.com`. I borrowed the preceding sample from `https://realpython.com/python-requests/`, which is part of a large and very complete tutorial on using this powerful library.

The point of all this is to point out that a system of third-party code libraries is necessary, or at least useful, in the context of Python—a language that strives to include everything you could ever need, but never will. The standard library may come close, but it will never include everything I could ever want.

Another important example of necessary third-party libraries is with respect to scientific and financial work. The standard math capabilities in Python are about the same as you would find in any other language. Most languages are not incredibly precise at handling floating-point calculations. They are also not very nuanced at handling matrices of numeric data, which represents a common requirement. Thankfully, third-party libraries such as `numpy` and `pandas` exist to fill this void. These libraries open new possibilities to Python developers and are one of the main reasons Python continues to attract new users.

Adding third-party libraries in PyCharm

PyCharm includes a UI screen that allows you to manage the packages in your current project. However, if an IDE were not in use, you could use a package manager to do it manually. For example, to install `numpy` into your project, you could use the `pip` package manager with a command such as this:

```
pip install numpy
```

You should make sure you have activated the virtual environment for the project in order for this to work correctly. Otherwise, `numpy` will be installed globally. The `pip` installer isn't the only installer available. There's `easy_install`, `pipenv`, `poetry`, and of course, `conda`. I'm not going to debate the relative merits of each since this is a matter of preference. PyCharm supports them all.

PyCharm's package manager invokes the package manager set in your environment settings. It presents a graphical interface where you can search for packages, view their descriptions, and install, update, and uninstall any package in your project. Let's take a look.

Going back to PyCharm, let's return to our project settings. Click on **Python Interpreter**, as shown in *Figure 3.15*:

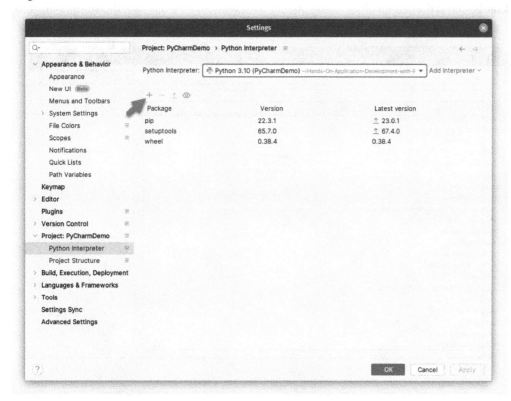

Figure 3.15: The interpreter settings show not only your interpreter
but also a list of packages available to that interpreter

The screen shows the interpreter in use for the current project. We saw earlier that we can change this environment at any time. Now, we are going to focus on the empty package list that takes up most of the screen. This is where you will be able to work with packages once we've installed them.

Let's install the numpy package. Start by clicking the + button, indicated by the arrow, at the top of the package list, as shown in *Figure 3.15*. This brings up yet another dialog that allows you to search for packages. In the search textbox, shown in *Figure 3.16*, type in numpy. As you type, you will see a list of packages from PyPI that satisfy your search. Click on the numpy entry and view the description.

It is a good idea to scrutinize the description since if you misspell your search term, you might wind up with the wrong packages. This is definitely the numpy library, so I'll install it by clicking the **Install Package** button at the bottom of the dialog. After a short wait, I'll see a message, shown in *Figure 3.16* (just above the grayed-out **Install Package** button), stating the package was successfully installed:

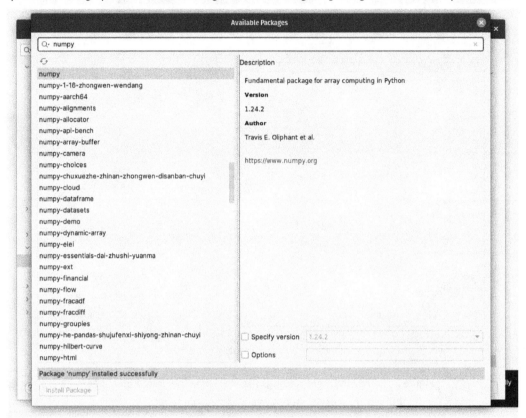

Figure 3.16: The display at the bottom indicates the package was installed successfully

Go ahead and close the dialog box to go back to the project settings.

Removing third-party libraries in PyCharm

Next to the + button we just used to search for and install the numpy package, we see a few more buttons near the arrow in *Figure 3.17*:

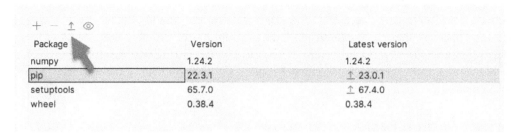

Figure 3.17: Tools for managing your package installations

You can likely guess what they do. The – button will remove a selected package. The up-arrow button will allow you to upgrade a package to a newer version. In *Figure 3.17*, we can see pip can be upgraded to version 23.0.1. Clicking the up arrow will accomplish this. The eye button will show you pre-release package versions should you want to try out the bleeding-edge versions of the packages.

Now that we understand what the UI for package management does, I'd like to digress for a moment and talk about something that it does not do well. The present release of PyCharm does not have a good way, in my opinion, to work with a requirements.txt file.

Using a requirements.txt file

A best practice in using Python projects is to use a file named requirements.txt to list the third-party library dependencies for your project. If you're starting your project from scratch, you can generate a requirements.txt file using pip in your terminal with this command:

```
pip freeze > requirements.txt
```

Figure 3.18 shows an example of the contents of the requirements.txt file we just generated. You might have to look hard to see it since it is only one line long. You can see the package name as well as the version requirements for numpy==1.24.2. If you are using a different package manager, review the specific process for generating your requirements.txt file:

```
bruce@maddevskilz: ~/Hands-On-Application-Development-with-...

(venv) bruce@maddevskilz:~/Hands-On-Application-Development-with-PyCharm---Sec
ond-Edition/chapter-01/PyCharmDemo$ pip freeze > requirements.txt
(venv) bruce@maddevskilz:~/Hands-On-Application-Development-with-PyCharm---Sec
ond-Edition/chapter-01/PyCharmDemo$ cat requirements.txt
numpy==1.24.2
(venv) bruce@maddevskilz:~/Hands-On-Application-Development-with-PyCharm---Sec
ond-Edition/chapter-01/PyCharmDemo$
```

Figure 3.18: The contents of a sample requirements.txt file showing
the third-party dependencies for our project

If you have cloned an existing project and it has a `requirements.txt` file, PyCharm will recognize it when you open the project and offer to install the contents to your virtual environment. PyCharm will also monitor your project as you work. If you add new dependencies, either through the GUI we've discussed or manually from the terminal, PyCharm will offer to add those dependencies to your `requirements.txt` file automatically.

The new Python Packages window

New to the latest releases of PyCharm which uses the new UI is a **Python Packages** window. It adds similar functionality to the interpreter settings window in a different location and layout. Clearly, they were reading over my shoulder when I wrote earlier about how the Python environment settings being inside the general settings window is unintuitive. I doubt I'll get credit for pointing it out, though. You'll find the new **Python Packages** window in the **More Tool Windows** ellipsis, indicated in *Figure 3.19*:

Figure 3.19: The More Tools menu contains the new Python Packages window

When you click the **Python Packages** icon, a new window will appear, as seen in *Figure 3.20*:

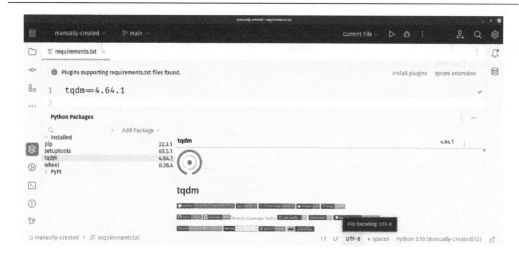

Figure 3.20: The new Python Packages window in PyCharm

As with the **Environment Settings** window, the **Python Packages** window shows a list of packages installed in the virtual environment, along with the accompanying version number. There is an **Add Package** button that allows you to add a package from PyPI or from a repository. You can search for packages using the search dialog, which shows a list of matching packages. Clicking one will show the documentation for that package. This is a step up from the **Environment Settings** window since this one displays the project's markdown documentation. You can see an example in *Figure 3.21*:

Figure 3.21: Searching for the numpy package in the new Python Package window

As you can see, I've searched for a package that was found on PyPI with 184 matches. I've selected the numpy package, and PyCharm displays the documentation for the project. There's a nice big **Install package** button and a selector to pick the version I'd like to install.

I can delete an installed package by clicking an installed package in the list. The version number is displayed along with the packages' documentation. Beneath the ellipsis next to the installed version number is a **Delete Package** button, as seen in *Figure 3.22*:

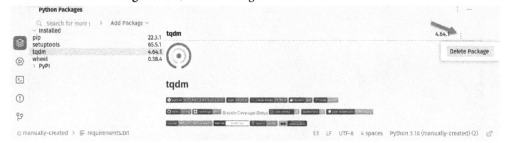

Figure 3.22: Deleting a package can be done using the menu option beneath
the ellipsis next to the version number in the Python Package window

This feature is so new as I write this that it almost didn't make it into the chapter. I happened to notice it while at work the other day. It presents, in my opinion, a less confusing and more convenient way to work with Python packages.

Professional features important to virtual environments

One major feature of the Professional edition of PyCharm is the ease of project creation compared to the more manual approach. Consider the Professional edition's new project window, which has a set of project types, as seen in *Figure 3.23*:

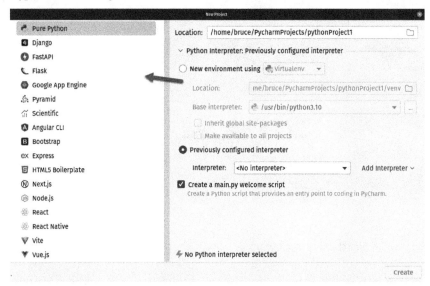

Figure 3.23: The Professional edition lists many project templates in the New Project dialog

The Community edition of Python does not have any of these project options. You can only create pure Python projects, but to be fair, you can still create a Flask project or any of the other project types listed using the Community edition. However, the IDE isn't going to help you do it.

Let's look at the steps to create a Flask project. Flask is a library that allows us to easily create a dynamic web application. We'll cover it extensively in *Chapter 8, Building a Dynamic Web Application in Flask*. For now, we're going to compare the level of work needed to do this without the Professional edition (that is, with no IDE at all).

These are the steps to manually set up the project:

1. Create a new folder for your project.
2. Create a new virtual environment for your project.
3. Activate the virtual environment.
4. Use your favorite package manager to install the Flask library along with its dependencies.
5. Create a Python file to hold your starting code.
6. Research the web and find an example of a simple "Hello world" sample and put that in your Python file.
7. Create a script that can set any necessary environment variables such as PYTHONPATH, then run your program.

I'll bet many of you can do this in about 20-30 minutes, tops. Here's my problem with that: when are you most fired up about your new project idea? It's at the beginning of the project! You are ready to roll but then must stop and spend 30 minutes doing this tedious setup. It isn't a lot of time, but it is an interruption. There is a chance of hitting some unexpected snags, which can zap your enthusiasm. In extreme cases, sometimes, unexpected snags delay you hours or days. PyCharm automates the entire process. You step through a couple of dialog screens, usually accepting the defaults, and your project is ready in fewer than 30 seconds. You can immediately start banging out your idea in code by modifying the starting boilerplate generated by the IDE.

The Professional edition will help you generate more complicated projects with very little effort on your part. The IDE will create your folder structure, a basic set of files with edit prompts to get started, and a virtual environment. PyCharm will even install the requirements for you.

Importing projects into PyCharm

Perhaps it goes without saying, but I'm going to say it anyway. You can import existing projects created either manually or with another IDE into PyCharm. This seems obvious because, after all, it is just a matter of opening a folder on your computer. The import process really is as simple as opening a folder in PyCharm. However, there's more to the story than that. PyCharm is your intelligent ally when it comes to working on getting a project running on your machine that was started, or entirely authored, on another without PyCharm involved. Let's see this in action.

Within this book's source code we cloned at the end of *Chapter 2, Installation and Configuration*, and within the chapter-03 folder, there is a project that I created entirely from the command line. You can see the process I used in *Figure 3.24*:

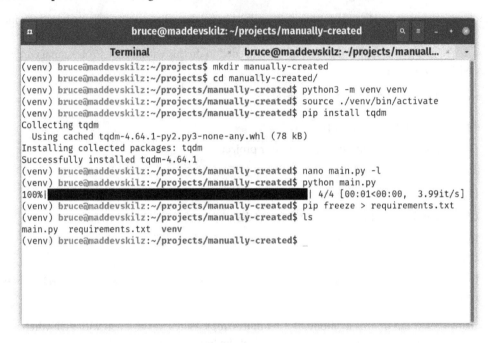

Figure 3.24: The terminal window I used to create a Python project entirely outside of PyCharm

The process I followed is clearly shown, as described here:

1. Within a new project folder called manually-created, I created a new virtual environment with the python3 -m venv venv command.

2. I activated the virtual environment with the source venv/bin/activate command. In this case, I am working in Linux. This same command will work on a Mac. If I were using Windows, it would be .\venv\Scripts\activate.

3. Next, I installed a third-party module called tqdm. You can find out more at https://pypi. org/project/tqdm/. The short version of this module is used to easily format the terminal output of a program to include a nice-looking progress bar. You can see the blocky progress bar a little further down in *Figure 3.24* after I run the program. I'm getting ahead of myself.

4. I used nano to add some code to a new file called main.py. I'll show you the contents in a moment, but all I did was copy and paste an example from the tqdm documentation on the https://pypi.org page I linked earlier. If you're wondering what the -l switch does, it displays line numbers in the nano editor, which makes nano a quick, easy-to-use code editor.

5. I ran the program using the `python main.py` command.

6. Having verified that it all worked, I created a `requirements.txt` file to document my program's dependence on the `tqdm` module. The `pip freeze` command will output a dependency graph to the screen. In order to turn that into a text file I can include in my Git repository, I piped the output with `> requirements.txt`, making the full command look like this:

```
pip freeze > requirements.txt.
```

This kind of command-line setup work is beneath us. In fact, I recommend you celebrate this by buying yourself a new pair of cargo pants and carrying yourself with a new air of swagger! If you identify as a non-cargo-pants-wearing sentient being, I hope you'll use your imagination to translate my intent. On second thoughts, at the risk of generalizing, you probably should take neither wardrobe nor social behavior advice from me. Traditionally, *wardrobe advice* is not my *strong suit*.

> **Warning**
>
> If this is the first of my books you are reading, one ground rule I keep is that all puns are intended.

Thankfully, working with projects created outside of PyCharm is a strong suit of PyCharm. Since the project has already been created outside of PyCharm, let's see what PyCharm makes of it. Let's open the `chapter-03/manually-created` folder in PyCharm. To make things crystal clear, I'm showing you the project's open dialog in *Figure 3.25*:

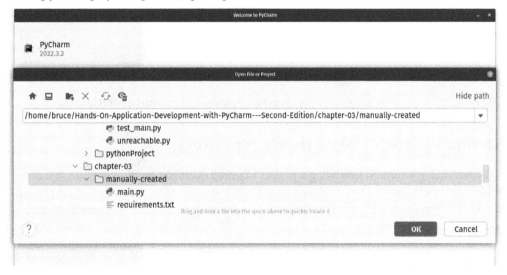

Figure 3.25: Opening the manually-created project that was created outside of PyCharm

For this project, I did something I would not usually do. The virtual environment (venv) folder is included in the git repository. Normally, it shouldn't be, but it needs to be there for you to see the next little bit of magic.

Open the project folder and watch what happens. If you're looking for a big display of software-empowered awesomeness, it might seem a little underwhelming. It isn't even worthy of a screenshot. The project opened, and it's just sitting there. That's the cool part. PyCharm can see your virtual environment folder, so it automatically sets up your project for you. You can verify all this in your project settings, as seen in *Figure 3.26*:

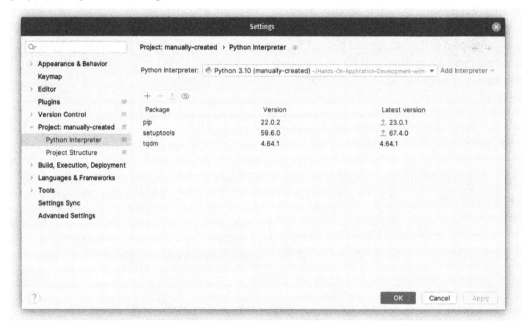

Figure 3.26: The imported project has the correct interpreter settings with no effort on our part

Importing a project cloned from a repository

Our previous example showed importing a project I created manually on my computer. It is more likely you will import a project you've cloned from GitHub or some other repository. These projects when cloned will not have the virtual environment folder present. As such, you have to do a little more work to set up the project.

I'm going to reuse the same project, but I'm going to delete a few files so that PyCharm won't remember anything about the project.

First, close the project in PyCharm, as seen in *Figure 3.27*:

Figure 3.27: Closing the project

Next, use your operating system to delete the folders shown in *Figure 3.28*:

Figure 3.28: Deleting the venv and .idea folders to simulate a project you
might have cloned from a version control system (VCS)

We are getting rid of the `venv` folder and the `.idea` folder. The latter will be hidden on macOS and Linux systems, so make sure you turn on the ability to view hidden folders. The `.idea` folder is the PyCharm project folder, which was automatically created when you opened the project folder. With those two folders gone, PyCharm is now virtually ignorant of having ever opened the project.

The folder will still show up in your **Recent** projects folder, but that is OK. Open the folder again with PyCharm. The result of opening the project in PyCharm is shown in *Figure 3.29*:

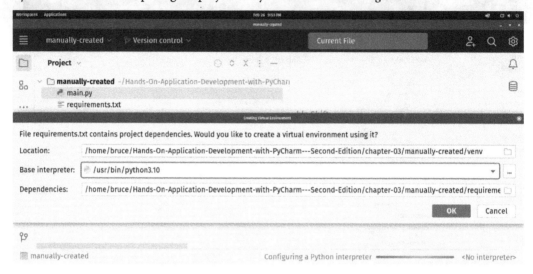

Figure 3.29: Importing a project created outside of PyCharm prompts to create a virtual environment

PyCharm sees the requirements.txt file but it can't find a suitable virtual environment because there isn't a subfolder in the project containing a Python executable. PyCharm will prompt you to create an environment for your project. In my case, the default is to a local folder called venv. It is going to use the Python 3.10 executable it found at /usr/bin/python3.10 as the base for the virtual environment, and it sees the requirements.txt file. If I hit **OK**, PyCharm will set up a virtual environment and then install my dependencies for me.

Dealing with invalid interpreters

No IDE is perfect. Sometimes, PyCharm can get confused about which virtual environment to use. This really only happens when you set up a new project with code not created in PyCharm. This is a corner case, but sooner or later, you're going to see it, so I want to spend a minute talking about this scenario. Maybe you're preparing to write a book on PyCharm. OK—that probably mostly happens to me. Say you're preparing a demo. Maybe you are setting up a training session and you've fiddled around with things a little too much or a few too many times. If you are like me, you like things to be perfect. You've worked toward setting up a project, and you see listings for invalid environments such as the one in *Figure 3.30*:

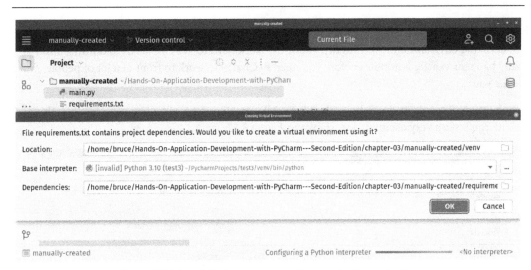

Figure 3.30: Invalid interpreter errors happen to the best of us

Gross! There's an ugly red message saying the base interpreter is invalid. We need to fix this. The good news is you know what to do! First, let's solve your immediate problem. You need to set the base interpreter so that PyCharm can finish importing your project. The first thing to try is the drop-down list for the base interpreter. In all likelihood, your global Python installation will appear in the list. If it does, pick it then click **OK**, and PyCharm will do its thing.

If you can't find one, you can still make a valid environment. You just need to create a virtual environment the same way we did when we were creating our project from scratch. You'd need to cancel out of the dialog you're seeing in *Figure 3.32* and use the project settings to add a new environment.

Click **File | Settings** to get into the **Settings** dialog and find the project settings, as shown in *Figure 3.31*:

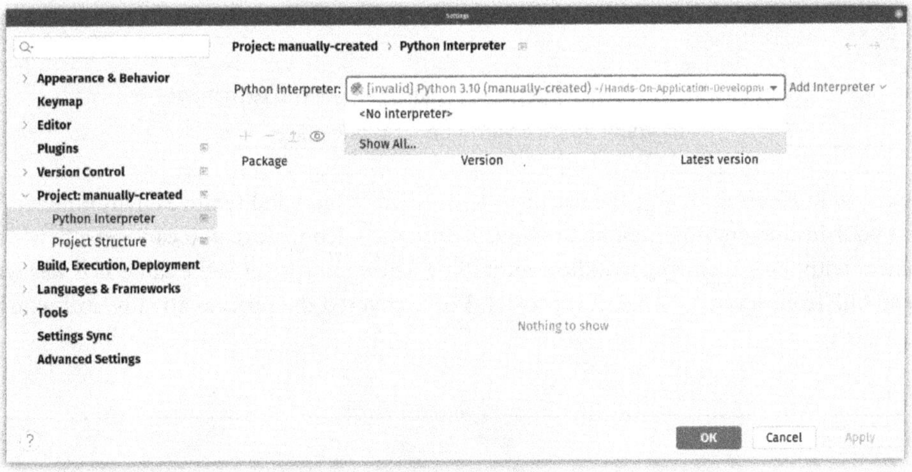

Figure 3.31: The worst-case scenario (it doesn't happen often, but it does happen)

This is the worst-case scenario! The list doesn't show the base interpreter, and the only option is our invalid virtual environment. Admittedly, you must work hard to get PyCharm to do this, but this usually happens exactly 5 minutes before you need PyCharm to work in front of a lot of people. I'm here for you.

At the bottom of the drop-down list is the **Show All…** option. This will allow us to fix everything! Click it! You'll see a very useful dialog, shown in *Figure 3.32*:

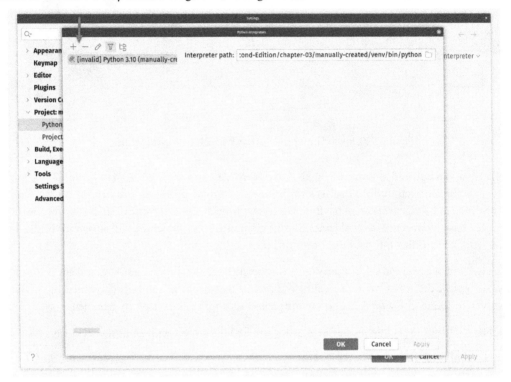

Figure 3.32: The Python interpreters dialog allows you to manage
all your Python environments in one place

Note the arrow in *Figure 3.32*. You can use the + and – icons to add and remove environments. You can select your invalid environment and remove it with the – icon. Next, you can add a new, valid environment with the + icon. The workflow for adding a new interpreter is the same as it was when we created one from scratch with a new project. We've covered the process already, so I won't go through it again.

Working with run configurations

Run configurations in PyCharm allow you to set up different ways to run your programs from the IDE. The heart of the run configurations is a cluster of blue buttons toward the top of the main window. Follow the arrow in *Figure 3.33*:

Figure 3.33: There are several run buttons at the top of the screen along with a drop-down list that allows you to work with various run configurations

Since we have the `manually-created` project already open from earlier, why don't we continue exploring using that project? That cluster of buttons I pointed to in *Figure 3.33* consists of a **Run** button, a **Debug** button, and a dropdown that lets you set and manage your run configurations. When we imported the project, it generated a run configuration called **Current File**.

With this set in the drop-down menu, the file in the **Focused** tab will be executed when you click either the run or debug button:

1. This is the regular **Run** button. It just runs whatever is indicated by the currently selected run configuration. In this case, it would run the `main.py` script because that is in the currently focused tab.

2. This is the **Run** (debug) button. Clicking this will run your selected run configuration with an attached debugger. We'll see this in action in *Chapter 6, Seamless Testing, Debugging, and Profiling*.

3. The ellipsis button contains more options for running a profiler and checking your test coverage. We'll cover these in later chapters.

4.   The **Run configuration** dropdown lets you select a run configuration. There is an option to create and edit existing configurations as well as create new ones.

For now, let's focus on the run configurations themselves since these have their own environment settings independent from the rest of the project.

Click the drop-down menu where it says **Current File** and click **Edit Configurations…**, as shown in *Figure 3.34*. This brings up a dialog for managing your run configurations. You can add, edit, and delete your configurations here. Note the Professional edition will have more tooling available in this window than will the Community edition. I will focus on the Professional edition:

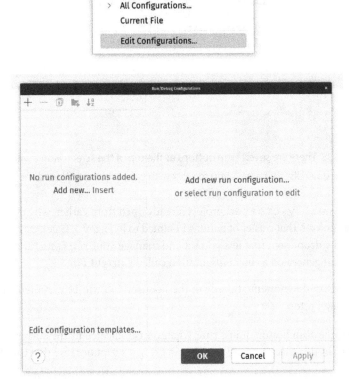

Figure 3.34: Adding a new run configuration for our manually-created project

There are plenty of prompts in the dialog that allow you to create a new run configuration. Let's ignore those because once you add one, those options will go away. Click the + icon at the top of the dialog, as shown in *Figure 3.35*:

Figure 3.35: Clicking the + button to add a new run configuration (the list shown is for the Professional edition, and you'll need to scroll down to find the Python item shown)

If you are running the Professional edition, you'll see a long list of options, as in *Figure 3.35*. The Community edition list is considerably shorter since it only has tooling for pure Python projects.

I'm going to pick the Pure Python project type since that's one we can all use. Each option may present a different dialog box with different settings based on what is appropriate for your selection. The Pure Python options look like what is shown in *Figure 3.36*:

Figure 3.36: The options for a run configuration using the Pure Python template

There are a lot of settings here. Let's review the most important settings by the numbers provided in *Figure 3.36*:

1. You should give the run configuration a name. If you don't, it will default to the name of the script. You can use a human-friendly name here; it doesn't have to relate to the running file in any way.

2. This setting is probably the most obvious. It lets you select the script you'd like to run. You can browse to it or type the path. You can also change this from a script file to a module name by clicking the triangle next to the script path text entry box. If you change the setting to run a module, the folder **Browse** button will change to an ellipsis, and you'll be able to browse the modules in your program to find the one you'd like to run.

3. The **Parameters** setting allows you to pass in arguments. If your program expects arguments using a library such as `argparse`, you can pass them here. This textbox is fairly interactive. Note the + icon. Clicking this allows you to invoke some macros available in the tool. For example, if you need the path for the current directory, you'll find an option for that in the macro list.

4. These are the environment settings. The default uses the project settings. You can set a different virtual environment for your run configurations than for your project if you need to test-run your software in different environments. You can also set environment variables here without jumping out to your operating system. This is handy if you rely on environment variables for your program settings. If you use OS-level environment variables for sensitive data such as passwords or connection strings, I recommend against setting them here. These settings can wind up in the project configuration files, which means they could make it into your source repository. There's nothing worse than realizing your hackathon project files contain your personal password or access tokens for your favorite cloud provider. `SuperH4xr1337@some-evil-hacker-org.darkweb.net` (*note*: hopefully not a real address) loves it when you do this. There are bots that troll GitHub looking for this stuff, so be careful. Personally, I use configuration files for this using one of the many `env` libraries. I'll put a link in the *Further reading* section if you're interested in this.

5. You can set a working directory should any part of your script rely on relative file paths.

6. This checkbox controls whether the content roots from your project are injected into the `PYTHONPATH` environment variable when you run your program. The `PYTHONPATH` environment variable controls where the Python interpreter searches for modules. Content roots refer to project structure settings where you define content folders. This is generally only used with web projects. A content folder might contain images or other static content. The **Add source roots to PYTHONPATH** option allows you to inject project-configured source folders into the `PYTHONPATH` environment variable. I've worked on microservice architecture projects where this was useful. Sometimes, you might have a module in another project that you need to leverage, but it belongs in its own separate project rather than being directly managed in the current project. You can set your source roots to include other projects with dependencies, and checking this box will make those available to your running program.

As you can see, there are a lot of options and ways you can customize the way a program is run using PyCharm. If your application has several executable scripts, you can set each one up with its own run configuration.

PyCharm's project files

Most IDEs have some sort of project file designed to contain project-level settings. If you've ever used any of Microsoft's IDEs, you might remember folders such as `.vscode` for Visual Studio Code and `.vs` in a Visual Studio project. Java IDEs such as NetBeans and Eclipse also use a set of files to contain their project settings. PyCharm too has a set of files stored in a folder within each project, called .idea. This might seem like a strange name until you remember that JetBrains began with only one IDE project, IntelliJ IDEA. IntelliJ IDEA garnered a reputation for being the best IDE for Java development, bar none. It is so good that Google contracted with JetBrains to create Android Studio; a natural fit given Android applications are written entirely in Java. All the IDEs from JetBrains have the same lineage. They are all descendants of IntelliJ IDEA, and that's why the project folder is called .idea. Remember—Windows users will plainly see this folder, while on Linux and Mac, any folder name beginning with a dot (.) is hidden.

By default, there isn't anything particularly interesting inside these folders should you ever be tempted to try to edit them. In fact, if you were to delete them, PyCharm would simply recreate them when you reopen the project.

That said, there are options in PyCharm that let you store your run configurations within these files, as shown in *Figure 3.37*:

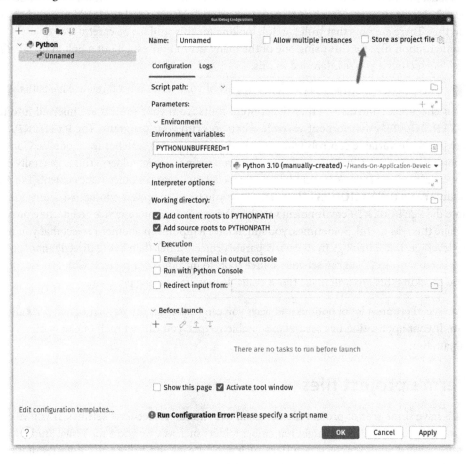

Figure 3.37: You can opt to store run configurations as part of the project files in the .idea folder

If you opt to do this, you have the capability to check the `.idea` files into your VCS repository and share them with your team. This means everybody will have the same configurations, so you might want to have a meeting and standardize your project structure so that you're not stepping on each other.

Summary

This chapter was all about setting up your virtual environment for a Python project. Each project typically has its own virtual environment. We use virtual environments to insulate our projects from the requirements of other projects and to keep our global Python installation from becoming polluted with lots of global packages that were used for only one project.

A virtual environment is a copy of a Python interpreter along with all supporting tools such as a package manager and third-party libraries needed for your project. PyCharm has features built in for creating and managing virtual environments.

We first see these tools during the creation of a new project. PyCharm prompts us to create a new virtual environment every time. We can also select an existing environment if that is appropriate. PyCharm gives us the ability to change the virtual environment for the project at any time.

Our virtual environments also house all the third-party libraries needed for our project. You can find thousands of ready-made modules at `https://pypi.org`. These modules can be installed and used in your projects by means of a package manager. The most common package manager is `pip`, but others exist, such as `conda`, `pipenv`, and `poetry`. PyCharm supports all of these tools, and you are afforded the opportunity to select your tool of choice when you create your virtual environment.

Having selected your package manager, PyCharm has a GUI that allows you to see, add, remove, and update your library dependencies from PyPI. You'll find this GUI within your project settings, which are bundled inside the general settings for PyCharm itself.

PyCharm can easily import projects created outside of PyCharm. All you need to do is open the folder where the code resides. PyCharm creates a set of project files within that folder called `.idea`, then prompts you to set an interpreter if it couldn't find one within the project folder. PyCharm will also look for a `requirements.txt` file and offer to install your dependencies for you.

When you are ready to run some code within the IDE, PyCharm offers a powerful run system that uses run configurations created in the GUI. PyCharm Professional ships with many project types, and each one has its own run configuration settings. We covered the extensive settings found in a pure Python project since that is available to Community edition users. The run configuration can manage—and in some cases mimic—a wide gamut of settings you would normally have to set manually at the operating system level.

All totaled, PyCharm gives you a very complete set of tools for managing virtual environments for development and running your code. In the next chapter, we'll switch our focus to the primary tools you'll use every day to manage, write, and edit your code.

Questions

1. What are virtual environments and why are they important?

2. What are the tools used by the Python community to create virtual environments?

3. Which virtual environment tools are supported in PyCharm?

4. Can a run configuration use a different virtual environment from the main project? How might this be useful?

5. Where does PyCharm keep its project configuration files?

Further reading

*   *Alternative Python Implementations*: `https://www.python.org/download/alternatives/`

*   The env library: `https://pypi.org/project/env/`

*   *Ajitsaria, A. What is the Python Global Interpreter Lock (GIL)?*: `https://realpython.com/python-gil/`

*   Be sure to check out the companion website for the book at `https://www.pycharm-book.com`.

4

Editing and Formatting with Ease in PyCharm

Leonardo Da Vinci, the great painter and sculptor, mused that his sculptures were fully formed in the blocks of stone from the quarry before he even saw the marble. Da Vinci explained that all he did was remove the pieces of marble that were not required for the form. In other words, his masterpieces were completed in his mind before a chisel touched the crude stone. In many ways, you are Da Vinci. You have a project in your head, fully formed, and you are eager to show the world your masterpiece. Instead of using a hammer and chisel to write your code, you are using PyCharm. In the previous chapters, we worked through the installation process and configuration of PyCharm. We also set up an interpreter for your project. Next up: the exploration of the main tools that you will use to craft your masterpiece, which mainly reside in the editor.

By now, you have discovered many of the obvious features of the editor. We know it handles a lot of the PEP-8 syntax rules automatically. We know we get the color-coded syntax. We also have observed that the **integrated development environment (IDE)** will make suggestions on several different areas of coding, ranging from linting style rules to auto-completion.

This chapter will focus on the features of the editor that are less obvious. The product's documentation provides keyboard shortcuts and editor basics that will not be discussed in this chapter. Instead, the following topics will be covered:

- Real-time code inspection with automated fixes, which allows you to focus on development goals rather than on the rules of Python coding.

- Various code-completion support features in PyCharm and how to leverage them. By using these, you'll be able to code more quickly and more accurately. We will only focus on those tools that ship with PyCharm versus third-party **artificial intelligence (AI)** enhancements that require plugins such as Kite or GitHub Copilot. These will be covered in *Chapter 15*.

- Refactoring tools that allow you to polish and refine your code into the masterpiece that it can become through patience, discipline, and good tooling.

- Documentation tools that will take you from the level of "good developer" to the level of "master developer." It's one thing to invent an amazing work of code. Documenting it so others can benefit from it takes your work to another level.

Technical requirements

In order to proceed through this chapter and the rest of the book, you will need the following:

- An installed and working Python interpreter. I'll be using the latest from `https://python.org`.

- Installed copies of `pip` and `virtualenv`. You get these automatically when you install Python on Windows, and MacOS has them included on every system. If you are using Linux, you need to install the package managers, such as `pip`, and virtual environment tools, such as `virtualenv`, separately. Our examples will use `pip` and `virtualenv`.

- An installed and working copy of PyCharm. Installation was covered in *Chapter 2*.

- This book's sample source code from GitHub can be found at `https://github.com/PacktPublishing/Hands-On-Application-Development-with-PyCharm---Second-Edition/tree/main/chapter-04`. We covered cloning the code in *Chapter 2, Installation and Configuration*.

Code analysis, inspection, and suggestion

Intelligent code completion is essential to any programming tool's adoption. The definition of a good code completion engine is one that is aware of high-level aspects of programming, including specifics of language syntax. The engine also must be aware of the lower-level specifics of the program you write. Many enhanced text editors support code completion but lack this level of sophistication. PyCharm stands out as an exceptionally sophisticated code editor, encompassing both the historical and modern aspects of code editors and offering a level of sophistication that surpasses many other enhanced text editors in terms of intelligent code completion.

The most common form of code completion is a large picklist of words that are matched as you type. The list of possibilities narrows as more letters are typed. Notepad++ is an enhanced text editor widely used by developers. I consider it a must-have tool for quick and easy edits when I am too impatient to wait on an IDE to fully load. *Figure 4.1* shows a session where I began typing some Python code:

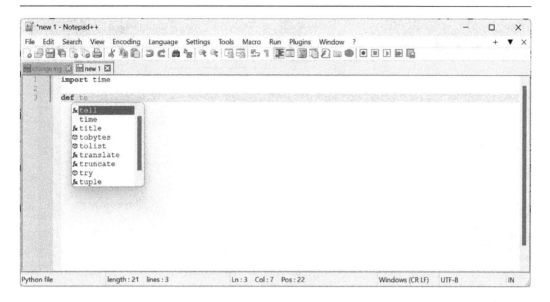

Figure 4.1: Notepad++ uses a very simple mechanism for code highlighting and completion

The tool does not intuitively know what is being typed; therefore, I must tell it that I am coding in Python. After the language is set, it will attempt to autocomplete everything, even though such an exercise is clearly futile. In *Figure 4.1*, I was going to type the following:

```
import time

def test_code():
    pass
```

This clearly isn't going to win me any Jolt awards. You see in the screenshot that the list is filtering a known list of words. Its only contextual point of reference is knowing that the file is a Python file. This isn't very effective, but it is better than nothing.

Systems like these are little more than spell checkers. While a seasoned pro might scoff at the usefulness of such a simple system, the earliest IDEs that displayed this level of wizardry pioneered a feature we are now unwilling to live without: code completion.

PyCharm lies at the opposite end of the spectrum with respect to sophistication. Like Notepad++, PyCharm is aware of the keywords that comprise PyCharm. PyCharm, though, is able to glean insight into the structure of the objects that make up the standard library. *Figure 4.2* shows me typing some code into PyCharm, having created a simple file for this example:

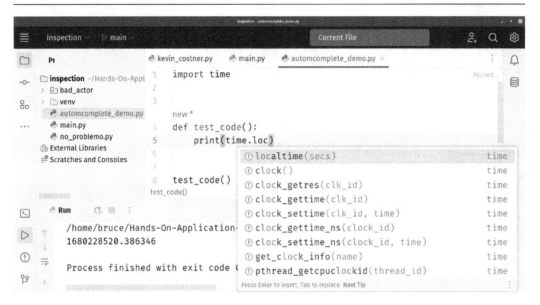

Figure 4.2: PyCharm auto-completes based on its understanding of the time library

In this case, I have imported the time library just as I did in the Notepad++ example from *Figure 4.1*. I'm a little further along here. I have my function defined, and I'm going to simply print the current local time using the time library I had already imported. As you can see in *Figure 4.2*, PyCharm is offering completion against the contents of the time library.

> **Completing the auto-completion**
>
> Once the auto-completion list appears, you can press *Tab* or *Enter* to select the highlighted option. You can use the up and down arrow keys to move through the list, or you can click any of the list items with your mouse. You'll work fastest, though, if you keep your fingers on the keyboard.

By now, you are starting to appreciate the code completion system offered by PyCharm. Let us further explore the capabilities of this important tool.

It duzunt assewm yew cna spel

Our simplistic word-list example from Notepad++ earlier already stands in sharp contrast to the more sophisticated features of PyCharm's auto-completion engine. Let's dig a little deeper. If your tool relies on a word list, then the second your spelling steps out of line, your suggestion list dries up. In effect, the word-list method requires you to know what it is you are looking for while requiring it to be spelled correctly.

In *Figure 4.3*, you will see something a little different:

Figure 4.3: PyCharm finds all possibilities containing the text you've typed

PyCharm is designed to offer suggestions based on the letters that are typed. In other words, as you type cl, the word *clock* might appear. The word *clock* will also appear if you type lo, ck, or any consecutive letters contained in the list of keywords matched. Perfectly spelled words are not necessary. Just get in the ballpark, and the word you are searching for will likely pop up.

It understands your code

Good code completion is able to understand and autocomplete based on the language and the libraries in use. In our case, that's Python, which has an enormous standard library compared to other languages. Python is designed around a "batteries included" philosophy. Contrast that with JavaScript as implemented in Node.js, where the only libraries you get are file and HTTP libraries. The .NET languages give you a small core. You can say the same about Golang. Most languages require you to use the package manager. The fact that PyCharm can do this is spectacular by itself.

PyCharm, being a great IDE, can also understand the code you've written. *Figure 4.4* shows the autocomplete_demo.py file, where I have added an import to the no_problemo.py file. The no_problemo.py file has one function in it called perfection(). As you can see, PyCharm is able to see inside the file and provide autocompletion on the code I have written versus simply doing auto-complete from a language-based word list:

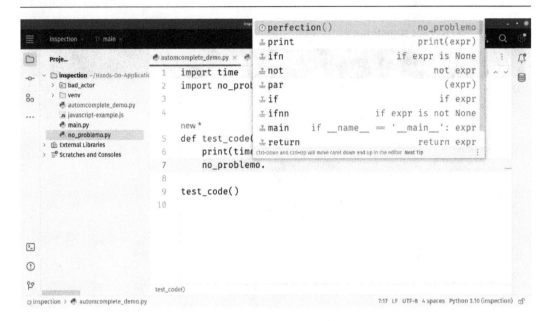

Figure 4.4: PyCharm provides autocompletion suggestions on the code you've
written, as well as standard Python language and the standard library

I am offered auto-completion on the function name, as well as hints on the **method signature**. If you're unfamiliar with the term *method signature*, it simply refers to the name, argument list, and return values for a function or method. If you've included type hints, PyCharm will remind you of the argument names and types the function or method requires. This works with modules as well as classes if you're using **object-oriented programming (OOP)**.

Postfix code completion

Traditional code completion has been taken to the next level in PyCharm, but we are far from finished. Usually, hitting the period (.) key on your keyboard triggers a list to appear. We are now used to that list containing what might come after the dot. However, what if PyCharm could give you suggestions on what might come *before* the dot? In *Figure 4.5*, we see an example of postfix code completion, which you will find in the postfix_example.py file in the *Chapter 4* sample code:

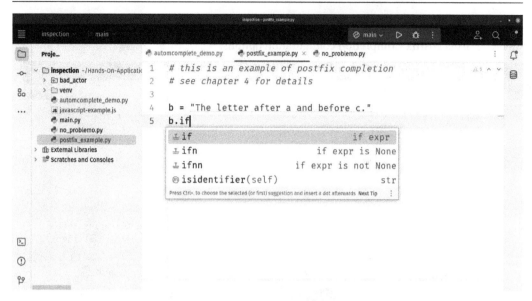

Figure 4.5: Postfix completion in PyCharm can suggest what might come
before the dot rather than simply what might come after

I can't blame you if you are confused by seeing `.if` (if expr) as a possibility following what is clearly a string-typed variable. The `.if` suggestion is not part of Python. It is a **postfix suggestion**. If you complete this suggestion your code is transformed. The following code isn't viable Python syntax:

```
b.if
```

Therefore, it is converted to the following:

```
if b:
```

Just imagine the possibilities! However, if you're not the imaginative type, check out *Figure 4.6*, which shows PyCharm's **Postfix Completion** configuration options:

Figure 4.6: PyCharm's Postfix Completion configuration options

Naturally, these options are fully configurable. You can even add your own! The templates are not limited to Python. You can see in the list that there are configurations for TypeScript, JavaScript, and **Structured Query Language** (**SQL**). This is important because application development is rarely limited to the scope of just the Python language.

Hippie completion

Hey, man! You wanna see something that is like totally far out? It's called **cyclic word expansion**. Only total squares call it that, though. If you wanna be *hip*, you'll call it **hippie completion**!

Hippie completion is invoked by pressing *Alt* + / (Windows and Linux) or ⌥ + / on macOS. Once triggered, PyCharm will index all the files you currently have open and provide auto-completion suggestions based on words within that context. In effect, you are using the simplest form of auto-complete; a word list. The word list is generated on the fly from the words in the files you have open. They don't have to be code. Plain text files, markup, markdown, or really any text will show up in the suggestions list based on a simple forward match. As you type, the list narrows. You can see an example in *Figure 4.7*:

Figure 4.7: Hippie completion is totally far-out!

The text file on the right contains a list of words I generated at https://fungenerators.com/lorem-ipsum/hippie/. Unfortunately, it turns out, a lot of the iconic words from the hippie generation in the United States cannot be printed in a book of this caliber. We have the highest standards! So, I edited the list, and this was all that was left. These words are random, so please don't try to construe any meaning from them, despite all the allegations about there being secret backward messages on albums by The Beatles. The code on the right can expand from that list using hippie completion. To make this work, I typed print("pat then pressed *Alt + /*. The word *patchouli* magically appeared! I hope this example was worth it for you. I may never get that smell out of my keyboard!

You can use *Alt + Shift + /* or ⌥ + *Shift + /* to enable backward cyclic word expansion, which matches from the end of the words backward to the beginning. If the powers that be had asked me (and they didn't, because they never do) I'd have called this **Ginger Rogers Completion**. Everyone thinks Fred Astaire was an amazing dancer in all the great Hollywood movies of the 1940s. Never forget, though, that his dance partner, Ginger Rogers, had to do everything Fred did, except she did it backward and in heels. That's my suggestion. Who knows? If enough of you tweet #GingerRogersCompletion and reference this book, it might catch on!

Pro hippie tip

Repeatedly pressing *Alt + /* (Windows and Linux) or ⌥ + / on macOS cycles through the list. You can just keep hitting the key combination until the word you are looking for appears.

Indexing

There are various engines at work in powering PyCharm's various code completion techniques. You might be wondering how it works. It isn't dark sorcery, I assure you. The key to understanding it is to pay attention when PyCharm loads a project. *Figure 4.8* calls your attention to the bottom of the PyCharm application window. PyCharm kicks off several background processes that comb through your code and index every character. The index is then converted into an in-memory database that is used by the various engines at play:

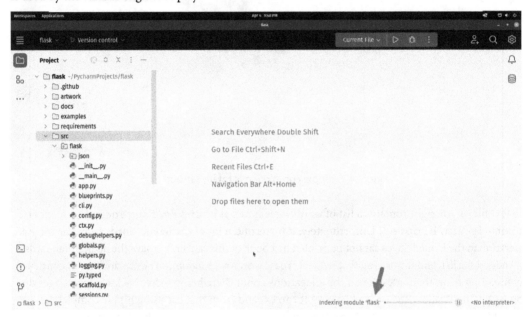

Figure 4.8: Keep an eye on the bottom of the PyCharm window to know
when background processes such as indexing are running

Normally, I don't really care how the magic works, but it is worth bringing up because there will be times when PyCharm seems slow or unresponsive. When PyCharm seems slow or if auto-completion isn't working, check the area of the screen indicated in *Figure 4.8* and see whether there are indexing processes running. You'll probably notice your CPU spike as well if you monitor such things. This is temporary. Once the indexing process completes, PyCharm will become responsive again.

Power Save Mode

One of the more cryptic entries in the PyCharm menu, shown in *Figure 4.9*, is **Power Save Mode**:

Figure 4.9: The Power Save Mode menu option can be found under the File menu

I remember the first time I clicked it. The streetlights throughout the city block where I live instantly got brighter. My electric meter that was spinning like a buzzsaw mere minutes ago was now lazily spinning slower than an abandoned top. Once, a guy at the power company even called and thanked me for doing my part in saving the planet.

OK, I'm making all that up, except for the part about the guy from the power company. That totally happened. The **Power Save Mode** option is designed to limit PyCharm's power consumption by turning off all those background processes, including the indexing used to generate code completion suggestions. PyCharm will remind you of this using a message, as shown in *Figure 4.10*. Not only can you see the warning message, but you can also see I don't get any completion on line 5. I would have at least expected b.if from the earlier example:

Figure 4.10: A message reminds you that power save mode is on and that you
will not be receiving the usual level of assistance from PyCharm

Personally, I consider this utterly barbaric! How are we supposed to work like this? Next, you'll be telling me I don't have access to the internet, Kite, GitHub Copilot, ChatGPT, or Stack Overflow! You'll strip me of my very reasonably priced subscription to packtpub.com, where I can get all the e-books I can read for one low price. Then you'll take away my Herman Miller Aeron Chair and limit me to only one $14 mezzo-Grande half-fat triple foam double shot latte with rainbow jasmine-infused sprinkles per day! Why don't you enact a dress code while you're at it? Strike! Strike! Strike!

Sorry. I got a little carried away. Needless to say, this is probably the least favorite feature of the IDE. Maybe it is useful if you chewed up your laptop's battery playing *Ghost Recon: Breakpoint* on an overseas flight, and upon landing, you suddenly get a call from the boss who needs something fixed right away. Suddenly, you need to squeeze every second out of that 5% battery level you have left. I hate it when that happens.

Customizing code completion

Customization within PyCharm is an ongoing theme. It might have been easier to show you what you can't customize, except that I haven't actually found anything yet. Code completion is no different. Whether you prefer a very lightweight experience with little to no help or you want your handheld on every line of code, there is a way to make PyCharm into the editor you want to use every day.

To open the settings for code completion, venture back to the settings dialog we explored in *Chapter 2, Installation and Configuration*. You can reach it easily by clicking the **File** menu item and selecting **Settings**. That brings up the settings dialog. If you recall from *Chapter 2, Installation and Configuration*, this dialog is massive! We're looking for **Editor** | **General** | **Code Completion**, as shown in *Figure 4.11*:

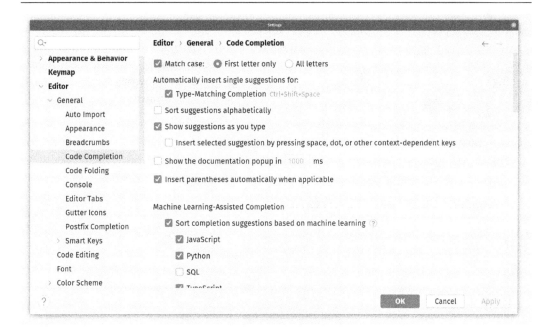

Figure 4.11: The Code Completion settings allow you to customize
the behavior of PyCharm's Code Completion engine

You should spend a moment going through everything you can do on this screen. PyCharm gives you a great deal of control! I promised this wouldn't be a tedious accounting of every option. Instead, draw your attention to the most popular and potentially most useful settings available.

Match case

Located at the top of the window, this option specifies whether items in the suggestion list should match the case of whatever you are typing. For example, if I wanted to type in an exception expression for the KeyboardInterrupt exception in Python and the **Match case** option is enabled, I would have to type a capital letter K for the correct class name to be included in the suggestion list. Next to the **Match case** checkbox, you can also choose only the first letter's case should be matched or whether this should apply to all the letters.

I personally always disable this checkbox so that I only have to type in, for example, a lowercase k to take advantage of code completion. When I am learning a new language or API, this setting can help me with a practice I call *property shopping*. I don't know what properties and methods are available, so an alphabetized list can be helpful. For example, every programming language has some sort of string-handling class or library. It is a very safe bet that the said library will have functions for trimming, which is to remove extra spaces from the front, end, or both ends of a string. There is always some sort of toUpper and toLower methods. These are all vital parts of defensive programming. A password input where a user accidentally includes a space at the beginning or end of the password makes for a frustrating user experience. Any conditional logic you use involving user input is easier to handle if you make everything upper or lowercase. Given these are so fundamental to our work, we know they will be on the list, but every language calls them something different. I work on projects that require switching between two or three languages, and it is very easy to type in the wrong function name. Take the method that converts a string to uppercase. In JavaScript, such a function looks like this:

```
let foo = "some user option";
if(foo.toUpperCase() === "SOME USER OPTION"){
  console.log("It matched!");
}
```

The same code in PyCharm, which I might be creating only minutes later, would look like this:

```
foo = "some user option"
if foo.upper() == "SOME USER OPTION":
  print("It matched")
```

In order to be effective, I need the word upper to be a match regardless of whether it is uppercase or lowercase.

Like everything we have seen in code completion, and for that matter, like everything in programming, there is a trade-off to this practice. Specifically, if **Match case** is disabled, sometimes the suggestion list might be populated by many more irrelevant options, which makes finding the correct API more difficult. At the same time, though, you will see a full list of what is possible, which can help you learn your way around and sometimes discover features in an API you had not imagined were available.

Sorting suggestions alphabetically

As its name suggests, this option allows you to sort the items in the suggestion list in alphabetical order. This feature is useful for long suggestion lists that require the developer to scroll through them carefully to find what they are looking for if they were not ordered alphabetically.

On multiple occasions, we have seen the dynamic nature of PyCharm, and it is once again demonstrated in this feature. Specifically, while interacting with a suggestion list in the editor, you can change the order of the items in the list at any time by clicking on the icon located in the bottom-right corner of the suggestion window, as shown in *Figure 4.12*:

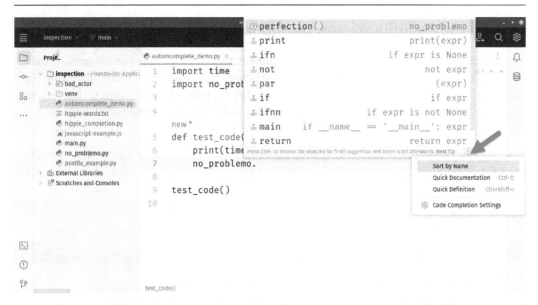

Figure 4.12: You can change the way suggestions are sorted within the list itself

Clicking the **...** (ellipsis) element allows you to change how the suggestions are sorted: by relevance or alphabetically by name.

Machine learning assisted completions

This newer option is simultaneously magical and scary. Enabled by default, PyCharm will train a machine learning model based on your code. This allows PyCharm to make suggestions based not only on your code but also that of thousands of other developers. Traditional code completion usually gives you suggestions for the next keyword, property, method name, or parameter you are about to type. Do not be surprised if PyCharm offers complete entire functions or blocks of code for you with machine learning assisted completions. You will see this for common tasks such as connecting to databases, working with pandas data frames, or validating user input.

The settings merely allow you to turn on various languages supported by PyCharm. Python, JavaScript, and TypeScript are enabled by default. Only SQL, a special-purpose language used for working with relational databases, is not enabled by default. I suspect this is because there are additional settings around your preferred SQL dialect both at the global and project level that contribute to suggestions. It would be awkward to expect a tight list of suggestions given the number of databases PyCharm supports and the differences in their implementation of language elements not defined by standardized SQL. We'll look at SQL and relational databases later in *Chapter 11, Understanding Database Management with PyCharm*. I promise the experience will not leave you bankrupt.

Showing the documentation popup in [...] ms

When you enable this feature, you will see the documentation in addition to the suggestion code. You will be able to understand what the code you are typing does rather than blindly accepting the suggestions. This is great for new developers, whether they are totally new to coding or just new to Python. The advantage of this feature is that you can go through the documentation of all the suggested items dynamically as you simply move the cursor down the items.

This is especially beneficial when working with classes and methods that have similar APIs. We will discuss this feature, along with other documentation-related functionalities, in the last section of this chapter.

Parameter info

Scroll down past the JavaScript section, as seen in *Figure 4.13*, and you'll find an option for suggesting parameter information:

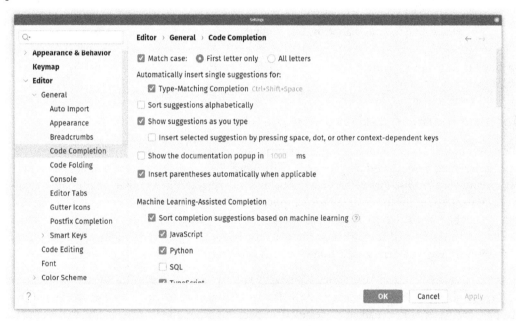

Figure 4.13: Scroll down past JavaScript to find options for showing parameter information

The first option is straightforward. It controls the amount of time that must elapse before a suggestion appears. In general, suggestions are great unless you are teaching, doing a code review, or doing some sort of demo, in which case they can clutter up your screen. Sometimes it's a good idea to raise the time limit so the suggestions or documentation are shown only if you linger for a few seconds.

The second option allows you to toggle, showing the full method signature. I love this feature. The code hint will show you the whole method signature so you can see all the arguments at once.

A method signature uniquely defines a function or method within the scope where it is declared. It consists of a name for the function. Along with the names, and preferably hints, for the type of the function's arguments with some hints about the return type. These are not unique to Python. In fact, they are a little bit fuzzy in Python. Now compare it with a static language such as C#, which uses more strict programming structures. In Python, you can use type hints, which help developers to remember the expected types of the arguments being passed. Let's look at an example of a method signature without hints:

```
a = 5
b = 6

def add_two_ints(first, second):
    return a + b
```

This is OK. This code will work as intended, and the intention of the developer is clear. Let's look at the same function with hints:

```
a = 5
b = 6

def add_two_ints(first: int, second: int) -> int:
    return a + b
```

This is much better! Now we know for certain the types that are expected as input parameters, and we know the type that is going to be returned. I said earlier that method signatures are "fuzzy" in Python. I said this because both code samples will work. Python ignores the hints entirely during compilation. The hints are just used by the tooling and make your Python code easier to read and understand. Adding hints to your code whenever possible will enhance the way you, and your teammates, see your method signatures if you turn on the **Show full method signatures** option.

Code analysis and automated fixes

Code completion is a standard feature of most code editors and IDEs. As we've seen, not all completion engines are created equally. The same can be true for analysis engines. A code analysis engine is an extension of code completion in concept, if not in implementation. Code completion tries to predict the code you are writing and helps you finish more quickly. Code analysis examines the code you've written and attempts to determine whether or not the code will work when you run it. Just as with code completion, there are differing levels of complexity at play here and different processes examining different things.

The simplest form of analysis is called *linting*. Pretty much every programming language has a linting tool, and Python is no exception. While there are many to choose from, PyCharm uses the popular `pylint` library by default.

A linter runs a tacit analysis of your code through a process of pattern matching. There are two linting operations: **logical lint** and **stylistic lint**. A logical lint looks for code errors, code with potentially unintentional results or side effects, and dangerous code patterns. A stylistic lint looks for code that doesn't conform to common conventions. This is less of a problem with Python since the language already has a strict set of code formatting rules called **Python Enhancement Proposal #8**. Nobody calls it that. Those in the know simply call it **PEP-8**.

Combined, you can think of `pylint` and, by extension, all linters, much like a spelling and grammar checker for regular text. The linter looks for misspelled keywords, malformed code, and obvious syntax errors. A linter can also enforce style guidelines, though really Python is already designed to enforce rules to make your code as human-readable as possible.

While it's one thing to point out problems in your code, it is entirely more useful if the tool also suggests and even implements fixes to those problems. The same is true of humans. It is easy to point out flaws. Anybody can do that. Good advice on how to fix your flaws is more useful than criticism. So, in addition to linting, PyCharm offers a system that will offer to help you fix the problems exposed by the linter.

Problem detection

Problem detection is performed by PyCharm in real time as you type your code. The indexing process we've mentioned before plays a role here, but we'll come back to that. First, let's focus on the visible interface in the editor that shows you where your problems lie. There are four places to look, as shown in *Figure 4.14*:

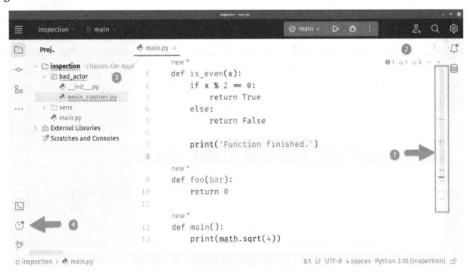

Figure 4.14: Four places in the user interface tell you that you have problems

The right gutter of the editor (1) will show you where all the problematic lines lie in the currently open file. This gutter is a compressed, miniature representation of your file. It is pretty common for a file to have hundreds or maybe even thousands of lines. You can click on the area in the gutter where you see the colored marks, and the editor will scroll to that location.

PyCharm will classify the problems into three basic categories: errors (red), warnings (yellow), and weak warnings (gray). This is reported for the whole file at the top of the gutter column with counts of each problem type (2). In addition to colors, this area gives you different shapes. The error icon is a round red circle with an exclamation point within it. Warnings are a triangle with an exclamation point. Weak warnings are also depicted using a triangle with an exclamation, but they appear considerably dimmer. If no problems are detected, you are rewarded with a green check mark. *Figure 4.15* shows two files. One has no problems (1), while the other has a number of issues in different categories (2):

Figure 4.15: The file on the bottom is devoid of any problems, while the one on top isn't quite as lucky

Anything marked in red is an error that will probably prevent your program from running correctly or at all. A warning means your code will probably run, but there are some obvious cases where it won't perform as expected. A weak warning is usually a minor flaw, such as a variable name that doesn't conform to an English dictionary word. If your locale is set to a language other than English, PyCharm will flag words from your local language.

The second place to look for problems is within the editor window itself. Look back at *Figure 4.15* at line 13. You'll see a squiggly red (trust me) underline beneath the word math. The colors of the lines correspond with the severity of the problem. The right-hand gutter shows you where the problem is located, while the underlines show you the problem directly on the offending line. If you hover your mouse over whatever is underlined, you'll get a description of the problem. I'll go into more depth on this later in this chapter when we talk about **intentions**, which are suggestions about how to fix problems in your code.

The third place you'll find indicators of problems is the project explorer. Refer back to *Figure 4.15*, area 3. There is a Python package called bad_actor. That file isn't open in *Figure 4.15*, but I opened it when I created it, typed in some incomplete code, then closed the file. You can see the file open in *Figure 4.16*:

Figure 4.16: Silly me! I started typing in the file but never finished

If there is an error in the file you aren't currently working on, you'll find it flagged in the file list. The warning will bubble up through the directory system. There's a red squiggly line at the top project folder, another in the folder for the package, and still another underline beneath the file where the problem lies. PyCharm doesn't examine closed files. It only examines files you open, but once it finds the problem, it will remember where it is and continue to warn you until you fix the problem.

> **Bad actor**
>
> I needed an exemplary bad actor for the previous visual pun. Kevin Costner is a bad American actor. He certainly isn't the worst, but he's easily in the top 10. If you don't believe me, watch the movie *Dances with Wolves*. If you still don't believe me, watch *The Bodyguard*. If you still think he's great, watch *Waterworld* and realize he financed that movie out of his own pocket because he was convinced it would be a mega-hit.

The fourth place is the problems window. In *Figure 4.17*, you can see a red dot over an icon in area 4 in the screenshot. Click the icon, and the problems window will open and show you a list of faults, as seen in *Figure 4.17*:

Figure 4.17: Open the problem window to see a list of all your problems. Only your code problems are displayed. Life problems are not shown

Syntax errors

Syntax errors are usually the shallowest errors exposed by an IDE. We've seen a few already. *Figure 4.17* shows an incomplete function definition, so it is flagged in red as a syntax error. In *Figure 4.14*, line 13 has a red underline beneath the word math. PyCharm recognizes this as a reference to the Python math library, which I have neglected to import. This throws an unresolved reference error. These kinds of errors are always marked in red as severe errors because they will prevent the program from running.

Duplicated code

If you make a habit of copying and pasting code within your project or even between different projects, you can expect a warning from PyCharm. Duplicated code is a sign your project is in trouble.

The best practice is to follow the concept called **Don't Repeat Yourself** (**DRY**). I'll say it again. You want your code to always be DRY. Never repeat your code by copying and pasting. Make sure it's DRY. OK, I'll stop if you promise to heed PyCharm's warnings about code not being DRY.

When you find this problem within a single project, you can usually fix it by hoisting the duplicated code into a function and calling the function from the parts of your code where the duplicates lie.

If you get flagged for copying and pasting between projects, you should turn the duplicated code into a Python package that can be shared between projects.

PEP-8 problems

PyCharm's linter alerts you to styling problems in your code that violate PEP-8. The biggest problem for developers new to Python is dealing with the rules around white space. Indentions and empty lines between functions are all part of the PEP-8 rules designed to keep your code very readable. Most PEP-8 problems are flagged as warnings.

Dead code

This is my personal pet peeve. Someone writes some code, which ultimately gets replaced with a different function. Both the old and the unused function are sitting in the code file, along with the new one. They might have similar names. They might even be in different files. When I was a kid, I had a poster on my wall titled Murphy's Laws of Technology. The poster espoused a pessimistic but, in my experience (and probably yours if you've been doing this for a while), totally accurate worldview. Here's a sampling of Murphy's Laws with respect to technology:

- You can never tell which direction the train traveled by looking at the track

- Logic is a systematic method of coming to the wrong conclusion with confidence

- Whenever a system becomes completely defined, some fool discovers something which either abolishes the system or expands it beyond recognition

- Technology is dominated by those who manage what they don't understand: if builders built buildings the way programmers wrote programs, then the first woodpecker that came along would destroy civilization

- The attention span of a computer is only as long as its electrical cord

- An expert is one who knows more and more about less and less until he knows absolutely everything about nothing

This is relevant because, at least for me, the likelihood that I will find and attempt to modify dead code (thinking it to be very much alive and the obvious source of all my problems) in a software system asymptotically approaches 100%. The tiny degree of variance somewhere between 99% and 100% seems to be affected by my present level of caffeination and whether I skipped breakfast. These effects appear to be inversely proportional.

I thank goodness for a system that warns me that I'm looking at dead code. My usual rant is that you should take dead code out. You won't need it, and if you do, that's what revision control systems are for.

Method signature mismatches

A method signature mismatch happens when a function requires more or fewer arguments than the number you supplied. PyCharm will warn you when this happens.

The road to good code is paved with PyCharm's intentions

Now that we've spent time learning about our flaws, let's look at some tools that help us fix them. PyCharm features a mechanism called intentions designed to automate fixing and improving your code. Take a look at *Figure 4.18*:

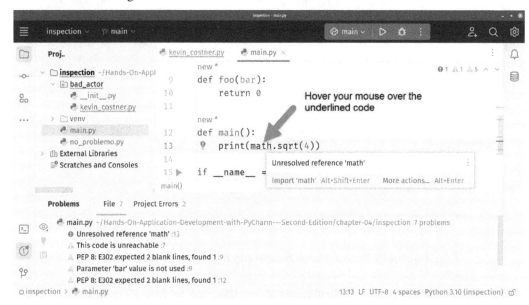

Figure 4.18: Hover your mouse over any underlined code to see
why it is underlined, along with possible fixes

In the case of the code shown, the problem is I invoked the `sqrt()` method, which finds the square root. The method is a static method in the `math` class. The problem is I failed to import that class. The description of the problem appears just below the underline when I hover. Below the problem description is the most likely fix. Pressing *Alt + Shift + Enter* will automatically fix the problem by adding `import math` to the top of the file.

If you'd like to try this out, you can use the `inspection` project in the `chapter-04` folder of the sample code we cloned in *Chapter 2, Installation and Configuration*.

Note this might not be the only possible fix. In *Figure 4.18*, we can also see **More actions…** prompting us to either click the link or press *Alt + Enter* to see more possibilities.

Truly astute readers might have noticed the lightbulb. This is an alternate vector to the same feature. Check out *Figure 4.19* to see the lightbulb in action:

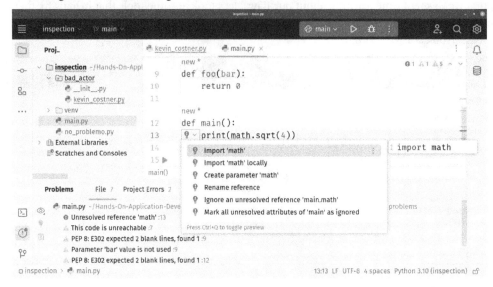

Figure 4.19: The lightbulb is another way to get the intentions

Clicking the lightbulb shows a list of possible intentions. This time, we see a preview. The intention is going to add `import math` at line 1 of the file.

The lightbulbs can be tricky sometimes because they have a tendency to disappear if you move off the line where they originally appeared. If you'd like to use the lightbulb, just click anywhere within the underline and wait for a tick. It will appear at the beginning of the line where the problem lies.

In the case we're exploring, the problem is a legitimate error. The program won't run until we fix the problem. You can't see it in the previous two figures, but the lightbulb is red. You'll also see yellow lightbulbs for less egregious problems.

Now if you're like me, you want to see a clean file with a green check and no underlines. Let me tell you, that will probably never happen. PyCharm will almost always find something to change. Sometimes the suggested changes are not very useful. You might heed a suggestion that changes your code in some minor way. Right after you do this, the lightbulb comes back, and PyCharm offers to change the code back to the way it was. Yellow light bulbs are not your enemy unless they have an exclamation point in them.

Refactoring

Most good IDEs, and development-focused text editors, for that matter, feature some level of tooling for refactoring. Refactoring is a very important practice that is often neglected. In my book, which is available on Amazon (or wherever the finest technical books are sold), *Real-World Implementation of C# Design Patterns*, I cover some of the entropic forces that lead a well-intended coding project to ruin. Your code starts off pristine, and the whole team commits to maintaining zero technical debt. But it never lasts. Factors such as time pressure, developer skill level, inevitable change, visibility, and complexity cause a process of devolution. Your code goes from a well-constructed, perfectly architected masterpiece to a big ball of mud on a plate of spaghetti!

I realize that I am pointing to a C# book here, but if you have a Packt subscription, I urge you to read the first two chapters of the book. The chapters discuss the common problems and preventions of work degradation. One thing you can do is to be vigilant and never dismiss the value of refactoring your code as a regular part of the development practice.

What is refactoring?

Simply put, refactoring is improving code without changing its functionality. If you have unit tests (you do, RIGHT!?!??!), they should pass before and after refactoring without any changes to the tests themselves. You are looking for ways to optimize your code in terms of readability and performance. Maybe you skipped some code niceties, such as adding **docstrings**, which we'll cover later in this chapter. Maybe you didn't add type hints to your method signatures. Perhaps there are opportunities to leverage design patterns or SOLID principles to make your code more flexible.

The idea behind refactoring is that you are taking a second look at your code, preferably after a little time has passed. Have you ever looked at code you wrote a month or even a year ago and wondered what possessed you to type that horrible function body? Why in the world did you _____? (Fill in the blank with something silly you did.) You can't believe that was you. You are smarter than that. Consider having regular peer reviews of your code. This can happen at any time during the writing process. Also, having someone less invested in your work will be able to spot unrealized opportunities for improvement. Almost always, this will involve refactoring. Flip things around. How many times have you been handed some code written by another developer? Maybe the person that has left the company? You look it over and conclude that whoever wrote the code was clearly a recent escapee from the local asylum. It must be totally rewritten. This is you refactoring someone else's code.

Refactoring tools in PyCharm

PyCharm has a set of menu options dedicated to refactoring. There are a few that are not explicitly called out as refactoring tools.

Cleaning up your code

PyCharm has a very thorough **Code Cleanup** tool. This tool, in effect, runs the same inspections you have seen so far, but it does them in bulk. You can have PyCharm try to fix all the problems as well. This feature is useful when you import a project created outside of PyCharm, say with a tool that doesn't offer the kind of assistance you have seen in PyCharm.

You can clean up an open file or all files in your project. To be honest, I don't recommend you do this at the project level since you can't really predict what the engine will do to a large set of files you haven't even opened. *Figure 4.20* shows the menu location for **Code Cleanup…**:

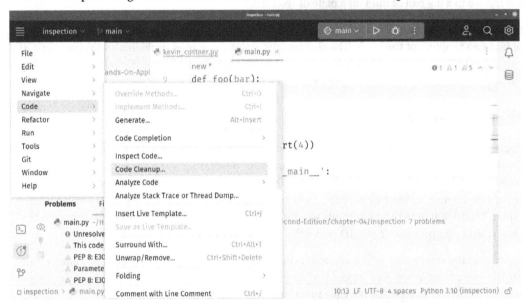

Figure 4.20: The Code Cleanup tools can be found in the Code menu

Once you click the menu option, you'll see a dialog asking about the scope of the clean-up, as seen in *Figure 4.21*:

Figure 4.21: Specify the scope of the code cleanup

You can clean up the whole project, uncommitted files, the current file (which for me is `main.py` from the `inspection` project in the `chapter-04` folder of the sample source code), or a custom scope. My recommendation is not to try to boil the ocean. Do not do a whole project cleanup on a massive project. It is usually smarter to let PyCharm work its magic on small batches of files. The **Uncommitted files** option is a nice step you can take before you commit changes to your version control system.

Renaming

Donald Knuth, one of the most respected software developers of all time, wrote in his book *The Art of Computer Programming*, that there are two things in programming that are hard: naming things (e.g., variables, functions, classes, files, and so on) well, and invalidating your caches. How true this is! It is an art form to write meaningful variable definitions that are self-documenting while making your intentions clear. It usually takes several tries to get it right. PyCharm has a tool that easily allows a name change. You can right-click on anything you've named and select **Rename**. Type the new name of the thing that is to be renamed. PyCharm will affect the change everywhere the named thing is referenced. It will even find and change references in comments and docstrings.

If the scope of the change is small, for example, you are renaming something scoped to a local function, the rename operation happens immediately. If you are attempting a rename with a broader scope, such as one that entails multiple files, PyCharm will preview the change for you by showing you all the files that will be affected. You can inspect all the changes before they are made to make sure the changes are appropriate. After you are satisfied, you can apply those changes.

> **There is no rename menu option for files!**
>
> This is confusing if you come from another tool such as Visual Studio Code, where renaming files is a simple matter of picking the file from the explorer view and clicking twice or pressing *F2*. You'll hunt for the rename option for files, and you will not find one. That's because it is in the **Refactor** menu. PyCharm considers renaming a file a refactor. Unlike other tools, PyCharm will make sure renaming the file doesn't affect your code.

Inlining variables

PyCharm gives you the ability to automatically inline your variables. In fact, this is among the more common suggestions PyCharm provides. Consider this code:

```
a = 5
b = 6

def add_two(num1: int, num2: int) -> int:
  sum = num1 + num2
  return sum

add_two(a, b)
```

The sum variable isn't really needed. If you inline the variable, the code becomes the following:

```
a = 5
b = 6

def add_two(num1: int, num2: int) -> int:
  return num1 + num2

add_two(a, b)
```

We've removed the line that declared the sum variable and assigned it the value of num1 + num2.

Extracting methods

Earlier, I mentioned a concept called DRY, or Don't Repeat Yourself. Yes, I realize that by mentioning it again, I am breaking the rule. I am doing so with a purpose. Remember, the IDE points out errors and then provides advice and tools to fix the problem. I'd like to present a very useful feature. PyCharm gives you a tool to easily extract code into a separate function. You will want to do this under a couple of circumstances. First, if you find yourself copying and pasting code within your project. You probably need to make that code a function and then call it from the places where you are pasting the copied code. Secondly, when you find a function that breaks the single responsibility principle. If you've never heard of this, you can guess what it means. A well-written program should contain functions that do only one thing. Written code that contains functions or methods that perform multiple responsibilities could be broken into separate functions.

Take a look at an easy example of such an opportunity. Open the chapter-04/not_dry.py file in the sample code. The code within is truly egregious! Sensitive viewers might want to sit down before opening the file. Behold! Something everybody has done at least once before they learned it was a bad idea:

```python
computer_science_grades = {
    "Guido van Rossum": 100,
    "Ewa Jodlwska": 99,
    "Fabrizio Romano": 88,
    "Henrich Kruger": 87,
    "Rick van Hattem": 83,
    "Steven Lott": 72,
    "Dusty Phillips": 72,
    "Quan Nguyen": 92
}
```

OK, so far, it is fine. We've got a dictionary of people who took a computer science class along with their grades. By the way, those aren't random names. After you finish this chapter, see whether you can figure out who these illustrious individuals might be. I apologize to some of the illustrious individuals for the numbers themselves. They are meant to be more or less random keys except for Mr. van Rossum, who would obviously have gotten a perfect grade. I'm sure they all did very well in real life. Following that, we have another set of class grades:

```python
advanced_theoretical_and_applied_recess_grades = {
    "Bruce Van Horn": 100,
    "Prajakta Naik": 92,
    "Kinnari Chohan": 88,
    "Pooja Yadiv": 86
}
```

While it is a different subject and a different group of people, it's the same idea. Now suppose we need to figure out the class average for each class. I can make a function for computing the average in the computer science class:

```python
def computer_science_average(grades: dict) -> float:
    raw_total = 0
    for grade in grades.values():
        raw_total += grade

    average = (raw_total / len(grades))
    return average
```

Our method signature gives lots of good hints. We have a descriptive function name. The function takes one parameter, and our hint tells us we're expecting a dictionary. The function is expected to return a float.

The function body creates a variable called `raw_total` and sets it to 0. Next, we loop through the values of `dict` and, on each iteration, add `value` to `raw_total`. Once we have the total, we divide it by the number of keys (`len`) in `dict`, and voila! We have the class average. Towards the bottom of the file, we can see where this function is called:

```
boring_class_average = computer_science_average(computer_science_
grades)
print(f"Boring average is {boring_class_average}")
```

Wonderful! We have a call to our `computer_science_average` function along with a highly judgmental (and probably inaccurate since it might have been your favorite class) variable assignment. So, what's wrong with any of this? Nothing. It's what comes next that presents a problem and an opportunity to extract a method. The next function computes a different class: advanced theoretical and applied recess. This is a field that I personally pioneered, and within this field, I have no rival. Unfortunately, since I spent more time on the playground perfecting my art and less time in computer science class, I have all but duplicated the function we wrote earlier:

```
def advanced_recess_average(grades: dict) -> float:
    raw_total = 0
    for grade in grades.values():
        raw_total += grade

    average = (raw_total / len(grades))
    return average
```

It's the same function with a different name! We need to consolidate! To do this, you need to highlight everything between the colon that ends the method signature and the `return` statement. Refer to *Figure 4.22*. Don't include the `return` statement, or PyCharm won't generate a `return` statement in your extracted function:

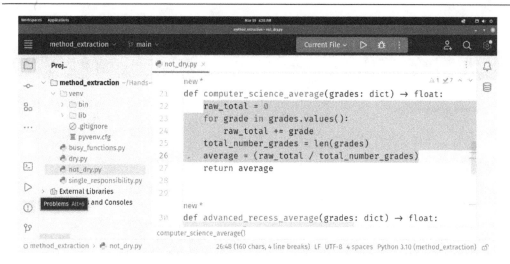

Figure 4.22: Select the code to extract into a new function or method

Next, right-click the selected code and click **Refactor | Extract Method**, as shown in *Figure 4.23*:

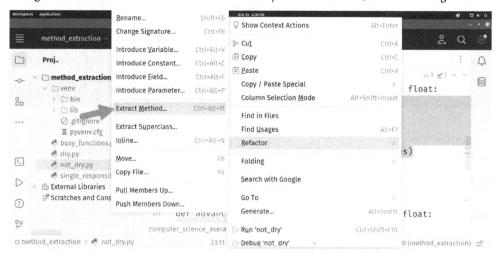

Figure 4.23: Right-click the selected code, then click Refactor, then Extract Method

This brings up a user interface that allows you to define the new method, as seen in *Figure 4.24*:

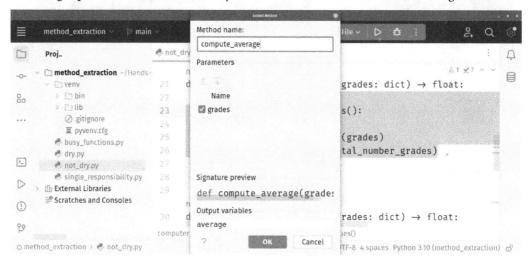

Figure 4.24: The Extract Method dialog in PyCharm

Set the name of the extract method. I set mine to `compute_average`. PyCharm has filled in the rest automatically. Click **OK**, and your code will change. *Figure 4.25* shows the result of my refactoring:

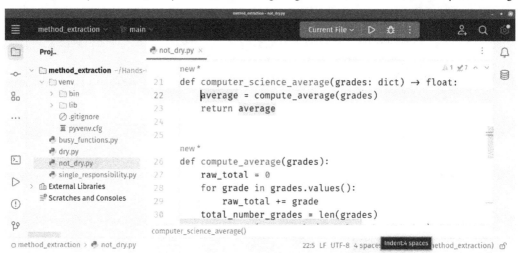

Figure 4.25: The result of the refactoring. Note the compute_average
function was generated automatically from the selected code

Let's look at the resulting code PyCharm generated from the refactor. First, `computer_science_average` has changed to this:

```python
def computer_science_average(grades: dict) -> float:
    average = compute_average(grades)
    return average
```

This function is now calling the extracted function. The extracted function looks like this:

```python
def compute_average(grades):
    raw_total = 0
    for grade in grades.values():
        raw_total += grade
    total_number_grades = len(grades)
    average = (raw_total / total_number_grades)
    return average
```

This is the code we selected for extraction. PyCharm generated the function for me. I must tell you, at this point, that I'm usually wary of generated code. It is rarely perfect. Here, I would have preferred a type hint on the `grades` parameter and a hint on the return type. Those are minor issues, though, and the result saved me some typing.

One lingering question might remain. Why didn't PyCharm detect and flag the duplicated code? The quick answer: our sample code is too short. If I were to add a few more lines to the duplicated functions, it would appear as a duplicate. Let's try it out. Modify the code in both functions so it looks like this:

```python
def computer_science_average(grades: dict) -> float:
    raw_total = 0
    fake_var_1 = 1
    fake_var_2 = 2
    fake_var_3 = 3
    fake_var_4 = 4
    fake_var_5 = 5
    fake_var_6 = 6
    fake_var_7 = 7
    print(f"{fake_var_1}{fake_var_2}{fake_var_3}{fake_var_4}")
    print(f"{fake_var_5}{fake_var_6}{fake_var_7}")
    for grade in grades.values():
        raw_total += grade

    average = (raw_total / len(grades))
    return average
```

All I did was add a bunch of fake variable declarations. They don't do anything important except make the duplicate code fragment longer. By default, PyCharm only looks for duplicated fragments that are 10 lines or longer. Short duplications don't make the cut. I bring this up because the magic of method extraction handles duplicates automatically. Let's do the same exercise. First, look at PyCharm with the changes in place. You should see some indicators that we have problems, as shown in *Figure 4.26*:

Figure 4.26: Now that our duplicated code is longer, it gets detected and flagged

We can see that PyCharm has noticed our duplicated code. Highlight the code for extraction, as shown in *Figure 4.27*:

Figure 4.27: Mark the code for extraction

Right-click the highlighted code and click **Refactor | Extract Method**, as shown in *Figure 4.28*:

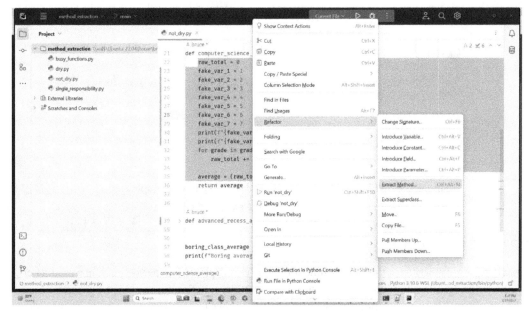

Figure 4.28: Extract the method by right-clicking, clicking Refactor, then Extract Method

Name the extracted function `compute_average`, as shown in *Figure 4.29*:

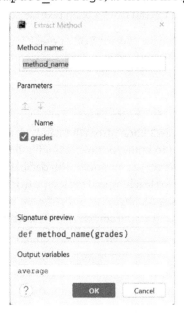

Figure 4.29: Name the extracted function compute_average

Click **OK**. This time things are a little different. You'll find that PyCharm creates the function extraction as before, but this time you are prompted to replace the duplicate code as well, as shown in *Figure 4.30*:

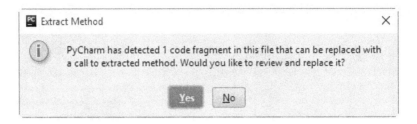

Figure 4.30: PyCharm asks whether you'd like to replace the duplicated
fragment with a reference to the extracted function

Exporting a function to another file

How often have you written a nifty utility function in the wrong place? Maybe you put it in a module or class that is designed to do something specific, but your utility function turns out to be generally used in lots of places. The single responsibility principle that applies to functions also applies to modules and classes. Having a function that connects to a database is a great example. Let's say you just got a job working for Billy Blanca's Candy Factory. They need you to write some scripts that will import lists of candies they make from several different text formats and store them in a database. The first requirement comes in, and you need to read from a plain text file and write to an SQLite database.

Open the project in `chapter-04/move_function/read_input_file_a.py`. Let's review the contents:

```
import sqlite3
CANDY_DB = "candy.db"
```

These first two lines import the `sqlite3` library from the standard library. If you haven't worked with `sqlite3` before, here's all you need to know for now: it is a file-based relational database. By this, we mean you don't need to install a server as you would with databases such as Postgres or MariaDB. This makes it a good database to use for teaching and prototype work. We'll cover databases in detail in *Chapter 11, Understanding Database Management in PyCharm*. Let's continue with the definition for the function that will open the file, read the contents, and insert them into the database:

```
def read_input_file_type_a(file_path: str) -> None:
    with open(file_path, "r") as data:
        for line in data:
            cleaned = line.strip("\n")
            write_to_database(cleaned)
```

```
print("Processing Complete!")
```

We've opened the file. For each line in the file, we are reading it in as text and removing the newline character. This is necessary for the database insert to work properly. Once the string is cleaned, we are calling a function that writes to the database:

```
def write_to_database(datum: str) -> None:
    connection = sqlite3.connect(CANDY_DB)
    cursor = connection.cursor()
    sql = f"INSERT INTO candy(name) VALUES ('{datum}')"
    print(sql)
    cursor.execute(sql)
    cursor.close()
    connection.close()
```

I've included the database file in the code repository, so there is no code needed to create the database. This function just opens the database, then creates a cursor. A cursor is used to execute commands against the database using SQL. Even if you don't know SQL, I'm sure you can figure out what is happening. There is a table in the database called candy. The table has only one field: name. We're keeping it very simple here. I have neglected to create a primary key because, for now, the database doesn't really matter. We should be focused on the function more than how it works.

Having generated a SQL statement to insert the candy name from the candy name in the current line of the text file, I execute the SQL statement, which will insert one row into the candy table.

As a general rule in programming, whatever you create, you should destroy, and whatever you open, you should always close. So, I close my cursor and my database connection to avoid any resource locks later down the road. Finally, I use the common dunder-name convention to run the file for testing:

```
if __name__ == "__main__":
    read_input_file_type_a("../input_file_a.txt")
```

In PyCharm, I can execute this by setting my run configuration to **Current File** and clicking the **Run** button. It works! The file is read, and we get no errors.

> **Dunderscores**
>
> A **double underscore (dundersore)** refers to an element in Python code preceded and
> proceeded by two underscore characters. This solves a pronunciation problem when talking
> about code. How would you talk about a method called __init__? You could say, "*underscore
> underscore init underscore underscore.*" But that is cumbersome. If you just say, "init" you're not
> being specific enough since there could be another function or method called init without
> the underscores. So, you say "*dundersore init*" or even just "*dunder init*", and everybody knows
> what you're talking about.

The next day we come to work and learn of a new requirement. We need another script that reads
data from a **JavaScript Object Notation (JSON)** file. The JSON file just contains an array like this:

```
{
 "data": [
  "truffles",
  "turtles",
  "dark chocolate bark"
 ]
}
```

It's still just a list of candy, but we need to process it differently. Open up chapter-04/move_
function/input/read_input_file_b.py. You'll find its code is similar to the other code:

```
import json
from read_input_file_a import write_to_database
```

We know we need to work with JSON, so I've imported the json package. I also know I'll need to
write to the same database as before. I know code reuse is a good thing, so I import the function from
the other script. Then I set to creating a version of the code that reads JSON files:

```
def read_input_file_type_b(file_path: str) -> None:
  with open(file_path, "r") as json_data:
    data = json.load(json_data)
    candies = data["data"]
    for candy in candies:
      write_to_database(candy)

  print("Processing Complete!")


if __name__ == "__main__":
  read_input_file_type_b("../input_file_b.json")
```

The `json.load` method takes the raw text and converts it into a regular Python 3 `dict`. As you can see from the preceding file listing, `dict` will have one thing in it: an array of candy with the key of data. So, I grab that and put it in the `candies` variable, then I loop over that array and call the `write_to_database` function for each `candy` in the array. Wow! It's not even lunchtime! Maybe I can walk around the factory? I hear they've got some little girl testing some gum that turns people into a raspberry.

Not so fast! This code could be improved. Our input scripts are really designed to read data from text. It doesn't make sense to have one of the scripts contain the database function because it simply doesn't belong inside the script that reads text input files. It really should be in its own package. Let's extract it to its own file.

Open `chapter-04/move_function/input/read_input_file_a.py`. Right-click on the name of the function we're going to move, as shown in *Figure 4.31*:

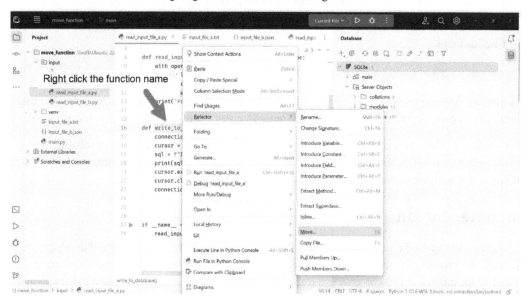

Figure 4.31: Right-click the function you want to move, then click Refactor, then Move

In the context menu, click **Refactor | Move**. You'll see a dialog asking for the target file name. I've entered a `database_helper.py` filename. Click **OK**. Watch carefully because a lot is about to happen.

I get a new file called `database_helper.py`:

```
import sqlite3

from input.read_input_file_a import CANDY_DB
```

```python
def write_to_database(datum: str) -> None:
    connection = sqlite3.connect(CANDY_DB)
    cursor = connection.cursor()
    sql = f"INSERT INTO candy(name) VALUES ('{datum}')"
    print(sql)
    cursor.execute(sql)
    cursor.close()
    connection.close()
```

This is the extracted function moved to its own file. PyCharm discovered the relevant import statement and moved that here as well. I had a constant for the file name called CANDY_DB. It didn't move that, which would be my preference. Unfortunately, the current release of PyCharm is not psychic. I'll just have to move that myself. Other than that, this file looks perfect.

If you check the contents of input_file_a.py, you'll see it has changed. The first line in the file now reads as follows:

```python
from input.database_helper import write_to_database
```

Likewise, if I open input_file_b.py, I'll find the input there as well. PyCharm extracted the function to its own file, then changed every reference in every file to point to the new location.

Now, I realize I probably should have put this in its own module, and I realize you probably would have done this totally differently. Before you go bashing me on Twitter, remember this book is about PyCharm, not software architecture. I'm trying to keep it simple on purpose.

Documentation

No programmer can doubt the importance of documentation in software engineering and development. That said, the process of creating documentation for a program can be quite tedious. Furthermore, the end result might not even be effective if the person doing the documentation was not following standard practices.

Keeping that in mind, PyCharm looks to streamline this process of documentation and make it as straightforward and seamless as possible. Regarding documentation, there are two components we will consider for this process: viewing and creating documentation. We will learn that PyCharm offers great support for both processes.

Working with docstrings

Documentation in Python is known as docstrings, defined as a string literal that is placed before any of the statements in a module, function, class, or method in Python. You can look at examples of Python docstrings by going into the source code of the various built-in Python functions. It is also recommended that any custom API you write also has the appropriate docstrings for readability and maintainability.

The most noteworthy subtlety in creating docstrings is the practice of using triple-double quotes to surround a docstring (which we will see examples of in the next subsection). For more details about docstring conventions, take a look at this PEP article: www.python.org/dev/peps/pep-0257/.

Creating documentation

In this subsection, we will look into the process of writing a docstring for functions with the help of PyCharm. Let's get started.

Open the project in the sample source code in chapter-04/documentation. Open the prime_test.py file, which looks like this:

```
import sys
from math import sqrt

def prime_check(n: int) -> bool:
  # TODO: docstring goes here

  if n < 2:
    return False

  limit = int(sqrt(n)) + 1
  for i in range(2, limit):
    if n % i == 0:
      return False # return False if a divisor is found

  return True # return True if no divisor is found
```

The file goes on after that, but the part I need you to focus on is the line right below the method signature for the prime_check function. There is a TODO there. If you're from a Spanish-speaking country, realize this doesn't mean *all*. It refers to a "to-do" item in the code. In this case, the original developer, who happens to be Quan Nguyen, the author of the first edition of this book, is stating he didn't write the docstring for this function. He is signaling here that he knows that, and he intends to come back and fix this later. Let's help him out with a little PyCharm magic. Before you get too excited, I'm sad to report that there isn't a tool in PyCharm that can read your code and generate the docstring. Given how much developers hate writing documentation, I'll wager there is a fast-and-furious effort underway somewhere to have AI do this. But we're sticking with what PyCharm lets us do out of the box.

Delete the # TODO line and, in its place, type three double quotation marks (" " ") and press *Enter*. You'll find a generated docstring template appears:

```
"""

:param n:
:return:
"""
```

This template needs some filling-in in order to become a proper docstring. Note the gap beneath the first set of triple quotes. Here, you are expected to write about what the function does. Maybe something like this:

```
"""
Check whether an integer is a prime number of not.
Generally, the function goes through all odd numbers
less than the square root of the input integer, and
checks to see if the input is divisible by that number.

:param n:
:return:
"""
```

Below that is a section for the parameters expected by the function. Here, the function takes one argument called n. We should write a little bit about that parameter, including its type:

```
"""
Check whether an integer is a prime number of not.
Generally, the function goes through all odd numbers
less than the square root of the input integer, and
checks to see if the input is divisible by that number.

:param n: the integer to prime check
:return:
"""
```

The last part is the documentation for the return value:

```
"""
Check whether an integer is a prime number of not.
Generally, the function goes through all odd numbers
less than the square root of the input integer, and
```

```
checks to see if the input is divisible by that number.

:param n: the integer to prime check
:return: boolean
"""
```

Consider the generated template of the docstring after we hit *Return/Enter* to expand the pair of triple-double quotes. `:param` and `:return:` are part of the template and will be included every time we expand a docstring in the same way. PyCharm allows us to change this format of docstring templates, making it highly customizable and accommodating.

Customizing the docstring templates

As usual, the docstring templates are highly customizable. You'll find the customization settings by going into the **Settings** window, covered extensively in *Chapter 3, Customizing Interpreters and Virtual Environments*. Just search on docstring, and you'll find the areas that should capture your attention. The first is shown in *Figure 4.32*:

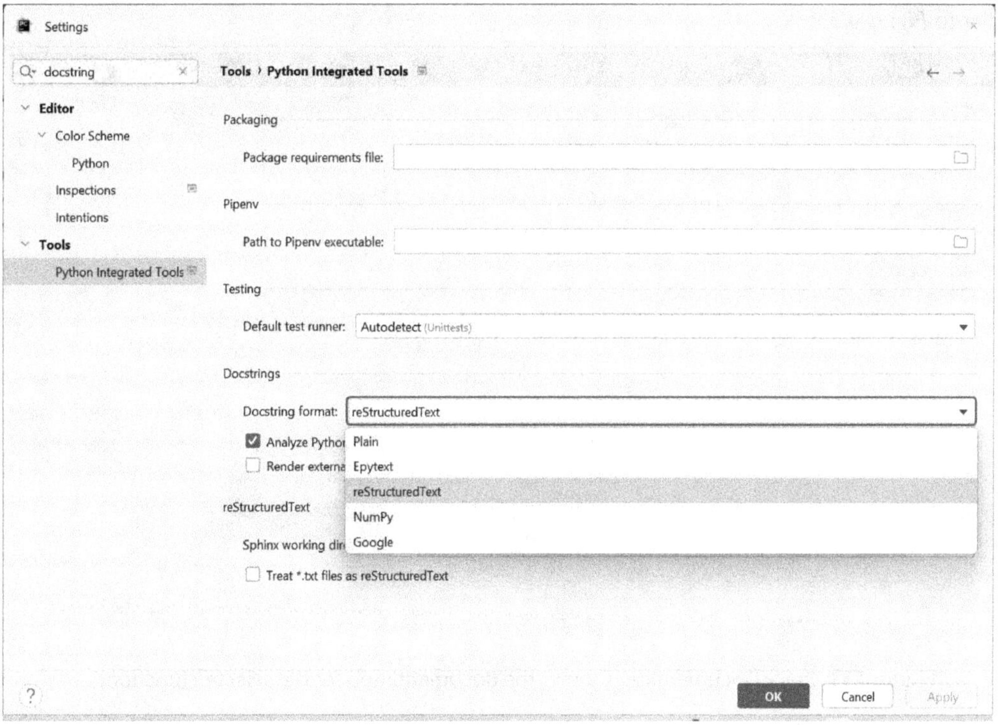

Figure 4.32: You can change the general format used to render your docstrings to one of several industry-standard formats

The other group of settings is part of the color scheme settings, which allow you to customize the color used to render the docstring in the PyCharm editor.

Viewing documentation

Imagine a situation where you are using a specific method from one package, but you are not entirely sure which parameters the method takes in and/or what its return type is. Therefore, you need to go online and look into the documentation of the package for that specific method.

As a PyCharm user, you can achieve the same thing with two simple actions: **Quick Definition** and **Quick Documentation**. Still using the prime_check.py script from the previous section, move your cursor to the line where we use the math.sqrt() function in the prime_check() function; it should be around line 19.

Quick Documentation

Let's say we'd like to see the documentation of this function. You can simply hover your mouse over the function call and wait a moment. Alternatively, you can choose **View** | **Quick Documentation** for this or its corresponding keyboard shortcut. You will see a pop-up window showing documentation similar to *Figure 4.33*:

Figure 4.33: Quick Documentation shows the documentation for the selected function

What's more, you can also view the documentation for your own functions, methods, classes, and so on using the same action. PyCharm's indexing process finds and generates this information when you open the project.

If you move your cursor to the call to `prime_check()` in the main scope in the following line (which should be around line 38):

```
if prime_check(num):
```

After waiting a moment, you will be able to see the same docstring that we entered earlier, as shown in *Figure 4.34*:

Figure 4.34: Quick Documentation shows the documentation for the selected function on line 38

Note the format of the docstring in the documentation matches the documentation shown in the window.

Quick definition

Quick Definition operates in the same manner as **Quick Documentation**. This is useful when the documentation does not provide enough information, and you would like to see how a specific function is defined within the source code. To do this, place your cursor at a specific API call, and go to **View | Quick Definition** to evoke the action.

For example, *Figure 4.35* shows the quick definition evoked on the call to `prime_check()` in our example:

Figure 4.35: Quick Definition shows the actual code definition for the
function, which naturally includes the docstring if one is present

Overall PyCharm provides powerful options when it comes to dynamically viewing documentation and definitions within the IDE. Significant time and energy can be saved when programmers do not have to switch from their development environment to look for documentation.

Summary

Throughout this chapter, we examined PyCharm's features regarding various aspects of programming, including code analysis, code completion, refactoring, and documenting. In all of these processes, PyCharm's intelligent code analyzer provides smart and convenient options for editing and fixing problems in your code in real time and in a dynamic way.

Aside from a wide number of options the intelligent code analyzer can support, PyCharm also allows users to customize the behavior of the analyzer to their liking. This can be achieved in various sections of the general settings. Overall, these support features look to improve your productivity as a developer in a way that is customized and beneficial to you.

In the next chapter, we will focus on a particular aspect of programming: version control. We will learn about the specifics of the version control process with Git and how PyCharm supports and streamlines this process.

Questions

1.   What levels of severity in terms of problems in a Python program are determined by PyCharm's code analyzer?

2.   What are some common problems that PyCharm can detect and help fix via its intelligent code analyzer?

3.   How is PyCharm's code completion support different from others?

4.   What are some common code completion options that PyCharm offers?

5.   What are the common causes for PyCharm's code completion support not working?

6.   What are some common refactoring options that PyCharm offers?

Further reading

- Jolt Awards: *The Best Books For Developers* (informationweek.com)

- Pylint home page: https://www.pylint.org/

- Murphy's laws on technology: https://www.netlingo.com/word/murphys-laws-on-technology.php

- Be sure to check out the companion website for the book at https://www.pycharm-book.com.

5

Version Control with Git in PyCharm

Version control is an essential best practice in the field of software development. The mechanics of the process, though, are daunting for new developers. It is easy to make mistakes. As a bootcamp instructor at Southern Methodist University (Go Ponies!), I have seen quite a few blunders, such as accidentally adding your entire home folder to a Git repository, creating repositories inside of other repositories, and wiping out the product of hard work by pushing and pulling out of order. I prefer my students to master Git on the command line. In fact, it is the very first skill I teach, and in my opinion, it is one of the most difficult.

After a developer gains confidence with the whole Git process, it is something of an annoyance to have to constantly jump out of the IDE to perform four or five commands, then jump back into the IDE to continue work. It is true you could use the built-in terminal window available in PyCharm, but the IDE offers a better option: a built-in version control GUI.

PyCharm supports a number of the major **version control systems (VCSs)**, including the following:

- Git
- Mercurial
- Subversion
- Perforce
- Microsoft **Team Foundation Server**

While there are many other VCSs available, these are easily the most popular, and among those in this list, Git has become the de facto standard in the industry.

This chapter will first cover some basic information about version control and VCSs just in case you are new to the concept. Following this introduction, we will focus entirely on the tooling for Git, since as I just hinted, it has a capital lead in terms of market share.

By the end of the chapter, you will come to understand the following:

- The merits of using a VCS

- Working with Git to perform adding, committing, pushing, merging, and branching operations

- Creating and maintaining a `.gitignore` file

- Working with the Git tooling in the IDE, which may be referenced from several vectors

Technical requirements

To be successful with this chapter, you will need the following:

- A working installation of Python 3.10 or later.

- A working installation of PyCharm.

- Git client software for your computer. Mac and Linux systems usually have this installed as standard. Windows users can visit `https://gitforwindows.org` to download the free software.

- A free GitHub account. Register at `https://github.com`. Note that while there are paid features of GitHub, we won't be using them

Version control and Git essentials

Software industry icon **Joel Spolsky**, who created Stack Overflow, wrote a famous blog back in the year 2000. One of his many influential posts included one titled *The Joel Test: 12 Steps to Better Code*. The post was designed to give software developers an easy assessment to rate any software development organization's maturity level. He asked 12 questions, with one point per question. A good software development group should have a score of 11 or higher. The very first item on the list is the concern of this chapter: Do you use source control? If you are curious about the rest, there is a link to the blog post, as well as a reference to Mr. Spolsky's book *Joel on Software*, in the *Further reading* section of this chapter.

Joel called it **source control**. I call it **version control**. The terms are interchangeable. I will call it *version control* in order to be consistent with the UI in PyCharm, which refers to the group of features we're talking about as a **version control system**, or **VCS**. Strictly speaking, version control is a process used to track changes to the files that make up your program over time. The objectives of a VCS include the following:

- The ability to revert to any previously saved version of any file in your project.

- The ability to automatically merge the work of multiple developers on a team so long as their work does not conflict. A conflict occurs when two developers change the same file in the same place.

- Provide an easy means to review conflicts and resolve them through collaboration.

- The ability to track which developers made each change in the code over time.

- Provide a branching system to allow bug fixes, enhancements, and experimentation without sacrificing the stability of your production code.

A VCS, then, is a software system designed to enable that process. VCSs come in two varieties, depending on how revisions are stored. **Centralized VCSs** work a little like your local public library. Your project is checked into a **repository**. Developers can then check out the code in order to work on creating a new revision. Doing so will retrieve the latest version of the project. Some systems, such as **Perforce**, traditionally require you to explicitly check out the files you want to work with just like you'd check out a book from a library. While you have those files checked out, nobody else is allowed to modify them until you check them back in with your changes. Other systems, such as **Subversion**, don't have this requirement. Anybody can work on their local working copy. When work is done, the developer **commits** their work to the central repository. During the commit process, the VCS checks for **conflicts**. If no conflicts exist, the incoming work is **merged** and a new version is stored on the VCS server, which is then available for other developers through an update process. If conflicts are detected, the commit is rejected, and the developer must work with other developers on the team to resolve the conflict before the work can be merged and finally committed. In all centralized systems, each developer on a team has only the latest version of the code on their local computer.

In contrast, **distributed version control systems** (**DVCSs**) such as **Git** and **Mercurial** keep every revision ever performed on the project on each developer's computer. The advantage here is there is no single point of failure that might result in a total loss of the project code. In a centralized system, if the server is compromised, the project's revision history might be lost. In a distributed system, there isn't a central system to store the project's revision history. Every developer has the project's entire history on their computer, so the loss of any one computer isn't a big deal beyond the usual pain of replacing the equipment.

With that said, distributed systems do use a central **hub** or **remote** to allow easy synchronization between the working copies on each developer's computer. The hub server allows additional functionality, such as managing who is allowed to view or change the code, as well as collaborative features such as code reviews, bug tracking, documentation, and discussion. A DVCS also presents an easy way to control the publication of new releases of web-based applications. Many continuous deployment systems, such as **Travis CI**, **CircleCI**, and **Beanstalk**, are simply leveraging features of the DVCS to control the release management process.

The most famous DVCS is Git, created by **Linus Torvalds**, who also created the **Linux** operating system. The most famous DVCS hub is, you guessed it, GitHub, which is owned by Microsoft. Many people use the terms *Git* and *GitHub* interchangeably. This is a mistake. GitHub is a place on the internet. The software used to access *GitHub* is called *Git*. Many projects that use Git as their DVCS host their repository hub in services other than GitHub, such as **GitLab**, **Microsoft Azure DevOps**, **Atlassian Bitbucket**, and **Beanstalk** (`https://beanstalkapp.com`, not to be confused with the Beanstalk service on **Amazon Web Services**, which has nothing to do with version control).

As developers make changes to their working copy, they can commit changes to their local copy. They can later synchronize their code by pulling changes from the central hub, reconciling any conflicts, and then pushing their merged work. Again, the big difference is in a DVCS; everything happens on the developer's computer versus on a server with a centralized system.

Setting up Git on your computer

Whether you installed Git for Windows on your Windows computer, or you are working with a pre-installed Git client on your Mac or Linux computer, you need to perform some additional setup beyond simply installing the software. The setup tasks ahead include the following:

1. Set your default username and email address.

2. Create a **Secure Shell** (**SSH**) key so you can securely communicate with remote hubs such as GitHub.

3. Add the SSH key to your account on GitHub.

Let's go through the process for each.

To get started, you need to launch a terminal. If you are using Mac or Linux, you should be able to find an app on your system, simply called *Terminal*. The commands I'll present are going to be using the **Bash shell**. Mac's terminal program defaults to a shell called the **Z shell** (**zsh**), which is directly compatible with Bash. Most Linux installations default to Bash, so you are all set. If you are in Windows, you need to have installed the Git software from `https://gitforwindows.org`. One of the programs installed is called *gitbash*. Launching **gitbash** will allow us all to use the same commands regardless of which operating system we're using.

Setting your default username and email address

Having launched your terminal, you need to execute the following command to set your default username:

```
git config --global user.name "FIRST_NAME LAST_NAME"
```

Naturally, you'll fill in your actual name. Next, fill in your email address. If you work for a corporation, I strongly recommend creating a separate GitHub account to keep your work separate from your employers to avoid any nasty intellectual property disputes. Keeping that in mind, use an appropriate email address for your work with the following command:

```
git config --global user.email "MY_NAME@example.com"
```

There are more extensive configuration options beyond using these two globals, but this is the most common way to set up Git, and you won't be able to push code to GitHub without these settings. If you'd like more in-depth information on working with Git, I recommend checking out the additional reading in the *Further reading* section of this chapter.

Generating an SSH key

One objective of a remote hub is to keep your code secure from malicious tampering. One of the ways this happens is to ensure all communications between your computer and the remote are encrypted. You can work with HTTPS encryption or SSH. While both are valid encryption tools, SSH is considered far superior and is the mark of a real pro. In order to work with SSH, you need to generate a unique pair of encryption keys: one public key and a matching private key. I won't go into how SSH works here, but if you're curious, I'll leave some reading suggestions in the *Further reading* section of this chapter.

Generating a key is pretty simple. Having opened a Bash session, simply type the following:

```
ssh-keygen
```

The key generation program will ask you some questions, such as where to store your key files and what to call them. By default, they are called `id_rsa` (the private key) and `id_rsa.pub` (the public key), both of which are stored in your home folder in a sub-folder called `.ssh`.

The last question asked is the passphrase for the key. You can enter a password for the key for extra security, or just press *Enter* for an empty passphrase. This is generally not advisable, since security is tighter when you create a passphrase. The drawback to having a passphrase is you are constantly challenged to enter the passphrase. An empty passphrase bypasses these interruptions but puts security at risk by making your key easier to compromise. I recommend entering a passphrase because one of the advantages of using PyCharm's tooling is that it stores your passphrase in its own encrypted database. PyCharm will answer all your challenges for you, eliminating the inconvenience of working with a passphrase-protected encryption key.

After the passkey is entered, you'll get some additional feedback. You can check your key by typing the following:

```
ls ~/.ssh -a
```

This lists (`ls`) the files in your home folder (`~/`) under the `.ssh` sub-folder including any hidden files (`-a` for "all files"). You should see, at a minimum, the `id_rsa` and `id_rsa.pub` files. You are going to need the contents of the `id_rsa.pub` file in just a moment as you are going to paste its contents onto a screen on GitHub.

We've come to the part in the book where I offer a fatherly lecture on security. Never ever, ever, ever (times infinity to the googleth power plus one) paste your private key into anything. Never ever (ad nauseam) allow anybody to copy your private key. Don't put it on a thumb drive. Don't copy it to a network drive or cloud file share for safekeeping. For the love of everything holy, never check it into a repository! That goes for any passwords for any system. Your repos might ultimately become public, if not to the whole world, then at least to the rest of your team.

The public key is for sharing. The private key is to be kept secret and hidden. If your private key is compromised, only your passphrase protects your work. If you left the passphrase blank, then you have no further protection!

To display the contents of your public key, type the following:

```
cat ~/.ssh/id_rsa.pub
```

The contents of your public key will appear in your terminal window. Select the entire key, right-click, and click **Copy**.

Adding your SSH key to your GitHub account

I'm going to cover this pretty quickly since I suspect many of you have done this before. If you need a better tutorial on adding an SSH key to your GitHub account, see the *Further reading* section at the end of this chapter for an explicit list of steps specific to Git.

Log in to GitHub and click your face. By that, I mean the avatar on GitHub in the upper-right corner, assuming they haven't re-designed their site since going to press. Find the option for working with your profile and find **Settings**. Inside your profile settings is an option to manage your SSH keys. Click that link, then find the option to add an SSH key. Paste in the public key you copied a moment ago, give it a name that is easy to remember, and click the **Add** button.

Congratulations! You are fully set up for secure communications between your computer and GitHub remotes. It is possible to reuse your SSH key between different computers you own. Just copy the `.ssh` folder between computers. Just be careful not to compromise the key by keeping it on a portable drive you might lose, or a cloud file share that might be compromised.

Setting up a repository manually

In *Chapter 3, Customizing Interpreters and Virtual Environments*, we created a virtual environment manually in order to become familiar with the process. We'll do the same thing here. Let's use the command line to create a repository and perform all the basic functions available in Git. Afterward, we'll see where PyCharm's tooling allows us to perform the same operations right from the IDE in a convenient GUI.

> **Don't use spaces in any file or folder name**
>
> I'm going to bring this up often since I know a lot of readers skip around in books like this one. If you are new to software development, you may not know that using filenames with spaces can cause problems. Avoid using file and folder names with spaces, including any folders created by your operating system. Instead, use separators in place of spaces, such as dashes or underscores, or use camelCase names, which omit spaces and present word boundaries with a capital letter.

With your Bash terminal session open, the first thing we're going to do is create a folder for our project. We'll do this in your home folder with this command:

```
mkdir first-repository
```

Next, let's change the directory to the newly created folder:

```
cd first-repository
```

This is where our code is going to live! Before we go any further though, we need to talk about a sensitive subject.

Master versus main branches in GitHub

For the first 12 years after GitHub was established, whenever one created a new repository in GitHub, the tool established a default starting branch called *master*. In 2020, an organization called *The Software Freedom Conservancy* advised GitHub to change the name of the default branch from *master* to *main* owing to the association of the term *master* with slavery. While Git doesn't force you to use any particular name, the default on GitHub has been changed to *main*. Since GitHub doesn't control Git, this name change is only the default on repositories created by GitHub. We've been creating our repositories using the Git command line, which is leveraged by PyCharm's Git tools. Whether you use the Git command or PyCharm's integration, there's a solid chance you're going to get a repository initialized with a branch called *master*. When you create a remote on GitHub, that repo will be created with a default branch called *main*.

You should take care to match the names of the default branches so that when you perform your first push, your branches synchronize properly. You can either change the name in GitHub or set the Git command on your computer to use *main* for the default.

If you want to change it on GitHub, you can go into your profile settings and click **Repositories**. You'll find the setting at the top, as shown in *Figure 5.1*.

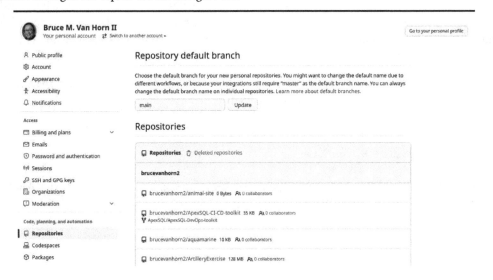

Figure 5.1: You can set the default name of repositories in GitHub to match the default on your computer

You can also set a global setting on your computer with this command:

```
git config --global init.defaultBranch main
```

If you intend to do a lot of work with GitHub as your remote, it is a good idea to synchronize the default branch name. If you don't, the first time you try to push the repository you created on your computer to the remote created on GitHub, you'll encounter an error. The default locally is *master*, while the default on the remote is *main*. The remote won't have a branch called *master*, so you'll get a message stating there is no upstream branch called *master*. You'll have to do some work to get this settled. I'll leave a link to an article on how to resolve this situation should you encounter it. I encourage you to just avoid it entirely by using the preceding Git command to set your local global setting to *main* so it matches GitHub.

Manually initializing the repository

Let's create our repository. It is entirely possible, and even normal, to create a repository after you have created a code project. However, we will start with the repository since this will be a very simple demonstration. To create a new Git repository, or repo for short, type the following:

```
git init
```

That was easy! It might look like nothing much happened. You'll get a message stating the repository was created. Let's look at the changes to the folder:

```
ls -a
```

The `ls` command lists all the files. The `-a` switch shows hidden files and folders. When you initialized the Git repository, the Git software created a folder called `.git`. Since the folder name starts with a period (`.`), the folder is hidden in Linux-like systems. If you perform these steps in Windows with PowerShell, you'll be able to see the folder, but it's hidden in the other operating systems.

The `.git` folder is where all your revisions are stored, along with all your project's settings. In general, you should never need to alter the contents of this folder.

We have a repository on our local computer. Let's add a new file. Type the following:

```
echo "hello world" > test.txt
```

This created a new file called `test.txt`. Within that file is the line `hello world`. What a great way to start, right? You can check the contents of the file by typing the following:

```
cat test.txt
```

Who needs an IDE, right? Wait, no, forget I said that. The order of the next few steps is important. The process is as follows:

1. Add the file(s) to the repository. The files you are adding are the files you have either created or modified since your last commit. We don't have one of those yet. Adding your files to the repo is also called staging your files. We are making the repository aware of new and changed files. You shouldn't always add every file to your project. There are some you should keep out of your repository. We'll cover that a little later.

2. Commit your files. This creates a new version of your code on your local computer. The commit action requires you to include a comment that explains the nature of the changes you've made. This is vital! You should endeavor to write a concise summary of your changes, and you should write these comments as though your most important customer will one day read all these comments. This is not a place to vent your frustrations! Trust me on this one. I've seen projects fall under unexpected audits where mean or inappropriate comments surfaced and working relationships were ruined. Assume everything you write will be read and judged by the whole world.

3. Pull changes from the remote hub. You always want to pull before you push. This allows you to find any conflicts between your work, and any work that might have been pushed by another developer on the project. This is important! If you don't pull before your push, it is possible to overwrite another developer's revision! This is certainly not catastrophic since all revisions are held in the repo. It will, however, make tomorrow's stand-up meeting very awkward for you as the other developer will likely not be happy with you for making extra work for the group! It's simple. Just remember to pull before you push. Do this even if you are the only person working on the project and just make it a habit!

4. Assuming there are no conflicts, push your work to the remote hub.

Your revisions are now available to the rest of the team and stored securely on the remote server. Let's go through the commands for this process.

First, add your new and changed files to Git. Remember, this is also called **staging** your files:

```
git add test.txt
```

If you have a bunch of files in your project, it is possible to add them all at once with the following:

```
git add .
```

With your latest changes staged, you can now commit them to the local repo. This creates a new version of your project on your computer. You need to include a comment that summarizes your changes:

```
git commit -m "initialized repository and added test.txt which might
be the best code in the world."
```

The -m switch is our comment, which is enclosed in double quotes. Just remember it as a *commit message* and the -m switch is easy to remember. Of course, by the end of the chapter, you won't need to remember all this command-line stuff since you'll have a nifty GUI.

Working with remotes

It is possible to work with a project entirely on your local computer. Naturally, you'd lose all the collaborative benefits provided by a remote hub, including the benefits of a remote backup of your change history. Earlier, I presented a four-step process:

1. Add or stage your changed files.
2. Commit your changes to create a new revision.
3. Pull changes from the remote.
4. Push your merged work to the remote.

We're halfway through the list, having completed the first two steps on our local copy of the repository. We must interrupt the process at this point because we don't presently have a remote. We're going to create one on GitHub, but naturally, you can use any compatible service.

Adding a remote on GitHub

Log on to GitHub and find the **Add Repository** button. It is usually a very obvious green button. With my luck, they'll redo the site at press time. Nevertheless, they usually make the **Create repository** button very obvious on the UI.

Let's create a repository to match the one we created locally. I'll make mine public, which means everybody can see it. If you're bashful, you can make it private. It won't matter for this exercise.

Once you have created the repository, GitHub will display instructions for adding the GitHub version of the repo as a remote. Just copy and paste the code GitHub generated into your terminal, making sure that your terminal is currently in the repository folder as the present working directory.

You can verify the remote by typing the following:

```
git remote -a
```

The command generated by GitHub sets the name of the GitHub copy of the repo as *origin*. You should have one remote called *origin*, while the local version of the repository is referred to by the current branch, which is usually *main*, as described earlier.

The first push

Now that you have a remote, you can push your local repo to the remote. Type the following:

```
git push origin main -u
```

This pushes your copy of the main branch to the remote and sets upstream tracking for the main branch. This is just a fancy way of saying both the remote and the local repository are aware of the main branch, and any push here will result in the remote main branch being updated. If the remote doesn't have a branch called main, one will be created and everything will synchronize nicely.

Making, committing, and pushing a change

Now that we have a fully working repository, complete with a remote on GitHub, let's make one full round of changes to our code. We'll cover the four-step process this time without interruption. This is the process you'll follow many times per day for the duration of your project.

The next step is very important. Make this a habit!

```
git pull
```

This pulls any changes sitting on the remote and allows you to fix any conflicts before they go out into the world! Naturally, in this situation, there won't be any conflicts since only we are working on the project.

Next, let's change the contents of our text file. Type the following:

```
echo "this is the best code in the world" > test.txt
```

You can check the result with the following:

```
cat test.txt
```

You should see the changed file. Now let's do a full cycle of add, commit, pull, and push. Type each of the following lines, one at a time, and press *Enter* at the end of each one:

```
git add test.txt
git commit -m "changed the text in test.txt"
git pull
git push origin main
```

Switch to your browser where you created your repository, and refresh the page. You should see your code. You can click the test.txt file in the browser to verify the new contents were pushed. You should also see there are two revisions.

Your repo is set up and working properly! Let's switch our focus from the command line to working in the IDE.

Working with Git in the IDE

We have already gone through some of the Git workflows in PyCharm. In *Chapter 2, Installation and Configuration*, we used PyCharm to clone the sample code repository for this book. Since we've covered cloning, we won't do it again. Instead, let's consider all we did manually a moment ago:

1. We used `git init` to initialize a new local repository.
2. We made a change to our code.
3. We used `git add` to add the changes as staged files in preparation for a commit.
4. We committed our changes to the local repository.
5. We pulled from the remote to make sure we have the latest code on this branch and that no conflicts exist between what we have in our working copy and what exists on the remote. The remote could have recently changed owing to some other developer pushing their changes.
6. Finally, we pushed our changes to the remote.

This list represents the most basic workflow for capturing and managing revisions on a project. We can do all of this and more in PyCharm's GUI. It is also fairly common to do some work in PyCharm and some in the command line. Using one or the other doesn't preclude anything. For example, I often branch and merge in the command line because it's quick and easy for me. If there is a conflict, I find resolving it in PyCharm to be superior in every way versus a manual approach. The GUI for this task is outstanding. We'll get to all this in good time. For now, open the folder you've been using in PyCharm, and let's explore what the IDE can do for us regarding these first steps we've taken manually.

Version control in PyCharm

PyCharm has several places in the UI that allow you to access your VCS, which for us is Git. They aren't redundant, but instead, each area provides a visual tool for a particular task. The first is the main menu, as seen in *Figure 5.2*.

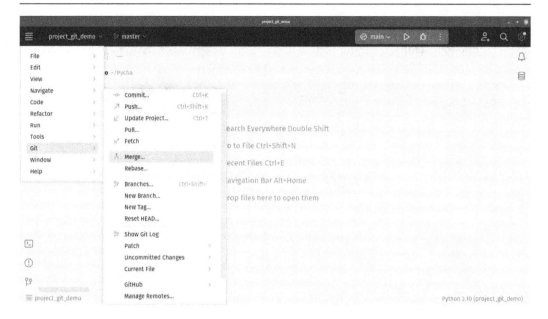

Figure 5.2: The Git menu allows you to access all the commands
you might normally use at the command line

The second provides a fast and easy way to commit files. This can be found in the sidebar menu, as seen in *Figure 5.3*:

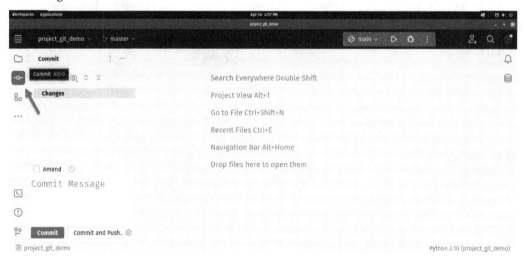

Figure 5.3: The Git commit tools can be found in the sidebar

The third allows visualization of the branch and commit history. This can be found in the tool window located at the bottom of the screen. This section of the screen collapses, but the tool window selector is always available at the bottom of the sidebar, as seen in *Figure 5.4*.

Figure 5.4: Clicking the Git tool window will open a window that shows
you the commit history, along with all the branches

The fourth is on the top toolbar next to the main menu. This area shows you the branch you are currently working on and allows easy branch management. You can see this in *Figure 5.5*.

Figure 5.5: The current branch is displayed near the main menu.
Clicking here allows you access to a few commands

The fifth is the VCS operations popup, as shown in *Figure 5.6*. This has been around for quite a while and I would consider it legacy even though it's still there. You can get to the popup using *Ctrl + `*. Please note that isn't a quotation mark. The ` key, called the gravure mark, is located to the left of the *1* (one) key on the US keyboard layout.

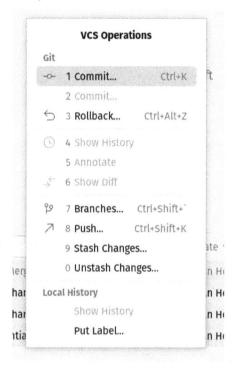

Figure 5.6: The VCS operations pop-up window is activated with Ctrl/Cmd + `.

Finally, you can right-click the editor window or a tab in the editor window to access the same Git menu found in the main menu, as shown in *Figure 5.7*.

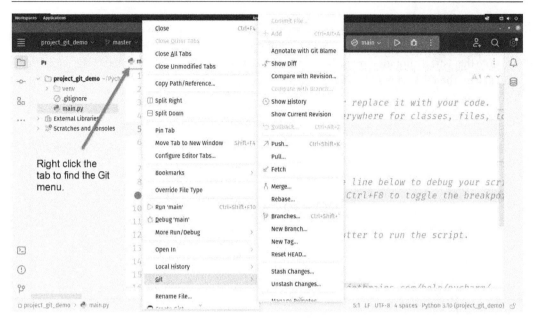

Figure 5.7: You can right-click in the editor window or on a tab to see the Git menu

As you can see, tooling for revision control is neatly woven into the IDE in an organized and intelligent fashion. Since we opened a folder that already had a Git repository in place, PyCharm simply recognizes that fact and presents the interface. When you open a folder or create a project without a GitHub repo, most of the tooling will still be visible, but it won't be Git specific. Since PyCharm supports many VCSs, a project that hasn't been initialized using Git or any other VCS will present generic tooling until such initialization is complete.

Creating a new project from scratch using VCS tooling in PyCharm

Let's make a new project. The code for this project is in the repo for the book, but you don't really want to just open that copy because it will already be associated with a repository, and you won't see everything I'm about to show you. For this exercise, you should create a new project from scratch as I am about to do.

Click the hamburger icon in the top-left corner of the application to activate the main menu, then click **File | New Project**. I'm going to call my project project_git_demo. I'll leave everything else as default. You can see my project creation dialog in *Figure 5.8*.

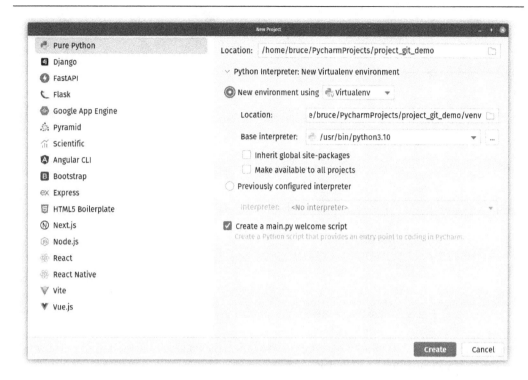

Figure 5.8: My demo project settings

We now have a project with which we can work.

Initializing the local Git repository

After my project has been created, I need to initialize a Git repository. Manually, we did this with the `git init` command. In PyCharm, we can use the main menu's **VCS** option. Right now, it says **VCS** because we haven't initialized a repository with any VCS yet, so the terminology in the UI is generic. As you can see in *Figure 5.9*, we have options for revision control in Mercurial, Git, GitHub, Perforce, and Subversion. There is a new option for sharing a project on JetBrains' new collaboration product called **Space**, which contains a Git hosting service. Naturally, as the Space product grows, you can expect to see more and more integration appear in all the IDEs. I'm going to click **Create Git Repository...**, as shown in *Figure 5.9*.

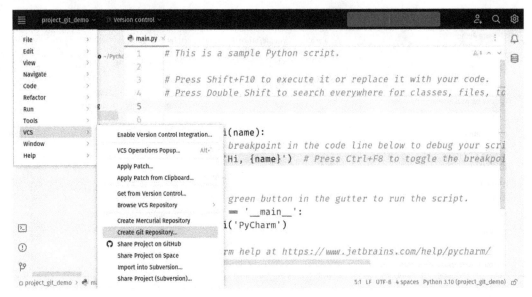

Figure 5.9: Creating a Git repository from the PyCharm VCS menu

As you can see in *Figure 5.10*, you are next prompted to select the folder where you'd like to create the repository. It defaults to the current folder, which is correct.

Figure 5.10: Select the folder where you'd like to create the Git repository

Clicking the **OK** button creates the repository in the selected folder. You can verify that it worked by checking whether the default branch (master) appears in the top toolbar with a dropdown that contains a few Git operations. Now that we have initialized a Git repository, the menus no longer use the term **VCS** but instead list options specifically for Git.

Adding a remote on GitHub

There isn't tooling in PyCharm for creating a remote. You need to log in to GitHub and create a repository just as you did earlier. *Figure 5.11* shows me setting up the remote repository in my personal account. Note this is distinct from the book's repository, which is meant to house all the code in the book rather than serve as a demonstration of creating a repository.

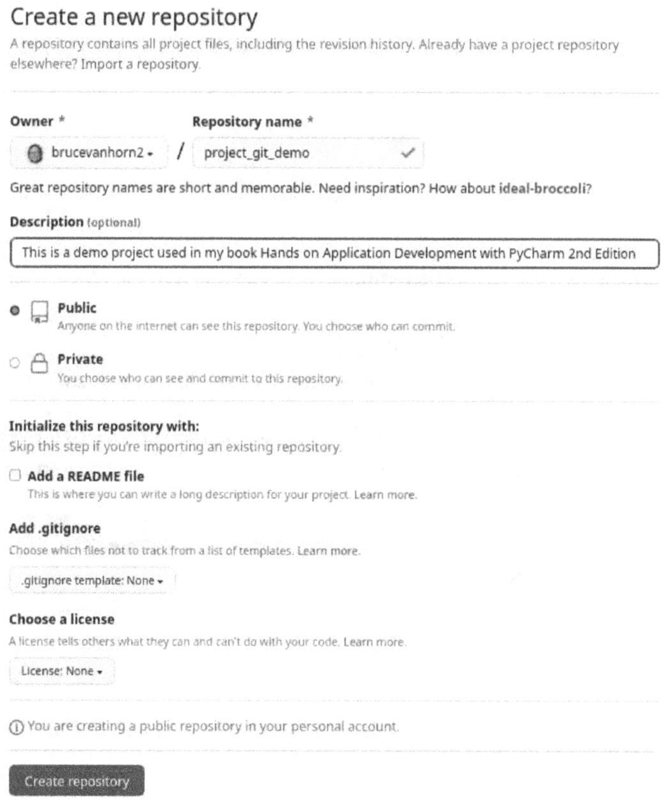

Figure 5.11: The settings for my remote

Note that only the bare minimum is set. No `.gitignore` file, no README file, and so on. I'm going to add all those in PyCharm. When I click the **Create repository** button, GitHub generates the URL I need for adding the remote. I've pointed this out in *Figure 5.12*.

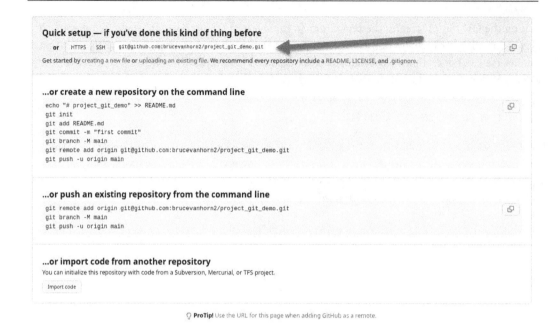

Figure 5.12: You need the URL for the remote in order to add it to your local repository

Next, switch back to PyCharm and find the **git** menu within the main menu. Remember, a minute ago, the menu said **VCS** because we had not defined a repository, but now it says **git**.

Within the **git** menu, you'll find an option called **Manage Remotes**. Click that and you'll see a modal dialog, shown in *Figure 5.13*, which allows you to add the remote you just created on GitHub.

Figure 5.13: The Git Remotes dialog allows you to add the remote you created on GitHub

Click the + button to add a remote. You get yet another dialog on top of this one, as seen in *Figure 5.14*.

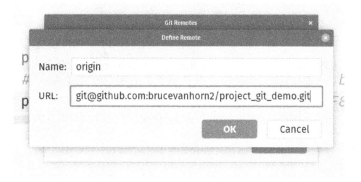

Figure 5.14: Add the URL you copied from the GitHub page

Click **OK** on the **Define Remote** dialog, and again on the **Manage Remotes** dialog. You'll see some subtle changes. The main.py file is red.. You'll just have to trust me. It's red because it is an untracked file. We need to add our files to our repository so we can track them.

Adding project files

Setting up the project and the remote is something you generally only do once for the duration of the project. If you're joining an existing team, it may have been done long before you joined. This next set of actions, though, is something you'll work with every day.

When you are working with changes you've made to the project, you'll find the **Commit** window very useful. Refer back to *Figure 5.3* if you have forgotten how to locate the **Commit** window.

Adding a .gitignore file

If you're not familiar, a .gitignore file defines files and folders you don't want to include in your repository. As a general rule, anything that can be generated from your code doesn't need to be in your repository. When working with Python projects, a short list of things you don't want in your repo might include the following:

- The venv folder since this is generated by running pip
- Python cache folders (you'll see them as __pycache__ folders)
- Byte-compiled DLL files
- C extensions
- Build files from distribution and packaging

- PyInstaller manifests

- Application log files

- Test coverage reports

This is by no means an exhaustive list. The list will really depend on what kind of application you are building and exactly what gets generated during a run of your project. There are plenty of suggestions on the contents of a `.gitignore` file. GitHub has such a list in a gist. You can get this file at `https://githubgitm/github/gigitnore/blgitmain/Python.gitignore`. It is also the `.gitignore` file in the book's Git repository. You can use this `.gitignore` file if you'd like, but to keep this short and easy, I'm just going to include a few entries in a `.gitignore` file we will create.

Switch back to the file view, as shown in *Figure 5.15*. You do this by clicking the folder icon (**1**). Then, right-click on the `project_git_demo` project title (**2**) and create a new file. Call it `.gitignore`. No creativity is allowed here. It must be called `.gitignore`, all lowercase.

Figure 5.15: Switch back to the file view and create a new file called .gitignore

When you create the new file, PyCharm will prompt you to add the file to Git, as shown in *Figure 5.16*. If you want to add new files to become the default, you can click the **Don't ask again** checkbox and all files you create will be added to GitHub automatically.

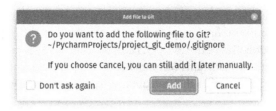

Figure 5.16: Each time you create a file in PyCharm, you are prompted to add it to the repository

Regardless of what you do with the checkbox, click the **Add** button to add the file. You'll notice the `.gitignore` file shows green in the project explorer since it was added and nothing has yet changed. Within the `.gitignore` file, add these lines:

```
venv
__pycache__
```

This will exclude the entire `venv` folder and any cache folders generated by Python. PyCharm saves your files as we go, so let's add this file and the `main.py` file to the repository. Switch to the **Commit** window and you'll see something like *Figure 5.17*.

Figure 5.17: The commit window after we've added our .gitignore file

Wow! Where did all that come from? We just added one file! As you can see, the `.gitignore` file was added in response to the dialog we saw when we created the file. The only other code file in the project is the `main.py` file generated by PyCharm when we created the project. What about the rest? Why is there a second `.gitignore` file listed in the unversioned files list?

These all come from the .idea folder created by PyCharm. There is some debate on whether this folder belongs in source control. JetBrains has a page in their documentation at https://intellij-support.jetbrains.com/hc/en-us/articles/206544839 discussing their ideas on the subject. To sum up the article, JetBrains recommends storing the contents of the .idea folder pertaining to the project, but not any files that contain user-specific settings, which are the following:

- workspace.xml

- usage.statistics.xml

- Anything in the shelf directory

The article is meant to cover all **IntelliJ IDEA**-based IDEs, so much of the article will pertain to things not relevant to Python work, such as artifacts from Android coding projects. Since I haven't done anything so far that would generate these files or folders, they are not on the list. I might, though, in the future. Anyone on my team might also contribute to the project and they might add the files to the repo without realizing it, which might change the way PyCharm acts according to someone else's preferences. Since that might be disturbing, it is a good idea to add these to the .gitignore file. We haven't committed anything yet, so add these lines to your .gitignore file:

```
.idea/workspace.xml
.idea/usage.statistics.xml
.idea/shelf
```

Let's check all the boxes to get all those files added, as shown in *Figure 5.18*.

Figure 5.18: Everything is added and we're ready to commit

Add a commit message in the box. You can click the **Commit** button to commit to your local repository or **Commit and Push…** to send the changes straight to GitHub. As a general rule, you should not use the **Commit and Push…** button unless you are completely certain that no one could have pushed changes since the last push. It is probably safe because we have never pushed; however, I'm going to hit the **Commit** button to demonstrate the whole process laid out earlier. You add your changes, commit, pull, and then push. So far, we've added our changes, and now we're committing.

If all goes well, a toast will appear in the lower-right corner of your screen stating that your files were successfully committed. If you didn't set your global username and email address during the manual exercise, you will be prompted via a dialog to set them up.

Pulling and pushing

Now that the first commit is out of the way, we are set to do the last half of the process. We always pull before pushing to ensure we have the latest revision on the current branch. This allows us a chance to resolve any conflicts that might have arisen since our last pull. In Git, the command we used was `pull`. There is a `pull` option in the Git tools, but before we go there, I will point out another option: **Update Project…**. This is found in the dropdown in the toolbar denoted by the current branch, as shown in *Figure 5.19*.

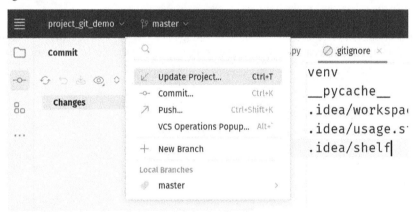

Figure 5.19: The Update Project… command isn't really a Git command. It refers to an update strategy

When you click **Update Project…**, you'll be asked to set your preference for updating your local Git repository. There are two possibilities depicted in the ensuing dialog box, as shown in *Figure 5.20*.

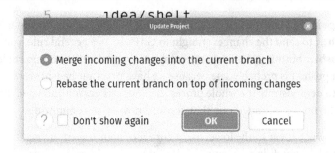

Figure 5.20: There are two update strategies from which to choose

The `git pull` command we executed earlier embodies the first option. The pull operation will *fetch* any changes from the remote and automatically *merge* those changes into our local copy. The `rebase` operation is a different strategy. It changes the structure of your repository in order to show a cleaner timeline of changes. I won't get into the arguments of which strategy to use, but I will include a link in the *Further reading* section of this chapter should you desire to dive deeper.

Personally, I prefer the first option since it is simpler and safer. I only have to click the **OK** button. I can click the **Don't show again** checkbox if I do not want to be prompted before use. PyCharm will forevermore use the selection I make here and now.

If you have problems with commitment, I don't mean generally, but technically, when it comes to executing `git commit`, you can skip this dialog entirely. Just use the **Pull…** menu item on the Git menu, as shown in *Figure 5.21*.

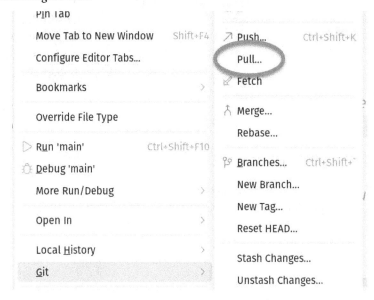

Figure 5.21: You can do a traditional Git pull from any of the Git menus

There is nothing left to do but push. Perhaps the quickest way was shown previously in *Figure 5.19*, where we encountered the **Update Project…** command.

Branching and merging

We have discussed the most basic functions of any VCS, which protects the project's code by tracking revisions over time. A second set of very important functions entails segregating the project work into several copies. This practice is called **branching**. There are many benefits to branching; I can't cover them all here. If you'd like more details on version control with Git, check out the Packt book *Git for Programmers* listed in the *Further reading* section of this chapter. However, I'll offer what I consider to be the most important benefits.

Consider a typical web start-up that goes through a cycle of creating a repository and iterating development to its first release. The release is sitting on a production server somewhere in the cloud and customers have started using the app. The start-up company not only wants to enhance their offering with additional features, but they will also encounter bugs and problems that must be fixed. Let's pretend the development and quality assurance teams did such an amazing job that there are virtually no bugs in the release. Pleased with themselves, the company wants to start adding new features. All work is being done in the main branch because that is the only one that exists. In order to add a new feature, we need to change something deep within the code. The moment you start the change, you need a week to finish it, and during that time, the development version of the product is very unstable.

All of a sudden, reality sets in. It is nigh impossible to have a software release with no bugs, unless, of course, the software was written by unicorns or Chuck Norris. Let's say it's not just a bug. It's a bad bug. Something like someone forgot a WHERE customer_id=@customerId on a SQL statement and your app erroneously displays all customer data to all customers. That's a career-ender! I've seen it happen and it isn't pretty. You need to fix it *immediately*! Except you can't without backing out all those changes you've made that might render the app unstable. That is one option. Another option is that you could revert to the code you released, then implement the fix and save your career. You would then spend a lot of time trying to cherry-pick the commits to salvage your feature work. You could also elect to write all of your code in Notepad using a keyboard set to the Dvorak layout with totally blank keys. You could do it, but it wouldn't be a productive use of your time.

This is where branching comes into play. The start-up can do all its work on the main branch. They shouldn't, but let's keep the story constrained to what we have so far. Once the software is released, they could make a new branch and maybe call it *development-branch*. The name isn't important. The branching operation creates a copy of what was released. It is in that branch that our intrepid development team starts to make changes that might have rendered the development version unstable.

Boom! The bad thing happens. You can switch from *development-branch* back to *main*. You now have the code that was released, and you can fix the problem. After the fix is in place, you can merge the fix into your development branch and continue working on your unstable app in *development-branch*. Keeping the work segregated allows you to work on new features independently of emergency bug fixes.

I am grossly over-simplifying the typical branching strategy used by most teams in this illustration. I would prefer to leave coverage of that topic to works dedicated to version control. I'll leave suggestions for further reading on branching strategies in the *Further reading* section of this chapter. Let's continue with the mechanics of working with branches. They are vital to your daily practice of software development.

Creating a branch

Creating a new branch is very easy. Click the branch menu on the top menu bar and click **New Branch**. You'll see the dialog shown in *Figure 5.22*.

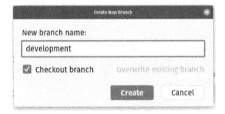

Figure 5.22: The Create New Branch dialog allows you to create a new Git branch

Type a name for your new branch. The branch is created locally, and you are automatically switched to the new branch.

Switching between branches

This is also very easy. Go back to the branch menu. The local branches are listed in the branch dropdown, as shown in *Figure 5.23*.

Figure 5.23: Local branches are listed in the branch menu

Switching to a different branch is just a matter of clicking the desired branch from the list and then clicking **Checkout**. As you can see, there are other operations you can perform on the branch.

Merging

When you're ready to merge a branch back into main, or any other branch for that matter, simply switch to that branch, then use the **Merge** command in the branch menu, as shown in *Figure 5.24*.

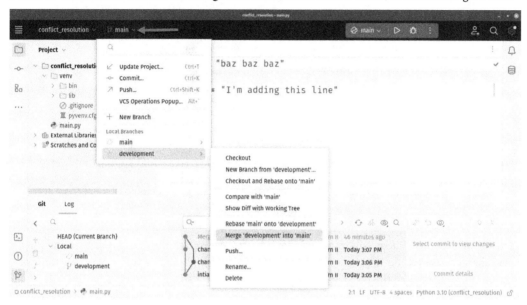

Figure 5.24: The Merge command can be found in the branch menu

The **Merge** dialog, shown in *Figure 5.24*, will allow you to select the branch you'd like to merge into the currently selected branch.

If you need something more exotic than the standard merge operation, there is a **Modify options** dropdown, which allows you to do the equivalent of several command-line switches normally employed during the manual merge process.

Viewing the branch diagram

The Git tool in the tool window provides a graphical view of the various branches in your repository. You can see it in *Figure 5.25*. This can be useful when you need to review what has recently changed in the repository. It's the kind of thing you might do first thing in the morning so you can review your team's changes in the last 24 hours.

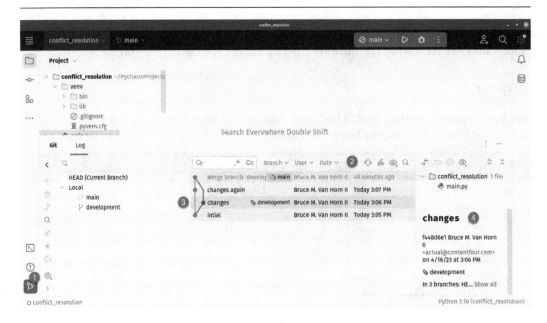

Figure 5.25: The Git tool can be activated by clicking on the toolbar
on the lower-left edge of the PyCharm window

To activate it, click the Git icon in the tool window (**1**). You can search the revision history and filter it using the various tools on the toolbar (**2**). Selecting a commit (**3**) allows you to see the details of that commit (**4**) along with the commit message.

Diffs and conflict resolution

Sooner or later, you're going to perform a pull prior to pushing some changes only to discover a conflict exists. This can be intimidating and stressful even for experienced developers because you are running the risk of breaking someone else's recent contribution. Nevertheless, it happens and you need a way to deal with the problem. This leads us to one of my favorite features in PyCharm. In *Chapter 1, Introduction to PyCharm – the Most Popular IDE for Python*, I told you about my experience with Microsoft's debugger. Having experienced it early in my career, to me, nothing else will do. I have the same regard for PyCharm's merge tool. Resolving a conflicted merge in anything else feels painful.

There is only one file in the project. By now, you'll recognize it as the main.py file PyCharm generates with new projects. We're going to generate a conflict using the following steps:

1. Create a new project in PyCharm.

2. Change the contents of the main.py file to a single line of code to ensure we generate a conflict.

3. Initialize a Git repository in the project folder.

4. Add and commit all project files.

5. Create a new branch called *development*.

6. Change the line of code that renders the *Hello World* message.

7. Commit the change to the branch.

8. Switch back to the main branch.

9. Make a different change to the one line of code.

10. Commit the change.

11. Now try to merge the development branch into the main branch.

The result of these 11 steps will be a conflict. Let's resolve it!

First, create a new project called `conflict_resolution` in PyCharm, as shown in *Figure 5.26*. Make sure you create the project in a location on your drive outside of the folder structure for the book's repository. Remember, the book's code is already in a repository. You can't create a new repo inside another repo.

Figure 5.26: My conflict_resolution project settings. They're just defaults

PyCharm generates a project with a `main.py` file. Delete all the lines in `main.py` and replace them with this code:

```
foo = "foo"
```

Just so we're clear, your PyCharm window should look just like mine in *Figure 5.27*.

Figure 5.27: The main.py file has been reduced to one line of code

Click the **VCS** menu in the **File** menu and click **Create Git repository**. If you don't remember where in the menu to find this, refer back to *Figure 5.9*. Make note of the default branch that was created. We don't need a remote for this exercise, so it doesn't matter whether it's *main*, *master*, or something else; you just need to remember its name. I'll assume it's called *main*.

Use the commit window to add the files for the project to the repository. *Figure 5.3* will remind you if you have forgotten how. Go ahead and commit the files by entering a commit message.

Next, we need to create a branch. Click the branch dropdown and click **Create branch**. *Figure 5.4* displays the menu location if you need a refresher. I'll call my branch `development`.

Open the `main.py` file. Replace the code with this one line:

```
foo = "bar"
```

By limiting ourselves to a single line, we can be positive our actions will result in a conflict. Commit this change to the `development` branch.

Switch back to the main branch using the branch dropdown. Change the contents of `main.py` to this code:

```python
foo = "baz baz baz"
```

Commit this change to the main branch. You've just simulated two developers changing the same file, in the same area. There will be no way for Git to reconcile the differences. With the main branch active, click the branch dropdown, click the development branch, and click **Merge development into main**. You will see a conflict message, as shown in *Figure 5.28*.

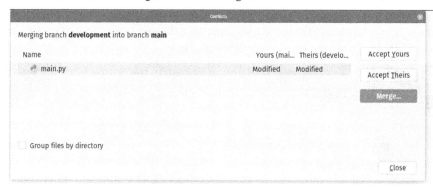

Figure 5.28: We have a conflict that needs to be resolved before we can merge

You generally have three options when resolving a conflict. You can choose to ignore the incoming changes and select your local work as the correct code by clicking the **Accept Yours** button. Likewise, you can select the incoming code changes and discard your local copy by clicking **Accept Theirs**. Often, though, you will need to merge parts of your local revision with the incoming changes. For this, you will need to activate the merge tool, as shown in *Figure 5.29*, by clicking the **Merge...** button.

Figure 5.29: Activate the merge tool to pick parts from the incoming code to merge with yours

With the merge tool active, you can see three panes. The pane on the left (1) represents the conflicting code from the main branch. The code on the right (2) is the revision coming from the development branch. The pane in the middle (3) represents the amalgamation of the two. You can pick parts of your code and parts of the incoming code to make the best possible combination. Experiment with the >> buttons (4), which copy the code into the central merged result. The buttons labeled **X** (4) will ignore the conflicted line. You can use the up and down arrows (5) to jump to the next unresolved conflict in the file.

Let's pretend the best resolution to my conflict is to have a line from the left pane and a line from the right pane together. In real life, this wouldn't work because we're going to wind up with two variable assignments next to each other, but it does demonstrate how the tool works. To use the line from the left pane, I can click the button indicated by the arrow in *Figure 5.30*.

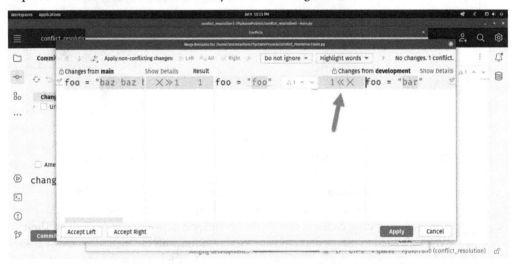

Figure 5.30: This button will move the code from the left pane into the working merge solution

Next, I'd like to place the line from the right pane below the line I just moved. Often, you want to use some of the code from both sides rather than it simply being right or wrong from one side. Click the button indicated by the arrow in *Figure 5.31* to copy the code from the left pane below the current line in the middle pane.

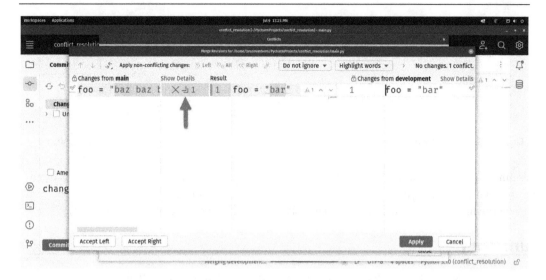

Figure 5.31: Clicking the double arrow copies this line below the one we selected from the right side

Once you complete this action, you have resolved the conflict! You are rewarded with a nice green message telling you as much.

Your objective is to use the left and right panes to create the best version of the code in the middle pane, which represents the resolution of the conflict. When you're finished, you can click the **Apply** button. If you have unresolved conflicts remaining in the file, PyCharm will tell you that. If you got them all, the merge you attempted is completed. If you are working with a remote, you should push the resulting conflict resolution once the commit is successful.

Viewing diffs

You don't need a conflict to use the diff window we just saw. A diff window is a window that shows two or more versions of code side by side. You can diff between branches, or between revisions. Say I make a quick change to our merged code by adding this line:

```
text = "I'm adding this line"
```

I also take out line 2, which reads as follows:

```
foo = "bar"
```

My code is now very different. If I want to compare my new code with the latest in the branch, I can right-click the main.py tab and click **Git | Show Diff**. I'll see a side-by-side diff of the two files, as shown in *Figure 5.32*.

Figure 5.32: The diff view between what you've got in your editor versus the last committed version

This diff is appearing in a side-by-side format. You can change it to an in-line view, which is often shown on GitHub when you view commits, by changing the drop-down setting labeled (**1**). You can also edit the file using the same line-moving tools you just saw in the merge indicated by (**2**).

Summary

In this chapter, we have covered two main topics—the idea of version control in application development and programming and its importance, as well as how to practice it using Git and GitHub within PyCharm. Specifically, we have learned how to carry out version control using Git and GitHub in two different ways: manually and with PyCharm.

With this knowledge, PyCharm users can apply version control to their own projects in a flexible way, skipping over the manual and tedious process in the terminal/command line. We see that, by offering these features, PyCharm allows us to focus on the actual development process in any given software engineering project.

Aside from version control, there are other practices in application development— which PyCharm provides intuitive, straightforward commands to facilitate. Without these commands, application development be quite complex and intimidating. These processes are testing, debugging, and profiling, all of which will be discussed in the next chapter.

Questions

1. What does the term *version control* entail, specifically in the context of programming?

2. What are the benefits of using version control?

3. What are the basic steps to version control for your own projects with Git and GitHub?

4. What is *branching* and why is it important?

5. Name the various windows and tool locations throughout PyCharm that give you access to Git and other VCS commands.

Further reading

- Be sure to check out the companion website for the book at `https://www.pycharm-book.com`.

- *Merging vs. Rebasing*: `https://www.atlassian.com/git/tutorials/merging-vs-rebasing`

- How Secure Shell (SSH) works: `https://en.wikipedia.org/wiki/Secure_Shell`

- *Adding a new SSH key to your GitHub account*: `https://docs.github.com/en/authentication/connecting-to-github-with-ssh/adding-a-new-ssh-key-to-your-github-account`

- *Why GitHub renamed its master branch to main*: `https://www.theserverside.com/feature/Why-GitHub-renamed-its-master-branch-to-main`

- *Git Merge Strategy Options and Examples*: `https://www.atlassian.com/git/tutorials/using-branches/merge-strategy`

- Git branching guidance: `https://learn.microsoft.com/en-us/azure/devops/repos/git/git-branching-guidance`

- Git Essentials for Beginners: `https://www.packtpub.com/product/mastering-git/9781783553754`

- Liberty, J. (2021). *Git for Programmers: Master Git for effective implementation of version control for your programming projects*. Packt Publishing Limited.

- Narebski, J. (2016). *Mastering Git*. Packt Publishing Ltd.

- *The Joel Test: 12 Steps to Better Code*: `https://www.joelonsoftware.com/2000/08/09/the-joel-test-12-steps-to-better-code/`

- Be sure to check out the companion website for the book at `https://www.pycharm-book.com`.

6

Seamless Testing, Debugging, and Profiling

In *Chapter 5, Version Control with Git in PyCharm*, I talked about *The Joel Test*. This test is just a list of best practices. At the top of the list is the use of version control, which was the subject of the previous chapter. If you looked up the list, you were probably not surprised to see testing was also on the list. Formalized software testing practices such as **test-driven development (TDD)** and **behavior-driven development (BDD)** are the cornerstones of software quality control. Working with these methodologies helps you create software that is less likely to fail in production. Done correctly, it also has side benefits, such as preventing scope creep and allowing for effective refactoring on projects that might have neglected best practices and taken on a lot of technical debt.

Several levels of testing are in practice today, including the following:

- **Unit testing**, which aims to test basic low-level functionality at the level of functions or classes
- **Integration testing**, which aims to test how components within a larger system work together
- **User interface testing**, which aims to test how interactive elements of a system work
- **End-to-end testing**, which tests an entire system in a production-like environment

Like all well-established programming languages, Python has a rich set of testing libraries available. And since Python is "batteries included," there are some fine testing tools built into the standard library. Naturally, third-party solutions have evolved and are available via `PyPi.org`.

I cut my teeth on Java's **JUnit** library, and later on its .NET port called **NUnit**. I found it made software development very enjoyable. There's just something fun about starting your day with a set of tests that don't pass, and throughout the day, writing the code to make each one pass. If you're disciplined, you will write the bare minimum code needed, and gradually you will see progress as your testing tool changes color from red to green. You shouldn't take shortcuts, and you shouldn't be tempted to write in functionality that seems cool but that you might not need later. When I made the leap to Python years ago, I was pleased to see so many options regarding testing libraries and frameworks. I was equally pleased to see that PyCharm supports most of the popular ones right in the IDE.

In this chapter, we'll be looking at creating unit tests in Python code while following the tenets of TDD. In TDD, you generally create a set of tests designed to prove your software meets a set of requirements. These tests are written before you create any functionality in your program, and they start as failures. Your job is to make the tests pass with the simplest code possible.

Along the way, you'll need to use a debugger to step through problematic code that either inexplicably fails, or perhaps worse, inexplicably works. Once your code works and passes tests, you usually want to consider the speed of execution. The **National Health Service** (**NHS**) in Great Britain developed an algorithm that matched organ donations to patients in the system. The complex algorithm had to be fast because there is a limited window of time during which a harvested organ is viable for transplant. Similar time constraints exist in many other types of applications. As developers, we need tools to help us pinpoint efficiency bottlenecks.

The following topics will be covered in this chapter:

- Unit testing in Python with PyCharm

- Using PyCharm's powerful visual debugger

- Working with PyCharm's profiling tools to find performance bottlenecks in your code

Technical requirements

The following are the prerequisites for this chapter:

- A working installation of Python 3.10 or later

- A working installation of PyCharm

- The sample code for this chapter, which can be found at `https://github.com/ PacktPublishing/Hands-On-Application-Development-with-PyCharm- -Second-Edition/tree/main/chapter-06`

Testing, testing, 1-2-3

Unit testing is a practice designed to prove your code works as designed. A good set of tests will match a functional specification. A great set of tests will do that but also account for any obvious paths of failure. To get started, let's get our feet wet with something simple: your bank account. OK, it doesn't have to be yours. Consider a typical transaction where you buy something at a store using your ATM card.

You visit your favorite brick-and-mortar bookstore to pick up your next excellent read in the field of software development. Let's say you find a copy of my first book, *Real World Implementation of C# Design Patterns*, published by Packt. Given its status as an instant classic, you can't resist picking up a copy at any price. You tap your card on the bookstore's point-of-sale system and two things happen:

1. The equivalent of $39.95 – which is an absolute steal by the way – is taken out of your bank account.

2. The same amount is transferred into the bank account of the bookstore.

This is a transactional operation. Formally speaking, a transaction is a multi-step operation where every step must complete without errors. It should be an all-or-nothing set of operations. If the first step completes but the second fails, then $39.95 just vanishes from your bank account and you don't get to go home with your book. If the second step works but the first fails, you get a free book, but the local bookseller goes broke. We need both steps to complete, or at worst, fail completely so that no money changes hands.

This level of criticality is a good scenario for learning about unit testing.

Unit testing in Python using PyCharm

Create a new project in PyCharm using the plain Python project template. Let's call it `bank_account`. You'll find the completed example in the source repository for this chapter, but if you'd like to practice creating and testing the necessary code, just follow along.

PyCharm created a file called `main.py`. We'll use it in a moment, but let's put our bank transaction code in a separate module. One of the tenets of writing good code is writing **testable code**, and the best way to write testable code is to follow the **single-responsibility principle** (**SRP**), where you create units of code that have only one responsibility. SRP is part of a larger set of rules for creating a resilient coding architecture called **SOLID**, which is an acronym for the following principles:

- **Single-responsibility principle (SRP)**

- **Open-closed principle (OCP)**

- **Liskov substitution principle (LSP)**

- **Interface segregation principle (ISP)**

- **Dependency inversion principle (DIP)**

SOLID is normally considered when developing a **fully object-oriented** (**FOO**) architecture using static languages that are strictly object-oriented. Java, C++, and C# are classic examples of such languages. Python allows for many different development paradigms, and its implementation of **object-oriented programming** (**OOP**) isn't as complete, or maybe not as traditional, as many others. If you've never heard of SOLID as a Python developer, that's probably why. Books and blogs exist where people have tried to shoehorn Python code to fit, but in my opinion, it often feels forced.

SRP is one you should absolutely follow. It fits into any language and any paradigm. Simply put, the elements you make, be they functions, Python packages, or objects, should do only one thing, and do it well. By breaking up the responsibilities of your code, you can create reusable elements that can easily be unit tested, and therefore easily maintained. Everything should do one thing. Of course, there will be something tying it all together – maybe a `main` function in a program whose only purpose is to call everything else and provide a flow for your program.

OCP states that once you have shipped a class to production, you should never change it. You should write your code in such a way that your classes are open to extension, but closed for modification. This principle is designed to protect the functionality you've already tested and shipped. If you open the class and change it, then you introduce the risk of bugs and you have to retest your entire program. If you limit your changes to an extension, then you only need to worry about testing the extension.

LSP doesn't translate easily to Python. It states that any sub-class should be able to replace its superclass without affecting the correctness of the program. In other words, if a program is using a base class, it should be able to work correctly when you substitute a derived class for the base class. When you adhere to LSP, you are promoting the concept of polymorphism within your classes. This allows different objects to be treated uniformly through their common supertype, which leads to more flexible and modular designs. Implementing LSP is hard in dynamic languages such as Python since these languages allow for dynamic typing and late binding of method calls. For this reason, LSP is even more crucial than it is in static, strongly typed languages. The challenge comes with the lack of a strict compile type check you get in C#, C++, or Java. Any design mistakes you make will not surface until runtime. As a Python developer, you must design very carefully, and test with more intensity than you might in other languages.

ISP states that classes or modules should have interfaces that are tailored to their specific needs. An interface that specifies the structure and behavior of a class should not contain anything that is not needed by that class. This doesn't translate well into Python since Python lacks the traditional interfaces found in languages such as Java and C#. The word interface can be taken to mean a regular superclass, in which case the superclass shouldn't contain properties and methods that are never used within a subclass.

DIP is a fundamental principle in object-oriented programming that deals with the dependencies between classes and modules. It states that high-level modules should not depend on low-level modules, but both should depend on abstractions. Additionally, it emphasizes that abstractions should not depend on details; rather, details should depend on abstractions.

Here are the key ideas of DIP:

- **High-level modules should not depend on low-level modules**: High-level modules represent the higher-level logic or functionality of an application, while low-level modules deal with the implementation details and lower-level operations. According to DIP, high-level modules should not directly depend on low-level modules. Instead, both should depend on abstractions.

- **Abstractions should not depend on details**: Abstractions, such as interfaces or abstract classes, define contracts that specify the behavior and functionality expected from the collaborating objects. DIP states that these abstractions should not depend on the specific implementation details of the lower-level modules. It promotes the idea of programming to interfaces rather than concrete implementations.

To adhere to DIP, it is essential to introduce abstractions, such as interfaces or abstract classes, and program against those abstractions rather than concrete implementations. This promotes loose coupling and allows for greater flexibility and maintainability in the code base. Ensure you don't confuse this with **dependency injection (DI)**. They are related, but not the same thing.

DI is a design pattern or technique that facilitates the implementation of DIP. DI is a way to provide the dependencies required by a class from an external source, rather than having the class create or manage its dependencies internally.

In DI, the responsibility of creating and providing dependencies is delegated to an external entity, typically called an "injector" or "container." The container is responsible for creating instances of classes and injecting their dependencies. This allows for better decoupling and flexibility and easier testing since dependencies can easily be substituted or mocked during unit testing.

DI can be seen as an implementation strategy for achieving the principles outlined in DIP. It helps in adhering to DIP by providing a mechanism that inverts the control of dependencies and separates the creation of objects from their usage.

In summary, DIP is a guideline for designing modular, loosely coupled systems, while DI is a technique or pattern that's used to implement DIP, which it does by externalizing the responsibility of managing dependencies.

If you are interested in this kind of architecture, you should check out that book I plugged earlier as SOLID is covered extensively throughout, albeit with C# as the language. SRP, however, fits nicely with any language or paradigm, Python included.

When you stick with functions and classes that only do one thing, and do it well, testing them is a breeze because the functionality is isolated. Functions or classes that try to do too much are harder to test because of the interplay between dependencies. Let's build something to make this clear.

Choosing a test library

Several popular unit testing libraries are available for Python 3. Some of the most widely used include the following:

- unittest: This is Python's built-in unit testing framework, often referred to as unittest. It provides a set of classes and methods for writing and running tests. unittest follows the xUnit style of unit testing and offers features such as test discovery, test fixtures, and assertion methods.

- pytest: pytest is a popular, feature-rich testing framework that provides a more concise and expressive way of writing tests compared to unittest. It supports test discovery, fixtures, parameterized tests, and powerful assertion methods. pytest is known for its simplicity and flexibility.

- nose: nose is another popular testing framework that extends the capabilities of unittest. It provides additional features, such as automatic test discovery, test generators, plugins, and advanced test selection and filtering options. While nose is widely used, its popularity has declined in recent years in favor of pytest.

- doctest: doctest is a unique testing framework that allows you to write tests in the form of interactive examples within docstrings or documentation comments. It extracts and executes the examples as tests, verifying that the actual output matches the expected output. doctest is well-suited for testing code documentation and examples.

These are just a few examples of popular unit testing libraries in Python. Each library has its own features, style, and strengths, so it's worth exploring them to find the one that aligns best with your project's requirements and your personal preferences. The neat thing about working with PyCharm is that it supports all of these testing libraries, and the UI for running tests and viewing the results is always the same.

Since this is a book on PyCharm rather than an exposition on testing frameworks, I'm going to be using the unittest library, which is part of Python's standard library. This will keep our sample code free of external dependencies.

Adding a bank account class

Right-click the project title in the project window and select **New** | **Python File**. Name the file bank_ account.py.

Next, add the following code:

```python
class BankAccount:
    def __init__(self, name: str, account_number: str, \
      balance: float):
        self.name = name
        self.account_number = account_number
        self.balance = balance
```

So far, we've created a class called BankAccount, created a constructor, and initialized three member variables called name, account number, and balance. Next, we'll add a method designed to handle withdrawing money, but only if the amount is less than the balance:

```python
def withdraw(self, amount: float) -> None:
    new_balance = self.balance - amount
    if new_balance > 0:
        self.balance = new_balance
    else:
        raise ValueError("Account overdrawn!")
```

If the amount that's withdrawn is more than `balance`, we throw a `ValueError` and issue a message stating `Account overdrawn!`. Next, we need a method to add money to the account. It needs to be a positive number; otherwise, we'll be doing a withdrawal, not a deposit:

```
def deposit(self, amount: float):
    if amount > 0:
        self.balance += amount
    else:
        raise ValueError("Deposit amount must be greater \
            than 0.")
```

So far, so good, right? Since our methods have some business logic in them, we should create a unit test for them.

Testing the bank account class

Right-click the title of the project in the project window and select **New | Python File**, but this time, make it a Python unit test, as shown in *Figure 6.1*:

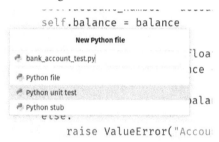

Figure 6.1: There are several templates for a new Python file

There are several conventions for working with test files. Some think it's a good idea to have a folder that contains just tests. Others think the test file should be right next to the file it is testing. I like this convention because it allows me to easily see which files in my project lack testing. Per a similar convention, I'm going to name the file `back_account_test.py`. Conventions dictate I either start or end the name of my file with the word *test*. I have put it at the end because if I don't, the test file won't be next to the file it is testing within the file explorer.

PyCharm creates the file, but it isn't empty. The code in the file looks like this:

```
import unittest
class MyTestCase(unittest.TestCase):
    def test_something(self):
        self.assertEqual(True, False) # add assertion here
if __name__ == '__main__':
    unittest.main()
```

The IDE has presented us with a template containing a testing class that inherits from Python's built-in unit testing framework. The framework is simply but unimaginatively called `unittest`. The template contains the required import at the top of the file, a testing class, one test method, and a dunder-main block that allows the script to run standalone. To get the test working, you need to modify this file. Start by adding an import to the file containing the class you want to test. The added line is in bold:

```
import unittest
from bank_account import BankAccount
```

Next, change the name of the class to `BankAccountTestCase`. Then, take out the `test_something(self)` method entirely and replace it with this one:

```
def test_init(self):
    test_account = BankAccount("Bruce Van Horn", \
        "123355-23434", 4000)
    self.assertEqual(test_account.name, "Bruce Van Horn")
    self.assertEqual(test_account.account_number, \
        "123355-23434")
    self.assertEqual(test_account.balance, 4000)
```

To be honest, this is kind of a silly test because the constructor logic is extremely simple. Even I would be tempted to skip it. That isn't always the case, though. If you're doing something complicated in the constructor, you should unit-test it. Here, the example serves as a simple one to get us moving. All we did here was create a new instance of the `BankAccount` class and pass in a name, an account number, and an initial balance. Then, we used the `unittest` class' `assertEqual` method to check each of the member variables to make sure they were set properly. There's pretty much no way they weren't unless you made a mistake, which is exactly the point.

Beware of the pesky self-typing self):

Having done a whole chapter on the miracles of auto-completion, I have to admit that sometimes, it can be annoying. This is one of those times. The instant you type the opening parenthesis of your test method, PyCharm is going to fill in the word `self`, along with the closing parenthesis and the colon for the end of the line. Because I type rapidly, I used to often wind up with something like `test_init(selfsel):` before I caught what happened. I've trained my right hand to find the *End* key on the keyboard as soon as I hit the opening parenthesis. This jumps you to the end of the auto-completed line. Hit *Enter*, and you'll be right where you want to be.

We're going to add two more tests below the first one. The first test will test the `withdraw` method. Type in the new method below the first test, but above the line with the dunder-main test:

```
def test_withdraw(self):
    self.fail()
```

Type the test for the deposit below the `test_withdraw` method:

```
def test_deposit(self):
    self.fail()
```

If you haven't guessed yet, these two tests are going to fail. That's OK. I like to see them fail so that I know the whole testing setup is working. One of the benefits and side effects of being a long-time software developer is you don't just assume anything will just work, regardless of who wrote it or how much the thing costs. Call it a survival instinct. If you skip this step, then may the odds be ever in your favor.

Running the tests

Let's run our tests. Like many things, there are lots of ways to run the tests. You have no doubt noticed the appearance of green arrows in your test code, as seen in *Figure 6.2*:

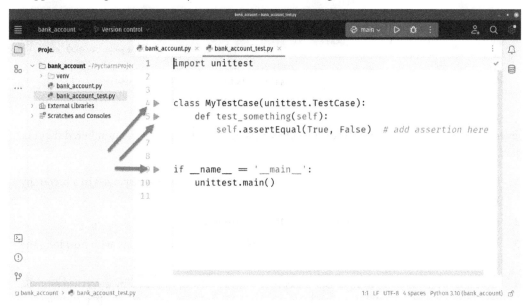

Figure 6.2: Green run arrows will appear in the IDE as you create your tests

These green arrows trigger a menu when you click them. For now, we'll click the first item, which is **Run 'Python tests for…'**. Clicking the green arrow next to the test class definition will run all the tests in this class. Clicking the green arrow next to any of the three test methods will run just that test.

If you click the green arrow next to `BankAccountTestCase`, the test runner will appear in the tool window at the bottom of the IDE window. You can see mine in *Figure 6.3*:

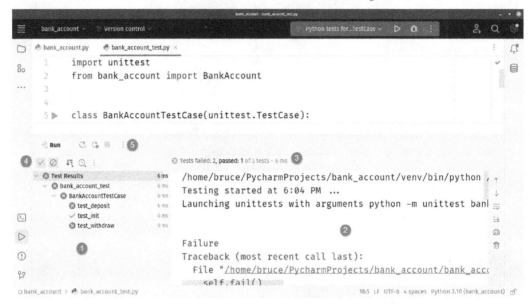

Figure 6.3: The test runner shows the tests that run, including those
that passed and failed, and the console output

The test runner itself has a complete set of tools integrated into its window. I've numbered them in *Figure 6.3*:

1. This pane shows the tests that passed and those that failed. They are displayed in a hierarchy that matches the call hierarchy.

2. This pane shows the console output from the test run itself.

3. Above the output pane is a summary of the number of passing tests, along with how long the test suite ran.

4. To the left on the same toolbar is a collection of five buttons, followed by a vertical ellipsis. The ✓ and ⊘ buttons will filter out all the passed and failed tests, respectively. Filtering out the passed tests lets you focus solely on what failed. Filtering out the failed tests reduces the general malaise and utter hopelessness that you'll feel when you have 5 out of 100 tests that passed. When this happens, I usually eat a sandwich and I feel better. Look at it this way: so long as you have failing tests, your job is probably safe because it would take longer to train a replacement than it would to wait until everything starts working. See it as a glass half-full. The next three before the ellipsis allow you to sort your test results, import tests from another file, and review your test run history. Say you have a test that was passing, then it failed and you wanted to go

back and look at the last time it passed. That history is there if you need it. The ellipsis holds a few more options, including some miscellaneous settings for the test runner itself.

5.   This toolbar allows you to rerun all the tests, rerun only those that failed, and stop a long-running test. Again, we have a vertical ellipsis, but this one has an interesting option for toggling **Auto Test**. Turning this option on will continually run your tests, for those of you who can't stand the cursor travel time back down to the rerun button.

When you run tests for the first time, PyCharm will create run configurations for you automatically. You can see them in the **Run configuration** dropdown on the top toolbar.

Fixing the failing tests

We have two tests that will always fail, no matter what we do. Let's start by altering the `test_ withdraw(self)` method in the `bank_account_test.py` file. Change it to this:

```
def test_withdraw(self):
  test_account = BankAccount("Bruce Van Horn", "123355-23434", 4000)
  test_account.withdraw(2000)
  self.assertEqual(test_account.balance, 2000)
```

The first line instantiates the `BankAccount` class with some testable values. Next, we invoke the `withdraw` method and withdraw $2,000. I hope it is for something fun! Usually, it is my daughters borrowing my wallet to either shop for clothes or maybe buy raw materials for an engineering project. I can hope, right? I now expect my balance to drop from $4,000 to $2,000. So, I use the `assertEqual` method on the `unittest` class, which is the superclass for my `BankAccountTestCase` class. I pass in `test_account.balance`, which will be compared with the expected result.

I fully expect this test to pass! Click the rerun failed tests button shown in *Figure 6.3*. It passed! Now, let's write the `test_deposit` method:

```
def test_deposit(self):
  test_account = BankAccount("Bruce Van Horn", "123355-23434", 4000)
  test_account.deposit(5000)
  self.assertEqual(test_account.balance, 9000)
```

The explanation here is the same as the last one, except this time, we are depositing $5,000 into my account. This rarely happens in real life, so give me a moment while I celebrate.

Rerun the failed tests. They should all pass now! But we're not done yet, are we?

So far, these tests have followed the no-fault path. This means that so far, I've only tested the methods while running them as I designed them. Users in the real world will never do this. We need to test fault paths as well.

Testing the fault paths

There is one obvious fault path we designed into the system: the overdraft. What will happen if we try to take out more money than is available in the current balance? Or as my daughters might say, how do we generate a signal that tells us it's time to come home from the mall and hide the receipts?

We account for this in our code:

```
def withdraw(self, amount: float) -> None:
    new_balance = self.balance - amount
    if new_balance > 0:
      self.balance = new_balance
    else:
      raise ValueError("Account overdrawn!")
```

As you can see, we check if the new balance will be a negative number. If it is, we throw a `ValueError`. This test is going to be a little different. Instead of using `assertEquals` to test a no-fault result, we want to verify that when this condition exists, we not only throw an error but that we throw the right kind of error. This is important because we expect `ValueError`, but if some other error is produced, the tests will give us a false positive if we only test for a generic `Exception`. Add the following test `BankAccountTestCase` class:

```
def test_overdraft(self):
  test_account = BankAccount("Bruce Van Horn", "123355-23434", 4000)
  self.assertRaises(ValueError, test_account.withdraw, 5000)]
```

As before, we instantiate the `BankAccount` class with some testable values. For the test, we want to assert that the withdraw method raises a `ValueError` if we pass in more money than what exists in the balance. Here, we use `self.assertRaises`, which takes three arguments. The first argument is the type of error we expect.

The second argument is the method under test. Note that we're passing a reference to the function lambda-style. We aren't executing the function since we need the `assertRaises` function to do that. Finally, we need to pass in the value of any arguments – in this case, some numbers that are bigger than the four grand I used for instantiation. In this case, I pass in `5000`. When I run this test, it should pass because the function will fail with the `ValueError` exception I expect.

There is just one test left: we need to be sure that when we pass a negative number into the `deposit` method, we get a `ValueError`. I'll leave this one for you to practice with. The full working code is in the repository code for this chapter.

Generating tests automatically

So far, we've spent some time writing the BankAccout class, but think back to our original idea for a use case for unit testing: a financial transaction. This time, we're going to write some code that needs to be tested, but instead of a generic test template, we're going to generate a more exact test.

Let's start with the code we will be testing. Create a new file in your project called transaction. py. The contents of this file should look as follows:

```
from bank_account import BankAccount
```

We'll need the BankAccount class since the whole idea is to write code that transfers money from one account to another in response to the sale of an item. Speaking of *item*, let's make a class to represent what we'll be buying:

```
class Item:
    def __init__(self, name: str, price: float):
        self.name = name
        self.price = price
```

There's nothing too crazy here – just two instance variables called name and price. Now for the hard part: we need a class to represent a transaction. Remember, a transaction is an atomic operation. All the steps should be completed. If there are any errors along the way, everything that happened before the error needs to be rolled back:

```
class Transaction:
    def __init__(self, buyer: BankAccount, seller: \
    BankAccount, item: Item):
        self.buyer = buyer
        self.seller = seller
        self.item = item
```

We started the class with a constructor that initializes two bank accounts and an item. After this comes the logic for the transaction itself:

```
def do_transaction(self):
    original_buyer_balance = self.buyer.balance
    original_seller_balance = self.seller.balance
```

We need to store the original balances. If anything goes awry, we'll need this information to put everything back the way it was. Next comes the part where money changes hands. I'll wrap it in a try:

```
try:
    self.buyer.withdraw(self.item.price)
    self.seller.deposit(self.item.price)
except ValueError:
```

```
self.buyer.balance = original_buyer_balance
self.seller.balance = original_seller_balance
raise ValueError("Transaction failed and was \
    rolled back")
```

We attempt to withdraw money from the buyer's account, then deposit the same amount into the seller's account. If a `ValueError` is thrown, we put all the money back by restoring the balances to their original values. Once the money has been restored, we should still raise an error so that the primary application knows the error occurred. This function will need to report the result to a user interface to let the user know what happened with the transaction. The last line handles this for us. In a real application, you might want to create your own custom error that might yield more information, but this one serves us well for demonstrative purposes.

Generating the transaction test

Earlier, we created a new test using the **File** menu. This gave us a very generic test that had nothing to do with our work up to that point. This time, we'll generate a test from the class definition itself. Right-click the line that starts with `class Transaction`. Then, click the **Generate...** menu option, as seen in *Figure 6.4*:

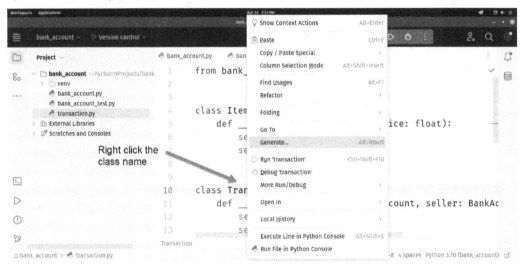

Figure 6.4: The Generate... menu item can be found when you right-click your class definition

Next, click **Test...**, as seen in *Figure 6.5*:

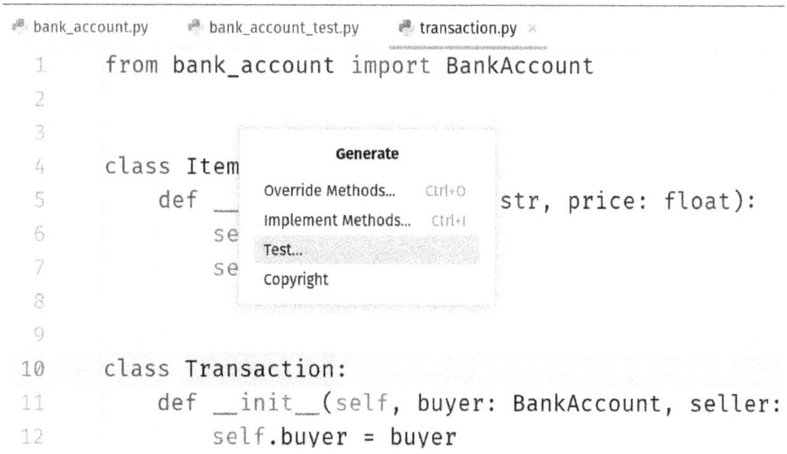

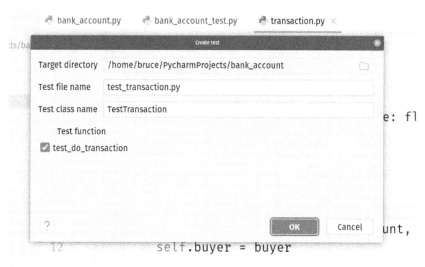

Figure 6.5: Click the Test... button to generate your test

At this point, a dialog box will appear where you can control the test that will be generated, as seen in *Figure 6.6*:

Figure 6.6: PyCharm is about to generate a unit test file based on these settings

PyCharm is about to create a file called `test_transaction.py`. Within that file, instead of a generic test class name, there will be a class definition called `TestTransaction`. Finally, within the file, assuming you leave the checkbox ticked, a test method stub will be generated called `test_do_transaction`.

The resulting file contains this code:

```
from unittest import TestCase
class TestTransaction(TestCase):
  def test_do_transaction(self):
    self.fail()
```

Way back in *Chapter 1*, I told you that one of the benefits of an IDE is that it can reduce boilerplate. The first time, PyCharm generated some generic boilerplate for us. At least we didn't have to type it in, but it was almost as much effort to change what it generated. This time, there is even less work to do. If I had many methods in my class, there would be a correctly named stub for each of them.

All I must do now is write the code that makes the `test_do_transaction` method pass. Behold!

```
from unittest import TestCase
from bank_account import BankAccount
from transaction import Transaction, Item
```

We started with the required imports. I know I'm going to need two tests, rather than just the one PyCharm generated. PyCharm generated one test method, which I'm using for the no-fault path. I'll pass in something that works the way the method is intended to work. Since I know I have two tests, I can reuse the seller account to keep my test **DRY**. If you're not familiar with the acronym, it stands for **Don't Repeat Yourself**. By hoisting this code to the top of the file, I only need to type it once. This code will initialize a seller's bank account with a balance of $4,000. It also sets up the item we will be purchasing, which will not change between tests:

```
initial_seller_balance = 4000
seller_account = BankAccount("PacktPub", "839423-38402",
                 initial_seller_balance)
item = Item("Python book", 39.95)
```

Next, we will move on to the test class itself, which was generated for us. We already have this part:

```
class TestTransaction(TestCase):
  def test_do_transaction(self):
```

I'm replacing the generated `self.fail()` with code that I hope will cause the test to pass:

```
    buyer_account = BankAccount("Bruce Van Horn", "123355-23434", 99)
    item = Item("Python book", 39.95)
    test_transaction = Transaction(buyer_account, \
    seller_account, item)
```

As usual, I instantiate the classes I'll be using in the test. So far, I've made two accounts and an item with a price. Next, I'll run the method under test:

```
test_transaction.do_transaction()
```

Then, I'll check my results:

```
self.assertEqual(buyer_account.balance, 99 - 39.95)
self.assertEqual(seller_account.balance,\
                initial_seller_balance + 39.95)
```

You might be tempted to get fancy with the test code. Be careful with this. Fancy test code is as likely to break as the purposefully fancy code it is meant to test. If you are testing complicated math, please don't duplicate the calculation in the test and then compare it to the code under test. You should be plugging in known inputs and checking for known outputs. Nothing more!

This test represents the no-fault path. I fully expect this to pass since this exercise merely entails everything working under ideal conditions. Let's see if I'm right. Click any of the green run buttons. My result is shown in *Figure 6.7*:

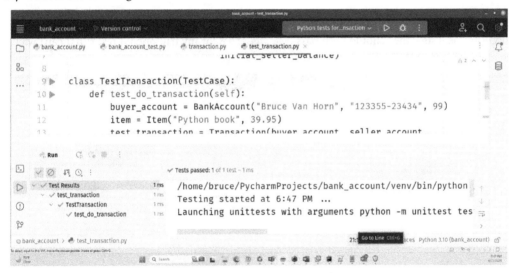

Figure 6.7: So far, so good! My test is passing!

We need a test for at least one fault path. In this case, it will be to test what happens when I don't have enough in my account to cover buying a book.

Here's my test for that case:

```
def test_transaction_overdraw_fault(self):
  initial_buyer_balance = 5
  buyer_account = BankAccount("Bruce Van Horn", \
    "123355-23434", initial_buyer_balance)
```

```
test_transaction = Transaction(buyer_account, \
  seller_account, item)
```

When I left for work today, I had at least $9,000 in my account. But my daughter Phoebe "borrowed" my card out of my jacket pocket. She said she was going to create a robotic bicycle factory. I thought nothing of it. She was kidding, right? So, I go to the bookstore after work, intent on picking up the latest masterpiece:

```
test_transaction.do_transaction()
```

The transaction occurs. Do you know that sound that Pac-Man makes when he gets eaten by a ghost? I'm making that sound now. The sale will fail; let's see if the transaction rolls back correctly:

```
self.assertEqual(buyer_account.balance, initial_buyer_balance)
self.assertEqual(seller_account.balance, initial_seller_balance)
```

This last piece of code verifies that both the buyer and seller balances are returned to their original values. Run the tests – they should both pass! See *Figure 6.8* for my triumphant test run. I can't wait to go home and relax!

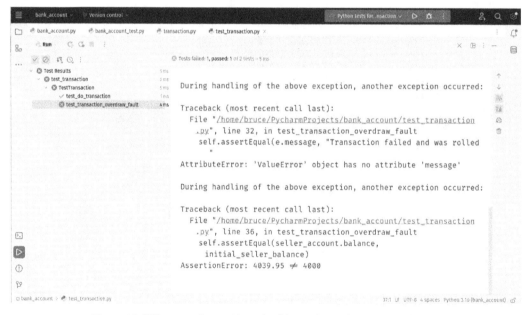

Figure 6.8: I'd better call my wife and tell her to keep dinner warm for me

It looks like I was a little overconfident. The output window shows a set of stack traces for everything that went wrong. It's so long that I had to scroll down quite a bit to get to the good part of this screenshot. In the trace (which is not shown), I can see that a few of the errors I thought would be thrown were, and that's fine. The two we can see here are not. First, I intended to verify that the message coming from the exception matched the value I assigned in the definition. Again, I'm doing this to make sure the error I threw is the one we're seeing and not some other error resulting from a mistake. It looks like I didn't understand the structure of the error, and in fact, there is no attribute called message. I coulda swore! Wait – that's probably from some other language. OK, I can look that up.

The other, more disturbing error is that my transaction didn't roll back! As you look at the trace, you'll see that there are hyperlinks throughout that allow you to navigate directly to the fault code mentioned in the trace. It is very easy to move around and look for problems. I can find the line for the first problem in the list of stack traces, as shown in *Figure 6.9*:

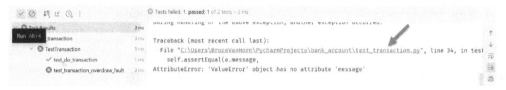

Figure 6.9: The stack traces are riddled with hyperlinks that will
jump you to the offending section of your code

Clicking this link takes me to the problematic code shown in *Figure 6.10*:

```
31          try:
32              test_transaction.do_transaction()
33          except ValueError as e:
34              self.assertEqual(e.message,
35                              "Transaction failed and was rolled back")
36          finally:
37              self.assertEqual(buyer_account.balance, initial_buyer_balance)
38              self.assertEqual(seller_account.balance, initial_seller_balance)
39
```

Figure 6.10: Fiddlesticks! The IDE even told me line 34 was wrong, but I didn't listen

I have a few options here, don't I? I could use the documentation features in PyCharm by hovering over the e variable. We talked about automatic documentation features in *Chapter 4*. *Figure 6.11* shows what this looks like in case you've been skipping around:

```
31              try:
32                  test_transaction.do_transaction()
33              except ValueError as e:
34                  self.assertEqual(e.message,
35                                                                          )
                              builtins
36              finally:          class ValueError(_StandardError)
37                  self.assertEqual(b                                      ance)
38                  self.assertEqual(s  Inappropriate argument value (of correct type).   alance)
39                                     `ValueError(_StandardError)` on docs.python.org ↗
```

Figure 6.11: The auto-documentation feature will give me a link to the official documentation

There's no easy answer here, is there? Sure, I could click on the link at the bottom and go to the Python site and read the documentation. If I do that, though, I'll lose any credibility with you, the reader. Read the manual with y'all watching? No chance! I'm sure I'd find the answer but at the expense of my pride.

I have another idea! I've talked about PyCharm's console before. I'd like to try something out. Check out *Figure 6.12*:

Figure 6.12: If the PyCharm Console button (2) isn't on your toolbar, click the ellipses (1) to turn it on

The arrow pointing to *2* will open the PyCharm console. If you've never done this, that icon won't be on the toolbar. You'll need to click the ellipsis at *1* and click the **Python Console** area. This will add it to your toolbar. My console session is shown in *Figure 6.13*:

Figure 6.13: Revisiting the console allows us to do a quick experiment to solve our error

In the console, I first hit *Enter* on the first line. I did that for you. If I hadn't, the console would have bunched everything up and it wouldn't look as pretty. Next, I typed the following:

```
check = ValueError("This is a test")
```

I suspect that if I convert the check into a string, I will get the message I am looking for. Call it intuition. Or call it "I looked it up with **ChatGPT** while your back was turned." I'm going with intuition.

If I type in `str(check)`, the Python REPL will evaluate the expression and print the result. The idea works. I can correct my code. Line 34 in `test_transaction.py` will now be as follows:

```
self.assertEqual(str(e), "Transaction failed and was rolled back")
```

Now, if I run the test again, it will fail, as shown in *Figure 6.14*:

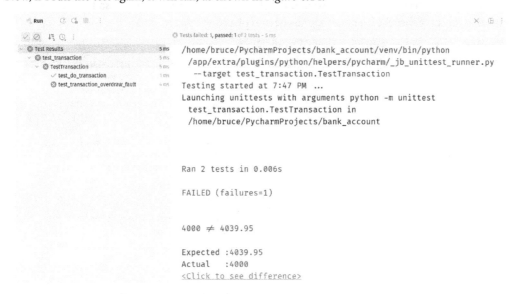

Figure 6.14: Progress can be measured in software development
by the rate at which the list of errors is reduced

We expected this. The list of problems got shorter, so it's a victory! Let's clear out the last problem. The transaction is failing to correctly reset the value of the seller's account after the transaction fails. We could stare at it for a while, or we could take a more proactive approach by firing up PyCharm's debugger and stepping through the whole test.

Working with PyCharm's debugger

In *Chapter 1*, I lauded PyCharm's debugger as the single biggest reason to use an IDE versus a command-line debugger such as the standard Python debugger, which is called **pdb**. Don't get me wrong – you should learn to use pdb because there will be times when the IDE isn't available. However, I suspect that once you use PyCharm's, you'll prefer it over anything else. Let's see if I'm right.

We have a problem in our `Transaction` class that isn't quite accurate. When it comes to testing, there are always two possibilities:

- The code is failing because of a flaw in the code under test.
- The code is failing because of the test code.

Since we don't know which possibility is correct at this point, the debugger is going to allow us to step through our code one line at a time and inspect its inner workings. To do this, we need to set a breakpoint. A breakpoint marks a spot in your code where you would like to halt its execution and inspect the contents of the variables, the stack, and so on. You can create a breakpoint by clicking the line number in the gutter within the editor, as shown in *Figure 6.15*. I'm going to add a breakpoint to the beginning of the test so that we can walk through it. The test starts on line 25, so I'll click on that line number; observe that the line number has been replaced with a red dot:

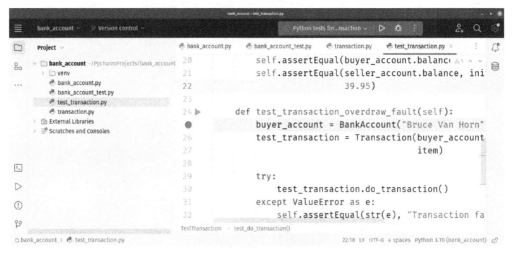

Figure 6.15: Click a line number to create a breakpoint, which will replace the number with a red dot

Next, we need to run the debugger. Click the green arrow in the editor window next to the method definition for the test_transaction_overdraw_fault(self) method. This time, click the **Debug 'Python tests for tes...'** option, shown in *Figure 6.16*, to run the failed test:

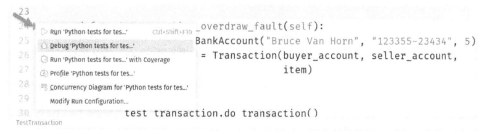

Figure 6.16: Clicking the green arrows provides a menu that can be used to
make variations to a running test, including running the debugger

When the debugger is run, the program will start, then stop on line 25 of our test. The IDE transformed significantly. Let's look at *Figure 6.17*:

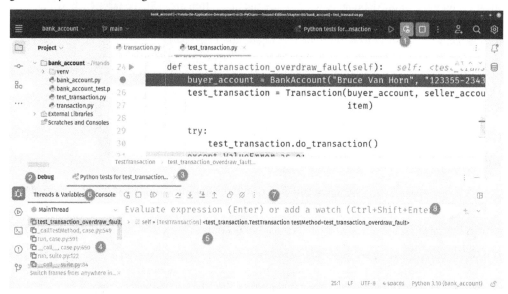

Figure 6.17: The paused debugger in PyCharm

There are a few things you might notice right away. First, the run buttons at the top of the IDE are now green, and the red stop button is illuminated (*1*). These are all visual clues showing that something is running, which of course we do.

The bottom half of the IDE is now taken up by the debugger tools (*2*). There is also a tab bar present (*3*), which allows you to run multiple debugging sessions at the same time. This can be handy when developing RESTful microservice architectures, which we'll talk about in several of the upcoming chapters, most notably in *Chapter 9, Creating a RESTful API with FastAPI*.

There is a list of threads on the right-hand side (*4*), which allows you to switch between and inspect the various threads at play. However, most of the time, you're going to land in the right place and might use this only rarely. The area at location *5* shows everything that is currently in scope. Right now, that is just `self`, which you can see is an instance of the `TestTransaction` class.

6 shows two tabs that allow you to switch between the view we're seeing right now, which allows you to inspect the state of the program at area *5*. If you switch this tab to **Console**, area 5 will display the Terminal output from your program. Any output or `print` statements will appear so that you can review the output as the program runs.

The toolbar marked with *7* houses a set of very useful tools, while the expression window (*8*) allows you to add a watch or evaluate an expression using whatever is currently in scope.

The most useful parts of the debugging window are the inspection area (*5*), the tab switch, which you can use to swap between the variable and thread inspector and console output (*6*), and the debugging toolbar (*7*). Let's take a closer look at the debugging toolbar:

Figure 6.18: The debugging toolbar in PyCharm

I've numbered each button. Let's review them:

1. This button restarts the debugging run. You can find a duplicate restart button at the top of the IDE window near the run button.

2. This button stops the debugging run. You can find a duplicate stop button at the top of the IDE window near the restart button.

3. This is the **Continue** button. The debugger will stop at any breakpoint it hits and wait until you use one of the step buttons (*5 – 8*) or you hit this button to continue the run.

4. The **Pause** button will pause the run. This can be useful if you're running a loop or an algorithm that takes a while and you want to pause the run.

5. The **Step Over** button will execute the current line where the debugger has paused. If that line is a function call to a function in your program, the function will execute normally and return, after which you'll be taken to the next line of your code, where the debugger will remain paused. Here, you're stepping over the execution of the next line.

6. In contrast, this is the **Step Into** button. If your debugger has paused on a line containing a function call, clicking this button will allow you to step into that function and step through as if you had placed a breakpoint at the beginning of the function. **Step Over** skips past this execution, while this button steps into it.

7. **Step Into My Code** is a game changer! This button is just like the **Step Into** button (6), except this one will not step into code that you didn't create. By that, I mean the **Step Into** button will happily step you into the bowels of your third-party library code, or into the code comprising Python itself. This is rarely useful. The **Step Into My Code** button will only step into code that is part of your project.

8. This is the **Step Out** button. If you find yourself stepping into some code that clearly isn't a problem, or maybe you've taken into library code you didn't create, the step-out code will jump you back out to the point where you entered.

Attention Visual Studio users

The buttons in the PyCharm debugger work differently than they do in Visual Studio! This took some getting used to for me. In Visual Studio, you can click the green button on the top toolbar to start the debugging session. When you hit a breakpoint, you can hit the same button to continue. In PyCharm, the continue button is in the debugging toolbar, in area 3 in *Figure 6.18*. If you were to click the same button you used to launch the debugger, you would launch a second debug session. PyCharm will generally complain when you do this unless you've checked the box in the run configuration that allows multiple runs at the same time.

Using the debugger to find and fix our test problem

Our unit test revealed a problem in our code. When our transaction fails due to an overdraft error, we expect the balances of our buyer and seller to revert to their original values. At this point, the seller is getting $39.95 in credit following a failed transaction. Let's use the debugger to step through and see if we can figure out why this is happening.

Per *Figure 6.19*, we've started the debugger on our unit test and we've stopped at line 25 in `test_transaction.py`. At this stage, nothing in the test method has run. When you're looking at a highlighted line in PyCharm's debugger, you need to remember that the highlighted line has not been executed yet. To execute the line, click the **Step Over** button, which is labeled as *5* in *Figure 6.18*. The debugger variable window will update now that `buyer_account` has been instantiated, and our highlight will move to and stop on line 26, as shown in *Figure 6.19*:

Figure 6.19: Having clicked the Step Over button, the debugger has been stopped on line 26

To see the content of the objects, you'll need to twirl open the caret, which I've circled in *Figure 6.19*. You can see that `buyer_account` has a balance of $5. However, what we're interested in here is the seller account since that's where the problem lies.

Click line 30 to add a breakpoint there, then click the **Continue** button. The debugger will stop on line 30. We're going to step into the `do_transaction()` method to watch it execute. Click the **Step Into My Code** button. Refer to *Figure 6.18* and look at *7* if you don't remember which button I mean.

This will take us to line 17 in `transaction.py`. Step over lines 17 and 18 to arrive at line 19 and inspect our state. You'll see the problem, which is shown in *Figure 6.20*:

Figure 6.20: The debugger reveals that the starting value of the seller balance is wrong

The debugger reveals that the original seller balance is $4,039.95, where we would expect it to be $4,000. You can see this value in two places. The variables window shows it to us (*1*), but you can also hover over any in-scope variable in the editor window (*2*) and see its value.

Now, why would our starting balance be wrong? It's a scope problem! Since I hoisted the `seller_account` variable to line 5 in `test_transaction.py` up to a global, the first test successfully changes the balance to $4,039.95 just like it should. Since it is global, that number remains. To fix this, we need to reset the balance of the seller account at the beginning of the `test_transaction_overdraw_fault(self)` method. We started our debugging efforts on line 25. Let's just make our change there. Click the stop button on the debugger toolbar, then add this line on line 25:

```
seller_account.balance = 4000
```

Rerun your tests without debugging. Be bold! Assume it worked! If you're not following along, kindly move to the edge of your seat and begin biting your nails nervously. Will our hero triumph in *Figure 6.21*? Cue organ music: duhn duhn duuuuuhn!

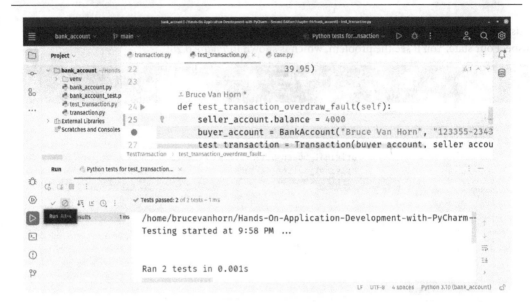

Figure 6.21: Victory!

It works! Now, it's time to head home and heat up dinner since we've restored everyone's faith in the international banking industry.

Checking test coverage

Unit tests are most effective when there are tests to cover every class, method, function, or module in your program. As your software code grows, it is easy to forget to write tests or maybe to put them off until you have more time. PyCharm has a tool that can tell you what your test coverage is and helps you find unexploited opportunities for testing more of your work than you might have on your own.

To check your test coverage, you just need to run your tests a little bit differently. We've been running our tests individually from within the test files. We need to run all the tests together so that we can have a comprehensive report of where we are missing coverage. For this, we will make a new run configuration. Click the run configurations dropdown on the toolbar and click **Edit Configurations**. Add a new configuration using the Python `unittest` template. Make sure you use my settings, as shown in *Figure 6.22*:

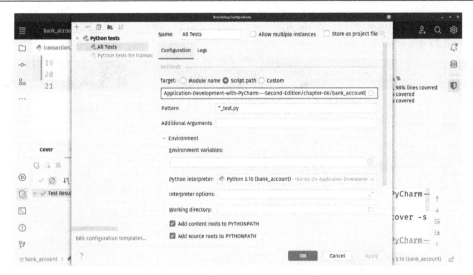

Figure 6.22: Create a run configuration that runs all your tests at once

For the script path, enter the folder where your tests are located. Set the pattern to `*_test.py`. This will make the test runner find all files that end with `_test.py`, which is different from the defaults. The defaults will look for files beginning with "test." I don't particularly like this because it bunches all the tests together in the project file window instead of putting the test right next to the file it is testing.

By setting the pattern and setting the test runner to a folder rather than a single file, the runner will find all files matching the pattern and run them as tests. Speaking of running, you can do that by clicking the ellipsis next to the run and debug buttons. See *Figure 6.23* to locate the **Run 'All Tests' with Coverage** menu item:

Figure 6.23: Run 'All Tests' with Coverage allows you to run your tests and
find out how much of your application isn't covered by unit tests

The first time you do this, you'll likely see an error message – not from your code, but from PyCharm. See *Figure 6.24* to see what I mean:

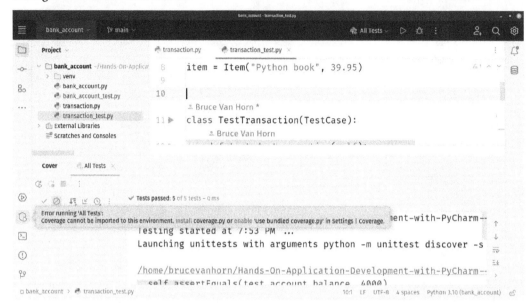

Figure 6.24: The first time you run test coverage, you'll be warned if you haven't installed the coverage software or enabled the bundled copy

Running with coverage requires some software, coverage.py, which we haven't installed. You have two options here: you can either add coverage.py to your project, or you can use the bundled version that ships with PyCharm. I prefer using the bundled version. You can click the word *enable* in the error message, which is displayed as a blue hyperlink, and PyCharm will turn on this setting for you. If you'd like to manage this setting yourself, see *Figure 6.25* to see where the setting can be found:

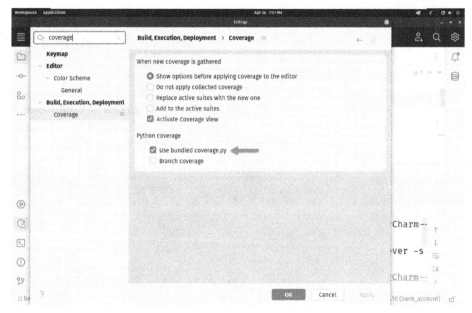

Figure 6.25: The setting for using the bundled coverage.py file allows you to use coverage.py without you having to add it to your project

With `coverage.py` enabled, rerun your coverage test. Let's see how we do:

Figure 6.26: I wish my grades in college were this good!

Holy smokes! We have 100% coverage in the transaction tests, but a miserable failure in the `bank_account_test.py` file – that is, if you consider 94% coverage a failure. Being a perfectionist, I would like to see how I missed those points. I can double-click the line showing the 94% in `bank_account_test.py` and I'll be treated to a color-coded gutter. Here, again, I must apologize for the book being printed in black and white. Area *1* in *Figure 6.26* is colored red. These are the lines that are not covered by the tests. To be truthful, I don't remember typing these in. I don't need them since my test runner is executing my tests for me. I can simply remove these lines and re-format my file with *Ctrl + Alt + L/Cmd + Opt + L*. Rerun the test with coverage. My results in *Figure 6.27* show that we're close:

Figure 6.27: We have achieved 100% coverage! Keep this up and you might get a raise

The `bank_account_test.py` file now has 100% coverage, but at the top, I can still see that the `bank_account` folder only has 98% coverage. This simply will not stand! Right now, I have my project explorer window closed to maximize space for the editor and coverage window. If I open it back up, having run with coverage, I will get some more information. *Figure 6.28* shows where we should look. The `bank_account.py` file only has 92% coverage. Upon double-clicking to open it, I'll see the lines I'm missing colored red, as seen in *Figure 6.28*:

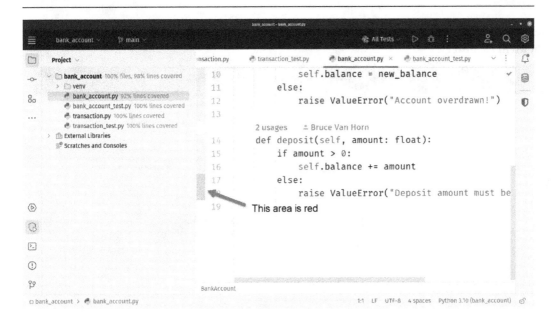

Figure 6.28: The grayish-red area in the gutter indicates that
lines 17 and 18 are not covered by any unit test

It looks like we have another unit test to write. I forgot to write a test for the error condition. This is legitimate! As you may recall, I left the deposit test as a challenge for you. I wrote it in my code for this book, but I forgot to write the error test. Coverage saves the day!

Open bank_account_test.py and add the following test, which will cover the case of trying to deposit a negative number:

```
def test_deposit_negative_number_fail(self):
  test_account = BankAccount("Bruce Van Horn", "123355-23434", 4000)
  self.assertRaises(ValueError, test_account.deposit, -2000)
```

Run the test and verify it passes, then rerun the **All Tests** configuration with coverage. My result is shown in *Figure 6.29*:

Figure 6.29: We have achieved 100% coverage for all files

This time, we should have a perfect score! Now that we're feeling fine, I'll point out the coverage window on the right-hand side of the screen. It shows a list of the results, which we've already seen. Note the shield icon in the right toolbar. You can show or hide the coverage window by clicking this shield.

Test coverage output

In addition to the graphical display, PyCharm outputs a report for the coverage run. You will see the output mentioned in the output window alongside the usual test output. Mine states the following:

```
Wrote XML report to /home/brucevanhorn/.cache/JetBrains/PyCharm2023.1/
coverage/bank_account&All_Test.xml
```

The XML file is generated by `coverage.py`, which we enabled earlier. As you might have guessed, `coverage.py` is a popular Python tool for measuring code coverage during test runs. It is an open source tool that helps you identify which parts of your Python code are being exercised by your tests and which parts are not. The tool works by collecting information about which lines of code are executed during a test run and then generating a report that shows the percentage of code coverage. The XML output is used by PyCharm to render the color-coded UI displays we've been using. The XML output can also be used by your **continuous integration** (**CI**) system to generate reports and displays.

JetBrains has created an excellent CI system called **TeamCity**, which can leverage coverage.py to fail a build if test coverage is below a set threshold.

Profiling performance

The first step in creating a great program is getting the program fully working. The second step is to perform automated testing to prove that the program works as intended. The final step ought to be tweaking the code so that the program runs as fast and as efficiently as possible. Poorly performing programs run the risk of having a low adoption rate at best, and may simply be unusable at worst. In England, the NHS has an algorithm that was designed to match organ transplant recipients to recently harvested organs. The algorithm is complicated but extremely time-sensitive. Harvested organs must be transplanted quickly; otherwise, their tissues will die and become useless. In short, the algorithm must be extremely accurate; otherwise, the transplanted organ may be rejected, resulting in the patient's death. It must also be fast since the organ will lose viability, which may also result in patient death. Suddenly, I'm very glad for my job dealing with hardware system capacity planning and forecasting. Nobody has ever died because my database queries were too slow. At least, not that I know of.

In addition to being able to run your tests with coverage, you can also run with performance profiling. While the coverage report tells you graphically which areas of your code remain untested, PyCharm's profiler gives you reports on which parts of your code are consuming the lion's share of the overall runtime. This allows you to spot bottlenecks so that you can focus your refactoring efforts toward making the code, and its execution, more efficient.

Similar to there being several testing libraries that are widely used by Python developers, there is also a variety of profiling tools, including Yappi, cProfile, and VMProf. PyCharm supports them all, but they do not work the same. cProfile is built into Python, and so is the default profiler. Yappi is an improvement over cProfile because it allows you to profile multithreaded applications and supports CPU time profiling. VMProf supports statistical sampling. When you profile using this tool, it won't simply time a single run of your program; instead, it will run and sample multiple runs, providing you with a more realistic performance profile. PyCharm will use VMProf if it is available. If not, it will look for Yappi. If it can't find Yappi, then it will use the cProfile solution built into Python. For this book, I will stick to the default cProfile tool.

Profiling in PyCharm

The code we'll be profiling can be found in this book's repository, in the chapter-06 folder. The profiling.py file contains the following code:

```
def custom_sum(n=1000000):
    result = 0
    for i in range(n):
        result += i
    return result
```

```
def built_in_sum(n=1000000):
    result = sum(range(n))
    return result


if __name__ == '__main__':
    print(custom_sum())
    # print(built_in_sum())
```

This code will compare two ways of computing the sum of the integers, ranging from one to an upper limit expressed as *n*, whose default value is 1,000,000. The `custom_sum` function loops through all the elements, adding each to a running sum. The `built_in_sum` function utilizes the built-in `sum()` method of Python.

In the main scope, we will use commenting to swap between the two function calls to test both methods. We will be looking at our custom summing function first, so the call to `built_in_sum` is commented out for now.

The typical claim is that built-in functions are generally faster than any code you might write. In this example, we will be able to fact-check that claim and further qualify it with runtime statistics through our profiling process. Let's get started.

As with testing and coverage, we can start a profiling run by using either the green arrows within the editor or the run button ellipsis at the top of the screen. *Figure 6.30* shows both options:

Figure 6.30: You can run a profile using either the ellipsis menu at the top right or
by clicking the green arrow next to the dunder-main entry point on line 14

When the profile run is complete, we will be provided with a performance report, as seen in *Figure 6.31*:

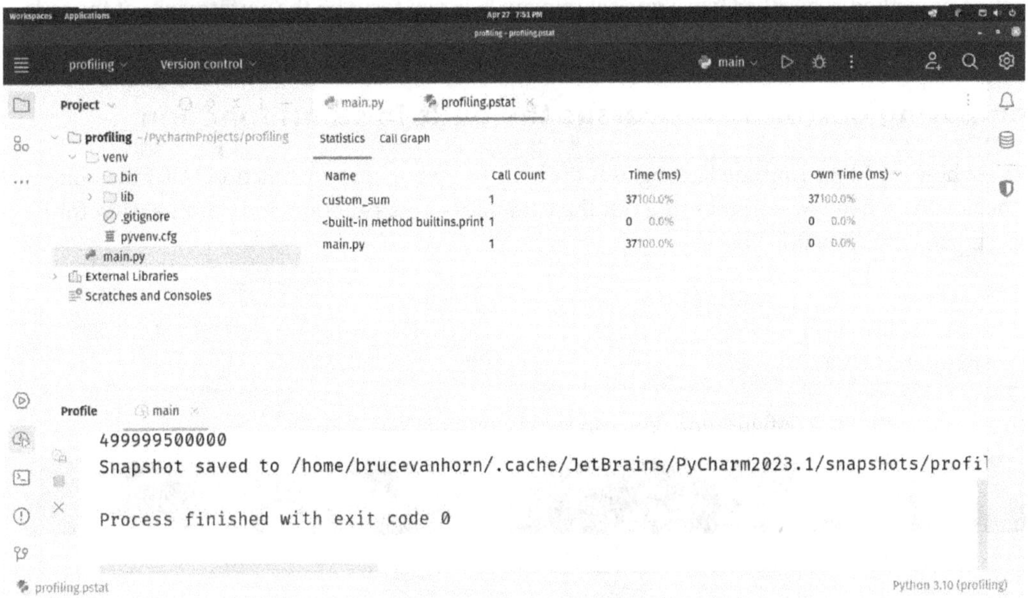

Figure 6.31: The performance profile for the custom_sum function

On my computer, which in this case is a VMWare virtual machine with a very modest configuration (2 cores, 4 GB of RAM, and a 7,200 RPM spinning disk), the custom_sum function completed in 41 ms. The time and the percentage are a little bunched together on my display, but we can see that 100% of the time was spent in the custom_sum function. If this were a more complicated program with many functions being called during the run, we'd see a full listing of each function and how much time was spent on each. Pay attention to the **Own Time** column versus the **Time** column.

In PyCharm's performance profiler, the **Time** column shows the total time spent executing a particular function or method, including the time spent executing any sub-functions or methods called within it.

On the other hand, the **Own Time** column shows the time spent executing only the code within the function or method itself, excluding any time spent executing sub-functions or methods. This means that the **Own Time** column can give you a better understanding of the performance of the code within a specific function or method, independent of any external factors such as the performance of other functions or methods it calls.

To illustrate the difference, consider a function, *A()*, that calls two other functions, *B()* and *C()*. If you look at the **Time** column for *A()*, it will include the time spent executing both *B()* and *C()* in addition to the time spent executing the code within *A()* itself. However, if you look at the **Own Time** column for *A()*, it will only show the time spent executing the code within *A()* and not the time spent executing *B()* and *C()*.

In general, the **Time** column can give you a sense of the overall performance impact of a particular function or method, while the **Own Time** column can help you focus on the performance of the code within that function or method.

Comparing performance versus the built-in sum() function

Let's see how my 72 ms runtime fares against the built-in Python sum() function. Alter the bottom of the main.py file by commenting out the custom_sum function and commenting in the built_in_sum function, like this:

```
if __name__ == '__main__':
    # print(custom_sum())
    print(built_in_sum())
```

Run a profile with this configuration. You can see my result in *Figure 6.32*:

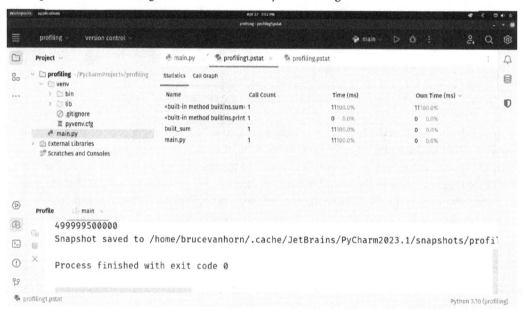

Figure 6.32: The built-in sum function appears to run significantly faster at 11 ms

Wow, there's no contest! On my computer, leveraging the built-in sum() function is seven times faster! In real life, I advise running each profile a few times and taking an average since the runtimes can vary. In my case, subsequent runs of the built_in_sum function ranged from 11 ms to 26 ms, which is a pretty wide variance.

Viewing the call graph

In addition to the statistics table, you can also view the profile as a call graph. This graph represents a tree-like view of your program's run, as shown in *Figure 6.33*:

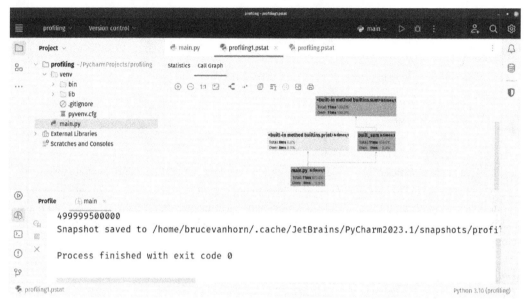

Figure 6.33: The call graph shows a tree-like view of the program run

The nodes in the call graph are shaded green and red. The darker the shade of red, the more time was spent on the function indicated by that node. In *Figure 6.33*, pretty much all of the time is being spent in the custom_sum function, which is as dark a red as it gets (trust me). The built-in print method takes up a tiny but non-zero amount of time when it prints the sum in the main function.

Navigating using the performance profile

You can navigate to a function using either the statistics table or the corresponding node in the call graph. Just right-click, as shown in *Figure 6.34*:

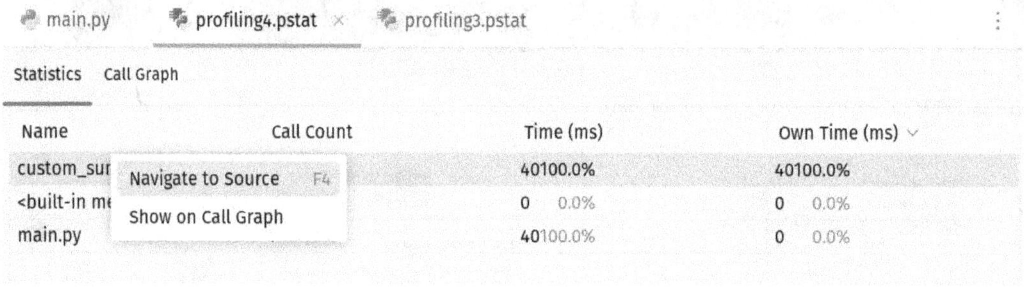

Name		Call Count	Time (ms)		Own Time (ms) ⌄	
custom_sur	Navigate to Source F4		40	100.0%	40	100.0%
<built-in me	Show on Call Graph		0	0.0%	0	0.0%
main.py			40	100.0%	0	0.0%

Figure 6.34: You can navigate to your code by right-clicking the function and selecting Navigate to Source

You can do the same thing on the call graph. Upon right-clicking a node on the call graph, you'll get the same navigation option to take you to the source. This can help you navigate straight to any code you might want to inspect.

Performance cProfile snapshots

When you do a profile run with cProfile, PyCharm will save a **cProfile snapshot**, or **pstat** file, for you. You can see this in the output window. In my case, the `.pstat` files are generated in my home folder:

```
Snapshot saved to /home/brucevanhorn/.cache/JetBrains/PyCharm2023.1/
snapshots/profiling4.pstat
```

When I'm doing serious profiling work, I will often copy these files into a more convenient folder and alter their names to indicate the conditions under which they were run. For example, in our example, I might call the first `.pstat` file something like `custom_sum_performance_1.pstat`; the second might be called `built_in_sum_performance_1.pstat`.

I'm doing this so that I have a baseline performance profile for each. In real life, I suspect you will rarely have such an easy alternative to what we've presented here. You'll more likely have several versions of a function using different approaches to algorithm design. In those cases, keeping your `.pstat` files so that you can compare them with future runs can be very handy, if for no other reason than to brag at your next employee review.

You can open your older `.pstat` files using the **Tools** menu, as shown in *Figure 6.35*:

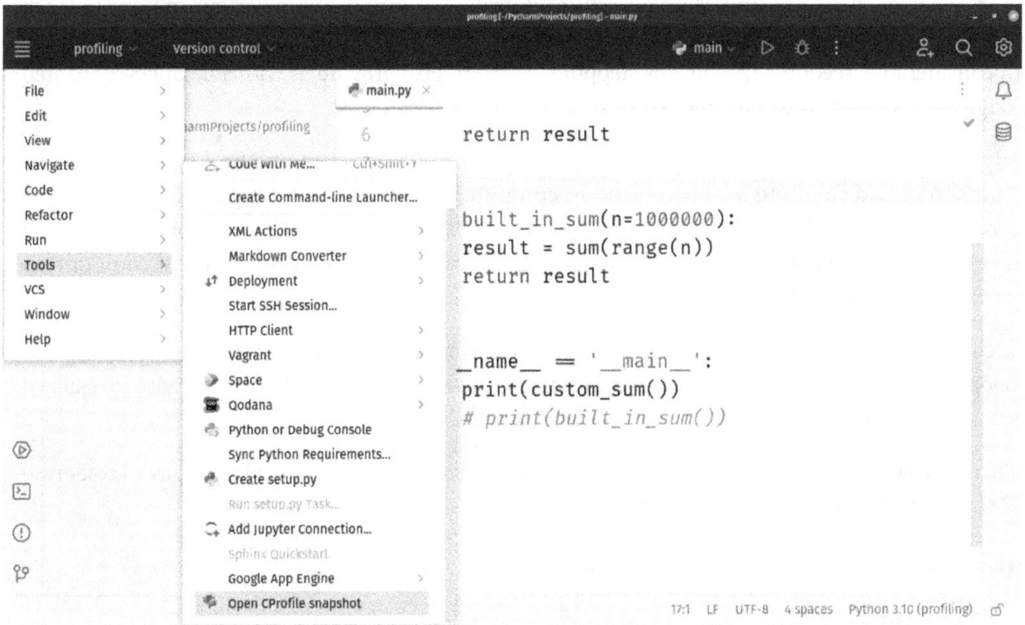

Figure 6.35: You can open your old snapshots via the Tools menu

Opening this `.pstat` file will show the statistics table and call graph. If you've refactored the names of the functions, then you shouldn't expect the navigation to still work; however, you can see the old results and compare them against a newer run.

Overall, PyCharm's ability to open and compare old `.pstat` files can be a useful tool for tracking the performance of your code over time and identifying areas where performance improvements can be made.

Summary

Testing, debugging, and profiling are high-level tasks we can use to analyze applications to look for improvements in correctness and performance, but they can be quite confusing to beginner developers. PyCharm offers straightforward and intuitive interfaces for these processes, making them more accessible and streamlined.

Unit testing is the process of making sure the individual components of a large system work as intended. PyCharm has convenient commands to generate test skeletons/boilerplate code that usually takes time for developers to write manually. While testing a program, it is important to consider expected faults, as well as the obvious tests for intended functionality.

In a debugging session, developers attempt to narrow down and identify the causes of bugs and errors that are detected during testing. With a graphical interface, combined with various options to track the values of variables throughout a program, PyCharm allows us to debug our programs dynamically with considerable freedom. The various stepping functions also provide us with a flexible way to step through the program we are trying to debug.

Lastly, the goal of profiling is to analyze the performance of a program and find ways to improve it. This can include looking for faster ways to compute a value or identifying a bottleneck in the program. With the ability to generate comprehensive statistics on the running time of each function that's executed, as well as call graphs, PyCharm helps developers navigate the different components of a profiled program with ease.

This chapter also marks the end of the second part of this book, where we focused on improving our development productivity. From here, we will be considering the usage of PyCharm in more specialized fields, namely web development and data science projects.

In the next chapter, we will cover the basics of three universal web development languages – JavaScript, HTML, and CSS – within the context of PyCharm.

Questions

Answer the following questions to test your knowledge of this chapter:

1. What is testing in the context of software development? What are the different testing methods?
2. How does PyCharm support testing processes?
3. What is debugging in the context of software development?
4. How does PyCharm support debugging processes?
5. What is profiling in the context of software development?
6. How does PyCharm support profiling processes?
7. What is the significance of run arrows in PyCharm's editor?

Further reading

To learn more about the topics that were covered in this chapter, take a look at the following resources:

- *Agile Software Development, Principles, Patterns, and Practices*, Martin, R. C. (2003). Prentice Hall.
- *Clean Architecture: A Craftsman's Guide to Software Structure and Design*, Martin, R. C. (2017). Prentice Hall.
- *Real-World Implementation of C# Design Patterns*, Van Horn, B and Symons, V. (2022). Packt Publishing.
- Be sure to check out the companion website for the book at https://www.pycharm-book.com

Part 3: Web Development in PyCharm

This part of the book focuses on web development processes in Python programming and what support PyCharm has in store for web projects. Readers will be able to use PyCharm and its features to efficiently develop their web applications.

This part has the following chapters:

- *Chapter 7, Web Development with JavaScript, HTML, and CSS*
- *Chapter 8, Building a Dynamic Web Application with Flask*
- *Chapter 9, Creating a RESTful API with FastAPI*
- *Chapter 10, More full stack frameworks: Django and Pyramid*
- *Chapter 11, Understanding Database Management in PyCharm*

7

Web Development with JavaScript, HTML, and CSS

This chapter marks the beginning of a series of five chapters on web programming with PyCharm, all of which will cover the development of general web applications. I have been looking forward to writing this section because this is my bread and butter. I have been developing web applications for as long as there has been a web. The professional edition of PyCharm contains something of a treat for web developers: a full copy of JetBrains' **WebStorm**, which is provided through a pre-installed plugin. This means we get a lot more than just syntax highlighting for **HTML**, **CSS**, and **JavaScript**! We also have full access to **Node.js** tooling and modern web UI frameworks such as **React**. I might be tempted to call it overkill, but it isn't. The product I work on every day has a mixture of **microservices** written in **Python 3**, **NodeJS**, and **React** for the frontend. I leverage three different databases: **Microsoft SQL Server**, **MongoDB**, and **Redis**. I never have to leave PyCharm! As I just mentioned, I have robust tooling for JavaScript, NodeJS, and React built-in. The databases are all supported in PyCharm, which we'll cover in *Chapter 11, Understanding Database Management with PyCharm*. I can create debug run configurations in PyCharm, run several services that communicate with each other via REST calls, and perform inter-service debugging. I can also place a breakpoint in the React frontend and another in a separate project using **Flask** or **FastAPI**; as I work through the application's workflow, my breakpoints stop, regardless of which project I'm in or which language the project is using. I would not attempt this in any other IDE. Did I mention how excited I was to start writing this set of chapters? I'm getting ahead of myself.

The topics that will be discussed in this chapter include integrating common web programming languages (JavaScript, HTML, and CSS) in PyCharm and how to develop with them in straightforward and intuitive ways. By the end of this chapter, you will have gained comprehensive knowledge of how to use the three languages so that you can start a web development project using PyCharm.

The following topics will be covered in this chapter:

- Introducing JavaScript, HTML, and CSS in the process of web development
- The options for working with JavaScript, HTML, and CSS code in PyCharm
- How to implement live editing and debugging for web projects
- How to work with HTML boilerplate options in PyCharm

Technical requirements

The following are the prerequisites for this chapter:

- A working installation of Python 3.10 or later.

- A working installation of PyCharm Professional. If you are using the community edition, most of what we'll cover in this chapter won't work since you'll only get limited HTML support. You can still work with CSS and JavaScript files, but the experience will be very limited compared to the professional edition.

- The Chrome web browser. You will need it if you want to debug JavaScript code running in the browser.

- A working installation of NodeJS and **node package manager** (**npm**). This is optional. You will only need these if you want to work with React or modern JavaScript frameworks such as Angular, Vue, or Express. React is an advanced topic and won't be covered extensively beyond setting up and working with a React project.

- I'll be showing you how to use PyCharm's deployment features. For this, I assume you understand how to deploy a web project to a remote host using a tool such as WinSCP or FileZilla, or how to transfer files using command-line tools such as **secure copy** (**SCP**) or **file transfer protocol** (**FTP**).

- You can find the sample code for this chapter at `https://github.com/PacktPublishing/ Hands-On-Application-Development-with-PyCharm---Second-Edition/ tree/main/chapter-07`. We covered how to clone the repository in *Chapter 2, Installation and Configuration.*

Introduction to HTML, JavaScript, and CSS

I call these *the triumvirate of web development*. They constitute the most basic skills you can learn as you progress toward becoming a full stack web developer. The term **full stack**, when referencing a full stack developer, just means you are skilled at developing the frontend portion of the application, along with the backend and the database. The next six chapters are devoted to full stack web development with PyCharm.

Strictly speaking, only one of the three languages we'll be covering here is a programming language. **Hypertext Markup Language** (**HTML**) is used to create the structure and layout of a web page or application UI. **Cascading Style Sheets** (**CSS**) is used to control the look of the UI while honoring the separation of concerns: we split the layout of buttons, text, and interactive elements from the definitions of visual appearance. Neither HTML nor CSS has any ability to create any level of interactivity by themselves beyond a few CSS tricks, such as changing a button's color when the user hovers their cursor over it.

The real interactivity in a web-based frontend comes from JavaScript, or as it is properly called, ECMAScript. About a million internet years ago, a company called Netscape was battling for the hearts and minds of the nascent web browser user community. It was David versus Goliath, where Goliath was Microsoft. Netscape's browser cost a small fee to license while Microsoft's Internet Explorer was free, built into the Windows operating system, and sported a set of tools that allowed IT managers to centrally customize their browser's behavior while rolling it out to large corporate user bases. Netscape's value proposition was non-existent. They needed a game-changer.

At about this time, Sun Microsystems was heavily marketing its new flagship programming language called **Java**. Like Netscape, Sun was plagued by competition from Microsoft, so the two teamed up. Netscape started creating what would become the in-browser programming language called ECMAScript, while Sun licensed the name Java with the understanding that the newly renamed JavaScript would never run anywhere but within a browser. Sun's end game was to make sure everyone was using Java to create their web application backends, with Netscape winning the market share for frontend rendering by offering an interactive experience. JavaScript has absolutely nothing to do with Java beyond marketing. They are very different languages and should never be confused.

I'm going to assume you have some knowledge of the vast world of HTML development. I also want to remind you that this is a book on PyCharm and not web development. Given this is how I earn my living, my experience here is deep, and I will move from "this is an HTML tag" (that is the absolute basics) to "and here's React" (that is, there be dragons if all you've ever done is Python work) pretty quickly. My only regret here is that Packt won't let me write "there be dragons" in a scary horror film-style font. I'll leave you references to books and other resources in the *Further reading* section of this chapter in case you want to learn more about frontend or full stack development in general.

Writing code with HTML

HTML, like any other code, is created within a text file. In the case of HTML, the text is highly structured using a set of HTML tags. You can think of the tags as being like keywords in a programming language, except these are set apart using angle brackets. Remember, HTML is for content structure and layout. It was created by Tim Berners-Lee (not Al Gore) as a way to present scientific journal articles on the internet's predecessor called the **Defense Advanced Research Projects Agency Network** (**DARPANET**). This is an adjunct of the United States Department of Defense. One problem in the scientific world with this was the time it took to publish a peer-reviewed journal article. In cases where science had to advance rapidly, we needed a format to electronically publish research without going through the peer review and print publication process, which can take months. HTML was designed to electronically mimic a paper publication. Since this is the case, it should be no surprise that the structure of HTML elements refers to a **document object model** (**DOM**). The document is organized into paragraphs, headers, sub-headers, sections, figures, images, and the like. Consider this example:

```
<html>
 <head>
  <title>Advances in the Application of Time Travel</title>
 <head>
 <body>
  <h1>Introduction</h1>
  <p> Lorem ipsum dolor sit amet, consectetur adipiscing
     elit. Vestibulum tincidunt tempus lectus vitae
     euismod.</p>
 </body>
</html>
```

This is an HTML document that is structured like a typical research paper. It has a title, which appears in the browser's tab. `<title>` is in the `<head>` tag of the document, which might also contain metadata and references to CSS files and JavaScript used on the page.

The `<body>` tag holds the document's contents. The head and body are enclosed within an HTML tag. Remember, the tags are enclosed in angle brackets; for example, `<body>`. Every tag has an opening tag and a closing tag with content in between. For example, the header opens with `<h1>`, the content, *Introduction*, is inserted, and the tag is closed with `</h1>`. The closing tag adds a forward slash to the matching element.

This structure enables the web browser to easily parse the document and display the content as an electronic page. In modern HTML, though, only the structure is defined. How the elements are laid out on the page, along with visual definitions for fonts, colors, sizes, and so on, are all controlled by an externally linked CSS document.

If we add this code to our earlier document, within the `<head>` tag, we get a page that looks very different in the browser:

```
<head>
 <title>Advances in the Application of Time Travel</title>
 <link rel="stylesheet" href="mystyle.css">
<head>
```

Note that the added link tag is a little different: it doesn't have a closing tag. There are a few exceptions in HTML like this. Additionally, the link tag has some attributes attached. You can think of attributes as being like arguments for a function. They define additional input used by the tag. In this case, several different types of link tags are possible in HTML. We are defining this one as a stylesheet using the `rel` attribute. The `href` attribute tells the HTML page where to find the CSS file. Here, the page will be looking for a file called `mystyle.css` in the same folder as the HTML file.

Creating HTML in PyCharm

The HTML frontend development experience is only available with PyCharm Professional. The community edition allows you to create HTML files in a Python project, but that's about all. I'll be strictly considering the professional edition in this chapter.

We're going to create a new project, but this time, we're not going to create a Python project. In fact, we're not going to create a new project in PyCharm at all. PyCharm used to have the option to create an empty project. At some point, it was removed, but that's OK. PyCharm projects are simply a folder with a .idea folder inside it.

Creating an empty project

Creating an empty project, which will bypass the process of setting up a virtual environment, which we don't need, is easy. Just make a folder somewhere on your computer. I created mine on the desktop and called it html-project. I like to name my projects that aren't using Python in kebab case instead of snake case so that I can easily spot the difference. Naturally, you can call it whatever you like.

Make sure PyCharm doesn't have an open project. If it does, use **File** | **Close** to close the current project.

Next, just drag your empty folder into PyCharm. You'll get the usual **Trust and Open Project** dialog, as shown in *Figure 7.1*:

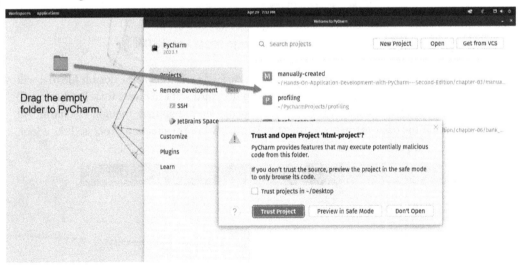

Figure 7.1: Drag an empty folder onto the PyCharm project window to
create an empty project with no Python environment

You may have noticed that there are HTML project types in PyCharm Professional's new project window and wonder why I am ignoring them. I would rather start you off with a basic example before I show you the HTML boilerplate project, which creates a whole site based on ideals established by Google. Let's walk before we fly. If you are already a full stack veteran, don't skip this section. Given this isn't a book on HTML, I don't intend to linger on the basics. I'm going to go over a few features in this simple example.

When you create a project in this way, it is effectively a Python project without an interpreter. You'll get a message stating that the default Python installation is being used as an environment, which is fine. We won't need it:

Figure 7.2: Right-click the project folder to create a new HTML file

You will be prompted to give the file a name. Call it index.html. This is the default file that will be displayed on a web server, so it is the most common file you'd want to create first. PyCharm will generate a basic HTML page structure based on a template. More than that, though, PyCharm will prompt you to fill in the basic elements of the template as part of the creation process. Take a look at *Figure 7.3*:

Figure 7.3: PyCharm presents a template for you to fill in

This template only has one template variable in it: `Title`. As you can see, line 5 is highlighted and the word `Title` is highlighted even more. PyCharm is expecting you to type a title, then press the *Tab* key. Doing this sets the title and then takes you straight down to the inside of the body tag.

Upon adding this code, a few things become evident:

1. All the autocompletion you've come to expect with Python is also applied to HTML tags. Valid attributes are also supplied in code completion. You'll notice this when you type in the link tag for the style sheet.

2. PyCharm will automatically create the closing tag for you. When you type `<h1>Introduction`, as soon as you complete the `<h1>` tag, PyCharm will insert the `</h1>` closer for you. Failure to close your tags can lead to layout issues or missing content.

3. The same documentation features for Python keywords and libraries exist for HTML. Hover over any element and you'll see documentation for that element.

4. The same linting we saw in Python code is at play in the HTML code too. *Figure 7.4* shows the same kind of warnings in the same areas we saw when we talked about these features in the editor for Python code:

Figure 7.4: We can see a lot of similarities between the editor's
treatment of Python and its treatment of HTML

The problem summary at the top of the screen (*1*) indicates that there are a few typographical errors. There aren't really any, it's just that the dictionary is assuming English, and my placeholder verbiage is in Latin. There is a warning, though. If you click the yellow triangle next to *1*, the problem window opens (*3*). I can also see a yellow warning marker at *2*. All these point to the fact that we have yet to create the CSS file referenced on line 6.

In addition to the usual things we normally see in the editor, we can see something new at *4*: there are a few icons that correspond to the web browsers PyCharm is aware of on your computer.

Previewing web pages

Clicking any of the browser icons will allow you to preview your code in that browser. In my case, I have three browsers: Chrome, Firefox, and PyCharm's built-in preview window. These icons will fade in and out as your mouse cursor approaches the top right of the editor window.

In honor of Netscape's shoutout at the beginning of this chapter, let's take a look at Firefox in *Figure 7.5* since it is Netscape's successor:

Figure 7.5: The browser launches and displays our page

There are three things worth noting in *Figure 7.5*:

- PyCharm didn't just open the page in the browser with a `file:///` URL. If you want to do that, you can hold down *Alt* or *Option* when clicking the browser icon. In our case, PyCharm launched its internal web server. This is handy because previewing your work in the browser with a `file:///` URL is very limiting. Many features simply won't work.

- The content in the `<title>` tag appears as the title on the tab in the browser.

- The year 1991 called and they want their website back. HTML just creates structure. This page is pretty ugly without the CSS. We should fix that.

Before we do, though, I want to point out a nifty feature that PyCharm gives us: auto-reloading.

Reloading the browser view on save

If you study the URL in the browser in *Figure 7.5*, you'll notice the RELOAD_ON_SAVE attribute. You can probably guess what this does, but let's cover it anyway. In *Figure 7.6*, I have tiled my windows so that PyCharm is on the left, and my browser is on the right. This is a common configuration used by web developers, though it usually plays out on several monitors:

Figure 7.6: PyCharm will automatically reload the page in the
browser every time you save changes to the file

I've added a second <p> tag that reads as follows:

```
<p>This is a paragraph I added later</p>
```

The moment I pressed *Ctrl + S* (*Cmd + S* on Mac), the browser updated with the new content. This seriously speeds up development! This is hardly revolutionary; most editors support this in some way, but so does PyCharm.

The Live Edit plugin

In older versions of JetBrains IDEs that support HTML development, you used to need a plugin called Live Edit to get this auto-reload feature. You don't need it anymore since the feature is integrated into the IDE.

Using the PyCharm HTML preview

If you'd rather keep 100% of your work in PyCharm rather than have an external browser, there is a new HTML preview feature, as shown in *Figure 7.7*, that launches an internal version of the Chromium browser:

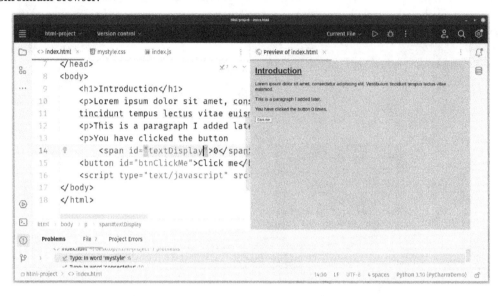

Figure 7.7: The PyCharm preview window allows you to view your work in a
Chromium browser window implemented as a PyCharm UI tab

If you're not familiar, Chromium is the open source version of Chrome. This is important to note since over the years, I've seen a lot of web development products with goofy preview products bundled in that bear little relevance to how your work will be displayed in a real browser.

Configuring the available browsers

The browser icons that appear as preview browsers are configurable. You can add or remove any browser on your computer to or from the configuration. You'll find this by going to **Settings** under **Tools | Web Browsers**, and then **Preview**, as shown in *Figure 7.8*:

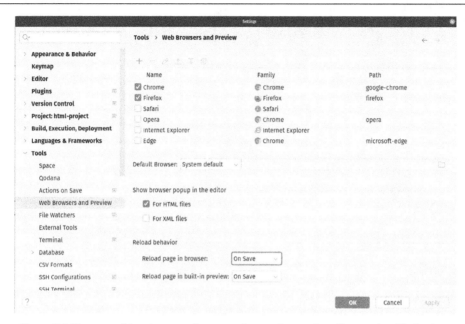

Figure 7.8: You can add and remove browsers for preview and configure reload behaviors

I think you'll find adding new browsers as easy as clicking the + icon and locating the browser's executable. If you'd like to remove the unsightly presence of Internet Explorer, just click it, and click the – icon.

Note the dropdown that allows you to set the default launch browser to the system default, which is the first in the list, or a custom path. You can also configure whether you see the launch icons for HTML files and/or XML files.

The reload behavior can be configured at the bottom of the screen. You can set the reload to happen on save, on change, or turn it off. In my opinion, the **On Change** setting fires too often. I leave it set to **On Save**.

Navigating structure code with the structure window

The structure window allows you to view the structure of your code. Most of the time, the structure window just shows a list of functions and global variables. If you open a class file, you'll see the properties and methods of the class. *Figure 7.09* shows what happens when you use the structure window with an HTML document:

Figure 7.9: The structure window allows you to see and navigate the DOM in the code window

When you open the structure view on an HTML page, you can see and easily navigate the entire DOM structure of the HTML document.

Adding the CSS

Right-click the project folder and add a Stylesheet file called `mystyle.css`, as shown in *Figure 7.10*. You will be prompted to choose a Stylesheet type. We're sticking to CSS files. The rest of the options are fancy, but they all transpile, usually via the **Babel** library and a **WebPack** build script, to regular CSS at the end of the day. If you are new to frontend work, I recommend learning plain CSS before branching off into exotic topics such as **Less** or **Sass**:

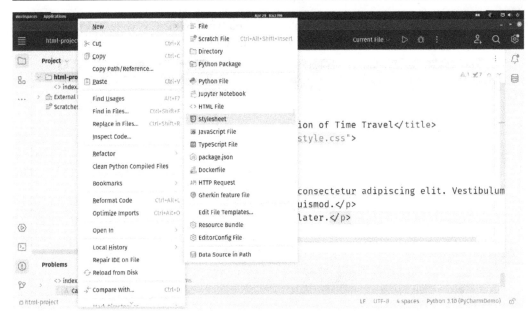

Figure 7.10: Create a new CSS file using File | New | Stylesheet

Be sure to name the file `mystyle.css` so that it matches what we have in the `<link>` tag in our HTML file. It also needs to be in the same folder as `index.html`. Add this code:

```
body {
  background-color: lightblue;
  margin: 20px;
  font-family: Arial, Helvetica, sans-serif;
  font-size: 18px;
}
h1 {
  font-size: 32px;
  color: navy;
  text-decoration: underline;
}
```

Save the file and return to your browser. Don't expect it to have updated; PyCharm's reload feature is watching the `index.html` file, not the newly created `mystyle.css` file. Hit the reload button in your browser. I won't bother with a black-and-white screenshot of a colored HTML page. The change should be immediately noticeable. Now that the browser has loaded the CSS, you can edit the CSS in PyCharm. With each save, the page will update, just as it did when you edited the HTML in the `index.html` page.

You no doubt noticed the excellent code completion as you typed in the CSS code. The color codes were all displayed by name, as well as hex value, as shown in *Figure 7.11*:

Figure 7.11: As you type CSS color names, you'll see the name, the hex value, and a preview of the color

There is a preview of the color next to the CSS color name as well so that you can see what color you're setting.

Using color selectors

You can set the color using a name or a hex value, or you can edit an existing color using the swatch, as shown in *Figure 7.12*. Here, I've clicked the color swatch in the gutter on line 10 of the mystyle. css file:

Figure 7.12: You can edit the color by clicking the swatch in the gutter and picking a new color

From here, I can pick the color using an RGBA or hex value or just drag the cursor around the color window. There's a hue slider as well as a slider for the alpha channel. This controls the opacity, which the UI is displaying as a percentage rather than the traditional 0-255 integer value.

You'll also notice that there is an eye dropper tool. You can use the eye dropper to select any color that's visible on your screen. This allows you to, for example, match a color to be used on your type with a color from an image that's visible on your screen.

Adding JavaScript

It's time to round out our experience with HTML, CSS, and JavaScript by adding some interactivity to our page. Right-click on the project folder and add a JavaScript file called index.js.

We're going to add a button to our HTML file, then have that button react when we click it using JavaScript. We'll write the JavaScript code first; then, we'll go back and add the button.

Adding some JavaScript code

Enter this code into your index.js file:

```
const btn = document.getElementById("btnClickMe");
const textDisplay = document.getElementById("textDisplay");
let clickCount = 0;
```

We'll add some elements to the HTML file that are referenced in this JavaScript in a minute. First, we'll add a button with an ID of btnClickMe. Then, we'll add a span tag inside a paragraph with an ID of textDisplay. Finally, we'll create a variable called clickCount. You can probably see where this is going. When you load the page, the value of clickCount will be 0. Each time you click the button, we increment the clickCount variable, then update the HTML within the span tag to reflect the new value.

To make this work, we need an onclick handler for the button. Add this code:

```
btn.onclick = function() {
    clickCount++;
    textDisplay.textContent = String(clickCount);
}
```

The button's onclick handler is assigned to the anonymous function, which increments clickCount and updates the display. I even went the extra mile and cast clickCount to a string.

With our JavaScript in place, let's update our HTML.

Adding the elements to the HTML file

Now, let's go back to the `index.html` file and add two new elements. First, we'll add a text area:

```
<p>You have clicked the button
  <span id="textDisplay">0</span>
times. </p>
```

Next, let's add a button:

```
<button id="btnClickMe">Click me</button>
```

The button has an ID attribute of `btnClickMe`, which I used in the JavaScript to the `onclick` event in the browser. Each time the **Click me** button is clicked, this event fires, and we run the anonymous function that updates the value of `clickCount`. Then, the function changes the text that appears in the span tag with an `id` of `textArea`.

We're almost done! We just need to add a script tag to the bottom of the HTML file. Add this line just above the closing body tag:

```
<script type="text/javascript" src="index.js"></script>
```

This line will load your JavaScript file after all the HTML has loaded into the browser window. Manually refresh your browser. You can click the **Click me** button and see the counter increment. You can see mine in *Figure 7.13*:

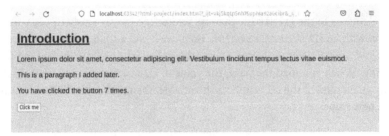

Figure 7.13: Our web page is now interactive!

As you were working, you no doubt took advantage of the usual code completion we've been discussing. That's pretty nice, right? But it gets even better! I'm going to show you how to debug from your IDE. Normally, you'd have to rely solely on the debugging tools in your browser, which means switching back and forth between the code display in your browser and your IDE. I have, at least once or twice, forgotten which tool I was in and found myself trying to directly edit in the browser's debugging tool. This works, except that it doesn't save your file back to the actual code file. Admittedly, this only happens when I'm really tired, but with two middle-school-aged daughters, a full-time job running a development team, and writing books, I'm pretty much always really tired. I did mention earlier that the debugger is my favorite feature, so without further ado, I give you client-side JavaScript debugging!

Debugging client-side JavaScript

You can debug the JavaScript that runs in your browser by setting up Google Chrome as your default browser. Chrome has a very good remote debugging server built into the browser. PyCharm can connect to it and display the debugging information directly in the PyCharm UI, just as it would appear when we debugged Python code back in *Chapter 6, Seamless Testing, Debugging, and Profiling*.

Open the index.js file and set a breakpoint in our click handler function on line 7, as shown in *Figure 7.14*:

Figure 7.14: By setting a breakpoint in your client-side code, you can debug your client-side JavaScript just as easily as you can debug Python code

To use the JavaScript debugger directly in PyCharm, you need to create a run configuration. We covered creating run configurations in detail in *Chapter 6, Seamless Testing, Debugging, and Profiling*. To create a run configuration that's capable of working with a JavaScript file loaded into HTML, create a run configuration using the JavaScript Debug template, as shown in *Figure 7.15*:

Figure 7.15: Use the JavaScript Debug template to set up a run configuration that allows you to debug your JavaScript code directly in PyCharm

Once you've selected the template, you'll see a settings screen, similar to the one in *Figure 7.16*:

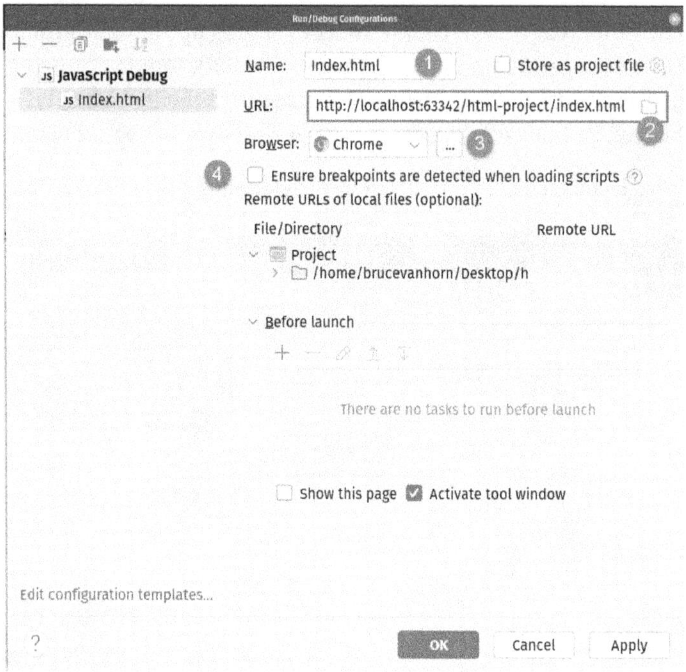

Figure 7.16: Fill in the settings to run your HTML page, which loads your JavaScript for debugging

The key settings fields are numbered in *Figure 7.16*.

At position *1*, you can fill in a name for the run configuration. It can be anything you like since the name doesn't affect the workings of the run configuration. For the URL, you want to click the folder icon at *2* and just browse to your `index.html` file. When you do that, PyCharm will fill in the localhost URL, along with the port number used by PyCharm's built-in web server. The selection at *3* determines which web browser is launched. PyCharm only supports debugging in browsers based on Chromium. For example, Chrome, Chromium, Edge, or Brave would work fine, but Safari or Firefox would not.

The setting at *4* is important since it loads your JavaScript breakpoints before the `OnPageLoad` event fires. If you are using JavaScript that loads based on an **Immediately Invoked Function Expression (IIFE)**, or even jQuery's `$(function())` call, you should check this box. Our script is very simple, so for me, it's fine to leave this unchecked. Note that checking this box will slow the load time for your debugger to start.

To start your debugging session, click the usual debugging button. If you don't remember where this is, refer back to *Chapter 6*. Chrome will launch with your web page. Upon clicking the **Click me** button we made earlier, the debugger in PyCharm should intercept the event. As with our debugger coverage in *Chapter 6*, you can use all the same features to inspect and step through your JavaScript code.

Working with Emmet templating

Emmet is a powerful and widely used plugin in PyCharm that provides an efficient and streamlined way of writing HTML, **JavaScript XML (JSX)**, and CSS code. It offers a range of templating features that significantly boost developer productivity and speed up the coding process. By leveraging the Emmet abbreviations and snippets, developers can write code snippets in a shorthand syntax and expand them into complete HTML or CSS structures with just a few keystrokes. The only downside is that you need to learn and memorize the Emmet abbreviations. I don't have the space to turn this into an Emmet tutorial. There is a cheat sheet available at `https://docs.emmet.io/cheat-sheet/`.

To use Emmet in PyCharm, you only need to type some Emmet shorthand into the editor window and press *Tab*. For instance, by typing `ul>li.item$*5`, followed by pressing the *Tab* key, Emmet can generate an unordered list with five list items, where the `$` symbol is automatically incremented for each item. This feature is particularly useful when dealing with repetitive HTML structures and eliminates the need to manually type out repetitive code blocks.

Another powerful feature of Emmet in PyCharm is that you can navigate and edit HTML and CSS code efficiently. With the **Go to Edit Point** feature, developers can navigate between predefined edit points within an expanded abbreviation, allowing for quick modifications and adjustments. Additionally, Emmet's automatic tag closing feature ensures that HTML tags are automatically closed, reducing the chance of syntax errors and saving time in the coding process. The **Go to Edit Point** feature effectively allows you to put placeholders in the code template. If you tried out the earlier example with the unordered list, you might have noticed that the code was generated, but your cursor was sitting inside the first list item tag, as seen in *Figure 7.17*:

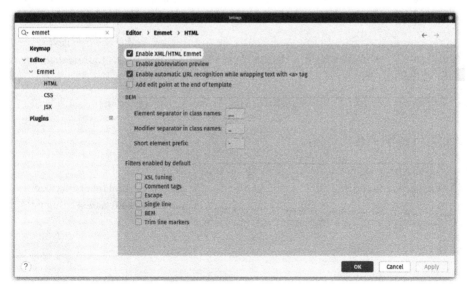

Figure 7.17: Emmet generated the unordered list thanks to the edit point defined in the template

Emmet also provides intelligent CSS abbreviations that simplify the process of writing and expanding CSS properties. By using shortcuts such as "bg" for "background" or "p" for "padding," developers can quickly generate CSS code snippets without having to remember the full property names. This feature speeds up the CSS development process and enhances code readability.

HTML project types in PyCharm Professional

Earlier, I mentioned that I wanted to start you off with a basic empty project with some simple HTML, CSS, and JavaScript code we created from scratch. PyCharm Professional offers new additional pure HTML project types. By pure, I mean they don't use any modern JavaScript frameworks such as React or Angular. These modern frameworks represent a paradigm shift in frontend development. A pure HTML project will continue to use very traditional DOM manipulation, as we did in our JavaScript example earlier. To change the content of our click counter span, we used this code:

```
Document.getElementById
```

Since client-side JavaScript like this runs in the browser, the code has access to the document object, which is effectively the browser window. JavaScript can manipulate the currently loaded document or even update the contents of the browser window itself.

Modern JavaScript frameworks no longer manipulate the DOM. Instead, they rely on a state change mechanism coupled with the idea of a shadow DOM. In the case of React, your program, which consists mainly of JavaScript, CSS, and HTML markup generated by JSX, maintains a component-driven state machine. Changes to the state trigger events within the React framework, which, in turn, trigger a re-render of the affected areas in the UI.

This is a fairly complicated paradigm to explain to the uninitiated, and since this isn't a book on modern JavaScript, I'll punt the idea of a deeper explanation to other books in the *Further reading* section at the end of this chapter.

There are two project types we can look at that are DOM-based. Let's check them out.

HTML 5 Boilerplate

The **HTML 5 Boilerplate (H5BP)** project can be found at `https://html5boilerplate.com/`. This project has been around since 2011, and it represents a site generation tool that epitomizes HTML development best practices. If you could generate a 100% by-the-book website as a starting point, and then alter it to make pretty much anything, you'd have H5BP.

Here are a few of its key features:

- A well-thought-out and structured `index.html` file replete with metadata tags and every optimization you could want. Just add content.

- `Normalize.css` and `Main.css` take care of your CSS resets and provide some base styles for helpers, media queries for responsive design, and even print-friendly options.

- Google Analytics baked in.

- The Modernizr library is included so that you can detect which browser is running your code and react accordingly.

- Server setting files so that you can deliver performance and security.

- Placeholder icons for mobile devices, favicons, and progressive web apps.

As I said, it is the ultimate HTML 5 starter kit for any website that doesn't lock you into a lot. Older versions use jQuery, but like so many other frameworks, more recent builds remove it as a dependency should you not want to use it.

Let's create an H5BP project in PyCharm. Click **File | New Project** and pick the **HTML 5 Boilerplate** project type. You will be asked which version you'd like to use. Just pick the latest one. For me, that's version 8.0.0. Next, just specify the location where you'd like the project to be generated, and what you'd like to call it. I'm calling mine h5bp and I'm just putting it in the default PyCharm `Projects` folder on my computer.

Behind the scenes, PyCharm will generate a large project using H5BP via npm. *Figure 7.18* shows my generated project:

Figure 7.18: My HTML 5 Boilerplate project with index.html open

Wow! Just look at all that code you didn't have to type, look up, or remember! With a more extensive project loaded, let's look at a few helpful features that I haven't pointed out yet.

Previewing and editing graphics with external tools

You can preview graphics in PyCharm by simply double-clicking the file. I'll open the tile.png file, as seen in *Figure 7.19*:

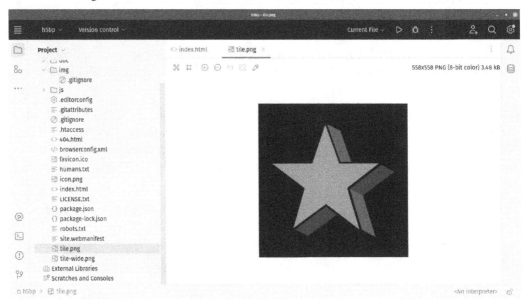

Figure 7.19: You can view graphics in PyCharm by simply opening them

I may have teased you a bit by implying that you can edit images in PyCharm. You can't. But you can configure an external editor that will launch when you open a graphic.

Launch the settings window and find **Tools | External Tools**. Click the + icon in the top toolbar. In *Figure 7.20*, I'm setting up the **Gnu Image Manipulation Program** (**GIMP**), which is an open source alternative to **Adobe Photoshop**:

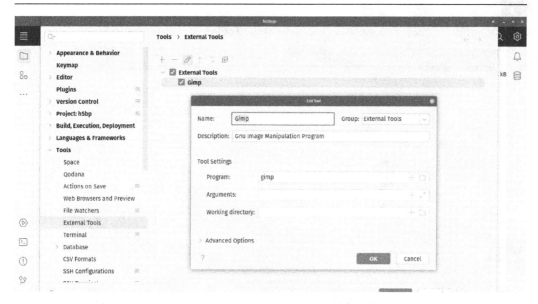

Figure 7.20: You can configure GIMP as an external editor to open images in your project

Don't get me wrong here: I prefer Photoshop. If you have it, use that. It doesn't run in Linux (to me, Wine doesn't count), so GIMP is the next best thing. Any kind of file that PyCharm can't edit can benefit from an external editor. Another good addition I often make is **Inkscape** or **Adobe Illustrator** for working with **Scalable Vector Graphics** (**SVG**) files. These are useful because they are resolution independent. Likewise, if you serve PDF files, adding **Adobe Acrobat** or some other program to manipulate PDFs is a good candidate for adding as an external tool.

To open a file in the external editor, just right-click the file, click the **External Tools** menu option, and select the appropriate external tool.

Uploading your site to a server

Many large sites and software projects use a continuous deployment system to deploy code to servers. If your project isn't that far along yet, or maybe you just need something simple, PyCharm has a publishing mechanism designed to help you easily publish a website or application. For that matter, it can be used to publish any kind of software, but I most often see it used to deploy web projects to web servers.

You'll find the deployment configuration and tools in the **Tools** menu, as shown in *Figure 7.21*:

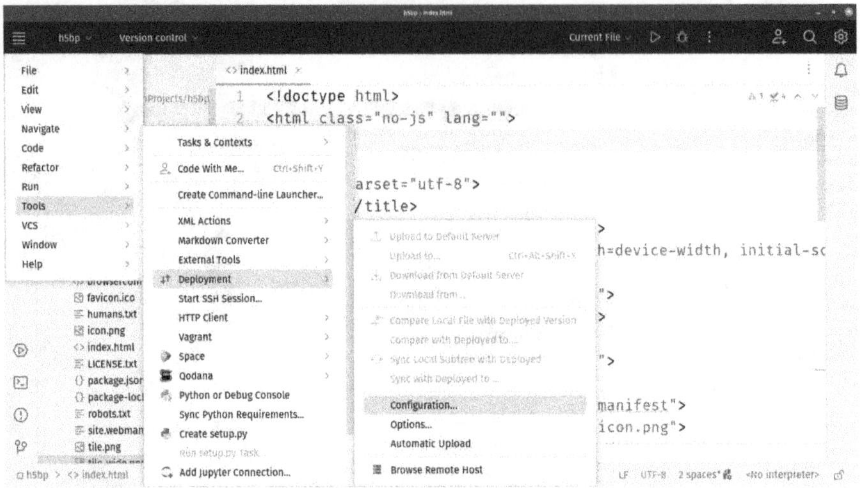

Figure 7.21: The deployment settings and tools can be found by going to Tools | Deployment

The process of setting up deployment entails configuring one or more remote servers. Let's take a look at how this is done.

Configuring the remote server

Click the **Configuration...** menu option shown in *Figure 7.21*. You'll be greeted by a plain gray window that says **Please add a web server to configure**. Click the + icon in the top-left corner of the window and select the type of connection you intend to use. You can see the choices in *Figure 7.22*:

Figure 7.22: Select the type of server connection you'd like to use

You have several connection protocols from which to choose:

- **Secure File Transfer Protocol (SFTP)**. This should be your go-to. Out of the options on the list, it is the most secure since it relies on the **Secure Shell Protocol (SSH)**.

- **File Transfer Protocol (FTP)**. In the real world, you should never use this option. FTP by itself sends all of its authentication data in an unencrypted text stream. Only use it if you want your site to be hacked.

- **File Transfer Protocol Secured (FTPS)** is FTP with **Secure Sockets Layer (SSL)** encryption. The same encryption certificates you'd use to secure your website with HTTPS can be used with FTP to become FTPS.

- **Web Distributed Authoring and Versioning (WebDAV)** was created back in the day when companies such as Microsoft and Macromedia (which were bought by Adobe) were selling web authoring tools for web designers – that is to say, people who write HTML but who aren't overly technical. Most of them died in the great developer rebellion of 1998. WebDAV allowed an authoring tool to connect to a server seamlessly with minimal fuss. Like FTP, though, it has its share of security issues. I don't recommend using it.

- **Local or mounted folder** is used when you have direct network access to the folder being used to serve your site or application.

- **In Place** allows you to copy your project files to a sub-folder of the current project. This reminds me of many build tools that create a folder called `build`, then copy the necessary files into that folder. I find the **Local or mounted folder** option to be more useful.

I'm going to walk you through connecting to a server using SFTP. When you click the **SFTP** option in the menu, shown in *Figure 7.22*, you will be prompted to name the server. This is a friendly name that helps you remember which server you're working with rather than a DNS name or IP address. I'm going to call mine Web Server, as seen in *Figure 7.23*:

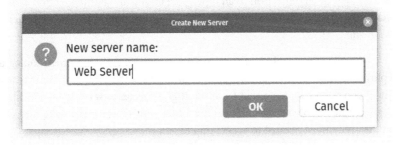

Figure 7.23: Give your server a descriptive name

Next, you'll need credentials. You generally get these from your friendly local system administrator or hosting service. These are entered into an SSH configuration, which is distinct from your deployment server configuration. The UI gets a little bit funky right here. To set up the SSH configuration, click the ellipsis button shown in *Figure 7.24*:

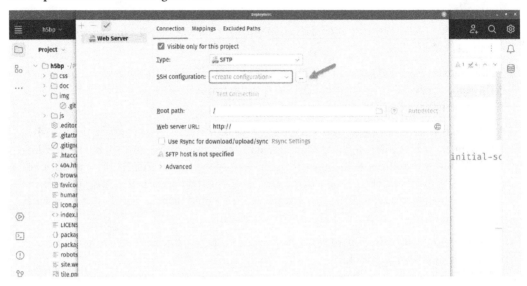

Figure 7.24: Creating a deployment requires you to also create an
SSH configuration by clicking the ellipsis shown here

This brings up yet another empty gray window. Click the + sign in the top corner of this window and you'll see a screen like mine, as shown in *Figure 7.25*.

Fill in your connection details – that is, your host, port, username, and password. Besides a password, you can also use SSH keys or a connection to an OpenSSH config and authentication agent. I'll keep it simple and stick with a password. Clicking the **Test Connection** button tells me whether or not my credentials are working.

Next, we need a root path. This should be the root of your web server's document folder, assuming you mean to deploy a website. There is an autodetect button there that will find the SSH user's home folder. This is fine if you're serving from that location. It is common to serve from a location such as /var/www/html on the remote server. If that is the folder your server uses, make sure your system admin gives you the credentials needed to access that location.

Below that, you'll see an entry for the web server's URL. The root path on the server should map to the web server URL. You can see my settings in *Figure 7.25*:

Figure 7.25: My deployment settings (so far)

Your next stop is the **Mappings** tab. *Figure 7.26* shows the **Mappings** tab with a mapping specified:

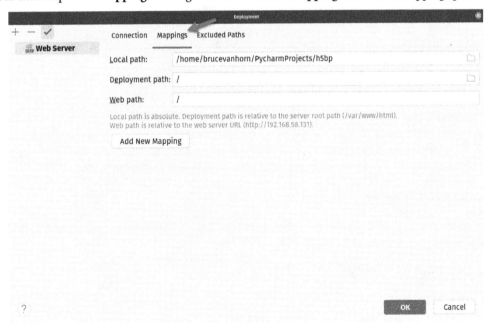

Figure 7.26: The Mappings tab specifies the mappings between the
folders on your computer and the folders on the server

For a web project, you usually just need one mapping between the folder containing your code on your computer, and the document root of the web server. Next, switch to the **Excluded Paths** tab, as shown in *Figure 7.27*:

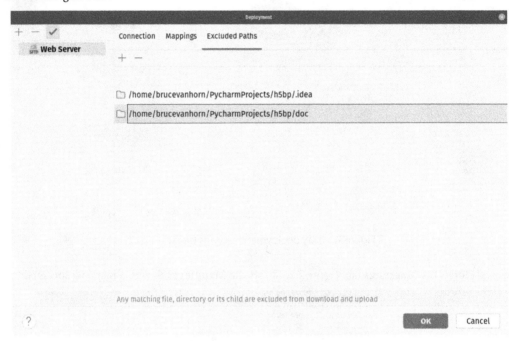

Figure 7.27: Exclude paths you don't need to copy to the server

Exclude any files you don't want to be copied. You can specify local files that shouldn't be copied to the server, and remote files that should not be copied down to your computer. I added the contents of the doc folder, which contains documentation for the developer, and the contents of the .idea folder, which is used by PyCharm. Click **OK**, and your deployment will be configured.

Uploading to the server

You are now ready to upload your project. Go back to the **Tools | Deployment** menu, and this time, click **Upload to Web Server**, as shown in *Figure 7.28*:

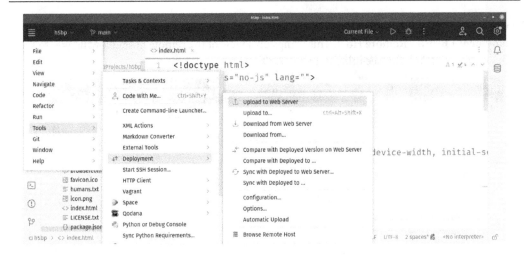

Figure 7.28: The upload controls are in the deployment menu

If you named your remote server something besides Web Server, that is what will appear in the menu. You will be asked to confirm the upload operation. PyCharm will display a message stating that the upload was successful, as seen in *Figure 7.29*:

Figure 7.29: The index.html file was successfully transferred

The upload operation only copied the open index.html file. We can check this by clicking **Tools | Deployment | Browse Remote Host**. This brings up a view of the remote host, allowing you to see the files on the host. You can see mine in *Figure 7.30*:

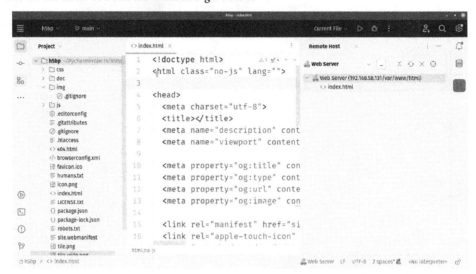

Figure 7.30: You can view the mapped project root folder on the server

You probably want to transfer the whole site rather than just the open file. Right-click inside the remote host window and click **Upload here**, as seen in *Figure 7.31*:

Figure 7.31: Right-click and then select Upload here to upload the whole site

As you can see from the menu, you have full graphical control over files on the server, including all file operations, such as rename, copy, or delete. You can compare operations that will diff the local file with the remote, and of course, the file operations are two-way, so you can synchronize work done directly on the server back to your computer.

All in all, this tool is more capable than a standalone file transport program such as FileZilla. It is integrated directly into the IDE, and there is even an auto-sync setting that uploads the local copy to the remote whenever you save a file. PyCharm has everything you need to work on the HTML frontend of a website or application, including the ability to publish right from PyCharm.

Creating a Bootstrap project

Bootstrap is another DOM-oriented HTML 5 project type you can use in PyCharm Professional. This one is more useful if you are building an application rather than a website. Bootstrap is a library of styled HTML components developed by Twitter that help users rapidly develop applications. Essentially, you can make a nice-looking application by simply generating this project, then copying and pasting Bootstrap snippets for elements such as buttons, card layouts, sliders, switches, and a mobile-first grid system.

You can create a Bootstrap project by clicking **File | New Project**, then picking **Bootstrap** from the templates on the right, as shown in *Figure 7.32*:

Figure 7.32: Creating a Bootstrap project

All this template does is create a js folder and a css folder. PyCharm then downloads Bootstrap and places the library files in their respective folders. That's it. It doesn't even generate an index. html file for you. It is just a quick way to set up a project with Bootstrap.

Working with modern JavaScript and NodeJS

PyCharm has all its features and templates available in the Web Storm product, which is designed for working with modern JavaScript projects. Since I assume you are mostly interested in Python projects, I won't spend a lot of time delving into the details of server-side JavaScript development since we will be covering the Python options, such as Flask, FastAPI, Pyramid, and Django, in the next few chapters.

However, you should know that if you have JavaScript projects and Python projects, there is no need to buy two separate products.

Creating a NodeJS project

To create a new Node JS project, just click **File | New Project** and select the NodeJS project template. This is the equivalent of generating a project with the npm init -y command. All you get is a generic package.json file. It is pretty bare-bones, but it does save you the trouble of firing up a terminal and running the init command.

In addition to a basic Node project, you can also generate a **Next.js** project or an **Express** project. Express is JavaScript's answer to Flask, which we'll cover in the next chapter. It is used to develop the backend of your project. Next.JS, on the other hand, is a fusion of frontend and backend development with an easy-to-use hosting service. For more on this, see https://nextjs.org.

Creating a React project

React is one of the most popular frontend frameworks available today. It represents a paradigm shift in frontend development as it doesn't use the DOM to manipulate the way a web UI looks. Instead of using the DOM to show and hide components in a **single-page application (SPA)** as appropriate, you instead manipulate a state object, which causes React to update the page.

React UIs are developed as a set of components that work together along with life cycle methods or hooks to handle traditional or even custom events. I'm showing a little more work with React here because it is what I use in my daily work, and because in a later chapter, I'll present how to use FastAPI with a React frontend.

Creating a React project is as easy as the others we've seen so far. Just click **File | New Project**, pick **React** from the templates, and give PyCharm the location. As you can see in *Figure 7.33*, PyCharm is leveraging create-react-app, which is normally executed from the command line:

Figure 7.33: Create React App can be run from the PyCharm GUI

PyCharm also gives you an easy way to select between JavaScript, which is the default, and TypeScript, which is the preference for many developers. TypeScript is a variant of JavaScript pioneered by Microsoft in the wake of Douglas Crockford's book titled *JavaScript, the Good Parts*. TypeScript aims to fix many of the bad parts, such as the lack of a strong type system.

Other frontend frameworks

PyCharm has support for several other modern frontend frameworks.

Angular is like React in that it uses components driven by a state machine. The biggest difference, besides being infamous for major releases not being backward compatible, is bi-directional communications between components. In React, properties drill down from top to bottom. In Angular, communications between components go both directions. This can make your applications harder to debug.

React Native is an offshoot of React that's designed to create native user experiences for mobile and desktop applications. The latest edition of the .NET framework from Microsoft includes a React Native variant for creating Windows user interfaces for desktop applications.

Vite is a modern framework that aims to solve performance problems associated with bloat. It is easy for a project in any other framework to require dozens or even hundreds of JavaScript module imports, which slows the performance of development and the application itself. Vite uses advanced bundling tools to streamline the frontend development process.

Vue is yet another frontend framework that provides a declarative component-based programming model. While React relies heavily on JSX, Vue uses standard HTML, CSS, and JavaScript and can be configured to include elements such as routing, server-side rendering, and more.

Summary

This chapter covered using PyCharm as a frontend development tool for web pages and applications. We discovered PyCharm has a very rich set of capabilities in this area because the JetBrains Web Storm product is integrated directly into PyCharm Professional as a pre-installed plugin.

This provides all the functionality of a robust, dedicated tool specializing in the development of HTML, JavaScript, and CSS. All the same debugging capabilities available to us in Python are also afforded in JavaScript code, whether it be client or server side. While we didn't spend any time talking about server-side JavaScript, the capability to work with NodeJS projects is there.

PyCharm Professional gives us a great many project templates in both traditional DOM-based development strategies, such as HTML 5 Boilerplate and Bootstrap, and modern state machine-based systems such as Angular and React.

We learned how to leverage PyCharm's deployment tools to upload sites and applications to remote servers. We also learned how to configure external tools such as image editors so that they're launched directly from PyCharm.

Having covered the frontend tooling, in the next chapter, we will discover how to develop a full stack web application using the Flask framework.

Be sure to check out the companion website for the book at `https://www.pycharm-book.com`.

Questions

Answer the following questions to test your knowledge of this chapter:

1. What is the purpose of HTML code? How is an HTML file structured?

2. What is the purpose of CSS code? How is a CSS file structured?

3. What is the purpose of JavaScript code? In general, what makes it one of the most popular web programming languages?

4. How can you include a CSS style sheet or a JavaScript script in an HTML file in PyCharm?

5. What is Emmet? How is it supported by PyCharm?

6. What options are available when it comes to debugging JavaScript in PyCharm?

7. What is the most secure way to deploy a web application from PyCharm?

Building a Dynamic Web Application with Flask

I am fortunate enough to have been around the field of web development since its inception. I was a software engineer before there was a World Wide Web, at least one used by the general public. I remember the first time someone asked me to build a web application. I had to ask what it was. The guy told me, and I remember thinking "Well that's dumb! Why wouldn't people just use CompuServe or **America Online (AOL)** for that?" I thought the internet was going to be, at best, a fad. It was complicated, loaded with jargon, the UI was terrible compared with online services of the day, and it all just seemed kind of janky. I guess I was wrong.

Once I figured that out, I learned HTML and JavaScript. CSS wasn't even a thing yet. It wasn't long before I hit a wall with HTML's capabilities. As you well know, HTML isn't a programming language. It is a content markup language that controls the presentation of static content. The earliest version of JavaScript wasn't very useful. You could validate forms. That's about it. Dynamic content generation with JavaScript wasn't a feature until HTML 3 came out.

Like I said, I hit a wall. I needed to take user interaction data from the browser and use it to interact with a database, generate files, and more. With HTML and JavaScript, this simply wasn't possible. I needed a backend language. Initially, that was the C language. Even that was limited. You had to write modules in C that could interoperate with the Apache web server using an interface called the **common gateway interface (CGI)**.

So that was it for the first few years. Writing dynamic web applications was hard, and nothing like the capabilities of today. New languages and paradigms emerged to make the practice of web development more accessible. My first good experience was with a product called **Cold Fusion**. This program consisted of a framework that effectively replaced the CGI development requirements and allowed you to create scripts in a custom language, called **Cold Fusion Markup Language (CFML)**. It was a mixture of HTML markup and specialized tags. The web server would recognize files with a `.cfml` extension and process those files differently than normal HTML files. I was able to access an Oracle database very easily and, coupled with a lot of long nights and the creativity of my youth, I created some graphics pipeline software that garnered my employer a software patent.

CFML was part of a growing trend. The same technology was employed by lots of other nascent companies and stacks, including the following:

- Microsoft created **Active Server Pages (ASP Classic)**

- Sun Microsystems introduced **Java Server Pages (JSP)**

- **Hypertext Preprocessor (PHP)**

- The **National Center for Supercomputing Applications (NCSA)** created **Server -side Includes (SSIs)**, which were not as feature-rich as the others in this list, but nevertheless existed as a way to generate dynamic content

In this chapter, we're going to take a quantum leap forward and look at a more modern framework for creating dynamic content, which is generated on the server side rather than the client side within the browser. Specifically, we'll be looking at a framework called **Flask**, a popular, unopinionated solution for creating web applications in Python. By the end of this chapter, you will understand the following:

- The basics of web development such as **client-server architecture**, and the stateless **request-response model** employed by the web

- What Flask is, and how it compares to other Python frameworks for web development

- How to create a Flask application in PyCharm

- How to work with **Jinja2** templates in PyCharm, which are used to serve dynamic content mixed with regular HTML markup, CSS styling, and JavaScript interactivity

- How to create a RESTful API endpoint that returns data in JSON format rather than content

- How to use PyCharm's HTTP Requests feature to test your API

Bear in mind, this chapter isn't meant to be a tutorial on Flask. It is a tutorial on how to use PyCharm to work with Flask. If you're looking for a full tutorial on Flask, visit my website at `https://www.maddevskilz.com`. There are several expanded tutorials on Flask that go into a deep dive and entail building entire projects.

Technical requirements

In order to proceed through this chapter, and indeed the rest of the book, you will need the following:

- An installed and working Python interpreter. I'll be using the latest from `https://python.org`.

- Installed copies of `pip` and `virtualenv`. You get these automatically when you install Python on Windows, and macOS has them included on every system. If you are using Linux, you need to install the package managers, such as `pip`, and virtual environment tools, such as `virtualenv`, separately. Our examples will use `pip` and `virtualenv`.

- An installed and working copy of PyCharm. Installation was covered in *Chapter 2, Installation and Configuration*, in case you are jumping into the middle of the book.

- This book's sample source code is from GitHub. We covered cloning the code in *Chapter 2, Installation and Configuration*. You'll find this chapter's relevant code at `https://github.com/PacktPublishing/Hands-On-Application-Development-with-PyCharm---Second-Edition/tree/main/chapter-08`.

Web basics – client-server architecture

When I began my career in IT back in 1991, I worked for a company called **Electronic Data Systems (EDS)**. It was a different era. Back then, any serious computing was performed by monolithic systems called **mainframes**. Imagine a mainframe computer as an incredibly powerful and large-scale computer that existed before the era of personal computers and smartphones. It was like a supercomputer, capable of handling massive amounts of data and performing complex computations.

Mainframe computers were typically housed in specially designed rooms or data centers because they required a lot of space and specialized power and cooling systems to function properly. The typical mainframe was usually about the size of a minivan while its separate **Power Distribution Unit** (PDU) was roughly twice the size of a typical clothes dryer. The **Direct Access Storage Device** (DASD) was in yet another similarly large rectangular metal box. Connecting these various components were heavy cables about the diameter of a spent paper towel roll. Models from IBM's Z14 series weighed between 2,500 and 4,000 kg (5,500 and 8,800 lbs).

In the past, mainframe computers were commonly used by large organizations, such as banks, government agencies, universities, and large corporations. They were responsible for processing and managing huge volumes of data, running critical business applications, and supporting the operations of entire enterprises. In my case, I worked with the IBM mainframe systems responsible for running the automotive assembly line operations for **General Motors** (GM), among others.

Mainframes were known for their reliability, security, and high-performance capabilities. They could handle multiple tasks simultaneously and provide fast response times, even when dealing with extensive workloads. People would access mainframes through terminals or other connected devices to perform tasks or retrieve information.

With the advancement of technology and the emergence of personal computers, the role of mainframes has evolved. While they still play a vital role in certain industries, many of the computing tasks that were once exclusive to mainframes are now handled by distributed systems, relatively cheap rack-mounted Intel and IBM Power-based systems, cloud computing, and smaller devices such as laptops and smartphones.

Mainframes were, and I suppose still are, very expensive to own and operate. Not only was the hardware expensive but it also generally took a team of expert computer operators and maintainers to keep the system running. The cost was out of reach for all but the largest corporations and universities.

Smaller companies and even smaller nations had to buy time on other people's mainframes to gain access to computing at scale. This, in fact, was the service rendered by EDS. We had acres of space in several very large data centers located throughout the world, and we sold time and provided services to nearly all of the Fortune 500 companies. The cost eventually, along with the implications of Moore's Law, led to the downfall of the mainframe.

Moore's Law is an observation and projection made by Gordon Moore, the co-founder of Intel Corporation, in 1965. It states that the number of transistors on a microchip doubles approximately every two years, leading to a significant increase in computing power and performance while reducing the cost of electronic devices.

Moore originally noted that this exponential growth in transistor density had been occurring since the invention of the integrated circuit, and he predicted that it would continue for the foreseeable future. Over the years, Moore's Law has held remarkably true, with advancements in semiconductor manufacturing technology allowing for increasingly smaller transistors and more complex integrated circuits.

The doubling of transistor density every two years has had profound implications for the field of computing. It has enabled the development of more powerful and efficient computers, with increased processing speed, memory capacity, and storage capabilities. As more transistors can be packed onto a chip, the overall performance of electronic devices has improved while their physical size has decreased.

As computers became smaller, and chip architectures such as **Reduced Instruction Set Computing** (**RISC**) and eventually Intel's x86 architecture appeared, a new model of computing emerged: **client-server**.

Mainframes were centralized and accessed using "dumb" terminals. These terminals had no compute capability, no storage, and only enough memory to maintain a communications buffer to send whatever you typed on the keyboard to the mainframe for processing.

Client-server architecture shifted some of the compute, storage, and memory to a local client, which was usually a PC. The client was connected via a **local area network** (**LAN**) to a server, which was generally more powerful than a PC and capable of running enterprise-grade computing loads. You typically had client software, which was composed of a desktop user interface running on the PC's operating system. The client software interfaced with centralized software running on the server.

Besides client and server hardware, one final piece came into existence around the same time: a standardized network protocol known as **Transmission Control Protocol/Internet Protocol** (**TCP/IP**). I was in college before TCP/IP and in order to interact with the University of Oklahoma's mainframe, I had to keep a stack of floppy disks on hand that held an odd, mismatched collection of communication protocols. Some systems used a protocol called **Kernel for Efficient, Remote, and Multiple Computer Interactions** (**KERMIT**). I also had disks for *XMODEM*, *YMODEM*, and *ZMODEM*. Depending on which type of computer I wanted to access, I had to employ a different protocol. TCP/IP changed all that with a standard set of protocols supported by everything from mainframes and PCs to modern smartphones and internet-connected toasters.

If this sounds like the internet to you, you'd be right – but with a few caveats:

- The client server was very slow, and often not even full duplex, meaning data could only flow in one direction at a time.

- Most client programs did not have a real GUI and didn't support mouse interactions. They were known as "green screen" interfaces because they were rendered using textual menus on monochrome screens that were often green. Later thick-client applications had real GUIs usually written in Java, Visual Basic, C++, or Delphi. They were called thick because the size of the program was large enough that downloading the GUI could take many hours over a typical connection. This sits in stark contrast to a typical web application running on the modern internet.

- The client software was always designed around a specialized set of use cases. In contrast, web browsers today, which comprise the client, can be used to run any kind of software from general word processing applications to specific lines of business applications.

The web is the natural evolution in client server architecture. Lightweight client software, the web browser, connects to a centralized server where the bulk of the real work is handled using universally accepted networking protocols.

Exploring the request-response mechanism in HTTP – how clients and servers communicate

One of the great accomplishments of the 1980s, besides CFC-laden hairspray, was the development of a universal set of networking protocols known as TCP/IP. In case you are new to this, the correct way to pronounce this is as letters: *tea sea pea eye pea*. The slash is silent, just like it is with ninjas.

It took a while for it to be universally adopted, but ultimately it was, and the protocols of TCP/IP form the basis of the modern web. While there are many useful protocols serving a myriad of functions, I want to focus your attention on the **Hypertext Transfer Protocol** (**HTTP**). You can go ahead and include the secure counterpart, *HTTPS*, where the *S* stands for *secure*. They effectively work the same way, except that HTTPS is encrypted.

The request-response mechanism entails a chain of events that describes a conversation that happens between the web browser or client, and the web server. You can watch this conversation unfold in *Figure 8.1*.

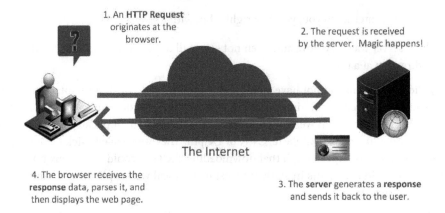

1. An **HTTP Request** originates at the browser.

2. The request is received by the server. Magic happens!

The Internet

4. The browser receives the **response** data, parses it, and then displays the web page.

3. The **server** generates a **response** and sends it back to the user.

Figure 8.1: The request-response mechanism in HTTP conveys a request from a browser to the server, which computes a response and sends it back to the browser

The request-response mechanism used by HTTP is the fundamental communication pattern between clients, such as web browsers or mobile applications, and servers on the World Wide Web. It works like this:

1. **An HTTP request originates from the browser**: The process begins when a client sends an HTTP request to a server. The request consists of a specific HTTP method, such as GET, POST, PUT, or DELETE, which indicates the desired action to be performed on the server's resources, along with additional headers and, in some cases, a request body that carries data.

2. **The request is received by the server**: Upon receiving the request, the server processes the information provided in the request. This may involve accessing databases, performing calculations, or executing other server-side operations based on the nature of the request. The simplest request is one for an HTML document, or other file that is simply returned.

3. **The server generates a response and sends it back to the user**: After processing the request, the server generates an HTTP response. The response contains an appropriate status code indicating the outcome of the request. For example, a request that is successful bears a status code in the response header of 200. If you request a resource on the server that isn't there, you'll get a 404 code signaling the resource was not found. The response header also includes additional fields providing more information and a response body that contains the requested data or any relevant information.

4. **The browser receives the response data**: The client receives the HTTP response from the server and processes the information contained within it. This could involve rendering HTML content, processing data, or performing other actions based on the response.

5. **Request-response cycle is complete**: With the response received, the request-response cycle is complete. The client may choose to send additional requests to the server to perform further interactions, or the process may end.

This request-response mechanism forms the basis of how information is exchanged between clients and servers over HTTP. It allows clients to request resources or perform actions on the server, and the server responds with the corresponding results or necessary information. This cycle enables the dynamic and interactive nature of web applications and services.

One thing to remember is that HTTP is stateless. This means that every request-response cycle is discrete. There is no native way in HTTP to share or retain data between requests.

What is Flask?

Flask is an unopinionated framework for working with the request-response mechanism found in HTTP. It does one thing and only one thing: it helps you receive requests into a simple Python object structure, then craft responses using Python code.

Let's go back to the word *unopinionated*. By this, I mean Flask by design only handles the request-response cycle. I realize I said that already, but it bears repeating. When you compare Flask to its virtual antithesis, which is Django, the difference is stark.

Django is extremely opinionated about how you create your web application. Django dictates the file structure, the application patterns, and the database to be used. It features its own object relational mapper, its own request response mechanism, and its own set of coding conventions. In short, Django will dictate your stack and most of the architectural details for your project.

Flask proffers some suggestions, but they are not set in stone, and you don't have to use them if you don't want to. A few years ago, I re-wrote my company's flagship software product, Visual Storage Intelligence (see `https://www.visualstorageintelligence.com`) as a Flask application strictly because it is unopinionated. I consider myself an expert at selecting the best stack given my knowledge, experience, and understanding of my company's business requirements.

For example, I pretty much never use an ORM. I have deep expertise in SQL and relational database systems. I can write and tune queries, stored procedures, and views to build a fast, responsive web application in a variety of commercial and open source databases. An ORM is designed to take all that out of your hands and give you a layer of abstraction above the database so a developer need only deal with objects.

An ORM is effectively a black box. Most developers don't know how it works or how to improve the performance of the queries the ORM generates. To me, it's just overhead. Personally, I would rather build and tweak those guts myself. Incidentally, if any of these database-related terms are mystifying to you, stay tuned. I'll talk a lot more about databases in *Chapter 11, Understanding Database Management with PyCharm*.

The point is, Flask doesn't care how I interact with my database. It doesn't care about how I structure my application, and it doesn't care what my stack looks like. It only does two things, and one of them is optional.

Request-response handling and routing with Werkzeug

The first thing Flask does for us is to make dealing with the request-response mechanism in HTTP very easy. Strictly speaking, an inbound request is binary in nature. As developers, we would really rather deal with text-like object abstractions of binary structures. Dealing with binary anything directly is soooo 1939. Thankfully, there is a Python library that handles this called Werkzeug.

The library's name, "Werkzeug," is derived from the German language, where it translates to "tool" or "instrument." The Flask framework, including its underlying utility library, Werkzeug, was originally developed by Armin Ronacher, a German software developer.

The name "Werkzeug" was chosen to reflect the nature of the library as a versatile and powerful toolset for building web applications. Just as a craftsperson relies on a set of tools to create and shape their work, developers can leverage Werkzeug to handle various aspects of web development, such as routing, request handling, and HTTP utilities. Flask builds on top of Werkzeug; it adds additional abstractions and features to provide a lightweight and user-friendly web framework.

Flask uses Werkzeug's functionalities to handle the low-level details of HTTP requests and responses, allowing developers to focus on building web applications quickly and efficiently. The effect is the ability to create web applications as simple as you would create any other Python application: you create functions to handle an incoming HTTP request, which returns a properly formatted HTTP response. If you can write a function in Python, you can create a web application.

The implementation in Flask looks like this:

```
@app.route('/hello')
def hello_world():
  return 'Hello, World!'
```

As you can see, this is a simple Python function that takes no arguments and returns a string. The only thing odd about it is the decoration above the function definition. We'll learn a lot more about this later. For now, understand that this decoration matches a route on your application's URL. You are used to typing in a URL with the usual syntax of `https://www.maddevskilz.com/`, which would take you to the root document of the website at that address. In the preceding code block, our function would answer any web request made to `https://www.maddevskilz.com/hello` with the string `'Hello, World!'`. Naturally, you'll learn to do more than deal with a simple request like this, but my point remains: if you can create a function in Python, you can write a web application!

Using this feature of Flask is non-negotiable. If you don't want to use this abstraction of Werkzeug, then you don't want to use Flask. Flask is, again, unopinionated, meaning this is really the only thing it "cares" about. We'll see a contrast in *Chapter 12, Building a Web Application in Django*. Django is highly opinionated. It wants you to use its pre-defined stack. Flask doesn't care. It does, however, make one strong suggestion that you can safely ignore if you'd like.

Templating with Jinja2

Flask does come with a default suggestion regarding a templating library called Jinja2. When you install Flask, you get Jinja2 as a dependency. Templating systems are designed to allow you to inject content into a markup document. Here is an example of a Jinja2 script that generates some items in an unordered list on an HTML page:

```
from jinja2 import Template

# Define the template
template_str = '''
<ul>
{% for item in items %}
  <li>{{ item }}</li>
{% endfor %}
</ul>
'''
```

The template is just a string that contains some special characters indicating where Python-like code is to be executed. This is how all templating languages work, from classic ASP to JSP to PHP. The Flask process gets the request from the web server. It parses the request, and here we're rendering the response with our template. The template itself is a markup fragment. A variable called `template_str` is created and set to an empty string. Remember, this isn't Python code, it's Python-like code because it exists within the context of markup. The single quotes are escaped by single quotes, meaning `` is interpreted as a single quote in the code.

As you can see, we have a `for` loop iterating over some list called `items`, which will be passed into the template as data. The code in the template is delineated with `{%` and `%}`. Each `<li>` has an expression bound in double curly braces. In this case, the expression is just the iterating variable item defined with the loop.

In my example, the template string is defined in the code, but in real life, the template is usually in a file since that is much easier to maintain. Next, we create the `template` object and pass the `template` string into the template constructor:

```
# Create the Jinja2 template object
template = Template(template_str)
```

Now, we're back to being in plain Python code. We'll make a list called `items` and populate it:

```
# Generate the list of items
items = ['Item 1', 'Item 2', 'Item 3', 'Item 4', 'Item 5', 'Item 6',
'Item 7', 'Item 8', 'Item 9', 'Item 10']
```

Now, we render `template`, which produces a new string set to a variable called `output`:

```
# Render the template with the items
output = template.render(items=items)
```

Here we are printing the output, but in the context of a Flask application, the output would be returned as the response:

```
# Print the rendered output
print(output)
```

Jijna2 has a robust set of language features common to most good templating systems. Remember though that Flask bills itself as *unopinionated*. You don't have to use Jinja2. There are other templating libraries out there, or you can forgo the use of a template system entirely. In my company's product, *Visual Storage Intelligence*, I used Jinja2 for version 4 of the product. At the time, I didn't know Python very well and was used to Microsoft's MVC template for C# web applications. I limited my learning curve to meet my deadline. Jinja2 is not difficult to learn at all. It is mostly HTML with some extra syntax. In version 5 of the product, I went back and replaced the UI layer of the application with a React frontend. This didn't require any changes to the Flask application beyond deleting the templates that I no longer used.

> **Reminder – this isn't a book on Flask**
>
> I've spent some time going over the high-level basics of Flask in case you are encountering this as a web development novice. While it may appear that I'm about to teach you Flask, I only intend to cover the features of Flask development as they relate to PyCharm. While we will be building a project, I won't be doing any really deep dives on how and why the code is what it is.
>
> As such, if you are indeed a novice and you are intrigued by the intentionally tacit coverage of Flask I'm providing here and you'd like a proper tutorial, I will include more in-depth resources in the *Further reading* section at the end of this chapter.

A note on naming files and folders

Before we get further into creating the next project, I want to give you some advice based on a principle I always point out to my students. **The internet abhors spaces**. Spaces are not allowed in URLs as-is because they are reserved characters. When you include a space in a URL, it needs to be URL-encoded as %20 to be considered valid. Web servers automatically handle this encoding, but manually encoding spaces can lead to readability issues in URLs, and it can cause issues when trying to run your projects on your local computer.

In a web project, most of your project paths will become URLs at some point. This can happen even when your project isn't even intended for the web. To add to the problem, different operating systems treat characters differently in their filesystems. Windows filenames are case insensitive. If you name your file or folder MyProject, and then try to create a folder called myproject, you'll get a collision since the folder already exists, despite the difference in upper and lowercase letters in the name. On Linux and macOS, file and folder names are case sensitive. It is totally fine to have MyProject and myproject together in the same folder.

My suggestion in all of this is to pick a standard you like and use it. For Python projects, the most common convention is to name your files with **snake_case**, so named for its use in Python. Snake case involves using all lowercase letters and substituting an underscore character wherever you would normally find a space. You would never create a project in a folder called `MyProject`. Instead, you would call it `my_project`.

With that said, most of my projects in this book are named with the PyCharm defaults, which are often rendered in camel or Pascal case. In these case standards, typically employed by Java and C# developers, spaces are omitted and the boundary between words is emphasized using capital letters. `myProject` and `MyProject` would be an example of camel and Pascal case respectively. I suspect the use of camel case in the project name defaults probably comes from the fact that PyCharm's ancestry is a Java IDE. Other strategies exist for eliminating spaces in code files. Kebab case is common in JavaScript development and uses dashes instead of underscores. `MyProject` becomes `my-project`.

I heartily recommend breaking any habit of using spaces in any of your folder or file names in your coding practice. This includes any upstream folders such as your operating system's home folder.

Creating a Flask application in PyCharm Professional

The tooling for Flask is a feature found only in the Professional edition of PyCharm. Naturally, you can make a Flask app in the free version of PyCharm, but you'll be on your own in terms of creating the files and setting up run profiles, special debugging, and so on.

To create a Flask App in PyCharm, just select **File | New Project** and select the **Flask** template, as shown in *Figure 8.2*.

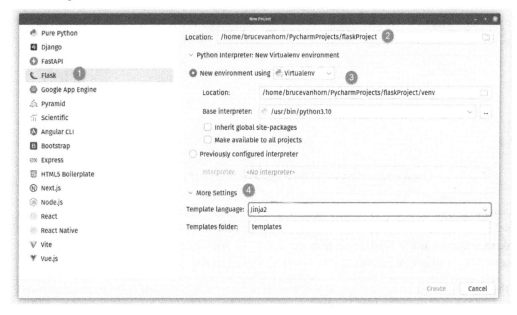

Figure 8.2: To create a new Flask project in PyCharm Professional,
choose the template from the New Project dialog

I've numbered the most important parts in *Figure 8.2*:

1. In the **New Project** dialog of PyCharm Professional, you'll find a template for **Flask** projects.

2. This part is no different than any project we've done so far. Fill in the location for the project.

3. Create your virtual environment. Once everything is filled in, PyCharm creates and activates the virtual environment and installs Flask and its dependencies.

4. This section is unique to Flask projects. I mentioned that Flask encourages the use of the Jinja2 templating engine. You can choose to leave it out and PyCharm will take care of that for you. There is also a setting for the folder you want to use for your Jinja2 templates. We're going to keep the defaults and I recommend if you are going to use Jinja2 templates that you leave the settings as they are because that is where most developers will expect them.

Once you have everything filled in, click the **Create** button at the bottom of the dialog and PyCharm will set up your project for you, including the creation of some starter code, as seen in *Figure 8.3*.

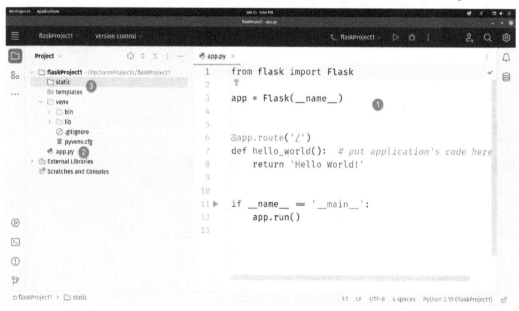

Figure 8.3: PyCharm generates your Flask project automatically

At position **(1)** we see the code PyCharm generated. It is basically the `Hello World` idiom from earlier, except this one is responding to the root route of your web application. At the top, we import Flask, then we instantiate Flask as the `app` variable. Now that you know that, the decoration for the route on *line 6* makes more sense; `app.route` is simply coming from the `app` instance of Flask.

All this code is contained in `app.py` at position **(2)** of *Figure 8.3*. The name isn't a requirement, and you can change it if you'd like. You can also see, at position **(3)**, that PyCharm has generated two folders for Jinja2 templates and static files such as your images, CSS, and JavaScript files.

Creating a dynamic web application

The Hello World program generated by PyCharm is a good starting point for new applications. It provides you with some nice cognitive prompting in case it's been a while since you created the Flask application from scratch. Naturally, we'll be wanting to replace Hello World with something a tad more useful.

Let's create a very simple application for cataloging new Python libraries! This kind of project is usually done with a database, but it doesn't have to be. Our app is going to hold a list of Python libraries along with their description and a rating from 1-5 on how useful we think they are. To accomplish the database part, we're going to simply use an in-memory array of lists. Using this approach prevents the need to do a deep dive on the database features of PyCharm, which isn't coming until *Chapter 11, Understanding Database Management with PyCharm*. We'll also exercise every excuse to cover some features we've covered earlier in a practical setting, such as using the HTML features from the last chapter.

Setting up the static parts

The easiest place to start when building a web application is to get the static parts working. I'm talking about the non-dynamic parts of the application such as the index.html page with its basic structure, any CSS, images, and JavaScript we might need.

Start off by right-clicking in the Templates folder and creating a new file called index.html. This is going to be a Jinja2 template, so it belongs in the Templates folder rather than the static folder.

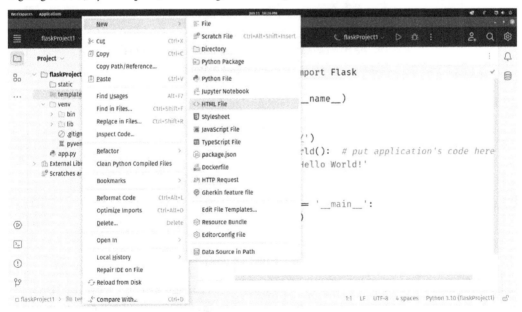

Figure 8.4: Right-clicking the Templates folder and creating a new HTML file

Note that we created a plain HTML file. There is no special file type for a Jinja2 file. The file is created using the Emmet templating system we covered in *Chapter 7, Web Development with JavaScript, HTML, and CSS*. As you hopefully remember, **Emmet** is a templating language for generating code, particularly HTML. It provides a design-time template that provides a "fill-in-the-blank" approach. When you added the HTML file, you found the code was generated but the IDE took you straight to the `title` attribute in the HTML file, allowing you to fill in that blank spot in the HTML template. You can see mine in *Figure 8.5*.

Figure 8.5: The HTML creation template puts your cursor in the
title tag so you can fill in that part of the page

Next, let's modify the contents of the `<head>` tag like this:

```
<head>
  <meta charset="UTF-8">
  <link href="https://cdn.jsdelivr.net/npm/bootstrap@5.3
  .0/dist/css/bootstrap.min.css" rel="stylesheet"
      integrity="sha384-9ndCyUaIbzAi2FUVXJi0CjmCapSmO7SnpJef0486qhLnuZ2
cdeRhO02iuK6FUUVM"
      crossorigin="anonymous">
  <title>Python Libraries R Us</title>
</head>
```

This brings in the bootstrap CSS and JavaScript libraries from a **content delivery network (CDN)**. If you don't want to type all that in, you can copy the code from the book's repository code, or you can go to `https://getbootstrap.com` and find the latest in the **Getting Started** section of their site, which usually includes copyable links to their CDN.

We're using the CDN so we don't need to keep these common files in our project. Besides, CDNs usually serve these kinds of files faster than will your own web server once you move your amazing app into production.

Next, change the contents of the `<body>` tag to the following:

```
<body>
   <h1>Python Libraries R Us</h1>
   <h2>All the libraries that are fit to use!</h2>
</body>
```

Next, we're going to use the Emmet feature we learned about in *Chapter 7, Web Development with JavaScript, HTML, and CSS,* to generate an HTML table header. Type this Emmet code into the editor on a new line just below the `<h2>` tag:

```
table>thead>tr>th*4
```

This abbreviation will generate a table, followed by a `thead` tag, with one table row (`tr`) and four table head fields (`th*4`). Press *Tab* to expand the abbreviation. PyCharm's Emmet plugin will generate your code and take you straight to the contents of the `th` tags, as shown in *Figure 8.6*.

Figure 8.6: Emmet expands the code into all the code you need for the table header

Once Emmet has expanded your code, you'll see the prompts inside the th tags allowing you to edit the content, as shown in *Figure 8.7*.

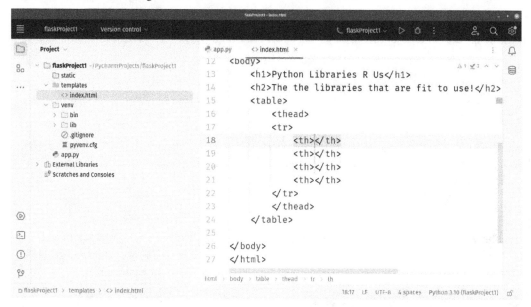

Figure 8.7: Emmet expands the shorthand in line 15 in Figure 8.6 to what we see here

Traditionally, you'd use **Tab** to move between the fields, but in PyCharm, the *Tab* key is bound to the action that expands Emmet, as we just saw. You can't use *Tab* to navigate as you'd expect if you're coming from a different Emmet-enabled editor. Instead, you'll need to find out what the shortcut is on your system since this will depend on which keyboard shortcut layout you configured when you installed PyCharm. I chose the Windows layout, so for me, moving between the fields is done using *Alt + Shift +]*.

Inside the first th tag, type Library Name. Then use *Alt + Shift +]* to move to the next field and change it to Description. The third field will be called Rating and the fourth is titled URL.

If *Alt + Shift +]* doesn't do it for you, let's find out what will. Go into PyCharm's settings and find the **Keymap** settings as shown in *Figure 8.8*.

I've typed Emmet into the search box and I can see that my **Navigate** > **Next / Previous Emmet Edit Point** settings are **Alt + Shift +]** and **Alt + Shift + [**, respectively. If yours are different, you'll see what they are here, and as we've learned, you can change them to anything you'd like so long as the change doesn't conflict with something else.

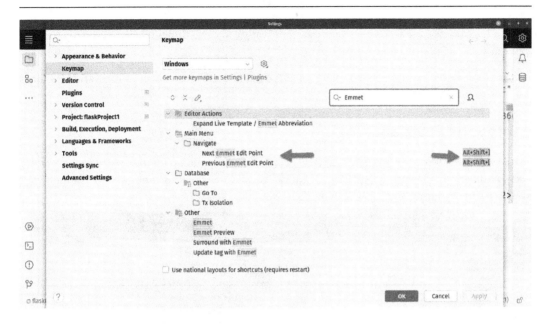

Figure 8.8: Your Emmet navigation settings are found and set here in Settings

At this stage, your HTML `table` code should look like this:

```
<table>
    <thead>
    <tr>
      <th>Library Name</th>
      <th>Description</th>
      <th>Rating</th>
      <th>URL</th>
    </tr>
    </thead>

    </table>
```

Let's add one more thing to the `table` code. Put this below the `</thead>` closure but before the `</table>` closure:

```
<tbody>
  <tr>
    <td colspan="4">No libraries to display</td>
  </tr>
</tbody>
```

If your code got messy, use PyCharm's reformat code feature to clean things up. This is usually *Ctrl + Alt + L*, or *Cmd + Opt + L* on a Mac.

We have a basic web page laid out. Before we make it dynamic, let's create a run configuration for the app so we can preview our handiwork.

Running the Flask app

When we created our project, PyCharm created a Flask run configuration for us. Let's take a look at it so we can understand how the app will be run by PyCharm. Click the **Run configuration** dropdown and click **Edit Configurations…**, as seen in *Figure 8.9*.

Figure 8.9: Editing the run configurations so we can see what they're made of

The settings look like those shown in *Figure 8.10*.

Figure 8.10: Flask run configuration generated by PyCharm

Most of these settings will be familiar now, so only a few are marked.

There are a couple of ways to run a Flask app. The easiest is to just run the app.py file, which is the **Script path** option at (**1**). Because PyCharm generated a dunder-main line that runs the app, this works just fine. Recall the code at the bottom of app.py:

```
if __name__ == '__main__':
    app.run()
```

You can also run it using the module name, but let's stick with what PyCharm generated for now.

At position (**2**), the FLASK_DEBUG environment variable gets its own checkbox. When you check this box, it puts the dedicated Flask development server into debug mode, which yields several benefits. The greatest of these is that the app server will restart whenever you change the code. This saves you from having to remember to stop and restart the server every time you make a change. Generally speaking, you want this box checked. Above the check is a commonly used FLASK_ENV environment variable that is also passed to the running app. It defaults to development. You can use this environment variable to turn on and off certain behaviors in your app, including setting log detail levels.

The two PYTHONPATH checkboxes at position (3) add your project folders to the PYTHONPATH folder, which prevents you from getting an error stating Python can't find your application. You want these checked.

Note that with all these checkboxes, PyCharm gives you the ability to set common environment variables that are passed into the running app. This is nice, because setting them at the OS level is extra work that we often forget, and changing environment variables often doesn't work as well as it should depending on your operating system. When you use environment variables at the OS level, you generally need to either reboot or log out and log back in to make sure the new values are active. PyCharm injects variables directly into the running development server, which saves a lot of time and frustration.

Click **OK** to close the run configuration dialog.

Before we fire it up, we need to make a code change to app.py. We need to alter our Hello World code to load and display our template. The altered code looks like this:

```python
from flask import Flask, render_template

app = Flask(__name__)


@app.route('/', methods=["GET"])
def root():
  return render_template("index.html")


if __name__ == '__main__':
  app.run()
```

First, I've added an import for the render_template method from Flask. We'll use this to, you guessed it, render our Jinja2 HTML template.

Next, I've added some code to the route decorator. Previously, we had @app.route('/'), which defines the root route for our site that will be handed by our root function. I've added a second argument, methods=["GET"]. Flask allows you to lock a route to one or more of the HTTP request methods I described earlier in the chapter. Locking Flask application endpoints to a particular HTTP method, such as GET or POST, is a fundamental practice in web development for several important reasons:

- **Security**: Different HTTP methods have different purposes and security implications. For example, GET requests are typically used for retrieving data, and they should not have any side effects on the server. In contrast, POST requests are used for submitting data to the server, and they can have side effects, such as creating, updating, or deleting resources. By restricting endpoints to specific HTTP methods, you can prevent unintended or malicious actions. This is known as "method-based access control."

- **Predictability**: Locking endpoints to specific HTTP methods makes your API or web application more predictable and self-documenting. Other developers (or even your future self) will have a clearer understanding of how to interact with your application. For example, if an endpoint is designed for GET requests, it's clear that it's meant for data retrieval.

- **Consistency**: Consistency in your API design can improve the user experience and reduce confusion. When users or clients know that a specific HTTP method is expected for an endpoint, they are less likely to make incorrect requests.

- **Preventing accidents**: Accidental misuse of an endpoint can lead to unintended consequences. By restricting the allowed HTTP methods, you reduce the chances of UI developers making mistakes, such as trying to delete data with a GET request.

- **Framework support**: Flask, along with many other web frameworks, provides built-in support for routing requests based on HTTP methods. This makes it easier to implement method-based access control, as you can define separate routes and handlers for each HTTP method.

If you look closely, the argument we're passing is an array. You can pass one or more methods allowing one route to handle one or several methods differently. Here, we're locking the `root` route function to the HTTP GET method, which is what your browser issues when you visit a site.

Next, we've added Flask's `render_template` method to our import. I changed the name of the function from `hello_world` to `root`, then I changed the return from the `'Hello World'` string to the result of the `render_template` function that takes the filename of a template. Flask knows to find `index.html` in the `Templates` folder.

Now we're ready to try it out. Make sure your Flask app is selected in the run configuration dropdown and click the green **Run** button. The **Run** tab will appear at the bottom of the PyCharm screen. Mine appears as shown in *Figure 8.11*.

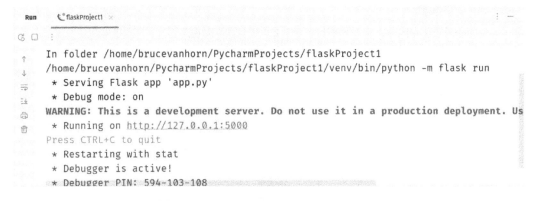

Figure 8.11: The Run window for our Flask app

There are a couple of remarkable elements to point out. The first is the big red warning message. I know, it's gray for you, but you'll see it the first time you try this out. We're running our app using Flask's built-in development web server. Please don't use this in production. Instead, you need to use a production-quality app server such as Green Unicorn. This falls outside the scope of developing with PyCharm, but it is such a huge mistake to deploy your app using the built-in server that I felt it needed to point out and justify this warning being in big red letters.

Second, it tells you the app is running at `http://127.0.0.1:5000`. The address is listed as a hyperlink, which you can click to open your browser. I have mine open in *Figure 8.12.*

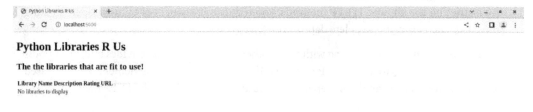

Figure 8.12: It worked, but 1991 just called on the phone and they want their web design back

It is awfully ugly, isn't it? We went to the trouble of adding Bootstrap, the least we can do is use it.

Let's make it look a little better

The page doesn't have much happening in terms of design, and while we won't be building some amazing user experience that might land you a design job at Apple, we can at least make this a little more presentable by adding some Bootstrap classes. We'll be doing this within the `body` tag inside our Jinja2 template, `index.html`.

First, let's set up Bootstrap's layout grid. This allows us to create apps that gracefully adjust to any size screen from the tiniest phone browser to the largest 8K display.

Add this code just inside the `body` tag. When you're done, it should bump up against the `table` code we created earlier:

```
<div class="container-fluid h-100">
  <div class="row">
    <div class="col-12">
      <h1>Python Libraries
        <span class="flipped-letter">R</span> Us</h1>
      <h2>All the libraries that are fit to use!</h2>
      <hr/>
    </div>
  </div>
</div>
```

```
<div class="row">
  <div class="col-8">
    <h5>Here are the libraries:</h5>
```

Here, we've added a `div` marked with the `container-fluid` class. This is going to give us some much-needed layout and padding so our content doesn't slam up against the edges of the browser window. I've also set this to take up the full height available in the browser window in anticipation of there being many useful libraries in our table. I did this with Bootstrap's `h-100` class.

After that, I added a `div` to act as a row followed by one acting as a column. I've set the class on the column to `col-12`, which in Bootstrap means it should take up the full width of the browser window with appropriate margins and padding defined by the `container-fluid` class in the ancestral `div` tag we added earlier.

The next three tags are just content additions – some labeling that explains what the user is seeing using H1 and H2 tags followed by a horizontal rule. I added a CSS class to flip the letter R so it is reminiscent of a popular, yet presently bankrupt toy shop in the US. One more icon from my childhood has bitten the dust. Bear in mind, we haven't created this CSS class yet. We'll do that in just a minute.

Let's add the Bootstrap `.table` class to the table. Change your `table` code by adding `class="table"`:

```
<h5>Here are the libraries:</h5>
        <table class="table">
            <thead>
            <tr>
                <th>Library Name</th>
                <th>Description</th>
                <th>Rating</th>
                <th>URL</th>
            </tr>
```

This will fix up the spacing in and around the table so everything isn't squished together.

To close all this out, we need to add all the necessary closing tags after our table is closed. That's just three nested `div` closures:

```
    </div>
  </div>
</div>
```

The first closes the column, the second closes the row, and the third closes the container. The last step is to add some CSS.

Adding some CSS

Right-click the `static` folder and create a new CSS file called `index.css`. Add the following code to the file:

```css
body {
    margin: 92px;
    height: 100%;
}

.flipped-letter {
  display: inline-block;
  transform: scaleX(-1);
}

.gold-star {
    color: gold;
}
```

In this CSS file, we're adding some extra margin around the page and setting the height to 100% so we don't wind up with a stubby little page that is fully dependent on how much content is in our table.

I added a `flipped-letter` class in `index.css` to flip the letter R in our imaginary site's title. We're going to be displaying a rating for each library. I thought, instead of just a boring old number, we'd put some stars in there. Not just any stars – gold stars! So, there's a class for that, which I called `.gold-star`. If you're new to CSS, the leading dot is significant. It flags the rest, `gold-star` as a custom class. In CSS, a class has nothing to do with object-oriented development, so if you've learned some Java or other class based language, the word *class* is not related to the concepts from those languages. You'll see in a minute when the class is used within the HTML, the dot will be absent. This is not an error.

Now that we have a CSS file in the `static` folder, we need to reference it in the HTML file. Since it is in the static folder, which has special meaning in a Flask app, our code is a little different than a straight CSS reference like those we saw earlier with plain HTML. Add this line of code inside your head tag:

```html
<link href="{{ url_for('static', filename='index.css') }}"
      rel="stylesheet"
      type="text/css">
```

Note the Jinja2 expression that resolves the location of the static folder.

I mentioned a moment ago that I want to use stars to show my ratings. I don't really want to use graphics for this. Instead, I'd rather use a font, specifically **Font Awesome**. Font Awesome is essentially agigantic web font that, instead of containing alphabetical characters, contains hundreds of useful graphical icons useful for making modern UI and website designs. For more information on Font Awesome, see `https://www.fontawesome.com`.

Rather than include Font Awesome in our project, which of course is an option, I'm going to link to a version of it hosted on a **content delivery network (CDN)**. CDNs are a desirable way to host content because they are designed to serve static content with great speed. They do this not only through normal server optimizations but also by strategically positioning servers all over the world. When your page loads static content from a CDN, the request for that content is routed to the closest server. Your users in India will reach a CDN server in India, while users in Kansas (the middle of the United States) will be served the content from a server much closer.

Font Awesome lists its CDN links on its website. I'm going to use a link I have copied from the Font Awesome website and add this to the `head` tag of our page. Since this is coming from a CDN instead of the static folder, I don't need any Jinja2 voodoo magic to resolve it:

```
<link rel="stylesheet"
      href="https://cdnjs.cloudflare.com/ajax/libs/font-awesome/5.15.3/
css/all.min.css">
```

Things should be looking much better! I'll hold off on the revealing screenshot until we've added the dynamic content. I don't want to spoil the big reveal! Don't forget, you can check the final code in the chapter's repository folder cloned from GitHub.

Making the page dynamic

We've created a Flask app and gotten a template working. Let's add dynamism to the page using Flask and Jinja2. We're going to simulate a database using a list of `dicts` with fields that correspond to the fields we've put in our table.

Switch to the `app.py` file and find this line, which should be near line number 3:

```
app = Flask(__name__)
```

This line, which was generated by PyCharm when we created the project, creates an instance of Flask and assigns that instance to a variable called app. We'll begin adding new code below this line. Let's start by creating a global variable to hold our data:

```
library_data = list()
library_data.append({"python_library": "Flask",
          "description": "An unopinionated web framework",
          "rating": 5,
          "url": "https://pypi.org/project/Flask"})
library_data.append({"python_library": "Jinja2",
          "description": "Templating library",
          "rating": 3,
          "url": "https://pypi.org/project/Jinja2"})
```

In general, global variables, especially in a large program, are to be avoided. In this case, we're using the global variable to simulate a database connection, which is generally an exception to the rule.

Here, we're adding a few records to our fake database. If you're a fan of Jinja2, please don't hate me. I rated it a 3 in the content just to have some visual difference between the two sample records.

There's just one more change. Add a second parameter to the `render_template` call:

```
return render_template("index.html", library_data=library_data)
```

The `render_template` method is a **variadic function**. You can pass as many parameters into it as you'd like. Jinja2 will be able to render the passed data in the template. Here, we're just adding one data variable.

We're done with `app.py`! The final code looks like this:

```
from flask import Flask, render_template

app = Flask(__name__)
library_data = list()

library_data.append({"python_library": "Flask",
        "description": "An unopinionated web framework",
        "rating": 5,
        "url": "https://pypi.org/project/Flask"})
library_data.append({"python_library": "Jinja2",
        "description": "Templating library",
        "rating": 3,
        "url": "https://pypi.org/project/Jinja2"})


@app.route('/', methods=['GET'])
def root(): # put application's code here
   return render_template("index.html", library_data=library_data)

if __name__ == '__main__':
   app.run()
```

Now that we're passing some data into the template, we need to go back and modify the `index.html` template to render the data. You need to change the contents of the `tbody` tag to this:

```
<tbody>
        {% if library_data|length > 0 %}
```

The {% and {{ markers in the template are marking out places where logic and content take place. Here, we are checking the length of the array. If it is greater than zero, we're rendering table rows using the contents of the array. Further down, there's an else that will render what we have now, which is a single row stating there is no data:

```
{% for data in library_data %}
  <tr>
    <td>{{ data.python_library }} </td>
    <td>{{ data.description }}</td>
    <td>
      {% for _ in range(data.rating) %}
        <i class="fas fa-star gold-star"></i>
      {% endfor %}
    </td>
    <td><a href="{{ data.url }}"
        target="_blank">View on pypi.org</a></td>
  </tr>
{% endfor %}
```

In the preceding code, we are looping through the library_data list and generating a table row (tr). The table row is then supplied with columns. The {{ }} placeholders denote where contents from the dict from the current list iteration should be placed. The first column shows the contents of data.python_library. The second shows the description.

The third is where we add some razzle-dazzle! We add a code block that loops using a range to generate stars in that column. If the rating is 3, the loop runs 3 times and we get 3 stars!

For the URL, I used the value of data.url as the href attribute on a hyperlink.

That just leaves the else statement I told you about:

```
{% else %}
  <tr>
    <td colspan="4">No libraries to display</td>
  </tr>
{% endif %}
</tbody>
```

To summarize, if we pass in an array with zero elements, Jinja2 will render the row we had before, which states there is no data. If there's data in the array, Jinja2 loops over the array and generates a table row for each row in the data.

Run the project and direct your browser to http://localhost:5000. You'll see a table rendered with two records, as seen in *Figure 8.13*.

Python Libraries Я Us
All the libraries that are fit to use!

Here are the libraries:

Library Name	Description	Rating	URL
Flask	An unopinionated web framework	★ ★ ★ ★ ☆	View on pypi.org
Jinja2	Templating library	★ ★ ★	View on pypi.org

Figure 8.13: The big reveal! Our page is now dynamic

Let's pause for a moment and take stock of how PyCharm has helped us.

Editor enhancements for working with Flask and Jinja2

You've been getting a lot of help during this exercise. If you don't believe me, try repeating this exercise with Vim or Notepad! By now, you're becoming accustomed to how much PyCharm takes off your plate in terms of lightening your cognitive load, and physically handling a lot of typing.

You might not have even noticed the following:

- The HTML editing features, such as syntax highlighting, automatic tag closures, and color-coded indicators for your nested opening and closing tags in the markup.

- We used Emmet to generate some of our markups.

- PyCharm understands Jinja2 syntax and the inspection doesn't freak out when you start putting curly braces everywhere.

- In fact, it auto-closes the curly braces for both `{{ expressions }}` and `{% code blocks %}`.

- If you made any mistakes along the way, you might have noticed that PyCharm's inspections and suggestions clearly understand how to use Flask. It's not simple introspective auto-completion. PyCharm will give you specific assistance tailored to Flask development.

Let's look at a few features that are not so obvious:

- Switch to `app.py`, put your cursor inside the template filename (`index.html`), then press *Ctrl / Cmd + B*. This activates the **Go to declaration** shortcut, which takes you directly to the template file. This also works the other way round. If you place your cursor on the `library_data` variable in the template and press *Ctrl / Cmd + B*, it will take you to the render template call, which passes that variable into Jinja2.

- It shouldn't surprise you that the debugger works in `app.py`. It also works in the Jinja2 template within the code blocks. Place a breakpoint in the `for` loop in the Jinja2 template, `index.html`. Start your app with debug, and the debugger will stop on the loop. You can use the same step-through capabilities as with anything else you are debugging. You can inspect template variables just as you would variables in a normal Python script. Considering Jinja2 is effectively a meta-language, completely distinct from Python, and specialized in what it can do, this is quite remarkable.

- If you made any mistakes, Werkzeug has a nifty error page with links to your stack trace, which includes a trace of your template. PyCharm captures this information and displays it, complete with hyperlinks in the **Run** window. The hyperlinks take you to the code in PyCharm rather than just displaying it as Werkzeug does in the browser window.

- You'll see the same level of support for popular Flask plugins as you do for Jinja2. Flask is designed to be extensible. There is a plethora of plugins to make your life easier in many areas of web development, from REST API development to database ORMs to session handling and authentication. You'll find PyCharm guiding you through development in any Flask development scenario in which you find yourself.

Summary

I've pointed out a few times now that this chapter is a poor tutorial on Flask. We just barely scratched the surface of what Flask can do, but we covered all the ways PyCharm can help you with Flask development and it is one of the few IDEs that provides the level of help and tooling we've seen as we developed this simple project.

For starters, Flask provides an easy way to generate a project structure and starter code for a Flask project. Like any other project, PyCharm sets up your virtual environment and gives you some starter code. When we use the Flask template in PyCharm Professional, PyCharm also installs your project dependencies for you and sets up a specialized run configuration for your project.

Once you get into editing your project, you find all the features we've covered in earlier chapters coming together. The HTML, CSS, and JavaScript-related features work not only with normal HTML projects but also with the Jinja2 templating language native to Flask. We get Flask-specific inspections, code hints, and documentation not just for Flask but also for the extended Flask ecosystem.

We even found we can debug Jinja2 templates as if they were actually Python code! Combine that with some very nice navigational enhancements to help you move between presentation logic and backend logic and you've got an unbeatable combination of power and functionality at your fingertips as a Flask developer.

Flask isn't the only game in town. Newer development models have become popular over the last few years: specifically **single-page apps** (**SPAs**) combined with pure RESTful APIs on the backend. The next chapter focuses on a fast, modern approach to building RESTful APIs using a framework called FastAPI.

As you will see, FastAPI bears some resemblence to Flask but with some important differences. Flask uses a worker model to serve content or data while FastAPI works a little more like NodeJS, which uses an asychronous programming model. FastAPI tends to focus solely on creating RESTful APIs and lacks the templating utilities found in Flask.

Further reading

Be sure to check out the companion website for the book at `https://www.pycharm-book.com`. The site allows me to list newer resources as they become available. The following resources will also be useful:

- Gaspar, D., & Stouffer, J. (2018). *Mastering Flask Web Development: Build Enterprise-grade, Scalable Python Web Applications.* Packt Publishing Ltd.

- Van Horn II, B. (2019). *Building RESTful APIs with Flask.* LinkedIn Learning: `https://www.linkedin.com/learning/building-restful-apis-with-flask/restful-apis-with-python-3-and-flask-4`.

- Van Horn II, B. (2021). MongoDB for Python Developers. MadDevSkilz.com. `https://www.maddevskilz.com/courses/mongodb-for-python-developers`. Note: Despite the title, this is a short tutorial on creating a Flask application that uses MongoDB. It is very similar to, and newer than, my LinkedIn course.

9

Creating a RESTful API with FastAPI

In the last chapter, we learned about a framework called Flask. Flask represents Python in a landscape of traditional web development frameworks designed to generate content on the server and send it back to the browser. This is how we have developed web applications for decades. The 2010s brought a paradigm shift, but it didn't happen overnight.

In 2004, the term **AJAX**, an acronym for **Asynchronous JavaScript and XML**, was coined by Jesse James Garrett in an article titled *Ajax: A New Approach to Web Applications*. This article helped popularize the concept and techniques of asynchronous web applications. By 2005, mainstream browsers all supported a new **XMLHttpRequest** (**XHR**) web API call. The feature allowed a developer to request pure data instead of a generated HTML page with the data integrated with markup.

The rise of **single-page applications** (**SPAs**) in the 2010s was closely associated with the advancement of JavaScript frameworks such as AngularJS (now Angular), React, and Vue.js. These provided developers with the tools and capabilities to build dynamic, interactive web applications differently from traditional applications, which make requests for HTML and data at the same time. SPAs load all their markup, CSS, and JavaScript in a single request. After that, the app uses XHR to request data, and in response to the data received and the user's interactions, the developer used JavaScript to show and hide different elements in the user experience rather than re-rendering the entire page each time there was a change in data or a user interaction.

AngularJS, released by Google in 2010, played a significant role in popularizing the concept of SPAs. It introduced a declarative approach to building web applications, allowing developers to create rich, responsive user interfaces without the need for full-page reloads. AngularJS provided a solid foundation for building SPAs, and its success inspired the development of other JavaScript frameworks that further refined and improved the SPA development experience.

React, developed by Facebook and released in 2013, also contributed to the popularity of SPAs. React introduced a component-based architecture that made it easier to manage the state and UI components of an application. React's virtual **DOM (Document Object Model)** diffing algorithm and efficient rendering mechanism made it well suited for building fast and scalable SPAs.

Vue.js, created by Evan You and released in 2014, gained popularity as a lightweight and approachable framework for building SPAs. It offered a gentle learning curve and provided a flexible and intuitive way to build user interfaces.

Overall, the combination of these JavaScript frameworks, along with advancements in browser technologies and APIs, led to the rise of SPAs in the early 2010s onward. SPAs today continue to provide a more seamless and responsive user experience by dynamically updating content on a single web page, eliminating the need for full page reloads, and providing a more app-like feel to web applications.

We could certainly create an SPA backend using Flask, but it might not be the best choice. This is especially true if you expect your application's user base to be large. Flask is criticized as being a bit slow when you have server requests at high volume. Thankfully, there are other players in the game, and in this chapter, we're going to focus on FastAPI.

The interesting thing about FastAPI is the way it handles web requests. Most products, including Flask, use a worker model. A pool of workers is responsible for servicing multiple incoming requests on separate processes managed by the operating system. FastAPI uses an **asynchronous programming** model. In the realm of asynchronous programming, functions are invoked, but the immediate return of outcomes is not guaranteed. Let's explore the following illustrative Python code:

```
async def add_two(a: int, b: int) -> int:
    return a + b
```

When calling add_two in a synchronous programming context, the execution thread halts until the function is completed and the outcome is furnished. However, the mechanics differ when employing asynchronous programming. An asynchronous invocation doesn't halt the invoking thread. Instead, the calling thread persists in execution after obtaining a **coroutine**, which is linked to an event. In simpler terms, a coroutine signifies that a certain task will be carried out later, subsequent to some triggering event. In our scenario, we pledge to provide the sum of a + b once this computation has been executed. It's important to acknowledge that this may not happen instantaneously, but during the computation, other operations remain unblocked. Naturally, performing an addition of integers is likely to conclude swiftly.

Consider an alternative scenario where a request is made to a networked resource, such as fetching a web page. The speed of response is no longer solely contingent on the processor's execution speed. It encompasses factors such as computer performance, network latency, and various other elements that might introduce delays ranging from seconds to even minutes. This is particularly true for those who don't reside in well-connected urban areas with high-speed internet access. Since the asynchronous software doesn't block, it can serve many requests serially since none of them are waiting for the previous function call or, in this case, web request, to finish. You can think of it as a restaurant with one waiter. You submit your order serially with other diners, but the cook only returns your food when it has been cooked. With this expectation set, the cook is free to cook as many dishes at once as their stove allows, and there is an implicit promise given that once your food is cooked, the waiter will bring it to you. Someone who orders a glass of juice might get their order back immediately, whereas your baked Alaska will take a little longer to produce.

A synchronous restaurant, by contrast, would employ, say, eight cooks. Eight orders can come in at once, but each cook is completely dedicated to fixing that one order until it is complete. As it turns out, the throughput, at least for computers, is often faster when employing the asynchronous model for typical web request workloads.

In Python 3.4, we got a new module called `asyncio`, which brought asynchronous programming features to our favorite language. Three years later, we found the first GitHub commit to a library project called **Starlette**. Starlette is an asynchronous web framework for building high-performance applications with Python. It provides the core functionality for handling HTTP requests and responses in an efficient manner. Starlette is known for its simplicity, speed, and support for modern Python features, making it an ideal foundation for building web applications. Like Werkzeug, though, which powers Flask, Starlette was only meant to be a foundation. This chapter covers **FastAPI**, a framework built on top of Starlette that represents a full implementation of a web framework specializing in the development of **RESTful Application Programming Interfaces** (**REST APIs**) Where Flask used a worker model, FastAPI uses an asynchronous model, and where Flask was designed to create traditional round trip, template-driven content generation, FastAPI normally used the SPAs to handle serving data in the form of **JavaScript Object Notation (JSON)**.

I realize we just introduced a lot of jargon, which may be new to Python developers who aren't normally web developers. We'll explain our terminology in context as we cover building a simple FastAPI project using PyCharm.

By the end of this chapter, you will be able to do the following:

- Explain the difference between a traditional template-driven content generation system such as Flask and one that strictly serves data

- Describe the stateless nature of HTTP (and HTTPS) along with how **representational state transfer** (**REST**) is used to mitigate the lack of state in HTTP

- Create a FastAPI project using the built-in template provided in PyCharm Professional

- Perform tests on your FastAPI project using PyCharm's HTTP REST client

- Create a React frontend application in a separate but connected (attached) project in PyCharm, allowing you to develop a full stack application without mingling the frontend JavaScript code with the backend Python code

- Manage multiple run configurations and debug the entire request-response pipeline in PyCharm's debugger

Bear in mind that this chapter isn't meant to be a full tutorial on either FastAPI or React. The core purpose of this book is to teach PyCharm within the context of creating applications. Our coverage of FastAPI might be tacit, whereas our coverage of PyCharm as a tool to make an application with FastAPI will be very complete.

Technical requirements

In order to proceed through this chapter, and indeed the rest of the book, you will need the following:

- An installed and working Python interpreter. I'll be using the latest from `https://python.org`.

- Installed copies of `pip` and `virtualenv`. You get these automatically when you install Python on Windows, and macOS has them included on every system. If you are using Linux, you need to install the package managers, such as `pip`, and virtual environment tools, such as `virtualenv`, separately. Our examples will be using `pip` and `virtualenv`.

- An installed and working copy of PyCharm. Installation was covered in *Chapter 2*, *Installation and Configuration*, in case you are jumping into the middle of the book.

- This book's sample source code is from GitHub. We covered cloning the code in *Chapter 2*, *Installation and Configuration*. You'll find this chapter's relevant code at `https://github.com/PacktPublishing/Hands-On-Application-Development-with-PyCharm---Second-Edition/tree/main/chapter-09`.

There is no REST in a wicked stateless world

I've heard it said that computers are the dumbest creatures on the planet. They only do exactly as they are told, and they take your instructions in an extremely literal way. This is what makes programming a computer so difficult. You must choose exactly the right syntax and structure your ideas precisely and succinctly because any ambiguity will result in a bug.

There is only one way to make our lives hard, and that is to base our work and our careers on a system with the attention span of a fruit fly. I'm talking about web servers, of course. The term web server can mean two different things: it can refer to hardware or software. The hardware is any computer system running the software. I've seen people build web server hardware that fits in a matchbox, and I've seen web server hardware fill expansive rack mount systems in specially cooled data centers. In truth, for us at least, the hardware is the boring part.

Web server software is a little more interesting to those of us who write code. Web server software, such as **Apache**, **Nginx** (pronounced "engine-ex"), **LightHTTPD**, and others, are designed to be simple yet robust implementations of a common specification for the HTTP protocol. These specifications are internationally agreed to by the **World Wide Web Consortium (W3C)**. The protocol itself is very straightforward. We've mentioned a few things about it already in earlier chapters, such as the following:

- **Client-server model**: HTTP follows a client-server model, where the client (typically a web browser) sends a request to the server, and the server responds with the requested data.

- **Request-response paradigm**: HTTP requests are made by clients to retrieve or send data. The request typically includes a method (such as GET, POST, PUT, or DELETE), a **Uniform Resource Identifier (URI)** that identifies the resource being accessed, and headers that provide additional information. The server responds with a status code indicating the success or failure of the request and includes the requested data in the response body. In case you missed it, there's a full discussion of the request-response paradigm (complete with pictures) in *Chapter 8, Building a Dynamic Web Application with Flask*.

- **Text-based protocol**: HTTP is a text-based protocol, meaning that both the request and response messages are human-readable. The messages follow a specific format called the HTTP message format, which consists of headers and an optional message body.

- **Secure variant**: HTTP can be augmented with encryption and security features using **HTTPS (HTTP Secure)**. HTTPS adds a layer of **Transport Layer Security (TLS)** or **Secure Sockets Layer (SSL)** encryption to protect the confidentiality and integrity of the data transmitted between the client and the server.

In our immediate discussion, I want to point out a nugget we have heretofore glossed over: HTTP is stateless. This means that each request from a client is treated independently, without any knowledge of previous requests. The server does not retain any information about the client's previous interactions. In the US, there is a famous advertising campaign for the city of Las Vegas, which states "What happens in Vegas stays in Vegas." Likewise, what happens within the request-response mechanism stays in that request-response life cycle. Once the response is received and acknowledged by the web browser, there is nothing other than a log entry somewhere that the request even took place.

In concert, what we have here is a dumb machine executing requests of which it has no memory. This can make our job somewhat frustrating. We want our users to be continually interacting with our application, but the server isn't going to help us do that without some form of cajoling.

Over the years, a number of mechanisms have been invented to help with the state in our application. If you're not sure what I mean by state, I like to describe it as a saved game in your favorite video game.

Imagine you are playing an adventure game. You've been playing for quite a while, and you've found the entrance to the dark castle, which is on level three. You've answered the gatekeeper's riddle, and you have obtained the vorpal sword of smiting. You have amassed 32,768 gold pieces and your character is at full health. Then your mom yells for you to go take out the trash. As we all know, this is "mom code" for "quit playing video games and do something productive." She'll never understand, will she? Naturally, you'd like to pick up where you left off, so you save your game. You can turn off your computer and turn it back on tomorrow, at which point you can load your game and it will behave as though you never stopped playing. This is because your saved game represents a saved state for the program. It is a snapshot of all the objects, variables, and data used by your game at the time you saved it. This is the program's state. This is what web applications intrinsically lack, at least at the protocol level.

The state can be managed using a few techniques. Server solutions such as Flask allow you to implement sticky sessions where HTTP requests generate a token. The request details can be stored between sessions with reference to the token. This is not handled by your web server, but by your application server, which leverages the web server for the communications part: the request-response mechanism. Sessions are generally not desirable because, in most cases, they don't scale. If you have a lot of web traffic, it is common practice to balance the traffic load between several servers. If your session is stored on server A on the first request, and a subsequent request goes to server B, it won't have your session. Naturally, we've come up with solutions for that too, but let's not get down in the weeds.

You can use cookies, which store the data on the client side. Unfortunately, cookies have a bad reputation as they have been highly abused over the years. The major browsers expose the cookies you are saving, and your ever-paranoid users can choose to not accept your request to store cookies.

The best answer is to store the state of your application in the application itself. The idea here is called representational state transfer, or REST for short. In a RESTful scenario, we maintain the program's state in memory on the client. We transfer any part of the state, or even (but not usually) the entire state using the request-response mechanism. The program essentially sends the parts of the state the server will need to fulfill the request. The server does whatever it is supposed to do, and then sends back the altered state in the response. If you are familiar with software design patterns, REST reminds me of the command pattern: the request encapsulates everything the server needs to complete the request.

Now that the stage is set, let's remember that SPAs are now responsible for maintaining their state, that all of the markup HTML, CSS, and JavaScript is loaded in the browser, and that all subsequent requests contain only the state data, which is sent to the server where it is altered and returned.

The format of the data transfer can be any form of text. Most often, it is JSON. Back in ye olde days of yore, we used XML, but we stopped because XML processing is ridiculously slow in a browser. JSON is faster since the browser already inherently understands JavaScript, so there is no parsing of the text required. Just in case this is your first rodeo, let's compare the two formats. First, here's some XML:

```
<person>
  <firstName>Bruce</firstName>
  <lastName>Van Horn</lastName>
  <dateOfBirth trueDate="Heck No">12/19/1987</dateOfBirth>
</person>
```

XML is tag-based markup like HTML, but you can define your own tags using an XML schema. This was the format originally used in browsers with the **XMLHttpRequest** (**XHR**) API call. The *X* actually stands for *XML*. XHR is still used, but almost nobody (Microsoft Azure API teams notwithstanding) still uses XML. Instead, for performance reasons already mentioned, I give you the same thing in JSON:

```
{
  "person": {
    "firstName": "Bruce",
    "lastName": "Van Horn",
    "dateOfBirth": {
      "date": "12/19/1987",
      "trueDate": false
    }
  }
}
```

The same data is represented as is the structure of that data. As a Python developer, you've no doubt recognized this as a dict. Instead of tags with content and attributes, we have key-value pairs stored within curly braces. It is a rule of JSON that keys and textual values be enclosed in double quotations. Be careful here. JavaScript and Python both consider single and double quotation marks to be interchangeable, but JSON does not. Only double quotes are acceptable! Thankfully, Python has a json library available within the standard library that will convert your structures to JSON, and back again, without any fuss:

```
import json

# Convert dictionary to JSON
data_dict = {"name": "John", "age": 30, "city": "New York"}
json_data = json.dumps(data_dict)
# Print the JSON data
print("JSON data:", json_data)
```

These first few lines import the json library, then convert it to a JSON object with the json.dumps method. Just remember, we're dumping to a string, hence dumps (the *s* is for *string*). Now let's convert the other direction:

```
# Convert JSON to dictionary
parsed_dict = json.loads(json_data)

# Access the dictionary
print("Name:", parsed_dict["name"])
print("Age:", parsed_dict["age"])
print("City:", parsed_dict["city"])
```

We used json.loads to convert the JSON back to a dict. Just remember it as "We're loading a JSON string," hence loads (the *s* is for *string*).

You now understand the basic mechanics of what we're going to be doing with FastAPI. Requests will be coming in like they did with Flask, but generally, instead of simple GET requests, which are intercepted and processed using the Jinja2 template engine, the requests will contain JSON payloads, which we will process. The results of the processing will be returned as JSON. The request-response mechanism will be handled using asynchronous functions, so the code will look a little different than it did with Flask.

Let's get our hands dirty so you can see what I mean!

Creating a FastAPI project in PyCharm Professional

By now, we've created many projects in PyCharm Professional and this isn't very different. I'll remind you that this set of features is only available in the Professional edition of PyCharm. If you need to use the Community edition, you can, but you're on your own in terms of setting up the project since you won't have access to the tooling we're about to use.

Create a new project in PyCharm by clicking **File | New Project**. Then, find **FastAPI** in the list of templates. You can see mine in *Figure 9.1*:

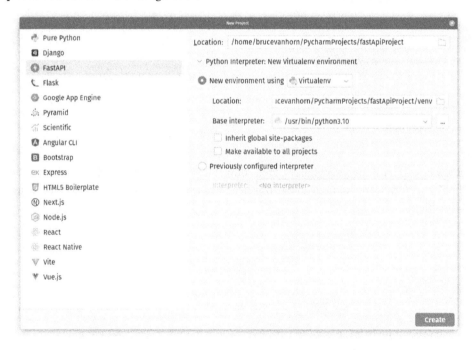

Figure 9.1: The PyCharm project menu contains a template for a FastAPI project

As with Flask, the FastAPI project template generates some starter code and a run configuration for us, as seen in *Figure 9.2*:

Figure 9.2: The template generates our FastAPI starter code and run configuration

There is a lot to talk about in *Figure 9.2*, so I've numbered the diagram for reference.

PyCharm has created a virtual environment, along with two files as seen at (1): `main.py` and `test_main.http`. We'll come back to the files in a moment. PyCharm generated a run configuration for us. You can tell because it is the currently selected run configuration at (2) where that menu would normally say **Current File** if PyCharm didn't have a run configuration set up.

At position (3), we can see an example of a `Hello World` endpoint for our FastAPI project. The power of these starter code templates is the psychological prompting they provide. If you have used any system for working with web routing and endpoints, regardless of language or framework, you can read this code and tell what is happening.

Lines 1 and 3 show us a typical constructor for the imported library instance of FastAPI. Line 6 shows us how FastAPI decorates endpoints. `@app` comes from the instantiation on line 3 and we're invoking the HTTP `GET` method here so requests coming in using that method will be received and processed. If a client makes a request using another HTTP verb such as `PUT` or `POST`, they'll receive an error since, currently, there is no code to handle that HTTP method.

Position (3) shows us our root route as indicated by the endpoint definition on line 6. As promised, all puns intended, we have an `async` function below the decorator on line 7, and we can see we are returning something that looks like a `dict`, which also looks like JSON.

Position **(4)** shows us another GET endpoint defined as /hello/{name}. The name variable offset in curly braces refers to part of the URL that can vary and is called a path parameter or a path variable. You can see it is duplicated in the async function definition on line 12. The contents of the branches (name) on line 11 should match the name of the parameter for the function on line 12.

Position **(5)** on line 13 shows us the path variable used in the return JSON where a Python f string expression fills the name into the data. There is no special templating mechanism other than a normal Python f string.

Running the FastAPI project

Naturally, we can run the FastAPI project by clicking the green arrowed run button near position **(2)** in *Figure 9.2*. If you've skipped the chapter on setting up and using run and debug configurations, you might want to peek at *Chapter 6, Seamless Testing, Debugging, and Profiling*, for details on how this feature works in PyCharm. You can see my program running in *Figure 9.3*:

Figure 9.3: I clicked the green run button, which spawned a tab
in the run window for my project in PyCharm

This looks similar to the runs in Flask, but there isn't a warning about the development server. This is because FastAPI runs in an application called uvicorn, which is a variant of Green Unicorn (gunicorn). Uvicorn is production ready, so there is no warning. You can develop using the same application server software you will use when you deploy your application to your customers. The difference between uvicorn and gunicorn, which is most often used as a production server for Flask applications, is that uvicorn handles the async programming model while gunicorn uses traditional workers, as described earlier in this chapter.

At this point, we are left with something of a quandary. When we did this with Flask, the app was generating some HTML for us to view. This one isn't. You can view the endpoint in a browser if you would like, as I am in *Figure 9.4*:

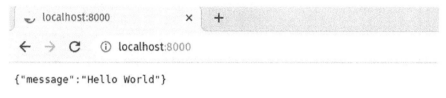

Figure 9.4: Visiting the root route isn't very exciting, but it works

I can also visit the other URL with the path parameter as part of the URL as shown in *Figure 9.5*:

Figure 9.5: Supplying a path parameter alters the data in the response

This time, I added the path parameter to the end of the URL, and as we saw in the code earlier, we're getting back the generated JSON data.

There's a problem with using the browser. The browser only allows you to submit HTTP GET requests. There are quite a few more HTTP methods typically used in a REST API project. In fact, the four most popular methods, sometimes referred to as verbs, map to the typical CRUD operations used in database applications. **CRUD** is an acronym for **Create, Read, Update, Delete**. The verbs map as shown in *Figure 9.6*. Your request is defined by these operations. You don't have to use these methods, but you should as a best practice. I've seen big, expensive, commercial applications only use GET and POST.

In addition to standards for your requests, your responses can be standardized via best practice by using proper HTTP status codes. These are documented in the HTTP specifications provided by the W3C. Reading the specification is a sure-fire cure for insomnia, so I'll refer you to the excellent **Mozilla Developer Network (MDN)** page for the status codes. This is a handy address to bookmark in your browser: https://developer.mozilla.org/en-US/docs/Web/HTTP/Status.

HTTP Verb / Method	CRUD Operation	HTTP Status for Successful Response	Explanation
GET	READ	200 (OK)	Used to retrieve or get information from the server or database. For example, getting a list of users in your application.
POST	CREATE	201 (Created)	Used to create a new record in a database. Use this anytime you are creating something on the server. For example, new user registration.
PUT	UPDATE	204 (No Content) or 200 (OK)	Use this method when you are sending an update to something that already exists, such as a database record. For example, updating a password.
DELETE	DELETE	204 (No Content) or 200 (OK)	Use this when you want to delete something.

Figure 9.6: HTTP methods map to CRUD operations 1:1 and have standard response codes to denote successful responses

With your browser limited to HTTP GET requests, and the 100% likelihood that we will want to use at least one of the other methods in our project, we need something better than just a browser for testing our API. We have a few options:

- There are browser plugins that allow you to send different kinds of requests. You can find them in your favorite browser's marketplace.

- Command-line tools such as cURL allow you to craft HTTP requests using any of the HTTP methods.

- Dedicated API testing tools such as Insomnia (https://www.insomnia.rest) or Postman (https://getpostman.com) allow you a graphical tool for working with API requests. These tools can be very bloated as they are meant to do a lot more than just allow you to make the various request types. With that said, I use both because of their wide adoption rate. Believe it or not, there are developers on my team who don't use PyCharm.

- PyCharm's built-in HTTP Requests feature.

Obviously, we're going to be focusing on the fourth option.

Working with PyCharm's HTTP Requests

When we generated our project, PyCharm created two files. It created `main.py`, which we have already examined. It also created a file called `test_main.http`. This file is unique to PyCharm. Let's examine the file shown in *Figure 9.7*:

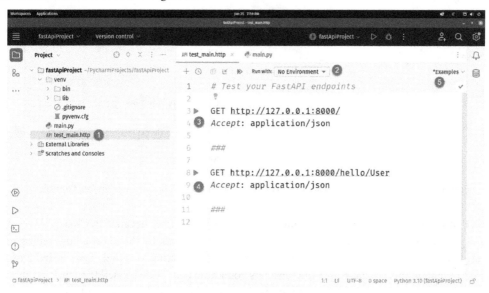

Figure 9.7: The HTTP test file generated by PyCharm as part of a FastAPI project

You'll find the file itself directly next to `main.py` **(1)**. We mentioned this as one of the popular conventions for the placement of test files – right next to the file we're testing. It is called `test-main.http`, which lets us know exactly what is being tested. The `main.py` file will contain endpoints and `test_main.http` will then contain tests for all the endpoints.

This `http` test file isn't code, as we saw in *Chapter 6, Seamless Testing, Debugging, and Profiling*. This is a specification for HTTP requests. Positions **(3)** and **(4)** reveal one test per endpoint in `main.py`, which is a good starting point. These tests are very simple, and like unit tests, they can be run individually using the green arrows. If you want to run all the tests in the file, you can use the toolbar **(2)**, which has a button with two green arrows. There is also an environment selector, which we'll come back to soon. Position **(5)** shows a link that gives you a set of examples that can be pasted into your test files. We'll come back to that too. First, let's exercise our test and see what it does. I'll click the double arrow run button shown by the top arrow in *Figure 9.8*:

Figure 9.8: Click the double arrow to run all the tests and you'll find they both fail! Oh no!

This isn't good. Both of the tests fail spectacularly. I say *spectacularly* because PyCharm leaves no ambiguity. I see a red banner telling me my test failed. I see red text, by the lower arrow, telling me two tests failed. I see red Xs next to the test list. I see a message stating **Stopped. Tests failed 2 of 2**. If that isn't enough, there is a log area that also lets you know your code missed the mark. In short, there are more red marks on this screen than there are on this chapter's manuscript after the editor made their first pass! Trust me, that's a lot! What in the world could be wrong? Why would PyCharm generate a failing test code like that in a *Hello World* example?

There's nothing wrong with the code! In *Chapter 6, Seamless Testing, Debugging, and Profiling*, we learned about unit testing. Unit tests comprise code that exercises the code you are testing using assertions. The HTTP file doesn't contain code, and this is not unit testing, this is integration testing. These tests require a running server in order to work. Let's try this again. Examine *Figure 9.9* and follow along if you like:

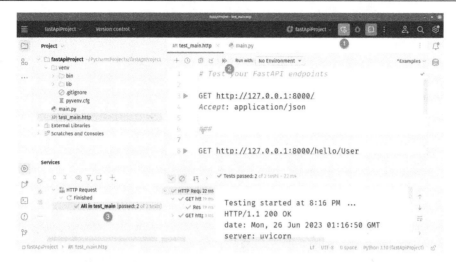

Figure 9.9: You have to run the development server before you run the HTTP tests

Click the run button for the API project (**1**). Then click the run button for the tests (**2**). With the server running, all the tests will pass (**3**). If they don't, call JetBrains and ask for your money back. That probably won't work, which is OK because your tests should pass.

Examining the details of the return

It isn't enough to know we passed, because all that really means is both requests were made against the local development server, and both came back with a status code of 200. What you really want, most of the time, is to be able to see the JSON data that came back on the response. Let's go find that. Locate the output for the test and scroll down until you see a mention of a JSON file like the one shown in *Figure 9.10*:

Figure 9.10: Scroll through the log and find the links to the JSON files.
Click them to open the data in the tabbed area in the editor

This section in the log window tells us all the details about the request and response made in the test. We can see the following:

- The version of HTTP being used (1.1)
- The status code of the response (200 OK)
- The date of the request
- The server that generated the result (uvicorn)
- The content type of the response (application/json)
- The location where the test result was saved

Yahtzee! PyCharm saved the result of the response in a JSON file that is date stamped, along with the status code, and presented it as a hyperlink in the log. If you click the link, the JSON file opens like any other text file in its own tab. In *Figure 9.10*, I had to expand the log to be large enough to make for a good screenshot, but this obscured the contents of the open tab, so check out *Figure 9.11* to see the return data in its tab having clicked the hyperlink in the log:

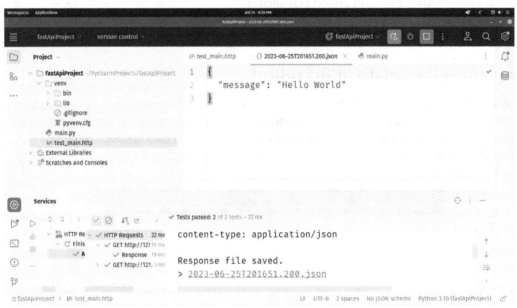

Figure 9.11: The returned data appears in its own tab when you click the hyperlink

If you notice, it says the file is saved, but it doesn't appear in the project files. If you are wondering where it was saved, you can right-click the tab as indicated in *Figure 9.12*:

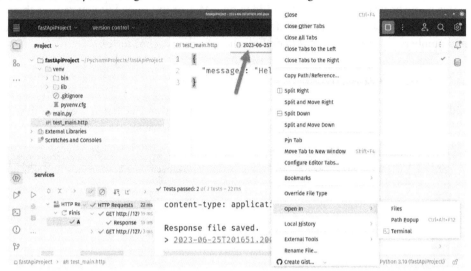

Figure 9.12: Right-click the tab and use the Open In menu to open the location of the test result JSON file

The contents of the menu will differ depending on your operating system. You're looking for the top option, which for me is **Files**, which is the default file manager in **Gnome 42**. Windows will have a reference to Explorer and macOS ought to have a reference to Finder. Clicking that option will show you the location in your OS-specific file manager. You can see mine in *Figure 9.13*:

Figure 9.13: My file manager reveals the location for the HTTP
response files, which is in the project's .idea folder

As you can see, the test results are stored in the PyCharm project folder: the hidden `.idea` folder the IDE creates when you either create a new project or open a folder in PyCharm. Remember, any folder with a name beginning with a dot is hidden on a Mac or in Linux, but you can see them in Windows because Bill likes to be different. If you test often, as you should, these files might begin to stack up in numbers. I personally prefer to exclude these from my repositories.

We just generated a new run configuration

A neat side effect of running all tests from the test window is that PyCharm creates a new run configuration, which you will find in the run configuration dropdown shown in *Figure 9.14*:

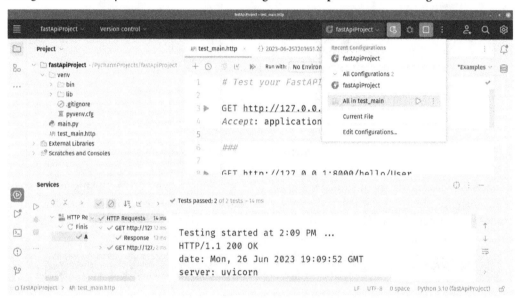

Figure 9.14: PyCharm created a new run configuration automatically
following the first time we ran the HTTP tests

If we edit the configuration, you can see more details, as seen in *Figure 9.15*:

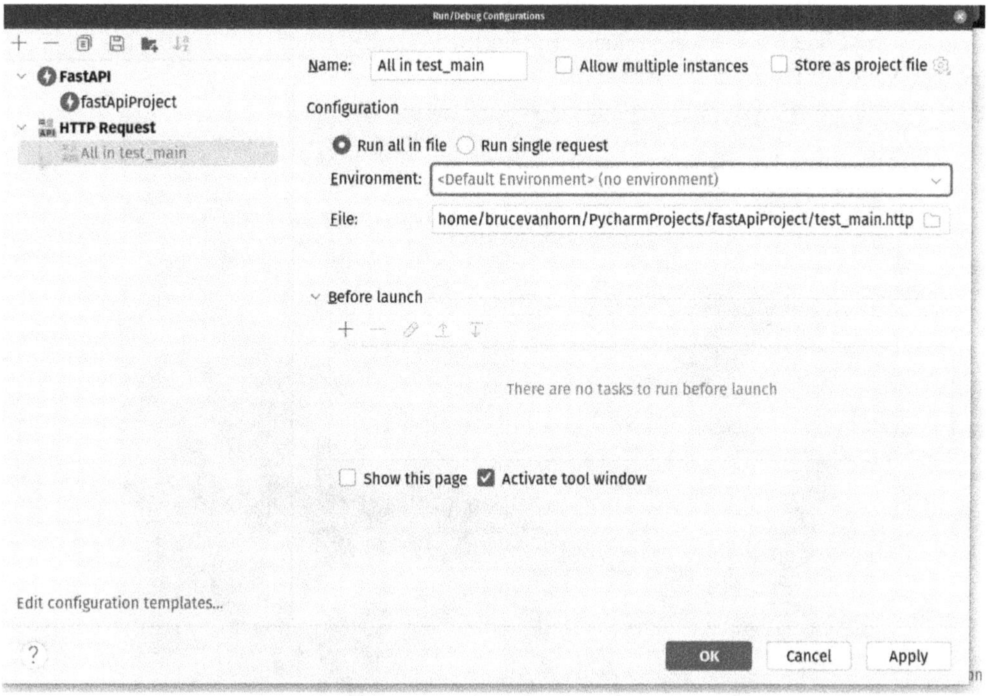

Figure 9.15: Options for HTTP Request test runs can be found in the run configuration editor

As you can see, you can opt to run individual requests or all the requests in the file. Running single requests is handy if you're focusing on the code for one endpoint and you need to run it over and over. If you had many endpoints in the test, your tests might take a while to complete.

Using Before launch actions in run configurations

We've seen that every run of our HTTP tests generates a new JSON file containing the response. This can fill up a folder pretty quickly with hundreds of files. Since PyCharm gives us a run configuration, we have the opportunity to set up some automation to delete older files. In this section, we'll explore some automation capabilities available in PyCharm's run configuration settings.

To do this you'll need a script to delete the JSON files as you see fit. Perhaps you want to delete everything older than a week, or maybe you just want to keep the last 25 runs. This part is up to you.

In order to automate this, you need to create a shell script for your operating system. If you aren't a shell scripting guru, that's OK, because modern artificial intelligence can come to your rescue. *Figure 9.16* shows me asking ChatGPT to create a shell script for the Bash shell that keeps only the last 25 JSON files generated by our test runs:

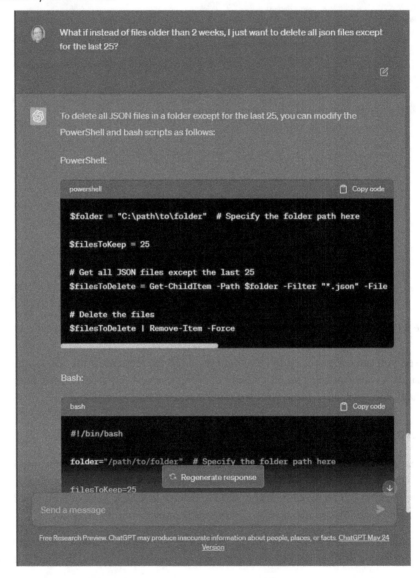

Figure 9.16: I've asked ChatGPT about a few different ways to
delete old files and it has generated a script for me

I realize you can't see the whole script for Bash in the figure, so I'll be sure to include it in the project source for this chapter.

Warning – never run generated scripts you don't understand!

You should never blindly run a script generated by ChatGPT or anything (or anyone) else, including or even especially me, without fully understanding how it works! ChatGPT will probably not give you the same result it gave me, so exercise caution when running any script it gives you. Be especially wary if the script includes anything like -Force switches, as in the PowerShell script in the figure. If you don't know what the script does, don't run it on your computer!

To use the generated code, you can just add a new file to your project as you would any other. I'm going to right-click my project in the Project window and create a new file called delete-old-http-test-results.sh. Naturally, if you are on Windows, you'll want to use PowerShell, which typically bears an extension of .ps1, so it would be delete-old-http-test-results.ps1. Copy the script generated by the AI once you fully understand the ramifications of running said script and save the file.

Make sure the script has run permissions

Make sure the script file you create has permission to run on your computer. Most editions of Windows heavily restrict running any PowerShell script, and your ability to do this might even be restricted by your employer's security policy.

On Mac and Linux, you might need to run this in a terminal before PyCharm will execute the script:

```
chmod +x delete-old-http-test-results.sh
```

If you can't run the script manually, it probably won't work in PyCharm either.

Next, we need to create a run configuration that executes the script. Click the run configuration dropdown and click **Edit Configurations**. If you don't remember how to do this, review *Chapter 3, Customizing Interpreters and Virtual Environments*. Add a new run configuration using the Shell Script template. You can see mine in *Figure 9.17*:

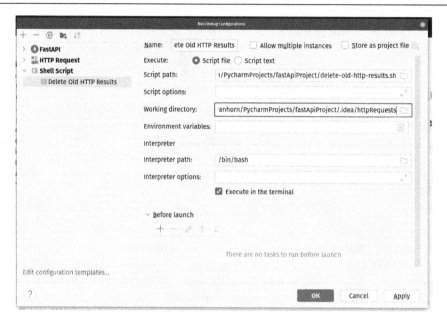

Figure 9.17: Create a run configuration for the shell script we just created

You can navigate to the shell script using the folder button in the **Script path** textbox. Be sure to set **Working directory** for the script; otherwise, you might delete files in your project! We saw earlier that these files live in the `httpRequests` folder inside the project's `.idea` folder. Click the folder icon in the **Working directory** textbox to browse this folder. If you are not on Windows, this will be a hidden folder, so be sure to turn on viewing hidden folders in the selection dialog as I did in *Figure 9.18*:

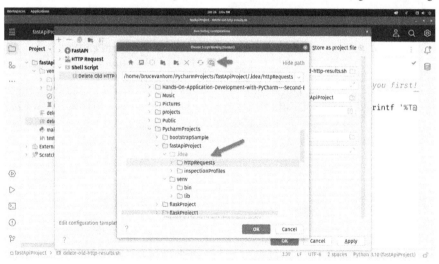

Figure 9.18: To find the httpRequests folder inside the .idea folder, you need to
turn on hidden folders by clicking the eyeball (ouch) on the top toolbar

You now have a run configuration that executes your `delete` script. You should test it. Run your tests 26 more times, and verify you only have the last 25 results in your `httpRequests` folder. I'll show you my results in the next 25 full-page color screenshots. Just kidding. Sometimes it's fun to scare my editors.

If it works, and you're happy, then there's one more thing you can do to make it extra awesome. You can chain your delete script run configuration with your test run configuration. Edit the run configuration for the tests and add a `Before build` condition. Click the + button to add a new condition. Click **Run another run configuration**. Click **Delete Old HTTP Results run configuration**. You should see something like *Figure 9.19*, which shows the deletion script will run before each new test run:

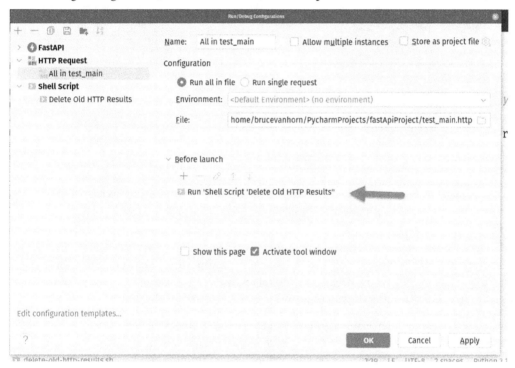

Figure 9.19: The deletion run configuration will now run before each launch of my tests

For the sake of the book, I changed my retention number to the last five JSON files and tried it out. After each run, I can look in my file browser, shown in *Figure 9.20*, and see whether it's working:

Figure 9.20: After my run, there are seven JSON files since the delete script reduces the
file count to five before the run, and the test produces results for two endpoints

You'll only ever have at most 25 results in your folder, or however many you specified in your script! Don't forget, though, the deletion script runs first and PyCharm will generate one new JSON file for each tested endpoint. If I set my delete script to retain five JSON files and I run the generated test script, I'll have seven files after the run since there are two endpoints being tested.

Using this technique, you can enable a great many automation scenarios for your code. Python doesn't generally have a build script, like many languages, so it's nice to know you have this level of automation available in the IDE itself. There were several options besides running another run configuration. I recommend you explore all the possibilities!

Working with HTTP Request environments

Most web projects begin their life on a developer's computer. When you test, you run your application locally on your laptop or PC, and all of your test requests are usually going to localhost, which is the loopback address assigned to every computer with a network card. The project starts out there, but assuming the app enjoys any level of success, it will not stay there.

Best practice dictates that applications intended for publication should use some sort of **continuous integration (CI)** environment where automated tests can be run. In fact, JetBrains makes a CI product called Team City. I used Team City for many years and can attest that it is an excellent CI system that is easy to set up, and it is free for small teams. These days, there is even a cloud version, so you needn't set up your own servers if that's not your thing. Team City, though, has the same plugin we've been using to create tests for our HTTP endpoints in our FastAPI project. This allows you to test your project automatically every time someone commits code to your source repository.

Once your code passes muster with the CI system, it is common for the code to be deployed to a testing server. This should be a server that is as much like production as you can manage. Some people call this a staging server, some call it **user acceptance test (UAT)**. No matter what you call it, it represents an environment. Production too is an environment. An environment is simply a configuration environment where you can run your code. To be clear, so far, we've mentioned four such environments:

- Your local computer (localhost)
- A CI environment, which these days is probably a Docker container
- A UAT/staging environment where you can test your app before you release it to production
- A production environment where your real customers use your app

Each of these environments might have different attributes. For example, your FastAPI app running on your laptop can be accessed using the IP address 127.0.0.1. By default, the app runs on port 8000, and also by default, the protocol used is HTTP and not HTTPS since few developers take the time to set up an SSL/TLS certificate on their laptops.

However, when you test your application in staging, all of those parameters are different. You probably will have an SSL certificate, so you'll use HTTPS as your protocol. You'll definitely have a different IP address. You might even have a domain name server resolving a nice test domain name for your app. You probably won't be using port 8000 since that would not be very production-like. Instead, you'll be using port 443 or 80, and in that case, you needn't necessarily fill in the port at all.

The production too will have different attributes again.

In our API tests, we are able to configure a set of variables to be used in our test script, which are assigned to an environment name. Make sure you have the `test_main.http` file, or any `.http` file. Click the environment dropdown shown in *Figure 9.21*:

Figure 9.21: You can select an environment for running your
tests each with it's own configuration variables

I'll be honest. I worked ahead and set one up, but we'll pretend I didn't. Right now, your only option is **No Environment**. How boring! Check out the two options at the bottom and click **Add Environment to Public File**. You'll find PyCharm adds a new file to your project called `http-client.env.json`. You can see mine in *Figure 9.22*:

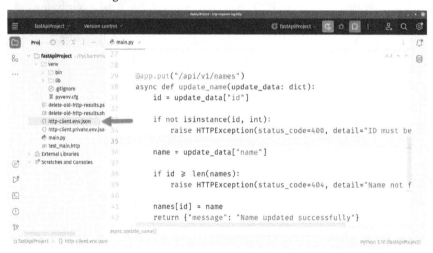

Figure 9.22: PyCharm created http-client.env.json, which will allow
me to set up different environments for testing

If you had chosen the **Private file** option, you'd have gotten `http-client-private.env.json`. The purpose of and difference between the two files isn't in the documentation as I write this, so we'll have to use our imaginations. Personally, I put environments I want to share with my development team in the public file. If I want to create some sort of private environment, maybe a virtual machine, Windows Subsystem for Linux, custom experiments in Docker, or maybe a Kubernetes cluster in a lab, I can use the private file, which I would likely put in my `.gitignore` file. Since the file contents are the same, I'll focus on the public file.

I'm going to add a definition for my local computer. Change the contents of `http-client.env.json` to this:

```
{
  "dev": {
    "protocol": "http://",
    "base_url": "localhost",
    "port": 8000,
    "api_version": "v1"
  }
}
```

We now have a dev environment set up with some environment variables. Let's use them in our `test_main.http` file. Your first endpoint definition looks like this:

To use the environment variables, replace the parts of your URL with mustache-formatted text. Mustache format entails putting the variables you want to resolve in double curly braces like {{ this }}:

```
GET {{protocol}}{{base_url}}:{{port}}
```

Taken together, the URL will resolve to the original, which is `http://localhost:8000`, or if you prefer, `http://127.0.0.1:8000`. Tomayto tomahto. The difference is, now you can create your other environments in the same way. You can switch the environment and run the tests unchanged, and the environment variables will resolve your URLs for you.

If you review my code in this chapter's sample code, you'll find I've tricked out the whole file this way.

Let's get CRUDdier and then get testier!

Right now, the only thing in our app is two pre-generated endpoints. Let's add some more to make this a little more interesting. We're going to make a fake list app as we did in *Chapter 8, Building a Dynamic Web Application with Flask*.

Open up `main.py` and let's add one endpoint for each CRUD operation, and in turn, each of the four main methods used in building RESTful APIs. We're going to make some sweeping changes, so I'll simply present them starting at the top of the file.

On the first line, where we have the import, change it to this:

```
from fastapi import FastAPI, status, HTTPException

app = FastAPI()
```

The app instantiate was unchanged. Below it, though, add this list of amazing people:

```
names = ["Bruce", "Karina", "Kitty", "Phoebe"]
```

This list will serve as a fake database, saving us the time of setting up servers and the blah blah blah, which would seriously bloat the book and not contribute to our soon-to-be champion-level PyCharm prowess. We're going to leave the first two generated endpoints alone, so just start your editing below the say_hello function's return. Our first CRUD endpoint is going to give us a list of names as if from a database query:

```
@app.get("/api/v1/names")
async def get_names():
    return [{"id": idx, "name": name} for idx, name in enumerate(names)]
```

It is best practice to start the endpoints in your project, which are expected to return JSON data, rather than markup, with a prefix of API followed by a version designation. Trust me when I say that you want to do this. As your API code matures, you may want to offer updated endpoints that may not necessarily be backward compatible, and this technique allows you to keep your API backward compatible and non-breaking with your older clients while introducing improved functionality for newer clients. As the code matures further, you can remove the v1 endpoints at a time of your choosing:

```
@app.post("/api/v1/names", status_code=status.HTTP_201_CREATED)
async def create_name(name: dict):
    new_name = name["name"]
    names.append(new_name)
    return {"message": "Name added successfully"}
```

On the preceding POST endpoint, it is a best practice for the successful call to return an HTTP status code of 201 indicating new data was created by the API. The FastAPI code works very differently from Flask. Instead of discrete request and response objects, everything is implicit. If you are expecting JSON to be posted as a payload to your API, you need only specify this using an argument type of dict. In this case, I am expecting data to be posted in this format:

```
{"name": "Igor"}
```

A real app would have a richer structure. We're keeping it simple. When this JSON comes in as the payload for POST, we extract the name and append it to our list. For the sake of simplicity, I am not doing any validation on this endpoint. You should always validate your incoming data to protect yourself against toxic data and injection attacks. That's the subject of another book. With that said, I won't be a total slouch. I'll do a little bit of this in the PUT endpoint, so you can see what some of this would look like. Remember, a PUT call is an UPDATE operation. We're taking an id value and a new name value and we'll change the existing value accordingly. Add these lines below your create_name function return:

```
@app.put("/api/v1/names")
async def update_name(update_data: dict):
    id = update_data["id"]
```

Now back to the code. Let's make sure the ID attribute submitted is a number, specifically an integer:

```
    if not isinstance(id, int):
        raise HTTPException(status_code=400, detail="ID must be an
integer")
```

What's happening here? If you submit an ID attribute that doesn't resolve to a number, I'm going to send you back an HTTP error status code of 400, which means your request is malformed. Just to be nice, I'm going to add a little message telling you what you did wrong. For example, say you use PUT on this data as follows:

```
{ "id": "2", "name": "Igor" }
```

Everything should work. But say you use PUT for the following:

```
{ "id": "this isn't a number", "name": "Igor" }
```

Your request will fail. Raising the HTTP extension will cause the response to be sent immediately, and the rest of this code isn't executed. So, let's continue. If you submitted good data, we can move on and grab the new name:

```
    name = update_data["name"]
```

Next, we detect whether the numeric ID you submitted isn't out of range. Our list starts off with four names in it. If you try to send an update to id 600, that shouldn't work unless you've added at least as many names to the list via the POST endpoint. In a PUT, if you present an invalid id value, it is customary to send back a 404 error stating you couldn't find that ID in your database (or list in our case):

```
if id >= len(names):
    raise HTTPException(status_code=404, detail="Name not found")

names[id] = name
return {"message": "Name updated successfully"}
```

That's three down and only one to go. For the DELETE endpoint, all I need is id. Sending a JSON payload for something this simple would be silly, so I'll just take the ID as a parameter on the endpoint URL. I still need to check to make sure it is within range of the length of the names list:

```
@app.delete("/api/v1/names/{id}")
async def delete_name(id: int):
    if id >= len(names):
        raise HTTPException(status_code=404, detail="Name not found")
```

If it is, then I'll just pop it out of the list and return a nice message:

```
deleted_name = names.pop(id)
return {"message": f"Deleted name: {deleted_name}"}
```

Run the app and make sure it starts. Make any adjustments needed. Remember, the final working code is in the chapter's sample code from the repository we checked out in *Chapter 2*.

Getting testier

If I were all cruddy, chances are I'd be pretty testy, right? Now that we have more varied endpoints, let's learn more about testing them with HTTP clients. As it turns out, the tool is extremely rich, as rich as dedicated tools such as Insomnia or Postman, just without all that UI in the way.

Open your test_main.http file and let us add tests. Not just simple ones, let's make some real ones and get a feel for how the PyCharm workflow helps you build RESTful APIs.

> **These testing features of PyCharm work with any framework**
>
> I should mention that while we're using FastAPI, these features are not unique or tied to that framework. These tools would work the same if you developed your API in Flask, or even in some other framework.

So far, you just have two tests, which were generated when you created your project:

```
# Test your FastAPI endpoints

GET {{protocol}}{{base_url}}:{{port}}
Accept: application/json


###


GET {{protocol}}{{base_url}}:{{port}}/hello/User
Accept: application/json
```

I didn't specifically tell you to modify the second test endpoint with the environment variables we made earlier, but I went ahead and did it since that seems like an obvious improvement. As you add code to the test file, there are a few things worth noting:

- Requests may be stored in files with either .http or .rest extensions. So far, we've worked with the .http file that was generated with the project. In the wild, you may see either extension and there is no fundamental difference between them other than the icons displayed in the IDE. This is purely cosmetic.

- Code highlighting and syntax completion are active. The syntax of these files is specialized, but you can expect the same level of tooling here as you would anywhere else.

- Inline documentation will also appear for the code in this file.

- Requests must be separated by three hashtag/pound signs: ###. If you fail to add these, the IDE will let you know with a sea of red squiggly lines.

- You can paste a command-line cURL command into this file, and it will automatically convert it to the syntax used by PyCharm.

- Templating is supported. We've already seen the environment variable substitution at work. Stay tuned, it's about to get amazing!

The test editor has a little bit of UI to it, but to be honest, once you learn the syntax, you probably won't use it. Let me show you. Refer to *Figure 9.23*:

Figure 9.23: The test editor has a minimal UI

Let's look at the numbers:

The + icon at **(1)** allows you to add another test. To be honest, this is easier to do directly in the editor, but if you like clicking things, here's your jam.

The clock icon **(2)** is actually very useful. It opens up the request history log, which contains the last 50 requests you've made. This opens as a normal project file would, and you'll find the file in the location we visited earlier in the `httpRequests` folder inside the `.idea` project folder. Since PyCharm automatically reloads files when they change, leaving this file open allows you to see everything that is happening without having to look at the individual response files. Earlier, we added automation to remove many of these response files since there are often so many of them. This doesn't affect the log file since the request information is appended from the log window instead of the response file itself. In fact, the log shows the response data too.

Pro tip – open the log in a split view so you can always see it

If you right-click the tab containing the log file and select one of the split options, such as **Split Right**, the tab will open in a separate tab group. If you have a nice wide 4K monitor, you have plenty of room to keep the log open alongside your code and test files so you can see it all together.

The document icon at **(3)** is there to make command-line mavens happy. If you select a request and click this button, you are able to generate a cURL command, which can then be pasted into a terminal window. The import icon at **(4)** gives you a UI where you can paste a cURL command whereupon it will be converted to the request format used by PyCharm. This isn't all that useful since you can paste a cURL command directly into the editor itself and the conversion happens automatically.

We've already seen the **Run All Tests** button at **(5)**, as well as the environment selection dropdown. Probably, the most useful item on this toolbar, apart from the history log, is the link to the examples at **(6)**. This is not fancy, but it is useful. Clicking this link will open a file that contains a slew of examples that you can copy, paste, and modify. Essentially, this is the same thing that happens when you click the UI button at position **(1)**. To me, opening the samples is faster and easier because you can see them all in one place. To use it, just click the *Examples link as shown in *Figure 9.24*:

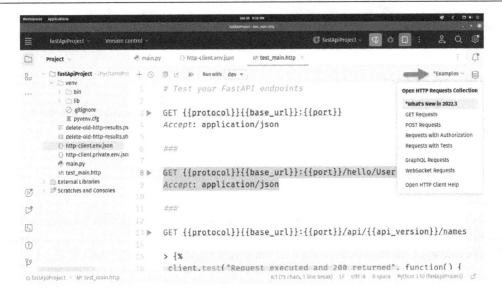

Figure 9.24: The test examples are broken out by category

I like to use the POST requests sample open to the side, as in *Figure 9.25*:

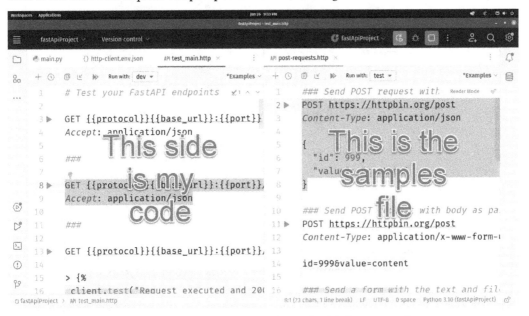

Figure 9.25: You can open the samples to the side for easy pasting

To split the files like this, just right-click the tab and click **Split Right**, or left, up, or down according to your preferences.

Creating the tests

Let's create those tests! Make sure you are working in `test_main.http`. Add these lines below your last test:

```
###

GET {{protocol}}{{base_url}}:{{port}}/api/{{api_version}}/names
```

The three hashtags are the separator between tests. The rest are variables coming from the environment variables we created earlier. This will translate to `http://localhost:8000/api/v1/names`. Make sure your app is running and run the test. You should see some results like those in *Figure 9.26*:

Figure 9.26: When you run the test, you can see the response data in the log
view. The left side of my results will normally look different than yours

This is nice, right? You can see you got back a good status code (`200`), and you can see your data. What if you could turn this into a proper test? You can! Go back to the `test_main.http` file. Every great moment in American, and perhaps world, history was preceded by the phrase I will utter next: *Hold my beer and watch this.*

Right below your test, add this code:

```
> {%
  client.test("Request executed and 200 returned", function() {
    client.assert(response.status === 200, `Response status is
${response.status} but should be 200`);
  });
```

The first character is crucial. You have to type a > followed by { %. If you don't, PyCharm will become quite cross! Just stare at the majesty for a moment. Take it all in. What we have here is a test. WRITTEN IN JAVASCRIPT! I'm sorry. I should have warned you to sit down or something. I did, however, mention that beer was involved. There is some magic here. There is a client object inherent in this test window, not unlike the window object that is ever-present in a browser window. We're invoking the .test method on that client object and we're passing it two arguments. The first is a string that describes the test. This can be anything you'd like. The contents do not affect the test in any way. The second argument is an anonymous function that actually executes the test. If you're not up on JavaScript's use of lambda-style functions, you're just going to have to roll with it and copy these tests from examples. I suppose you could also go learn JavaScript, but that might take a while. Thankfully, the client.assert part seems like the tests we wrote in *Chapter 6, Seamless Testing, Debugging, and Profiling*, so let's keep going. The assert takes an expression that will evaluate to true or false. JavaScript uses a triple equals sign for testing equality without coercion. If you have not heard of this, for now, just know you should always be using three equals signs because using two means something else and you don't want that. A double equals sign, which is the norm in Python, might yield a false failure in your JavaScript test code because JavaScript will attempt to force any data types it encounters to match. The triple equals avoid this.

After the conditional statement, we have a JavaScript template literal. This is the equivalent of a Python f-string. You use the gravure marks for quotes. The gravure mark is the shifted tilde (~) on a US keyboard, and it looks like a heavy single quote: `. Enclosing a string within the gravure marks specifies the string to be a template literal. You can substitute expressions or variable values using ${whever} in the curly braces. So, in Python, given the foo = bar variable, an f-string would be as follows:

```
f"I'd rather be at the {foo}."
```

In JavaScript, given const foo = "bar", it would be as follows:

```
`I'd rather be at the ${foo}`
```

Here, I've used the template literal to give a little more information since this second string literally exposes a message seen when the test fails.

This particular test checks to make sure that the HTTP response code for the request was 200, which indicates it was successful. If you don't include a test like this, then your results will always be green even if your endpoint code melted the server and summoned the great Cthulu from his deep slumber at the heart of the cosmos. This is a test that should be included every single time, though the expected code might change depending on what you're doing.

More tests you should always add

Checking your status code is the bare minimum. I assert (see what I did there?) that you should check as many things as you can think of. Here, I'll add a test to verify the returned data has a mime type of `application/json`, which is important to the way clients will consume this data. Add this below our earlier test:

```
client.test("Response should be json", function() {
  const type = response.contentType.mimeType;

  client.assert(type === "application/json", `Expected application/
json
  but got ${type}`);
});
%}
```

Remember, it's JavaScript! So here, I've added a constant called `type` and pulled the value from another magical object available in the test window. `response.contentType.mimeType` gives you exactly that. We test to make sure it is `"application/json"`. Personally, I think attention to detail is important, and I see APIs created by professionals as being very unprofessional if the content type isn't set correctly. As it happens, FastAPI does this for us, but not every framework will.

Now that you have the basics down, I invite you to explore my finished `test_main.http` file in the chapter's sample code. There are tests there for all the conditions we put into the `PUT` endpoint allowing you to make sure the `400` status is returned if your user sends a non-numeric ID. There is also a test to make sure you get a `404` error if your ID is beyond the acceptable range for the `names` list.

Editing and debugging a full stack app by attaching projects

PyCharm has the ability to attach multiple projects together allowing you to work on full stack applications in the same instance of the IDE. When you are running multiple attached projects in your PyCharm IDE, you can debug them together in a seamless fashion! This capability alone is probably reason enough to stop using vim or VS Code and never look back! While it is possible to do this in other IDEs or even VS Code, PyCharm makes it so easy you'll probably not want to.

Creating a React app in a separate project

To create a frontend for our FastAPI backend, we're going to leverage React. As usual, I won't have the space here to teach you a lot about React. I'll make sure there is some reference reading in the *Further reading* section at the end of this chapter.

To create a React app in PyCharm Professional, just use the usual **File | Project** operation to which you have hopefully become accustomed. There is a project template that leverages an open source product called **create-react-app** (**CRA**). This is a tool widely used by React developers because, in truth, setting up a full-on React app from scratch is tedious and time-consuming.

In order for this `create-react-app` script to work, you need to have Node.js installed. If you don't, PyCharm will attempt to install it for you, as you can see in *Figure 9.27*:

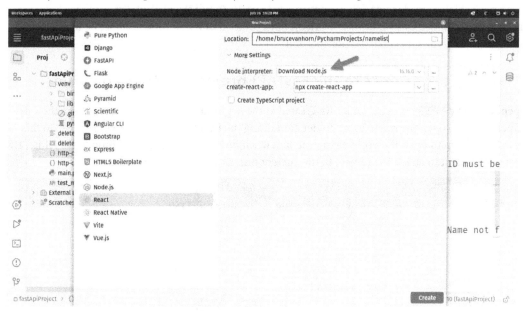

Figure 9.27: When creating a JavaScript project, such as a React project, you'll need
to have Node.js installed, otherwise PyCharm will try to install it for you

In my experience, this doesn't always work out. This same feature exists in Visual Studio, and I usually advise my students to install Node.js manually, rather than have an IDE do it. In general, the IDEs often don't point to the latest release of Node.js. I can see in *Figure 9.27* that PyCharm intends to install 16.16.0, which isn't the latest. Besides, looking at the right version, I further recommend you use the latest **long-term support** (**LTS**) version of Node.js rather than the version with the highest version number. The LTS product is guaranteed stable, whereas the absolute newest version isn't.

Another thing I recommend with Node.js, and Python too, for that matter, is to use a package manager such as **Chocolately** (`https://chocolatey.org/`) or **Homebrew** (`https://brew.sh/`). Package managers are standard affairs on Linux, and every distribution uses their own, so if you're using Linux, I'll assume you know which one you need. The reason I advocate using package managers for installing Node.js is that the package manager makes it very easy to update, or even fully remove, your software should you ever need to. If you want to try out Homebrew for Mac, there is a short, free course on my website that teaches you to set up an Apple computer for Node.js development. You can find it at `https://www.maddevskilz.com/courses/setting-up-a-nodejs-development-workstation-in-macos`. I'll look at making more of these after I finish writing this book, so check the site if you want to see the Windows version.

Having installed Node.js manually, let's get back to creating our React project. I called my project `namelist`. React is picky about names, so I picked one that I know will work. I'll leave fancier names to books about React. Click the **Create** button. CRA takes a while, but once it is finished, you should have a project folder ready to go. We are now ready to go 100% full stack! Next, I'm going to show you my favorite technique in PyCharm to work on both projects as if they were one, while maintaining full separation of the UI code from the backend.

Attaching the project to the FastAPI project we created earlier

Open the `fastAPIProject` folder we created at the beginning of this chapter. Now, use the **File | Open** menu to open the `namelist` folder containing the React project. Usually, when we do this, we tell PyCharm to open the project either in a new window or in the current window. This time, I want you to tell it to attach the project to the current one, as shown in *Figure 9.28*:

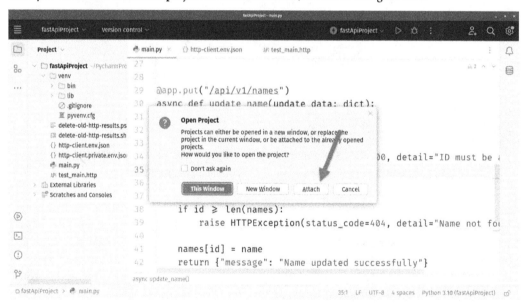

Figure 9.28: Pick the Attach option when you open the React project

You will find both projects open at the same time in the IDE. This is evident in the project window shown in *Figure 9.29*:

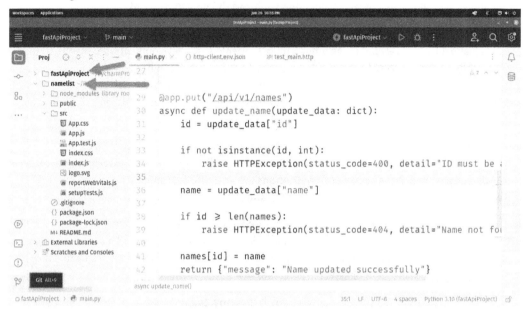

Figure 9.29: Both halves of a full stack app can be open at the same time,
allowing you to run and debug them as if they were one project

Working with attached projects makes for a very enjoyable experience in full stack development. Consider the benefits:

- Technically, they are separate projects in separate repositories.

- PyCharm allows you to create run and debug configurations for all attached projects. For example, it is possible to set a breakpoint in your React app to examine some form of data just before it is submitted. Then in your FastAPI project, you can set a breakpoint in the endpoint function to inspect the data received, making it easy to find errors in data formatting between the two projects.

- Other people who are not able to work full stack can still work on individual projects separately.

In *Chapter 11, Understanding Database Management with PyCharm*, we'll learn that you can work with the frontend, the backend, and databases, all from within one PyCharm window. For full stack development, PyCharm is hard to beat! But first, in the next chapter, let's look at a third web development framework supported by PyCharm: Pyramid.

Summary

In this chapter, we effectively covered everything you need to know in order to get started creating a RESTful API project using FastAPI in PyCharm.

FastAPI is distinct from Flask, and many other template-oriented web development frameworks, in that it is specifically designed to create only RESTful APIs. A RESTful API is a backend that is decoupled from any frontend markup, layout, interactivity, or display logic. Instead, the API focuses solely on receiving requests bearing user interaction data and returning processed data, such as that retrieved or processed in a relational database.

Since these types of applications focus on data, we learned that an SPA is normally used to serve as the frontend presentation layer. A number of modern frameworks support this paradigm, including React, Angular, and Vue. It is the frontend application's job to control the application state since HTTP is a stateless protocol, and any backend would be ill suited to this responsibility.

Creating the FastAPI project was easy using the template built into PyCharm Professional. It generated starting code as well as a special type of test file unique to PyCharm. The HTTP file contains a specification for a request, and a testing framework based on JavaScript, which allows us to validate the response with the same kind of assertion logic we saw in our earlier exposure to unit testing.

Finally, we created a React frontend in a separate, but connected (attached), project in PyCharm, allowing you to develop a full stack application without mingling the frontend JavaScript code with the backend Python code. In the next chapter, we will discuss Django and Pyramid.

Questions

1. What framework serves as the basis for FastAPI, and what makes it different from Flask and Werkzeug?
2. What is meant by "representational state transfer" and what problem does it solve?
3. Where is the application state stored in a RESTful API project using an SPA as its frontend?
4. What are the four most widely used HTTP methods?
5. What are CRUD methods, and how do the HTTP methods map to CRUD methods?
6. What are the benefits of keeping frontend and backend projects separate, and how does PyCharm make working with such full stack projects easier?

Further reading

- Garret, J. J. (2005). A new approach to web applications. `http://www.adaptivepath.com/publications/essays/archives/000385.php`.

- Pandey, R. (2023) Build Full Stack Projects with FARM Stack [Video]. Packtpub.com `https://www.packtpub.com/product/build-full-stack-projects-with-farm-stack-video/9781803236667`

- Van Horn, B. (2021) Setting Up a Python Development Workstation in Windows 10. maddevskilz.com `https://www.maddevskilz.com/courses/setting-up-a-python-development-workstation-in-windows`

- Van Horn, B. (2021) Setting Up a NodeJS Development Workstation in MacOS. maddevskilz.com `https://www.maddevskilz.com/courses/setting-up-a-nodejs-development-workstation-in-macos`

- Be sure to check out the companion website for the book at `https://www.pycharm-book.com`.

More Full Stack Frameworks – Django and Pyramid

The web frameworks we've covered so far were exemplary in the way they work. Flask is an unopinionated micro-framework. By this we mean Flask only handles endpoint routing and optionally, serving templated page content. FastAPI features a framework specifically for building RESTful APIs rather than serving content beyond data. It also features an asynchronous programming model reminiscent of modern JavaScript frameworks running in NodeJS.

There are two more frameworks you'll find on the **New Project** menu in PyCharm Professional, and we're going to cover them here. **Django** is a very popular framework that is, philosophically speaking, the diametric opposite of Flask. Django is a highly opinionated framework that attempts to make all your platform and framework choices for you.

The final framework we'll talk about is **Pyramid**. Pyramid aims for the middle ground between Flask and Django offering more bundled features than Flask, but more flexibility than Django.

In this chapter, you will learn the following:

- How to generate a Django project using PyCharm Professional's new project template
- How to identify the major files and folders present in the templated project generated by PyCharm
- How to use Django-specific tooling in PyCharm for `manage.py` tasks
- How to create a Pyramid project in PyCharm Professional

We've already covered a lot of theory on how web applications work in earlier chapters, so let's get straight into developing these two frameworks using PyCharm. As with other web development frameworks, these features are only available in the Professional edition of PyCharm.

Technical requirements

In order to proceed through this chapter, and indeed the rest of the book, you will need the following:

- An installed and working Python interpreter. I'll be using the latest from `https://python.org`.

- Installed copies of `pip` and `virtualenv`. You get these automatically when you install Python on Windows, and macOS has them included on every system. If you are using Linux, you need to install the package managers such as `pip` and virtual environment tools such as `virtualenv` separately. Our examples will use `pip` and `virtualenv`.

- An installed and working copy of PyCharm. Installation was covered in *Chapter 2, Installation and Configuration*, in case you are jumping into the middle of the book. I am using build PyCharm Professional 2023.1 (build #PY-231.8109.197) with the new UI turned on.

- This book's sample source code from GitHub. We covered cloning the code in *Chapter 2, Installation and Configuration*. You'll find this chapter's relevant code at `https://github.com/PacktPublishing/Hands-On-Application-Development-with-PyCharm---Second-Edition/tree/main/chapter-10`.

What's all this fuss about Django?

If you ask most Python developers which framework they prefer, I'll wager it is an even split between Flask and Django. I'll also wager that the Django crowd are raving fans of Django while Flask seems more like a thing you use to get stuff done. It's like getting excited about a screwdriver. Django is a lot more opinionated, and as such, a lot more "in your face." You barely notice Flask because it's just a piece of the puzzle. Django is all the pieces in one box, plus that glue you use to make puzzles into a picture, plus an expensive frame for the completed glued puzzle, plus a beach house so you have a place to hang your puzzle. There might even be little mints on the pillows in the beach house, but I make no promises.

Django, on the other hand, promises to be a web framework that handles the heavy lifting and repetitive aspects of web application development. Web developers are freed up to focus on the specific logic of their applications. Web frameworks usually implement common design patterns and good practices into their structure, so that a web application developed with a framework will be up to common standards by default, without its developer having to manually integrate those standards into the application.

Django aims to have everything you need to develop a web application baked into the framework. Since that is true, you shouldn't have to think about your stack at all. Django becomes more than a framework; it becomes an ethos. You become a fan of Django's way. You might even say *"This is the way,"* and Django might say it back. Here are some things Django is good at:

- **Speed**: Similar to Python itself, Django emphasizes the ease of developing and translating ideas into actual code. With straightforward yet extensive APIs, Django aims to accommodate a wide range of web applications and features.

- **Security**: Web development is one of the topics in programming in which security is the highest priority. The Django framework offers features that navigate web developers, beginners, and experts alike, away from security flaws in their applications.

- **Scalability**: When a website gains more clients, scalability becomes more and more important. Scalability in Django can be achieved in flexible and intuitive ways; in fact, some of the largest sites on the internet (Bitbucket, Instagram, Pinterest, and so on) are built with Django for that reason.

None of these are specifically addressed by Flask. In fact, Flask is not normally used for large web applications because it is relatively slow. Personally, I've moved all my product backend code away from Flask and into FastAPI because the performance is noticeably better.

So far, Django sounds much better than anything else we've talked about so far. Despite being a popular and powerful web framework, Django, like any technology, has its detractors. Some of the common criticisms and concerns raised about Django include the following:

- **Steep learning curve**: Some developers find Django's learning curve to be relatively steep, especially for beginners with limited experience in Python or web development. Its extensive feature set and comprehensive nature can be overwhelming for newcomers.

- **Magic and abstraction**: Django's emphasis on "batteries included" and abstraction can be a double-edged sword. While it saves development time, some developers argue that it can obscure the underlying mechanisms, making it harder to understand and troubleshoot complex issues.

- **Overhead for small projects**: For small projects or simple websites, some developers feel that Django's feature richness and structure can be overkill, adding unnecessary overhead and complexity.

- **Monolithic nature**: Critics argue that Django is a monolithic framework, and it may not be the best fit for microservices architectures or highly specialized applications where a lightweight framework might be more suitable.

- **Flexibility versus opinionated**: Django follows a particular design philosophy and enforces certain patterns, which some developers see as overly opinionated. This can lead to debates over the "Django way" of doing things versus alternative approaches.

- **Performance**: Although Django is reasonably performant, some developers claim that it may not be as fast as certain micro-frameworks or specialized tools. Performance-critical projects may require additional optimization efforts.

- **ORM limitations**: While Django's ORM is powerful and easy to use, it may not cover all edge cases or offer the same level of control as writing raw SQL queries. In certain scenarios, developers may prefer using other ORMs or query builders.

- **Version upgrades**: Upgrading between major versions of Django can sometimes be challenging, especially for older projects heavily reliant on deprecated features. This can lead to maintenance issues and additional development efforts.

- **Customization complexity**: While Django offers flexibility, some developers find it challenging to customize certain built-in components, such as the admin interface, to fit specific design requirements.

- **Community and ecosystem**: Although Django has a large and active community, it may not have as extensive an ecosystem or as many third-party packages available as some other web frameworks.

It's important to note that while these criticisms exist, Django has an extensive user base, and many developers appreciate its productivity, stability, and comprehensive feature set. Ultimately, the choice of a web framework depends on the specific needs and preferences of the project and development team.

Django framework components

Django includes an inclusive set of components that make it a comprehensive and feature-rich framework for web development. Here are some of the key components:

- **URL dispatching (routing)**: Django uses a URL dispatcher to route incoming HTTP requests to the appropriate view functions or class-based views. This enables clean and logical URL patterns for your web application.

- **View functions and class-based views**: Views in Django are responsible for processing user requests and returning HTTP responses. You can use simple functions as views or use Django's class-based views for more organized and reusable code.

- **Templates**: Django's template system allows you to define the structure and layout of your web pages using HTML templates with placeholders for dynamic content. This separation of concerns (logic and presentation) makes it easier to maintain and scale your web application.

- **Model-View-Template (MVT) architecture**: Similar to the **Model-View-Controller (MVC)** pattern, Django follows the MVT pattern. Models represent the data structures and the database schema, views handle the logic and processing, and templates take care of rendering the output.

- **Object-Relational Mapping (ORM)**: Django's ORM is one of its defining features. It provides a high-level, Pythonic way to interact with databases without having to write raw SQL queries. It allows you to define models as Python classes, and the ORM handles the mapping of these models to the database tables.

- **Forms**: Django includes a form-handling system that simplifies form creation, data validation, and handling user input. It helps in processing HTML forms and converting user-submitted data into Python data types.

- **Admin interface**: Django's admin interface is an automatic admin interface that can be used to manage your application's data models. It provides an out-of-the-box solution for managing model data and is customizable to fit your specific needs.

- **Middleware**: Middleware components in Django are hooks that allow you to process requests and responses globally before they reach the view or after they leave the view. It enables features including authentication, security checks, and request/response modification.

- **Static files**: Django has built-in support for managing static files such as CSS, JavaScript, and images. It simplifies the process of serving static content during development and deployment.

- **Authentication and authorization**: Django provides a robust authentication system for managing user accounts, permissions, and groups. It makes it easy to add user registration, login, and password management functionalities to your application.

- **Internationalization and localization**: Django supports internationalization and localization, allowing you to create applications that can be translated into multiple languages and adapted to various regions.

- **Testing framework**: Django comes with a testing framework that facilitates unit testing and integration testing of your application. You can write test cases to ensure that your code works as expected and avoid regressions.

With all that overhead, it's a good thing we have such a capable tool in PyCharm. Let's dive into creating a Django application.

Creating a Django project

The process is no different than most other projects. Click **File | New Project** then click the **Django** option as shown in *Figure 10.1*.

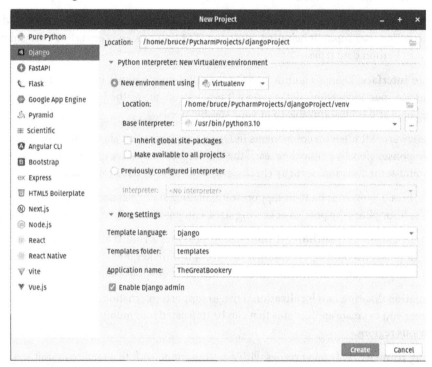

Figure 10.1: Creating a new Django project is much like any other project

Be sure to twirl down the **More Settings** section. Here you can set the template language. You can use either the **Django templating language** or **Jinja2**, which was what we used in *Chapter 9, Building a Dynamic Web Application with Flask*. Since we covered Jinja2 already, let's stick with Django. You can set the name of the folder you'll use for templates, and you absolutely should set a value for the **Application name** field as shown at the bottom of *Figure 10.1*.

> **Don't skip the application name**
>
> If you skip the **Application name** setting at the bottom of *Figure 10.1*, PyCharm will assume you want a Django project without any applications. Of course, you can add additional applications later using the manage.py tooling we'll cover later, but that's probably not what you want most of the time when you are creating a new project. Furthermore, you should not name the application the same as the PyCharm project as it can cause confusion in PyCharm's indexing, not to mention for the humans working on the project.

Django projects often have multiple applications within them, and the **Application name** setting here is used to create and name the first application within the project. We're going to be building a single library application in our project. Since the term *library* is ambiguous in a programming book, I'll clarify the name of the application so we understand the *library* is a place that serves books rather than a programming library.

The resulting newly created project is shown in *Figure 10.2*.

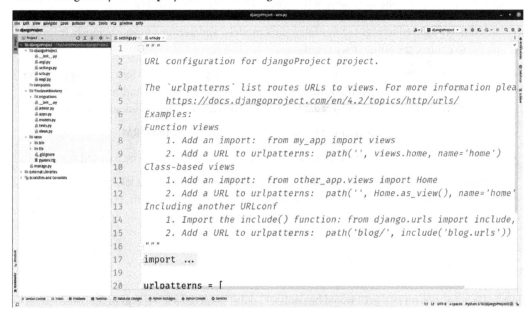

Figure 10.2: The Django project has been created and PyCharm opens
the urls.py and settings.py files as a starting point

Given the super long list of components, it is a little surprising how few files were created. PyCharm has automatically opened two as a starting point: `urls.py` and `settings.py`. Let's take a look at what these and the rest of the files and folders are for in our newly created application.

Structure of a Django project

The first thing you might notice is the project, which I just called `djangoProject`, has its own set of files distinct from the application, which is in the `TheGreatBookery` folder. All of the files inside of the `djangoProject` folder are used in the deployment of your application to production, as well as to run the built-in development server.

Inside the `TheGreatBookery` folder, we have a folder for database migrations. This is common for applications that use ORMs. You need a way to make changes to the production database as you roll new releases into production. You can't simply drop the database and rebuild it since that would erase all your application's data. There needs to be a system to migrate schema changes to the existing database while maintaining your existing production data. Django's system for migrations utilizes migration scripts stored in this folder.

The templates folder, which is technically outside the application's folder, is where we keep our HTML templates.

You might be able to guess the functions of the remaining files by their names:

- `admin.py` is used to register modules, data models, and perhaps most obviously from the name, to control the admin user interface.

- `apps.py` provides a central place to customize and configure the behavior of your application within the Django project. It allows you to specify various settings and metadata for your application, such as the human-readable name, default app configuration, and signals.

- `models.py` will contain your data model, which is affected by the ORM.

- `tests.py` will house your application's unit tests, which run using Django's own testing framework.

- `views.py` will contain view functions. These are Python functions that take an HTTP request as an argument and return an HTTP response. Within these functions, you can handle the request, process data from the models or other sources, and generate an appropriate HTTP response, often by rendering a template with dynamic data.

Initial configuration

While this is not a book on Django, I would be remiss if I didn't point out a few things in the `settings. py` file. Like Flask, Django has a built-in development web server that is not designed to be used in production. The `settings.py` file has some dangerous settings in it as hardcoded values that are appropriate for local development only. Open up `settings.py` and locate these lines:

```
# SECURITY WARNING: keep the secret key used in production secret!
SECRET_KEY = 'django-insecure-39u&w+cgs2t4*jwe3nuz4y4j^s!s65^xb7eq
tb_a3bl!a_s%tn'

# SECURITY WARNING: don't run with debug turned on in production!
DEBUG = True
```

Something you should do early is make sure to draw these values from outside your code. You should never hardcode a secret in your application code, and you should never commit secrets to a revision control system! You can externalize these values using environment variables, `.ini` files, or `.env` files using libraries from `PyPi.org`. Leaving the DEBUG setting hardcoded can be dangerous because errors thrown may be plainly visible along with the stack trace and other details that bad actors might be able to exploit.

Another setting you might want to review is the database engine. You'll find these lines toward the bottom of `settings.py`:

```
# Database
# https://docs.djangoproject.com/en/4.2/ref/settings/#databases

DATABASES = {
    'default': {
        'ENGINE': 'django.db.backends.sqlite3',
        'NAME': BASE_DIR / 'db.sqlite3',
    }
}
```

PyCharm has defaulted us to SQLite3, which is not really suitable for a production application. SQLite3 is a file-based database, and using it for local development is advantageous because it doesn't require the installation of a server. You shouldn't serve a production app with SQLite3, and in my opinion, you should develop using the same database you'll use in production.

That said, we won't be taking this app to production so I'm going to leave the settings as they are. Your database will appear in the project directory as a file called `db.sqlite3`. We will learn about PyCharm's database capabilities in *Chapter 11*. Know that PyCharm has a rich set of tools for viewing and working with databases, including SQLite3, which can help during development.

Running the Django project

When we created the project, PyCharm created a run configuration for us. We covered run configurations extensively in *Chapter 6*. We simply want to run the one PyCharm generated, so simply click the green **Run** button shown in *Figure 10.3*.

Figure 10.3: The Run button will start the development server

Running the project will open the **Run** panel at the bottom of the IDE window, as shown in *Figure 10.4*.

Figure 10.4: Our project is running and being served on localhost port 8000

We can see our project is running on port 8000, and there's a handy link that will open our default browser to the running app, as shown in *Figure 10.5*.

Figure 10.5: Clicking the link opens the browser and displays a nice
message letting you know everything is working

PyCharm has effectively created a minimal working application for us. In a real projects, this is usually where I address deployment via **continuous integration** (**CI**) and **continuous delivery** (**CD**). One piece of advice I always give new web developers is to get the production mechanics in place as early as possible. If you do it right, you won't have to mess with them again for quite a while.

JetBrains has a very good CI/CD server called TeamCity. I used it exclusively for the last 10 years, having only last year switched begrudgingly to Microsoft Azure DevOps. TeamCity is a much better system and its definitely worth your time and trouble if you're looking for a CI/CD server. JetBrains even offers plugins for PyCharm that allow you to control and monitor builds right from the IDE.

This, though, is a chapter on Django, so let's keep the party rolling and move on to working with data models.

Creating Django models

In a Django application, models play a central and crucial role. They are the backbone of the application's data structure and are responsible for defining the database schema and handling data operations. Models allow developers to interact with the underlying database in an object-oriented manner, making it easier to manage and manipulate data.

Models serve as an interface between the application and the database. They abstract away the complexities of SQL queries and provide a high-level API to perform **Create, Read, Update, Delete** (**CRUD**) operations. By using model methods and querysets, developers can interact with the database without having to write raw SQL code. Everything related to the database driving the application (including the things a lot of developers usually leave out, such as validation and constraints) can be found rolled into a Django model.

A prevalent anti-pattern that sometimes pops up with projects that forgo using ORMs is the use of the database to encapsulate business logic. The justification for this is usually that changing the database is quick, easy, and doesn't require a new compilation or a new deployment. This is a foolish economy, and in a modern era that requires governance and documented change control, it becomes anathema. The senior database developer on my team, who is also a technical reviewer for *Chapter 11*, describes this practice as changing the tires on a semi-truck while it is traveling down the highway at 100 mph. Django models, though, since they are technically objects, are able to handle business logic effectively and without taboo. This is because only the structure of the data model is translated into the database while the logic remains within the object.

The thing you need to remember about using an ORM, which is what we're doing when we create and manipulate models, is that we are working with an abstraction of our database. When we manipulate instances of our models we are altering data in the database. Likewise, when we change the structure of our classes, we are altering the structure of the database. There are differences between the way data types in your programming language work and the way they work in the database. We'll see this in action later, but right now I want you to think about the fact that Python is a dynamic language that uses duck typing. In Python, I can alter any structure or type in any way that suits me. Databases on the other hand are static and strongly typed. Django's ORM has its work cut out for it given the differences in paradigm between the way Python works with classes, types, and variables versus the way the database works with tables.

Let's look at creating an easy model. Locate the `models.py` file. You can find it displayed in *Figure 10.6*, or you can use the navigation features in PyCharm by pressing *Ctrl + Shift + N* (**Navigate** | **File** in the menu) and typing in the filename `models.py`.

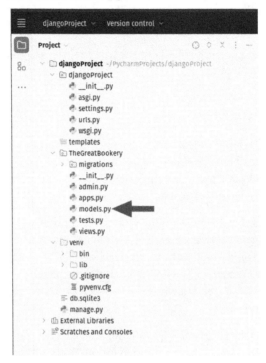

Figure 10.6: Open the models.py file so we can add a model

The generated code within will look like this:

```
from django.db import models


# Create your models here.
```

We're going to create two models for our Bookery application: `author` and `book`. To do this, let's alter the code in `models.py` as follows:

```
from django.db import models

import datetime
from django.utils import timezone
```

Here, we've added two imports both related to time and dates. We're going to use these libraries in some business logic that we will attach to the book model. Let's not get ahead of ourselves, though. Let's make a simple model to represent book authors:

```
# Create your models here.
class Author(models.Model):
    first_name = models.CharField(max_length=100)
    last_name = models.CharField(max_length=100)

    def __str__(self):
        return f'{self.last_name}, {self.first_name}'
```

The class is hopefully straightforward enough. The `Author` class inherits from Django's `model.Model` class. There are two fields for the author's first and last name and use the `models.CharField` type to represent what would be varchars in the database. Relational databases require to declare a strong type, and in the case of a varchar (a variable-length character field), we have to supply a maximum length. The dunder string method simply gives us a nice format should we request the contents of the model as a string. Here, we've elected to format the author's name as last name, comma, space, and first name.

Every ORM, regardless of platform, works the same way. Its aim is to allow developers to work only with native language objects. With that said, they usually need their own type system to allow the ORM to translate between the type system of the language (Python) and the database. You'll learn in *Chapter 11* that database data types are not the same as in their programming language counterparts. At a minimum, differences such as calling strings as varchars are apparent, and types including int and float exist in both contexts. Sometimes they are even different between database platforms. There are datatypes in SQLite3 that are not present in MySQL, and vice versa.

An ORM has to work everywhere, so having its own type system for models allows for a single type system for the developer that can be adapted to any database platform. It is a classic implementation of the Gang of Four's **adapter pattern**, which I cover in my book *Real-World Implementation of C# Design Patterns*, published by Packt.

The `author` class is not very fancy. Let's do some more interesting code in the Book model code:

```
class Book(models.Model):
    title = models.CharField(max_length=200)
    author = models.ForeignKey(Author, on_delete=models.CASCADE,)
    pub_date = models.DateTimeField('date published')
```

So far we have a `Book` class inheriting from `models.Model` as before. We have a title field with a maximum length of 200 characters. There is an `author` field, but rather than make this a string, we used the `Author` class to set up a **foreign key**. In database parlance, this means the data for the authors is represented in the `authors` table, which is controlled by the `Author` class we made a minute ago. A foreign key relationship specifies that any `Book` we add to the database must contain a related (it's a relational database) database to an existing author. Operationally, this means we have to make sure the author exists in the database before we can add the author's books to the database.

Foreign key constraints serve as a form of built-in data validation but they also help maintain data integrity in the database by enforcing rules. If I were to add an author to the database, and then add a bunch of books written by that author, we would have a nice relationship going on between the two tables. If I were to then delete the author from the `authors` table, we'd still have a bunch of book records without a related author. They would be orphan records. Orphan records are bad because they take up space in the database, and they break the integrity of the relationship between authors and books.

In this class, when we define the `author` field, we are defining it with a foreign key constraint with an actual rule covering what happens when you delete an author. The code that says `on_delete=models.CASCADE` tells the ORM that when an author is deleted, so are the records of the books they've written. It is called a cascading delete because the delete cascades from the author to the book records, which could in turn cascade to other tables that might have similar relationships to books. A well-constructed database can keep itself clean and devoid of orphan records regardless of how complex the database structure might be.

Lastly, we have a date to contain the publication date:

```
pub_date = models.DateTimeField('date published')
```

If the `foreign key` field didn't add enough spice for you, let's add one more thing. Since we are dealing with an object, and since objects can contain both data and functional logic, let's add a function to our `Book` model:

```
def was_published_recently(self):
    now = timezone.now()
    return now - datetime.timedelta(days=1) <= self.pub_date <= now
```

This adds a field to our model, but rather than this data being stored in the database, it is computed at the time the method is called. We're taking the static field for the publication date and computing the difference (delta) of the time to the current date. We're taking into account the time zone and we're presenting it as the number of days since the book was published. This allows us to show our users how old the book is in days, which might be used to prompt authors to produce new and updated editions of their books.

Performing migrations using manage.py

One of the files generated for your Django project is `manage.py`. You can see it in *Figure 10.7*.

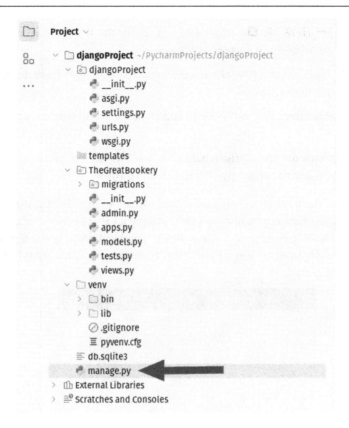

Figure 10.7: The manage.py file provides utilities for working with your Django
project so you don't have to type in long commands or remember full paths

The purpose of the manage.py task is to allow you to run Django-specific commands from the command line without having to remember the full path to your Django project or manually set up the Python environment. By using manage.py, you ensure that the commands are executed within the correct Django project context.

Some common tasks you can perform with manage.py include the following:

- **Running the development server**: You can start the Django development server using manage.py runserver. This allows you to test your application locally during development. Earlier, we ran the Django project using the generated run configuration. We could have also used manage.py for this.

- **Creating and applying database migrations**: With manage.py makemigrations and manage.py migrate, you can create and apply database migrations, respectively. This helps you manage changes to your models and keep your database schema up to date.

- **Creating a superuser**: You can create a superuser for the Django admin interface using `manage.py createsuperuser`.

- **Running tests**: You can execute your test suite using `manage.py test` to ensure that your application functions as expected.

- **Managing static files**: You can collect and manage static files using `manage.py collectstatic`.

- **Managing translations**: For internationalization and localization, you can use `manage.py makemessages` and `manage.py compilemessages`.

This is just a short list. There are many more utilities in `manage.py`. The `manage.py` file serves as an entry point to Django management commands, making it easy to perform administrative tasks without leaving your development environment. Before you head down to the terminal button in PyCharm, there is actually an easier way to work with `manage.py`. Click **Tools | Run manage.py task...** as shown in *Figure 10.8*.

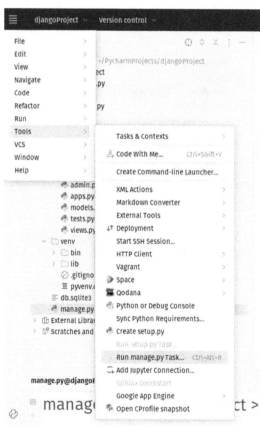

Figure 10.8: PyCharm has a dedicated tool panel for working with manage.py

This gives you a new panel, as shown in *Figure 10.9*.

Figure 10.9: The Run manage.py task panel is a dedicated command-line interface
that lets you easily invoke commands specific to Django's manage.py file

The manage.py panel opens at the bottom of the IDE as many do. At first glance, it looks like a terminal window, but this one is specific to Django and the manage.py file. As you can see, the panel provides auto-completion to help with the commands.

In order to create our migrations, you should type this command into the panel:

```
makemigrations TheGreatBookery
```

The result will resemble *Figure 10.10*.

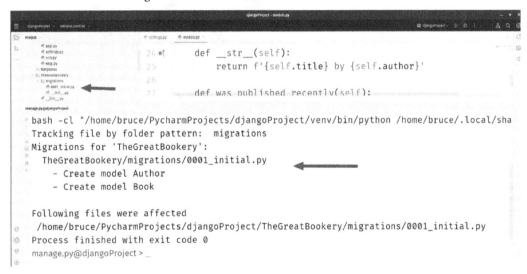

Figure 10.10: The result of the makemigrations command

You'll find some messages in the manage.py panel as well as a new file in the migrations folder called something like 0001_initial.py. The makemigrations command generated the code needed for the migration, but it hasn't performed the migration yet. Performing the migration is what affects the changes to the database. In order to run the migration, type this into the manage.py task panel:

```
sqlmigrate TheGreatBookery 0001
```

The output from the command, shown in *Figure 10.11*, indicates the database structure has been updated to match the models.

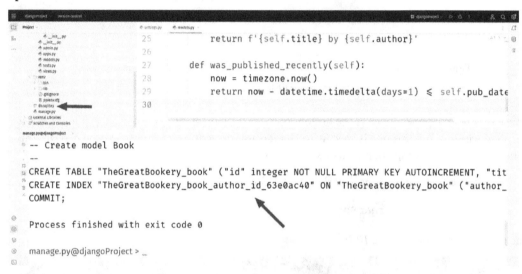

Figure 10.11: The result of the migration is a set of messages and the appearance of our database file

We see a bunch of SQL statements that were generated to bring the database structure up to match the structure of the models. We also see a new file for our database. If you remember, we saw earlier that the name and path of this file were set in the settings.py file. Since SQLite3 is a file database, this is the actual database itself. This is the kind of thing you might want to exclude from revision control on a real project.

The Django admin interface

This is one of the killer features of Django: it creates a web-based administrative panel for you. This means you don't have to build an interface for dealing with users, handling logins, or creating screens for simple data entry into your model structure. The first thing every app needs is an administrative user or superuser. It is common for applications to have role-based user access, and the super-user is the user who can do everything, including adding new users. This kind of thing might take a developer two or three days to get working, but with Django, it's already done.

Creating a superuser and logging in

Before users, logins, or any of the other goodies we're talking about here work, you need to apply a migration that was generated for you when you created the project.

Let's head back to our manage.py task panel and type this command:

```
migrate
```

Just like that, by itself. This adds all the base tables for the application. We probably should have done this first, but I didn't want to break the flow of what we were working on. OK, really I forgot, but it sounded better the other way.

With that migration run we now have all the tables and structures in the database to support Django's login and user administration feature. Next, let's create the superuser. In the panel, type the following:

```
createsuperuser
```

You are asked a set of questions designed to create a superuser for your application as shown in *Figure 10.12.*

```
manage.py@djangoProject > createsuperuser
bash -cl "/home/bruce/PycharmProjects/djangoProject/venv/bin/python /home/bruce/.local/sha
Tracking file by folder pattern:  migrations
Username (leave blank to use 'bruce'):  admin
Email address:  admin@myproject.com
Warning: Password input may be echoed.
Password:  P@ssw0rd
Warning: Password input may be echoed.
Password (again):  P@ssw0rd
This password is too common.
Bypass password validation and create user anyway? [y/N]:  y
Superuser created successfully.
manage.py@djangoProject > _
```

Figure 10.12: The manage.py panel interaction for creating a superuser

Let's try out the management interface! While you could just use the run configuration, let's see what it is like to run it from the manage.py task panel. Type the following:

```
runserver
```

Then click the link in the panel message shown in *Figure 10.13.*

```
manage.py@djangoProject
  manage.py@djangoProject > runserver
  bash -cl "/home/bruce/PycharmProjects/djangoProject/venv/bin/python /home/bruce/.local/sha
  Tracking file by folder pattern:  migrations
  Watching for file changes with StatReloader
  Performing system checks ...

  System check identified no issues (0 silenced).
  July 30, 2023 - 23:04:06
  Django version 4.2.3, using settings 'djangoProject.settings'
  Starting development server at http://127.0.0.1:8000/
  Quit the server with CONTROL-C.
```

Figure 10.13: This time, let's run from the panel!

In truth, it is the exact same thing you would have gotten by clicking the green run button as we did the first time we ran the app. After clicking the link, your browser opens to the same page we saw before. Change the URL in the browser to http://127.0.0.1:8000/admin. This will take you to the administrative login page shown in *Figure 10.14*.

Figure 10.14: The best kind of login system is the one you didn't have to make yourself!

Type in the superuser user name and password you specified in the task panel. *Figure 10.15* shows the admin screen that should appear.

Figure 10.15: Without writing any code, we can add users and groups to the application

Click around to see everything Django has generated for us. You can add users and groups to the application despite not having written any code for this – Django handled it for us. The downside here is that it was generated based on the Django project's ideas on what an admin panel should look like and how it should work. While it is possible to customize some of this functionality, remember that I keep saying that Django is *opinionated*. It has assumptions baked in. Less opinionated frameworks would require you to build this or use a plugin, but you would be in total control over how this feature was implemented.

Adding the Author and Book models to the admin interface

While you get users and groups for free, you do have to do a tiny bit of work to get authors and books to show up in the admin interface. Let's start with the `Author` model.

Open the `admin.py` file in `TheGreatBookery` folder and find a comment that says `# Register your models here`. Add the following code:

```
# Register your models here.
from .models import Author
admin.site.register(Author)
```

If your app stopped or crashed, go ahead and restart it, then navigate to the admin page as before. You should now see **Authors** appear on the admin page, as shown in *Figure 10.16*.

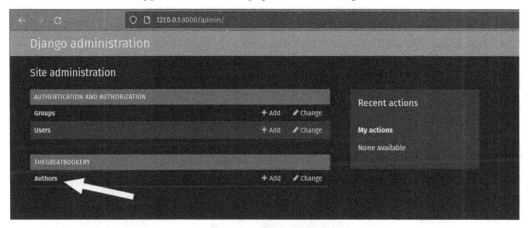

Figure 10.16: With very little effort, we can now add, edit, and delete authors

We have the Author model; let's add `Book`. This one is a little fancier. Remember, there is a relationship between Book and Author. Each Author can be related to many Books, or inversely, many Books are related to one Author.

Since this is so, we want the admin interface to not only reflect this relationship but enforce it at the UI layer. You can just slap an import for the book model in and expect it to work perfectly.

Go back to the admin.py file and add this code:

```python
from django.contrib import admin

# Register your models here.
from .models import Author, Book

class BookInLine(admin.TabularInline):
  model = Book
  extra = 1

  fieldsets = [
    (None, {'fields': ['title']}),
    ('Date information', {'fields': ['pub_date']})
  ]


class AuthorAdmin(admin.ModelAdmin):
  inlines = [BookInLine]

admin.site.register(Author, AuthorAdmin)
```

This code creates an addition to the Author UI that allows you to add books inline which is to say when you add an author, you will then have the opportunity to add books. You can't have books without first adding authors. Because we defined the relationship and the UI this way, the ability to add and edit books is part of administering the author. You'll never even have the chance to mess up by adding books before authors, or by somehow disassociating a book from an author.

Restart your server, and refresh your browser. Nothing changed! Hang on, that's OK. We haven't tried to add an author yet. Click **Authors** and then click **Add**, and you'll find the interface shown in *Figure 10.17*.

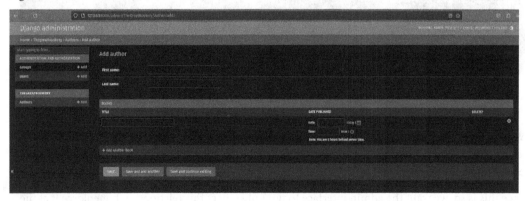

Figure 10.17: Our code added inline books to the UI for managing authors

As you can see, the form for adding books is now attached inline to the form for working with authors.

Creating Django views

The admin UI is pretty magical, but it is really only designed to create simple screens for managing data in a database. Sooner or later, you're going to have to actually make some real screens for the app itself.

We need to be careful about terminology here because the word *views* doesn't mean what you might expect if you are versed in more conventional web development design patterns. The prevailing industry pattern is called **Model-View-Controller (MVC)**. The pattern employed by Django is called **Model-View-Template (MVT)**. *View* doesn't mean the same thing between the two patterns. Let's compare the two.

MVC	MVT
Model refers to the data structure, usually from a database.	Model means the same thing as it does in MVC.
View refers to the visual elements which is usually the user interface.	View refers to the controller layer, which accepts incoming requests, performs logic, and returns content or data.
Controller refers to a layer that accepts incoming requests, performs logic, and returns content or data	Template refers to the View in MVC, which is the HTML or user interface elements in the application.

In summary, the Django View is really the Controller, and the Django Template would be the View in an MVC app. So here, when we are about to make the View, we're talking about the part of the app that receives requests, does something, then returns the response.

Open the `views.py` file in the `TheGreatBookery` folder. Change the code to this:

```
from django.shortcuts import render
from .models import Book


# Create your views here.
def index(request):
    latest_books = Book.objects.order_by('-pub_date')[:5]
    context = {'latest_books': latest_books}
    return render(request, 'TheGreatBookery/index.html', context)
```

Here, we've imported the `Book` model, then defined a method designed to accept a request, retrieve all the books in the database, and order them by the `pub_date` field in descending order indicated by the minus sign next to `pub_date`. We're only going to display the first five books we find as indicated by the slice `[:5]`.

Next, we create a variable called context ,which becomes a dictionary that will be used to pass data to the template during rendering. In this case, it creates a key-value pair where the key is `latest_books` and the value is the `QuerySet` of the latest books retrieved in the previous step.

The `return` line calls the `render` method imported at the top of the file. It passes the `request` object, a path to the template (which we have yet to create), and the `context` dictionary variable we just created.

This view function won't do all the work by itself. Before it can be used, it must be registered in the `urls.py` file so we have a route to employ this function.

Open `urls.py` and change the code to this:

```
from django.contrib import admin
from django.urls import path
from TheGreatBookery.views import index


urlpatterns = [
  path('admin/', admin.site.urls),
  path('', index, name='index')
]
```

We added an import to the `index` function we just created in the `views.py` file. Next, we added by way of the `path` function an empty string, which will map the root route for the app, a reference to the `index` function that will execute in response to requests at the root route, and a friendly name.

We're almost done. There's just one more thing. Go back to the `view.py` file and you'll see some problematic yellow highlighting. See *Figure 10.18*.

```
 settings.py    models.py    admin.py    views.py    urls.py
1   from django.shortcuts import render
2   from .models import Book
3
4
5   # Create your views here.
    2 usages
6   def index(request):
7       latest_books = Book.objects.order_by('-pub_date')[:5]
8       context = {'latest_books': latest_books}
9       return render(request, 'TheGreatBookery/index.html', context)
```
Template file 'index.html' not found
Create Template TheGreatBookery/index.html   Alt+Shift+Enter   More actions... Alt+Enter

Figure 10.18: We have a view and a URL mapped, but we haven't made the template yet

Hover your mouse over `index.html` and note that the tooltip has an action available to create the template for us. Either click the blue link text in the tool-tip window or use *Alt + Shift + Enter* as indicated. *Figure 10.19* shows the ensuing dialog.

Figure 10.19: The dialog you get when you use the in-line action to create the missing template is automatically filled in based on some obvious assumptions

When you click **OK**, you are prompted to create a folder in `Templates` called `TheGreatBookery`. It is possible to have multiple apps in your Django project. Since that is the case, you might want to segregate your templates. Go ahead and let PyCharm create the folder for you. After it does, you get an empty file called `index.html`.

This isn't a book on web page design, so we aren't even going to try to make this pretty. Enter this code into your `index.html` page:

```
{% if latest_books %}
  <ul>
    {% for book in latest_books %}
      <li>{{ book.title }} by {{ book.author }}</li>
    {% endfor %}
  </ul>
```

```
{% else %}
  <p>No books available.</p>
{% endif %}
```

This looks a lot like Jinja2 code we saw in *Chapter 8* with Flask. It is very similar. All this code does is check whether or not a dictionary key called `latest_books` exists on the data context that was passed in. If you go back and look at the `render` function we called in the view, it's passing this in.

If the key is there, we render the contents using the templates for loop syntax. This isn't exactly an amazing UI. It is just going to render an unordered list with each book as a list item. If the key were not there, then we'll be rendering a paragraph that says **No books available**.

What's with the weird Python icon in the template gutter?

You might have noticed a big, juicy Python icon in the gutter of the `index.html` file. Check out *Figure 18.20*.

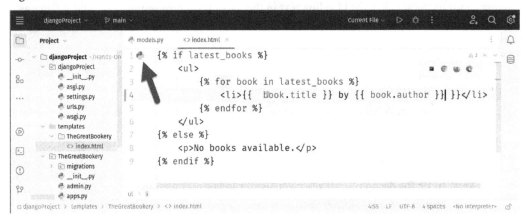

Figure 10.20: Look at that icon up there just begging to be clicked!

That Python icon is actually called a *Pythicon*.

OK, no it isn't, I just made that up. Still, you really want to click it, don't you? Go ahead, click it! It takes you to the Python code in `views.py` where we invoke it. Travel works both ways. In `views.py`, you'll notice a more subtle icon in the gutter where the template is invoked. See *Figure 18.21*.

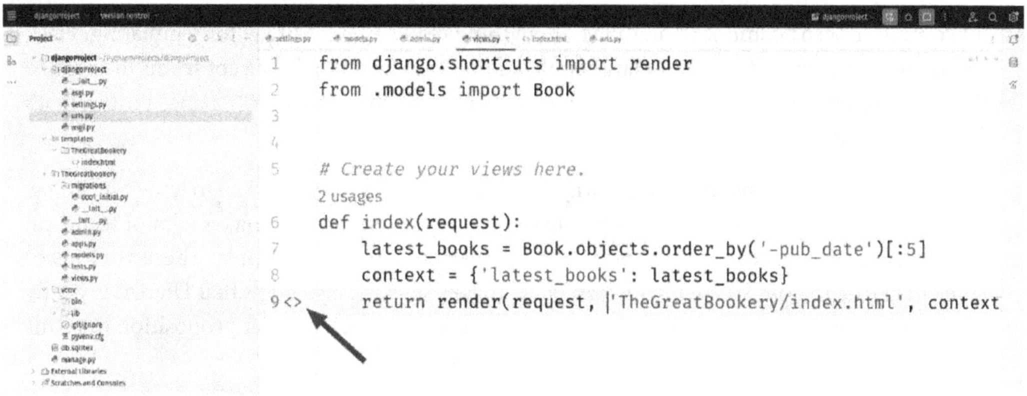

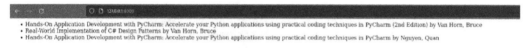

```
1    from django.shortcuts import render
2    from .models import Book
3
4
5    # Create your views here.
     2 usages
6    def index(request):
7        latest_books = Book.objects.order_by('-pub_date')[:5]
8        context = {'latest_books': latest_books}
9 <>     return render(request, 'TheGreatBookery/index.html', context
```

Figure 10.21: Click the HTML icon to navigate to the template

Again, just click the html icon, er, I mean HTML icon, to go to the template. I wouldn't blame you for clicking back and forth between the two while saying, *"Take that, vi and emacs!"*

Run it!

Start or restart your server and check the results as seen in *Figure 18.22.*

- Hands-On Application Development with PyCharm: Accelerate your Python applications using practical coding techniques in PyCharm (2nd Edition) by Van Horn, Bruce
- Real-World Implementation of C# Design Patterns by Van Horn, Bruce
- Hands-On Application Development with PyCharm: Accelerate your Python applications using practical coding techniques in PyCharm by Nguyen, Quan

Figure 10.22: This might be the best website ever!

If you direct your browser to `http://localhost:8000/` you should see either some books or a message stating there are no books. I added some obvious reading choices and so my run looks absolutely glorious!

Clearly, you could leverage the HTML tooling we learned in *Chapter 7* to make this nicer, but we still have more ground to cover, so I'll leave that up to you.

Building Pyramid applications with PyCharm

We've seen three popular web frameworks so far. There is one left that is listed in PyCharm's **New Project** menu: **Pyramid**. You can find details on Pyramid at `https://trypyramid.com/`.

The organization behind Pyramid bills it as a framework that allows you to start small, finish big, and stay finished. To my mind, this might be a little bit of a dig at its main competitors. Django is criticized as being overly opinionated, and for being overkill for small projects. This fits with the "start small" idea in Pyramid. You have more leeway in choosing the components for your application, and you can leave out what you don't need. For example, you can choose from a couple of ORM libraries, or simply choose not to use one. Django really wants you to use theirs.

Flask, in contrast, doesn't come with an ORM or anything really, besides Jinja2 for templating. Flask is criticized for not being performant in large applications. The "finish big" concept seems to speak to this criticism. I'm not sure what, if anything, the "stay finished" directive is criticizing. I think that's something we all want.

Having seen the first-rate tooling for Django, switching to Pyramid now is going to seem underwhelming. Django is a good candidate for custom tooling because it is complex, and it makes a lot of technical decisions for you. We can consider the `manage.py` task panel as an example. There are tons of commands in `manage.py`, so having its own panel makes sense. It also helps that Django is wildly popular. Pyramid isn't. So from a PyCharm perspective, this is a much simpler proposition in terms of tooling.

Creating a Pyramid project

Creating a Pyramid project is no different from any other. Just use **File | New Project**, and pick the **Pyramid** template, as shown in *Figure 10.23*.

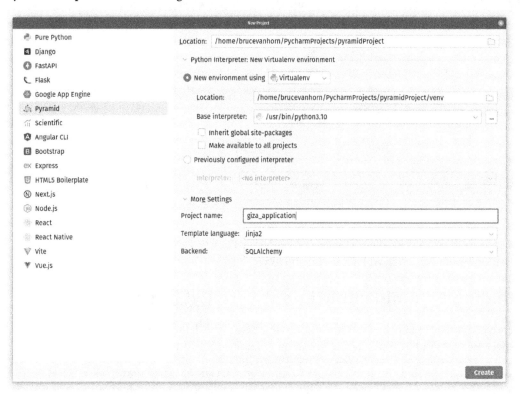

Figure 10.23: PyCharm has a project template for Pyramid

As with Django, you should twirl down the advanced settings, as shown in *Figure 10.23*. You are able to set a project name, as you were in Django. Be careful with this setting!

> **Pyramid project name**
>
> Make sure the project name is different than the PyCharm project name entered in the **Location** box.

When working with Pyramid, it's a best practice to have a PyCharm project name that is different from the project name you define within Pyramid. This separation of names is recommended to avoid potential conflicts and confusion between the two namespaced systems: PyCharm, an IDE, and Pyramid, a Python web framework.

Here's why it's advisable to keep them different:

- **Namespace clashes**: If your PyCharm project name matches your Pyramid project name exactly, you may encounter namespace clashes or naming conflicts. These conflicts can make it challenging for PyCharm to distinguish between project-specific settings, configurations, and files, and the Pyramid framework-specific files and configurations. This can lead to confusion and potential errors in your development process.

- **PyCharm project settings**: PyCharm uses the project name for its internal settings and configurations, including virtual environments, code analysis, and project-specific settings. If your PyCharm project name is the same as your Pyramid project name, PyCharm might overwrite or interfere with Pyramid-specific configurations and settings.

- **Clarity and maintainability**: Keeping distinct names for your PyCharm project and Pyramid project helps maintain clarity and organization in your development environment. It makes it easier to understand which aspects of your development are controlled by PyCharm and which are specific to your Pyramid web application.

- **Flexibility**: Having different names provides flexibility, especially if you work on multiple projects with Pyramid or use PyCharm for various other Python projects. It prevents potential conflicts when switching between projects.

I'm going to name my imaginary project `giza_application`, a nod to the location of the Great Pyramids of Egypt.

Having set the project name, you can select from two template engines: **Jinja2** and **Chameleon**. Finally, you have settings for the ORM, which here is specified as **Backend**. The two choices are **SQLAlchemy**, which is very popular, and **ZODB**, which is somewhat exotic.

SQL Alchemy is a straightforward ORM used for working with relational databases. You create models as we did with Django's ORM, and through a migration process, you can apply your database schema changes to a new or existing database.

ZODB refers to the Zope database. Generally speaking, Zope is an open source web application server written in Python. Less generally speaking, it is used as a content management system similar to WordPress. The database component, ZODB, has some interesting features that distinguish it from typical relational databases. It's a powerful tool that can be used in conjunction with the Pyramid web framework to manage data in a more Pythonic way. Here's how ZODB integrates into a Pyramid project and some of its features:

- **Python native**: ZODB lets you store Python objects without needing to serialize them into a different format. You can work with complex data structures directly, without having to map them to a relational database schema.

- **ACID transactions**: ZODB supports **Atomicity, Consistency, Isolation, Durability (ACID)** transactions. This ensures that your data remains consistent, even if something goes wrong during a transaction.

- **Integration with Pyramid**: ZODB can be easily integrated with Pyramid using the `pyramid_zodbconn` package. This provides a smooth way to get a ZODB connection within Pyramid's request handling.

- **Hierarchical storage**: ZODB allows you to organize your data in a tree-like structure. This can be particularly useful in a Pyramid application using traversal, where the URL structure often mirrors a hierarchical data structure.

- **Scalability**: ZODB can be scaled across multiple machines, allowing for more extensive and complex applications.

- **Versioning**: ZODB supports object versioning, allowing you to keep track of changes to objects over time. This can be useful for implementing features such as undo/redo.

- **Querying**: While ZODB does not provide a query language such as SQL, it offers ways to index and search objects using tools including the BTrees module or third-party packages such as `repoze.catalog`.

- **No schema required**: Unlike relational databases, ZODB doesn't require a fixed schema, offering flexibility in data modeling. You can modify the Python classes used for storage without needing to migrate data.

- **Blob support**: ZODB supports the storage of large binary objects (BLOBs), such as images or videos, alongside regular objects.

- **Persistence**: ZODB provides a straightforward persistence model. Any changes to persistent objects within a transaction are automatically saved to the database when the transaction is committed.

- **Compatibility**: ZODB works well with various WSGI servers and can be integrated into a Pyramid application running on different platforms.

ZODB can be a compelling choice for Pyramid developers looking for a database that aligns closely with Python's object-oriented paradigm. Its integration into a Pyramid project allows for intuitive data management without the need for complex SQL queries or ORM mapping, making it an attractive option for certain types of applications. If the hierarchical, object-oriented nature of ZODB fits the data model of your Pyramid application, it may be an excellent choice. From a PyCharm perspective though, there is no special tooling for this database.

Clicking the **OK** button will generate the project structure and the run configuration.

I really wish there was more to say here, but in truth, besides Djano, any other framework that could have been covered last would have the same problem. We've already covered PyCharm's tools for developing web applications in an unopinionated framework. We have seen the support for Jinja2 templates, working with an ORM, and obviously general Python project work.

Summary

In this chapter, we examined various PyCharm features regarding supporting and automating tasks in the process of web development with Django. While this list of features is in no way exhaustive, I hope it can offer you a solid starting point to continue discovering other powerful features for your web development process.

First, we see that, by specifying the PyCharm project type as Django, an extensive project skeleton will be generated with convenient boilerplate code already filled out. With the implementation of the `manage.py` panel inside the project window as well as its run/debug configuration, PyCharm additionally allows for a higher level of development, with various tasks traditionally achieved via the command line, such as running the server or making migrations. Finally, by acknowledging integrated views and templates in Django, PyCharm makes it as easy as possible for developers to work with them in the editor—be it generating a missing template, code completion even in HTML and Jinja, or even dynamically switching between views and templates.

We concluded with a short coverage of Pyramid. Pyramid is a framework that aims to be more flexible than Django but packs more features than Flask. It's a happy medium between the two. Unfortunately for Pyramid, we covered it last. PyCharm doesn't have any special tooling for Pyramid beyond the project template that creates the project structure. To be fair, if Flask had gone last, it would have suffered the same fate because most of PyCharm's web development tools are useful regardless of which framework you choose. Pyramid has some great features and is worthy of consideration for any project.

In the next chapter, we will tackle the last major component of any web application: the database. Buckle up, because the tooling for databases in PyCharm is extensive!

Questions

1. What are the major characteristics of Django, and how do they set Django apart from another popular Python web framework, Flask?

2. What is the purpose of the PyCharm `manage.py` panel in a Django project, and how does one open and utilize it?

3. What is the purpose of the Django admin interface? How does one create an instance of a model (that is, a new entry in a database table) in this interface? How does the process change if the model references another model?

4. What is the purpose of the run/debug configuration in PyCharm in the context of running a Django server?

5. Does PyCharm's code completion logic only apply to Python code in Django projects?

6. What is the significance of being able to switch between Django views and corresponding templates in PyCharm?

7. Describe the PyCharm tooling available for the Pyramid framework.

Further reading

Be sure to check out the companion website for the book at `https://www.pycharm-book.com`.

Check the following resources to expand on what was covered in this chapter:

- *Web Development with Django, Second Edition*
- *Hands-On RESTful Python Web Services, Second Edition*

11
Understanding Database Management in PyCharm

What do horseshoe crabs, coelacanths, crocodiles, and relational databases have in common? I'll wait while you go look up *coelacanth*. All four of these have been around for millions of years and yet have evolved very little. OK, databases haven't been around for millions of years, but they have been around for millions of internet years. Everybody knows that internet years are very short. JavaScript developers often joke that before lunchtime, anywhere in the world, dozens of new frameworks have been invented, risen to prominence, fallen out of favor, and then been abandoned all before you finish your noodles.

In the early 1970s, a researcher named E. F. Codd was working at IBM's San Jose Research Laboratory in California. He developed a revolutionary concept called **the relational model of data.** In his seminal paper titled *A Relational Model of Data for Large Shared Data Banks*, published in 1970, Codd outlined the principles and foundations of this new approach to organizing and retrieving data.

Codd's relational model proposed a way to represent data as a collection of tables, known as relations, with each table consisting of rows and columns. He introduced the concept of **relational algebra**, a mathematical framework for manipulating and querying data in these tables. The model emphasized the use of mathematical **set theory** and logic to define relationships and perform operations on the data.

Codd's ideas challenged the prevailing hierarchical and network database models of the time, which were more complex and less flexible. The relational model offered a simpler and more intuitive way to manage data, providing a foundation for **Structured Query Language** (**SQL**) and other tools used in relational databases.

In 1974, IBM released the first commercially available **relational database management system** (**RDBMS**), called *System R*, based on Codd's work. System R implemented many of the concepts outlined in Codd's research and became an influential precursor to subsequent relational database systems. In 1974, IBM released System R based on Codd's work, but the product wasn't aggressively marketed or sold because IBM executives were worried about cannibalizing sales on other database systems sold by the company. During that time, another start-up database company was born: **Oracle**. The initial release of Oracle was developed by Larry Ellison, Bob Miner, and Ed Oates. Released in 1983, Oracle is generally considered to be the first commercial success even though IBM had a serious head start.

Relational database technology evolved throughout the 80s and 90s, and along the way, it became a staple of corporate IT in every industry in every corner of the globe. In 1986, the SQL language became standardized. The standard evolved over time, but to be honest, 49 years after the invention of SQL, most development is done with the simplest and oldest set of language statements.

A moment ago, I stated that Codd's ideas challenged the prevailing hierarchical and network database models of the time, which were more complex and less flexible. It is interesting to note that in the early 2000s, there was a shift away from relational database technology toward what we call **NoSQL databases**. The world of IT often acts like a pendulum, forever swinging back and forth. We used to have relatively low-powered PCs capable of playing video files at 12 frames per second in a postage stamp-sized window. Technology improved to the point where we could watch a 4K high-definition video at full speed on a PC, but then we invented small hand-held devices, such as the iPod, and we were back to low-end processing and choppy, grainy video. Eventually, those improved into the iPhone, which can play video at high definition and high frame rates. Some iPhones are bigger than the TV I had in college.

Likewise, with databases, one day the world was using hierarchical and network-oriented databases. The next day everything swung to a new thing called *relational*. Today, we see a swing back in the other direction. More and more projects today favor non-relational databases, many of which support hierarchical data. Regardless of which technology you might favor, it is safe to say that just about any project you build, especially in the corporate IT world, will interact with some database in some big way.

In 2015, JetBrains created a new product aimed at becoming a popular IDE for database developers. **DataGrip** was created to provide a unified interface and robust toolset for working with various databases. It offers features such as intelligent code completion, advanced SQL editing capabilities, schema navigation, data analysis, and integration with version control systems. Like the web development product by JetBrains, WebStorm, the DataGrip product is integrated into the Professional edition of PyCharm through its plugin system. Consider that your 99 USD investment in PyCharm Professional gets you a Python IDE, a JavaScript IDE, an IDE for web frontend work in HTML and CSS, and now a fully fledged IDE for database work and you'll see you've gotten a solid deal!

In this chapter, we will cover the features of PyCharm related to databases. By the end of the chapter, you will have learned the following:

- Some database history and some basics just to make sure we're all on the same page in terms of terminology. If you've been developing software for a while, this might be a review. If you're new, I will endeavor to provide you with the best possible introduction to database technology.

- How to navigate to the database tools in PyCharm, which are hidden away in a tab on the right side of the interface. I have met many developers who have used PyCharm for years yet don't know these tools are even present.

- How to connect to different databases, including how to add the necessary connection drivers to PyCharm. JetBrains has made this very easy!

- How to configure SQL dialects for individual projects as well as globally.

- How to use SQL generation templates to help you write SQL queries more quickly.

- How to generate an **entity relationship diagram** (**ERD**).

- How to use the graphical designers to build tables easily.

- How to use consoles to create and run ad hoc queries against any database.

On a personal note, besides learning to code in BASIC when I was 12, relational technology was the first skill I mastered when I got into the IT field over 30 years ago. This is a skill set that has always been in demand, and will probably continue to be in demand for many years to come. It is a subject I have extensive experience in, and I am excited to share that experience with you in this chapter. So, let's get to it!

Technical requirements

In order to proceed with this chapter, and indeed the rest of the book, you will need the following:

An installed and working Python interpreter. I'll be using the latest from `https://python.org`.

An installed and working copy of PyCharm. Installation was covered in *Chapter 2, Installation and Configuration*, in case you are jumping into the middle of the book.

A database server is a nice-to-have in this chapter so you can practice on a real database. There are dozens of popular relational databases to choose from, so it is not practical for me to cover all of them. I will be running **MySQL** using **Docker Desktop**. If you plan on following along, you'll need to have Docker Desktop installed on your computer. You can find instructions for installation at `https://www.docker.com/products/docker-desktop/`.

This book's sample source code is from GitHub. We covered cloning the code in *Chapter 2, Installation and Configuration*. You'll find this chapter's relevant code at `https://github.com/PacktPublishing/Hands-On-Application-Development-with-PyCharm---Second-Edition/tree/main/chapter-11`.

Relational databases in a nutshell

The idea of relational data conceived by E. F. Codd is based on a few simple principles. Firstly, data can be represented in sets called *tables*. A **table** consists of **rows** and **columns**. For example, if we wanted to create a database to be used by an online bookstore, the first table we might want to think about is one called `books`. The `books` table will contain columns that define the data within those columns – maybe something like this:

Title	ISBN	Page Count	Author	Price
The Art of War	1599869772	68	Sun Tzu	4.99
Book of Five Rings	8387743849	43	Miyamoto Musashi	4.50

This table has five columns designed to structure data about books. We have two books, which are stored as rows in the table.

Structured Query Language

E. F. Codd's paper that defined relational algebra served as the basis for SQL. SQL is unlike any other coding language you will ever use because it is one of only a handful of languages that use a declarative paradigm. Most languages you use, including Python, use an imperative paradigm. In short, the language serves as a syntactical framework to give a computer instructions on what you want it to do. You are basically a micro-manager. You specify every input, every output and every step the program will take during the processing that happens to get the input to the output. You must be meticulous, as the computer will take you literally. If you leave out even a single detail, you are setting things up to malfunction.

Declarative programming, on the other hand, entails merely specifying the output you want from an implicit input. You have little to no control over the operations performed to derive the output from the input. Consider this SQL statement designed to get some rows from your bookstore database:

```
SELECT title AS Title, isbn AS ISBN, author AS Author, price AS Price
FROM books ORDER BY price DESC
```

This query will produce some output consisting of a table that has a few of the columns from your original database, which serves as the implicit input. You'll get the following columns:

```
Title
```

```
ISBN
```

```
Author
```

```
Price
```

But you won't get the page count because you didn't ask for it in the query. The input data source is implied in the `FROM books` section of the query. At the end, we have a request to order the results by price in descending order (`DESC`), which will make our resulting tabular list of books appear from the most expensive to the cheapest.

The two halves of SQL

SQL itself is split into two separate sets of syntax: **Data Definition Language** (**DDL**) and **Data Manipulation Language** (**DML**). DDL is used to define the structure of the database. DML is used to query the database and to perform the four basic **Create, Read, Update, Delete** (**CRUD**) operations we've referenced in early chapters. The SELECT statement presented earlier is an example of a read operation. SQL has keywords for INSERT, UPDATE, and DELETE operations for records which are straightforward, so I want to focus on DDL since this is going to be a big part of your work in PyCharm.

Our earlier example of a table to be used in a bookstore application had one table in it called books. That table contained a set of columns, which we would define using DDL like this:

```
CREATE TABLE books (
    title VARCHAR(255),
    isbn VARCHAR(255) UNIQUE,
    price DECIMAL(10, 2),
    author VARCHAR(255),
    page_count INT
);
```

If you are new to SQL, you might have noticed the keywords are capitalized. In fact, I'll bet you correctly assumed that the capitalized words were keywords. While it isn't a requirement to capitalize keywords, it is good practice – particularly if your project's database lead is a large man retired from the United States Marine Corps who is particular about the details of syntax in *his* database! In this case, good practice might become a matter of survival.

Most of what you read in the table's DDL is easy to figure out. We're creating a table called books. We already knew about the column names. SQL uses a strong type system, meaning you have to define the type of data that will go into a column, and violating that constraint might come with consequences. I've said many times before that a developer's job is to protect a program from entering an invalid state. Likewise, it is a database developer's job, as well as that of a **database administrator** (**DBA**), to limit the ability of a program to enter invalid data into a database. The first line of defense is the type system. The thing that confuses or even intimidates developers is the different names for the types. Looking at our preceding list, you might be able to guess that VARCHAR refers to a variable-length set of characters. Programmers call this a *string*. The number (255) after the type refers to the maximum length of VARCHAR. All of the VARCHAR (string) fields in the database are limited to 255 characters in length. The number 255 is very common because many of us old-timers grew up in the world of 8-bit computing. The number 255, being the maximum value of an 8-bit unsigned integer, was a common maximum for the length of the field. We'd set it to that when we weren't sure how long the data might be.

Naturally, today, we normally work in 32- and even 64-bit architectures, so the maximum can be much higher. It is normal to constrain ourselves to the old maximum because 255 characters are generally enough for most things. Specifying sane maximums helps keep your database storage and memory requirements reasonable.

Look at the `price` field. It is specified as the `DECIMAL` type, which is obviously like a float. Database systems have different names for their types, so you should always consult your database system's documentation to get the exact naming. `DECIMAL` is indeed a floating-point number, but we also specified the level of precision with `(10,2)`. This means we can have a 10-digit number with 2 decimal places. This is commonly used to specify prices. Some database systems have specialized types specifically for currency. SQL Server is an example of this with their `MONEY` and `SMALLMONEY` types. Again, check your database system's documentation for appropriate types since these specialized types aren't part of standard SQL.

Relationships

Consider our bookstore will naturally grow in size and complexity. Let's say we've added some different fields and removed some we weren't using. Our new table structure looks like this:

Title	Author_name	Author_email	Pages	Price
C Programming Language, 2nd Edition	Brian Kernighan and Dennis Ritchie	bkernigan@ notrealaddress.com	272	53.60
Real-World Implementation of C# Design Patterns	Bruce Van Horn	bvanhorn@ notrealaddress.com	442	44.99
Hands-On Application Development with PyCharm	Quan Nguyen	qnguyen@ notrealaddress.com	785	35.45
Hands-On Application Development with PyCharm, 2nd Edition	Bruce Van Horn	bvanhorn@ notrealaddress.com	840	44.99

Besides the complexity coming from more records, we've introduced some complexity in terms of design. At some point, it became important for us to track more information about the authors of any given book. We added fields for the name and email address, which seemed to solve our problems at first, but ultimately led to more issues.

The C book has two authors, but we only have one field. While it might be fine to store both authors as we did, there is also a field for the email address and this can only accommodate one address. This is not ideal since our objective might be to send royalty statements or sales reports to the authors. One address is a problem.

The email addresses will be duplicated in the event we store two books with the same author. If the author changes email addresses, all of the records have to be updated. This is the equivalent of hardcoded values kept in multiple places in a program. You have to remember to change it in lots of places. The problem is compounded if this email address data is duplicated in several different tables.

The solution to this is prescribed by SQL and the ideas behind relational algebra. You need a single source of truth for the author's data instead of mixing it in with other tables. So, we create a new table for authors:

```
CREATE TABLE authors (
    id SERIAL PRIMARY KEY,
    first_name VARCHAR(255),
    last_name VARCHAR(255),
    email_address VARCHAR(255)
);
```

This table has fields for the first and last names as well as the email address. It also has a field called id, which is going to the server as a primary key. A primary key is a field that can uniquely identify the information in that row. The idea here is that every author gets only one row to store their information. We need some piece of data to uniquely identify that row. Consider my own records. My first and last names make poor choices to uniquely define my record in the database. I know of at least three other people named Bruce Van Horn. One was my father, who published in the medical field. One is a motivational speaker who publishes books in that literary field. I found another Bruce Van Horn on LinkedIn, and believe it or not, he too is a software developer! So the name is a poor choice as a unique identifier.

Email addresses might work, except that we've already figured out that email addresses can change. I have no fewer than five email addresses and at least one of these is so overtaken with spam that I no longer even check it. Email isn't going to work.

The best practice is to use some piece of data that is unique but arbitrary, with no bearing at all on the rest of the data in the record. There are two ways to do this. The most common is to use a database sequence. A **sequence** is an automatically incrementing source of integers. Each time a record is inserted into a table, the sequencer generates a sequential number, which is guaranteed to be unique.

The other approach is to use **universally unique identifiers** (UUIDs). This approach uses an algorithm that presents a combination of data that will make a unique ID. For example, you might take the serial number of a user's processor, combine it with the current date stamp on the computer, and maybe lump in some information about the computer's BIOS serial number, or maybe the IP address or the MAC address on the user's network connection. If you take many factors, one of which involves time, the possibility of two computers generating the same UUID is effectively nil. UUIDs are a little harder to work with than plain integers. A UUID might look like this: `6f35e0e7-d99a-4437-b894-f73ff35bd3ad` versus a record with the `id` value of `16`. Which would you rather type into your queries?

Now that we have a field that uniquely identifies an author's record, we can adjust our book table structure like this:

Title	pages	price	author_id
Real-World Implementation of C# Design Patterns	442	44.99	2
Hands-On Application Development with PyCharm	785	35.45	1
Hands-On Application Development with PyCharm, 2nd Edition	840	44.99	2

Our `authors` table looks like this:

author_id	first_name	last_name	email
1	Quan	Nguyen	qnugyen@notrealaddress.com
2	Bruce	Van Horn	bvanhorn@notrealaddress.com

The author ID in the `authors` table is used as a related column in the `books` table using a one-to-many relationship. Each author will have one record, which is related to many records in the `books` table.

More relational structures

We've solved a big problem using our one-to-many table structure. We no longer have duplicate data in multiple records for our authors. We didn't, however, solve all of our problems. For example, the C book has multiple authors. How can we store authors in a way that allows each book to support multiple authors?

I'm afraid we've reached the point where I tell you that this isn't a book on SQL, nor is it a book on relational theory. If I've hooked you on this, I can recommend some excellent books that I used when I learned these things. We've presented enough relational database vocabulary to help you relate to what you will see in PyCharm's tooling and that was my real objective.

Since I am not a total degenerate, regardless of what you may read about me on Stack Overflow, I will give you the solution quickly and without many pages of explanation.

You'd solve it using what we call a mapping table. Your structure would require the addition of a table called `books_authors_map`:

Id	Book_id	Author_id
1	1	1
2	1	2

Your `books` table would look like this:

Book_id	Title	Pages	Price
1	The C Programming Language	442	44.99

We took out the `author_id` field and added a `book_id` field, which really should have been there all along. The `authors` table would look the same:

Author_id	First_name	Last_name	Email
1	Brian	Kernighan	bkernigan@ notrealaddress.com
2	Dennis	Ritchie	dritche@noterealaddress.com

The mapping table can map a **many-to-many relationship** between `books` and `authors`! If either author goes solo and publishes a book without their co-author, that will work! The `books` table's record will have one related record in the map, which has one related record in the `authors` table.

If a book has 10 authors, it will have 1 book record, 10 author records, and 10 mapping entries. Relational algebra is pretty cool! It is an underrated skill in today's world of **object relational mappers (ORMs)**, which abstract all of this into normal object structures. Developers today tend to lose this skill. If you do, you give up a lot. You can make fine-grained modifications in your DDL that lead to huge performance gains for your application.

Speaking of that, let's learn about PyCharm's tooling for database development.

Database terminology uses simple English plurals

As we go through some of the terminology used when talking about databases, I feel compelled to point out something that bothered me for a very long time. Many terms used when talking about databases come from Latin root words. For example, an **index** is an addition to a table that can speed up data retrieval at the cost of the speed of inserting new data. It is also a Latin word that refers to *a pointer, indicator, or signpost*. A **schema** refers to a way of partitioning off tables and other structures in a database. The word *schema* originated with the Greek word σχῆμα (*skema*) and in both languages means *shape, form, or plan*.

When talking about the plural forms, the words might not be as you expect if you received a classical education as I did. If you come from a country where your language is based on Latin, you might notice this issue as well.

I would expect the plural form of *schema* to be *schemata*, and the plural of *index* to be *indices*. If you expect this, you will always be disappointed. The industry has standardized simple plural forms such as *schemas* and *indexes*.

Database tooling in PyCharm

The database tooling in PyCharm is complete but generic. By this, I mean that PyCharm attempts to support every database out there, and as such, it generally supports features common to all. You may find yourself sometimes leaning on more specific tools, such as **SQL Server Management Studio** (**SSMS**) for SQL Server. However, for general development work, the tooling in PyCharm is more than sufficient. The starting point for working with databases in PyCharm is opening the database tools and creating a connection. For this, you also need a database. PyCharm supports dozens of the most popular database servers. Since this is true, it would be impossible for me to predict which one you prefer, so I'm going to fall back on one that I know well: MySQL. Regardless of your favorite, the tooling in PyCharm is generic, so as long as you pick a relational database that is standards-compliant, the processes are the same.

Setting up a MySQL database server with Docker

The easiest way to try out any database system, or pretty much any server technology at all, is to use Docker. I have more plans for Docker later in the book, and I will be using Docker Desktop, along with the command line. I like the desktop's GUI for seeing what is running graphically, but you should master Docker command-line skills in order to remain competitive. If you don't have Docker Desktop installed, you can find the installation instructions at `https://www.docker.com/products/docker-desktop/`. Naturally, there are other options, such as installing a database server on your computer. I personally rail against this because database servers are very complicated. Installing something such as SQL Server or Oracle will make modifications to your OS at a level that makes these software packages hard to uninstall. It used to be a rule of thumb that if you made any mistakes installing the database server, the smartest option was the wipe the OS and start over. I'm relatively sure that's no longer the case, but I still treat database servers with respect because of all the moving parts in your solution, this one is easily the most complicated. The last thing you want is a broken database server on your laptop while in the middle of developing an epic project. So, I recommend Docker. If something goes wrong, you delete the container and make a new one.

Likewise, you can create a VM using products such as **VMware Workstation** or **Oracle VirtualBox**. This is another fine way to work, though it takes up more space and resources than Docker will, and you must remember to keep your VMs up to date.

Another fine option is to spin up your database server of choice in your favorite cloud. I recommend **DigitalOcean** for this since their pricing and setup are both extremely easy to understand. I use this service to host the companion website for this book. If your computer isn't up for running a database server, VMware, or Docker, using a cloud provider is your best option.

All these options are great, but I need to pick one, so I'm going to be working with Docker. Remember, this isn't a book on Docker. My coverage is going to be tacit. Your objective is to get a database server up and running so you can practice. If you can do that with something besides Docker, go ahead and skip to the next section.

Installing and running the MySQL container

I'm assuming you have Docker running on your computer and that your Docker commands are available in your PATH. We can confirm this by opening our terminal and typing this command:

```
docker ps -a
```

This command will list all the containers currently running, or stopped. If you just installed Docker, you should see an empty list, which is to say, nothing at all. The test is really to make sure the command runs and doesn't throw any errors. If it doesn't, you're ready to grab MySQL using this command:

```
docker pull mysql
```

You'll see a nicely animated display of the installation, as shown in *Figure 11.1*.

```
root@photon-6d5886da020 [ ~ ]# docker pull mysql
Using default tag: latest
latest: Pulling from library/mysql
e2c03c89dcad: Pull complete
68eb43837bf8: Pull complete
796892ddf5ac: Pull complete
6bca45eb31e1: Pull complete
ebb53bc0dcca: Pull complete
2e2c6bdc7a40: Pull complete
6f27b5c76970: Pull complete
438533a24810: Pull complete
e5bdf19985e0: Pull complete
667fa148337b: Pull complete
5baa702110e4: Pull complete
Digest: sha256:232936eb036d444045da2b87a90d48241c60b68b376caf509051cb6cffea6fdc
Status: Downloaded newer image for mysql:latest
docker.io/library/mysql:latest
root@photon-6d5886da020 [ ~ ]#
```

Figure 11.1: The Docker command used to pull the images needed for MySQL

This command pulled all the requirements needed to run one or more containers for MySQL. Next, we need to create and run a container with this command:

```
docker run --name pycharm-mysql -e MYSQL_ROOT_PASSWORD=P@ssw0rd -p
3306:3306 -d mysql
```

This command will create and run a container named `pycharm-mysql`. It sets the root password for the MySQL database to `P@ssw0rd`. The –p flag maps port `3306`, which is the standard port for MySQL, to the same value between your container and the host. This will make it seem as though you are running the MySQL server directly on your computer. The -d flag tells Docker to run MySQL as a background process rather than waiting for it to exit. This is common with server software. I hope I don't need to remind you that *this is not production ready*. If you are in a small group where the developers are responsible for standing up a production environment, don't simply duplicate your development environment on a server open to the internet. You should at least map your database to more robust permanent storage, as well as harden MySQL, use non-privileged accounts for your app, and use a non-obvious root password.

We are now running the MySQL server. When you run the Docker command, your output is somewhat cryptic and unsatisfying. You can see mine in *Figure 11.2*.

```
bruce@bruce-workstation:~$ docker run --name pycharm-mysql -e MYSQL_ROOT_PASSWORD=P@ssw0rd -p 3306:3306 -d mysql
8d3076aa35fbe0c60bf57425e72f08a39bbccada3bb2d0fe61f8136bed358552
bruce@bruce-workstation:~$
```

Figure 11.2: A long string of seemingly random letters and numbers is Docker's way of saying "I love you," or at least that your container is running

There is an old saying that goes, *Tell a man there are a trillion stars in the galaxy, and he'll believe you. Tell him his container is successfully running in Docker and he'll run* `docker ps -a` *to be sure.* In truth, I might have just made that up. Nevertheless, let's make sure:

```
docker ps -a
```

You should see proof like mine in *Figure 11.3*. The `CONTAINER ID` value will be different for every run, so don't expect yours to match mine.

```
bruce@bruce-workstation:~$ docker run --name pycharm-mysql -e MYSQL_ROOT_PASSWORD=P@ssw0rd -p 3306:3306 -d mysql
8d3076aa35fbe0c60bf57425e72f08a39bbccada3bb2d0fe61f8136bed358552
bruce@bruce-workstation:~$ docker ps -a
CONTAINER ID   IMAGE    COMMAND               CREATED          STATUS          PORTS
NAMES
8d3076aa15fb   mysql    "docker-entrypoint.s…"  11 minutes ago   Up 11 minutes   0.0.0.0:3306->3306/tcp, 33060/tcp
pycharm-mysql
bruce@bruce-workstation:~$
```

Figure 11.3: I can see my container named pycharm-mysql is running and has exposed port 3306

Stopping and starting the container

When you're ready to retire for the day, you might want to stop the container:

```
docker stop pycharm-mysql
```

This stops the container. You can check with the same `docker ps -a` command we've been using to confirm the status changed from *Up* to *Stopped*. Tomorrow morning, when you come back, type the following:

```
docker start pycharm-mysql
```

This starts things up so you can pick up where you left off.

Connecting to data sources using PyCharm

Open PyCharm Professional and create a new Python project called `database_fun`. Now, locate the database tools. You can find them on the right side toolbar via the database icon that looks like a three-layer cake (yum!). Alternatively, you can find it via the hamburger (yum!) menu by clicking **View | Tool Windows | Database**. Both options are shown in *Figure 11.4*.

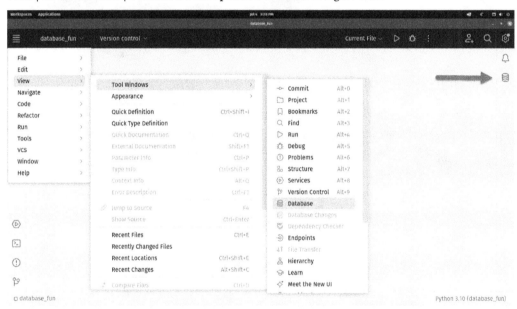

Figure 11.4: Two options for opening database tools – one from the menu, and the second by clicking the database tools icon

With the database tools open, you need to create a new **data source**. Note the generic terminology. PyCharm supports relational as well as non-relational databases, so the term *data source* is just a generic way of pointing that out. Click the + icon shown in *Figure 11.5*, then hover over **Data Source**. You'll see a long list of supported data sources. Find **MySQL** and click it.

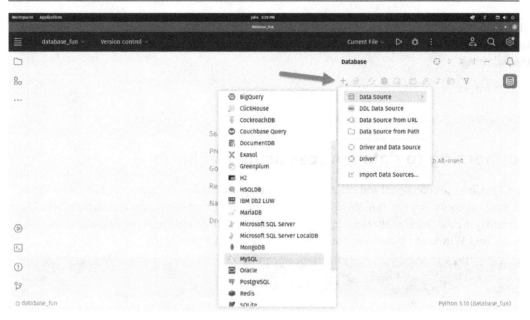

Figure 11.5: Supported data sources in PyCharm

You'll see a configuration window like mine in *Figure 11.6*.

Figure 11.6: Configuration window for a MySQL database

Each database server may have slightly different settings, but essentially they boil down to the IP address (or DNS name), port, security credentials, and, very often, the default database, which may not yet exist. We defined the root password for our MySQL server as P@ssw0rd, and we know since we're running in Docker our IP is just going to be localhost. You might also remember the port that was displayed in the output of the docker ps -a command we ran earlier is 3306. The arrow in the preceding figure points to an important aspect of database tooling in PyCharm.

PyCharm, like most JetBrains IDEs, is written in Java. As such, PyCharm relies on **Java Database Connectivity** (**JDBC**) drivers in order to work. Most JDBC drivers are written by the same company or group that publishes the database, which means it's generally not legal for JetBrains to bundle those drivers with PyCharm without getting lawyers involved. Nobody wants that! JetBrains did the next best thing. The IDE can download and install the driver automatically, but you have to initiate this by clicking the **Download missing driver files** link on this screen. This only needs to be done the first time you use the database driver. Once the drivers are installed, the option shown by the arrow in *Figure 11.6* no longer appears. You can test your connection by clicking the **Test Connection** link. If everything works, you'll get a confirmation message stating your database connection was successful. Click **OK** to close the connection dialog.

Once the connection dialog is closed, you'll see a list of data source connections for your project in the **Database** panel. There is a small toolbar visible at the top of the database panel, as shown in *Figure 11.7*.

Figure 11.7: The database panel has a small menu bar at the top

As usual, I've numbered the options in the figure. Let's review them:

1. The **Add Data Source** button, which we've already seen, allows you to add new data sources to your project.

2. The **Duplicate** button allows you to make a quick copy, presumably with some minor adjustments. Many of my projects entail multiple databases on one server. All I have to do is set up the first one, then duplicate the connection and change the name of the database. This option makes this a quick and easy process.

3. The **Refresh** button reloads the metadata for your connections. Remember this one. PyCharm doesn't automatically keep track of all your database changes, especially if they are made outside of PyCharm. You'll need to click the **Refresh** button periodically to make sure you're viewing the latest information on your data sources.

4. The **Data source properties** button will display a dialog that allows you to change the settings of the data source configuration.

5. The **Disconnect** button will disconnect you from a database server.

6. The **Edit data** button allows you to directly edit data in tables in your database using a graphical, spreadsheet-like UI. This is nice for quickly adding or changing test data.

7. The **Go To DDL** button will take you to the SQL definition of whatever you have currently selected. You need to have a DDL mapping for this to work properly.

8. **Compare Structure** lets us compare two database structures. This is usually used to help migrate one database structure to another after changes were made during the normal development process. Migration technology in PyCharm 2023 is only partially complete, so this feature might have changed at the time you are reading this book.

9. **Jump to Query Console** is pretty much your go-to tool for interacting with the database at the command line. A query console was opened automatically when you first connected to the database, but if you closed it, this button opens it and brings it into focus.

10. The filter button allows you to filter what you see in the data sources you have defined. By default, everything is turned on, which might be a bit much for most developers who are not usually accustomed to seeing all the guts of the database so explicitly displayed.

Besides these tools, there are others that pertain to setting up how you view and work with your data sources. These will be a little easier to explain once we have a database to play with. Let's take a moment to create one.

Creating a new database

Before we do anything else, we need a new database. Most database servers just call this "a new database." MySQL is a little different. They call a new database a new **schema**. To create a new database or schema, right-click the server (@localhost) and click **New** | **Schema**, as shown in *Figure 11.8*.

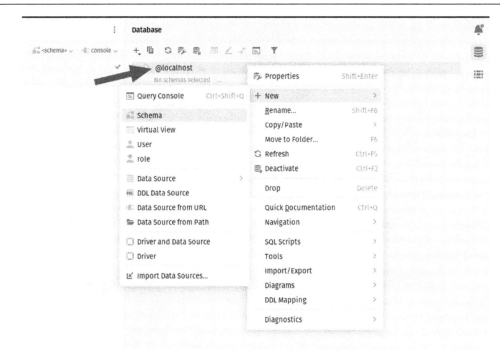

Figure 11.8: Create a new database by right-clicking the server
(indicated by the arrow), then New | Schema

When you do this, you are prompted to name the schema, as shown in *Figure 11.9*. I'll name my schema to match my project in PyCharm. I'll call it `database_fun`.

Figure 11.9: Name your schema using this dialog

Beneath the covers, PyCharm is just generating and executing DDL statements. This is how it is able to be so agnostic with respect to so many database options. You can see the preview of the command it will run in *Figure 11.9*. Click **OK** to execute the command, and the database window will update to show the new schema.

You've just created a new database! It is just as easy using any other database server software supported by PyCharm.

Before we get into working on the structure of our database, there are a few more setup options to consider.

Setting the SQL dialect (this is crucial)

Since PyCharm supports dozens of different databases, each with its own dialect of SQL, it stands to reason that you might need to tell PyCharm which SQL dialect you intend to use. You won't have any trouble remembering to do this because PyCharm nags you until you fill in the setting.

In your project window, right-click the project and create a new file called `test.sql`. It's the same process we've been using for Python files, except there isn't a template in the list. Right-click the project, then click **New File**, as shown in *Figure 11.10*.

Figure 11.10: There isn't a specific listing for SQL files, so just right-click and pick New | File

A small dialog will appear. Type the name of the file as `test.sql`. The moment you do this, the nagging begins. You'll see a message stating the SQL dialect is not configured, as shown in *Figure 11.11*.

Figure 11.11: PyCharm will hound you until you configure the SQL dialect

If PyCharm were me and the user of PyCharm were my 13-year-old daughter, there would be a lot of eye-rolling, an exasperated grunt, followed by, "Fine! I'll set the SQL dialog! But none of my friends do!" Then I'd say, "If you're friends all installed Windows 7 on their computers, would you follow their example?" Then she'd sag her head and say, "No, of course not."

Nobody wants this dialogue playing out, so we'd better make our IDE overlord happy. Click the link in *Figure 11.11* to set the dialect. You'll need to set it locally and globally. The configuration is shown in *Figure 11.12*.

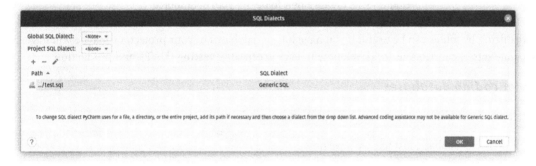

Figure 11.12: Set the SQL dialects globally and locally

The global setting carries across all projects, so if you're like me and you only ever use one database server type, you can set it globally here, and it will be set for all your projects. The project dialect is a little more nuanced. If you value your sanity, you really need to create a folder for your SQL files, then set the dialect for the folder. Here, I'm just showing you where the settings are. Go ahead and pick **MySQL** for your global and local dialect and we'll worry about the whole folder idea a little later.

Grouping and color coding data sources

My own work consists of creating the SaaS product sold by my employer. This means that for the first seven years of the project, I only had one database to deal with. As the product grew in capability, we added two more SQL databases, a MongoDB database, and several Redis data caches to the project. My project is still pretty tame compared to some I've worked on. If you have many databases to deal with, PyCharm allows you to organize them in several different ways.

Organizing by folders

You can organize your data sources by grouping them into folders. We only have one, but we'll go through the process anyway. Click the data source indicated by the arrow in *Figure 11.8*. Last time, we right-clicked; this time, just click the data source and press *F6* on your keyboard. This brings up a dialog, as shown in *Figure 11.13*.

Figure 11.13: Create a new folder for your data source

Organizing by folder can be useful if you have lots of databases in your project, or maybe you have separate sets of connections for development, **user acceptance testing** (UAT), and production.

Color coding databases

I'm fond of this feature since I have four environments:

- A local database, just like we have now
- A central development testing database where the development validates their designs before the product team is allowed to see our changes
- A staging database that is connected to a staged version of our application for UAT
- A production database

I always color code everything! You can set a color for the data source by opening up the **Data Source Properties** window. To do this, click the **Data Source Properties** button on the toolbar. I showed you this earlier in *Figure 11.7 (4)*. Clicking this button reveals a dialog box similar to the one you used to create the data source earlier. Look at mine in *Figure 11.14*.

Figure 11.14: Click the innocuous dot next to the data source name in
the properties window to set a color for your data source

You can probably figure it out from here. Once you dismiss the dialog, your database elements in the IDE become awash with lovely pastel hues. Personally, I set my local development environment to violet, the dev environment to green, staging to yellow, and production to red. Not rose from the selection, but a bright, obnoxious, over-the-top, fire engine red picked from the custom dialog at the bottom of the list. As the project's development lead, there are times when I need to go look at the project in production. I want to make sure I remember where I am! Color coding helps!

Sharing a data source between projects

If you have many projects that use the same data source, it would be tedious to have to set the same thing over and over for each project. Thankfully, you don't have to. PyCharm allows you to make a data source global, meaning it is available to all your projects in PyCharm. In the data source properties window shown in *Figure 11.15*, find the button indicated by the arrow.

Figure 11.15: You can make your data source configuration global so it is available to all your projects

If you click it, the dialog changes very subtly to indicate the data source is now global. If you want to check, just make a new project like we did earlier. Open the database tools and you'll find the data source is already there. I made a project called `more_database_fun`, and as you can see in *Figure 11.16*, the data source indeed carried over.

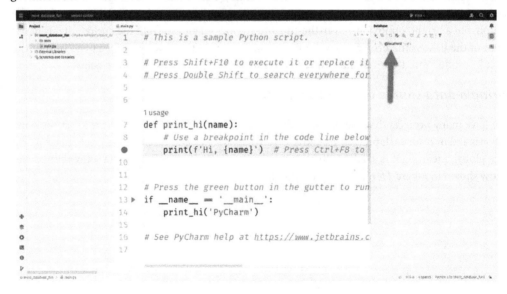

Figure 11.16: I made a new project and opened the database tools. The global data source is there

Since there is no code in this second project, I did not include it in the chapter source code.

Another fun feature is the global data sources are exported when you export your IDE settings. Refer back to *Chapter 2, Installation and Configuration*, if you need a refresher on importing and exporting settings, but I'll go ahead and point out the export settings I'm talking about here in *Figure 11.17*.

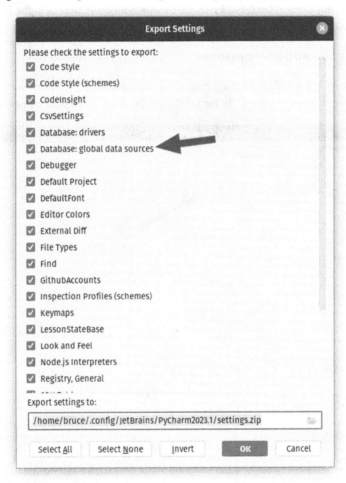

Figure 11.17: You can export your global data sources to the settings export
ZIP file, allowing others to simply import the relevant settings

If you are a development lead, you might consider creating an export of your IDE settings that does not include things such as color and font size. Those are likely more personal preferences and make sense when you want to copy your settings between a laptop and a workstation. But it does make sense to export more work-specific settings such as your data sources so your team can easily import them. If you do this, remember you are also potentially copying credentials! You should only make development data sources available as global exports lest your `settings.zip` file falls into the wrong hands. This is especially important in an age where more and more of us are using cloud database servers rather than locally installed servers.

If you need tight control over credentials, PyCharm can integrate with a product called *KeePass*. Since that is fairly niche, I'll not cover it here, but I will leave a link with more details in the *Further reading* section of this chapter.

Connecting with SSL and SSH options

For even more security, especially with respect to cloud data sources, PyCharm supports SSL and SSH configuration options. See *Figure 11.18* for your security setup options for your data sources.

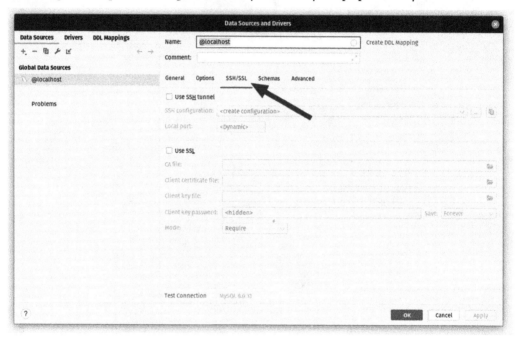

Figure 11.18: SSH and SSL security options can be found in the data source settings on the SSH/SSL tab

I won't go deep into this here, but you need to know where these settings lie in the IDE since you will need them for cloud providers such as Microsoft Azure.

Database design and manipulation

Let's move on to the part you've probably been waiting for: the part where we get to build a database! We already created the schema, but at the moment, we don't have any tables. Let's fix that first!

Creating a table

Right-click the schema, **database_fun**, which we created earlier, and click **New | Table**, as shown in *Figure 11.19*.

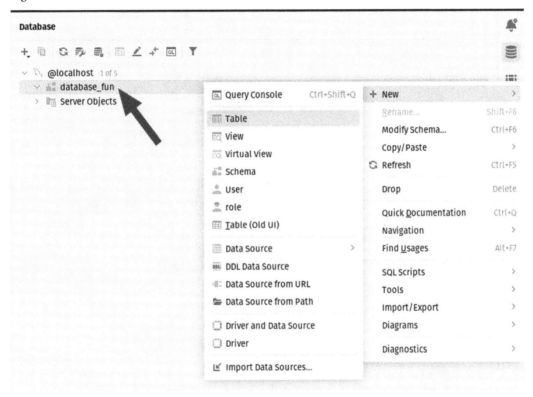

Figure 11.19: Right-click on the schema indicated by the arrow, then click New | Table

You'll get a new window, as shown in *Figure 11.20*.

Figure 11.20: New window

I had to stretch mine out a little to see it all, as shown in the figure. The next few steps will build our table. I went ahead and typed the table name in the **Name** field at the top. You can see what's going on here. As before, with the schema creation DDL, PyCharm is building a DDL script in the preview at the bottom of the window. Right now, we have a red squiggly line under the semicolon because we have yet to add any fields, so this DDL is invalid.

At the top left of the window is a button with a + icon. Click that to see a list of elements you can add to the table, as shown in *Figure 11.21*.

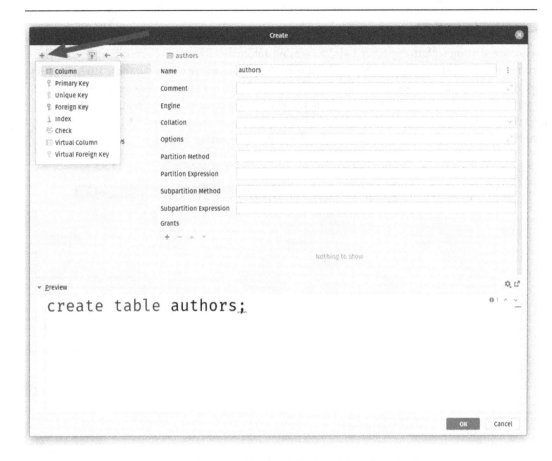

Figure 11.21: You can add to the table by clicking the + button

From here, you can pick whatever it is you need to add. We're going to add our primary key field first. If you're new to relational database design and you need a good primer, *Database Design for Mere Mortals* by Michael Hernandez is a must-read. I've used it as a textbook in my classes for over 20 years! Hernandez has an equally impactful book on SQL queries, as does another author, named Ben Forta. I'll leave the details in the *Further reading* section of this chapter.

In short, every table we create should have a field that can uniquely identify individual records. It should not consist of data that is related to the domain of data contained in the table. By this I mean we are making a table to hold information about book authors. We should not use any field related to the author as the primary key, the record's unique identifier. Instead, we should use something unrelated. With MySQL, the norm is to use an auto-incrementing integer field.

An auto-incrementing integer field refers to a field that will automatically populate a number from a sequence starting with the number 1 and increasing automatically with each record insertion. The increment is not something you should do in code. This is a feature of the database itself. This is important. Relational databases are designed to be atomic, meaning all transactions are isolated. This is important because it means the database will never generate the same value for the auto-incrementing key even if two record insertions happen within microseconds of one another. This is something you cannot guarantee with your own code. You need to rely on the server for this.

Using the menu shown in *Figure 11.21*, add a column and set it as shown in *Figure 11.22*.

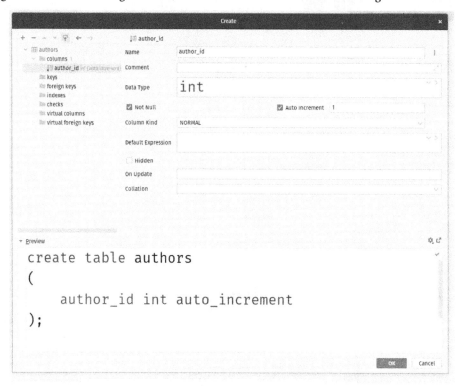

Figure 11.22: Add the first column with the settings shown here

Here, we've created an auto-incrementing integer field called author_id. I'm using snake case here, but this is not required. Use whatever naming conventions your project requires. Note I haven't yet officially made it the primary key. That's coming. First, let's finish out the rest of our columns.

This can be done quickly if you leave the author_id field selected, then click the plus button three times. When you have a column selected, or even when you have the columns folder selected in the window, PyCharm assumes that when you click the + button, you want a column. Likewise, you can select any of the other folders for things such as primary keys, foreign keys, and indexes. PyCharm will simply create it without making you use the menu we saw earlier.

Configure the three fields like so:

- `first_name: varchar(30)`
- `last_name: varchar(30)`
- `email: varchar(255) not null`

Figure 11.23 shows the last field configuration. I gave this one the `not null` constraint, which will prevent a record insertion from completing if the `email` field is left empty. This is done by clicking the checkbox titled **Not null**, as seen in *Figure 11.22*.

Figure 11.23: Configure the email field as shown

It's starting to look like a table, isn't it? There are just a couple more things we need. Let's go ahead and configure the `author_id` field to be a proper primary key.

Setting the primary key

Click on the `keys` folder, then click the + button. You're asked whether you want to create a primary or unique key, as shown in *Figure 11.24*.

Figure 11.24: Make sure the keys folder is selected, as shown in this
figure, then click the + icon and pick Primary Key

This will bring up a different window, as seen in *Figure 11.25*.

Figure 11.25: Adding a primary key entails clicking the + icon and
then selecting the field name from the dropdown

To add the key, click the + button shown by the arrow, then click the dropdown to reveal the fields. Click the `author_id` field to add it as the primary key. The relational theory allows for the creation of compound keys, which is why you could potentially add more than one field. It isn't used in general practice since if you stick to an auto-incrementing integer for your key, creating a compound primary key isn't needed. In fact, I consider a compound key to be a code smell.

Adding a unique key constraint

Next, let's constrain the `email` field so that the value of any inserted record must be unique. This prevents data toxicity problems arising from promiscuous inserts. There should really only be one record for each email address. Let's enforce it formally with a unique key.

The process is the same as with the primary key, except this time we'll pick a unique key instead of the primary key and we'll specify the `email` field. There's a trick though. This time, you'll need to right-click the `keys` folder to pick the **Unique Key**. If you just click the + icon, it will add another primary key field, which isn't what we want. *Figure 11.26* shows you what to do.

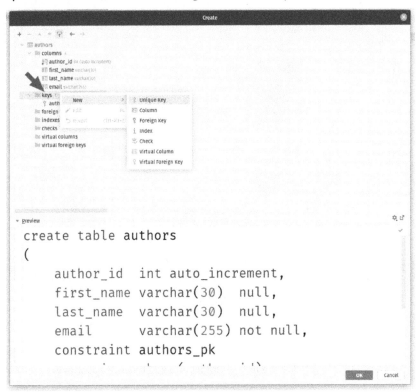

Figure 11.26: Right-click keys, then click New | Unique Key to avoid creating a second primary key

Right-click the keys folder, indicated by the arrow in the preceding figure, then click **New | Unique Key** to create the unique key constraint. Then, as before, click the dropdown, then click the email field. I would also change the name from the generated authors_pk2 value to authors_uq. This will tell you at a glance in the DDL that it is a unique field constraint.

Adding an index

Adding an index to a table will make filtered read operations more performant. It would be a reasonable requirement to expect an application to allow users to search for an author by their email address. Adding an index to the email field will make this search faster at the expense of making new record inserts slightly slower. The insert performance hit is small, but if you were to add an index to every single field, it would become noticeable, so pick the fields you want to index carefully.

The process is the same for creating the keys. Refer to *Figure 11.27*.

Figure 11.27: Right-click the indexes folder and add the index as shown

This time, we right-click the indexes folder and click **New | Index**. From here, the dialog is familiar, as shown in *Figure 11.28*.

Figure 11.28: We've added an index to the email field

At this point, our table code won't fit in a screenshot, so here's what we have:

```
create table authors
(
  author_id int auto_increment,
  first_name varchar(30) null,
  last_name varchar(30) null,
  email    varchar(255) not null,
  constraint authors_pk
    primary key (author_id)
);

create unique index authors_email_uindex
  on authors (email);

alter table authors
  add constraint authors_uq
    unique (email);
```

When you're happy with your table structure, click **OK** and PyCharm will apply the DDL code generated to the database. You can see the results in the data source. Check mine out in *Figure 11.29*.

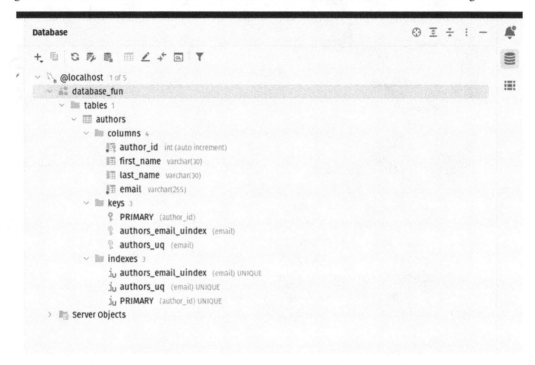

Figure 11.29: The results of our hard work are shown in the data source panel

Altering existing structures

I've seen a lot of tools over the years that are good at allowing you to graphically create a database structure, but when it comes to altering existing structures, they fall flat. Microsoft SSMS springs to mind! It will let you merrily design away only to tell you when you try to commit your changes that it can't do it.

PyCharm's not like that. PyCharm handles changes the way your company's DBA wants you to do it. If you're new to the field, a DBA is in charge of the database. They're the boss. If you are lucky enough to be granted the *privilege* of creating anything in their database, you will follow their rules. And they want you to alter structures using SQL `alter` statements.

Right-click the `authors` table and click **Modify Table...**, as shown in *Figure 11.30*.

Figure 11.30: You can alter existing tables by right-clicking the table

When you do this, you get a window like the one shown in *Figure 11.31*.

Figure 11.31: Changes you make here are generated as an alter statement,
which is a best practice in database development

In *Figure 11.31*, I've added a column called `date_of_birthd` with the type of date. As you can see in the preview window, PyCharm is generating an `alter` statement rather than trying to drop and recreate the table as many database editors do. If you wanted to drop the table, there was an option for that in the menu displayed in *Figure 11.30*.

Generating scripts

PyCharm has a very powerful utility for generating all kinds of SQL scripts. Since we're talking about DDL here, it makes sense to learn how to generate the full SQL script that will create the table we've been working on.

Right-click the database, as shown in *Figure 11.32*, and click the **SQL Scripts | SQL Generator...** menu item.

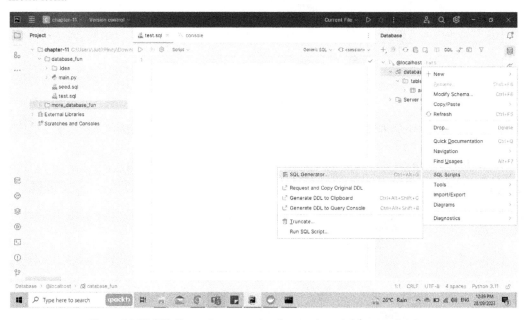

Figure 11.32: SQL Generator generates the create script for our database

The panel on the left allows you to set a few interesting options. As you click them, the generated SQL will change if applicable. I say *if applicable* because not every database platform supports every syntax option in the list. We're using MySQL, which supports the Use `CREATE IF NOT EXISTS` syntax but doesn't support the `CREATE OR REPLACE` syntax, which you would find in Postgres or Oracle. Clicking a syntax that isn't supported simply doesn't change the syntax in the preview window.

When the DDL script meets your needs, you can use the buttons on the far right (circled in *Figure 11.32*) to copy, save, or run the script in a query window.

Generating a database diagram

Very traditional database practices typically entail a design document such as a database schema diagram. In the good old days, we'd use dedicated tools for diagramming. PyCharm has a diagramming tool built in, and the best part is the diagram is generated based on the structure of the database, rather than being drawn from scratch.

To generate a diagram, just right-click your database, find the **Diagrams** menu item, and pick either option shown in *Figure 11.33*.

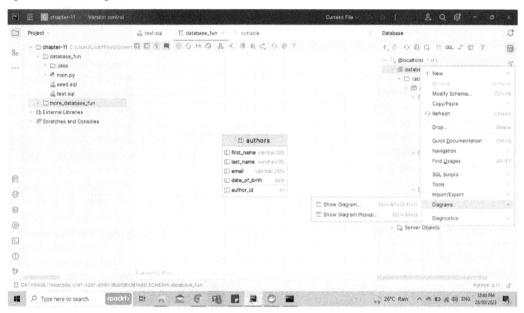

Figure 11.33: The Diagrams menu items are shown along with a generated diagram

The only difference between the two options is one draws the diagram directly in the content area of the IDE while the other generates it in a pop-up window. The pop-up window is useful for viewing the diagram on another monitor. You can navigate the diagram with zooming tools, as well as panning around by right-clicking within the diagram while dragging.

You'll also find export options on the top toolbar for exporting your diagram to image files, as well as data files that can be imported into dedicated diagramming tools.

Querying the data source using SQL

Querying the database is probably the second most useful feature of having database tooling built right into the IDE. As with many of the features in PyCharm, this one ensures you never need to leave PyCharm to get your work done.

There are several places that allow you to run queries. You can run ad hoc queries in a query console, or you can run queries directly from `.sql` files.

Ad hoc queries

Ad hoc queries are simply queries for an immediate purpose. An ad hoc query has a number of characteristics:

- **Unplanned**: Ad hoc queries are not part of a predefined set of queries. They are written on the spot to address a particular need.

- **Temporary**: They are used to retrieve data for a specific task or situation and are not saved for future use. They aren't part of your application, though after some experimentation and tweaking, you might formalize them in your code.

- **No optimization**: Ad hoc queries might not be optimized for efficiency, as they are quickly put together without the time for fine-tuning.

- **Variability**: The syntax and structure of ad hoc queries can vary depending on the user's knowledge and experience.

- **Not stored**: Unlike stored procedures or views, ad hoc queries are not stored in the database as with, say, a view or a stored procedure. This means they cannot be called or executed again later unless you save them to a file later.

Ad hoc queries are executed in a database console. A console window appears automatically when you complete your connection to the data source, but there are many places in the interface where you can create a new console view. Look at *Figure 11.34* and you'll see the data source window. A button labeled **QL**, for **Query Language**, is circled. It doesn't say *SQL* because, remember, PyCharm also supports NoSQL databases, such as MongoDB, Apache Cassandra, and Redis.

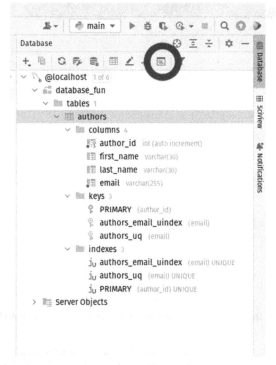

Figure 11.34: Any place you see a QL icon like this you can launch a console
window and query your data source using an ad hoc query

The **QL** button is sensitive to the database selected in the data source window, so if you have more than one data source, you can open a query source to any of them by selecting them in the data source window and then hitting the **QL** button. I actually closed the console that was automatically launched when I created the data source. To create a new console, I'll hit the **QL** button and select **New Console**.

The first console you open becomes the **default console**. PyCharm keeps track of your consoles in the **Scratches and Consoles** folder, as shown in *Figure 11.35*.

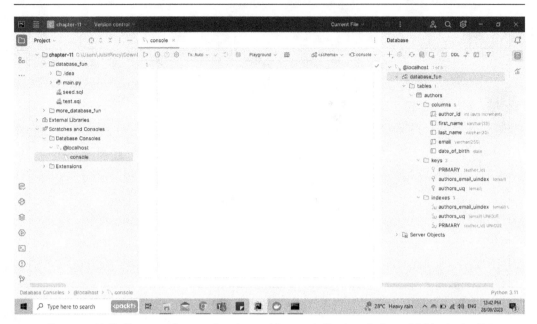

Figure 11.35: PyCharm tracks consoles along with scratch files in a dedicated folder in the IDE

If you've typed any SQL in the console, PyCharm will keep the contents even between sessions. Empty consoles will disappear when you exit PyCharm. This is handy for keeping track of your ad hoc work.

Generating SQL statements

We need to create some seed records, which will ultimately be saved as a seed script. A seed script is a script that can be used for testing an application by seeding the database with some initial test data. We're moving away from the strictly DDL statements we've used so far. We're going to be using more DML, which are the statements used to work with data rather than database structure. Seed scripts are also useful for filling in data tables with static data that rarely changes.

We're going to seed our `authors` table with a few records, but we're going to have PyCharm generate a lot of the SQL for us. Begin by creating a console if you don't have one open already. Right-click the `authors` table, hover over **SQL Scripts**, then find **Insert rows into a table**. Check out *Figure 11.36* to see it in action.

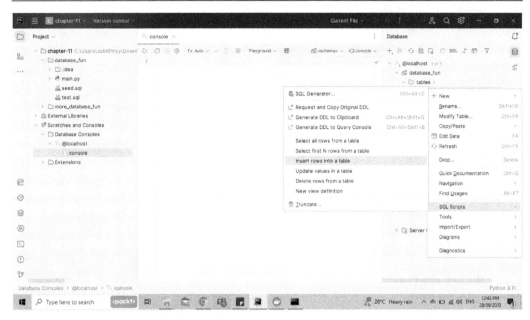

Figure 11.36: PyCharm will generate DML queries for you automatically!

Once you click the option, you'll find an `insert` statement has been inserted (oh yes!) directly into the console. You can see mine in *Figure 11.37*.

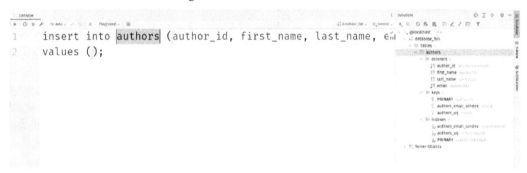

Figure 11.37: PyCharm generated an insert statement for the table we selected

Note the bounding box around the text. We've seen this before. You're looking at a template! This means we can tab from place to place in the templated text, which is why you shouldn't mess with the text as I did.

> **Copy-paste warning!**
>
> If you have an electronic copy of this book that allows you to copy and paste from the e-book itself, be careful with any code that relies on single quotation marks as the upcoming SQL statement does. The process of editing the book often turns them into special characters that won't work when you paste them into a console. Make sure the single quotation marks are really single quotation marks!

`insert` statements can be divided into two halves:

```
insert into authors (first_name, last_name, email)
values ('Bruce', 'Van Horn', 'bruce@test.com');
```

The halves I'm talking about are the parts of the statement that aren't boilerplate – the parts in the two sets of parentheses. The first set specifies which fields you'll be filling, and the second set is the values. You have to match the order and type of the fields in the first half when you type values for each field. If you hit the *Tab* key, you'll move between the two halves of the `insert` statement, allowing you to modify it as you see fit.

> **Unconventional generated SQL**
>
> PyCharm doesn't generate SQL keywords in all caps by default, which is the normal convention. You might notice that statements that I type are all caps, but generated ones aren't. I had to resist the temptation to fix that for the sake of the book, but I also need to explain why there are inconsistencies at play.

PyCharm generated a placeholder for the primary key, which is a field you wouldn't normally populate since the database fills that in automatically. Go ahead and take that first field out of the field set in the first parentheses as I did in the preceding code.

Next, tab over to the `values` section, and begin to fill in values. Remember, in SQL, `varchar` (`string`) values must be enclosed in single quotes. Python allows you to use either single or double quotes but SQL does not. As you type values, PyCharm will give you hints about the field you are matching for the value. It does this with a tooltip over the text in the editor, but it also color codes the current field in the top half of the statement. See *Figure 11.38* to see what I mean.

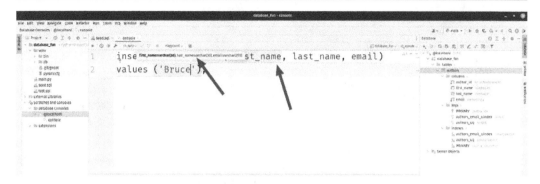

Figure 11.38: PyCharm gives tooltips for the field and type you are
currently filling in the second half of the query

This is huge! How many times have you written a long `insert` statement only to find that you have more values than fields? Or worse, you discover you've transposed a few fields and you enter a bunch of garbage data by mistake? PyCharm gives you a visual indicator to make sure you know exactly which field you're entering by showing you a tooltip with the field and type you are filling in. It also shades the field in the top half of the SQL statement.

Running the query

You probably don't need me to tell you this because, at this point, you're probably used to seeing green run arrows where it is appropriate to run something. You can run the contents of the console by clicking the green arrow at the top of the console's tab in the IDE. You can also highlight a section of the console's contents and run a portion of the query.

Change the contents of your console to match this code:

```
insert into authors (first_name, last_name, email)
values ('Bruce', 'Van Horn', 'bruce@test.com');
insert into authors (first_name, last_name, email)
values ('Kinnari', 'Chohan', 'kinnari@test.com');
insert into authors (first_name, last_name, email)
values ('Prajakta', 'Naik', 'prajakta@test.com');
insert into authors (first_name, last_name, email)
values ('Jubit', 'Pincy', 'jubit@test.com');
```

All I did was copy the same SQL four times, then I changed the names for a little variety, and to give a shout-out to my Packt crew (holla!). Next, highlight the first statement and run the query. The **Services** panel will open to show the results of the query. As you can see in *Figure 11.39*, only one record was inserted.

Figure 11.39: You can execute single statements by selecting them and clicking the Run button

If you select the remainder and run again, you'll find three insertions.

Now that we have some data, let's query with a SELECT statement. Add this code to your console:

```
SELECT * FROM authors;
```

I could have generated select, but this query is short. I wanted to show you how PyCharm displays the results. Take a look at *Figure 11.40*.

Figure 11.40: By default, select statements produce a nice, tabular output

This is a dense panel! You can do a lot here. By default, you see a tabular view of the data (**1**). You can double-click the cells and edit the data in place. You can also add and delete rows using this UI (**2**). After you've edited the data to your liking, you can submit your changes using the small green up arrow on the toolbar (**2**) in *Figure 11.40*.

If you'd rather change the output view from tabular to either raw text or a tree view (which makes more sense for querying hierarchical data), you can click the eyeball icon in the toolbar (**2**) in *Figure 11.41*.

Exporting query results

You can export the results of your `select` statements using the export button *Figure 11.41*. *Figure 11.41* shows what this looks like.

Figure 11.41: Exporting data is easy in PyCharm

The export format defaults to **comma-separated values** (**CSV**), which is a common format for tabular data exchange. PyCharm supports dozens of other useful formats, which you'll find in the **Extractor** drop-down list. Change the output file to something you like, then click the **Export to file** button.

Working with SQL files

PyCharm supports files with a `.sql` or `.ddl` file extension. Like other recognized file types, you'll get auto-completion, syntax highlighting, and so on. You can also run statements directly in the SQL file just like we can in the console.

Let's immortalize our console work so far as a proper script. Create a new file in PyCharm called seed.sql. Next, add this line to the top of the script file:

```
USE database_fun;
TRUNCATE TABLE authors;
```

The USE statement is MySQL-specific and ensures you have the database_fun database selected prior to executing the SQL statements. The TRUNCATE statement will delete all the records in the authors table and reset the auto-incrementor sequence on the table back to its initial value. This is useful for development testing since now the seed script can reset to a clean set of testing values. Just be careful to never run the seed script in production!

Next, cut and paste the contents of your console beneath the TRUNCATE statement. Note that I said cut. You want the console empty. The script should look like this:

```
USE database_fun;
TRUNCATE TABLE authors;
insert into authors (first_name, last_name, email)
values ('Bruce', 'Van Horn', 'bruce@test.com');

insert into authors (first_name, last_name, email)
values ('Kinnari', 'Chohan', 'kinnari@test.com');

insert into authors (first_name, last_name, email)
values ('Prajakta', 'Naik', 'prajakta@test.com');

insert into authors (first_name, last_name, email)
values ('Jubit', 'Pincy', 'jubit@test.com');

SELECT * FROM authors;
```

Save your seed script and run it. It should execute successfully.

Summary

I have this terrible feeling that I haven't covered everything. That's because I didn't. I could write a whole book just on the database features of PyCharm, but if I did, I might as well title it something like *Hands-On Database Programming with DataGrip*. Don't forget, we're seeing a whole other IDE crammed into the crevices of PyCharm much as we did with WebStorm in *Chapter 7, Web Development with JavaScript, HTML, and CSS*. The feature set is truly staggering and I didn't cover some of the really interesting features owing to either lack of space in this book or because some of the really cool features are still works in progress.

For example, you can set code as a data source and synchronize the code to the structure of the database. At present, it isn't 100% complete, which is why I left it out. As a database developer, I would expect to be able to have a round-trip experience where changes to the code are reflected in the database and changes to the database are copied back to the code. I think we're well on our way.

What we did cover, though, was pretty complete coverage for either full stack web development or a data science practitioner needing to tap multiple database platforms and data storage paradigms.

We started out with a little history. I like covering the history in this and previous chapters because I have the advantage of a long career behind me. I was around for most of what I'm describing, and I had a front-row seat. I was in the first grade when E. F. Codd formalized relational algebra. Part of me wishes I could brag about using his early work, but in truth, I was a bigger fan of watching the Saturday morning TV show *Lassie and the Rescue Rangers* in my footy pajamas than I was of SELECT statements. When I was older, I got to work on IBM mainframes, so I did eventually catch up.

Moving into more practical matters, we learned that PyCharm, using separately installed JDBC drivers, can connect to dozens of different database platforms. We learned it supports not only relational databases but NoSQL as well. After we learned how to open the database tools and connect our data source, we learned how to design a database using a host of tools that generate DDL for us.

Then we moved on to using PyCharm to generate the DML that would power our work once we got some data in our tables. Finally, after working in a console to create our initial work, we saved our SQL into a .sql file.

The positioning of this chapter in the book is very intentional. I've restrained myself from doing a lot of coding in the full stack frameworks we covered in the last few chapters. In real life, you would most assuredly have databases attached to such projects. While many developers rely on ORMs to handle the database work for them, it never hurts to at least be able to examine the database and its contents directly using a console.

If you're like me, and you forgo ORMs entirely, you now have the missing piece to the puzzle. You can create your database code using a marvelous set of tools without leaving PyCharm.

This chapter also offered a logical split as the next few chapters start coverage of PyCharm Professional's power data science feature set. It only makes sense to preface that set of chapters with coverage of these most ubiquitous engines for data storage and retrieval.

In the next chapter, we'll be turning on *science mode*! Go pick up your lab coat from the dry cleaners, grab yourself a big cup of $C_8H_{10}N_4O_2$, and I'll see you in the next chapter!

Further reading

Be sure to check out the companion website for the book at `https://www.pycharm-book.com`.

- Docker Desktop installation instructions: `https://www.docker.com/products/docker-desktop/`.

- Using KeePass in PyCharm: `https://www.jetbrains.com/help/pycharm/reference-ide-settings-password-safe.html`.

- Codd, E. F. (1983). A relational model of data for large shared data banks. *Communications of the ACM, 26*(1), 64-69.

- Forta, B. (2013). *Sams teach yourself SQL in 10 minutes*. Pearson Education.

- Hernandez, M. J. (2013). *Database Design for Mere Mortals: A Hands-On Guide to Relational Database Design*. Pearson Education.

- Pettit, T. and Cossetino, S. (2022). *The MySQL Workshop*. Packt Publishing.

- Poulton, N. (2023). *Docker Deep Dive – 2nd Edition*. Packt Publishing.

- Viescas, J. L. and Hernandez, M. J. (2014). *SQL Queries for Mere Mortals: A Hands-On Guide to Data Manipulation in SQL*. Pearson Education.

Part 4: Data Science with PyCharm

Similar to the previous part, this part of the book focuses on a specific application of Python programming, this time data analysis and data science. Readers will be able to use PyCharm and its features to efficiently work on their data science and scientific computing projects.

This part has the following chapters:

- *Chapter 12, Turning on Scientific Mode*
- *Chapter 13, Dynamic Data Viewing with SciView and Jupyter*
- *Chapter 14, Building a Data Pipeline in PyCharm*

12

Turning On Scientific Mode

Welcome to the third section of the book. One of my favorite video game franchises is Sid Meier's *Civilization*. It takes many days to complete a single game, which starts you off as the head of a civilization at the dawn of history. You progress through prehistoric eras, through medieval, renaissance, and industrial areas. With each new age comes unique challenges as players vie for various facets of global domination. The game truly speeds up once the players reach the information age. I can just hear my editor saying, *"Put down the video game, and type faster!"* OK, I will. Talking about the book, I feel like we've reached a similar milestone with this chapter. We've come a long way since our *hello world* message in `main.py` back in the first few chapters of this book.

PyCharm is aimed at Python developers, but PyCharm Professional really targets two groups: web developers and data scientists. The latter group seems like it is a little harder to nail down given JetBrains has multiple products for data science. Besides PyCharm Professional, JetBrains also makes a separate IDE called **DataSpell** which is billed as *The IDE for Professional Data Scientists*. What gives?

I wondered the same thing. According to the company's FAQ for DataSpell, PyCharm is supposed to support software developers who engage in data-sciency activities as part of their job as software developers. DataSpell is for professionals who are not developers, but who simply do analytics. There is some cross-over in terms of features, but unlike what we've seen with WebStorm and DataGrip which are fully embedded in PyCharm, DataSpell has features PyCharm doesn't, and there are no plans to change that. They are targeting two different sets of professionals.

Support for scientific and analytical workflows entails turning on scientific mode in PyCharm. This opens up new UI layouts and tool panels you wouldn't normally with scientific mode turned off. In this chapter, we'll be covering the following topics:

- Starting a scientific project in PyCharm

- Advanced features of PyCharm's scientific projects

By the end of this chapter, you will understand how these features can improve productivity in scientific computing projects. This chapter will serve as a general, high-level discussion on the various tools PyCharm offers and will help you understand scientific computing and how these tools are integrated and work with each other.

Technical requirements

In order to proceed through this chapter, and indeed the rest of the book, you will need the following:

- Since we're switching to the topic of data science, I'll be switching my preferred Python distribution to Anaconda, which is a Python distribution tailored to data science workloads. You can find it, along with installation instructions for your operating system at `https://anaconda.com`.

- Likewise, instead of the usual `pip`, I'll be leveraging `conda`, which is Anaconda's package manager. It is installed alongside Anaconda.

- An installed and working copy of PyCharm. Installation was covered in *Chapter 2, Installation and Configuration*, in case you are jumping into the middle of the book.

This book's sample source code from GitHub. We covered cloning the code in *Chapter 2, Installation and Configuration*. You'll find this chapter's relevant code at `https://github.com/PacktPublishing/Hands-On-Application-Development-with-PyCharm---Second-Edition/tree/main/chapter-12`.

Creating a scientific project in PyCharm

By now, you're intimately familiar with the New Project dialog in PyCharm. Let's create a science project! Click **File | New Project**, and you'll find a template called **Scientific**, as shown in *Figure 12.1*:

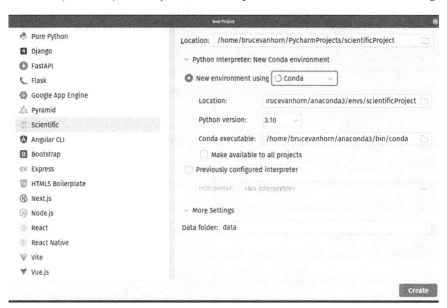

Figure 12.1: Stand back! We're about to do SCIENCE!

I mentioned earlier, I will be using Anaconda for this section of the book because this is what most data science pros use. The only interesting setting beyond the change in interpreter is the **Data folder** setting under **More Settings**. It is setting a folder in our soon-to-be-created project that will hold, you guessed it: data. More on this after we create the project. Go ahead and click **Create**.

Once the creation process is complete, you'll find a setup like mine in *Figure 12.2*:

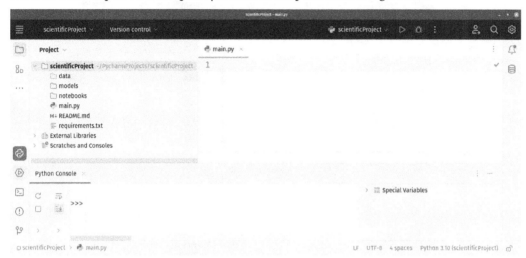

Figure 12.2: Behold! We have created a science project in PyCharm!

Let's talk about what just happened. We generated a project, per usual. We got a folder called data, which must be special because it is a different color than the rest. We got more empty folders for notebooks and models. We got a `main.py` file, a `requirements.txt` file, and a Markdown file called `README.md`, all of which are empty. We usually get some boilerplate code but not this time.

Each file and folder serves a purpose. As I mentioned, the data folder must be special because it is a different color. Mine is highlighted in yellow. This folder is important because it is meant to contain data files for your scientific analysis. Since it isn't code, and since your data files might be very large, PyCharm marks this folder as special to the project. You might have noticed the template folder in Flask and Django apps were also colored differently than the rest. There are special folders in many project types.

We can gain some clues about this in the project's properties. I have the project properties window up in *Figure 12.3*:

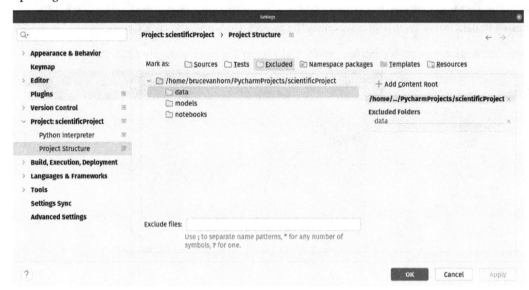

Figure 12.3: You can set several types of special folders in many of the
project types in PyCharm including scientific projects

In this case, the data folder is excluded from the rest of the project. PyCharm will not index or scan this folder in any way. We need this for the data folder because it is fairly normal for your data files to be very large. There is no code in this folder, so really, there is no reason to scan it for the purposes of providing the usual help and insights you've come to expect from code files. You might even consider having your revision control system disregard this folder as well, since it might not be appropriate to check your data into a repository for a number of reasons ranging from privacy issues, depending on the nature of the data, as well as file size. Git has limitations on the size of files it can handle, and GitHub will limit the size of your repository. The data folder is an obvious bloat that probably doesn't need to be in the repo.

With that mystery solved, let's look at the `requirements.txt` file. We have seen this before. This file is used by the Python project, regardless of which IDE you use, to track the library requirements for the project. Anytime you use a third-party library from PyPi, you need to include it in `requirements.txt`. This file should be checked into your repository so other developers can replicate your virtual environment. The file is empty, and we saw the tooling around `requirements.txt` in *Chapter 3*.

There is something here we have not seen before: the `README.md` file. The `.md` extension indicates this is a Markdown file. Markdown is an alternative to HTML, which is a markup language. See what they did there? Markdown allows you to create a formatted text file without all the overhead of HTML.

While you get rid of the overhead, you also lose a lot of capability. Markdown is just used to create documentation files. If you've ever browsed a repository on GitHub, and the project has a snazzy landing page, you're really looking at the README.md file rendered to HTML by GitHub and your browser. There's an example of a nice README.md page for one of my repos in *Figure 12.4*:

Figure 12.4: The README.md file gets rendered as the landing page on
GitHub and is used to document the contents of the repository

For this project, PyCharm has generated an empty README.md file. The main.py file is just a plain old Python file. Really, this is a very minimal project template.

Additional configuration for science projects in PyCharm

PyCharm's out-of-the-box configuration is normally very complete. For scientific projects, though, there are some plugins you might want to add. We have a whole chapter on some amazing plugins later in the book, but you need them right now, so let's take a look.

Plugins are installed using the PyCharm Marketplace. You can get to the Marketplace using the gear icon you normally use to get to settings. You'll recognize it in *Figure 12.5*:

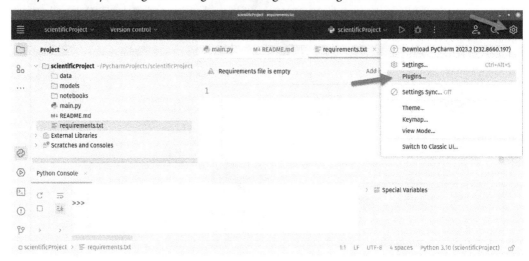

Figure 12.5: The plugins menu option will take you to the plugins
window which includes the PyCharm Marketplace

Open the **Plugins** window. You can see mine in *Figure 12.6*:

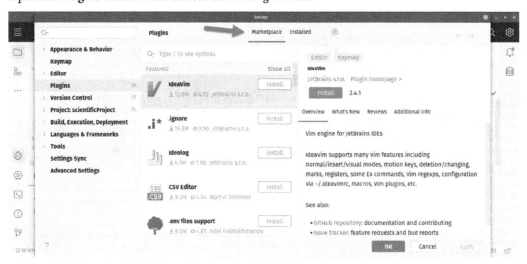

Figure 12.6: The Marketplace allows you to find all kinds of plugins for PyCharm and other JetBrains IDEs

Note it takes you straight to the **Marketplace** tab. This reminds me of the inevitable gift shop at the end of every museum tour I've ever taken. There's a tab to the right that lets you see what is already installed. That's boring though, right? It is more enticing to browse what we don't yet have. Many of the plugins here are free, and some are not. Likewise, many of the plugins here are well documented and supported by developers who carefully craft their Marketplace offering. Some are just short descriptions with a title. Let's go shopping!

Markdown plugins

Your first stop is to find a good Markdown plugin. Markdown isn't exactly rocket science, even though we find it in a science project. However, a good Markdown plugin will render your Markdown so you can see what it will look like when the Markdown code is converted to formatted text.

To find a Markdown plugin you need to search using the **Search** box indicated in *Figure 12.7*:

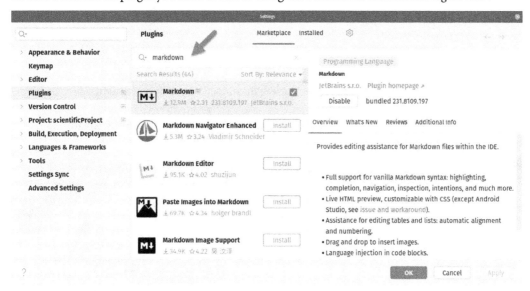

Figure 12.7: Search here for plugins and avoid the temptation of the search box that helps you find settings

As it happens, JetBrains now bundles a Markdown plugin in the default installation. They haven't always done that. You can see there are alternatives to explore. I'm just going to use the bundled one. If you have an older version of PyCharm, you might need to install this. In this case, there will be an **Install** button as you can see with the others.

Let's try it out. Exit the settings window and open the README.md file. Add the following code to your README.md file:

```
# The Science Project
Welcome to my science project!
```

You should see your Markdown code on the left, and the rendered preview on the right, as shown in *Figure 12.8*:

Figure 12.8: Markdown code is on the left; the rendered result is on the right

You can change the layout of the preview, or hide it altogether using the buttons on the top right of the Markdown editor as shown in *Figure 12.9*:

Figure 12.9: You can adjust the layout of the preview window

Clicking the left button hides the preview. Pushing the right one hides the code. You can click the button in the middle once to toggle the preview alongside the code. Click it again, and you'll get code and preview stacked on top of one another.

Adding images

A needed characteristic of a good Markdown editor is the ability to easily add images. In PyCharm, if you need images in your Markdown, start by making a folder in your project called assets. Copy your image files to this folder. Then, just drag the image and drop it in the editor. In *Figure 12.10*, I'm dragging an image from my assets folder and then dropping it in my Markdown editor:

Figure 12.10: Drag images from outside PyCharm and drop them
into the code to include them in your Markdown

The result can be seen in *Figure 12.11*:

Figure 12.11: The dragged image appears in your code and in the preview

All in all, the default plugin is pretty good. Some of the others have more advanced features, but really the only one I'd want is one that converts the Markdown to other formats. If you need that, a few of the plugins in the marketplace can do that.

Installing the CSV plugin

A common format for data storage is the **comma-separated values** (**CSV**) format. This is a format that is supported by every spreadsheet program ever devised. The marketplace has a CSV function that allows you to open CSVs and similar files such as **tab-separated values** (**TSV**) in a spreadsheet-like interface. You can see the Marketplace page for it in *Figure 12.12*:

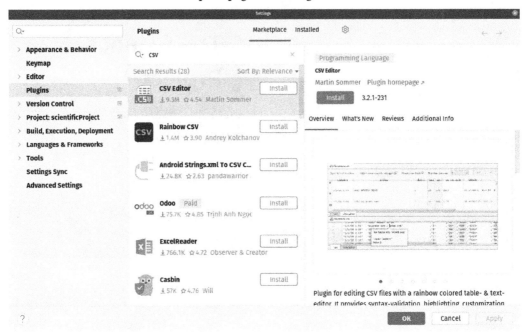

Figure 12.12: You'll probably be using CSV files at some point. Luckily, there's a plugin for that

After you click the install button for the CSV Editor plugin, you'll be prompted to restart the IDE. This is very common. After you restart, you can try it out with any of your own CSV files, or you can use my sample of FDA study data in the sample code's data folder. The CSV plugin renders my data in full color as seen in *Figure 12.13*:

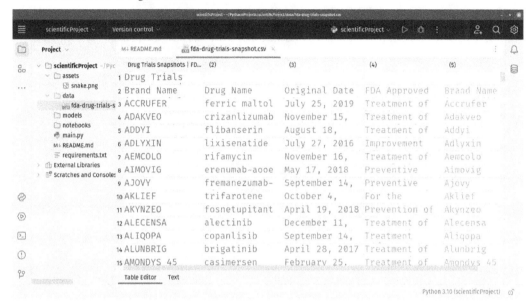

Figure 12.13: The CSV Editor plugin renders data in columns in different
colors. It's like having a pretty spreadsheet embedded in your IDE

Naturally, you can edit the data, but this isn't a spreadsheet. Don't expect to be able to add formulas and expressions to your cells. At the bottom you'll see you can switch between the **Table Editor** view the **Text view**.

There's one more you're going to want for sure and that's the cell mode plugin.

Installing the cell mode plugin

I'm not going into great depth on what the cell mode plugin does just yet. Just trust me when I say it is extremely handy when you are working with PyCharm code cells, which we'll be covering shortly. Since we're already in the Marketplace, let's grab it now. *Figure 12.14* shows the Marketplace page for the cell mode plugin:

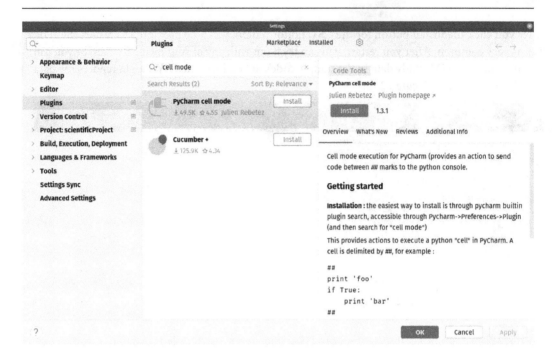

Figure 12.14: The cell mode plugin will make working with code cells easy a little later in this chapter

Install it by clicking the **Install** button. At this point, you have PyCharm fairly kitted out for data work.

Installing packages

We are getting ready to do some science, but first, we need to set some requirements for our project. We've covered this in earlier chapters, but we'll quickly review it here.

The newest way to add packages to any Python project is to use the **Python Packages** panel shown in *Figure 12.15*:

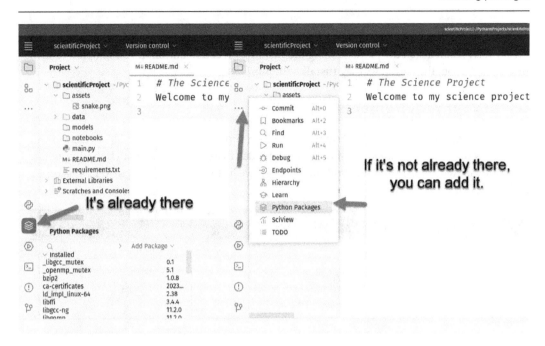

Figure 12.15: Use the Python Packages panel to manage Python
packages. If it isn't on the right-hand toolbar, you can add it

If you've used the panel before, it will be on the right-hand toolbar. If you haven't used it before, you can add it by clicking the three dots, and then picking the **Python Packages** option. Once you've located the button to open the panel, you'll find the **Search** box shown in *Figure 12.16*:

Figure 12.16: You can search packages from PyPI easily from this panel and add them using conda

We're going to add `numpy` and `matplotlib` to our project. Type each into the **Search** box indicated in *Figure 12.17*, then install the package using the **Install with conda** button. If you've opted to stick with vanilla Python, the button will say **Install with pip**.

Backfill your requirements.txt file

Now that you have the two packages installed, open the `requirements.txt` file. PyCharm will let you know that the requirements installed in the conda environment don't match the empty file. *Figure 12.17* shows you the option to add the packages we just installed to the `requirements.txt` file automatically.

Figure 12.17: PyCharm helps you keep your requirements.txt file up to date

Click the link button to update your requirements file.

Adding some sciency code

My editor keeps saying "sciency" isn't a word. A wise man once said, "Science isn't about why. It's about why not!?" I'm going to keep using it and if you're actually reading this, it means I got away with it.

We've set up the IDE, and installed our required packages. Let's open up `main.py` and add some code so we can see PyCharm strut its stuff! In `main.py`, add this code:

```
import numpy as np
import matplotlib.pyplot as plt
```

These first two imports just bring in `numpy` and `matplotlib` with aliases. It turns out scientists hate typing more than normal developers:

```
N = 100
x = np.random.normal(0, 1, N)
```

```
y = np.random.normal(2, 3, N)


#%% plot data in histograms
plt.hist(x, alpha=0.5, label='x')
plt.hist(y, alpha=0.5, label='y')
plt.legend(loc='upper right')
plt.show()
```

Using NumPy, we are simply creating two sample 100-element datasets from normal distributions. The values of x are created from a distribution with a mean of 0 and a standard deviation of 1, while y is from a distribution with a mean of 2 and a standard deviation of 3. Then, we draw their corresponding histograms using Matplotlib. Run the program per usual and note the results in *Figure 12.18*:

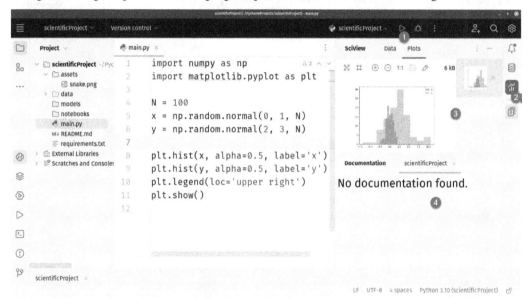

Figure 12.18: Click the run button (1) and the matplotlib graphical plot is displayed in SciView

Our Python script ran, but doing so triggered SciView to turn on. SciView is the centerpiece of PyCharm's data analytics feature set. It allows you to view plots alongside the complex API documentation common to libraries such as NumPy, pandas, and PyTorch.

I highlighted the run button at (1) in *Figure 12.18* in case you're joining us late, and you skipped the earlier chapters on running your code in the IDE. The icon at (2) indicates SciView is turned on. You can toggle it on or off just like any other panel. When SciView is turned on, you get a panel for visualizations (3) and a panel for documentation (4). We'll be working with these tools more over the next few chapters.

Toggling scientific mode

I have mentioned the term *scientific mode* a couple of times before; now, we will see the significance of this mode in PyCharm projects.

Scientific mode consists of multiple components that we will be exploring in this and the upcoming chapters, the most notable being the **SciView** and **Documentation** panels. It is important to note that this special mode in PyCharm is not equivalent to having a scientific project. Moreover, it is more of a configuration setting where various PyCharm features that support scientific computing are easier to access and use.

There are a great many programs that have different UI configurations depending on how you intend to use the software. Adobe Photoshop has different view sets for photographers versus web designers. Many browsers have chromeless options or modes optimized for distraction-free reading. PyCharm itself has a *Zen mode,* which removes all of the UI except for the editor. You can see it in *Figure 12.19*:

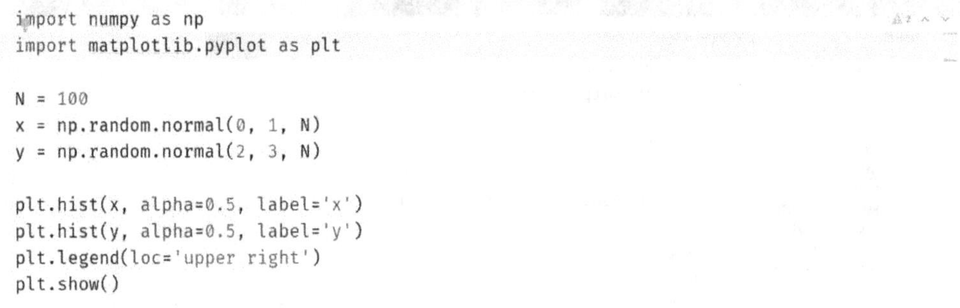

```python
import numpy as np
import matplotlib.pyplot as plt

N = 100
x = np.random.normal(0, 1, N)
y = np.random.normal(2, 3, N)

plt.hist(x, alpha=0.5, label='x')
plt.hist(y, alpha=0.5, label='y')
plt.legend(loc='upper right')
plt.show()
```

Figure 12.19: In Zen mode's embrace. PyCharm's code dances with peace. Clarity in lines

If you're interested in Zen mode, you'll find it by clicking **View** | **Appearance** | **Enter Zen** mode from the main menu. That's nice and all, but we're here for scientific mode and the point I was making is that this mode is more of a configuration of the appearance of PyCharm rather than being dedicated tool panels unique to the scientific project. You can enable scientific mode in any project type. To turn it in, click **View** | **Scientific Mode**, as shown in *Figure 12.20*:

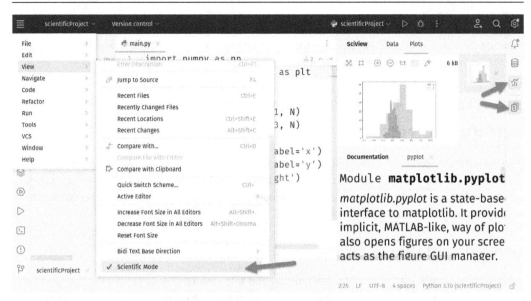

Figure 12.20: You can toggle Scientific Mode on the view menu. When scientific mode is on, you can toggle the two panels using the buttons on the toolbar to the right edge of the screen

PyCharm is also a little bit nosy. If it sees you are using NumPy, it prompts you to turn scientific mode on with a little toast in the bottom-right corner of the IDE. See *Figure 12.21*:

Figure 12.21: Your Pythonic big brother is watching you, but at least it's trying to be helpful

Overall, scientific mode offers an intuitive interface that can improve your productivity in scientific computing projects. In the next section, we will examine other advanced features within a scientific project in more detail, namely the **Documentation** panel and PyCharm's code cells.

Understanding the advanced features of PyCharm's scientific projects

Equipped with the features we discussed in the previous section, you can navigate and work with PyCharm's scientific projects efficiently and productively. However, there are still other subtle features that PyCharm offers that can prove to be useful in this context. First, we will consider the **Documentation** panel and its usage.

The documentation viewer

Documentation is an essential part of programming and software development, and PyCharm offers the most powerful and straightforward features to support the task of working with documentation in Python. We saw it in action first in *Chapter 4, Editing and Formatting with Ease in PyCharm*.

In a scientific project, the **Documentation** panel, as we have seen, is pinned as one of the main panels of the project window. This documentation viewer displays real-time documentation data in a dynamic way. Specifically, as you move your caret to a particular method or function call in the editor, the **Documentation** panel will show the official documentation corresponding to that method or function.

Go back into the code we wrote earlier, and place your cursor on line 10. Place your cursor in the word legend and the **Documentation** window will instantly display the documentation for that method, which is part of the Matplotlib library. You can see this in *Figure 12.22*:

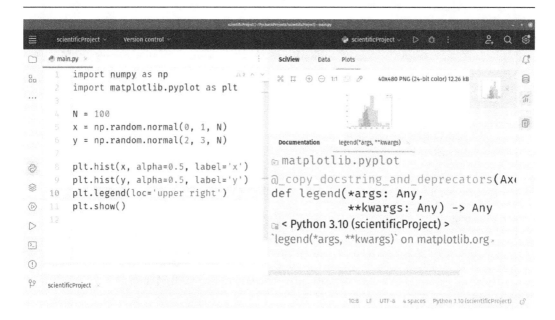

Figure 12.22: Click on pretty much anything, and the Documentation
panel will show documentation on any property or method

The thing with these scientific libraries that are popular with data science is they can have complicated data structures being used as arguments and return types. Having instance reference material is extremely useful. I'd recommend a larger screen to truly take advantage of it. My screenshot in *Figure 12.22* is a little crowded only because it's on a smaller screen with the fonts dialed up to make them clear for the printed book.

Besides showing you documentation for wherever you click, the **Documentation** panel will update as you type your code. Not only do you get the usual auto-completion, but you see the full documentation at the same time. The **Document** panel has a few configuration options reached by clicking the three vertical dots at the top of the panel, shown in *Figure 12.23*:

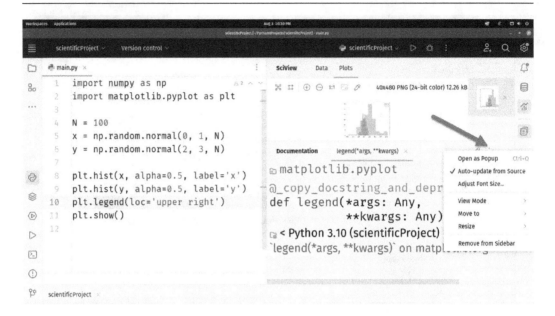

Figure 12.23: There are a few configuration options for the Documentation
panel found beneath the menu at the top of the panel

Next, we will examine a unique feature in PyCharm when it comes to executing Python code, that is, implementing code cells.

Using code cells in PyCharm

PyCharm's code cells are a way to separate and execute different portions of a large Python program sequentially. You'll recognize this feature if you have ever used the **Jupyter Notebook**. Code cells in PyCharm are basically a trimmed-down version of that tool. PyCharm also has direct support for Jupyter notebooks, but I'm saving that for the next chapter.

The needs of data science are different from the needs of a general software developer. A data scientist isn't worried about writing shipable code with the same architectural and scaling constraints as a software developer. They also don't deal with your typical variables that are mostly primitives, or smallish objects with a handful of properties and methods. They deal in volume, and the programs they write are algorithmic. Don't get overly wrapped up around the word **algorithm**. An *algorithm* is simply a set of steps that make up a process. Sure, the algorithm that powers Google's search business, PageRank, is an amazing feat of proprietary engineering. It's an algorithm, but so is the recipe for a good old peanut butter and jelly sandwich. Complexity isn't a requirement, in fact the best algorithms are usually simple.

Data scientists study problems by collecting, filtering, and processing large amounts of data using a series of aggregate steps. Each step is very discrete with an input and an output. Code cells make it easy to construct and work with these discrete steps rather than having to deal with complicated code structures the way a regular software developer would.

Using PyCharm code cells

Code cells in PyCharm are defined by lines of code that start with the following characters: #%%. These lines are treated as standard comments in the low-level execution of Python, but PyCharm will recognize them as code cell separators in its editor. Let's see this feature in action.

Let's go back to our demo code from earlier and make some small changes:

```
import numpy as np
import matplotlib.pyplot as plt


#%% generate random data
N = 100
x = np.random.normal(0, 1, N)
y = np.random.normal(2, 3, N)


#%% plot data in histograms
plt.hist(x, alpha=0.5, label='x')
plt.hist(y, alpha=0.5, label='y')
plt.legend(loc='upper right')
plt.show()
```

Note the addition of the two lines beginning with #%%. Those lines define our code cells. Moreover, they also serve as regular comments that explain what the code block is doing. Now look at how the PyCharm UI has changed. You should now see some run buttons appear in the gutter, as shown in *Figure 12.24*:

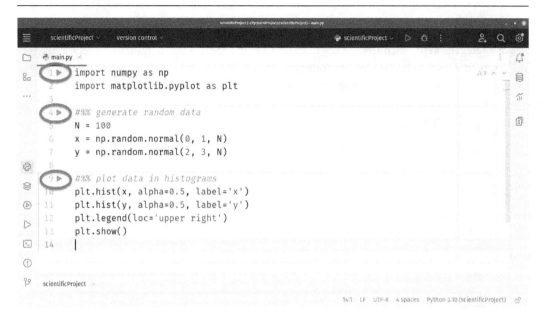

Figure 12.24: Run buttons appear in the gutter in response to the special comment format

Now, we can run each cell and review the result before running the next. If we need to make an adjustment in the middle cell, we can re-run that cell and those that are subsequent. When you click the run buttons, the code is being executed in the PyCharm console. If your console isn't visible, you can get to it by clicking **View | Tool Windows | Python Console**. With the **Python Console** panel open you can inspect the code as it runs, as shown in *Figure 12.25*:

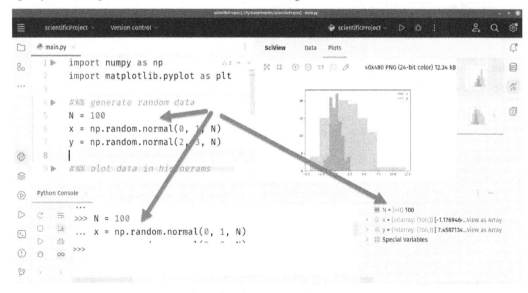

Figure 12.25: You can see the code is being run in the console. There is an inspection panel allowing you to see what happened after the cell executed

As each step runs, you can see the code execute in the console window. Remember, the console is accessing Python REPL, it isn't a terminal window. We discussed this in *Chapter 3*. The **Python Console** window has an inspection panel allowing you to inspect state much as you would if you were debugging.

Since it is a PyCharm console that is executing your code, if you need to start over, you can just kill the console and run your steps again. This will spawn a fresh console.

The cell mode plugin

Earlier, when we were discussing some cool plugins you can use for data science work, we installed a plugin called cell mode. The cell mode plugin extends the features of code cells.

For starters, with the cell mode plugin, you need to use double pound/hashtag signs (##) instead of the usual #%%. When you do this, the plugin takes over and gives you some extra run options. Take a look at *Figure 12.26*:

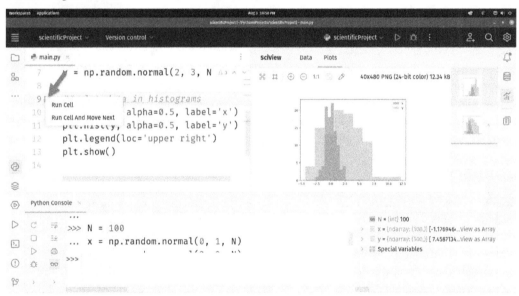

Figure 12.26: This time when you click you get some additional options

Your run buttons now allow you to run the cell and immediately jump to the next, rather than simply stopping at the bottom of the cell you just ran. *Figure 12.27* shows you have some additional control at the menu level:

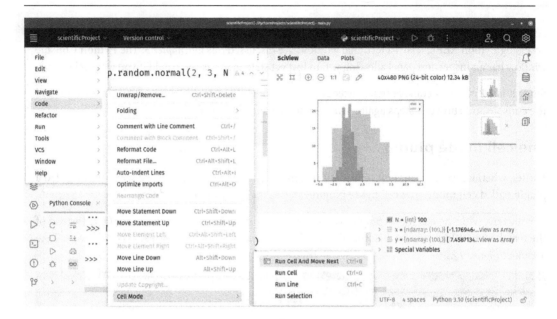

Figure 12.27: The cell mode plugin adds additional menu items to the Code menu

When you click **Code | Cell Mode** you get even more granular run options for your code cells. Overall, we can see that this plugin offers all the advantages of using Jupyter notebooks without having to actually switch to Jupyter applications.

Summary

A scientific project in PyCharm is created with a general structure that is common among projects in real life, including good practices such as a data folder that is excluded from version control, the README.md file, and the requirements.txt file. As you can imagine, having to manually create this setup for every project can prove to be difficult and time-consuming. This feature helps PyCharm users get right down to the development process after the project has been created so that they don't have to worry about taking care of miscellaneous details. This will allow us to be faster and more productive in our development workflow.

Additionally, PyCharm's Scientific mode includes various features that support the development process of scientific computing or data science projects, namely the Documentation and SciView panels. In combination with this mode, you can also take advantage of other powerful features, such as code cells and the CSV plugin, to streamline various tasks and effectively improve your productivity in data science projects.

However, these features only mark the beginning of what PyCharm has to offer when assisting us in data-related projects. Building on these topics, in the next chapter, we will look into the usage of the SciView panel and Jupyter notebooks, which are a big part of the Python data science ecosystem within PyCharm.

Be sure to check out the companion website for the book at `https://www.pycharm-book.com`.

Questions

1. What is the Markdown language? What purpose does a `README.md` file in a GitHub repository serve?

2. Why is the data folder in a scientific project in PyCharm excluded from version control?

3. How can you turn scientific mode on and off in PyCharm? What effect will this have on a given project window?

4. What features are available within PyCharm's **Documentation** panel?

5. What are code cells in PyCharm and how can you implement them?

6. What features are available within the CSV plugin in PyCharm?

13

Dynamic Data Viewing with SciView and Jupyter

In this chapter, we will continue our scientific voyage through the exploration of two vital features of PyCharm: **SciView** and integration with **Jupyter notebooks**. Both features give us integrated and usable interfaces, allowing us to view and work with data and variables in our science projects.

We'll begin by discussing the SciView panel, which was introduced tacitly in the last chapter. Here, we'll be going into more depth and realism by working with NumPy arrays and pandas DataFrames.

After that, we'll evolve our workflow even further to include coverage of working with interactive Python computing tools such as Jupyter notebooks within the context of our scientific projects in PyCharm.

By the end of this chapter, you should have gained understanding in the following areas:

- Viewing and interacting with data in the SciView panel in PyCharm
- The integration of **Interactive Python** (**IPython**) within PyCharm
- Using Jupyter notebook support for interactive programming within a PyCharm scientific project

By the time you're flipping the page to the next chapter, you'll be armed with the knowledge needed to wield the two most important weapons in the war to tame your data.

Technical requirements

Since we've switched to the topic of data science, I've switched my preferred Python distribution to Anaconda, which is a Python distribution tailored to data science workloads. You can find it, along with installation instructions for your operating system, at `https://anaconda.com`.

Likewise, instead of the usual `pip`, I'll be leveraging `conda`, which is Anaconda's package manager. It is installed alongside Anaconda.

You'll need an installed and working copy of PyCharm. Installation was covered in *Chapter 2, Installation and Configuration*, in case you are jumping into the middle of the book.

You'll also need this book's sample source code from GitHub. We covered cloning the code in *Chapter 2, Installation and Configuration*. You'll find this chapter's code at `https://github.com/PacktPublishing/Hands-On-Application-Development-with-PyCharm---Second-Edition/tree/main/chapter-13`.

Data viewing made easy with PyCharm's SciView panel

We took a 10,000-foot view of the SciView panel in *Chapter 12*, so we know what's coming. We know SciView is a panel that allows us to visualize our data graphically, alongside a second panel that allows us easy and integrated access to documentation for the more complex data science libraries at play in a typical scientific project.

In order to see this magic in action, we're going to revisit some code we wrote back in *Chapter 12*, with a small enhancement. Rather than having you go back into the code for *Chapter 12*, I've copied the project into the *Chapter 13* folder in the repository so everything is together. You can find it in the `chapter-13/sci_view_panel` project within the `main.py` file. Don't forget you'll need to install the requirements within the `requirements.txt` file in a virtual environment in order to use the sample project. If you need a refresher on how to do this, refer back to *Chapter 3*:

```
import numpy as np
import matplotlib.pyplot as plt


N = 100
for _ in range(5):
  x = np.random.normal(0, 1, N)
  y = np.random.normal(2, 3, N)

  plt.hist(x, alpha=0.5, label='x')
  plt.hist(y, alpha=0.5, label='y')
  plt.legend(loc='upper right')
  plt.show()
```

You'll recognize what this does from the last chapter. The code generates two sample sets of data and then plots the results as a histogram. The difference is that we've added `for _ in range(5)`. It's the same code; we're simply running it five times in succession, which will generate five different histograms.

Viewing and working with plots

For this example, you should take advantage of the ability to run your code in the console. The setting for this is probably already ticked, but you can double-check in the default run configuration as shown in *Figure 13.1*.

Figure 13.1: The pointed-to setting indicates this code will run in the console window, which is frequently used in scientific projects

You saw this plot in the graph in the previous chapter, but take a look at the results for this run in *Figure 13.2*.

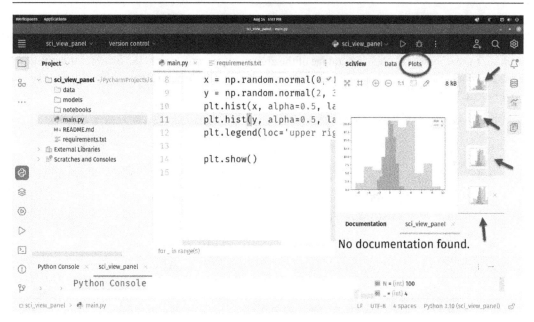

Figure 13.2: The SciView window shows us the latest plot but also
allows us to pick the plots from the other runs

You can already see a difference: there are five plots this time. Clicking each plot will change the histogram that changes in the viewer. This is an improvement over normal Python runs since the plot view would normally block execution while it displayed the histogram. You can normally only view one at a time, and the next is only generated when you hit the *Q* key to quit the current plot.

Instead of the default functionality, PyCharm grabbed all your plots to save you from having to individually export each image by hand. This is a huge time saver! You also have the option to zoom in and out using the toolbar at the top of the panel, remove the plot from view using the **X** button to the right of its icon, save the plot to an image file, or remove all the plots from view by right-clicking on the plot icon, as shown in *Figure 13.3*.

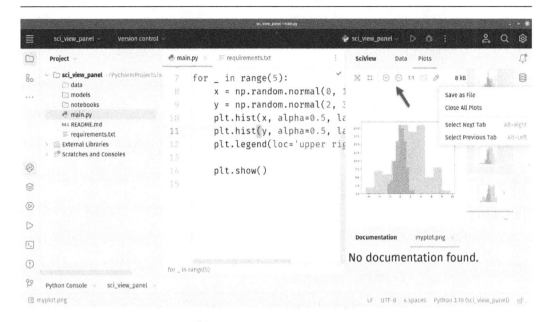

Figure 13.3: PyCharm gives you many options for working with plots

In addition to the ability to save the graphs that interest you, your viewer has some viewing options, such as the ability to zoom in, which is indicated by the arrow in the preceding figure.

Heatmaps and correlational data

PyCharm is able to color heatmap plots to help you easily spot correlations within a correlation matrix. To see this, let's generate some data that will have some data points that are correlated and some that are not. You'll find a file in the chapter source called `correlation_heatmap.py`. The substance of the code is this:

```
import pandas as pd
import numpy as np
import matplotlib.pyplot as plt

#%% generate sample data
# x and z are randomly generated
# y is loosely two times of x
x = np.random.rand(50,)
y = x * 2 + np.random.normal(0, 0.3, 50)
z = np.random.rand(50,)
```

```
df = pd.DataFrame({
    'x': x,
    'y': y,
    'z': z
})

#%% compute the correlation matrix
corr_mat = df.corr()

#%% plot the heatmap
plt.matshow(corr_mat)
plt.show()
```

Notice that the code contains cell separators delineated by #%% characters. We covered the special meaning of these characters to PyCharm in *Chapter 12*.

In this program, we are creating a **pandas DataFrame** with three different attributes (x, y, and z) that are randomly generated. We're adjusting these random numbers between x, y, and z so that there will be some level of correlation between them. Then, we compute the correlation matrix of this dataset using the corr() method. Finally, we display this correlation matrix as a heatmap using the matshow() method from Matplotlib.

On the theoretical side, a correlation matrix tells us how much an attribute in each dataset is correlated to another. A higher value means a higher correlation between a pair of attributes. Generally, knowing which attributes are highly correlated to each other will offer valuable insights into the dataset of a data science project.

To demonstrate this point, we generate the y attribute to be roughly two times the size of the x attribute, creating a correlation between these two attributes. The z attribute, on the other hand, is generated randomly and independently from x and y, so there should not be a high correlation between z and either of the other attributes.

The project should have a run configuration called correlation. The settings for the run configuration are shown in *Figure 13.4*.

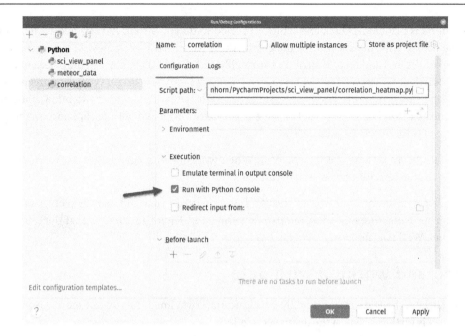

Figure 13.4: This is the run configuration for the correlation_heatmap.py file

Remember, it is important that we check the **Run with Python Console** checkbox. Go ahead and run the file and view the plot result. Mine is in *Figure 13.5*. Since the data is random, yours may appear differently than mine.

Figure 13.5: Correlational heatmaps are rendered using colors to indicate
the level of correlation within the correlational matrix

Since this book is printed in black and white, I've tried to do you a solid here by adding letters to indicate the colors. This isn't a feature of the graph. The cells labeled **Y** are yellow. **G** is for green and **P** is for purple. The first and second attributes are highly correlated, so the color in the corresponding cells in the correlation matrix (row 1 column 2 and row 2 column 1) is bright (yellow or green, each of similar brightness). The correlation between the third attribute with the other two is low, indicated by a dark purple color. Naturally, each attribute is perfectly correlated with itself, hence the bright yellow or green color in the diagonal cells.

The visual ramifications here are very helpful. When working with correlation matrices, we can instantly see the relationships between our variables.

The **Plots** tab in SciView gives us a lot of great tools we can use to view and manage plots in our data science projects. Note, too, that there are two tabs shown in *Figure 13.2* (circled) at the top of the SciView panel. We'll talk about the **Data** tab next.

Viewing and working with data

When you click on the **Data** tab, you might be a little underwhelmed. As you can see in *Figure 13.6*, the real action is further down in the debugger window.

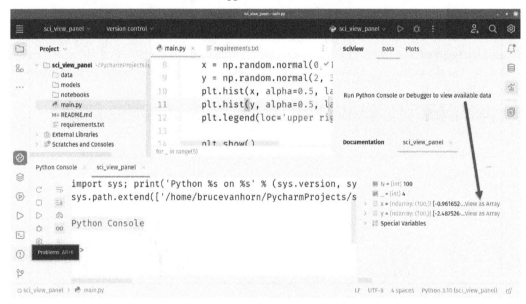

Figure 13.6: Nothing shows up in the Data tab until you select one of the sample sets to view as an array

Shift your attention to the **Python Console** panel, which appeared at the bottom of the project window when we ran our program in the console. On the right-hand side of the panel, indicated by the arrow, we can see a section that lists all the variables in our program and their respective values. For single variables such as N, this panel is sufficient. However, if you are using NumPy arrays, as we are, viewing the array in the context of a normal debugger window like this one is problematic.

If you click on the **View as Array** link, which can also be activated by right-clicking the variable, you can see a spreadsheet-like table in the **Data** panel. Check out *Figure 13.7*.

Figure 13.7: Having selected the X variable in the lower panel, the Data
tab now displays the elements of the NumPy array within X

As you can see, the **Data** panel fills with details on what you've selected in the lower console. I clicked on **View as Array** for X, and so I see X displayed as a long row of colored data. I can scroll to the right and inspect all 100 elements. Cells with high values are filled with warmer colors, while the ones with low values are filled with cooler colors. This provides you with contrast so you can visually detect differences between values without squinting at the decimal place.

The leftmost arrow in *Figure 13.7* shows you that X in the textbox above relates to X in the window below. You can change the value in the textbox to Y, or any other valid variable name present in the lower console, and see the data represented more graphically above. The key here is the word *valid*. The **Data** tab only shows NumPy arrays and pandas DataFrames. Clicking on the N variable will display an error in the **Data** tab.

To the right of the textbox is the formatter. This allows you to specify how the numbers in the **Data** tab appear. The formatting string uses the same format as normal Python string formatting.

When you select multiple variables in the console view, each variable will be displayed in its own tab as shown in *Figure 13.8*.

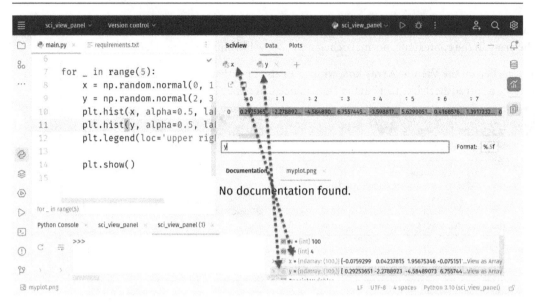

Figure 13.8: Picking multiple variables in the console will open a tab for each variable in the Data tab

Just remember, this only works for NumPy arrays and pandas DataFrames. This data is a little boring since there's just one row. Let's try something a little spicier, so we can see more of the features in the **Data** tab.

In the chapter code, you'll find a file called `meteor.py` that only has two lines in it:

```
import pandas as pd
meteor_data = pd.read_csv("./data/Meteorite_Langings.csv")
```

This data comes from the **National Aeronautical and Space Administration (NASA)** in the United States. You'll find it, along with thousands of other freely available datasets, at `https://data.gov`, all courtesy of me personally, since I pay a lot in taxes. Sure, others helped, but at least once per year, it feels like it is all up to me.

The data file contains NASA's data on meteorite landings. Specifics can be found at `https://catalog.data.gov/dataset/meteorite-landings`.

There should be a run configuration for `meteor_data.py` in the project from the repository, but just in case, my settings are in *Figure 13.9*. If you need a refresher on run configurations, we covered this topic in *Chapter 3*.

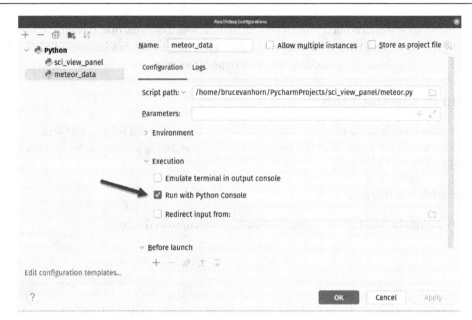

Figure 13.9: This is the run configuration settings dialog for the meteor.
py file. Be sure that Run with Python Console is checked

As before, the key here is to make sure the file runs in **Python Console** so you get the panel view needed for SciView. Go ahead and run the file. You can see the result of my run in *Figure 13.10*.

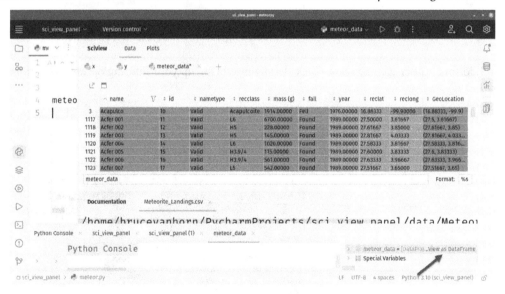

Figure 13.10: My run of the meteor data has to be squished and stretched so you can see everything

I had to seriously drag panels around to get it all to fit in the screenshot. Note that, this time, the button indicated by the arrow says **View as DataFrame** since this time we used pandas instead of NumPy. I've clicked it and the **Data** tab has loaded the DataFrame for viewing.

Filtering in the Data tab

The meteor dataset is a little more realistic. It contains a lot of values and it might make sense to filter on some of the fields. PyCharm gives you the ability to filter the data appearing in the data tab using either a wildcard or an expression.

Filtering with a wildcard

In *Figure 13.11*, you can see I am hovering over the name column in the **Data** tab.

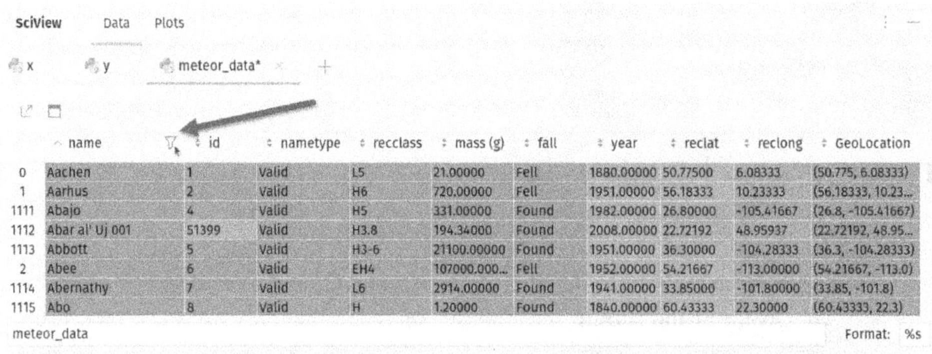

Figure 13.11: Hovering over a column reveals a filter icon, which resembles a funnel

When I do this, a filter icon appears. Click that icon to bring up your filtering options as seen in *Figure 13.12*.

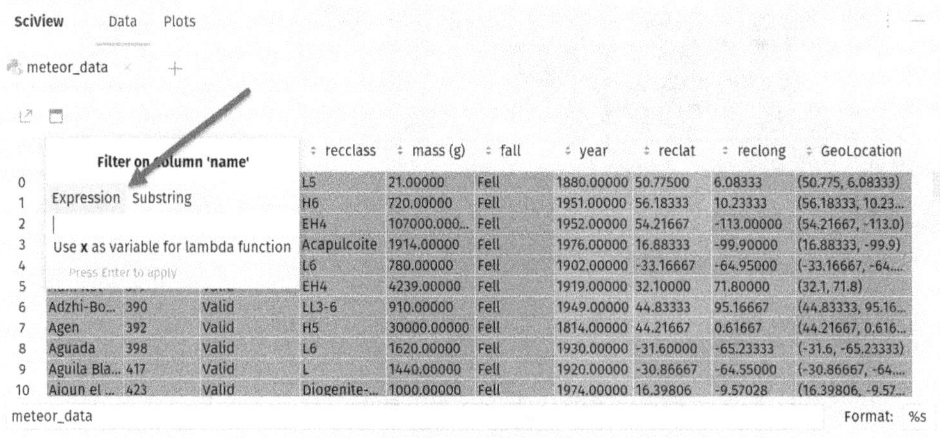

Figure 13.12: You can filter by expression or by substring (wildcard)

Click on the **Substring** tab and let's filter on `Bal`. You can see mine in *Figure 13.13*.

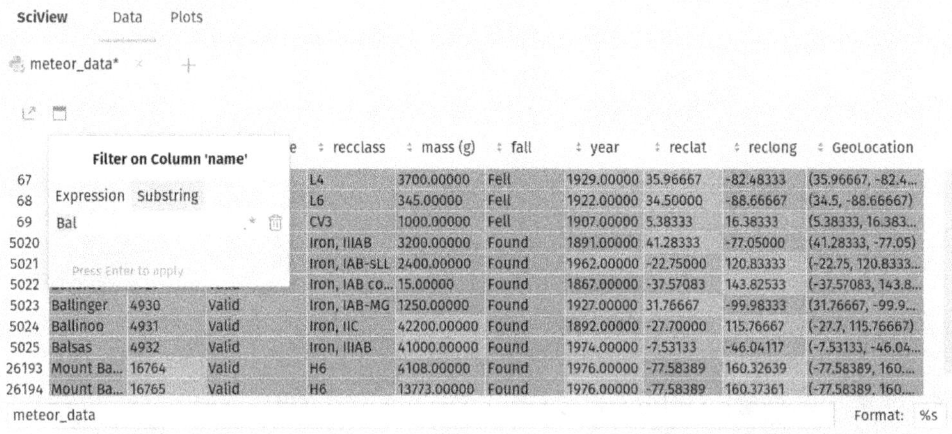

Figure 13.13: We're filtering the name column to show all names
with the characters Bal somewhere in the name

Note that the trashcan icon lets you remove the filter. While the substring filter can be useful, the expression filter is far more powerful and precise.

Filtering with expressions

Using expressions, you can be a little more selective. Meteors are pretty cool, but nobody is impressed by a tiny pebble. For example, let's filter meteors larger than 10kg in *Figure 13.14*.

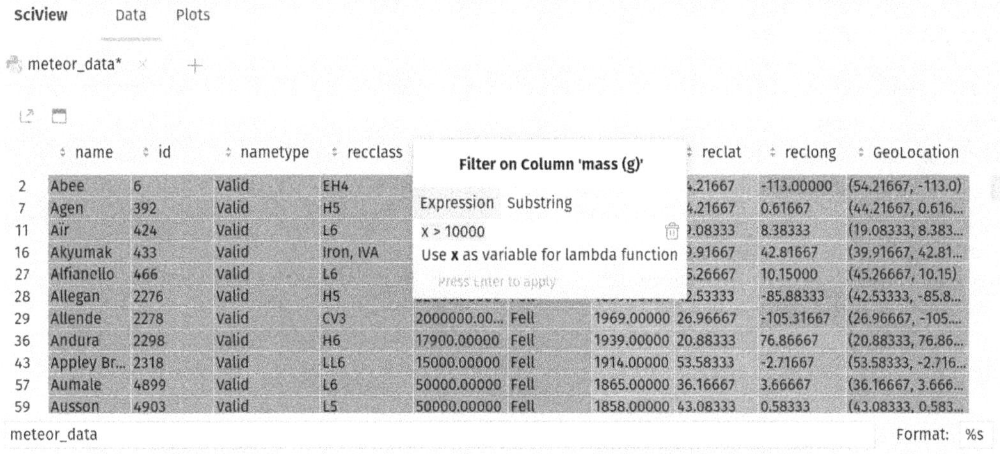

Figure 13.14: Filtering on the mass column where x (the value in the column) is greater than 10,000

There are quite a few! Now let's filter to more recent strikes by filtering to only those occurring from the year 2010 onward. Mine is in *Figure 13.15*.

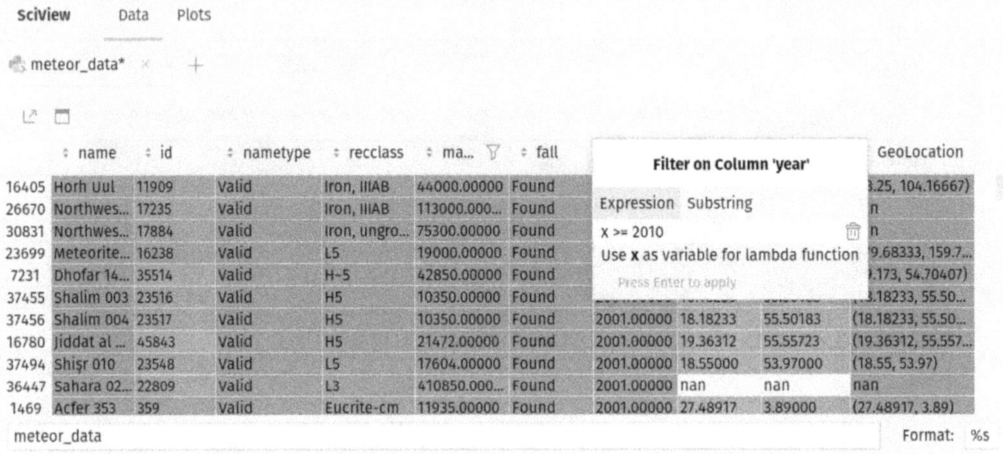

	name	id	nametype	recclass	ma...	fall				GeoLocation
							Filter on Column 'year'			
16405	Horh Uul	11909	Valid	Iron, IIIAB	44000.00000	Found				3.25, 104.16667)
26670	Northwes...	17235	Valid	Iron, IIIAB	113000.000...	Found	Expression Substring			n
30831	Northwes...	17884	Valid	Iron, ungro...	75300.00000	Found	x >= 2010		🗑	n
23699	Meteorite...	16238	Valid	L5	19000.00000	Found	Use **x** as variable for lambda function			9.68333, 159.7...
7231	Dhofar 14...	35514	Valid	H~5	42850.00000	Found	Press Enter to apply			.173, 54.70407)
37455	Shalim 003	23516	Valid	H5	10350.00000	Found				3.18233, 55.50...
37456	Shalim 004	23517	Valid	H5	10350.00000	Found	2001.00000	18.18233	55.50183	(18.18233, 55.50...
16780	Jiddat al ...	45843	Valid	H5	21472.00000	Found	2001.00000	19.36312	55.55723	(19.36312, 55.557...
37494	Shisr 010	23548	Valid	L5	17604.00000	Found	2001.00000	18.55000	53.97000	(18.55, 53.97)
36447	Sahara 02...	22809	Valid	L3	410850.000...	Found	2001.00000	nan	nan	nan
1469	Acfer 353	359	Valid	Eucrite-cm	11935.00000	Found	2001.00000	27.48917	3.89000	(27.48917, 3.89)

meteor_data   Format: %s

Figure 13.15: Limit data to just meteor strikes during and after 2010

Thankfully, there are not as many, and the data ends with only one strike in 2013. As coincidence would have it, that's the last year I paid my income taxes on time. I told you it was all me.

> **Dear Internal Revenue Service**
>
> That last line is what we in the writing biz call "a joke." I know this is a foreign concept to you all, but trust me, everybody else laughed.

I am so getting audited.

Anyway, another thing we can see through our filtering experiment is there is missing data in the `reclat`, `reclong`, and `GeoLocation` fields. These were no doubt recorded in Area 51 where geolocation data is illegal. Nevertheless, this can be a quick way to check your data for anomalies as part of creating a data pipeline, which we'll be covering in the next chapter.

Exporting to files or new tabs

Take a look at the top of the **Data** tab in *Figure 13.16*.

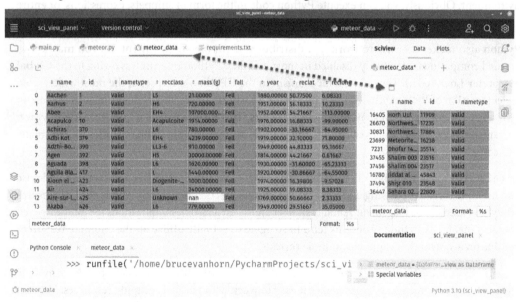

	name	id	nametype	recclass	ma... 🝖	fall	⌃ ye... 🝖	reclat	reclong	GeoLocation
16405	Horh Uul	11909	Valid	Iron, IIIAB	44000.00000	Found	2001.00000	43.25000	104.16667	(43.25, 104.16667)
26670	Northwes...	17235	Valid	Iron, IIIAB	113000.000...	Found	2001.00000	nan	nan	nan
30831	Northwes...	17884	Valid	Iron, ungro...	75300.00000	Found	2001.00000	nan	nan	nan
23699	Meteorite...	16238	Valid	L5	19000.00000	Found	2001.00000	-79.68333	159.75000	(-79.68333, 159.7...
7231	Dhofar 14...	35514	Valid	H-5	42850.00000	Found	2001.00000	19.17300	54.70407	(19.173, 54.70407)
37455	Shalim 003	23516	Valid	H5	10350.00000	Found	2001.00000	18.18233	55.50183	(18.18233, 55.50...
37456	Shalim 004	23517	Valid	H5	10350.00000	Found	2001.00000	18.18233	55.50183	(18.18233, 55.50...
16780	Jiddat al ...	45843	Valid	H5	21472.00000	Found	2001.00000	19.36312	55.55723	(19.36312, 55.557...
37494	Shişr 010	23548	Valid	L5	17604.00000	Found	2001.00000	18.55000	53.97000	(18.55, 53.97)
36447	Sahara 02...	22809	Valid	L3	410850.000...	Found	2001.00000	nan	nan	nan
1469	Acfer 353	359	Valid	Eucrite-cm	11935.00000	Found	2001.00000	27.48917	3.89000	(27.48917, 3.89)

meteor_data   Format: %s

Figure 13.16: You can export your data or pop it out into a new tab in the editor window

The **Data** tab allows you to export your data to a `.csv` or `.tsv` file. This is pretty straightforward, so I think you can live without a screenshot. You can also pop the contents of your data tab in SciView into the regular tab in your editor view. I've done this in *Figure 13.17*.

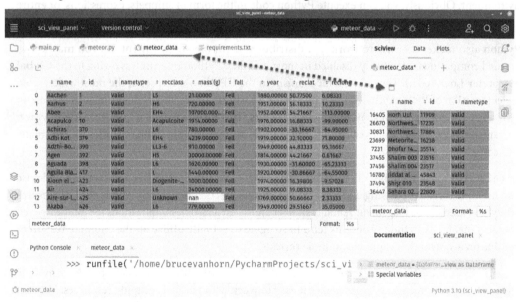

Figure 13.17: I've popped the SciView Data tab contents into a tab in the main editor window

All totaled, the **Data** tab in SciView contains a lot of useful features for performing explorations on your data, whether it be raw, as with the meteor data, or generated through calculation, as with our earlier random set. When you combine this graphical way to view input and output data with PyCharm's cell mode described in the last chapter, you start to see the power of the data science tools in PyCharm. They are just a few simple panels, but there is so much we can do with them!

Understanding IPython and magic commands

IPython is an enhanced interactive shell for the Python programming language. It provides a more feature-rich and user-friendly environment compared to the default Python interactive interpreter. IPython was developed to make interactive computing and data analysis tasks more convenient and efficient.

When working with IPython beyond the confines of PyCharm, you'll find some features you won't find in any standard console or REPL environment. The shell experienced is heavily enhanced to support features you'd expect within PyCharm, such as tab completion, syntax highlighting, and history navigation.

The tool allows for an array of rich display options. Imagine a command-line interface that includes the ability to work with images, videos, audio, and interactive widgets directly within the interactive environment. Obviously, you can execute Python code in the form of snippets, expressions, or entire scripts, and you do all of this in an interactive fashion.

IPython also makes it easier to work in a distributed compute environment. As you may know, threaded computing is effectively disabled in most mainline Python interpreters owing to the **Global Interpreter Lock (GIL)**. The GIL is a mechanism in the CPython interpreter, the most widely used implementation of Python. The GIL is a mutex (or a lock) that only allows one thread to execute in the interpreter at a time, even on multi-core systems. This means that in a multithreaded Python program, only one thread can execute Python bytecode at any given moment, regardless of how many CPU cores are available.

The GIL was introduced to simplify memory management and avoid potential conflicts that could arise from multiple threads accessing and modifying Python objects concurrently. While the GIL ensures that Python memory management remains simpler and safer, it also has implications for multithreaded programs insofar as Python programs tend to struggle to actually utilize all the compute resources available on a system that supports multiple threads.

While IPython doesn't have any secret sauce that defeats the GIL limitation, it does provide a module called `ipython.parallel` that makes it easy to work with parallel compute resources. You can create clusters of IPython engines that can run code in parallel across multiple processes or even multiple machines.

IPython seems like something we should be very interested in, given that it is obviously a powerful tool that more fully enables a mode of enriched stepwise data interaction that is the modus operandi of modern data science workflows. The standing question then is, how can we leverage IPython within PyCharm?

Installing and setting up IPython

Installing IPython is done like any other Python library. You can use `pip install ipython` from PyCharm's terminal, or you can use the package management screen we've been working with since *Chapter 3*. *Figure 13.18* shows me about to install using the **Python Packages** panel in PyCharm.

Figure 13.18: I've searched for ipython in the Python Packages pane
and I'm about to install it to my project using conda

If you plan to work with IPython often, you might consider installing this one globally so it is available to all your projects. You'd do this by simply installing IPython outside the confines of a virtual environment using `pip`, `conda`, or whichever tool you prefer for package management.

Once IPython is available, PyCharm will use it owing to the default settings in the IDE's **Build, Execution, Deployment** settings, as shown in *Figure 13.19*.

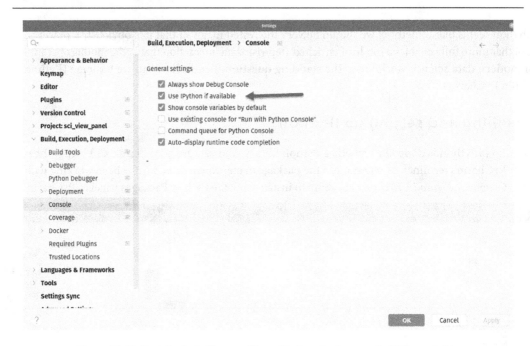

Figure 13.19: By default, PyCharm will use IPython for its console if it is available

We covered settings in great detail in *Chapter 2*, so if you've skipped to this chapter and you're not sure how to get to the settings, go review the earlier chapter. Once IPython is available in your project, you need to close or cycle any consoles that might be open. So far, we've run three programs that we intentionally set to run in the console, so you won't see any change to those since they were running before we installed IPython. *Figure 13.20* shows you what an IPython prompt looks like.

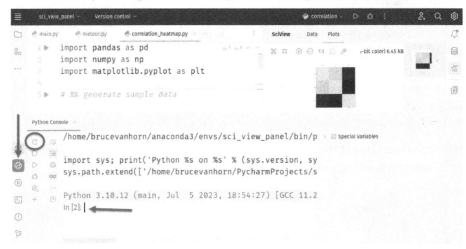

Figure 13.20: The IPython prompt appears after I close or restart my existing console

In *Figure 13.20*, I've drawn an arrow to remind you how to open the console, if it isn't already open. If you don't see that icon, try clicking the three-dot icon above the arrow. If you still can't find it, review *Chapter 2* where we talk about working with the console for the first time.

As I mentioned, if you already have consoles open, they need to be restarted. I've circled the button for this in *Figure 13.20*. When the console is restarted, you should see a different prompt beginning with the word In, in contrast to the normal prompt, which displayed >>> symbols. Following the word In, you'll see some square brackets containing a number. In *Figure 13.20*, it's showing 2. This number indicates the order of commands entered so far. If you look at the top of the new IPython console, you'll see a few commands were entered automatically, which import the sys library, print out the Python version, and extend our path. That's three commands, but remember we start at 0. The next command you enter will be the fourth command and will be labeled as 3.

If PyCharm were a video game, installing IPython would be like unlocking the super gun, sword, or magic power you can use to vanquish your unwitting and utterly unprepared foes. If this is your first time, you probably can't wait to explode some data zombies, so let's take a look at IPython's magic commands. Hyperbole aside, *magic commands* are literally what they are called!

Introducing IPython magic commands

In IPython, a **magic command** is a special command that starts with a % (for line magics) or %% (for cell magics) symbol and is used within an IPython session or Jupyter notebook cell. These magic commands provide shortcuts for performing various tasks, from running code with specific options to interacting with the environment or controlling IPython's behavior. Magic commands are a convenient way to execute common operations without writing extensive code.

There are two types of magic commands:

- **Line magics**: Line magics are prefixed with a single % symbol and are used on a single line. They typically take arguments and options to modify their behavior. For example, %run script.py can be used to run an external script within the IPython session.

- **Cell magics**: Cell magics are prefixed with %% and are used at the beginning of a cell. They allow you to affect the entire cell's content. For example, %%time can be used to measure the execution time of the entire cell's code.

Here are a few common examples of magic commands you'll use daily:

- %run script.py: Runs an external Python script in the IPython session.

- %timeit: Measures the execution time of a Python statement or expression.

- %matplotlib inline: Configures matplotlib to display plots directly in the notebook.

- `%%writefile filename.txt`: Writes the contents of a notebook cell to a file named `filename.txt`.

- `%load_ext extension_name`: Loads a specific IPython extension.

- `%%html`: Renders the content of a cell as HTML.

- `%reset`: Resets the namespace by removing all names defined by the user.

- `object_name?`: Don't take me literally on this one. You don't type *object_name?*. Instead, you type the name of an object you've instantiated. Maybe we should just do this in just a moment, so you understand.

By now, you're starting to smell what we're cooking up here. We've seen cell mode in *Chapter 12*, but now, with IPython, there is a lot more we can do with a cell using these magic commands. Like any good magic spell from the movies, there is just enough cryptic but short syntax to learn, which adds to the mystique and makes you feel just a little more elite than your non-magic-using colleagues.

Let's try a few out, shall we?

In your IPython console, type a = 1. Now, let's try the `object_name?` magic. You don't type *object_name?*; instead, you type a?. The name of the object is a and you follow it with a question mark as if you were Canadian or Australian. Whatever object name you use, assuming it is valid, you'll get back information about that object. You can see my result in *Figure 13.21*.

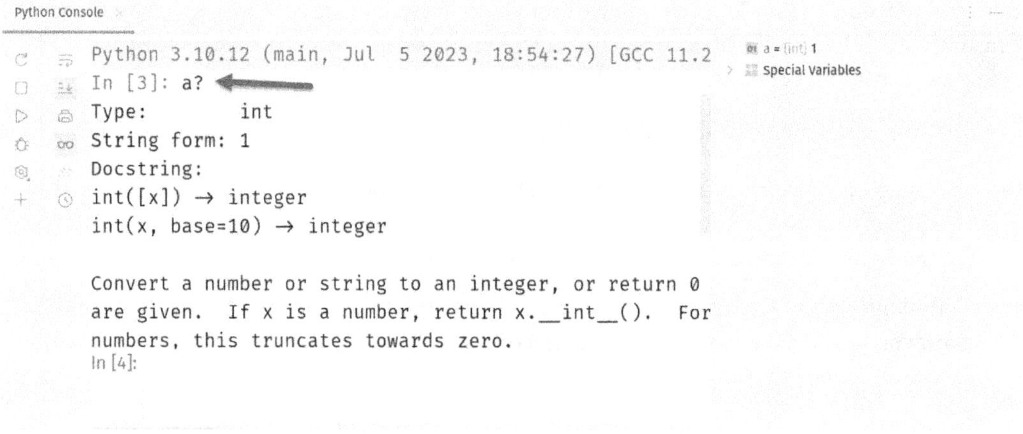

```
Python Console

Python 3.10.12 (main, Jul  5 2023, 18:54:27) [GCC 11.2          a = (int) 1
In [3]: a?                                                     Special variables
Type:         int
String form: 1
Docstring:
int([x]) → integer
int(x, base=10) → integer

Convert a number or string to an integer, or return 0
are given.  If x is a number, return x.__int__().  For
numbers, this truncates towards zero.
In [4]:
```

Figure 13.21: How's it goin, a?

We've learned a lot about a, eh? Okay, eh, let's try another one. Type `%precision 4`. The result should be `'%.4f'`. This tells us we've set our session to four decimals of precision. Let's test that by typing in this code:

```
import math
math.e
```

Lowercase e is a reference to **Euler's constant**, which is the base for the natural logarithm. It is similar to pi in that it is a repeating decimal with no terminus. The constant e to 10 places is 2.7182818285. We, though, are set for 4 decimal places of precision, so the result from IPython should show 2.7183, as shown in *Figure 13.22*.

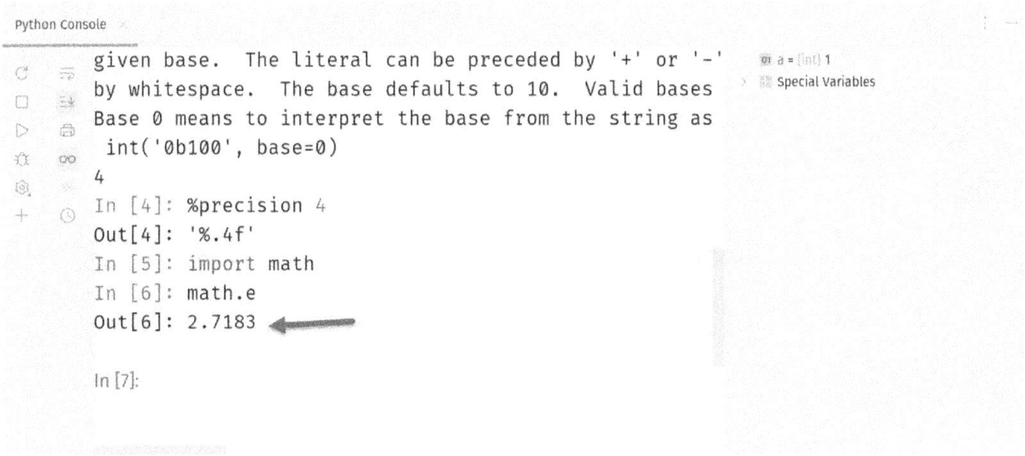

```
Python Console

      given base.   The literal can be preceded by '+' or '-'        a = [int] 1
      by whitespace.   The base defaults to 10.   Valid bases      Special Variables
      Base 0 means to interpret the base from the string as
       int('0b100', base=0)

      4

      In [4]: %precision 4
      Out[4]: '%.4f'
      In [5]: import math
      In [6]: math.e
      Out[6]: 2.7183  ⟵

      In [7]:
```

Figure 13.22: Having set our precision to four decimal places,
we can see the constant e is rendered properly

Let's try one more. The %%timeit magic is very useful during the creation of algorithms. Algorithms are simply repeatable sets of instructions; however, in order to be useful, an algorithm needs to be efficient. Efficiency is judged by two vectors: time needed to complete and space required to work. For example, the **National Health System (NHS)** in England has devised an algorithm that matches organ donors to recipients based on a number of complicated factors. It is meant to match an organ to a donor in a way that minimizes risks of tissue rejection, among other factors. As you can imagine, this is a complicated algorithm that has to operate against a dataset containing thousands of registered donors and thousands of registered recipients. When an organ becomes available, it has a limited shelf life. If the matching algorithm takes too long to generate a match, the organ becomes unviable for transplant, and the algorithm is effectively useless. We covered profiling in *Chapter 6*, but this was really meant for software engineering workflows to help find bottlenecks in execution.

In data science, we're operating outside the confines of a typical software project, so it makes sense to time individual steps to at least gain some insight into how a step of our calculations might scale. Even if our objective isn't to create an algorithm, we still have to deal with practical limitations on time and compute space (such as memory and storage) in our regular exploratory work.

The %%timeit magic then becomes an integral part of our work. Now that I've spent all this time building up a huge example, let's try it out with something laughably trivial in *Figure 13.23*.

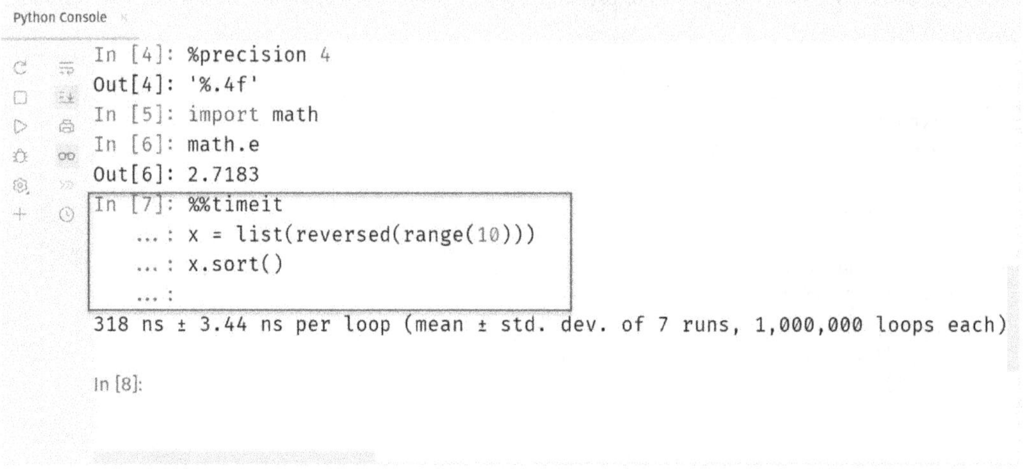

```
Python Console

In [4]: %precision 4
Out[4]: '%.4f'
In [5]: import math
In [6]: math.e
Out[6]: 2.7183
In [7]: %%timeit
   ...: x = list(reversed(range(10)))
   ...: x.sort()
   ...:
318 ns ± 3.44 ns per loop (mean ± std. dev. of 7 runs, 1,000,000 loops each)

In [8]:
```

Figure 13.23: We're trying out %%timeit with a simple sort to
find the operation completes in around 318 ns

This truly was a trivial task. Start by typing %%timeit in the IPython console. When you press *Enter*, it takes you to the next line. In the second line, we're creating a list with the numbers 0 through 9 in reverse order. On the last line, we're sorting them back into their normal order. This is super boring! Hit *Enter* on the last blank line to run the code. Look at what %%timeit did! It could have just started a clock, run the script, then stopped the clock and reported the delta. Instead, %%timeit ran this code over and over to gain a sample size where it can compute a mean and standard deviation. This gives us better and more accurate insight into how long this code will take to run. Naturally, different computers will perform differently. For me, it ran in 318 nanoseconds plus or minus 3.44 nanoseconds.

Here, we have considered three of the most common magic commands in IPython. Of course, there are many other useful commands that you can take advantage of, which can be found in IPython's official documentation: https://ipython.readthedocs.io/en/stable/index.html.

With that said, the main purpose of IPython is not simply the ability to utilize convenient APIs to facilitate specific tasks such as variable inspection, formatting, or profiling—IPython actually uses those functionalities to power its underlying interactive characteristics. In the context of data science projects, IPython, when used in PyCharm, offers a great way for us to inspect and test small blocks of code before using them in a large program.

With that, let's move on to the next section, where we will consider the other notable support PyCharm offers for scientific computing—Jupyter notebooks.

Leveraging Jupyter notebooks

Jupyter notebooks are arguably the most-used tool in Python scientific computing and data science projects. In this section, we will briefly discuss the basics of Jupyter notebooks as well as the reasons why they are a great tool for data analysis purposes. Then, we will consider the way PyCharm supports the usage of these notebooks.

We will be working with the `jupyter_notebooks` project in the chapter source. Don't forget you'll need to install the requirements within the `requirements.txt` file in a virtual environment in order to use the sample project. If you need a refresher on how to do this, refer back to *Chapter 3.*

Even though we will be writing code in Jupyter notebooks, it is beneficial to first consider a bare-bones program in a traditional Python script so that we can fully appreciate the advantages of using a notebook later on. Let's look at the `main.py` file and see how we can work with it. We can see that this file contains the same program from the previous section, where we randomly generate a dataset of three attributes (x, y, and z) and consider their correlation matrix:

```python
import pandas as pd
import numpy as np
import matplotlib.pyplot as plt


# Generate sample data
x = np.random.rand(50,)
y = x * 2 + np.random.normal(0, 0.3, 50)
z = np.random.rand(50,)

df = pd.DataFrame({
'x': x,
'y': y,
'z': z
})

# Compute and show correlation matrix
corr_mat = df.corr()

plt.matshow(corr_mat)
plt.show()
```

This is roughly the same code we used earlier in this chapter when we wanted to expose the heatmap features in PyCharm when reviewing a correlational matrix. Here, we have added the last two lines, which are different. Instead of a heatmap, this time we're drawing a scatter plot. I explained earlier that we have intentionally and artificially introduced correlation into our otherwise randomly generated data. Examine where we set y and you'll see we multiplied the matrix from x by 2, then added some small numbers from another random sample generation. This will make y appear to be roughly, but not exactly, correlated to x allowing us to see a plausible, though contrived, correlation matrix. This proves out when we run the file. My result is shown in *Figure 13.24*. Don't forget that our data is random, so yours will not precisely match mine.

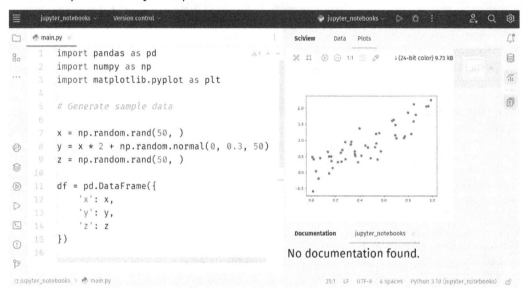

Figure 13.24: This is the scatter plot produced by our code

Like I said, there's nothing new or amazing here besides the change from a heatmap to a scattelot. We ran this as a point of comparison for our discussion of Jupyter notebooks.

Understanding Jupyter basics

Jupyter notebooks are built on the idea of iterative development. In any development effort regardless of what you are creating, breaking a large project into smaller pieces always yields rewards. Nobody at the Ford Motor Company just builds a car. They build millions of pieces that are later assembled into a car. Each piece can be designed, produced, tested, and inspected as individual pieces.

Similarly, by separating a given program into individual sections that can be written and run independently from each other, programmers in general and data scientists specifically can work on the logic of their programs in an incremental way.

The idea of iterative development

Most practitioners in the world of software development are used to the ideals behind agile methodologies. There are dozens of agile frameworks designed to help you manage software, or really, any project with the aim of creating some useful product. One thing they consistently have in common is the idea of iterative development. The development effort is broken down into smaller, simpler tasks called an iteration. At the end of each iteration, we should have some usable product. This is important!

You might think about making a car, but think truly about the research and development that went into the first cars. Our main concern at that time was to produce a vehicle to take us from point A to some distant point B in a manner that was faster and more efficient than using a domesticated animal.

We already know about the wheel, so let's entertain at a somewhat comical level the process your average software developer might use if they were going to create the world's first automobile. Remember, each iteration must produce some usable means of traveling from place to place. Our development team might start with a skateboard. This is something simple we could make in a short iteration. The next iteration might produce a scooter, the next a bicycle, the next might be a powered tricycle, then eventually, a rudimentary car. See *Figure 13.25*.

Figure 13.25: An iterative process realizes a goal one step at a time

Each iteration produces a usable result, and we can point to this as continuous progress. At the end of each iteration, you should reflect upon the next because, with each iteration, your understanding of the final objective becomes clearer. You learn a lot from each iteration, and if you keep your iterations small, you have the flexibility to change direction when you discover you need to.

This happens all the time in traditional software development and in data science work. You may set out with a particular research objective in mind, but ultimately, you have to go where the data leads you rather than succumbing to your own bias. Iterative processes make this possible.

We can apply this to the ideas behind Jupyter notebooks since these involve building up your work one cell, or iteration, at a time. During each iteration, you add or make the appropriate changes in the code cell that reads in the dataset and rerun the subsequent cells, as opposed to rerunning the code before it. As a tribute to its users, Jupyter notebooks were named after the three most common scientific programming languages: **Julia**, **Python**, and **R**.

Another integral part of Jupyter notebooks is the support for the Markdown language. As we mentioned previously, at the beginning of the previous chapter, Markdown is a markup language that's commonly used in README.md files in GitHub. Furthermore, because of its ability to work with LaTeX (which is typically used for writing mathematical equations and scientific papers in general), Markdown is heavily favored by the data science community.

Next, let's see how we can use a Jupyter notebook in a regular PyCharm project

Jupyter notebooks in PyCharm

For this task, we will be translating the program we have in the main.py file into a Jupyter notebook so that we can see the interface that Jupyter offers compared to a traditional Python script. I'll be leveraging my existing jupyter_notebooks project we started with. You can find it in the chapter's sample code. If you don't have that repository, we cover cloning it in *Chapter 2*. If you'd like to start from scratch, you can simply create a new scientific project, which was covered in *Chapter 12*.

Creating a notebook and adding our code

To add a new Jupyter notebook in a PyCharm project, create it as though it were just a file. Click **File | New | Jupyter Notebook** as shown in *Figure 13.26*.

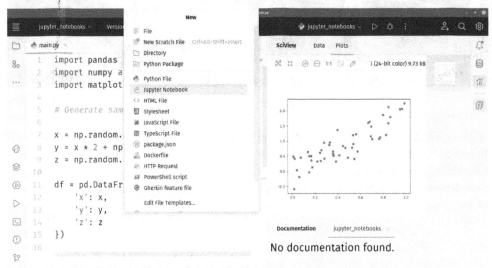

Figure 13.26: Create a new Jupyter notebook using the File | New menu option

You are immediately prompted to name your notebook. I called mine `basic.ipynb`. The file was created in the root folder of my project, but I went ahead and dragged it into the `notebooks` folder. You can see my starting point in *Figure 13.27*.

Figure 13.27: My new notebook is ready!

Let's begin by typing some documentation along with some known imports. At the prompt, type this code:

```
### Importing libraries
import pandas as pd
import numpy as np
import matplotlib.pyplot as plt
#%%
```

When you type the last `#%%`, you'll find PyCharm starts a new cell for you. In the second cell, let's enter some of the code we had earlier in our illustrative Python script:

```
x = np.random.rand(50,)
y = x * 2 + np.random.normal(0, 0.3, 50)
z = np.random.rand(50,)

df = pd.DataFrame({
    'x': x,
    'y': y,
    'z': z
})
```

```
#%%
```

I've explained this code earlier in this chapter, so I won't do that again. As before, the last #%% will create a new cell. See *Figure 13.28* to see what I have so far.

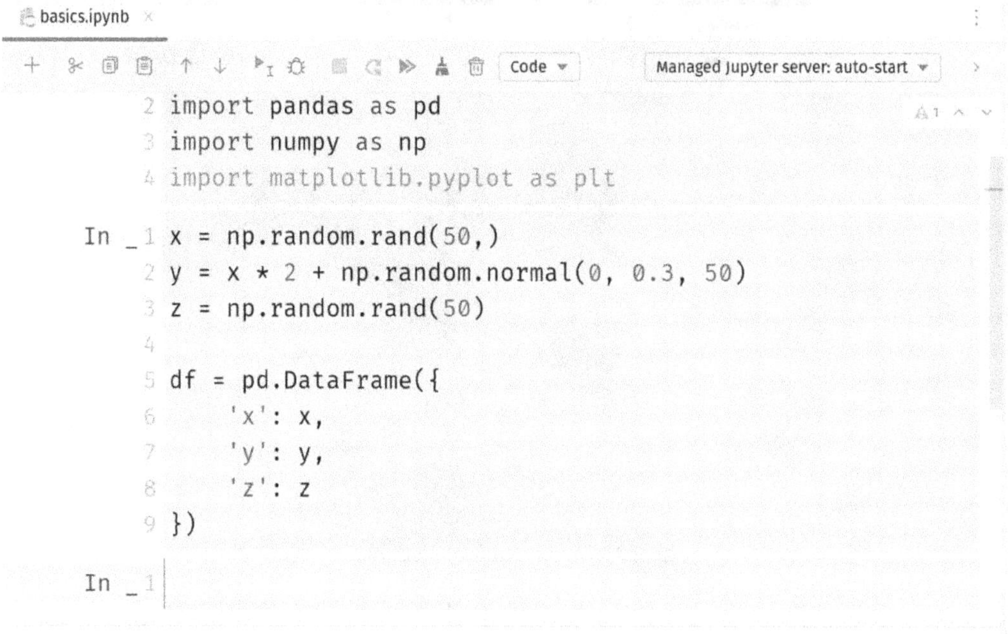

```
basics.ipynb  ×

+  ✂  ▣  ▤  ↑  ↓  ▶ᵢ  ⟳  ▦  ↺  ≫  ⚓  🗑   Code ▼        Managed Jupyter server: auto-start ▼        >

         2  import pandas as pd                                                      A 1  ∧  ∨
         3  import numpy as np
         4  import matplotlib.pyplot as plt

   In _ 1  x = np.random.rand(50,)
         2  y = x * 2 + np.random.normal(0, 0.3, 50)
         3  z = np.random.rand(50)
         4
         5  df = pd.DataFrame({
         6       'x': x,
         7       'y': y,
         8       'z': z
         9  })

   In _ 1
```

Figure 13.28: I now have two cells containing our code from our earlier program

So far so good! I have my imports and a cell that generates my dataset for me just as I had in my Python script. I've been breaking my program up into small, iterative steps. First, my imports, then my dataset. Next, I can look at doing something with my data. We know from earlier discussions that this is going to be a correlative matrix. What if this is a university project, and our professor wants us to document the formulae we use? That's probably a good idea even if you're out of school. Let's take a moment to look at a cool documentation feature we can use. We know we can have code cells. We can also have documentation cells that leverage not only Markdown but also LaTeX.

Documenting with Markdown and LaTeX

Markdown is something we've already seen. It is a simple markup language that lets you create HTML-like documents, but instead of a rich set of tags, you use symbols to mark your documentation. Markdown only covers basics, such as headings, lists, and simple images. We covered the use of PyCharm's integrated Markdown plugin in *Chapter 12*.

Working with Markdown in our notebooks allows us some simple formatting to enhance the look and readability of our notebooks.

LaTeX, which is pronounced "LAY-tech" or "LAH-tech," depending on where your math professor studied, is a typesetting convention used in the fields of science and mathematics. This kind of thing is needed in academic journals because you can't very well type complicated formulas easily on a keyboard, and not many math professors can bust out Adobe Illustrator and do their own illustration work. Instead of a graphical tool, they instead invented a terse, hard-to-understand, and impossible-to-remember convention for marking up their formulas in their journal articles. Then they named it a common English word but insisted we all mispronounce it.

Let's try it out!

First, I haven't been totally up-front with you on how to create cells. Sure, you can just start typing stuff in, and using #%% to separate cells works just fine. You can also hover over the space between cells, or where the division would be if you're at the top or bottom of the notebook. Check out *Figure 13.29*.

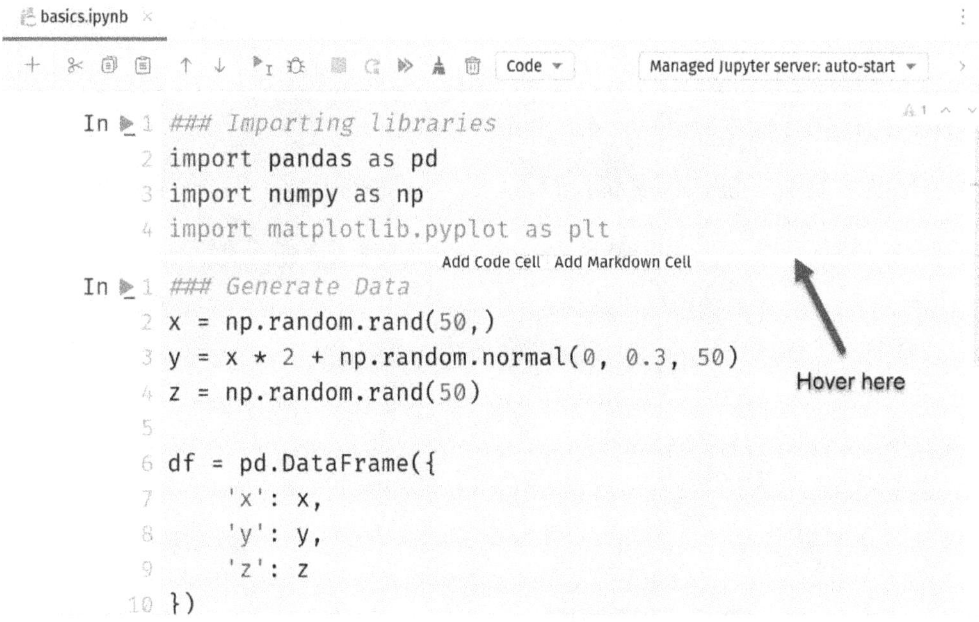

Figure 13.29: You can hover in the space between cells to get a little GUI help with adding new cells

When you click these buttons between cells, it triggers a process of cell division called mitosis. Wait, no, that's biology. It does split the cells by adding a new one between the two we have. I'm going to add a cell below my last one by hovering just below the last cell and clicking **Add Markdown Cell**. See *Figure 13.30*.

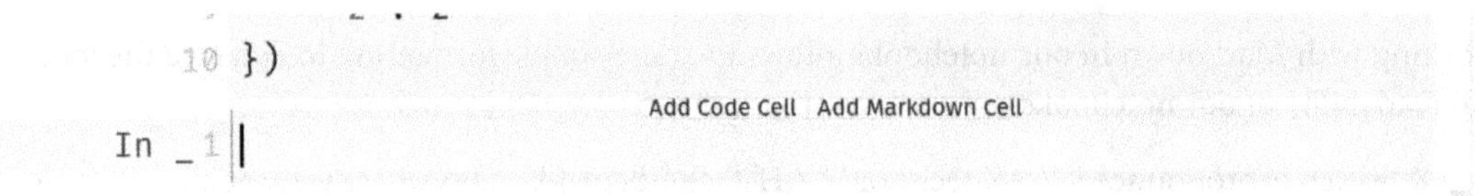

```
10 })
In _ 1
```
Add Code Cell   Add Markdown Cell

Figure 13.30: Hover above the last empty cell and click Add Markdown Cell

This will create a light blue cell without the IPython prompt. Since it's a Markdown cell, PyCharm isn't expecting code, so there's no need for the prompt. Now, within the cell, type this absolute nonsense:

```
### Pearson's correlation
$r_{XY}
= \frac{\sum^n_{i=1}{(X_i - \bar{X})(Y_i - \bar{Y})}}
{\sqrt{\sum^n_{i=1}{(X_i - \bar{X})^2}}\sqrt{\sum^n_{i=1}{(Y_i - \
bar{Y})^2}}}$
```

This is LaTeX markup syntax that will convey Pearson's formula for correlation. Trust me, it will be quite impressive in just a moment when we run our notebook. Let's go ahead and add our two plots from earlier.

Adding our plots

Add a new code cell below the last one and add this code for our heatmap:

```
# Compute and show correlation matrix
corr_mat = df.corr()

plt.matshow(corr_mat)
plt.show()
```

Next, add another code cell for our scattelot:

```
# Scatterplot
plt.scatter(df['x'], df(['y']))
plt.show()
```

Our implementation of our code as a Jupyter notebook is complete.

Executing the cells

You can execute the notebook by clicking the run button at the top of the notebook as shown in *Figure 13.31*.

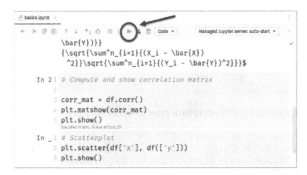

Figure 13.31: Run all the cells in the notebook using the double green arrow button

This triggers a marvelous transformation in PyCharm. *Figure 13.32* is a good starting place.

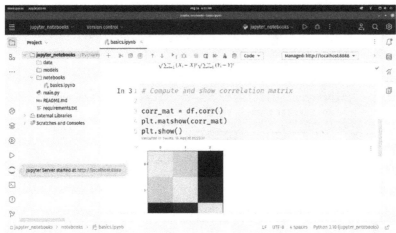

Figure 13.32: We've run the notebook, which causes a lot of changes in the PyCharm UI

First, notice there is a new tool on the left sidebar for Jupyter. We can see we've started a Jupyter server running on port 8888. If you were using Jupyter independently of PyCharm, this would be the normal mode of operation. You'd have run the Jupyter server from the command line and navigated to the notebook in your browser. PyCharm is replacing that experience within the IDE, but we still need to run the server to get the results.

If you scroll up, you'll see the LaTeX markup has been rendered in our Markdown cell shown in *Figure 13.33.*

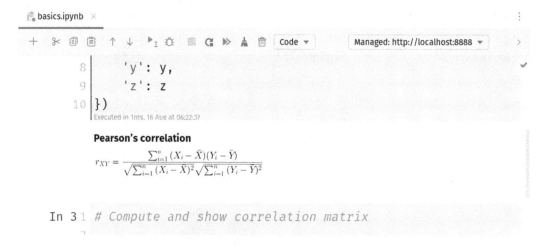

Figure 13.33: The nonsense now looks absolutely stunning!

If you scroll down to inspect the scatterplot, we see... Well phooey! There's an error! See *Figure 13.34.*

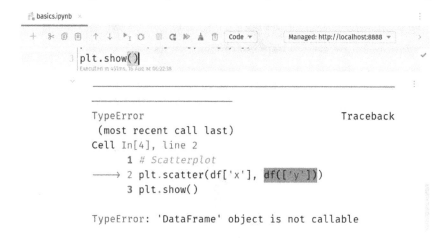

Figure 13:34: The error message shows us exactly what is wrong

I messed up. I put parentheses alongside the DataFrame object, df. I need to take those off so it looks like it's a neighbor:

```
# Scatterplot
plt.scatter(df['x'], df['y'])
plt.show()
```

Now, I could rerun the whole notebook, but I don't need to. The problem was in the last cell, so I could just put my cursor in the last cell and click the single green run arrow. See *Figure 13.35*.

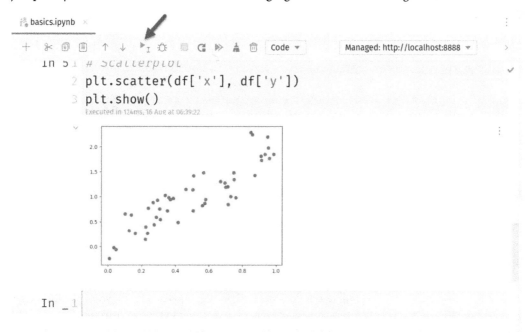

Figure 13.35: Yes, that's much better!

Let's finish up our coverage of Jupyter with a few odds and ends.

Odds and ends

At present, we're running a Jupyter server. We saw a moment ago this created a new tool icon on the left side menu. Let's click that and see what's up. See *Figure 13.36*.

Figure 13.36: The Jupyter panel opens and we can see the output
from the running server on the Server tab

Scrolling to the top of this window will reveal the local URL for the Jupyter server if you'd like to work with your notebook in the browser. But why would you do that when PyCharm is so much better?

Note the stop button that allows you to stop the running Jupyter server. Next to the **Server** tab is the **Variables** tab shown in *Figure 13.37*.

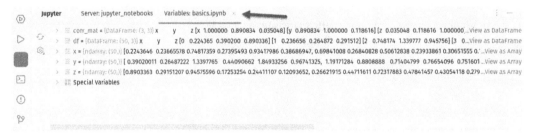

Figure 13.37: The Variables tab in the Jupyter pane allows for deep
inspection into variables within your notebook

In the **Variables** tab, you get the inspections that allow you to drill down into any variable within the notebook. Notice, too, that the **View as Array** and **View as DataFrame** options are there so you can also use the SciView panel to see and filter your array contents.

We didn't really talk much about the toolbar at the top of the notebook tab, as shown in *Figure 13.38*.

Figure 13.38: Controls for manipulating cells in your notebook

There is a set of tools for cutting, copying, and pasting your cells (**1**). The arrows at (**2**) allow you to reorder the cells in the notebook by shifting them up or down. There is a broad set of run and debug tools at (**3**) that you no doubt recognize as a common theme.

The broom icon will clear the output from a cell, which is handy if you're working on salary projections based on the raise you're about to ask for just as your boss walks up behind you. The trashcan deletes a cell entirely. There is also a dropdown here, marked **Code**, that allows you to change the type of cell, maybe from a code cell to a markup cell, or vice versa.

We have gone through the main features of PyCharm in the context of Jupyter notebooks. In general, one of the biggest drawbacks of using traditional Jupyter notebooks is the lack of code completion while writing code in individual code cells. Specifically, when we write code in Jupyter notebooks in our browser, the process is very similar to writing code in a simple text editor with limited support.

However, as we work with Jupyter notebooks directly inside the PyCharm editor, we will see that all the code-writing support features that are available to regular Python scripts are also available here. In other words, when using PyCharm to write Jupyter notebooks, we get the best of both worlds—powerful, intelligent support from PyCharm and an iterative development style from Jupyter.

Summary

A Python programmer typically works on a data science project in two ways—writing a traditional Python script or using a Jupyter notebook, both of which are heavily supported by PyCharm. Specifically, the SciView panel in PyCharm is a comprehensive and dynamic way to view, manage, and inspect data within a data science project. It offers a great way for us to display visualizations that have been produced by Python scripts as well as to inspect the values within pandas DataFrames and NumPy arrays.

On the other hand, Jupyter notebooks are a great tool for facilitating iterative development in Python, allowing users to make incremental steps toward analyzing and extracting insights from their datasets. Jupyter notebooks are also well supported by PyCharm, being able to be edited directly inside the PyCharm editor. This allows us to skip the middle step of using a web browser to run our Jupyter notebooks while being able to utilize the powerful code-writing support features that PyCharm provides.

By going in depth into what PyCharm helps with regarding the process of viewing and working with data, either via the SciView panel or with Jupyter notebooks, we have learned how to use PyCharm to facilitate various data science tasks in Python. With this, we have equipped ourselves with enough knowledge and tools to tackle real-life projects using PyCharm.

In the next chapter, we will combine all the knowledge we have learned so far regarding the topic of data science and scientific computing and walk through the process of building a data science pipeline in PyCharm.

Be sure to check out the companion website for the book at `https://www.pycharm-book.com`.

Questions

1. What two main features does the SciView panel contain?
2. What is the advantage of using the plot viewer in the SciView panel when multiple visualizations are generated by a Python program?
3. What kind of data structures does the data viewer in the SciView panel support?
4. What is the idea of iterative development and how do Jupyter notebooks support that?
5. What are Markdown and LaTeX? Why is it beneficial to have support for them in Jupyter notebooks?
6. How is a Jupyter code cell represented in the PyCharm editor?
7. What are the benefits of writing Jupyter notebooks in the PyCharm editor?

14
Building a Data Pipeline in PyCharm

The term *data pipeline* generally denotes a step-wise procedure that entails collecting, processing, and analyzing data. This term is widely used in the industry to express the need for a reliable workflow that takes raw data and converts it into actionable insights. Some data pipelines work at massive scales, such as a **marketing technology (MarTech)** company ingesting millions of data points from Kafka streams, storing them in large data stores such as **Hadoop** or **Clickhouse**, and then cleansing, enriching, and visualizing that data. Other times, the data is smaller but far more impactful, such as the project we'll be working on in this chapter.

In this chapter, we will learn about the following topics:

- How to work with and maintain datasets
- How to clean and preprocess data
- How to visualize data
- How to utilize **machine learning (ML)**

Throughout this chapter, you will be able to apply what you have learned about the topic of scientific computing so far to a real project with PyCharm. This serves as a hands-on discussion to conclude this topic of working with scientific computing and data science projects.

I want to specifically point out that I am heavily leveraging the text, code, and data from the first edition, which was written by a different author, Quan Nguyen. In this second edition, my main job was to update the existing content. Quan's treatment in this chapter was excellent, so most of what I did to update this chapter was use the newer version of PyCharm, update the libraries used to the latest versions, and then re-write this chapter in my own words so that the writing style matches the rest of this book. There is no way I could have pulled this off without Quan's original work and I wanted to tip my hat to the original Python data science kung fu master.

Technical requirements

To proceed through this chapter, you will need the following:

- Anaconda, which is a Python distribution tailored to data science workloads. You can find it, along with installation instructions for your OS, at `https://anaconda.com`.

- Likewise, instead of the usual `pip`, I'll be leveraging `conda`, which is Anaconda's package manager. It is installed alongside Anaconda.

- An installed and working copy of PyCharm. Its installation was covered in *Chapter 2, Installation and Configuration*, in case you are jumping into the middle of this book.

- This book's sample source code from GitHub. We covered cloning the code in *Chapter 2, Installation and Configuration*. You'll find this chapter's code at `https://github.com/PacktPublishing/Hands-On-Application-Development-with-PyCharm---Second-Edition/tree/main/chapter-14`.

Working with datasets

Datasets are the backbone of any data science project. With a good, well-structured dataset, we have the opportunity to explore, ideate, and discover important insights from the data. The terms *good* and *well-structured* are key. In the real world, this rarely happens by accident. I am the lead developer on a project that does data science every day. We ingest diagnostic, utilization, and performance data from various hardware platforms such as storage arrays, switches, virtualization nodes (such as VMware), backup devices, and more. We collect it for the entire enterprise; every device in every data center. Our software then turns that raw data into visualizations that provide insights, allowing organizations to effectively manage their IT estate through consolidating health monitoring, utilization and performance reporting, and capacity planning.

I've been at it for 10 years now and we're always looking to support new devices and systems. Our challenge, though, is getting the data we need. When I started 10 years ago, getting data out of a NetApp storage array was very hard because its diagnostic data is dumped as unstructured text. Contrast that with more modern arrays, which dump data in XML or JSON, or even better, have their own SDKs for interfacing with hardware and extracting the data we need.

A great deal of effort goes into taking data from various sources and working to mold the raw data into something useful. Sometimes it's easy, and sometimes it is very difficult. Poorly formatted data can lead to erroneous conclusions and false insights.

A great cautionary tale comes from a large shoe manufacturer. About 20 years ago, I worked for a company that sold software designed to manage factory production. We consulted with the shoe company and told them exactly how to model their data for the best results. They ignored us and went a different way. We told them it wouldn't work. They thanked us for our input. Their projections were galactically wrong, so they did what any big company with boards and shareholders would do – they blamed the software. Our CEO did the circuit on the business shows, but the damage was done. Our company stock tanked and a lot of people lost their jobs that year, including me. To this day, I won't wear their shoes. Bad data can cost livelihoods, reputations, and, beyond the context of shoes, even lives. We must have tools and processes at our disposal that help us get things right.

Let's go over a few steps of that process.

Starting with a question

Everything in science starts with a question. For our purposes, we'll consider two possible scenarios:

- We have a specific question in mind and we need to collect and analyze appropriate data to answer that question
- We already have data, and during exploration, a question has arisen

In our case, we're going to recreate the data analysis phase of a potentially important breakthrough in the field of medical diagnosis. I'll be presenting an example from Kaggle taken from a paper titled *High-accuracy detection of early Parkinson's Disease using multiple characteristics of finger movement while typing*, which was conducted by Warwick Adams in 2017. You'll find the full study paper and the dataset links in the *Further reading* section of this chapter.

> **Note**
>
> Kaggle is an online data community designed for data scientists and ML engineers. The site provides competitions, datasets, playgrounds, and other educational activities to promote the growth of data science, both in academia and the industry. More information about the website can be found on its home page: `https://www.kaggle.com/`.

Parkinson's Disease (**PD**) is a condition that affects the brain and causes problems with movement. It's a progressive disease, which means it gets worse over time. More than 6 million people around the world have this disease. In PD, a specific type of brain cell that produces a chemical called *dopamine* starts to die off. This leads to a variety of symptoms, including difficulty with movement and other non-movement-related issues.

At the time of writing, doctors don't have a definite test to diagnose PD, especially in the early stages when the symptoms might not be very obvious. This results in mistakes in diagnosing the disease, with up to 25% of cases being misdiagnosed by doctors who aren't specialists in PD. Some people can have PD for many years before they are correctly diagnosed.

> **This leads us to a question…**
>
> How can we effectively and accurately diagnose PD using some test, metric, or diagnostic data point without specialized clinical training?

Adams suggested a test that uses computer typing data collected over time. Since typing involves fine motor movement, and since this fine motor movement is the first thing to go during the early onset of PD, Adams hoped it would be possible to use the mundane task of typing as a diagnostic tool. The researchers tested this method on 103 people; 32 of them had mild PD and the rest, the control group, didn't have PD. The computer analysis of their typing patterns was able to tell the difference between the people with early-stage PD and those without it. This method correctly identified PD with 96% accuracy in detecting those who had it, and 97% accuracy in correctly identifying those who didn't. This suggests that this method might be good at distinguishing between the two groups. Let's see whether we can draw the same conclusion given their study's data.

Archived user data

Within this chapter's source code, you'll find a data science project called `pipeline`. The project contains a data folder containing our datasets in two folders: `Archived users` and `Tappy Data`.

The data within the `Archived users` folder is in text file format and appears like this:

```
BirthYear: 1952
Gender: Female
Parkinsons: True
Tremors: True
DiagnosisYear: 2000
Sided: Left
UPDRS: Don't know
Impact: Severe
Levodopa: True
DA: True
MAOB: False
Other: False
```

For the sake of immersion, let's demystify this a little bit. These are the fields we have in each record:

- `Birth Year: 1952`: This person was born in 1952.

- `Gender: Female`: This person identifies as female.

- `Parkinsons: True`: The person has been diagnosed with PD.

- `Tremors: True`: Tremors, which are involuntary shaking movements, are present in this person. Tremors are a common symptom of PD.

- `DiagnosisYear: 2000`: The person was diagnosed with PD in 2000.

- `Sided: Left`: The term *sided* in this context likely refers to the side of the body where the symptoms are more pronounced. In this case, the symptoms are more noticeable on the left-hand side of the body.

- `UPDRS: Don't know`: The **Unified Parkinson's Disease Rating Scale (UPDRS)** is a tool that's used to assess the severity of PD. In this case, it's not known what the specific UPDRS score is for this individual.

- `Impact: Severe`: The impact of PD on this person's life is considered severe, indicating that the symptoms have a significant effect on their daily activities and quality of life.

- `Levodopa: True`: Levodopa is a common medication used to manage the symptoms of PD. This person is taking Levodopa as part of their treatment.

- `DA: True`: **Dopamine agonists (DAs)** are another type of medication used to manage Parkinson's symptoms. This person is taking dopamine agonists as part of their treatment.

- `MAOB: False`: **Monoamine oxidase B inhibitors (MOABs)** are medications that can help manage Parkinson's symptoms by increasing dopamine levels in the brain. In this case, the person is not taking MAOBs.

- `Other: False`: If I were recreating this study for real, I would likely contact the original researcher if this data point wasn't explained directly in the publication. Since I'm not, I'll guess that it won't affect our project. This likely refers to other specific medications or treatments for PD, indicating that the person is not undergoing any other specialized treatments beyond Levodopa and DAs.

In summary, this individual was a 65-year-old woman at the time of the study who was diagnosed with PD in 2000. She experiences tremors, particularly on the left-hand side of her body. The impact of the disease on her life is severe. She is undergoing treatment with Levodopa and DAs to manage her symptoms, but she is not using MAOBs or any other specialized treatments. The specific severity of her symptoms, as measured by the UPDRS, is not provided in the given information.

The filenames in the folder are important. It isn't ethical to publish **personally identifiable information (PII)**. In many countries, it is explicitly illegal. So, each subject in the study is assigned an ID number, which is reflected in the filename. This data sample came from the `User_0EA27ICBLF.txt` file.

Tappy data

The study methodology uses an application called Tappy, which runs on Windows and records each subject's keypress timing, along with positional data about each key. If you remember from our earlier discussion of the user data, the sidedness is a factor. The motor cortex is the region of the brain that is responsible for planning, controlling, and executing voluntary movements. It's located in the cerebral cortex, which is the outermost layer of the brain.

The motor cortex, along with most of the rest of the brain, is divided into two hemispheres: the left hemisphere and the right hemisphere. Each hemisphere controls the voluntary movements of the opposite side of the body. In other words, the left hemisphere of the motor cortex controls movements on the right-hand side of the body, and the right hemisphere controls movements on the left-hand side of the body. Since this is true, knowing which side of the keyboard the keypress data is coming from is potentially of diagnostic importance.

Let's open a Tappy dataset and see what's inside:

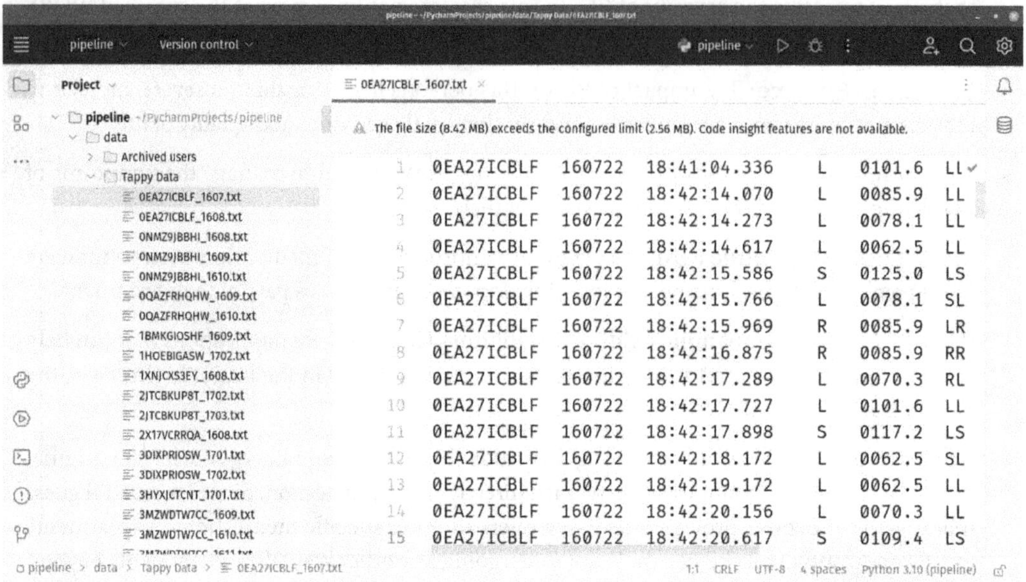

Figure 14.1: I've opened the first file in the Tappy data folder and I can see it is tab-separated data

I can see a warning at the top stating the file is large, by code editor standards, and that code insight is not available. This is spurious since the data folder in a scientific project in PyCharm is excluded from indexing and code insights anyway. You can safely ignore the warning.

I can also see that the file is tab-delimited, which will play nicely in a data pipeline. It is always encouraging to see your data come to you in an easily parsable format. This is effectively structured data that would be suitable for import into a spreadsheet or database table. That isn't necessarily what we will do with this data, but if we can do those kinds of imports with a given data file, we can pretty much do anything with the data.

As before, the filenames are significant. The first part of the file, delineated by an underscore, is the ID of the subject from the `Archived users` folder. We will be able to relate each subject's performance data found in the `Tappy Data` folder with their demographical data found in the `Archived users` folder.

The fields from the Tappy data file are as follows:

- Patient ID
- The date of data collection
- The timestamp of each keystroke
- Which hand performed the keystroke (*L* for left and *R* for right)

- Hold time (time between press and release, in milliseconds)

- The transition from the last keystroke

- Latency time (time from pressing the previous key, in milliseconds)

- Flight time (time from releasing the previous key, in milliseconds)

We have established that we have raw data in a workable format. Honestly, I'd call this a good day. It isn't completely perfect; we'll still need to do some munging, but it's a very good starting point.

> **Jargon alert – munging**
>
> **Munging** is a colloquial term used in computer programming and data processing to describe the process of manipulating, cleaning, or transforming data from one format into another. It often involves altering the structure or content of data to make it more suitable for a particular purpose, such as analysis, storage, or presentation. Munging can include activities such as the following:
>
> - **Data cleaning**: Removing errors, inconsistencies, or irrelevant information from datasets
>
> - **Data transformation**: Changing the format, structure, or representation of data to fit a specific requirement
>
> - **Data parsing**: Extracting specific pieces of information from a larger dataset
>
> - **Data aggregation**: Combining multiple sets of data into a single dataset
>
> - **Data filtering**: Selecting or excluding data based on certain criteria
>
> - **Data formatting**: Changing the way data is presented or encoded for compatibility with a certain system or software
>
> The term *munging* is informal and comes from a blend of *mangle* and *modify*. It's often used in a context where data needs to be prepared or adjusted for analysis, integration, or some other data-related task.

We have a good start for our project, but we have a question: can we detect early-onset PD using a typing test? We have raw data from a study that implemented such a typing test. We're ready to roll up our sleeves and get into it!

Data collection

We're lucky. I've already found our data and included it for your consideration. In the real world, we would have needed to have performed the normal step of data collection. While there are entire tomes on this topic – most 4-year scientific university degree programs focus heavily on this topic – I don't plan on doing a deep dive here. However, I will at least give you an overview should you be new to what we're trying to accomplish.

Downloading from an external source

This is the case for our example dataset since I downloaded it from Kaggle. When using a dataset downloaded from the internet, we should always make sure to check its copyright license. Most of the time, if it is in the public domain, we can freely use and distribute it without any worry. The example dataset we are using is an instance of this. On the other hand, if the dataset is copyrighted, we might still be able to use it by asking for permission from the author/owner of the dataset. I have found that, after reaching out to them via email and explaining how their datasets will be used in detail, dataset owners are often willing to share their data with others.

Manually collecting/web scraping

If the data we want is available online but not formatted in tables or CSV files, most of the time, we need to collect it and manually put it in a dataset ourselves. At most, we can write a web scraper that can send requests to the websites containing the target data and parse the returned HTML text. When you have to collect your data this way, it is also important to ensure that you are not doing it illegally. For example, it is against the law to have a program scrape data off some websites; sometimes, you might need to design the scraper so that only a certain number of requests are made at a given point. An example of this was when LinkedIn filed a lawsuit against many people who anonymously scraped their data in 2016. For this reason, it is always a good practice to find the terms of use for the data you are trying to collect this way.

Collecting data via third parties

Students and researchers who find that the data they are looking for in their study cannot be collected online often rely on third-party services to collect that data for them (for example, via crowd-sourcing). Amazon **Mechanical Turk (MTurk)** is one such service – you can enter any type of question to make a survey and MTurk will introduce that survey to its users. Participants receive money for taking the survey, which is paid by the owner of the survey. This option is, again, specifically applicable when you want a representative dataset that is not available online anywhere.

Database exports

This is most likely the case if you are working with data from your company or organization. Luckily, PyCharm offers many useful features in terms of working with databases and their data sources. This process was discussed in *Chapter 11*, and I highly recommend you check it out if you haven't already.

Version control for datasets

Since we took a quick little side journey to discuss data collection, I hope you'll indulge me once more while we talk about using data in a version control system such as Git. A little earlier, we opened a data file and PyCharm immediately complained about the size of the file. By modern standards, an 8 MB file isn't very big. However, consider that most code files, PyCharm's raison d'être, are on average well under 100K in size. If your files are very large, that's a code smell and you should figure out what you're doing wrong.

Here, we're presenting PyCharm with a file that is about 8,000% bigger than what it is used to. Git is also primarily used to deal with small files coming out of an IDE. I'm bringing this up because there is somewhat of a crisis of reproducibility in the data science and scientific computing community. This is when one data team can extract a specific insight from a dataset but others cannot, even when using the same methods. Many instances of this are because the data used across these different teams is not compatible with each other. Some might be using the same but outdated dataset, while other datasets might have been collected from a different source.

Version control for datasets is an important topic to consider. Git normally has a hard limit of 100 MB for any file, and I can tell you from experience there is an upper limit to the total size of your projects in total on GitHub. The same limitations exist in other version control systems. I used to teach game development with a tool called Unity 3D, and we were always struggling with these limitations since video games typically have very large assets in the projects that aren't necessarily code, but that could benefit from revision control.

Using Git Large File Support

Since the problem is endemic, Git (and others) have added the ability to track larger assets through **Git Large File Support (Git LFS)**. When we add a file using Git LFS, the system will replace that file with a pointer that simply references it. When the file is placed under version control, Git will only have a reference to the actual file, which is now stored in an external filesystem, possibly on another server. Git LFS allows us to apply version control to large files (in this case, datasets) with Git, without actually storing the files in Git.

This feature is normally installed with modern Git installers. *Figure 14.2* shows me installing Git for Windows, where LFS is part of the default installation:

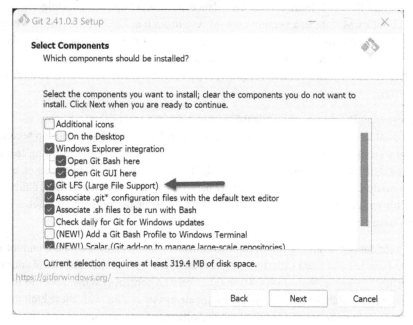

Figure 14.2: LFS is installed by default in Windows

You can check your installation, regardless of which OS you use, using the command line:

```
git lfs version
```

My result from running this command in GitBash in Windows 11 is shown in *Figure 14.3*:

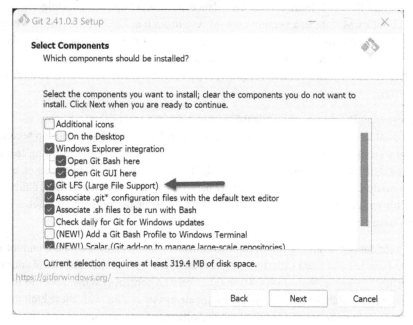

Figure 14.3: If LFS is installed, it should tell you the version number

The only reason I have Windows (besides Ghost Recon and Steam in general) is so I can use Microsoft Word to write this book. This wasn't my idea. I was going to write the whole thing in raw LaTeX using vi. Not vim. Not neovim. Original gangsta vi, which I naturally would be compiling from source. My editor said no. She's so super polite! If our roles were reversed, who knows what would have been said? Anyway, the rest of my real work is done on **Pop_OS**, which is a variant of Ubuntu Linux. When I throw the command into that environment, I get a less hospitable answer, as shown in *Figure 14.4*:

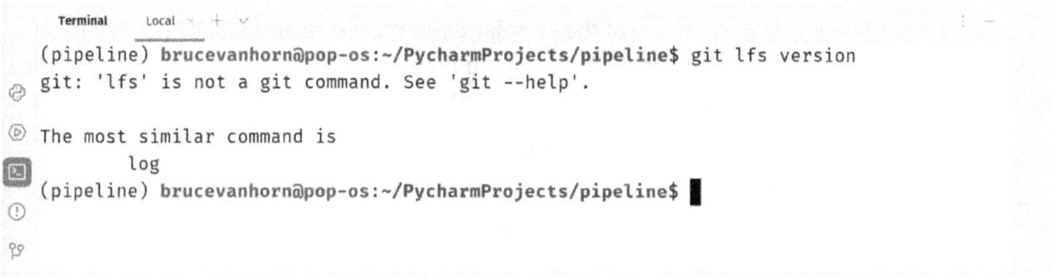

```
Terminal     Local ×  +  ∨
(pipeline) brucevanhorn@pop-os:~/PycharmProjects/pipeline$ git lfs version
git: 'lfs' is not a git command. See 'git --help'.

The most similar command is
        log
(pipeline) brucevanhorn@pop-os:~/PycharmProjects/pipeline$ █
```

Figure 14.4: My installer is not modern enough to have LFS pre-installed

I don't have it! I have to install it using these commands:

```
sudo apt update
sudo apt install git-lfs
```

With that done, I can test again:

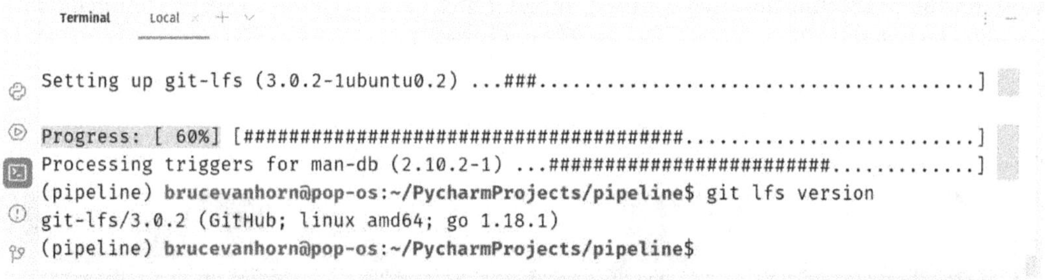

```
Terminal     Local ×  +  ∨

Setting up git-lfs (3.0.2-1ubuntu0.2) ...###....................................]
Progress: [ 60%] [#######################################...................]
Processing triggers for man-db (2.10.2-1) ...##########################............]
(pipeline) brucevanhorn@pop-os:~/PycharmProjects/pipeline$ git lfs version
git-lfs/3.0.2 (GitHub; linux amd64; go 1.18.1)
(pipeline) brucevanhorn@pop-os:~/PycharmProjects/pipeline$
```

Figure 14.5: Success! If you use some other Linux distribution, check your package
management system for the git-lfs package if your installation lacks it

The **apt** installer is unique to Ubuntu and other Debian variants of Linux. If you're using something such as CentOS, Arch, SUSE, or Photon (just kidding), check your package manager and locate the git-lfs package specific to your Linux distribution.

Using Git LFS

We're getting a little ahead of ourselves. If you're going to follow along in this little sidetrack exercise, it would be best if you made a new folder somewhere outside of this book's code repository. Let's assume you've something like this in your OS's terminal:

```
cd ~/
mkdir git-lfs-test
cd git-lfs-test
git init
```

This series of commands will work in any of the popular OSs (Windows, macOS, or Linux). If you are using Windows, this series of commands can be run in PowerShell and assumes you have the Git client for Windows installed. The installer is available at `https://git-scm.com/downloads`.

The first command takes you to your home folder. The second creates a new folder called `git-lfs-test`. Next, we change the directory to the `git-lfs-test` folder we just made and we initialize a new repository. Now, we are ready to set up support for Git LFS.

> **Don't forget the chapter files are already in a Git repo**
>
> If you're following along with this chapter's source, don't forget that the files are already in a Git repo. Creating a second repo within the existing repo won't work. If you want to practice, make a completely separate folder outside of this book's repo, and copy the project files into your folder. When you copy, you specifically want to avoid copying the `.git` folder into your target.

In our project, we're going to use Git LFS to track files of a given extension, specifically text files with the `.txt` extension. Given these files are naturally plain text, you could get creative with the extension without affecting how they are used, but we'll stick to just `.txt`. I'll run this command in my terminal window:

```
git lfs track "*.txt"
```

You can see my test run in *Figure 14.6*:

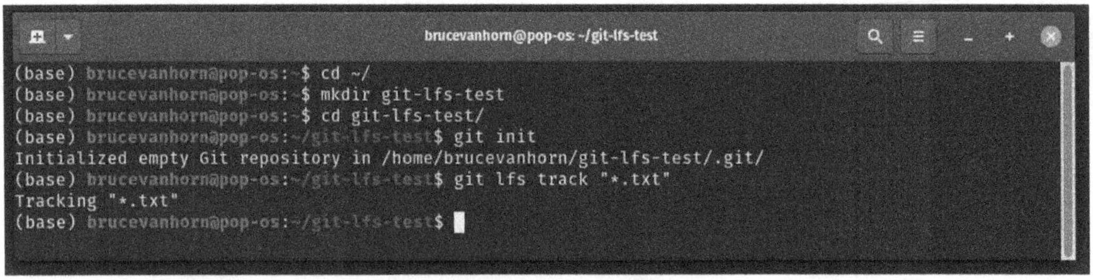

Figure 14.6: Git LFS is now tracking all files with the .txt extension

To complete my LFS test, I'll copy the file we examined earlier, `0EA27ICBLF_1607.txt`, from the `Tappy Data` folder into the `git-lfs-test` folder we're using for the experiment. Just to be clear, *Figure 14.7* shows my folder. We're not doing this within any sub-folder within this book's code repository since creating a repository inside another repository is a big no-no:

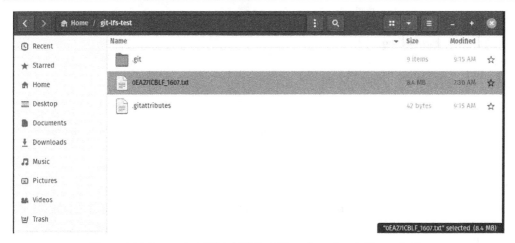

Figure 14.7: I've copied 0EA27ICBLF_1607.txt into the git-lfs-test folder

Now, let's add the newly copied text file to the repository:

```
git add 0EA27ICBLF_1607.txt
git commit -m "adding big file"
git lfs ls-files
```

We covered the first two Git commands extensively in *Chapter 5*. The last command will list all files being tracked by LFS in this repository. You can see my output in *Figure 14.8*:

Figure 14.8: I can see that my text file is being tracked by LFS

You now understand how to use Git LFS to track large files. If this were a real repository we were interested in keeping, there's one last thing we'd need to do. When we commanded Git to track our text files, a special file called .gitattributes was created on our behalf. We should add and commit that file:

```
Git add .gitattributes
Git commit -m "Added .gitattributes to repo"
```

You're all set! Let's move on to our next formal step in the process of data analysis, which entails data cleansing and preprocessing.

Data cleansing and preprocessing

As I mentioned earlier, we've been pretty lucky. Some of the data my team works with can be downright filthy. When we use terms such as "dirty," "filthy," and "cleansing" concerning data, what we're talking about is addressing the format of the data, as well as the fitness of the data for processing. Data is only useful if it's in a format we can work with. Structured data is what we always prefer.

Structured data refers to data that is split into identifiable fields. We've seen comma-separated and tab-separated text. Other examples of structured data include formats such as XML, JSON, Parquet, and HDF5. The first two, XML and JSON, are very common and have the advantage of being text formats. The latter two, Parquet and HDF5, are binary files and are specialized for storing larger datasets than would be comfortable when working with text. As we've seen, most tools, including PyCharm, buckle when they try to read very large text files. You need tools specialized for working with large files if you want to peruse or edit them in place.

When I talk about dirty versus clean data, I'm looking for things such as missing or invalid field data. Recall our earlier data sample:

```
BirthYear: 1952
Gender: Female
Parkinsons: True
Tremors: True
DiagnosisYear: 2000
Sided: Left
UPDRS: Don't know
Impact: Severe
Levadopa: True
DA: True
MAOB: False
Other: False
```

The UPDRS field is marked as unknown. This isn't ideal. If the field is included, I'd like to see a value there. In this case, there's no way to backfill it, but in a perfect world, that might be a candidate for an exercise in data cleansing.

A toxic data example peripherally involving ninjas

The most relatable example I've ever encountered with dirty – or in this case, toxic – data came from the corporate world rather than from a data science experiment. My company was consulting for a large aviation company, which is also a contractor for the US Department of Defense. I won't be naming real names here because I am generally averse to government ninjas kicking in my door at

2 A.M., or worse, being flagged for a tax audit for what I've written here. So, we'll keep this more or less theoretical.

The aviation company did business with lots of vendors, and when you do business with vendors at scale, it isn't uncommon to see discounts applied to whatever you might be buying based on volume. If you or I go to Hammers R Us and buy a hammer, we might pay $12.95 for a hammer. But if the aviation company buys 5,000 hammers across many orders in a single quarter, they might get a discount of up to 60%. It is the aviation company's job to track what they buy and from whom so that they can cash in on whatever bulk purchasing deals their company has negotiated with their suppliers.

When it's time to run the discount reports, an accounting analyst might query a database filled with data entered by hundreds or even thousands of people working in the field on behalf of the aviation company. Since these operatives are human, their ability to enter clean, standardized data into a poorly designed system without any kind of validation is virtually nil. In this case, the software used for order entry allowed users to type the name of the company into a text field, which was never validated against any sort of approved vendors list.

One guy enters a purchase with the vendor listed as "Hammers R Us." Another enters it as "HRUS" (naturally that's the stock symbol), and another as "H.R.U.S." Someone else misspells it as "Hammers Are Us" and yet another as "Hammers-R-Us." Now, we have five different references to the same company, which dilutes our ability to figure out how much of a discount we can ask for. If there are 5 spellings and the purchase quantities are even across 5 orders, each order will only be for 1,000 hammers and our discount is only 20% instead of 60%. Our toxic data problem is costing the company serious money!

The aviation company hired my company to do **data cleansing**. It was our job to clean all the data up and standardize all the references to Hammers R Us. The project was successful for us because all we had to do was charge the client a few dollars less than what they were losing, which was substantial. Then, we helped them fix their software to make it impossible to enter toxic data after that. It was a win for everyone! I even got a free hammer from Hammers R Us, at least in my version of the story that entails me not getting audited or visited by ninjas.

Exploratory analysis in PyCharm

While data cleansing in a data science project isn't usually financially profitable, it is a very necessary step. As you begin to examine your data for the first time, you will often hear this process referred to as **exploratory data analysis**, where we are exploring and analyzing the data at the same time. What we're doing though is taking stock to see what we can do with our data. It would be very difficult to perform a tabulation, such as computing sums, means, and standard deviations, without first making sure all our necessary data is both there and in a usable numerical format. We might also look for outliers. Maybe a hammer order was misentered and we have an order for a million hammers that was canceled via a separate transaction. These kinds of outliers would likely need to be removed before we begin our analysis in earnest.

In the case of our data, a few things are bothering me:

- The study says it examined 103 subjects; however, there are 277 user files in the `Archived users` folder. I suspect that not every user has matching collected data. We'll need a way to check that each user in the `Archived users` folder has a related dataset in the `Tappy Data` folder.

- Our raw data is purely textual, which means when we import it into Python by reading the files, the data will be expressed as strings. This is not ideal for data analysis. I'd like numbers to be converted into number types, dates into date types, Booleans into Boolean, and so on.

- The `Impact` column should be fully standardized to account for missing values in the data. Naturally, this applies to any other column where I can see or suspect the data might contain missing values.

- We can convert some of the fields in the user datasets into a binary format to make analysis easier. Specific examples include `Parkinsons`, `Tremors`, `Levadopa`, `DA`, `MAOB`, and `Other`.

- We can use a process called one-hot encoding to more easily process the fields labeled `Sided`, `UPDRS`, and `Impact`. I'll go into detail on one-hot encoding once we're ready to perform this process.

This is just what I see at first glance. There may be other opportunities for cleansing that present themselves once we get underway.

Reading the data from text files

Let's look at what we need to do with preprocessing our data. If you open the `data_clean.py` file, you'll see our clean-up script, which uses the cell mode discussed in *Chapter 12*. Our first cell handles our imports:

```
import pandas as pd
import numpy as np
import os
import gc
```

If you're following along with this chapter's code, don't forget to create a virtual environment using the `requirements.txt` file. Here we're importing a few old friends. `numpy` and `pandas` are standard analysis libraries. The `os` package will be needed for working with the file directories, and the `gc` package allows us to control the **garbage collection (GC)** process. If you've never heard of this before, it is because most programming languages, including Python, handle GC automatically. One common occurrence of GC happens when a variable, which will have memory allocated to store its value, goes out of scope and is no longer needed. In the C programming language, you would need to allocate that memory yourself before you could use the variable. When you were finished with the variable, you'd need to deallocate that memory "by hand." If you didn't, you'd be using more memory than you needed, and that's the kind of thing that gets you uninvited to the Pi Day pizza party.

Most modern languages handle this allocation and deallocation automatically in a process called GC. However, there are times, especially when you are loading and manipulating large amounts of data, that it makes sense to take a more active role when the garbage gets taken out, which frees up memory for further exploits.

With our imports out of the way, let's read some data with the following cell:

```
#%% Read in data


user_file_list = os.listdir('data/Archived users/')
user_set_v1 = set(map(lambda x: x[5: 15], user_file_list)) # [5: 15]
to return just the user IDs
```

The os.listdir method takes our data/Archived users/ folder and gives us an iterable list of files from that folder. This is important because we need a list of the IDs for each user, which is contained in the filename.

We create a variable called user_set_v1, and we instantiate a set. In Python, a set is a built-in data type that represents an unordered collection of unique elements. This means that a set cannot contain duplicate values, and the order in which elements are stored is not guaranteed to be the same as the order in which they were added.

We fill this set with data using a map statement, which iterates over our list of files in the Archived users folder. For each iteration of the map, we use a lambda function to extract a portion of each filename in user_file_list. Specifically, it takes a substring from the 5th to the 15th character of each filename. This is intended to extract user IDs from the filenames. Next, we'll need to do roughly the same thing to the Tappy Data files:

```
tappy_file_list = os.listdir('data/Tappy Data/')
user_set_v2 = set(map(lambda x: x[: 10], tappy_file_list)) # [: 10] to
return just the user IDs
```

Now, we have two sets, one from the user files and one from the Tappy data files. We need to find the intersection between the sets.

In **set theory**, the term *intersection* refers to an operation that combines two sets to create a new set containing only the elements that are common to both of the original sets. The intersection of two sets, often denoted by the ∩ symbol, represents the overlap or shared elements between the sets.

Mathematically, if you have two sets, A and B, the intersection of A and B is a new set that contains all the elements that are both in set A and set B.

I know all you math geeks out there love your symbols, and I also know that your brains are wired to scan for patterns rather than word-for-word reading, so I'll help you out. Symbolically, it is represented as $A \cap B = \{x \mid x \in A \text{ and } x \in B\}$.

In the context of programming in Python, the `intersection()` method of `set` performs this mathematical operation. Given two sets, it returns a new set containing only the elements that exist in both sets.

For example, let's say you have the following two sets:

- Set A = {1,2,3,4}

- Set B = {3,4,5,6}

The intersection of A and B would be $A \cap B = \{3,4\}$ since 3 and 4 are in both sets. In our case, it is important to get the intersection because the study text stated it examined 103 subjects, yet there are 227 subjects listed in the `Archived users` folder. I could make a list, and then go through and visually compare the contents of the `Tappy Data` folder to make sure everyone is accounted for, but that would be boring, time-consuming, and error-prone. I'll just have Python do it for me:

```
user_set = user_set_v1.intersection(user_set_v2)
```

Don't you just love Python's one-liners? Sure, there was some setup (hee hee, **set** up), but then bada-bing with the `intersection` method and we have our new set, which is all funk and no junk! Let's see what we've got by printing out the length:

```
print(len(user_set))
```

I'm going to run the first two cells using the green arrows indicated in *Figure 14.9*:

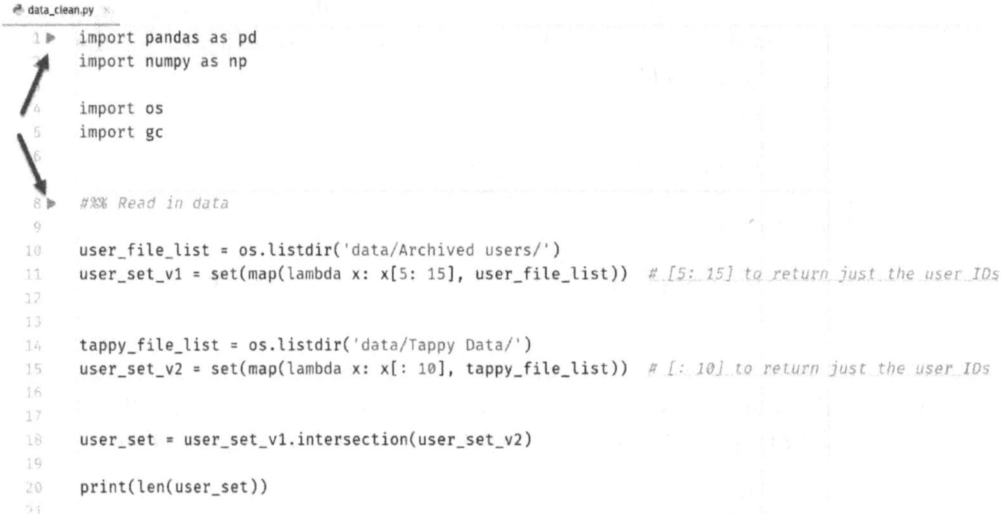

```
data_clean.py ×
1 ▶  import pandas as pd
     import numpy as np

     import os
5    import gc


8 ▶  #%% Read in data
9
10   user_file_list = os.listdir('data/Archived users/')
11   user_set_v1 = set(map(lambda x: x[5: 15], user_file_list))   # [5: 15] to return just the user IDs
12
13
14   tappy_file_list = os.listdir('data/Tappy Data/')
15   user_set_v2 = set(map(lambda x: x[: 10], tappy_file_list))   # [: 10] to return just the user IDs
16
17
18   user_set = user_set_v1.intersection(user_set_v2)
19
20   print(len(user_set))
21
```

Figure 14.9: I'm running the first two cells we've covered so far
using the green arrows at the top of each cell

The result of the run is shown in *Figure 14.10*:

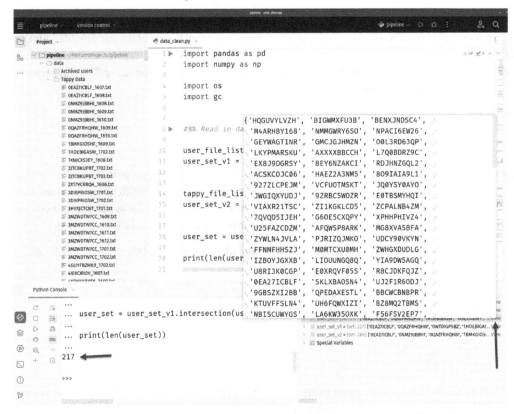

Figure 14.10: I have a relatively clean list of users after our first steps of cleaning the data

We got 217 users with correlated data between the two sets, so we've managed to eliminate 60 user files we aren't going to use. The number doesn't match the 103 subjects reported in the test, but that's OK – the day is still young, and we might eliminate more later. Even if we don't, there might be other reasons to eliminate properly matched data later on. Our new set can be used to iterate over data in either data folder since the filenames in both use the ID as a major part of the filename. This will be very useful in the next step in our data preparation process.

In *Figure 14.10*, I'm clicking on the view link to see my list with the **SciView** panel. It isn't particularly exciting since it's just a list of IDs, but the ability to easily inspect as we work without performing additional prints is very useful.

Getting our data into a pandas DataFrame

Our next cell contains code designed to take our loaded dataset and pull that data into a pandas DataFrame. pandas is a library that allows for easy analysis of tabular data and even provides a lot of very useful methods for loading data directly into a DataFrame, which is a tabular structure within pandas. A DataFrame object is a lot like an in-memory spreadsheet without the editor. You can perform all kinds of calculations with minimal effort.

Let's examine the code from the next cell:

```
#%% Format into a Pandas dataframe
```

Don't forget that #%% is a special formatting comment in PyCharm. It isn't part of Python. We covered this back in *Chapter 13*. These characters are used to split cells in our code, which allows us to use one script but operate step-wise from one cell to the next. At the end of the day, it is still a comment, so we should include some documentation to explain what is happening in the cell.

Next, we'll create a function that reads the data from the files in the Archived users folder:

```
def read_user_file(file_name):
    f = open('data/Archived users/' + file_name)
    data = [line.split(': ')[1][:-1] for line in f.readlines()]
    f.close()


    return data
```

The function simply takes a filename as an argument and opens the file. It then reads the file line by line. For each line, we're using the split string function to split the line into chunks as a list. This allows us to grab only the parts we need. As you may recall, a few lines of data for these files look like this:

```
BirthYear: 1952
Gender: Female
Parkinsons: True
```

The separation between the field name and the data is a colon and a space (:). We're using that as our splitter, so if you split "BirthYear: 1952".split(': '), you'll get back a list: ["BirthYear", "1952"]. We don't care about the field name right now, we care about the value. To get that, we grab [1], which gives us "1952", which is the value, but there is a newline character at the end of each line, and that was included in our split. The last thing we do, then, before moving on with the next iteration, is clear off the newline character with the Python split operator, [:-1], which effectively says "go to the end of the string," as evidenced by the fact that the number is after the colon, "and slice off one character from the end," as denoted by the negative number. Rather than using a loop, we've used list comprehension, which is an alternative way to iterate a list. These are generally more performant than a normal for loop. The result of the list comprehension is a new list that contains only the data we want.

The next few lines are setting us up for filling in a pandas DataFrame. First, we get a list of files in the `Archived users` folder:

```
files = os.listdir('data/Archived users/')
```

Next, we create a list of fields. We've already set up a function to rip the data out of the files without the field name. Ripping the names at the same time might add a lot of time since it is the same thing over and over; this is simply more efficient:

```
columns = [
    'BirthYear', 'Gender', 'Parkinsons', 'Tremors', 'DiagnosisYear',
    'Sided', 'UPDRS', 'Impact', 'Levadopa', 'DA', 'MAOB', 'Other'
]
```

Next, we make an empty DataFrame as a starting point using our `columns` list. Think of this like making a new spreadsheet, and filling in the first row of your sheet with your column names:

```
user_df = pd.DataFrame(columns=columns) # empty Data Frame for now
```

Next, let's loop through `user_set`, which we created in the previous cell. Remember, this is the list of user IDs that have data in the `Tappy Data` folder. Recall that the structure of the filename for this file is the word `User` followed by an underscore followed by the user ID and appended with the `.txt` file extension:

```
for user_id in user_set:
    temp_file_name = 'User_' + user_id + '.txt'
```

Next, we make sure that the file is there. It should be since we did our `set` operation earlier, but it is a good idea to check. If the file isn't there, our analysis set will crash. This isn't a big deal for a few hundred files, but it can be heartbreaking if you're going through tens of thousands. Assuming the file is there, we read it into a variable called `temp_data` using the function we created earlier. Remember, that function returns a list of data values that look just like the cells in a row of a spreadsheet. Then, we insert that data into the DataFrame using the user ID as the index for the row:

```
    if temp_file_name in files:
        temp_data = read_user_file(temp_file_name)
        user_df.loc[user_id] = temp_data
```

Naturally, we want to check, but we don't want every row – we just want the first few to make sure they are formatted as we expect:

```
print(user_df.head())
```

When I run this cell, I get the following output:

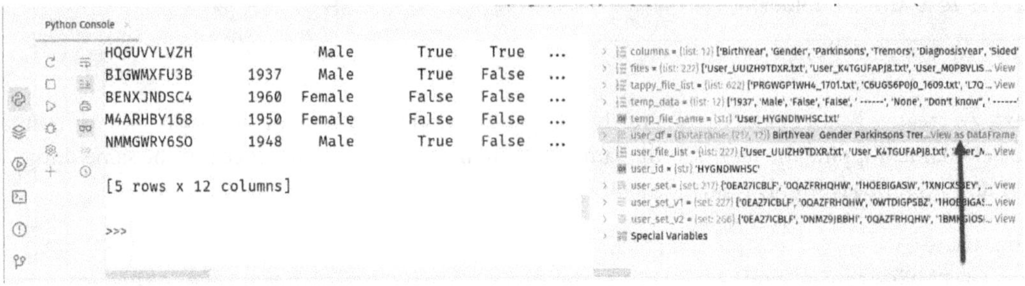

Figure 14.11: My run of our latest cell shows we have a populated pandas DataFrame

Remember, you can view the DataFrame in **SciView** by clicking the **View as DataFrame** button indicated by the arrow in *Figure 14.11*. Mine is shown in *Figure 14.12*:

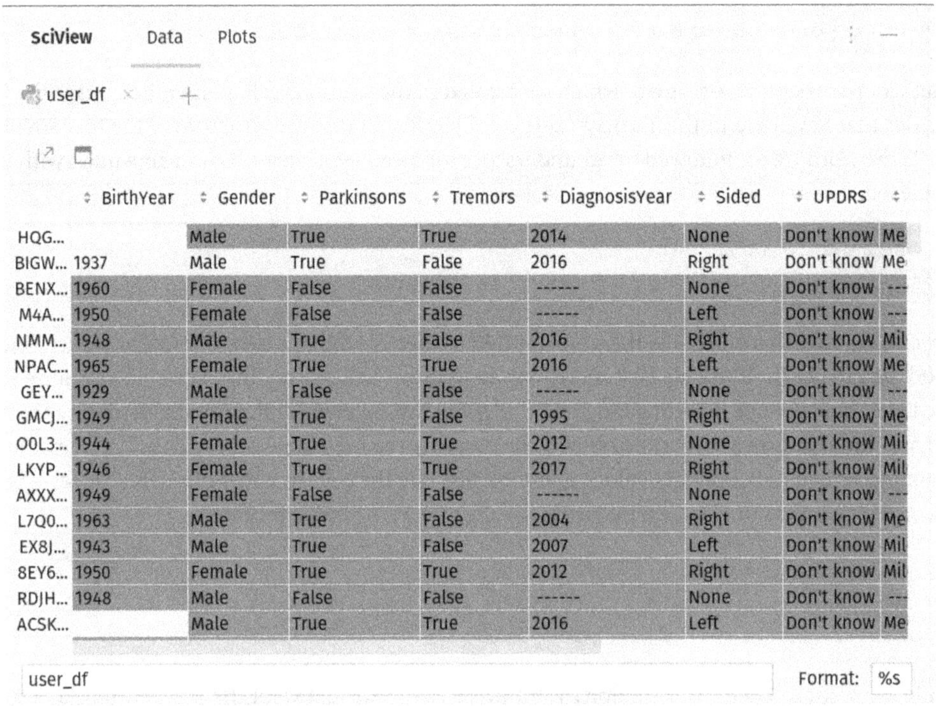

Figure 14.12: Viewing the DataFrame I created in the previous step is easy and colorful in PyCharm

I can see from this that I still have work to do. The diagnosis year is messy, as are a few of the other fields. Let's keep chipping away at it.

Data cleansing

Now that we can see our data in a tabular format, there are some ways we can improve the format of this data with the express purpose of performing numerical analysis across any dimensions we might choose.

Changing numeric data into actual numbers

Our next cell contains a few lines of code designed to convert numeric values into numeric types. Remember, everything is coming in as text and is treated like a string until you tell pandas otherwise. Here's the code for the cell:

```
#%% Change numeric data into appropriate format

# force some columns to have numeric data type
user_df['BirthYear'] = pd.to_numeric(user_df['BirthYear'],
errors='coerce')
user_df['DiagnosisYear'] = pd.to_numeric(user_df['DiagnosisYear'],
errors='coerce')
```

An application programmer would be tempted to process the data line by line and handle type conversions field by field. The neat thing about pandas is that once you have your data in a DataFrame, you can operate on entire rows and columns.

In this code, we're doing just that. `BirthYear` and `DiagnosisYear` are being converted into numbers using the `pd.to_numeric` method. The second argument, `errors='coerce'`, will attempt to force a data conversion to a numeric type. If this is impossible, such as with a value of "-------" (a bunch of dashes), which we saw in the **SciView** panel from the previous step, the dashes are replaced in the DataFrame with a bottom condition value of NaN, or "not a number." While NaN isn't computationally valuable, it does at least standardize all non-numeric values to just this one, which will make these rows easier to ignore should we choose.

The mention of NaN also indicates it's time to bake some delicious bread in your mom's tandoori oven. Some authors do Patreon, and I do bread, but it has to be your mom's recipe. That means you have to call her and tell her you love her. Do it now, even if she doesn't have a tandoori oven and can't bake bread! I'll wait.

While you were on the phone, I ran the cell; my result is shown in *Figure 14.13*:

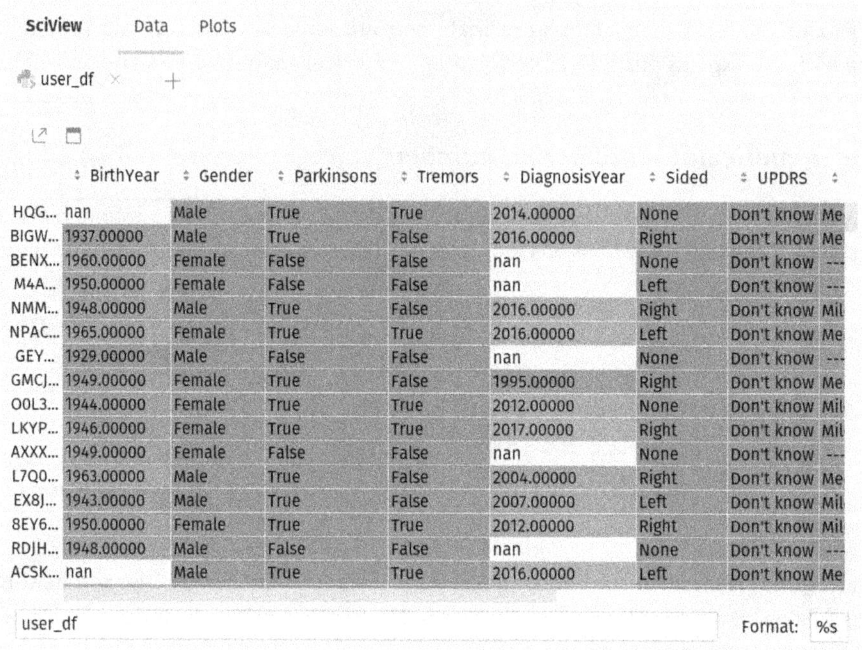

	BirthYear	Gender	Parkinsons	Tremors	DiagnosisYear	Sided	UPDRS
HQG...	nan	Male	True	True	2014.00000	None	Don't know Me
BIGW...	1937.00000	Male	True	False	2016.00000	Right	Don't know Me
BENX...	1960.00000	Female	False	False	nan	None	Don't know ---
M4A...	1950.00000	Female	False	False	nan	Left	Don't know ---
NMM...	1948.00000	Male	True	False	2016.00000	Right	Don't know Mil
NPAC...	1965.00000	Female	True	True	2016.00000	Left	Don't know Me
GEY...	1929.00000	Male	False	False	nan	None	Don't know ---
GMCJ...	1949.00000	Female	True	False	1995.00000	Right	Don't know Me
OOL3...	1944.00000	Female	True	True	2012.00000	None	Don't know Mil
LKYP...	1946.00000	Female	True	True	2017.00000	Right	Don't know Mil
AXXX...	1949.00000	Female	False	False	nan	None	Don't know ---
L7Q0...	1963.00000	Male	True	False	2004.00000	Right	Don't know Me
EX8J...	1943.00000	Male	True	False	2007.00000	Left	Don't know Mil
8EY6...	1950.00000	Female	True	True	2012.00000	Right	Don't know Mil
RDJH...	1948.00000	Male	False	False	nan	None	Don't know ---
ACSK...	nan	Male	True	True	2016.00000	Left	Don't know Me

Figure 14.13: The year fields are not actual numbers. Wherever there
was invalid data, we now see a standardized value of nan

Binarizing data

Any place where we can convert data that is essentially binary, we should. Within our data, gender is
reported with two possible values, male and female, representing a possibility of representing it in a
binary format. Likewise, many of the fields are presented as binaries, as shown here:

```
Parkinsons: True
Tremors: True
Levodopa: True
DA: True
MAOB: False
Other: False
```

In these cases, we just need to standardize the values as actual binaries, which may result in renaming
or expanding our list of field names. Let's look at the cell code:

```
#%% "Binarize" true-false data

user_df = user_df.rename(index=str, columns={'Gender': 'Female'})
```

```
user_df['Female'] = user_df['Female'] == 'Female'
user_df['Female'] = user_df['Female'].astype(int)
```

In the preceding code, we renamed the column in our DataFrame from `Gender` to `Female`. The second line changes the value in each row for the newly renamed column to the result of an expression comparing the current value versus the word `Female`. It either is or isn't `Female`, so we get back a `True` or `False` value. The third line converts the Boolean type into an integer, making it more amenable to analysis.

Next, we'll turn our attention to the previously listed columns and do the same conversion. This time, we're checking for the word "True" in our expression. The value is either `True` or it isn't, which results in a Boolean value:

```
str_to_binary_columns = ['Parkinsons', 'Tremors', 'Levadopa', 'DA',
'MAOB', 'Other'] # columns to be converted to binary data

for column in str_to_binary_columns:
    user_df[column] = user_df[column] == 'True'
    user_df[column] = user_df[column].astype(int)
```

Running this code yields changes to our DataFrame, as shown in *Figure 14.14*:

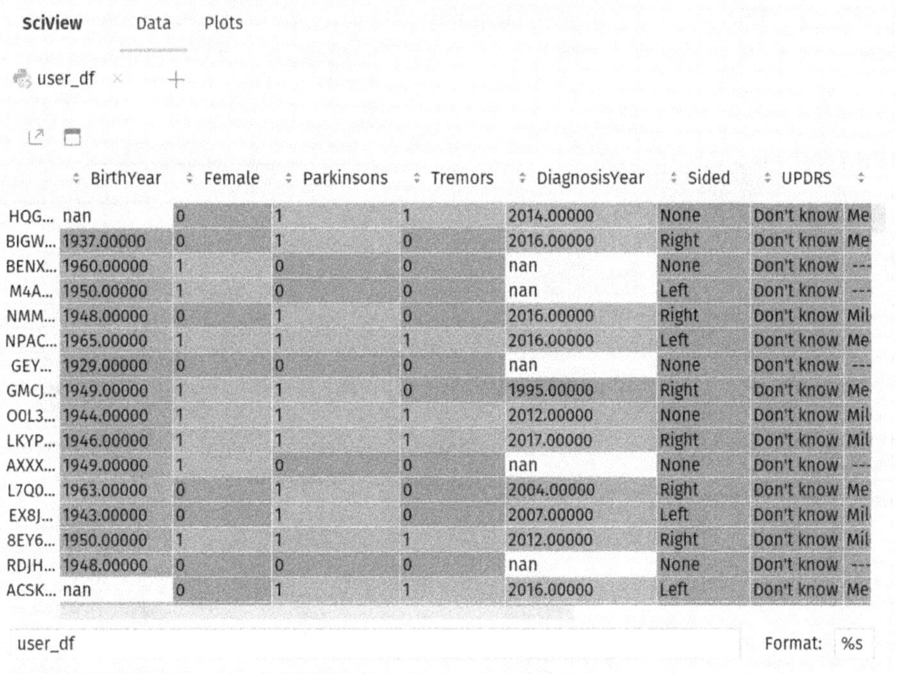

	BirthYear	Female	Parkinsons	Tremors	DiagnosisYear	Sided	UPDRS
HQG...	nan	0	1	1	2014.00000	None	Don't know Me
BIGW...	1937.00000	0	1	0	2016.00000	Right	Don't know Me
BENX...	1960.00000	1	0	0	nan	None	Don't know ---
M4A...	1950.00000	1	0	0	nan	Left	Don't know ---
NMM...	1948.00000	0	1	0	2016.00000	Right	Don't know Mil
NPAC...	1965.00000	1	1	1	2016.00000	Left	Don't know Me
GEY...	1929.00000	0	0	0	nan	None	Don't know ---
GMCJ...	1949.00000	1	1	0	1995.00000	Right	Don't know Me
OOL3...	1944.00000	1	1	1	2012.00000	None	Don't know Mil
LKYP...	1946.00000	1	1	1	2017.00000	Right	Don't know Mil
AXXX...	1949.00000	1	0	0	nan	None	Don't know ---
L7Q0...	1963.00000	0	1	0	2004.00000	Right	Don't know Me
EX8J...	1943.00000	0	1	0	2007.00000	Left	Don't know Mil
8EY6...	1950.00000	1	1	1	2012.00000	Right	Don't know Mil
RDJH...	1948.00000	0	0	0	nan	None	Don't know ---
ACSK...	nan	0	1	1	2016.00000	Left	Don't know Me

Figure 14.14: We've successfully binarized our fields

We can see that our fields are now binary numbers! This is going to make things easier later!

Let's jump into the next cell since the first part of the code is doing some more cleanup, similar to what we have done so far. In the first part of the cell, we are cleaning up the `Impact` field. We're standardizing any value that isn't `Mild`, `Medium`, or `Severe` as None:

```
# prior processing for `Impact` column
user_df.loc[
    (user_df['Impact'] != 'Medium') &
    (user_df['Impact'] != 'Mild') &
    (user_df['Impact'] != 'Severe'), 'Impact'] = 'None'
```

Next, while staying in the same cell, we're going to explore a powerful and popular technique that is used by an ML algorithm when preparing data for analysis.

One-hot encoding

For some reason, when I first heard the term **one-hot encoding**, I immediately thought of hot dogs and how I would love to encode one with mustard and sweet relish on a nice steamed bun, or maybe the NaN y'all are doing to send me. For the record, I know that's not how the bread is spelled, and I don't care. The joke only works if I spell it incorrectly. I don't know why I'm telling you that, but here we are.

One-hot coding is a technique that allows you to take data that isn't inherently Boolean, and make it so. When I was in the market for a new Jeep Wrangler, there were only a few colors I considered:

- Firecracker Red

- Ocean Blue Metallic

- Mojito!

- Hellayella

There are more colors than that, but they are all boring variants of black, white, or gray. I can't get an orange Jeep because people will think I went to Oklahoma State University, and we can't have that. I can ignore those colors, leaving me with a list that will fit on the page. Now, let's one-hot encode that list:

Color_Firecracker_Red	Color_Ocean_Blue_Metallic	Color_Mojito	Color_Hellayella
1	0	0	0
0	1	0	0
0	0	1	0
0	0	0	0
0	0	0	1

You can easily see how one-hot encoding works – it pivots the fields and then makes them binary. If you're a relational database guru, you have probably just lost your lunch. Data scientists do things a little differently. In the one-hot encoded representation, each observation gets a "1" in the column corresponding to its category and a "0" in all other columns. This encoding ensures that the categorical information is preserved in a way that ML algorithms can understand and use effectively. For the record, I went with *Hellayella* based on the idea that if I got my Jeep stuck somewhere inaccessible, such as the deserts of Big Bend National Park, or deep in the Piney Woods region of east Texas, the rescue helicopters would easily find my corpse.

One-hot encoding is commonly used for features such as categorical variables, which can't be directly used as numerical inputs in many ML algorithms. It's an important step in data preprocessing to convert such variables into a suitable format for training models.

Let's go back to our code for the current cell. We've explained the first few lines, so let's move on to setting up for one-hot encoding on several fields:

```
to_dummy_column_indices = ['Sided', 'UPDRS', 'Impact'] # columns to be
one-hot encoded
```

We're going to encode these three columns. One of the columns under consideration is the `Impact` column, which we just standardized as a lead-in for this step. We'll perform the one-hot encoding for all three columns here:

```
for column in to_dummy_column_indices:
  user_df = pd.concat([
    user_df.iloc[:, : user_df.columns.get_loc(column)],
    pd.get_dummies(user_df[column], prefix=str(column)),
    user_df.iloc[:, user_df.columns.get_loc(column) + 1 :]
  ], axis=1)
print(user_df.head())
```

Within the loop, the code performs the following steps:

1. `user_df.iloc[:, : user_df.columns.get_loc(column)]`: Selects the columns to the left of the current column being processed. This preserves the columns before the one being one-hot encoded.

2. `pd.get_dummies(user_df[column], prefix=str(column))`: Applies one-hot encoding to the current column using the `pd.get_dummies()` method. It creates a DataFrame with binary columns representing the different categories in the column. The `prefix` parameter adds a prefix to the column names to indicate which original column they were derived from.

3. `user_df.iloc[:, user_df.columns.get_loc(column) + 1 :]`: Selects the columns to the right of the current column being processed. This preserves the columns after the one being one-hot encoded.

When fed into the `pd.concat` method, these steps effectively replace each of the three categorical columns with one-hot encoded binary columns while keeping the rest of the DataFrame intact. When you run the cell, you should see results like mine, as shown in *Figure 14.15*:

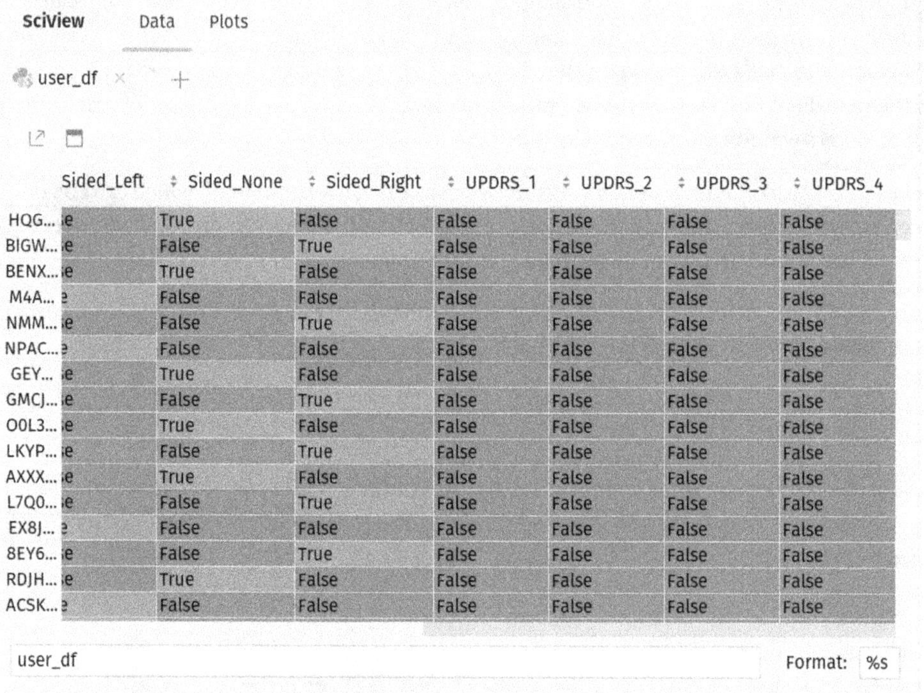

	Sided_Left	Sided_None	Sided_Right	UPDRS_1	UPDRS_2	UPDRS_3	UPDRS_4
HQG... e	True	False	False	False	False	False	False
BIGW... e	False	True	False	False	False	False	False
BENX... e	True	False	False	False	False	False	False
M4A... e	False	False	False	False	False	False	False
NMM... e	False	True	False	False	False	False	False
NPAC... e	False	False	False	False	False	False	False
GEY... e	True	False	False	False	False	False	False
GMCJ... e	False	True	False	False	False	False	False
OOL3... e	True	False	False	False	False	False	False
LKYP... e	False	True	False	False	False	False	False
AXXX... e	True	False	False	False	False	False	False
L7Q0... e	False	True	False	False	False	False	False
EX8J... e	False	False	False	False	False	False	False
8EY6... e	False	True	False	False	False	False	False
RDJH... e	True	False	False	False	False	False	False
ACSK... e	False	False	False	False	False	False	False

user_df   Format: %s

Figure 14.15: I've scrolled to the right so that you can see the newly
added one-hot encoded columns that were added

One-hot encoding will have added many new columns to the DataFrame, so you might need to scroll to the right to see them all.

Exploring the second dataset

With our user data fairly well-cleaned up and sitting in a pandas DataFrame, we are now ready to tackle the Tappy data. To keep things relatable, I'm going to arbitrarily pick one file from the `Tappy Data` set. Let's look at the code in our next cell:

```
#%% Explore the second dataset

file_name = '0EA27ICBLF_1607.txt'
```

As I said, I picked one arbitrary file to examine. We opened one of these files earlier and noted they were all in tab-separated format. pandas has a method that will easily read this file directly into a

DataFrame. Despite the method being called `read_csv`, you get to specify a delimiter, which doesn't have to be a comma. The method will read any kind of delimited file:

```
df = pd.read_csv(
  'data/Tappy Data/' + file_name,
  delimiter = '\t',
  index_col = False,
  names = ['UserKey', 'Date', 'Timestamp', 'Hand', 'Hold time',
'Direction', 'Latency time', 'Flight time']
)
```

For our purposes, we don't need the `UserKey` field:

```
df = df.drop('UserKey', axis=1)


print(df.head())
```

When we run this cell, we create a new DataFrame called `df`. Be sure to pick it from the console variables panel shown in *Figure 14.16*:

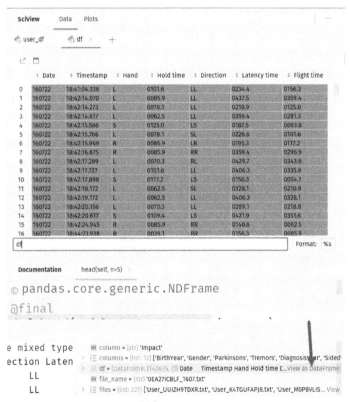

Figure 14.16: Our new DataFrame can be viewed by clicking the View as DataFrame button

Formatting datetime data

The next cell fixes our `datetime` data:

```
#%% Format datetime data
```

This first line tries to force the values in the `Date` column to be dates. If the coercion doesn't work, we'll see NaT (not a time), which is disappointing since there's no food joke to be made. Next, we'll do some more coercion on the `Hold time`, `Latency time`, and `Flight time` fields:

```
df['Date'] = pd.to_datetime(df['Date'], errors='coerce',
format='%y%M%d').dt.date
# converting time data to numeric
for column in ['Hold time', 'Latency time', 'Flight time']:
  df[column] = pd.to_numeric(df[column], errors='coerce')
```

Any observations lacking time data should be dropped:

```
df = df.dropna(axis=0)
```

Let's print the result for inspection:

```
print(df.head())
```

Let's run it! My cell run results are shown in *Figure 14.17*:

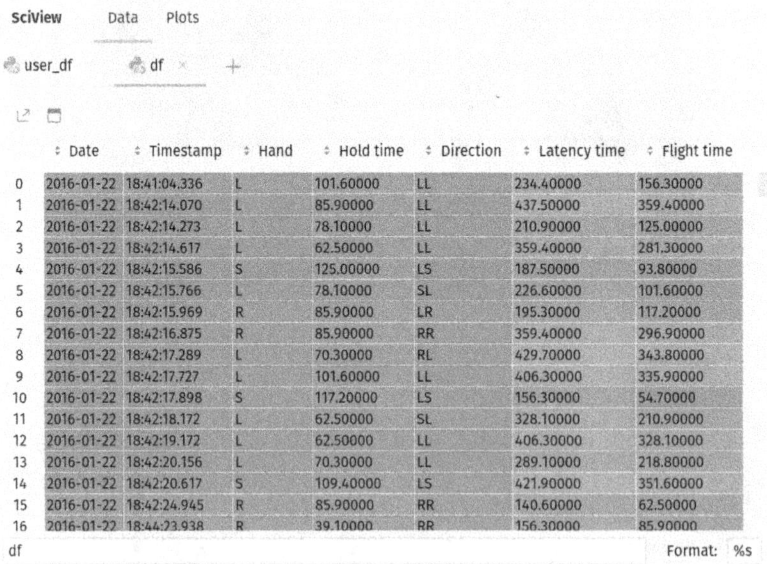

	SciView	Data	Plots				
	user_df		df ×	+			

	Date	Timestamp	Hand	Hold time	Direction	Latency time	Flight time
0	2016-01-22	18:41:04.336	L	101.60000	LL	234.40000	156.30000
1	2016-01-22	18:42:14.070	L	85.90000	LL	437.50000	359.40000
2	2016-01-22	18:42:14.273	L	78.10000	LL	210.90000	125.00000
3	2016-01-22	18:42:14.617	L	62.50000	LL	359.40000	281.30000
4	2016-01-22	18:42:15.586	S	125.00000	LS	187.50000	93.80000
5	2016-01-22	18:42:15.766	L	78.10000	SL	226.60000	101.60000
6	2016-01-22	18:42:15.969	R	85.90000	LR	195.30000	117.20000
7	2016-01-22	18:42:16.875	R	85.90000	RR	359.40000	296.90000
8	2016-01-22	18:42:17.289	L	70.30000	RL	429.70000	343.80000
9	2016-01-22	18:42:17.727	L	101.60000	LL	406.30000	335.90000
10	2016-01-22	18:42:17.898	S	117.20000	LS	156.30000	54.70000
11	2016-01-22	18:42:18.172	L	62.50000	SL	328.10000	210.90000
12	2016-01-22	18:42:19.172	L	62.50000	LL	406.30000	328.10000
13	2016-01-22	18:42:20.156	L	70.30000	LL	289.10000	218.80000
14	2016-01-22	18:42:20.617	S	109.40000	LS	421.90000	351.60000
15	2016-01-22	18:42:24.945	R	85.90000	RR	140.60000	62.50000
16	2016-01-22	18:44:23.938	R	39.10000	RR	156.30000	85.90000

df   Format: %s

Figure 14.17: Our datetime data is now numeric and any observation
with missing time data, being useless, has been dropped

Washing hands and fixing direction

The next cell cleans up the hand and direction columns:

```
# cleaning data in Hand
df = df[
    (df['Hand'] == 'L') |
    (df['Hand'] == 'R') |
    (df['Hand'] == 'S')
]
```

This code uses a logical OR to filter out anything that doesn't have a value of L, R, or S. Since it is presented as an OR, anything outside the three desirable possibilities will return as `false`, and be excluded.

Let's do the same thing with direction, which has more possibilities:

```
# cleaning data in Direction
df = df[
    (df['Direction'] == 'LL') |
    (df['Direction'] == 'LR') |
    (df['Direction'] == 'LS') |
    (df['Direction'] == 'RL') |
    (df['Direction'] == 'RR') |
    (df['Direction'] == 'RS') |
    (df['Direction'] == 'SL') |
    (df['Direction'] == 'SR') |
    (df['Direction'] == 'SS')
]
```

Of course, we'll print the result:

```
print(df.head())
```

Go ahead and run the cell. All rows containing invalid data have been removed. This result isn't as visual as most have been, so I don't think we need a screenshot for this one.

Summarizing data

Our next cell provides an example of how to summarize our data, which we have been working so hard to set up for analysis. We're ready! Let's try something simple. As usual, the first line of code in the cell just marks the beginning of the cell:

```
#%% Group by direction (hand transition)
```

Recall that the data we have been working with so far is typing speed data for a specific subject at a given time. A subject (`User`) is simply a single data point within our first dataset, and we would like to combine the two datasets somehow, so we need a way to aggregate our current data into a single data point.

Since we are working with numerical data (typing time), we can take the average (mean) of the time data across different columns as a way to summarize the data of a given user. We can achieve this with the `groupby()` function from pandas:

```
direction_grouped_df = df.groupby('Direction')[numeric_columns].
mean()
```

Of course, we should print it:

```
print(direction_grouped_df)
```

The result of the run is shown in *Figure 14.18*. The code puts the results in a new DataFrame called `direction_group_df`, so be sure you select it as shown in the figure:

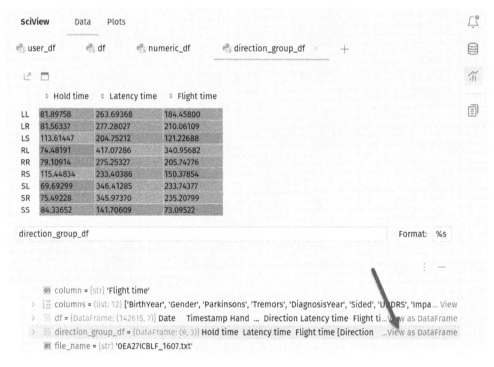

Figure 14.18: Hooray! We have our first calculated insight!

This is exciting! We have the mechanics working, but now, we need to concentrate on making this work with many data files instead of just one.

Refactoring for scale

Our exploration of the Tappy data has focused on one file to establish in an easily verifiable way that our code is working. We've determined that it is, so now, we should refactor our code so that we can process thousands of files. To do this, we should consolidate some of our cells into a function. The code in the next cell is long but familiar since it is just all the code we've written so far combined into one function. If you're an application developer, and you understand the design principle known as the **single responsibility principle** (**SRP**), you know this is an antipattern. Remember, though, this isn't application code. Nobody will run this beyond performing the analysis, so the rigors of SOLID principles that normally apply to software development are not observed in data science work.

Processing the Tappy data with one function

Here's the function:

```
#%% Combine into one function


def read_tappy(file_name):
```

Here, we're reading in the CSV filename passed as an argument to our function. We enrich the data with hardcoded field names:

```
df = pd.read_csv(
    'data/Tappy Data/' + file_name,
    delimiter='\t',
    index_col=False,
    names=['UserKey', 'Date', 'Timestamp', 'Hand', 'Hold time',
        'Direction', 'Latency time', 'Flight time']
)
```

We drop the unneeded column:

```
df = df.drop('UserKey', axis=1)
```

We fix the dates:

```
df['Date'] = pd.to_datetime(df['Date'], errors='coerce',
format='%y%M%d').dt.date

# Convert time data to numeric
for column in ['Hold time', 'Latency time', 'Flight time']:
    df[column] = pd.to_numeric(df[column], errors='coerce')
df = df.dropna(axis=0)
```

Always wash your hands by getting rid of invalid values:

```
# Clean data in `Hand`
df = df[
  (df['Hand'] == 'L') |
  (df['Hand'] == 'R') |
  (df['Hand'] == 'S')
]
```

Do the same with direction data values:

```
# Clean data in `Direction`
df = df[
  (df['Direction'] == 'LL') |
  (df['Direction'] == 'LR') |
  (df['Direction'] == 'LS') |
  (df['Direction'] == 'RL') |
  (df['Direction'] == 'RR') |
  (df['Direction'] == 'RS') |
  (df['Direction'] == 'SL') |
  (df['Direction'] == 'SR') |
  (df['Direction'] == 'SS')
]
```

We're doing our math! This is where the manual GC process comes in. It's a good thing we washed our hands, right? In the following code, we're doing our calculations. The results are being returned as a new DataFrame, so to save memory, we're deleting the old DataFrames as we go. This frees up memory since this kind of work is memory intensive:

```
    direction_group_df = df.groupby('Direction')[numeric_
columns][numeric_columns][numeric_columns] direction_group_df =
df.groupby('Direction')[numeric_columns].mean()
  del df
  gc.collect()
```

With our new result, we re-index and then sort:

```
  direction_group_df = direction_group_df.reindex(
    ['LL', 'LR', 'LS', 'RL', 'RR', 'RS', 'SL', 'SR', 'SS'])
  direction_group_df = direction_group_df.sort_index() # to ensure
correct order of data
```

This line returns the flattened NumPy array, which contains the mean values of the grouped data. The `.values.flatten()` method converts the DataFrame into a two-dimensional NumPy array and then flattens it into a one-dimensional array for ease of use:

```
  return direction_group_df.values.flatten()
```

Processing the users with a function

Within the same cell is a second function:

```
def process_user(user_id, filenames):
    running_user_data = np.array([])
```

This line initializes an empty NumPy array named `running_user_data`. This array will be used to accumulate data as the function iterates through filenames, which is what the following block does:

```
    for filename in filenames:
        if user_id in filename:
            running_user_data = np.append(running_user_data, read_
tappy(filename))
```

This loop iterates through the list of filenames. If the provided user ID is found in the filename, it calls the `read_tappy()` function (which returns a flattened NumPy array of mean values) and appends its contents to the `running_user_data` array.

After iterating through the filenames and appending the data, the following line reshapes the `running_user_data` array into a two-dimensional array, with each row containing 27 columns. This flattening of time data allows for further analysis:

```
    running_user_data = np.reshape(running_user_data, (-1, 27))
```

The last line calculates the mean values along the rows (`axis=0`) of the `running_user_data` array using `np.nanmean()`. The `np.nanmean()` function ignores NaN values while calculating the mean:

```
    return np.nanmean(running_user_data, axis=0)
```

To summarize, the `process_user` function processes data for a specific user by iterating through relevant filenames, aggregating the data using the `read_tappy` function, reshaping the data, and calculating the mean values while ignoring NaN values. The final result is an array of mean values for each column of the data.

Processing all the data

This one's for all the marbles! The following cell processes the data for all available users by aggregating and calculating mean values based on the Tappy data. First, there's a little housekeeping. We're going to ignore any warnings:

```
#%% Run through all available data

import warnings
warnings.filterwarnings("ignore")
```

We'll make one more trip through the `Tappy Data` folder:

```
filenames = os.listdir('data/Tappy Data/')
```

Next, we'll make some column names for the final DataFrame:

```
column_names = [first_hand + second_hand + '_' + time
        for first_hand in ['L', 'R', 'S']
        for second_hand in ['L', 'R', 'S']
        for time in ['Hold time', 'Latency time', 'Flight time']]

user_tappy_df = pd.DataFrame(columns=column_names)
```

Next, let's loop through the user indexes and use our `process_user` function:

```
for user_id in user_df.index:
    user_tappy_data = process_user(str(user_id), filenames)
    user_tappy_df.loc[user_id] = user_tappy_data
```

These next few lines do a little interim cleaning by ensuring any NaN values are substituted with zeros, and any negative numeric data is also normalized to zero:

```
user_tappy_df = user_tappy_df.fillna(0)
user_tappy_df[user_tappy_df < 0] = 0
```

And then, we print like we've never printed before! OK, that's not true – we've done this a lot:

```
print(user_tappy_df.head())
```

Saving the processed data

The last code cell likely doesn't need much explanation:

```
#%% Save processed data
```

First, we concatenate the two DataFrames together:

```
combined_user_df = pd.concat([user_df, user_tappy_df], axis=1)
print(combined_user_df.head())
```

Finally, we save it to a CSV file:

```
combined_user_df.to_csv('data/combined_user.csv')
```

This is generally a good practice in a given data pipeline. Saving the processed, cleaned version of a dataset can save data engineers a lot of effort if something goes wrong along the way. It also offers flexibility, if and when we want to change or extend our pipeline further.

I'll open the CSV file in PyCharm for one last look before we start doing the real analysis work. You can see mine in *Figure 14.19*:

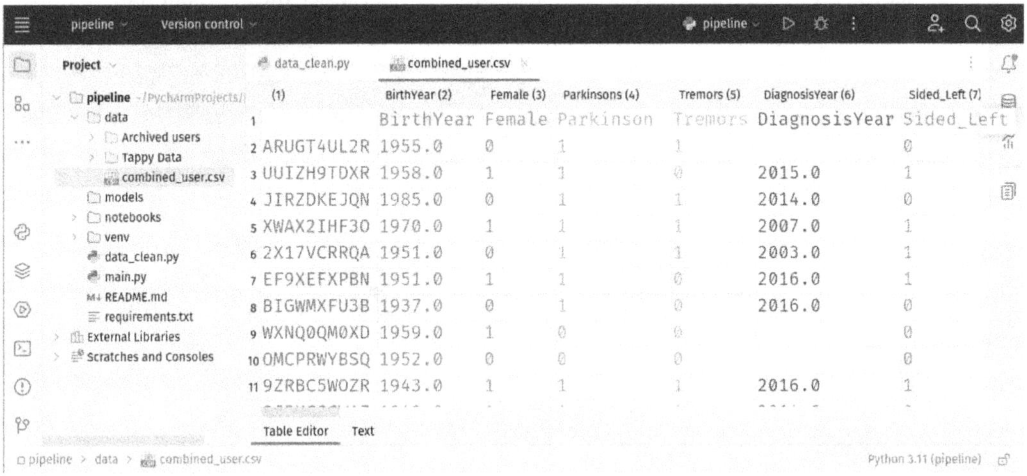

Figure 14.19: Our hard work has paid off! Our data is ready for analysis

With that, we are ready to start exploring our dataset and searching for insights.

Data analysis and insights

Remember what we said about the importance of having a question in mind when starting to work on a data science project? This is especially true during this phase, where we explore our dataset and extract insights, which should revolve around our initial question – the connection between typing speed and whether a patient has PD or not.

Throughout this section, we will be working with the EDA.ipynb file, located in the notebooks folder of our current project. In the following subsections, we will be looking at the code included in this notebooks folder. Go ahead and open this Jupyter notebook in your PyCharm editor, or, if you are following our discussions and entering your own code, create a new Jupyter notebook.

Starting the notebook and reading in our processed data

Remember that when you open a Jupyter notebook in Python, you can see the code, but Jupyter won't run unless you click the **Run** button. You can see PyCharm ready for this in *Figure 14.20*:

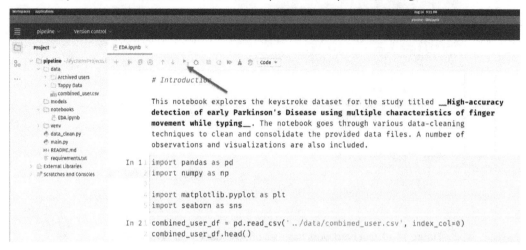

Figure 14.20: The notebook is open, I've clicked in the first cell (In 1),
and I'll now click the Run button indicated by the arrow

Once you click the **Run** button, a Jupyter server will start and run the first cell in the notebook, which handles our imports and reads in our cleaned dataset:

```python
import pandas as pd
import numpy as np

import matplotlib.pyplot as plt
import seaborn as sns


combined_user_df = pd.read_csv('../data/combined_user.csv', index_col=0)
combined_user_df.head()
```

Since the last line has us printing the first five lines of our output, you'll see them appear below the code and next to a marker that says **Out 2**, as shown in *Figure 14.21*:

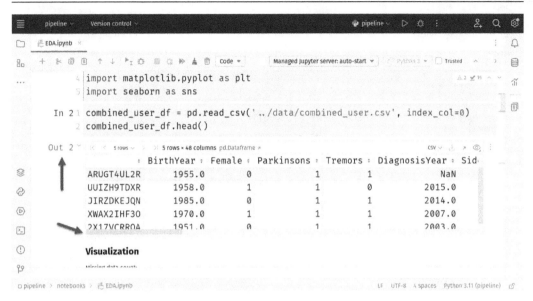

Figure 14.21: The output from the head statement in In 2 is shown in Out 2 and is horizontally scrollable

Now that our cleaned data has been loaded up, we can move on to analysis techniques.

Using charts and graphs

Visualization is normally the end goal for most of my work, so for me, this is a natural next step. I'm going to start by creating a bar graph that will show me the distribution of the counts of unique values within the data. I think this might give us some insight into which factor would affect the dependent variable in this study, which is whether a subject has early-onset PD. However, there's still a problem. As shown in *Figure 14.21*, there are still some holes in the data I will need to account for before I begin analysis in earnest.

What I'm going to do first is create a bar chart to visualize our missing data. The following code cell handles this:

```
#%%

missing_data = combined_user_df.isnull().sum()

g = sns.barplot(x=missing_data.index, y=missing_data)
g.set_xticklabels(labels=missing_data.index, rotation=90)

plt.show()
```

Running this code produces the visualization shown in *Figure 14.22*:

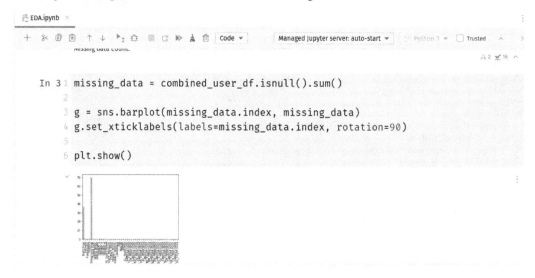

Figure 14.22: The missing data is visualized in the bar chart

Thankfully, our chart is very sparse. There is only a small amount of data that is missing, or incomplete. There are some missing values for `BirthYear` and `DiagnosisYear`. You can even see one in the preview shown in *Figure 14.21*. Analyzing missing values is important, and we will come back to the process of filling in these values later on. But for now, let's continue with the visualization process.

A great feature in Matplotlib is subplots, which allow us to generate multiple visualizations side by side. In the following code cell, we are creating multiple visualizations with this feature to highlight potential differences between patients with and without Parkinson's:

```
#%%

f, ax = plt.subplots(2, 2, figsize=(20, 10))


sns.distplot(
combined_user_df.loc[combined_user_df['Parkinsons'] == 0,
'BirthYear'].dropna(axis=0),
kde_kws = {'label': "Without Parkinson's"},
ax = ax[0][0]
)
sns.distplot(
combined_user_df.loc[combined_user_df['Parkinsons'] == 1,
'BirthYear'].dropna(axis=0),
```

```
kde_kws = {'label': "With Parkinson's"},
ax = ax[0][1]
)

sns.countplot(x='Female', hue='Parkinsons', data=combined_user_df,
ax=ax[1][0])
sns.countplot(x='Tremors', hue='Parkinsons', data=combined_user_df,
ax=ax[1][1])

plt.show()
```

After running this code cell, a visualization will be generated, as shown in *Figure 14.23*:

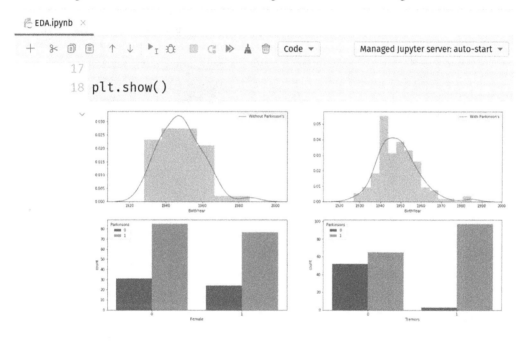

Figure 14.23: Four plots drawn together from the previous cell

The top two visualizations represent the distribution in the year of birth of people with (top right) and without (top left) Parkinson's. We can see that these distributions roughly follow the normal bell curve. If you were to encounter a distribution that is skewed or in a strange shape, it might be worth digging into that data further. Note that we can also apply the same visualization for the DiagnosisYear column.

In the bottom-left visualization, we have a bar chart representing the count of male patients (two bars on the left) and female patients (two bars on the right). Patients with Parkinson's are counted with the orange bars, and patients without are counted with the blue bars. In this visualization, we can see that while there are more patients with the disease than the ones without, the breakdown across the two genders is roughly the same.

The bottom-right visualization, on the other hand, illustrates the breakdown between patients with tremors (two bars on the right) and those without tremors (two bars on the left). From this visualization, we can see that tremors are significantly more common in patients with Parkinson's, which is quite intuitive and can serve as a sanity check for our analyses so far.

Next, we will move on to box plots. Specifically, we will use box plots to visualize the distributions of different time data (Hold time, Latency time, and Flight time) among patients with and without Parkinson's. Once again, we will use the subplots feature to generate multiple visualizations at the same time:

```
#%%

column_names = [first_hand + second_hand + '_' + time
for first_hand in ['L', 'R', 'S']
for second_hand in ['L', 'R', 'S']
for time in ['Hold time', 'Latency time', 'Flight time']]


f, ax = plt.subplots(3, 3, figsize=(10, 5))

plt.subplots_adjust(
right = 3,
top = 3
)

for i in range(9):
temp_columns = column_names[3 * i : 3 * i + 3]
stacked_df = combined_user_df[temp_columns].stack().reset_index()

stacked_df = stacked_df.rename(
columns={'level_0': 'index', 'level_1': 'Type', 0: 'Time'})
stacked_df = stacked_df.set_index('index')

for index in stacked_df.index:
stacked_df.loc[index, 'Parkinsons'] = combined_user_df.loc[index,
'Parkinsons']

sns.boxplot(x='Type', y='Time',
```

```
hue='Parkinsons',
data=stacked_df,
ax=ax[i // 3][i % 3]
).set_title(column_names[i * 3][: 2], fontsize=20)

plt.show()
```

In this code cell, each subplot will visualize data of a specific direction type (LL, LR, LS, and so on) and will contain different splits denoting patients with and without the disease. You should obtain the visualization shown in *Figure 14.24*:

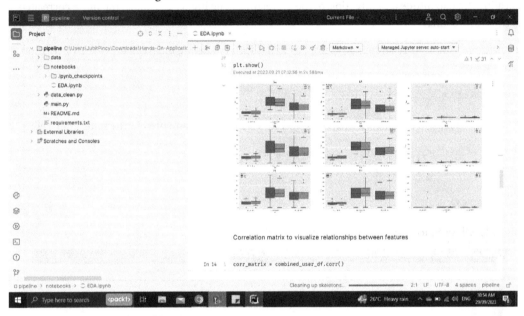

Figure 14.24: The plots from the previous run cell

What we can gather from this visualization is that, surprisingly, the distribution of typing speed among patients without Parkinson's can span across higher values and have more variance than that among patients with Parkinson's, which might contradict the intuition some might have that patients with Parkinson's take more time to press keystrokes.

Overall, bar charts, distribution plots, and box plots are some of the most common visualization techniques in data science tasks, mostly because they are both simple to understand and powerful enough to highlight important patterns in our datasets. In the next and final subsection on the topic of data analysis, we will consider more advanced techniques – namely, the correlation matrix between attributes and leveraging ML models.

Machine learning-based insights

Unlike the previous analysis methods, the methods discussed in this subsection and other similar ones are based on more complex mathematical models and ML algorithms. Given the scope of this book, we will not be going into the specific theoretical details for these models, but it's still worth seeing some of them in action by applying them to our dataset.

First, let's consider the feature correlation matrix for our dataset. As the name suggests, this model is a matrix (a 2D table) that contains the correlation between each pair of numerical attributes (or features) within our dataset. A correlation between two features is a real number between -1 and 1, indicating the magnitude and direction of the correlation. The higher the value, the more correlated the two features are.

To obtain the feature correlation matrix from a pandas DataFrame, we must call the `corr()` method, as shown here:

```
corr_matrix = combined_user_df.corr()
```

We usually visualize a correlation matrix using a heat map, as implemented in the same code cell:

```
f, ax = plt.subplots(1, 1, figsize=(15, 10))
sns.heatmap(corr_matrix)

plt.show()
```

This code will produce the visualization shown in *Figure 14.25*:

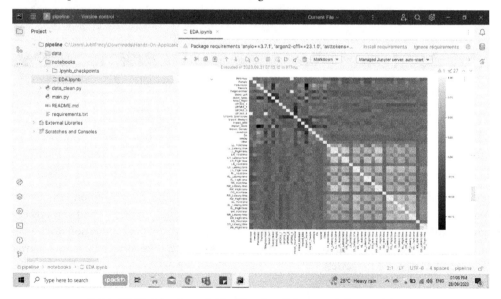

Figure 14.25: A heatmap is ideal for visualizing correlation matrices

Next, we will try applying an ML model to our dataset. Contrary to popular belief, in many data science projects, we don't take advantage of ML models for predictive tasks, where we train our models to be able to predict future data. Instead, we feed our dataset to a specific model so that we can extract more insights from that current dataset.

Here, we are using the linear **support vector classifier (SVC)** model from scikit-learn to analyze the data we have and return the feature importance list:

```
#%%

from sklearn.svm import LinearSVC


combined_user_df['BirthYear'].fillna(combined_user_df['BirthYear'].
mode(dropna=True)[0], inplace=True)
combined_user_df['DiagnosisYear'].fillna(combined_user_
df['DiagnosisYear'].mode(dropna=True)[0], inplace=True)

X_train = combined_user_df.drop(['Parkinsons'], axis=1)
y_train = combined_user_df['Parkinsons']

clf = LinearSVC()
clf.fit(X_train, y_train)


nfeatures = 10

coef = clf.coef_.ravel()
top_positive_coefs = np.argsort(coef)[-nfeatures :]
top_negative_coefs = np.argsort(coef)[: nfeatures]
top_coefs = np.hstack([top_negative_coefs, top_positive_coefs])
```

Note that before we feed the data we have to the ML model, we need to fill in the missing values we have in the two columns we identified earlier – BirthYear and DiagnosisYear. Most ML models cannot handle missing values very well, and it is up to the data engineers to choose how these values should be filled.

Here, we are using the **mode**, or the most commonly occurring data point, of these two columns to fill in the missing values. This is because the mode is one of the statistics that tends to represent the range of different kinds of data well, especially for discrete or nominal attributes, which is what we have here. If you are working with numerical and continuous data such as length or area, it is also common practice to use the mean of a given attribute. Finally, getting back to our current process, this code trains the model on our dataset and obtains the coef_ attribute of the model afterward.

This attribute contains the feature importance list, which is visualized by the last section of the code:

```
plt.figure(figsize=(15, 5))
colors = ['red' if c < 0 else 'blue' for c in coef[top_coefs]]
plt.bar(np.arange(2 * nfeatures), coef[top_coefs], color=colors)
feature_names = np.array(X_train.columns)
# Make sure the number of tick locations matches the number of tick
labels.
plt.xticks(np.arange(0, 2 * nfeatures), feature_names[top_coefs],
rotation=60, ha='right')

plt.show()
```

Running this code produces the visualization shown in *Figure 14.26*:

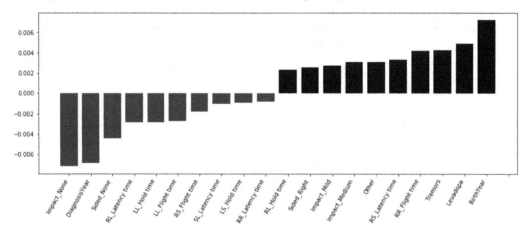

Figure 14.26: A graph of the feature important list identifies features
used extensively while training an ML model

From the feature importance list, we can identify any features that were used extensively by the ML model while training. A feature with a very high importance value could be correlated with the target attribute (whether someone has Parkinson's or not) in some interesting way. For example, we can see that `Tremors` (which we know is quite correlated to our target attribute) is the third most important feature of our current ML model.

That's our last discussion point regarding analyzing our dataset. In the last section of this chapter, we will have a brief discussion on deciding how to write a script for a Python data science project.

Scripts versus notebooks in data science

In the preceding data science pipeline, there are two main sections: data cleaning, where we remove inconsistent data, fill in missing data, and appropriately encode the attributes, and data analysis, where we generate visualizations and insights from our cleaned dataset.

The data cleaning process was implemented by a Python script while the data analysis process was done with a Jupyter notebook. In general, deciding whether a Python program should be done in a script or a notebook is quite an important, yet often overlooked, aspect while working on a data science project.

As we discussed in the previous chapter, Jupyter notebooks are perfect for iterative development processes, where we can transform and manipulate our data as we go. A Python script, on the other hand, offers no such dynamism. We need to enter all of the code necessary in the script and run it as a complete program.

However, as illustrated in the *Data cleansing and preprocessing* section, PyCharm allows us to divide a traditional Python script into separate code cells and inspect the data we have as we go using the **SciView** panel. The dynamism offered by Jupyter notebooks can also be found within PyCharm.

Now, another core difference between regular Python scripts and Jupyter notebooks is the fact that printed output and visualizations are included inside a notebook, together with the code cells that generated them. While looking at this from the perspective of data scientists, we can see that this feature is considerably useful when making reports and presentations.

Say you are tasked with finding actionable insights from a dataset in a company project, and you need to present your final findings, as well as how you came across them with your team. A Jupyter notebook can effectively serve as the main platform for your presentation. Not only will people be able to see which specific commands were used to process and manipulate the original data but you will also be able to include Markdown texts to further explain any subtle discussion points.

Regular Python scripts can simply be used for low-level tasks where the general workflow has already been agreed upon, and you will not need to present it to anyone else. In our current example, I chose to clean the dataset using a Python script as most of the cleaning and formatting changes we applied to the dataset don't generate any actionable insights that can address our initial question. I only used a notebook for data analysis tasks, where there were many visualizations and insights worthy of further discussion.

Overall, the decision to use either a traditional Python script or a Jupyter notebook solely depends on your tasks and purposes. We simply need to remember that, for whichever tool we would like to use, PyCharm offers incredible support that can streamline our workflow.

Summary

In this chapter, we walked through the hands-on process of working on a data science pipeline. First, we discussed the importance of having version control for not just our code and project-related files but also our datasets; we then learned how to use Git LFS to apply version control to large files and datasets.

Next, we looked at various data cleaning and preprocessing techniques that are specific to the example dataset. Using the **SciView** panel in PyCharm, we can dynamically inspect the current state of our data and variables and see how they change after each command.

Finally, we considered several techniques to generate visualizations and extract insights from our dataset. Using the Jupyter editor in PyCharm, we were able to avoid working with a Jupyter server and work on our notebook entirely within PyCharm. Having walked through this process, you are now ready to tackle real-life data science problems and projects using the same tools and functionalities that we have discussed so far.

So, we have finished our discussion on using PyCharm in the context of scientific computing and data science. In the next chapter, we will finally consider a topic that we have mentioned multiple times through our previous chapters – PyCharm plugins.

Questions

Answer the following questions to test your knowledge of this chapter:

1. What are some of the main ways of collecting datasets for a data science project?
2. Can Git LFS be used with Git? If so, what is the overall process?
3. Which type of attribute can have its missing values filled out with the mean? What about the mode?
4. What problem does one-hot encoding address? What problem can arise from using one-hot encoding?
5. Which type of attribute can benefit from bar charts? What about distribution plots?
6. Why is it important to consider the feature correlation matrix for a dataset?
7. Aside from predictive tasks, what can we use ML models for (like we did in this chapter)?

Further reading

Be sure to check out the companion website for this book at `https://www.pycharm-book.com`.

More information can be found in the following articles and reading materials:

- Adams, W. R. (2017). *High-accuracy detection of early Parkinson's Disease using multiple characteristics of finger movement while typing*. PloS one, *12*(11), e0188226.

- The *Tappy Keystroke Data with Parkinson's Patients* data, uploaded by Patrick DeKelly: `https://www.kaggle.com/valkling/tappy-keystroke-data-with-parkinsons-patients`.

- *Building a Data Pipeline from Scratch*, by Alan Marazzi: `https://medium.com/the-data-experience/building-a-data-pipeline-from-scratch-32b712cfb1db`.

- *A Business Perspective to Designing an Enterprise-Level Data Science Pipeline*, by Vikram Reddy: `https://www.datascience.com/blog/designing-an-enterprise-level-data-science-pipeline`.

- *Data Science for Startups: Data Pipelines*, by Ben Weber: `https://towardsdatascience.com/data-science-for-startups-data-pipelines-786f6746a59a`.

- Documentation for the pandas library: `https://pandas.pydata.org/pandas-docs/stable/`.

Part 5: Plugins and Conclusion

This part will introduce readers to the concept of PyCharm plugins and walk through the process of downloading plugins and adding them to their PyCharm environment. It will also go into details regarding the most popular plugins and how they can optimize a programmer's productivity even further. We'll also gloss over important topics discussed in previous chapters of the book and offers a comprehensive view on PyCharm's most popular features.

This part has the following chapters:

- *Chapter 15, More Possibilities with PyCharm Plugins*
- *Chapter 16, Future Developments*

15

More Possibilities with Plugins

Any IDE worth its salt is extensible via a plugin architecture. The big names from Microsoft, Eclipse, and JetBrains support plugins as do the smaller, free, and open source IDE projects such as Geany and Ninja IDE. Even vim, which is as bare bones as it gets given it has no GUI, has a plethora of plugins available that allow you to customize your experience beyond the capabilities of the shipped product. In the case of JetBrains IDEs, the plugin architecture is at the heart of everything they build.

Consider that JetBrains started with IntelliJ and from that, built a dozen or so specialty IDEs. The reason this was possible is that their architecture is based on plugins. PyCharm Professional includes all the core functionality of two other IDEs, WebStorm and DataGrip, because those features are simply sets of plugins.

In this chapter, we're going to discuss some important plugins both from JetBrains and from third-party developers. By the end of this chapter, you will know the following:

- How to leverage JetBrains remote development features that allow you to work on your local laptop while leveraging a remote environment such as a virtual machine, workstation, or server

- How to work collaboratively with JetBrains *Code With Me*

- How to work with Docker using the JetBrains Docker plugin

- How to leverage development infrastructure as code using HashiCorp Vagrant within PyCharm

- I'll also cover some smaller, quality-of-life plugins including themes, specialized highlighters, additional languages, and of course, the Black code formatter

Technical requirements

In order to proceed through this chapter, and indeed the rest of the book, you will need the following:

- An installed and working copy of PyCharm. Installation was covered in *Chapter 2, Installation and Configuration*, if are jumping into the middle of the book.

- Many of the sections in this chapter require connecting to services on the internet. A high-speed connection or a lot of patience is required for some of the demonstrations.

- For the section on remote development, you'll need a remote computer accessible via SSH and running a Linux operating system. This can be a physical machine or a virtual machine running via a cloud provider. I only cover connecting to a remote. I won't go into a deep dive on setting up a Linux computer or virtual machine to serve as a remote.

- For the section on Docker, I'll be using Docker Desktop. You can find the installation instructions for your computer's operating system at `https://www.docker.com/products/docker-desktop/`.

- This book's example source code from GitHub. We covered cloning the code in *Chapter 2, Installation and Configuration*. You'll find this chapter's relevant code at `https://github.com/PacktPublishing/Hands-On-Application-Development-with-PyCharm---Second-Edition/tree/main/chapter-15`.

Bundled plugins and JetBrains Marketplace

There have been several cases throughout the book where I pointed out useful plugins. I just couldn't wait, and the plugins I showed you were either highly relevant to the particular chapter in play or just really cool and exciting. In the interest of being a responsible PyCharm mentor, I will collect myself, contain my enthusiasm (as much as I can), and pretend that you skipped immediately to this chapter, which might just be the best chapter in the book. Or not, you decide.

A great many features throughout JetBrains IDE products are built as plugins. You're going to encounter two types of plugins: plugins made by JetBrains, and third-party plugins available in JetBrains Marketplace. Many plugins made by JetBrains are bundled in the various IDEs they make, but some have to be added or activated. Let's start by exploring the **Plugins** panel available in the IDE's settings.

The plugins window

There are several ways to get to the **Plugins** window. Perhaps the simplest is to just close whatever project you might have open in PyCharm, which gives you the window we started with 15 chapters ago in *Figure 15.1*.

Figure 15.1: The Plugins window contains all the tools you need to manage plugins in PyCharm

At the top of the **Plugins** window, you'll find two important tabs: one shows you the plugins you have installed (**2**) and the other takes you to Marketplace where you can buy and install new plugins (**1**). Many of the plugins in Marketplace are free, but many of the better ones are not.

The gear icon (**3**) allows you to configure additional plugin repositories. I've never needed this, but it's there if you do. You can also install a plugin from a local folder using the relevant menu found under the gear.

The search box (**4**) allows you to find plugins in the list. When you select a plugin you'll usually get some information about it on the right side (**5**). Plugins can be enabled and disabled (**6**), so if your IDE behaves erratically after installing a plugin, you can turn it off temporarily or uninstall it completely.

Bundled plugins

If you study the list in *Figure 15.2*, you'll find that most of the plugins on this screen are bundled with PyCharm. These are plugins created by JetBrains and included in the normal PyCharm installation. It's not a bad idea to examine this list and disable plugins you aren't likely to use. For example, I use **Terraform** and **Ansible** for my DevOps and **Infrastructure as Code** (**IaC**). I am not likely to use Puppet, so I should disable that plugin.

As you do this, you might find PyCharm warning you about dependent plugins. For example, there is a plugin for Less, which is a CSS meta-framework. I don't use it, so it's tempting to disable it. However, the JSX Styled Components plugin, which I do use in React projects, is dependent on Less. See *Figure 15.2*.

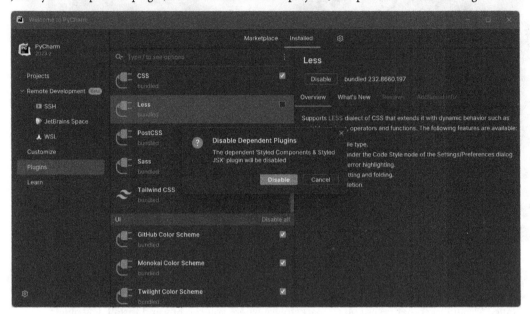

Figure 15.2: I am warned when I try to disable a plugin that is needed by another plugin

In this case, I'd better leave **Less** enabled.

JetBrains Marketplace

If you're up for some retail IDE therapy, you can click the **Marketplace** tab and go shopping. Some plugins are free, some aren't. You can search for and install plugins from Marketplace easily from this screen. If you buy one, you'll likely be routed to the JetBrains Marketplace website so you can control your license.

Making your own plugins

Anyone can make an IDE plugin using the Java programming language and IntelliJ Community or Ultimate editions. I won't cover how to make a plugin, I'll at least show you how to get started. In *Figure 15.3*, I have IntelliJ Community Edition open on the new project dialog. Given you have extensive experience with creating projects in PyCharm, I'll tell you that all the IDEs are identical. IntelliJ is the original flagship IDE product from JetBrains.

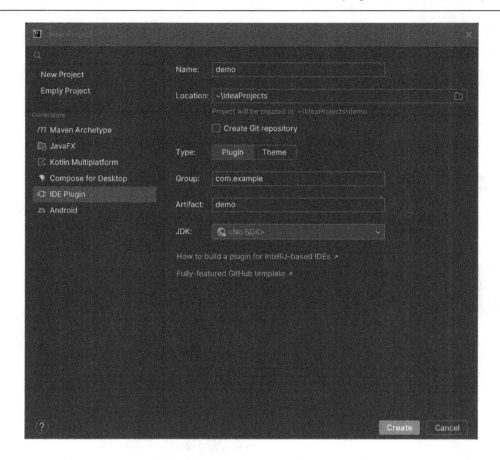

Figure 15.3: IntelliJ Community Edition has a project template for creating your own IDE plugins

In addition to the project template, there is also a hyperlink to a tutorial on building your plugin project.

Requiring plugins for your projects

Just as we have a `requirements.txt` text file to list the names and versions of the packages necessary for a given Python project, we can specify particular plugins as requirements for a PyCharm project. This will ensure other developers have access to any plugin functionality you deem crucial to their success in collaborating on your project. *Figure 15.4* shows you how to set the required plugins for your project.

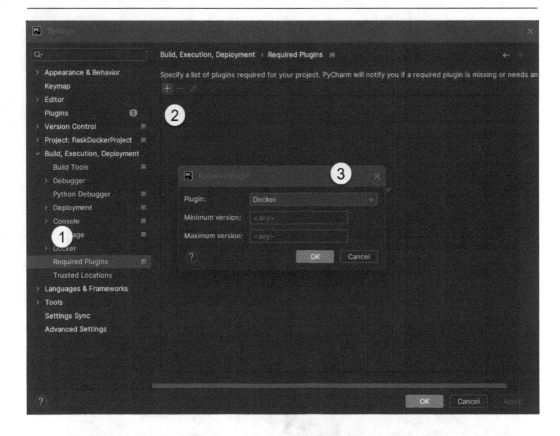

Figure 15.4: The steps for requiring plugins

First, having gone into your project's settings and located **Build, Execution, Deployment**, find the **Required Plugins** menu item (**1**) and click it. Next, click the + icon (**2**) and select your required plugins from the dialog box that appears (**3**). Click **OK**.

Useful miscellaneous plugins

I want to devote the bulk of this chapter to some very impactful plugins that are packed with complex features. Before I do that, though, let's get the easy stuff out of the way. I'll cover the small, interesting plugins you're most likely going to think of when you search for IDE plugins. Some of these we have seen in other chapters:

- The CSV plugin was covered in *Chapter 13*.

- The Markdown plugin. This didn't used to come bundled, but now it does and it definitely makes the cut.

- The cell mode plugin, which we also covered in *Chapter 13*.

Let's talk about a few more, which I'll group based on what they do.

Theme plugins

You spend 8 to 16 hours a day staring at the IDE. You might as well spend some time making it look cool. There are lots of color themes available. *Figure 15.5* shows my current favorite: the dark purple theme.

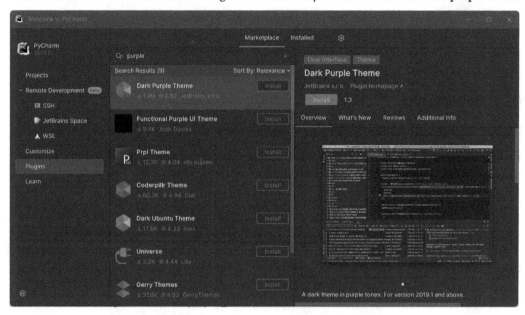

Figure 15.5: The Dark Purple Theme is one of my favorites because
it's different than the standard VS Code dark theme

When people walk by and see the IDE up, they'll immediately know you aren't one of those VS Code slaves with their ubiquitous out-of-the-box Microsoft dark theme. You could use the stock Darcula theme that comes with PyCharm, but for a University of Oklahoma grad like me, that theme has entirely too much orange in it. Pick something you don't see every day and soon everyone at the cube farm will know you are the real deal!

I also like the Material Theme UI in a nice solarized blue. This plugin comes in a lite (free) and a paid version. If you look around, you'll find a color theme that suits you as there are many from which to choose. The easy way to find your new favorite is to type a tag into the search box shown in *Figure 15.6*.

Figure 15.6: You can filter your plugin search using tags such as "Theme"

I recommend you try this because for whatever reason, leaving the search box blank doesn't yield a very long list of options.

File handler plugins

This class of plugins provides colored highlighting for some of the non-code files we use every day.

The .ignore plugin provides some nice formatting for any of the common ignore files such as .gitignore and .dockerignore.

Tools integration plugins

Paul Everitt, one of the developer advocates for PyCharm, often reminds us that the I in IDE stands for *Integrated*. You should never need to leave PyCharm for any reason. Besides writing code, developers need to interact with issue trackers, VCSs, continuous build environments, and potentially a plethora of infrastructure tooling. It is no surprise there are plugins to help with these types of integration. *Figure 15.7* shows the tag used to find these plugins.

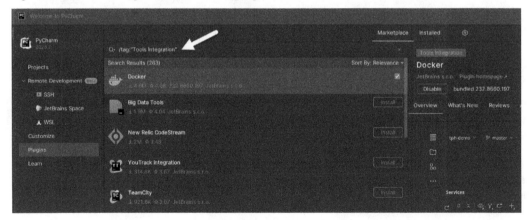

Figure 15.7: Use the Tools Integration tag to find integrations to
your favorite infrastructure and DevOps tools

I used to be a heavy TeamCity user. If you use TeamCity, or any of the other JetBrains team tools, you'll find plugins that allow you to monitor your builds, deal with issues, and more right from your IDE. For the record, Team City is still my favorite **continuous integration** (**CI**) server.

Productivity plugins

Developer productivity is the main reason to use an IDE in the first place. There are many additional features and integrations you'll find under this tag. *Figure 15.8* shows this tag in action.

Figure 15.8: Use the productivity tag to find tools to make you more productive

My favorite DevOps plugin by far is GitToolbox. Take a look at one of my projects open in PyCharm with GitToolbox enabled.

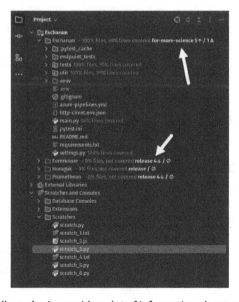

Figure 15.9: The GitToolbox plugin provides a lot of information about your project's repository

At a glance, I can see the branch I am currently using along with how many commits ahead or behind I am relative to my remote. The plugin will help you clean up old branches you haven't used in a while, perform regular fetches at timed intervals, and validate your commit messages. My favorite feature might be that you see the `git blame` information for each line. I'm not the blaming type, but I find it very useful as a lead developer to see which of my colleagues has worked on a particular file. It definitely helps code reviews go a little bit faster.

Completion plugins

AI has become a game-changing integral part of software development. Using the `/tag: Completion` tag will list dozens of traditional and AI-powered code completion plugins, as seen in *Figure 15.10*.

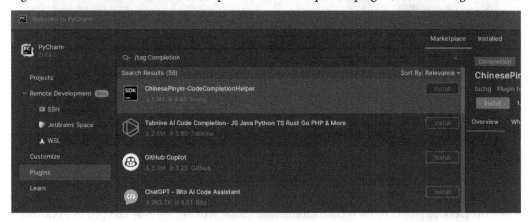

Figure 15.10: Completion plugins including the most popular AI implementations

At the moment, GitHub Copilot and any of the dozens of ChatGPT plugins are very popular autocompletion plugins. Before you pay money for them though, check out my discussion of JetBrains **AI Assistant** plugin in *Chapter 17*. It is currently in closed beta, so I can't really include it here, but it is really good and more tightly integrated than any of these plugins.

Code with me (and never be lonely again)

Pair programming is a popular practice introduced many years ago via the agile methodology known as **Extreme Programming** (**XP**). While not as well known as Scrum or Kanban, XP has many of the same practices and goals, but with pair programming as a mandatory component. In XP, two programmers sit in front of one computer and write code together. One person types while the other watches, coaches, looks things up, and generally contributes by helping out. At fixed intervals the programmers trade places. Adherents to the practice swear by it, claiming it eliminates the need for code reviews and generally leads to better code. Detractors, which include every non-technical manager alive, say it doesn't make sense to have two expensive, specialized workers doing half as much work as they should.

Love it or hate it, you have to admit there is a great deal of utility in direct collaboration. The real issue is in a post-Covid world where a great many developers work remotely, the idea of two developers at one screen is no longer feasible, at least until now.

JetBrains has an integrated tool called *Code With Me*. This tool allows multiple developers to join a shared session online, where everybody works on a project at the same time on one computer. This plugin comes bundled with all JetBrains IDEs including PyCharm. You can activate this by clicking the icon shown in *Figure 15.11*.

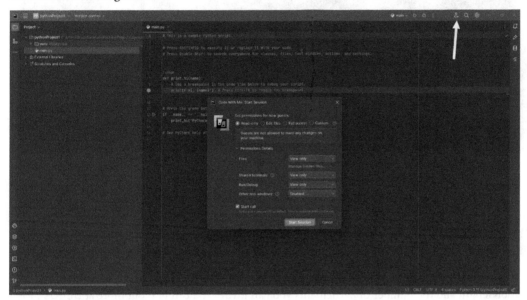

Figure 15.11: To start a Code With Me session, click the icon indicated with the arrow

You can set permissions for your guests. Remember, you are granting access to your computer! You should engage in sessions only with people you trust, and likewise only send your session links to people you trust.

Once you click **Start Session**, PyCharm creates a hyperlink you can share as you see fit. You can email it, but I most often see it sent to other developers via Slack or similar private chat services. Anyone who has the link can click to join the session. In addition to sharing the IDE, you also have normal conferencing tools. Participants can see and hear each other like you'd expect on a product such as Zoom or WebEx. *Figure 15.12* shows me conferencing with nobody, but it gives you an idea of what to expect.

Figure 15.12: A Code With Me session in progress. Unfortunately, since I spend all
my time writing books, I don't have any friends to call, so it's just me

This feature is useful in a lot of scenarios beyond the obvious pair programming use case. You can use this for each class, or conduct a coding interview using something more realistic than a Google Doc.

If you intend to use this service often, you will need a subscription since there are limitations on session length and the number of participants you can invite. You can find out more at `https://www.jetbrains.com/code-with-me/buy/#commercial`.

Remote development

At my office I have a large, powerful, 60 lb full-tower HP workstation with dual Intel Xeon processors (a total of 48 cores), 128 GB of memory, a professional-grade NVidia GPU, and 24 GB GPU accelerator! It even has a **serially attached small computer system interface (SAS)** for running enterprise-grade storage! You really can't get this kind of power in a laptop and there are days when I push it to its limits.

> **Our industry loves alphabet soup!**
>
> I'm just going to clear this up for all you engineering types who are trying to figure out how the **three letter acronym (TLA)** *SAS* stands for no fewer than six words. It's because the acronym *SAS* contains one letter that itself stands for another acronym. It's **Serially Attached SCSI (SAS)**. **SCSI** stands for *small computer system interface*. SAS drives are spinning disks that are capable of higher rotational speeds than your standard **serial advanced technology attachment (SATA)** drives, but they are still nowhere near as fast as a **solid-state drive (SSD)** or **non-volatile memory express (NVME)** drives that feature **NOT-AND** or **NAND** memory. SAS drives are, however, designed to be used in **redundant arrays of inexpensive disks (RAID)**, which makes them useful for inexpensively storing very large files in a fault-tolerant way.
>
> All these acronyms and jargon are part of an industry-wide conspiracy designed to make your relatives, who have no idea what you do, both proud and uncomfortable at family gatherings and holidays.

But like probably every other developer out there, I'd also like to be able to work from home. Obviously, I'm not willing to lug my 60 lb workstation around with me. Even if I were, our security team isn't going to like our source code leaving the building. True, I could use a remote technology such as VNC Viewer or Microsoft Remote Desktop, but those can be laggy and lack the creature comforts, such as support for four monitors, to which I have become accustomed.

I could also just work over SSH using **neovim**. But I think you and I, we're past that, right? If you think that's a good idea, skip back to *Chapter 1* where I talked about it being a bad idea. So, what am I to do?

Thankfully, JetBrains has me covered. Using its remote plugins, which are pre-installed on PyCharm Professional, I can run my IDE on my PC at home, but operate on my workstation in my office. This is done using **secure shell (SSH)**, which is an encrypted communications protocol typically used to administer Linux and Unix-based servers.

Simply put, you can configure PyCharm to use a virtual environment (`venv`) that is installed and configured on your remote PC, along with the code on the remote hard drive. Everything runs on the remote except for the IDE itself. Your run configurations will execute your code on the remote. When you debug, the debugger is running on the remote rather than your local machine. It is fairly seamless, but there are a couple of downsides.

Firstly, you have to be somewhat knowledgeable about networking to configure a project to do this. You need to have the IP address of the remote, and you need to have valid access credentials that allow you access to the remote computer. In my case, I also need a **virtual private network (VPN)** client running in order to access the network in my office, and this is external to PyCharm. While a VPN isn't technically a requirement, in most scenarios, it should be.

The second trade-off is performance. PyCharm isn't exactly zippy on a good day. We have to wait for indexing to take place before we can use any of those amazing features we've been talking about throughout the book. It isn't uncommon to get out-of-memory errors from PyCharm, which requires you to increase the amount of memory PyCharm is allowed to use. Updating or installing plugins requires you to restart the IDE, and even the initial loading screen hangs there longer than many of us would like. All in all, sometimes PyCharm can be a little clunky, but we put up with it because of the value it brings in easing our overall workflow.

I tend to think of PyCharm like a diesel truck. Such a truck isn't going to win a quarter-mile sprint race against a Porsche or a Tesla Model 3. Being from rural Oklahoma, I can tell you nobody owns sports cars where I'm from because our diesel trucks are more than transportation, they are part of our livelihood. I can't use a Tesla to tow a load of cows to auction, nor can I use a Porsche to haul hay to the back 40 to feed the horses. Likewise, we use heavy IDEs because we are willing to trade the "zippiness" of a minimal editor such as VS Code for some pretty extreme value presented by PyCharm's indexing. The ability to find usages, jump directly to function definitions, and have such a tightly integrated set of tools covering everything from editing to database management is worth a little lag.

With that said, that lag can become more evident when you are working on a remote project. You can expect your indexing times to be longer because the indexing is happening remotely and is then transmitted back to you. Network latency and VPNs will always make things slower, and that isn't PyCharm's fault. We put up with it because you get to work from home in your pajamas, with your music turned up, close to your own kitchen and snacks, and you can limit your interaction with other humans, which normally just slows people like us down. It's worth it. Now that your expectations have been set, let's look at how to make this work.

Configuring remote development in PyCharm

In all my books and courses, I pride myself on keeping everything as realistic as possible. For example in *Chapter 7*, I had trouble with the PyCharm feature that is supposed to download Node.js for me automatically. I didn't hide it, because that legitimately happened to me, which means it might also happen to you. There is value in learning to work around these kinds of issues.

By now, you might have noticed this chapter's screen captures look different that those in previous chapters. I am writing this chapter on a day when I am working at home, and I'm using a Windows 11 PC that has not been configured to work remotely before today. Since this is my home computer, the screenshots might look a little different than those from previous chapters, particularly with respect to dark mode. I turned dark mode off for most of the book because the light mode is easier to read in a printed book, and I'm saving my publisher money on ink. Not today though. Because I'm keeping it real.

The first thing I'll do is install and open PyCharm. Obviously, we've covered that already in *Chapter 2*, so there's no need to do that again. The welcome screen provides the option for opening a remote project, as shown in *Figure 15.13*.

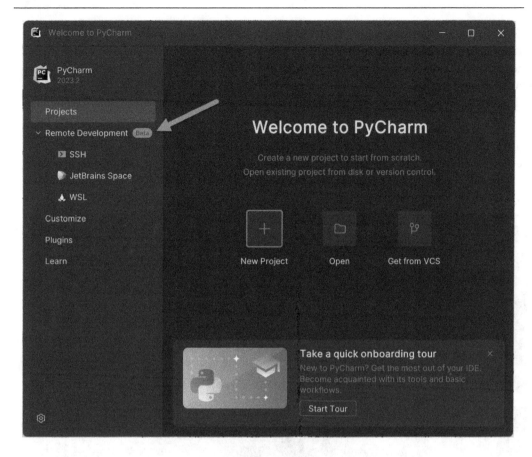

Figure 15.13: The remote development options are clearly available
on the right side of the welcome window

There are several options here including SSH, which is what I'll be using. JetBrains Space is a separate product, and I don't own it, so I can't really cover it. **WSL**, or **Windows Subsystem for Linux**, is likely only going to show up if you're using Windows. WSL allows you to run a Linux virtual machine directly in Windows without using an obvious hypervisor such as VMware or Virtual Box. I say *obvious*, because of course there is a hypervisor at play here – it is Microsoft's **HyperV**, which is built in to the professional editions of Windows 11 and Windows Server products. Windows 11 makes it seamless by allowing you to select one or more Linux installations via the Windows Terminal program that is new in Windows 11.

Since WSL is technically a virtual machine, it counts as remote development even though it happens on your local computer. For now, I'm going to focus on real remote development by accessing my workstation, currently about 12 miles away, over SSH. To be clear, my local computer is running Windows 11, but my workstation is running **Pop_OS! 22**, which is a variant of Ubuntu Linux. You've seen it in the screenshots throughout the book. This adds to the magic! I can use a consumer-grade OS such as Windows or macOS to connect to a professional-grade Linux workhorse.

Before you jump on Twitter (now called X) to flame me for disrespecting your favorite OS, realize that this is the only possible combination. You have to connect to a Linux remote as Windows and Macs are not yet supported. I'm not sure what the hold-up is on macOS since it comes with an SSH server preinstalled. This workflow would make sense for a use case where you have a Mac Pro at work and something else at home. The setup screens that follow do indicate this functionality is intended for future releases.

Figure 15.14 starts us off by showing what happens when we click the SSH option shown in *Figure 15.13*. We are given a screen that allows us to create a new project on our remote, but only after we first configure our connection. This is going to be like creating an SSH connection for publishing our web projects, which we covered in *Chapter 7*.

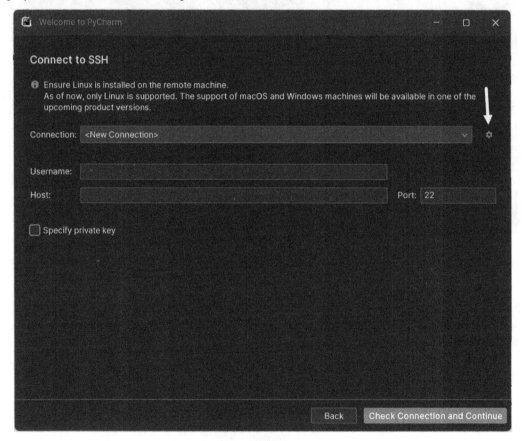

Figure 15.14: The remote configuration dialog could only be improved
by stacking another configuration dialog on top of it

Before you can do anything, you need to configure an SSH connection by clicking the gear icon indicated by the arrow in *Figure 15.14*. This brings us to yet another dialog, shown in *Figure 15.5*.

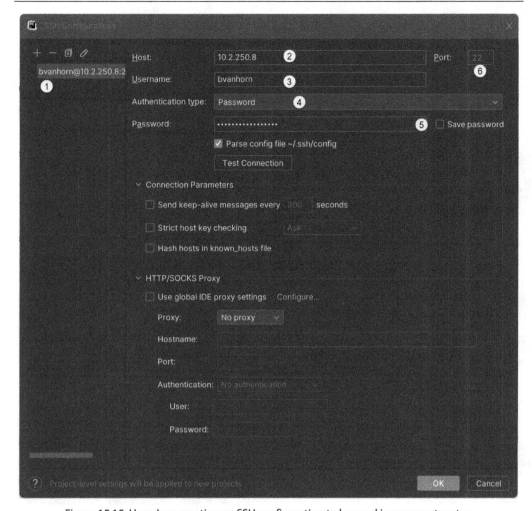

Figure 15.15: Here, I am creating an SSH configuration to be used in my remote setup

I've gone ahead and clicked the + button indicated at position **1**, which gave me the rest of the form I'm filling out. We need to fill in our host IP or **fully qualified domain name** (**FQDN**) should you have one. That's rare; you'll more likely use an IP address. The address in the figure is a private IP so don't bother trying to access it. This is realistic since your remote IP will also probably be private on a remote network secured by VPN. I've entered my username (**3**) and for authentication, I'm using a password (**4**). Having typed in my password, I can opt to save it (**5**). The default port for SSH is 22, so I've left the default set (**6**).

If you go back to the first position (**1**), you can click that pencil icon and give it a different name if you don't like the aesthetics of a username and an IP. I'm renaming mine in *Figure 15.16* to something a little more appropriate given its hardware specifications.

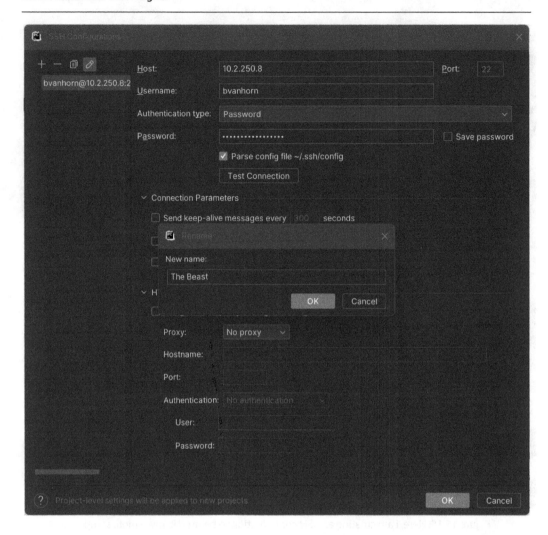

Figure 15.16: The Beast is the name for my remote workstation

The rest of the options aren't important to me because I don't have to go through a proxy to get to my workstation. I went ahead and expanded all the closed options in *Figure 15.15* so you can see any additional settings you might need.

Click **OK**, which takes you back to the earlier dialog. You'll need to select the connection you just created from the dropdown. For me, the re-naming didn't stick so it's back to the username and IP as shown in *Figure 15.17*.

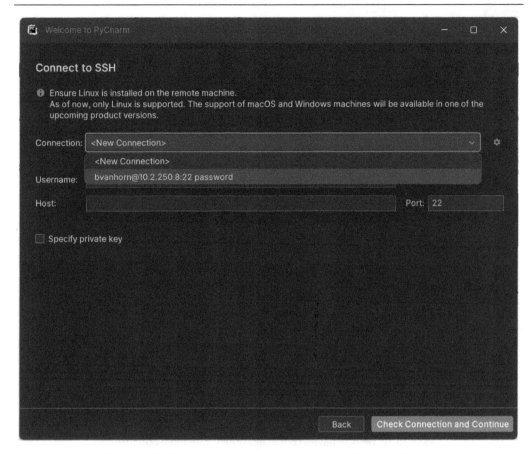

Figure 15.17: Having created a connection, you need to select it here
and the username and host fields will be filled in for you

Note that you have the option here to go passwordless and use a private key. Using the SSH keys potentially limits the need for a password, but you can still be challenged to unlock the key. In either case, PyCharm can remember your password or your SSH key phrase for you if you'd like. If you work for a security-conscious company, you might check your guidelines to understand where it is considered appropriate for an application to store your passwords and key phrases.

Click the button labeled **Check Connection and Continue**. Assuming you gain access, PyCharm copies some software and settings over to the host and then presents you with our original dialog box, as shown in *Figure 15.18*.

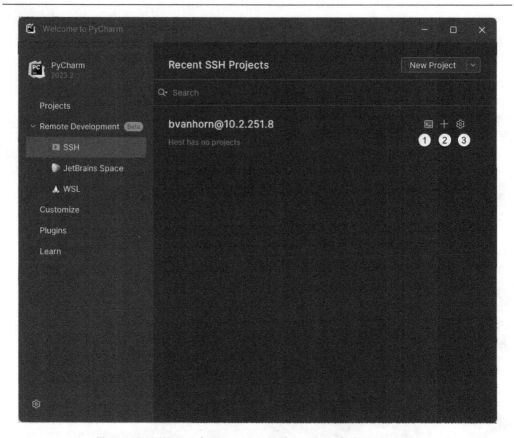

Figure 15.18: We now have a connected system with three options!

From here, we have three options. You can connect to the host with a terminal session by clicking it icon shown at (**1**). Clicking the + icon at (**2**) allows you to create or open a project on the remote. The gear (**2**) allows you to either remove the host or manage the backends on the host. This latter option is explained by my earlier remark. When we connected for the first time, I told you that PyCharm copied some software to the host. The software in question is a lot like our toolbox application. It's going to help us manage the IDE backends we'll upload as part of our project creation process. There are several other IDEs you can use in this way and you have the ability to manage these backends here. If you click it right now, there won't be any, because we haven't created any projects yet. Let's rectify that.

Creating a remote project

Click the + button indicated at position (**2**) in *Figure 15.18*. You'll be rewarded with the screen shown in *Figure 15.19*.

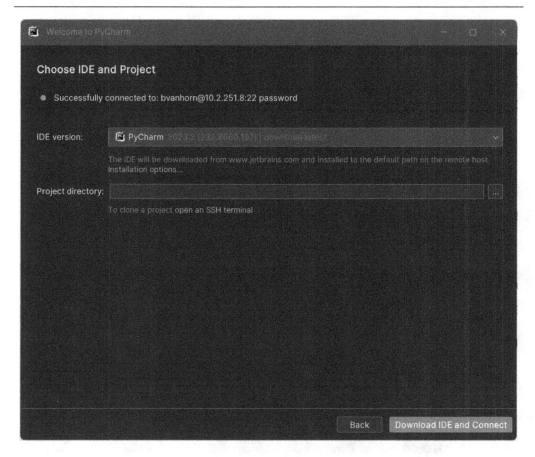

Figure 15.19: We're about to create a new remote project, which requires
downloading the IDE backend and selecting a project folder on the remote

Remote project creation requires you to specify which IDE you want to use and where you'd like to store your code on the remote hard drive. Given we're invoking PyCharm to create the project, it might seem odd that it is asking us to choose which IDE we need. Remember, though, this isn't really PyCharm. It is a plugin that can be leveraged by many of the JetBrains IDEs. Right now, you are really interacting with a different piece of software that just happens to be hosted in PyCharm.

We do get PyCharm as the default, so that's something. Pay attention to the version. Mine is defaulting to the EAP version, which might not be what you want. Personally, I don't use EAP unless I'm just testing them for backward project compatibility. I use the stable release in my day-to-day work. Pick the appropriate entry from the dropdown as shown in *Figure 15.20*.

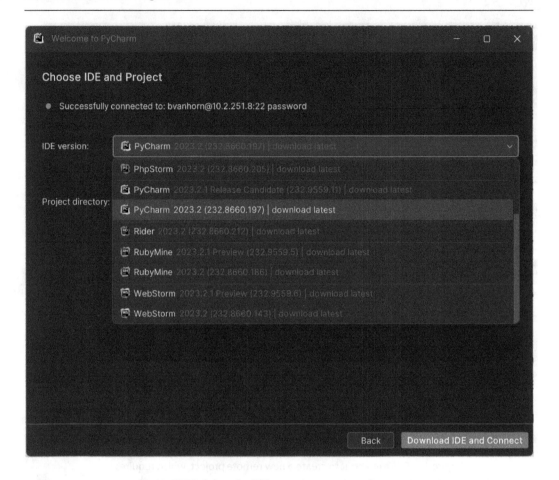

Figure 15.20: Select the IDE you want to use on the remote

The other, perhaps obvious consideration is you will need to have a license for whichever IDE you choose. Next, we need to pick a location. This can be confusing since the layout of a Linux filesystem is different than what you encounter in Windows. Linux doesn't use drive letters, and it uses forward slashes to separate path elements while Windows uses backslashes. Thankfully, I can just browse by clicking the three dots next to the project directory setting. Check out *Figure 15.21*.

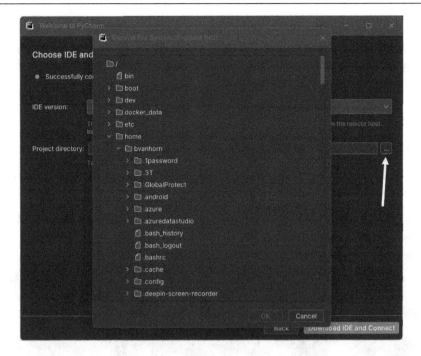

Figure 15.21: Click the three dots to browse the filesystem on the remote to pick your project directory

By default, the directory browser will display your home folder on the remote. You can browse to the folder of your choosing. Unfortunately at the moment, one big missing feature is an option to create a new folder for your project. I'm sure that's coming, but right now it is absent. We're going to have to work around this. Click **Cancel**, then **Back** to navigate back to the screen shown in *Figure 15.5*. Click the terminal button to launch an SSH terminal session on the host, as shown in *Figure 15.22*.

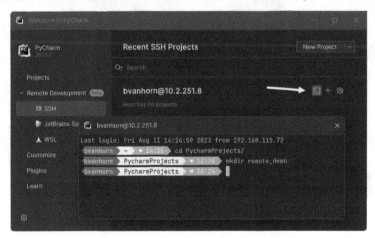

Figure 15.22: Use a terminal session to create your folder

Use the commands shown to create a new folder. I already had a `PyCharmProjects` folder on the remote in my home folder. This is because PyCharm is actually installed on the remote since it's my daily-use computer. You can make any folder that suits you within your home folder on the remote. You can exit the terminal session by typing `exit`.

Let's try that again

Like before, click the + icon, pick your IDE from the dropdown, and browse to the folder you just created.

Just think of this as being PyCharm without the UI. We're connecting the frontend on our computer with the uploaded PyCharm backend on the remote.

Let's bring our focus back to working on a project on the remote. Click the **Download IDE and Connect** button shown in *Figure 15.23*.

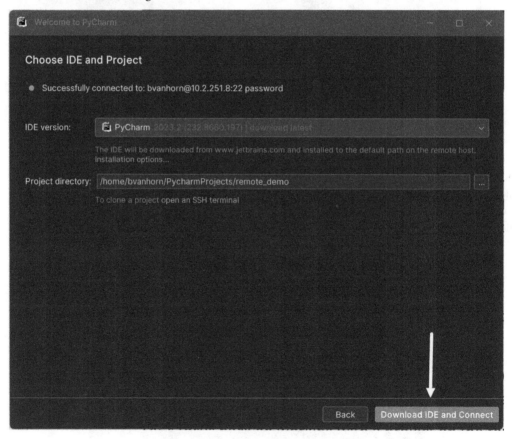

Figure 15.23: Click the button to create the project on the remote

This next part takes a few minutes. After you click the **Download IDE and Connect** button, a delightful orchestration of commands runs on your remote. The result is a running IDE backend, as shown in *Figure 15.24*.

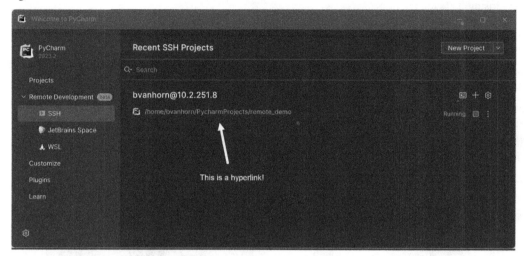

Figure 15.24: You now have an IDE backend server running on the remote

Click the link shown back in *Figure 15.11* to connect to your remote IDE. You will likely see password challenges, and maybe a note from Windows asking whether it's OK to let the traffic through the firewall, but eventually, you'll be live on the remote like I am in *Figure 15.25*.

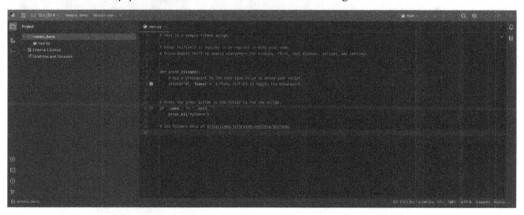

Figure 15.25: Magical! It looks the same as working locally!

From here, you mostly know what to do. Your IDE will function normally except for one step that was skipped: you were never prompted to create a virtual environment.

Creating a virtual environment on the remote

We've done this before, in *Chapter 3*, so I won't do another deep dive here, but there is one point that is confusing. Let's look at it.

To create a virtual environment you need to go to the project settings and locate the setting for the project's interpreter. Mine is shown in *Figure 15.26*.

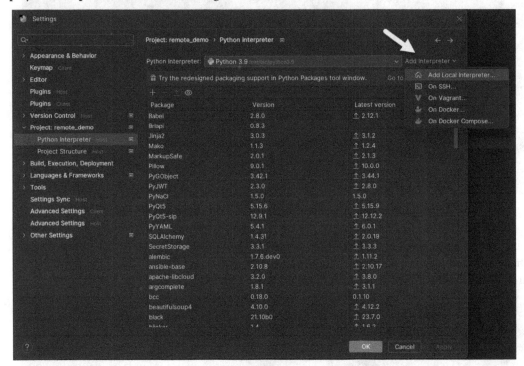

Figure 15.26: When you add the interpreter, remember that while it is remote, it is treated as local

The interpreter has defaulted to `/usr/bin/python3.9`, which is the global instance and not what I want. When I click the **Add Interpreter** button it gets a little confusing. You might be tempted to use **On SSH** because, well, we're using SSH to connect to the remote. However, we are connected to the remote already, so PyCharm is running on the remote, which makes it a local interpreter. When you click **Add Local Interpreter**, you'll note like in *Figure 15.14*, the path is Linux-like rather than a Windows path. This would be less obvious to macOS users since the pathing looks the same.

Other considerations

Now that you have this setup, you are effectively running PyCharm on the remote computer. All your file paths will show as Linux paths. Git and other revision control clients work with the remote folder. If you use SSH keys to authenticate with GitHub or your revision control host, you will need to configure the keys from the remote rather than just using your local public keys. Essentially, forget about your local computer entirely. You are operating completely on the remote.

Figure 15.27: Even though we picked the local option, everything happens on the remote

Click **OK**, and you'll find a proper `venv` has been created for the project. You are now ready to start working on your project!

Working with Docker

Container technology is one of the most important advances in DevOps technology since the virtual machine. **Docker** and similar container technologies have revolutionized the way software applications are developed, deployed, and managed. Imagine containers as lightweight, standalone units that encapsulate all the necessary components to run an application, including code, runtime, system libraries, and settings. This encapsulation ensures that the application runs consistently across different environments, from a developer's laptop to production servers.

Docker, in particular, is a widely used platform for building, shipping, and running containers. It provides a standardized way to package applications and their dependencies, isolating them from the underlying host system. This isolation enables developers to avoid the notorious "*it works on my machine*" issue, as containers behave consistently across various environments.

Another major advantage of containers is their portability. Developers can package an application and all its dependencies into a container image, which can then easily be shared with others. This makes collaboration more efficient and reduces the chances of compatibility issues. Furthermore, containers are highly scalable. They can be quickly replicated to handle increased workloads, offering an excellent solution for modern, dynamic, and resource-demanding applications.

Docker also brings about improved resource utilization. Since containers share the host operating system's kernel, they are more lightweight than traditional virtual machines, which require separate operating systems. This translates to faster startup times, lower memory overhead, and a higher density of containerized applications on a single host.

The bundled Docker plugin

PyCharm Professional comes with the JetBrains Docker plugin already bundled and enabled. You don't have to do anything further to use the Docker plugin. You do, however, need to install Docker. On my development computers, I usually run Docker Desktop because I find the product's GUI useful. It will be useful today as I show you how much you can do in PyCharm with Docker.

Let's create a Flask project and run it in Docker.

Create the project

In PyCharm Professional, create a new Flask project. If you're skipping around, I showed you how to do this in *Chapter 8*. You can see my project settings in *Figure 15.28*.

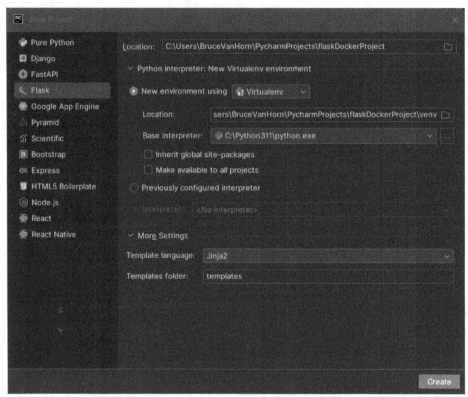

Figure 15.28: Create a Flask project so we can run it in Docker

We won't be making any changes to the generated project except for adding a **Dockerfile**. *Figure 15.29* shows me doing this.

Figure 15.29: Right-click the project and click New | Dockerfile

In the preceding figure, I'm right-clicking the project, hovering over **New**, and clicking the **Dockerfile** menu option. This generates a Dockerfile template for me with the following contents:

```
FROM ubuntu:latest
LABEL authors="BruceVanHorn"

ENTRYPOINT ["top", "-b"]
```

The first line indicates which Linux kernel will serve as the basis for our container image. I'm a pretty big fan of Ubuntu, but there are other possibilities. Alpine Linux is also very popular.

The second line is just what it says: a label for the image containing the author's names. We don't really need this, nor do we need the last line, at least in its current form. Let's replace the generated template with something more useful. The corporation behind Docker maintains a large registry of pre-made containers you can use as a starting point for your work. Among them is a container with any given version of Python 3 already installed. I'm going to use Python 3.9, even though that isn't the most current, because I happened to notice 3.9 is the version on my PC when I generated the sample project:

```
# Use the official Python 3.9 image as the base image
FROM python:3.9
```

On the next line, I'll set the working directory inside the container. The container has a minimal file system with limited space. This is where our app code will live:

```
WORKDIR /app
```

Next, I need to instruct Docker to copy my requirements text file and use `pip` to install my project's requirements:

```
# Copy the requirements file and install the necessary packages
COPY requirements.txt requirements.txt
RUN pip install -r requirements.txt
```

Next, I'll copy my code to the container:

```
# Copy the Flask application code into the container
COPY . .
```

The `COPY` instruction will copy the entire contents of my project folder, which would include the `venv` folder. Since the `pip` command will install our requirements, we don't need a `venv` folder. I'll fix this in just a moment. My next step in this file is to expose port `5000` on the container's firewall so I can access the app:

```
# Expose the port on which the Flask app will run
EXPOSE 5000
```

Finally, I'll define the command to run the Flask app when the container starts:

```
CMD ["python", "app.py"]
```

To fix the copy problem, I'll make a file in the project folder called `.dockerignore`. This works the same way a `.gitignore` works, except obviously it is used to set file exclusions for Docker. The contents of the `.dockerignore` file are simply this:

```
venv
```

Incidentally, you can find a plugin in Marketplace called `.ignore` that adds formatting to an array of ignore files.

Add a Docker run configuration

We covered creating and using run configurations in *Chapter 3*, so we won't cover it again here. I'll merely point out the option for creating a run configuration using Docker as seen in *Figure 15.30*.

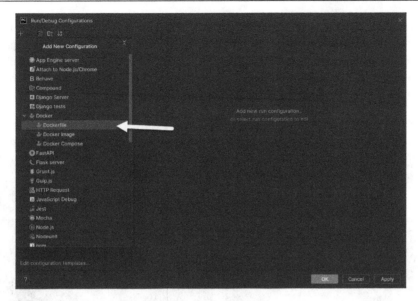

Figure 15.30: Use the Dockerfile option to create a run configuration that uses Docker

Much of your run configuration will be filled in for you. PyCharm will see your Dockerfile and use that as the default. My settings are shown in *Figure 15.31*.

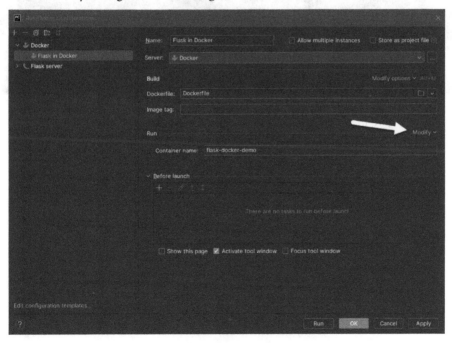

Figure 15.31: My Docker configuration

If we were to run this, Docker would pull the Python 3.9 image, make a container, and run the app. If we actually want to use the app, there's one more thing we need to do. The arrow in *Figure 15.31* points to a menu that allows you to tailor your `docker run` command. There are normally things you'll want to do here depending on your app, such as mapping persistent storage volumes, or in our case mapping the port in the container to the port on our local computer.

Click **Modify** | **Bind ports**, as shown in *Figure 15.32*.

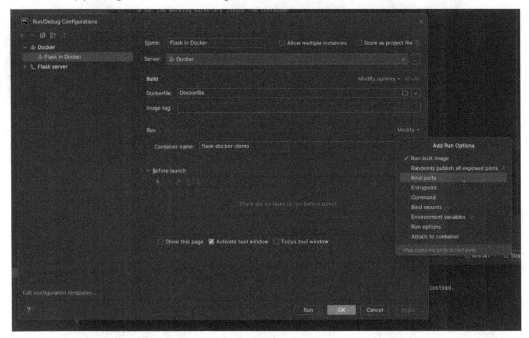

Figure 15.32: You have to add a bind port for the Docker container in order to see the application running from your browser

Once you click the **Bind ports** option, PyCharm adds a configuration parameter for **Bind ports**. Oddly, there is a folder icon indicated by the right arrow in *Figure 15.33*.

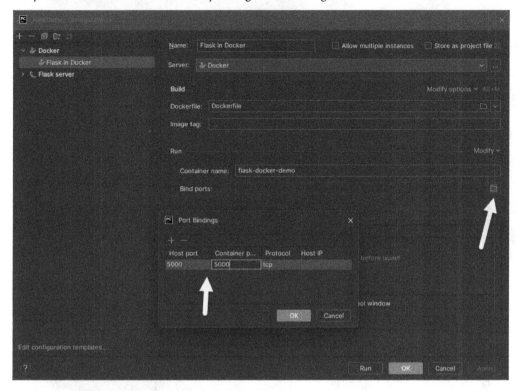

Figure 15.33: Click the folder to bring up the Port Bindings dialog and set the port mapping

It's odd because we won't be browsing for a file or folder. When you click it, you get a **Port Bindings** dialog. By default your Flask app runs on port 5000, so all you need to do is specify a binding between 5000 on the container and 5000 on your computer. Click **OK** until you're out of the run configuration. Run the run configuration. We explained run configurations way back in *Chapter 3*, so if you're joining us late, go back and review.

You should be treated to a textual light-show as Docker downloads the chunks to the container image, builds the container, and finally runs the app. You can see mine running in *Figure 15.34*.

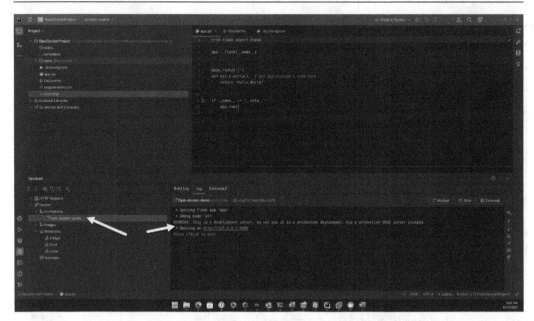

Figure 15.34: My Flask app is running in a Docker container

If you care to compare the UI for Docker versus Docker Desktop, you'll see many of the same features exist. A quick tour is shown in *Figure 15.35*.

Figure 15.35: PyCharm has many of the features you'd expect from a competent Docker UI

At position (**1**) we can see three tabs. **Build Log** allows us to examine the output generated when Docker built the container from our Dockerfile. We have some basic controls to stop and restart the container at (**2**). Naturally, when the container is stopped, the option to start it will appear here as well. Then perhaps most usefully, you can use the **Terminal** button (**3**) to start a terminal session inside the container.

On the left side (**4**) we see a full display showing all our running containers, downloaded images, networks, and mounted volumes.

In sum, you can really do almost anything in PyCharm that you can do in Docker Desktop. Once again, PyCharm's mission to give you an integrated experience with one of the most important technologies in use today is fully realized!

Summary

PyCharm plugins are customized add-ons that can further add to the list of features and functionalities one can take advantage of while using PyCharm. We have seen how to browse through, download, and manage different plugins in the PyCharm environment. By taking advantage of these plugins, we can further customize our workspace and improve our own productivity. Plugin management in PyCharm can be done in the **Plugins** tab in the settings.

We looked at some simple plugins to enhance your quality of life while coding, such as theme plugins and some useful file handlers. We looked at one of my favorites, GitToolbox, which allows you to see a lot more details from your Git repository right in your IDE window.

We then branched out and looked at some very big-feature plugins that are fairly new to PyCharm 2023. Remote development is very useful in a post-pandemic world where more and more of us find ourselves working remotely. Even if you're not, chances are you're finding yourself working increasingly with cloud servers and virtual machines rather than always using the hard drive on your local laptop.

Another big advance is PyCharm's support for Docker. The bundled Docker plugin provides full integration, from giving you autocomplete and syntax highlighting in Dockerfiles and composer files to a full GUI for managing your containers. You'll find yourself never needing to leave PyCharm to jump over to Docker Desktop to handle your Docker operations. Naturally, if you'd like to, you'll find both environments fully synchronized, and you could also use the **Terminal** window in PyCharm to interact with your containers that way if that is your preference.

Plugins are responsible for adding a lot of very cool and very useful features to our IDE. There are a few plugins that I didn't cover because, to be honest, they're not quite ready yet. I have some access to some closed beta features and some buried gems I want to cover in the next chapter. I can't wait to show you some of the things that are coming up in future releases!

Your Next Steps with PyCharm

PyCharm's features are so extensive, and improvements from JetBrains come so rapidly that it's been hard to keep up.

In this, my parting chapter, I want to do a few more things to try to do justice to this amazing piece of software. In this chapter, we'll cover the following:

- I'll do the obligatory wrap-up by briefly summarizing and commenting on our journey together so far.

- I'll cover a few cool features to help with your productivity that just didn't fit neatly into the chapter topics presented so far.

- I'll cover some cool new features that were introduced over the course of the 8 months it took me to write the book. I've been covering version 2023.1, and I have avoided updating it so I can stay consistent with screenshots of the UI used throughout the book. The 2023.2 release is out and there are some amazing changes, including a beta of the new **AI Assistant**!

- I'll raise a glass and shed a tear as we part company until the next book comes out.

I'll do my best not to get emotional on you. We've been together for a while now and it's going to be hard to take this victory lap with you knowing the book is almost finished. I'm getting a little misty over here just thinking about it, so let's keep moving.

In order to proceed through this chapter, you will need the following:

- An installed and working Python interpreter. I'll be using the latest from `https://python. org`.

- Installed copies of `pip` and `virtualenv`. You get these automatically when you install Python on Windows, and macOS includes them on every system. If you are using Linux, you need to install the package managers (such as `pip`) and the virtual environment tools (e.g., `virtualenv`) separately. Our examples will use `pip` and `virtualenv`.

- An installed and working copy of PyCharm. Installation was covered in *Chapter 2*. The screenshots in this chapter come from version 2023.2.1.

This book's sample source code from GitHub can be found at `https://github.com/PacktPublishing/Hands-On-Application-Development-with-PyCharm---Second-Edition/tree/main/chapter-16`. We covered cloning the code in *Chapter 2, Installation and Configuration*.

Miscellaneous topics in PyCharm

As I said, the sheer volume of features in this IDE is staggering. In this section, I'll cover a few things that didn't fit neatly into other chapters. I'll be presenting them more in the spirit of my saying "Hey, look at this!", rather than presenting a full tutorial on each feature.

Remote virtual environments

We've had this feature for a while now, and I think it is likely outshined by the newer remote development features we covered in *Chapter 15*. This feature allows you to work with an interpreter on another computer accessible via SSH. There are a couple of use cases for this. I have used this feature to debug a copy of an application using the virtual environment on the production server. I have a copy of the production code on my computer, but the venv is on the production system. This allows me to reproduce a bug and fix it locally using the exact environment where it normally lives. This was especially effective back when I used Mac and Windows laptops as my main development environment while the production environment ran in Linux. As we've pointed out, lots of packages deploy differently based on the operating system. I've always had challenges with **NumPy**, **pandas**, and **pymssql** (the Microsoft supported driver for SQL Server), which work very differently in these different environments, especially Windows. To build your third-party packages that leverage C code, you need a compiler. In Linux it's *cmake*. On Windows, it is the Microsoft C++ compiler. There is a big difference between the two, and testing an application only on Windows doesn't cut it for me. I want a more realistic test, and using this feature I can use the exact environment where it will run.

You can create or use a virtual environment on a remote computer by setting up an SSH connection to it. We covered creating an SSH connection back in *Chapter 15*, so I won't repeat the instructions here. The options for using a remote environment are alongside the normal options in the project interpreter settings shown in *Figure 16.1*.

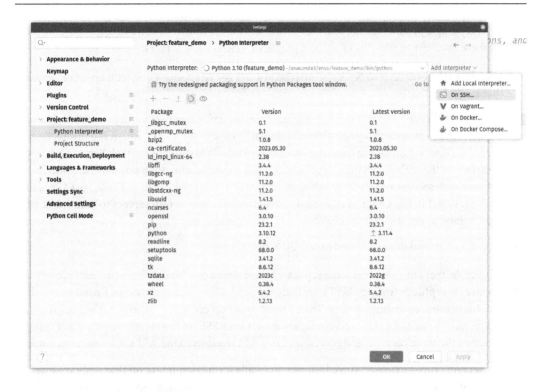

Figure 16.1: Use the interpreter settings dialog along with a previously configured
SSH connection to set up your virtual environment on a remote Linux system

Naturally there is going to be a pretty big performance hit when you work this way; at least there was for me. For my use case, it was well worth it!

You'll note there is also an option for **On Vagrant**, which is effectively the same option, but instead of a random remote server it's on a local virtual machine managed by **HashiCorp's Vagrant**. What is Vagrant you ask?

Working with HashiCorp Vagrant

Within the field of DevOps, a movement called **Infrastructure as Code** (**IaC**) has become very important. The idea is that nobody really runs anything on bare metal anymore; everything is run on a virtual machine. Regardless, one of the challenges I've faced over the years is when I go to set up my testing and production environments, I have to do it all by hand and it takes quite a while. My objective is to set up at least two or three nearly identical environments.

Let's say I'm creating a product using Flask that uses React for the frontend, and Microsoft SQL Server as the database. In order to run this using best practices, I need a few servers:

- I need a web server such as Nginx or Apache to serve my React app along with any static assets that might be needed.

- I need an application server. Flask's development server isn't going to cut it in production. I need a server that runs something like **Green Unicorn** (*gunicorn* for short), which is a production-grade WSGI server capable of handling production loads. **WSGI** stands for **Web Server Gateway Interface** in the realm of Python development. It is a specification for a standardized interface between web servers and Python web applications or frameworks such as Flask, FastAPI, and Django. WSGI defines a set of rules and conventions that allow web servers to communicate with Python applications in a consistent and interoperable way.

- I need a dedicated database server for SQL Server.

Keeping it simple, that's three servers, each replicated three times: one for development testing, one for staging or **user acceptance testing** (**UAT**), and one for production. For each server, I need to install, patch, and harden the operating system. Then I need to set up each type of server. The web server is easy, I just need to install nginx and configure it so it uses SSL, redirects any requests not using HTTPS, caches the static content, and reverse-proxies API requests to the API server running Flask.

The Flask server is more involved since best practice calls for having nginx on that system as well, forwarding traffic to Green Unicorn. I'll usually set up firewall rules on this server to reject any traffic not coming from the web server, and block any ports that are not needed.

The database server is the toughest one. Ideally, I need separate partitions for OS, logging, and data to prevent IO performance bottlenecks. All totaled, it can easily take a week for me to set up and validate a small environment.

If I were to use IaC, I could write a script that automates setting up and tearing down each of the three environments. It would take just as long to write the script as it does to manually set everything up, but when it comes time to scale or update my infrastructure, having it in code will be very helpful. Since it is in the code, everything is documented. If I want to update the OS, say from Ubuntu 20 to 22, I just change a variable and I can rebuild all new servers or update the ones I have. IaC is worth the time investment in every single case beyond a throw-away prototype.

One of the more popular IaC frameworks is **HashiCorp's Terraform**. You'll find plugins for the **HashiCorp language** (**HCL**) in JetBrains Marketplace that allow you to work with Terraform files with the usual syntax coloring and auto-complete functionality. Terraform is designed to help you configure virtual machines by way of providers. There's a provider for VMware and that's what converts your IaC into actual virtual machines. There are providers for cloud services too, including Azure, AWS, and Digital Ocean.

HashiCorp also makes a product called **Vagrant**. Vagrant is designed to be IaC for your local computer. I've been saying all along that you should use Linux for development if you plan to run your final application on a Linux server. But most people would rather not give up working on Windows or Mac. Since Mac is based on a Linux-like operating system, the Mac is at least close, but it won't be identical if you're running your work in Ubuntu, Red Hat, or Fedora.

Vagrant is a program that, when coupled with a local hypervisor such as VMware Workstation, Oracle VirtualBox, or Microsoft's Hyper-V, allows you to create a script that generates a local virtual machine, called a *box*, that can match your production environment. Essentially you are automating the creation and maintenance of virtual machines on your local computer the same way you'd use Terraform for your servers. Vagrant does some neat things, such as automatically mapping your project's folder to the virtual machine, so you don't need to constantly copy your code to the VM manually. Your terminal in PyCharm is automatically connected to the VM using SSH, so when you execute commands you are using your local terminal in the IDE, but the VM is handling the execution. You could do this with **Windows Subsystem for Linux** (**WSL**), but there would be more effort involved and WSL is pretty limited in how it can be used compared to making individual VMs for each project.

While Vagrant is very useful, most developers are shifting to Docker for these kinds of workflows, but I still see developers, especially in the cybersecurity fields and in educational settings, still working with virtual machines. Vagrant has an advantage in that Docker containers are immutable, meaning they can't be changed once they are created. While this is operationally superior, since immutability of a deployed application provides a very stable system, it might be less desirable for daily development since it is useful for a developer to be able to fiddle with the environment without restrictions.

Vagrant creates a box, which is just a virtual machine, and represents a full server experience with a complete operating system. You can do anything you want to it, and since it's on your laptop, if your machinations break the system you can just kill the box and make another reset to its original state in minutes.

Vagrant gives you the ability to build web applications using a real IP address instead of using the loopback address, also known as localhost. This provides local testing advantages since applications working on localhost often behave differently than applications bound to a real IP address. Furthermore, you can choose to make your Vagrant box's IP address shareable not only on the local network but also on the public internet. When you're ready to show off your progress, you can invite others to your shared Vagrant box, elicit feedback, and then turn sharing off.

You'll find the tooling for Vagrant in the **Tools** menu shown in *Figure 16.2*.

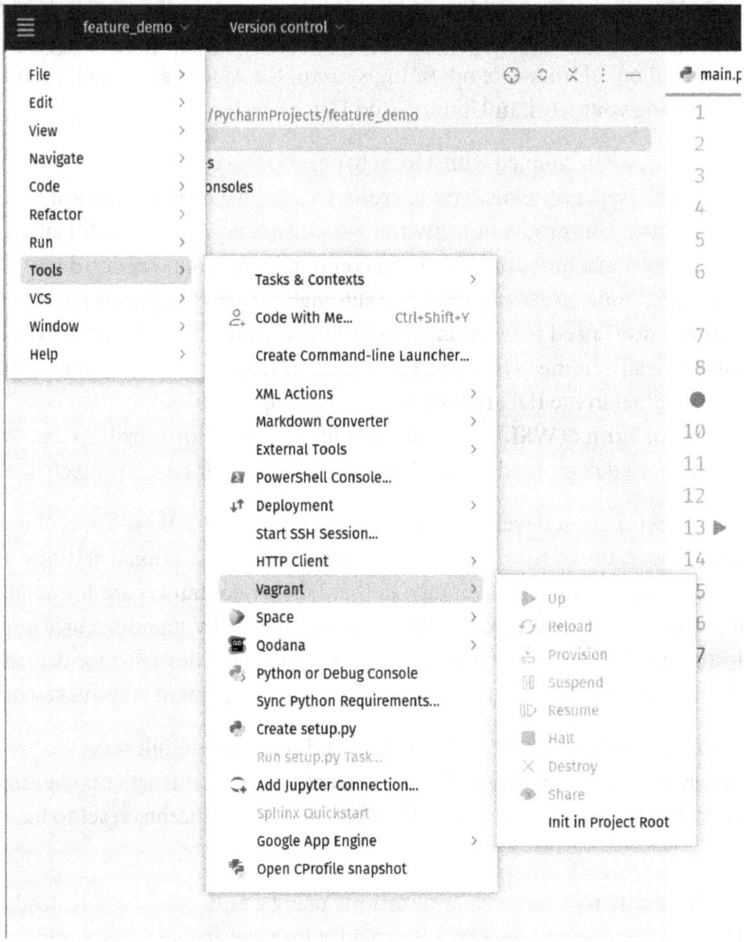

Figure 16.2: PyCharm supports all the Vagrant commands directly via menu options

In order to use Vagrant, you need to install it along with a supported hypervisor. You can find the installation instructions at `https://developer.hashicorp.com/vagrant/tutorials/getting-started/getting-started-install`. As for the hypervisor, the default is Oracle VirtualBox. You can find more about VirtualBox at `https://www.virtualbox.org/wiki/Downloads`.

Once you have these programs installed you can use the **Init in Project Root** option shown in *Figure 16.2*.

This will prompt you to create a file called `Vagrantfile` at the root of your project by selecting a name for your Vagrant box and providing the image URL. The dialog is shown in *Figure 16.3*.

Add Vagrant Box

| Box name: | lucid32 |
| Box URL: | http://files.vagrantup.com/lucid32.box |

OK   Cancel

Figure 16.3: You are prompted to create a Vagrant box with a very old default

It is clear that this is a very old default since `lucid32` refers to Ubuntu 10. At the time of writing, the current version of Ubuntu is 23 while the long-term support edition is 22.

You should probably find a newer box definition if you're serious about using a more current virtual machine. You can find box definitions at `https://app.vagrantup.com`. I've done this in *Figure 16.4* where I've searched for `Jammy Jellyfish`, the project codename for **Ubuntu 22**, which is what I use for all my current production projects.

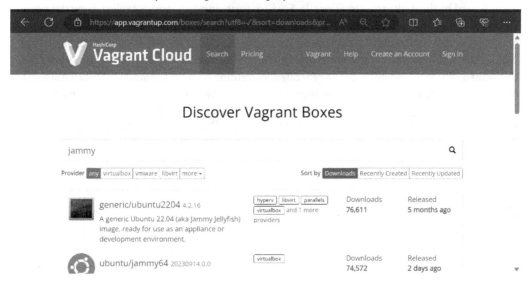

Figure 16.4: You can find a wide variety of predefined boxes on the Vagrant Cloud registry

Once you find one you want to use, click on it. In *Figure 16.5*, I'm clicking on the second entry in the list.

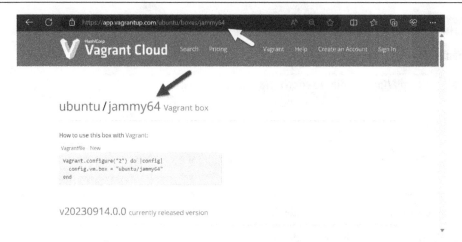

Figure 16.5: This is the box definition for Ubuntu Jammy 64

Now that we have a box definition, refer back to *Figure 16.3*. In the first field, you need to type the box name indicated by the dark arrow in *Figure 16.5*, which is `ubuntu/jammy64`. Next, copy the name of the box definition's URL, indicated by the light arrow in *Figure 16.5*, which in our case is `https://app.vagrantup.com/ubuntu/boxes/jammy64`. Clicking **OK** will download the box image and create the VM. Once it is ready, you'll find the rest of the Vagrant tools are no longer grayed out in the menu as shown in *Figure 16.6*. The generated Vagrantfile is open (not automatically, I did that), and you can even see that PyCharm is prompting me to add the new file to the Git repository.

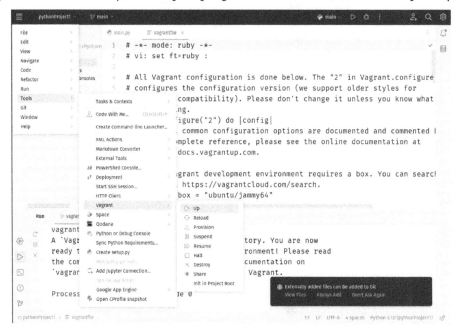

Figure 16.6: The Vagrant tool options are now available

If you dive more deeply into using Vagrant, you'll find that like many of PyCharm's integrations, the IDE gives you a graphical way to perform what would otherwise be a command-line workflow. You can run the commands using the menu in *Figure 16.6*, or you can type the commands in your terminal to achieve the same result. Packt has some good books on developing with Vagrant. I'll be sure to leave a few suggestions in the *Further reading* section of this chapter.

There are some big benefits to using Vagrant. You can have your whole development team use identical environments for developing and testing your application using the same environment you'll use in production. No more "*It works on my machine*", which implies the code is fine and a configuration issue is to blame. Since the environment configuration is standardized, and maintained as part of the code base, the project should work the same everywhere assuming the code and any external configuration files (such as .ini or .env files) or environment variables are also identical.

Using IaC in Vagrant shields less experienced developers who don't know how to set up virtual machines, and it also standardizes the build so everybody's VM is the same. The configuration is tracked in your revision control system and so it tracks and updates just like application code.

Tracking your time

Over the course of my long career, I've worked for the United States Government on several occasions, and I've run my own freelancing practice. In each case, I've needed a way to track my time. In the case of government contracts, I have to track a set of billing codes down to 7-minute intervals. Time tracking can be used in more reasonable environments as well. I try to keep time-tracking data to correlate the ever-elusive story point used in agile development methodologies such as Scrum with how much time it will take to complete a task. According to most agile methodologies, people are really bad at estimating time. But they are pretty good at estimating relative size. In *Figure 16.3*, you would have a hard time telling exactly how tall, in inches or centimeters, the soy milk carton is next to the cup of latte.

Figure 16.7: How tall is the soy milk carton?

Is it 8 inches tall or 20? But if you try estimating the size using the coffee cup as your unit of measure, you can be more precise. The carton is about two and a half coffee cups tall. So it is with story points, but at the end of the day, the boss really wants to know how long something will take. You can't tell her you'll have her feature done in two coffee cups and expect her to be happy about it. This could invite the obvious reply, "Great, so it will be done after my second cup of coffee!"

I do my normal story point estimate, then I track my time to see how long it really took so I can both give the boss her answer and be better at estimating next time.

To use the time tracking features in PyCharm, you need to connect to a server. By server, in this case, I mean one of the project tracking services supported by PyCharm, as shown in *Figure 16.4*.

Figure 16.8: Click the Configure Servers menu item to configure your project tracker

When you click this menu item, you should see the screen shown in *Figure 16.5*.

Figure 16.9: Pick whichever project tracking service you use from the list

Once your server is registered, you'll be able to pick a backlog item or issue that is assigned to you. *Figure 16.6* shows my YouTrack server integration with the issue number **DEMO-20: Finish Chapter 16 in PyCharm Book**.

Figure 16.10: The time I've spent on this issue is automatically tracked

As you switch between tasks throughout the day, you can switch from right in your IDE, which will track how much time you spend on each task. You can then synchronize your work times up to the server to keep an accurate tally of how you are spending your time.

TODO list

This may sound like it is related to the time tracking feature, but it really isn't. The TODO list panel shows you all those TODO comments in your code as a list. You can see an example in *Figure 16.7.*

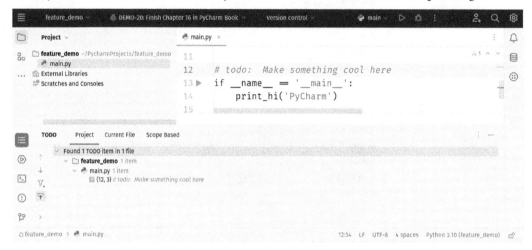

Figure 16.11: The TODO panel in PyCharm lists all the to-do comments in your
code and takes you right to the given line when you double-click

You can double-click the TODO item to go right to that line in the code, allowing you to quickly find your way back to whatever you had to temporarily abandon.

Macros

A macro is a script of recorded keystrokes that can be played back in order to create useful automation. In my opinion, learning to use these is a necessary survival skill in the jungles of software development.

Let's say we need a list of things that don't change to populate a drop-down list box in HTML. For this example, I'm going to create a SELECT tag with all 50 states of the US. This is something that hasn't changed since 1959, although if I'm ever elected Emperor, Canada and Mexico are first on my list. They'll never see it coming.

Back in reality, I need to get this done and I darn sure don't want to type all this out. I asked my best friend ChatGPT to give me a list of the 50 states in alphabetical order. The result is in the us-states.txt file in the chapter source.

You'll also find an HTML file called `states.html` in the source. I've included the code as follows:

```
<form>
    <p>Pick a state:</p>
    <select id="state" name="state">

    </select>
</form>
```

As you can see, there is nothing in the `<select>` tag, which is meant to render a drop-down selection list in the HTML page defined by the rest of the code in that file. I need to add the states so they look like this:

```
<option>Alabama</option>
<option>Arkansas</option>
```

And so on for all 50. I can do this with a macro. Sure, I could also just have ChatGPT generate it for me, but that would be anti-climactic since this is a book on PyCharm and not a book on ChatGPT.

Open the project called `feature_demo` in the chapter source code, then open the `united-states.txt file`. Start by placing your cursor in front of `Alabama` in the `united-states.txt` file, as shown in *Figure 16.9*.

Figure 16.12: Put your cursor in front of Alabama

Next, click **Edit | Macro | Start Macro Recording** as seen in *Figure 16.10*.

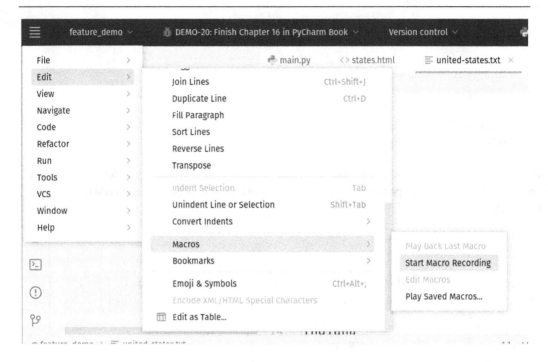

Figure 16.13: Start recording your macro

With the macro recording, type <option>. Then hit the *End* (*Cmd + Right Arrow* on a Mac) key on your keyboard to go to the end of the line, then type </option>. Press the *down arrow* key on your keyboard, followed by the *Home* key (*Cmd + Left Arrow* on Mac). The cursor should now be at the beginning of the second line, Arkansas. Go back to the same menu item shown in *Figure 16.10*, but note **Start Macro Recording** now says **Stop Macro Recording**. Click it. You are prompted to name your macro or leave it blank if it is just temporary. I called mine option-list.

Return to the menu shown in *Figure 16.10* again and you'll see either your saved macro name listed or just **Play Back Last Macro**. Either will work. When you click either option, your keystrokes will be replayed and you'll be on the next line having converted Arkansas to an option tag.

You can map your macro to a key combination and repeat your actions with a keyboard shortcut, making it easy to do over and over.

If I'm being honest, the macro feature in PyCharm is okay, but it isn't as good as in some other tools. Ultraedit and Notepad++, while not IDEs, both have very sophisticated macro features such as the ability to replay a macro until it reaches the end of the file, or to run the macro a specific number of times. PyCharm's macros are fine for small jobs, but for bigger ones you might look to other tools.

Notifications

Sometimes PyCharm will present notifications as toast windows in the lower-right corner of the screen. These messages will usually disappear within a few seconds, but you can see them in the notifications panel. You'll find this panel on the right-hand toolbar, as seen in *Figure 16.11*.

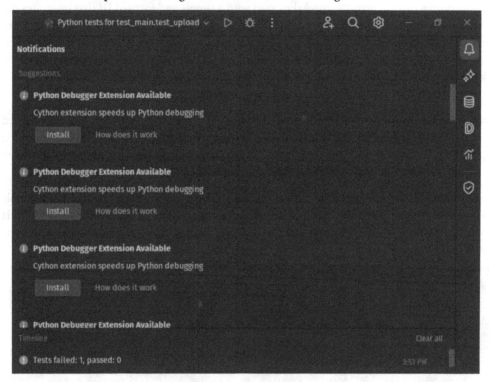

Figure 16.14: The notifications panel

You can toggle the panel by clicking the *bell* icon on the right-hand toolbar. The panel has a **Timeline** option that allows you to list notifications by recency. You can choose to dismiss any notifications you no longer need, or clear them all.

New features in 2023.2

During the course of writing this book, a lot has changed, especially in the UI. I used build #PY-231.8109.197, or as I like to call it, *the fightin' 197th*. I kept the same release in play for the entire time, neglecting to install any updates because I wanted things to be consistent. Right about the time I started working on *Chapter 13*, JetBrains held an online event revealing a new point release, 2023.2. The new release is packed with new features, but today as I write *Chapter 16* (this chapter), two more point releases have come out. This pace is probably due in large part to JetBrain's re-vamp of the UI.

If you remember at the beginning of the book, we had to turn the "new UI" on in the settings. By the time you read this, the new UI will be the default. JetBrains didn't stop there. The UI has always been highly configurable, and we covered that thoroughly in the early chapters of this book.

One of the main pushes in the new UI effort has been to streamline the development process. Most IDEs go through a cycle of growth where they start with a simple and focused UI that integrates the minimal features needed to be considered an IDE versus an enhanced text editor. Over time, more and more features are added with the aim of giving you a tool that does everything you might need. It occurred to me just the other day that on days when I am 100% focused on Python development, or even JavaScript, web, or database development, all I'd really need is a lightweight OS and PyCharm. I wouldn't even need a window manager beyond what is needed to run PyCharm!

The problem caused by the richness of such a tool is it becomes daunting for new users, and disorganized for veteran users. We learned in *Chapter 15* that most new features of any JetBrains IDE are implemented as plugins. This can lead to a disorganized UI and it can make the IDE feel like it is a bunch of unrelated pieces cobbled together in a sub-optimal overall user experience.

The new UI aims to take care of this by compacting the UI, exposing the most commonly used tools and hiding (but not removing) the more complicated options. The build I used for the book did this very well. As newer point releases come out, I'm noticing further efforts to hide complexity. Take look at *Figure 16.13*.

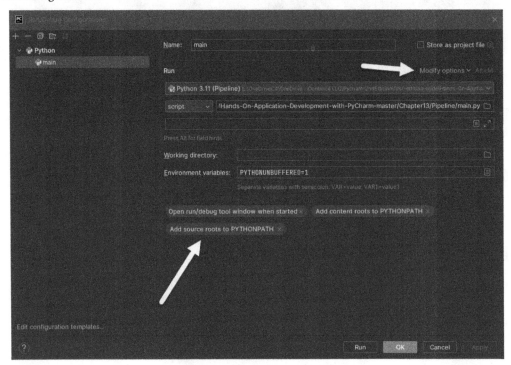

Figure 16.15: JetBrains has moved a lot of settings into tags instead of having dozens of checkboxes

This is a run configuration from the latest update released only days ago, labeled as Build #PY-232.9559.58 built August 22, 2023. There are two visible differences. There is a set of tags at the bottom and a **Modify Options** dropdown both indicated by arrows in *Figure 16.13*. Compare this to *Figure 16.14*.

Figure 16.16: This is the old dialog from Chapter 3

All those options are still there, but they've been rolled up into the **Modify Options** dropdown. The settings you've actually used appear as tags at the bottom of *Figure 16.13*. The amount of change over only a few months is staggering!

In addition to product changes, there are some interesting new feature additions and improvements.

Black integration

First presented at PyCon 2019, Black is an uncompromising code formatter. It has gained a great deal of attention and popularity since its release, and JetBrains has added support to PyCharm. Black needs to be installed in order for this feature to work. You can find details on installation and more at `https://github.com/psf/black`. If you are using Linux, check your package manager. I use Pop_OS, which is based on Ubuntu. *Figure 16.15* shows I've found Black as a package and I prefer to install it that way.

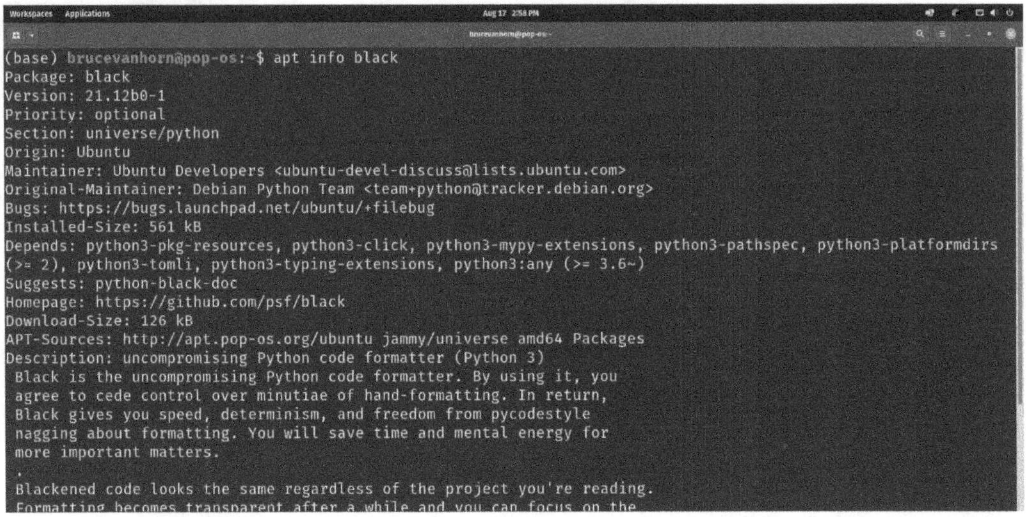

Figure 16.17: In Linux, you can probably install Black using your package manager

Once Black is installed, you need to turn it on on a per-project basis. You'll find this option when you search for Black in the **Settings** dialog shown in *Figure 16.16*.

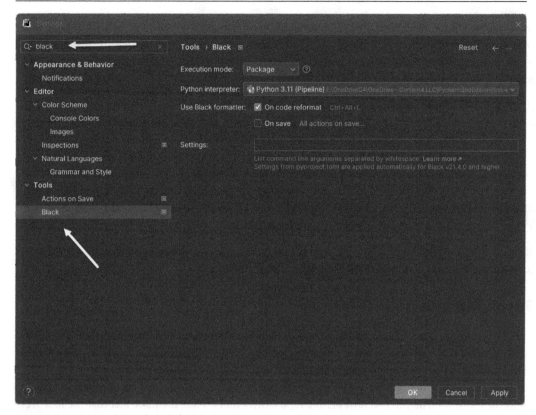

Figure 16.18: Search for Black in the Settings dialog and you'll find it under Tools

Your options for formatting are **On code reformat** and **On save**. If you work on a team, and you have an existing code base, use this with a little bit of caution. One of the design goals of Black is to format your code consistently to reduce diffs during merges and code reviews. The first day you use it, you will likely encounter huge diffs. I'll explain why. Let's say I have a branch in Git called development. On my team, we individually branch off development into feature branches. If I'm working on some new feature, I'll branch off development and make a new branch called feature/amazing-thing. Next, I'll create my amazing thing, but I'll need to touch some other files written by other developers along the way. Naturally, before I commit, muscle memory automatically uses the *Ctrl + Alt + L* (reformat code) command to reformat. Black will reformat the whole file. When you go to merge, you may find other developers have changed some of the same files you re-formatted, but they were less conscientious about reformatting. You are presented with the challenge of an ugly merge even if there were only a few lines actually changed between the two developers, and they might not have otherwise collided.

This is no fault of the Black formatter! The same thing will happen if you use PyCharm's default code formatter. The Black formatter, though, is a better solution since it aims for determinism, which is a fancy coder word that means the results of an operation always produce the same output. A non-compromising deterministic formatter should yield very consistent results every time it is used.

My advice, then, if you want to start using Black is to get together as a team. Have everyone push their work, merge it into a branch, and then apply Black to the whole project. In my example, I would resolve my conflicts, and then merge back into the development branch. Then I would have all my colleagues do the same. Once development has everyone's changes, freeze the code and use Black on all your source files. During the freeze, nobody is allowed to work on any individual file until the formatting has been applied and pushed. If you have a very large code base, you might have to organize your efforts over time. The results will be worth it! Your code will be PEP-8 compliant, and you should see fewer merge conflicts, especially those caused by formatting.

Black can be configured to run on save, and beyond the scope of PyCharm, Black can be used as a hook in your revision control, as well as in your CI/CD process.

GitLab integration

GitHub is easily the most popular and widely used cloud-based solution for managing code. Its Achilles heel is the fact that it is cloud-based. Organizations that are serious about security, such as those whose trading partners require a certification such as the **Service Organization Control 2** (**SOC2**) certification are often not satisfied with their intellectual property being hosted on a publicly available platform. While it's true you can host private repositories on GitHub, the mere fact that the files are not on a server controlled by the certified organization can be a problem.

Thankfully, it is possible to host your own private GitHub server using GitLab. You can run GitLab on-premises behind your firewall and exercise total control over your security and infrastructure while still using what is in every other sense, the GitHub experience. You'll find GitLab integration in the **Version Control** settings as shown in *Figure 16.17*.

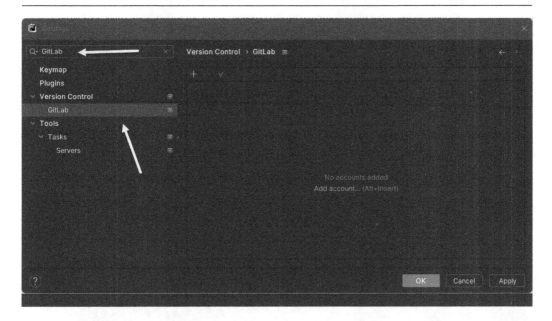

Figure 16.19: GitLab settings can be found alongside the other VCS settings

The integration is fairly deep. Beyond the basics we covered in *Chapter 5*, you can handle all your pull requests, approvals, and more right from the IDE.

Run anywhere

We've had **Search everywhere** for quite a while. In case you missed it, you can double-tap the **Shift** key and get a dialog that allows you to find anything anywhere in your project. This works even if what you're looking for isn't in code. It could be in documentation, settings, or elsewhere.

New to PyCharm, though not necessarily new to IntelliJ is **Run Anything**, activated by double-tapping the *Ctrl* key. You'll also find hints throughout the UI illuminating this new (to PyCharm) feature. In *Figure 16.18*, you'll see I've double-tapped the *Ctrl* key, which brings up a small dialog. Since I'm new to this feature, I've typed a question mark (?) in the dialog.

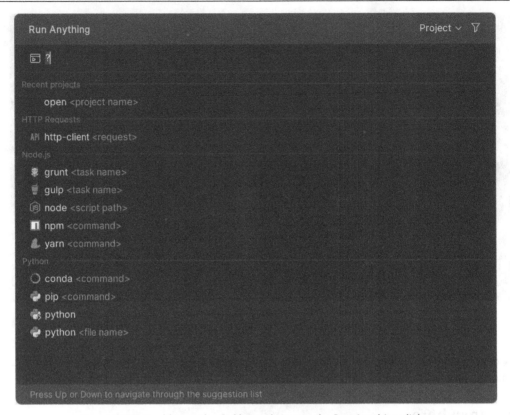

Figure 16.20: Double-tap the Ctrl key to bring up the Run Anything dialog

It's nice enough to say, *"You can run ANYTHING!"* But all you critical thinkers out there will immediately follow up with, *"What do you mean by ANYTHING?"* Here, the answer to my question mark tells me what can be run. I can see I can run any Python script in my project by simply typing its name. I can see I can run `pip` and `conda` commands as well. Web developers can run the HTTP request test code we covered in *Chapter 9*. They can also run all the popular package managers such as **npm** and **yarn**, as well as common build tools including **gulp** and **grunt**. These two tools have been displaced by **webpack** in most modern toolchains, but we don't really need a configuration for that since most people run webpack from a configuration in the `package.json` file via npm, which is visibly supported. Naturally, we can also run any **Node** process as easily as we can run Python.

AI Assistant

The show stealer at most of the recent events featuring PyCharm is the AI Assistant. As I write this, the feature is in closed beta, meaning you have to sign up and be approved in order to try out the feature. Bear in mind that anything I show here will probably change.

The easiest thing to implement, and there are numerous plugins that do this, is to just provide an integrated frontend experience for some online AI API.

In contrast, you'll find the AI Assistant integrated throughout PyCharm. To use the AI Assistant, use the right-hand menu shown in *Figure 16.19*.

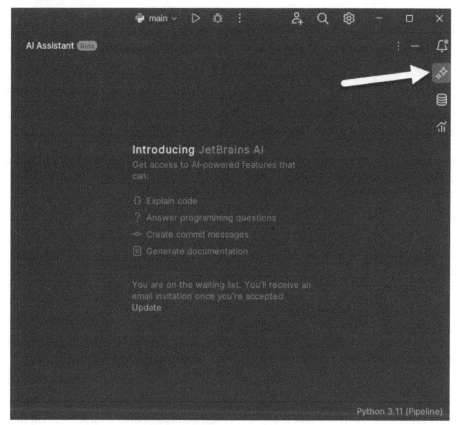

Figure 16.21: The AI Assistant can be activated using the button on the right-hand menu

The preceding dialog summarizes the features available. Let's take a look.

> **This feature is not local**
>
> If your company or environment has a restriction on sending code out to an API such as ChatGPT, you need to know that this feature does exactly that. The functionality is not self-contained within PyCharm and **any code or information you enter will be sent out to various external third-party APIs**. This is documented in the agreement you blindly scrolled through and ignored so you could get to use PyCharm and the cool new AI features.

Explain code

There are many circumstances where you might encounter code you don't understand. My normal mode of describing these circumstances is pretty colorful, especially at 2 A.M. the day before a deadline. I'll endeavor to keep it professional:

- It was written by someone else who clearly has no idea what they are doing.
- It was written by someone else who is clearly better at this than you are. Sometimes this might be the same person depending on the time of day.
- It was written by someone who loves terse code despite it being an anti-pattern in Python.
- The code contains a regular expression you have not committed to memory, since no normal human understands regular expressions even though they pretend otherwise.

In circumstances such as these, help is a mouse-click away. Highlight the code in question, right-click, and select **AI Assistant Action | Explain code**. Seconds later, the AI will give you a breakdown of the selected code.

> **Note**
> Bear in mind that the AI Assistant is not always correct, and doesn't always give completely sound advice.

Answer programming questions

In truth, the AI Assistant will answer any question you ask. I've asked it questions about nginx configuration, Docker, and general networking questions. Of course, it also answers programming questions.

Create commit messages

This one is really neat! I'm a huge fan of the XKCD online comic and their treatment of Git in many comics is spot-on. This one comes to mind right now: `https://xkcd.com/1296/`.

Since the IDE can see your change list, it can generate a commit message for you as shown in *Figure 16.20*.

Figure 16.22: Commit messages are generated that are more deep
and meaningful than "I changed a bunch of stuff"

Maybe you don't put much stock in your commit messages. I've worked on US Government projects where the commit messages were audited. This wasn't generally known by the development team who, upon learning of this, opted to rebase and re-create every commit to remove their more colorful language within the commit messages. The audit wasn't really looking for that; it was being used to validate the change control process. My team is currently going through SOC2 certification, and I can tell you firsthand that complete and descriptive commit messages are seriously helpful. As cybersecurity continues to invade developer workflows, you can bet this feature will prove its value to you sooner or later.

Generate documentation

Do you hate writing docstrings? That's a trick question. If you're a software developer, you probably think that the code itself is all the documentation anyone could ever need. But you've also seen the power of well-documented code when using the documentation features both in the main UI and in SciView. Wouldn't it be nice if your own functions were as well documented without the need for you to write that documentation yourself? *Figure 16.21* shows me generating a docstring for a function in one of my projects.

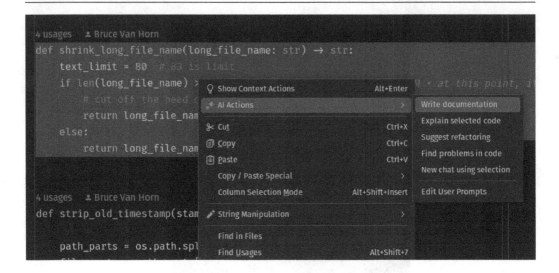

Figure 16.23: Don't write documentation, generate it

Documentation in this case is really just another form of boilerplate. You should let the IDE generate that for you, then maybe improve on what it creates if needed.

Jupyter Notebook support for Polars

While pandas is great, for big data, it is too slow. Spark and other big data frameworks can help but only by scaling horizontally, which involves setting up multiple compute nodes on your network. **Polars** is a data science library designed to allow you to work with large data without resorting to using multiple computers and has long been a requested feature in PyCharm. If your DataFrame fits in your computer's memory, you can use it in Polars and view it in PyCharm just as you would any other DataFrame.

Furthermore, PyCharm supports the **Plotly** library for visualization, which uniquely works with Polars DataFrames. When you combine PyCharm's support for these advanced libraries, you can overcome many of the obstacles that are normally cited as detractors for using Polars.

Summary and closing remarks

We have covered a great deal in a short time! At least it feels this way for me since in many of these chapters it was extremely tempting to jump into a tutorial on the subject we were covering. For example, in the Flask and Django chapters, I felt "wrong" about not giving you a tutorial on Flask and Django. I didn't do so because those are quite literally books unto themselves both within and outside of the Packt library.

We learned that the point of an IDE is to offer you a full suite of tools for every development task you might perform on a daily basis. When viewed through that lens, PyCharm is an amazing IDE that really has very few competitors.

We saw how the basics around setting up a simple Python project are made easy by automating processes such as creating a virtual environment. The Professional edition of PyCharm has many additional features for project creation, mostly centered around project templates for the most popular types of projects in the areas of general software development, full stack web development, and data science. There is even a special edition for educational use, which allows you to create interactive lessons that play out directly in the IDE. We didn't talk about that one, but if you're interested, I'll leave a link in the *Further reading* section.

Full stack web developers have a huge chunk of PyCharm's tooling dedicated just to their work. We saw all the major frameworks supported, and the support isn't even limited to Python. PyCharm can do anything WebStorm can do with respect the JavaScript development and working with modern JavaScript UI frameworks such as Angular, Vue, Vite, and React.

PyCharm has truly complete tooling for interacting with relational and non-relational databases. This feature set is mainly from DataGrip, a different IDE from JetBrains focused completely on databases, in particular on creating and development relational structures. It has full support for MongoDB and Redis, which are two that I use daily. Where I would normally need to flip to tools such as Studio 3T or Redis Insights, I can instead just stay in PyCharm. The diversity of platforms supported is staggering! There are dozens of supported databases, and sometimes it can be fun to just look at the list and go look up the ones you've never heard of.

After covering databases, we learned about the boon that PyCharm brings to the field of data science. You can use what I'll call a light version of Jupyter Notebooks by leveraging code cells in IPython. I'm not a daily data science guy at work, but sometimes I like to pretend that I am. The code cell features covered in *Chapters 12* and *13* are useful for tasks such as integrating multiple APIs or microservices together. I can create a prototype script using cells that draw data from different APIs or microservices, toss them into a pandas DataFrame, and I can use SciView to see the results even if I don't need to keep the DataFrame calls in my real program. Just being able to visualize the data in several easy tables rendered next to each other can be a big help.

If you are a data science practitioner, your support grows with tools such as Jupyter Notebooks integration making PyCharm a one-stop tool for your whole workflow. That's the point of the tool for its three different audiences.

When Packt asked me to write this book, I was excited and daunted. I was excited because I had just learned that LinkedIn Learning had taken down my PyCharm course, and that was one of my personal favorites. This book offered me the opportunity to do a deeper dive than you can do in a 2-hour video course. If 2-hour video courses are your thing I have one left on LinkedIn covering developing APIs with Flask. I doubt they'll keep it up much longer, so if you're interested, be sure to check it out before they take it down. I'll put a link in the *Further reading* section. My newer video courses can be found on my course website, `https://maddevskilz.com`. Naturally, anything about Python will feature PyCharm as the IDE.

The idea (.idea?) of writing this book was daunting because there is so much packed (Packt?) into this IDE and I actually do know what I don't know. I don't know everything. I definitely found features I didn't know were there when I started. I probably got some things wrong. That's OK (I hope). Ending this book is a single point in time on a journey that, for me, started seven years ago when I got fed up with Visual Studio and web development in C# in general. When I saw how easy it was to create applications in Flask, and then again how easy PyCharm made it for a total n00b like me to actually get real work done, I was hooked. Writing a book like this is a huge responsibility with potentially a huge impact. Coding is a legitimate superpower. Unlike most superpowers in the movies, it is a superpower that can be taught. There is no need to come from a far-away planet, get bitten by a radioactive spider, or get injected with an experimental serum. While some of that might help, all you really need is grit, curiosity, and to put in the hard work. If you master this craft even a little bit, you can do great things.

I've had the opportunity to create software that helps choose treatment modalities for prostate cancer patients. The project didn't wind up going anywhere, but a year after I had shelved the project my father called and told me he had just gotten a diagnosis for prostate cancer. The extra moral of this story is to never delete your old repos! My father was a pathologist himself, and with the help of the doctor who created the algorithm, we ran my dad's numbers through the program and the resulting treatment gave me another 8 years with him.

I've also been part of projects designed to help keep my country safe, train pilots in the US Marine Corps, and to manage IT assets. When I was working on these projects, they were just projects. They were deadlines I had to meet, and they were sources of stress. But every piece of software published, indeed every line of code we write has the potential to help make the world around us a better place! Sometimes the benefits are obvious, as with the cancer treatment software. Even software with a mundane purpose, such as enterprise storage capacity planning, can have far-reaching benefits since this too is a tool for enabling others to do what they do and build what they build.

Consider too, our superpower works at scale. Superman can only be in one place at one time; a fact too frequently exploited by various supervillains. We are not limited in this way. There are apps in multiple app stores that can help dyslexic children learn to read. That one app downloaded tens of thousands of times can educate generations that would be marginalized or ignored by the public education systems of most countries, which value test scores and funding over outcomes.

You have a superpower! Use it! These tools make it easier! If I've hooked even one person and they get the benefit from this tool and this language that I have gotten since I started, then for me, this book is a wild success.

Further reading

Be sure to check out the companion website for the book at `https://www.pycharm-book.com`, along with the following useful resources:

- Braunton, A. (2018) *Hands-On DevOps with Vagrant*. Packt.

- RESTful APIs with Python 3 and Flask (linkedin.com): `https://www.linkedin.com/learning/building-restful-apis-with-flask/restful-apis-with-python-3-and-flask-4`

- Polars library: `https://www.pola.rs/`

- The Plotly Library for Python: `https://plotly.com/python/`

- Educational edition of PyCharm: `https://www.jetbrains.com/pycharm-edu/`

- HashiCorp Vagrant: `https://www.vagrantup.com/`

- HashiCorp Terraform: `https://www.terraform.io/`

- Docker Desktop: `https://www.docker.com/products/docker-desktop/`

- Oracle VirtualBox: `https://www.virtualbox.org/`

- JetBrains AI Assistant: `https://blog.jetbrains.com/idea/2023/06/ai-assistant-in-jetbrains-ides/`

Index

Packtpub.com

Subscribe to our online digital library for full access to over 7,000 books and videos, as well as industry leading tools to help you plan your personal development and advance your career. For more information, please visit our website.

Why subscribe?

- Spend less time learning and more time coding with practical eBooks and Videos from over 4,000 industry professionals

- Improve your learning with Skill Plans built especially for you

- Get a free eBook or video every month

- Fully searchable for easy access to vital information

- Copy and paste, print, and bookmark content

Did you know that Packt offers eBook versions of every book published, with PDF and ePub files available? You can upgrade to the eBook version at packtpub.com and as a print book customer, you are entitled to a discount on the eBook copy. Get in touch with us at customercare@packtpub.com for more details.

At www.packtpub.com, you can also read a collection of free technical articles, sign up for a range of free newsletters, and receive exclusive discounts and offers on Packt books and eBooks.

Other Books You May Enjoy

If you enjoyed this book, you may be interested in these other books by Packt:

Learn Python Programming - Third Edition

Fabrizio Romano, Heinrich Kruger

ISBN: 978-1-80181-509-3

- Get Python up and running on Windows, Mac, and Linux
- Write elegant, reusable, and efficient code in any situation
- Avoid common pitfalls like duplication, complicated design, and over-engineering
- Understand when to use the functional or object-oriented approach to programming
- Build a simple API with FastAPI and program GUI applications with Tkinter
- Get an initial overview of more complex topics such as data persistence and cryptography
- Fetch, clean, and manipulate data, making efficient use of Python's built-in data structures

Python Real-World Projects

Steven F. Lott

ISBN: 978-1-80324-676-5

- Explore core deliverables for an application including documentation and test cases
- Discover approaches to data acquisition such as file processing, RESTful APIs, and SQL queries
- Create a data inspection notebook to establish properties of source data
- Write applications to validate, clean, convert, and normalize source data
- Use foundational graphical analysis techniques to visualize data
- Build basic univariate and multivariate statistical analysis tools
- Create reports from raw data using JupyterLab publication tools

Packt is searching for authors like you

If you're interested in becoming an author for Packt, please visit `authors.packtpub.com` and apply today. We have worked with thousands of developers and tech professionals, just like you, to help them share their insight with the global tech community. You can make a general application, apply for a specific hot topic that we are recruiting an author for, or submit your own idea.

Share Your Thoughts

Now you've finished *Hands-On Application Development with PyCharm*, we'd love to hear your thoughts! Scan the QR code below to go straight to the Amazon review page for this book and share your feedback or leave a review on the site that you purchased it from.

`https://packt.link/r/1837632359`

Your review is important to us and the tech community and will help us make sure we're delivering excellent quality content.

Download a free PDF copy of this book

Thanks for purchasing this book!

Do you like to read on the go but are unable to carry your print books everywhere?

Is your eBook purchase not compatible with the device of your choice?

Don't worry, now with every Packt book you get a DRM-free PDF version of that book at no cost.

Read anywhere, any place, on any device. Search, copy, and paste code from your favorite technical books directly into your application.

The perks don't stop there, you can get exclusive access to discounts, newsletters, and great free content in your inbox daily

Follow these simple steps to get the benefits:

1. Scan the QR code or visit the link below

https://packt.link/free-ebook/9781837632350

2. Submit your proof of purchase
3. That's it! We'll send your free PDF and other benefits to your email directly

www.ingramcontent.com/pod-product-compliance
Lightning Source LLC
Chambersburg PA
CBHW060634060326
40690CB00020B/4396